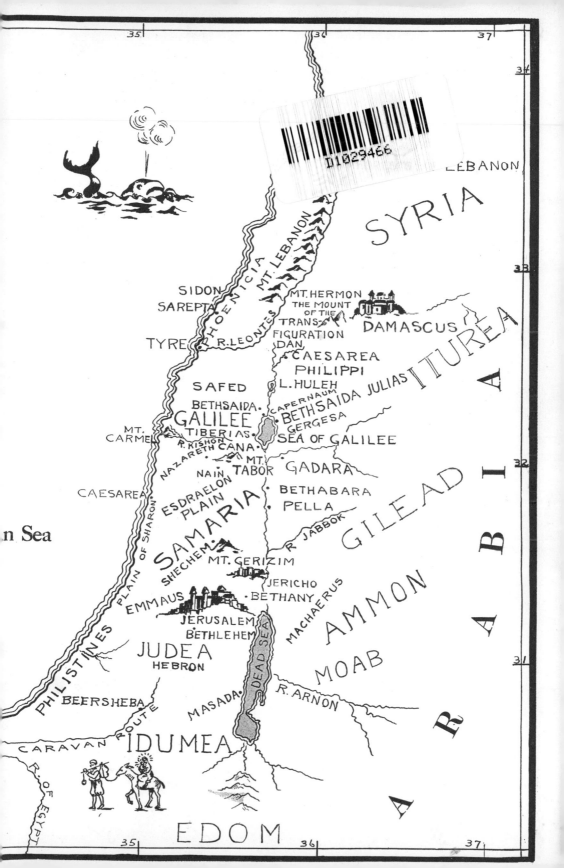

35　　　　　　36　　　　　　37

37

SYRIA

LEBANON

33

MT. LEBANON

PHOENICIA

SIDON
SAREPTA

MT. HERMON
THE MOUNT
OF THE
TRANS-
FIGURATION

DAMASCUS

ITUREA

TYRE
R. LEONTES

DAN

CAESAREA
PHILIPPI

SAFED

L. HULEH

CAPERNAUM

BETHSAIDA

BETHSAIDA JULIAS

GALILEE

GERGESA

MT.
CARMEL

TIBERIAS
R. KISHON

CANA

SEA OF GALILEE

NAZARETH

MT.
TABOR

GADARA

32

NAIN

CAESAREA

ESDRAELON
PLAIN

BETHABARA
PELLA

SAMARIA

R. JABBOK

GILEAD

A
R
A
B
I
A

n Sea

PLAIN OF SHARON

SHECHEM

MT. GERIZIM

JERICHO

MACHAERUS

AMMON

EMMAUS

BETHANY

JERUSALEM
BETHLEHEM

DEAD SEA

PHILISTINES

JUDEA
HEBRON

MOAB

31

BEERSHEBA

MASADA

R. ARNON

CARAVAN ROUTE

IDUMEA

R. OF EGYPT

EDOM

35　　　　　　36　　　　　　37

THE
LIFE OF CHRIST

By

ADAM FAHLING

Κατὰ τὴν ἀναλογίαν τῆς πίστεως.
Rom. 12, 6.

Sᴛ. Louɪs, Mo.
CONCORDIA PUBLISHING HOUSE

PRINTED IN U. S. A.

DEDICATED TO THE CHRISTIAN PASTOR, TEACHER, AND STUDENT WHO SEEKS, BUT CANNOT ALWAYS QUICKLY FIND, DETAILED, AUTHENTIC, SATISFACTORY, SCRIPTURAL, AND COLLATERAL INFORMATION ON THE LIFE OF CHRIST.

PREFACE.

The subject needs no introduction. It concerns the earthly life of our Lord Jesus Christ, after the date of whose birth practically the whole civilized world numbers its years; who is Himself the Son of God, the Light, the Life, and the Truth; the First and the Last; the One and All; and the Way to life everlasting. "Neither is there salvation in any other; for there is none other name under heaven given among men whereby we must be saved."

The book is written from the standpoint of a believer. The existence of miracles, the verbal inspiration and the interpretation of Holy Scriptures according to the intended sense of the holy writers, are taken for granted, for which no apologies are offered. This is not done in ignorance of the many charges of inaccuracy raised against the statements of Holy Writ, but rather with the knowledge that the charges cannot be successfully maintained.

The author is indebted to the best Biblical scholarship of ancient and modern times. While the general structure and scope of the work is his own, he was guided by the books listed in the bibliography and among these is especially indebted to Farrar, Edersheim, Andrews, Schuerer, Bruce, Dods, Meyer, and others, not only for the subject-matter, but also for literary expression.

The encouragement to begin the work grew out of a succession of manuscripts on related subjects, which led to the appointment to write this book. The consideration with which the present manuscript was received in its original, revised, and rewritten form is herewith gratefully acknowledged. Particular thanks for their kindness, advice, and assistance are extended to the Rev. L. Buchheimer of the Synodical Literature Board, Dr. W. Arndt of Concordia Seminary, the Rev. E. Eckhardt, Dr. F. Rupprecht,

Dr. Edmund Seuel, and his able assistants at the Concordia Publishing House.

The reader is naturally interested in the result, not in the process, of an author's investigation. A tremendous amount of work and study awaits him who attempts to write a book on the life and time of Christ. An immense amount of material must be examined. The wide fields of ancient history, archeology, geography, chronology, the Greek New Testament, the ancient manuscripts, the transmission of the sacred text, the harmony of the gospels, the synoptic problem, and the like, must be investigated. All this the reader is spared. The author prays that God's blessings will accompany this volume, written to glorify our divine Savior. A. F.

FOREWORD TO SECOND EDITION.

The publishers take pleasure in making this new, revised edition of Adam Fahling's *The Life of Christ* available to all who are looking for additional information on the life and times of our Savior.

Ever since its first appearance, in 1936, this book has been a valuable source of reliable information for the pastor, for the Sunday-school and Bible-class teacher, and for the lay student of the Scriptures — giving life and color to many otherwise black-and-white impressions of the earthly ministry of our Lord.

This new edition incorporates improvements and revisions which were suggested by the author shortly before he went to be with Him of whom he wrote so much, so well. May this new edition of Adam Fahling's greatest work continue to exalt the Savior in the hearts and lives of men. CONCORDIA PUBLISHING HOUSE

CONTENTS.

X   *Contents.*

THE FOURFOLD GOSPEL.

(The outline *Harmony of the Gospels,* upon which this work is based.)

The marks of parentheses indicate that the passage has been taken out of its order.

Description	Matthew	Mark	Luke	John	Chapter
252. After the Departure of Judas, Jesus Indicates His Glorification	26—29	22—25	19. 20	31—35	No. 15
253. Institution of the Lord's Supper. (1 Cor. 11, 23—26.)					,, 16
(Here follow in the order of Luke: —					
The Traitor is Revealed			(21—23)		
The Contention of the Disciples)			(24—30)		
XXXII. The Passion Week — Thursday Night — Farewell Discourses.					**XXXII**
254. Peter's Denials are Foretold	26, 30—35	14, 26—31	22, 31—39	13, 36—38	No. 1
255. Farewell Discourses: Jesus Comforts His Disciples and Promises the Comforter				14, 1—31	,, 4
256. Farewell Discourses: Christ the True Vine				15, 1—27	,, 8
257. Farewell Discourses: The Disciples Warned of Persecutions.				16, 1—33	,, 10
258. The Holy Spirit Promised				17, 1—26	,, 12
The Great Intercessory Prayer					
XXXIII. The Passion Week — Thursday Night to Friday Morning.					**XXXIII**
259. The Agony in Gethsemane	26, 36—46	14, 32—42	22, 39—46	18, 1—9	No. 1
260. The Arrival and Betrayal of Judas	47—50	43—46	47. 48		,, 4
261. Peter's Untimely Zeal	51—54	47	49—51	10. 11	,, 7
262. The Arrest of Jesus	55—56a	48. 49	52—54a	12	,, 8
263. The Disciples Flee	56b	50—52			,, 9
264. Jesus is First Taken to Annas	57	53	54a	13. 14 (19—23) (24)	,, 10
265. Jesus is Next Led to Caiaphas	59—66	55—64	54b	15—18	,, 14
266. The Denials of Peter	69—75	54 / 66—72	54c—62	25—27	,, 17
267. Jesus Maltreated during the Night	58 (67—68)	(65)	63—65		,, 22
268. Formally Condemned by the Sanhedrin	27, 1	15, 1a	22, 66—71		,, 23
XXXIV. The Passion Week — Friday Morning. "Suffered under Pontius Pilate."					**XXXIV**
269. Jesus Brought before Pilate	27, 2	15, 1b	23, 1	18, 28a	No. 1
270. Remorse and Suicide of Judas. (Acts 1, 18.19.)	3—10				,, 2
271. Jesus before Pilate, the First Time	11—14	2—5	2—5	28b—38	,, 4
272. Jesus before Herod			6—12		,, 10
273. Jesus before Pilate, the Second Time	15—31a	6—20a	13—25	39—40 / 19, 1—15	,, 14 / ,, 20
XXXV. The Passion Week — Friday. "Crucified."					**XXXV**
274. Jesus on the Way to Golgotha	27, 31b	15, 20b	23, 26a	19. 16. 17a	No. 1
275. Simon of Cyrene Compelled to Bear the Cross	32	21	26b		,, 2
276. Lamentation of the Daughters of Jerusalem			27—31		,, 4

INTRODUCTORY.

THE RECORDS.

The principal, and practically the only, sources of our knowledge of the life of Christ are the four canonical gospels, the first three of which are called the synoptic gospels. Very little, either in the few notices of Christ in the writings of non-Christian authors, in the references made to Christ in the other books of the New Testament, or in later Christian literature, adds to the information which the gospels already supply. The few additional sayings of Jesus and supposed incidents of His life found in the so-called apocryphal gospels are not only of questionable character, but altogether worthless as authority.

Of authors without the pale of Christendom who referred to Christ the following may be mentioned: —

1) *Josephus,* 94 A. D. There is the famous passage in Josephus, *Ant.,* XVIII, III, 3: "Now, about this time lived Jesus, a wise man, if indeed He should be called a man. For He was a doer of marvelous acts, a teacher of such men as receive the truth with pleasure; and He won over to Himself many Jews and many also of the Greek nation. He was the Christ. And when, on the indictment of the principal men among us, Pilate had sentenced Him to the cross, yet did not those who had loved Him at the first cease [to do so]; for He appeared to them alive again on the third day, as the divine prophets had declared — these and ten thousand other wonderful things — concerning Him. And even now the race of Christians, so named after Him, is not extinct." It is very likely that Josephus made some reference to Jesus, but most writers agree that the passage, if not entirely spurious, has been the subject of Christian revision. The present writer is inclined to accept its authenticity; but this is not the place to enter into the argument.

2) *Pliny the Younger,* 112 A. D. Pliny, writing from Bithynia to Trajan, refers to the Christians as meeting on certain days and singing hymns "to Christ as to a god." *Letters,* X, 96.

3) *Tacitus,* 117 A. D. The well-known Roman historian, in a passage relating to the persecution of Nero, tells how the Christians, already a great multitude, derived their name "from one

Christus, who was executed in the reign of Tiberius by the procurator of Judea, Pontius Pilate." *Annals,* XV, 44.

4) *Suetonius,* 120 A. D. In his *Lives of the Caesars* (Claudius, XXV, 4), Suetonius speaks of the Jews as expelled from Rome for the raising of tumults at the instigation of one "Chrestus," plainly a mistake for "Christus." Of course, Suetonius was mistaken about the cause of the disturbance, but the incident is doubtless that referred to in Acts 18, 2.

Of the ancient Christian apologists mention may be made of the following: —

1) *Quadratus,* 125 A. D. This missionary of apostolic times wrote an apology of the Christian faith and presented it to the Emperor Hadrian. The work has been lost; only a fragment has been preserved. Here is an interesting passage, which is found in the *Church History* of Eusebius: "But the works of our Savior were always present, for they were genuine. Those that were healed and those that were raised from the dead, who were seen not only when they were healed and when they were raised, but were also always present, — and not merely while the Savior was on earth, but also after His death, — they were alive for quite a while, so that some of them lived even to our day." Eusebius, *H. E.,* IV, 3.

2) *Aristides,* 125 A. D. In his *Apology,* likewise addressed to the Emperor Hadrian, Aristides has the following beautiful reference to Jesus: "Now, the Christians trace their origin from the Lord Jesus Christ. And He is acknowledged by the Holy Spirit to be the Son of the Most High, who came down from heaven for the salvation of men. And being born of a pure virgin, unbegotten and immaculate, He assumed flesh and revealed Himself among men that He might recall them Himself from their wandering after many gods. And having accomplished this wonderful dispensation, by a voluntary choice He tasted death on the cross, fulfilling an august dispensation. And after three days He came to life again and ascended into heaven." *Ante-Nicene Library,* Additional Volume, p. 259 ff.

3) *Justin Martyr,* 150 A. D. His *Apology,* addressed to the Emperor Antoninus Pius, contains the following references to the time, birth, and life of Christ: —

"Christ was born one hundred and fifty years ago under Cyrenius and subsequently, in the time of Pontius Pilate, taught what He said He taught." *First Apology,* XLVI.

"Our teacher of these things is Jesus Christ, who also was born for this purpose and was crucified under Pontius Pilate, proconsul of Judea, in the time of Tiberius Caesar." *Ibid.,* XIII.

"Now, there is a village in the land of the Jews [Bethlehem, mentioned before], thirty-five stadia from Jerusalem, in which Jesus was born, as you can ascertain also from the register of the taxing made under Cyrenius, your first procurator in Judea." *Ibid.,* XXXIV. We are giving these quotations without comment.

"And after He was crucified, they cast lots upon His vesture, and they that crucified Him parted it among them. And that these things did happen you can ascertain from the *Acts of Pontius Pilate." Ibid.,* XXXV.

"In these books, then, of the prophets we found Jesus, our Christ, foretold as coming, born of a virgin, growing up to man's estate, and healing every disease and every sickness, and raising the dead, and being hated, and unrecognized, and crucified, and dying, and rising again, and ascending into heaven, and being called the Son of God." *Ibid.,* XXXI.

THE WRITERS OF THE FOUR GOSPELS.

MATTHEW.

We do not know much about the writer of the Gospel according to St. Matthew. From the beginning of the postapostolic age he has been universally identified with the Apostle Matthew, and his gospel was placed first in order among the books of the New Testament. He was a disciple and apostle of the Lord, also called Levi, Matt. 10, 3; Luke 5, 27. When Jesus passed forth from Capernaum, "He saw a man named Matthew sitting at the receipt of custom and saith unto him, Follow Me. And he arose and followed Him," Matt. 9, 9. Matthew was a publican, a tax-collector, and as such belonged to that class of men whom the Jews mentioned in one breath with sinners. Tradition relates that he preached in Palestine for fifteen years and then went to the Ethiopians, Syrians, Persians, Parthians, and Medes. There is also a tradition which says that he died a natural death.

The apostolic origin and canonicity of the gospel which bears his name was accepted by the early Church. Barnabas (IV, also V), himself an apostolic father, quotes him distinctly with the formula: "It is written." Matt. 22, 14. And Origen refers to his book as the first of the four gospels which was received without doubt by the Church of God. Eusebius, *H. E.*, VI, 25. Its identity with our Matthew is confirmed by the undoubted presence of the gospel in the first gospel harmony, the *Diatessaron* of Tatian, Justin's pupil, which was written in Rome about 155 A. D. *Ante-Nicene Fathers,* Additional Vol., p. 43 ff.

The purpose of Matthew's gospel is indicated in almost every section of the book. His object was to prove to his fellow-countrymen that the entire life as well as the Passion, death, and resurrection of Jesus Christ is the fulfilment of the Old Testament prophecies concerning the Messiah. The continual repetition of the phrase "that it might be fulfilled" is abundant evidence of this.

The date of composition is probably 60—70 A. D. But it is unknown where this gospel was written. Ancient tradition has it that Matthew wrote it originally in Hebrew, rather Aramaic. Papias, Bishop of Hierapolis in Phrygia, wrote about 140 A. D.: "Matthew composed the Logia in the Hebrew dialect, and each

[4]

one interpreted them as he was able." Eusebius, *H. E.*, III, 39, 16. But this is a debatable question. It may be fairly inferred that Papias himself had this gospel in Greek. And there is no evidence that he had ever seen a copy of Matthew in Aramaic. Barnabas, who wrote before Papias, quotes the gospel of Matthew in Greek. If Matthew originally wrote in Aramaic, we must assume that he himself composed his gospel in Greek, too, for it strikes one as altogether an independent composition and not as a mere translation.

From a closer examination of the gospel itself, as compared with Mark and Luke, it is clear that the principle of arrangement of the material is not strictly chronological, but that of similarity of material. This is a problem which has always troubled the harmonists, especially in the arrangement of the material as contained between Matt. 8, 14, to 13, 58, some even supposing a shifting of pages in some ancient manuscripts. However, the supposition of a topical arrangement of this portion of the gospel best explains the matter.

MARK.

The writer of our second and shortest gospel has from the earliest times till now been identified with John Mark of Jerusalem, the son of a well-to-do woman by the name of Mary, in whose house the disciples were wont to gather, Acts 12, 12—17. He was a companion of Paul and Barnabas on their first mission journey, Acts 13, 5. His intimacy with Barnabas is explained by the fact that he was either his cousin or his nephew, Col. 4, 10. Through Barnabas he came in contact with Paul. But at that time he still lacked Christian fortitude and constancy; for at Perga, in Pamphylia, he left the two apostolic missionaries and returned to Jerusalem, much to the displeasure of Paul, Acts 13, 5. 13. When on the next journey Paul refused to take him along and Barnabas was willing to overlook the temporary weakness, there was a sharp contention over the matter between the two, with the result that Paul and Barnabas parted company, Barnabas taking Mark to Cyprus and Paul choosing Silas, Acts 15, 36—40. But later we find Mark again as one of the fellow-workers of Paul, who said he was of great assistance to him, Col. 4, 10. 11; Philemon 24; 2 Tim. 4, 11.

We, however, find Mark connected especially with Peter, whom he assisted in his work, whom he accompanied to "Babylon," 1 Pet. 5, 13, and as whose attendant and assistant he is particularly remembered in the early Christian Church. According to the earliest patristic statement, "Mark, having become the interpreter of Peter, wrote accurately what he remembered of the things said or done by Christ." Papias, in Eusebius, *H. E.*, III, 39. Mark is said to have lost one finger and that the nickname "stump-fingered" was given him on that account. Zahn, *Introduction to N. T.*, III, 428. He is represented as having been present at the death of Barnabas on Cyprus and then to have gone to Alexandria and there to have founded the first Church of St. Mark, of which he became the first bishop.

The gospel which bears his name was most likely written at Rome before the destruction of Jerusalem. Cf. Eusebius, *H. E.*, II, 14. 15. An outstanding characteristic of Mark is his realism, and his pithy style and vivid flashes of portrayal confirm the historicity of his gospel. All this is a guarantee of a first-hand historical record, a record such as might be expected from so lively a character as Peter, since, as Papias would have it, Mark neither saw the Lord nor followed Him. Eusebius, *H. E.*, II, 14. 15. The commentators speak of the "Petrine character" of his gospel.

As to the canonicity and the authenticity of this gospel there can be no doubt; for it is supported by the unanimous testimony of the ancient Church, as represented by writers from practically every quarter of the Roman world. Eusebius, quoting Origen, *H. E.*, VI, 25. With the theory which would make of Mark the first writer of the synoptic gospels, — the other writers following his lead, — we are not here concerned. The more we study the gospels in Greek, especially when we compare again and again every word of each account, the more we are convinced that the three Synoptists wrote independently of one another.

LUKE.

According to the testimony of early writers, Luke was, in a way, the interpreter of Paul as Mark was of Peter. While Luke does not mention his name, there is no reason to doubt the tradition transmitted by Eusebius that "the beloved physician" and companion of Paul is the author of the Acts of the Apostles and also of the gospel which bears his name. Eusebius, *H. E.*, III, 4. 28; V, 8; VI, 25. Cf. Col. 4, 14.

Of his personal history little is known. He had not known Jesus personally, but purposes to set forth faithfully "a declaration of those things which are most surely believed among us, even as they delivered them unto us which from the beginning were eye-witnesses and ministers of the Word," Luke 1, 1. 2.

By birth he seems to have been a Greek from Antioch and by profession a physician. He was probably converted by St. Paul in Antioch, where the disciples were first called Christians, and we find him connected with the great apostle in a lifelong, intimate friendship, 2 Tim. 4, 11. When Paul set out on his second missionary journey, Luke joined him at Troas and accompanied him to Philippi, Acts 16, 10—17 (the "we" passages). On the third missionary journey he was again with Paul, Acts 20, 5 ff. Afterwards he went with the now captive Paul to Rome, Acts 27, 1 ff.; and during the apostle's second captivity he was again with him, for which the apostle was duly thankful, 2 Tim. 4, 11.

Beyond these facts nothing definite is known as to circumstances either of his life or of his death. But from his own writings we may gather that Luke had received a good education, writing, as he does, in an easy, flowing, and elegant style, colored at points by the language of his profession, Luke 8, 43; Acts 28, 8, etc.; and he was a historian of the highest order.

That the early Church regarded the Book of Acts and the gospel of St. Luke as authentic is established by the fact that the Muratorian Canon, a Latin list of New Testament books, ca. 170 A. D., both names Luke the physician as the author and lists his gospel and Acts as Scripture and that his gospel was used as one of the four recognized gospels in the earliest Life of Christ, the *Diatessaron* of Tatian.

The date of writing of this gospel cannot be definitely fixed. But in order to meet the argument that Luke used the *Antiquities* of Josephus, which were published about 93 A. D., it might be said that Luke surely wrote his gospel before the year 70 A. D., since there is no reference to the destruction of Jerusalem, concerning which a complete prophecy is given in Luke 21. From the last verses in Acts it is probable that this book was written before the death of St. Paul, 67 or 68 A. D. And Luke's gospel preceded his Acts. Cf. Acts 1, 1.

In spite of the difficulties that for a long time puzzled historians we now find that Luke is not only reliable, but that he is *the* historian among the New Testament writers. Luke cannot only be checked up with history, but history ought to be compared with Luke.

JOHN.

We have no right to declare one Biblical writer more reliable than another or where one account is apparently out of harmony with another to credit one writer at the expense of the other. But there are qualities in John's gospel on account of which his book, being that of "the beloved disciple," has won first place in the hearts of many Christian readers. Looking at the matter from the point of view of the historian, we have to say that as an eye-witness from the beginning to the end he was singularly able to tell the truth. In addition, we must consider his remarkably long life and the fact that he who heard the Lord formed the connecting link between the apostolic generation and other remarkable men living well along into the second century. All this confirms the reliability and trustworthiness of his account. There is Irenaeus, since 177 A. D. bishop of Lyons, who had spent his early childhood in Asia Minor, where he heard the preaching of the aged bishop Polycarp of Smyrna (died 156 A. D.). And Polycarp had heard John, who had heard the Lord. Eusebius, *H. E.,* V, 20; III, 14.

Although the writer of our fourth gospel does not expressly mention his name, he describes himself with sufficient clearness, so that there is no doubt that he is one of the sons of the Galilean fisherman Zebedee and his wife Salome and "the beloved disciple" of the Lord, John 13, 23. 25; 19, 26. A close comparison of a few passages has suggested the inference — although some do not accept it — that Mary, the mother of Jesus, and Salome, the wife of Zebedee, were sisters, which made John a cousin of Jesus, placed him all the nearer to the Lord, and commends him to us all the more as a reliable and trustworthy biographer of Christ, Matt. 27, 56; Mark 15, 40; John 19, 25.

In his earlier days John had been a disciple of John the Baptist, by whom he was directed to Christ. This was an experience which he never forgot; for he records for us even the hour of the day when he first met Jesus, John 1, 39. Together with Peter and his own brother James he later became one of the most confidential disciples of Christ, and he was with the Lord as an eye- and ear-witness of all the Master's labors, journeyings, discourses, miracles, His crucifixion, resurrection, and ascension.

In contradistinction to the fiery character of Peter, — although in his earlier days he evinced a fiery temper himself, Mark 3, 17; Luke 9, 49. 54, — he was one of those quiet, modest, unassuming personalities, who avoid even the mention of their own name, and of a receptive nature, following every move and listening most intently to every word of the Lord.

It seems that John, writing later than the other three evangelists, was acquainted with the synoptic gospels. In fact, it seems that it was his purpose to supply what the other evangelists had omitted in their account. Thus we have in John the particulars of the early Judean ministry of Jesus and His various journeys to Jerusalem.

Of his later life, history reports that he went to Asia Minor, probably after the death of St. Paul, that Emperor Domitian, in 95 A. D., banished him to the island of Patmos, where he wrote the Apocalypse (cf. Rev. 1, 9), and that, after regaining his liberty, he returned to Ephesus, where he died about 100 A. D.

His gospel was evidently written shortly before the end of the century. It is undeniably present as one of the four interwoven gospels in the harmony of Tatian. This work, the *Diatessaron*, begins with the prolog and ends with the last verse in the appendix of St. John. The Gospel according to St. John is listed in the Muratorian Canon. And Eusebius says that the gospel of St. John has been known and accepted by all the Christian churches under the sun. Eusebius, *H. E.*, III, 24.

for grace." This statement can be made because "the Law was given by Moses, but grace and truth came by Jesus Christ." Thus "the Word" is formally identified with Jesus Christ. The Law conveys no knowledge of the grace of God, but in this wonderful incarnation the grace of God has been revealed. "No man hath seen God at any time; the only-begotten Son, which is in the bosom of the Father, He hath declared Him."

CHAPTER I.

THE STATE OF THE WORLD.

1.

The time was ripe for the coming of Christ. In all the world's history there never was such a combination of favorable circumstances for the birth of Christ and the introduction of Christianity — political, social, economic, intellectual, linguistic, religious, and moral — as that which Divine Providence itself had foreseen

The Roman Empire. and provided "in the fulness of the time." [1] Daniel's mighty kingdom of iron was reaching the height of its power.[2] In ever-widening circles the legions of Rome were extending her boundaries — from Rome to all of Italy, to the neighboring isles, to Carthage, to the right, to the left, until finally all the countries of the Mediterranean Basin were crushed under their iron heels or had voluntarily accepted the Roman peace. The whole world was at rest. From the wooded swamps of Britain to the sands of Egypt, from the Pillars of Hercules to far-off Mesopotamia, the famous *pax Romana* prevailed. And it was to prevail for centuries to come.

2.

There had been mighty empires in the ancient world. History relates, 'and archeology reveals, the glories of the early Babylonian, the Egyptian, the Assyrian, the Chaldean, the Persian, and the Macedonian past. And even Israel had had its brief spell of

Asiatic Monarchies. political glory. But in general these older empires owed their rise to the success and ability of some adventurous conqueror, and when the master-hand was withdrawn, they fell asunder or were swept away to make room for some new kingdom or dynasty which sprang up with the same rapidity and in its turn experienced the same fate.[1] This refers in particular to a number of ancient Asiatic kingdoms, but it is also true of the Greek monarchy established by Alexander, which, issuing from Europe, was broken up at his death into several conflicting kingdoms and yet survived in its influence and passed on to its heirs an heirloom of far-reaching importance.

1,　1) Gal. 4, 4.　　2) Dan. 2, 40.
2,　1) H. H. Milman, *History of Christianity*, 21.

3.

But with the coming of the Romans a new era began. The Roman monarchy was founded on principles hitherto unknown. Ruthless conquest was not followed by oppression, but by a government in which conscious strength was tempered with consideration for local customs and which insured military protection, public safety, and domestic peace.[1] This refers of course to the general policy, not to local tyranny, which was so often practised by the individual provincial governor. By this general policy the edifice of Roman power was gradually built up, and it was preserved by

Roman Principle of Moderation.
the wisdom of the ages. Here was the first empire that endured for a long period of time and whose yoke was rather endurable. In view of its size, its character, its composition, its lasting structure, and its success it can justly be called the grandest political achievement ever accomplished by man.[2] With it the monarchies of Alexander, of Charlemagne, and of Napoleon cannot be compared. Greeks, Romans, Gauls, Britons, Jews, Syrians, Egyptians, were all peacefully and seemingly permanently united in one *communis omnium patria*. The general principle of government was wise and yet simple as well as beneficent. The various nationalities, though differing among themselves, felt as one. Their obedience to the central government, upon the whole, was voluntary, uniform, and permanent. The vanquished nations, blended into one great people, resigned the hope, nay, even the wish of resuming their independence and scarcely considered their own existence as distinct from the existence of Rome.[3]

4.

Never before had so many nations been so bloodily conquered and so peacefully ruled. The established authority of the Caesars was exercised with the same facility on the Thames, the Orontes,

Voluntary Submission.
and the Nile as on the banks of the Tiber.[1] The Thracians were kept in subjection by two thousand Roman guards; the Dalmatians lived in peace under a single Roman legion. Nearly eighty years the tribes of Gaul had fought for independence, and now they sub-

---

3, 1) S. Angus, "Roman Empire and Christianity," in the *International Standard Bible Encyclopedia.*

2) Charles Merivale in Myers's *General History*, 200.

3) Edward Gibbon, *Decline and Fall of the Roman Empire*, I, 55.

4, 1) Josephus, *The Jewish War*, II, 16, 4. Agrippa's speech against Roman war.

mitted to the orders of twelve hundred men. A single legion sufficed to govern Spain. But one legion was quartered in Northern Africa. And a few legions curbed far-reaching Egypt and the proud nobility of Greece. While it was still necessary to keep the German peace with eight Roman legions and to pacify the Britons with four, generally speaking, the conquered nations bowed respectfully to the proud Roman mistress and believed their own best interests to coincide with the common interests of Rome.

5.

Thus Rome blended the nations and prepared them for the preaching of the Gospel among them. With the exception of a few inconsequential barbarian tribes beyond well-patrolled frontiers and outside the interest of the Roman horizon, now for the first time we may speak of "the world" as embracing universal humanity or the *genus humanum.*[1] For practical purposes it was 'H OIKOΥMENH. the whole then known world, united and largely at rest. With her enemies conquered, peace everywhere established, her program of expansion concluded, with Europe, Asia, and Africa firmly united, and her own civil wars ended, Rome finally settled down on January 16, 27 B. C., to put the principle of the empire formally into operation. This was the day when Gaius Octavius became *Imperator* Caesar Augustus and was invested with absolute power under republican titles. That was the best thing that could be done under the circumstances. For after the Battle of Actium, Augustus found himself at the head of nearly forty veteran Roman legions and the Roman world at his feet.

6.

Happily for the tranquillity of mankind and for the coming of the Prince of Peace, whose advent he was unwittingly to usher in, Caesar Augustus was himself a prince of peace. His imperial policy was not aggression, but firm, yet peaceful administration.[1] He was satisfied to relinquish the ambitious design of subduing the Caesar Augustus. whole earth and to preserve those dominions which had been won in the first seven centuries of the history of Rome. He concluded his last will and testament, written in his own hand, with the counsel to his successors never to aim at an extension of the empire.[2] And this

---

5, 1) Luke 2, 1.
6, 1) Gibbon, *Rome,* I, 2. 3.   2) Tacitus, *Annales,* I, XI.

policy was, on the whole, adhered to by the Julian-Claudian line
in the period with which we are now concerned, that is, during the
life of Christ and in the first days of the Christian Church. Three
times during the reign of Augustus the doors of the temple of
Janus Quirinus were closed.[3]

7.

Ever since the dawn of history there had been a gradual inter-
mingling of peoples around the shores of the Mediterranean Sea.
Early Phenician settlers formed colonies in Northern Africa and
Spain; but in the course of time many of them were made citizens
of Rome. The same honors were conferred upon Greek settlers of
Italy, Sicily, Sardinia, Corsica, and Southern Gaul. As a result
of the many wars, deportations, captivities, and colonizations the
Oriental peoples had already become thoroughly acquainted with
one another. After the Macedonian conquests the whole East was
covered with Greek colonies and cities. Greeks settled everywhere
as professors, merchants, physicians, artists, actors, and acrobats.
And now, with the coming of Rome, the East was to become
thoroughly and permanently acquainted with the West. The
members of each nationality discovered how much they really had
in common with one another. While the Greeks brought civilization and culture, the Romans brought law, order, and peace; and
the entire nation was to enjoy the blessings of both groups of gifts.

Cosmopolitanism. This peaceful and ordered state of affairs
in the empire contributed largely to the
spread of the cosmopolitanism already in progress. In an empire
which was international in character it was but natural that national
barriers were largely removed. The great cities of the empire,
Rome, Alexandria, Jerusalem, Antioch, and others, became meeting-
places of all races and languages. The polyglot character of the
legions recruited from every quarter of the empire was in itself
a contributing factor in the breaking up of national barriers. On
the front, soldiers of various nationalities fought their battles,
became companions in arms, and then returned to their distant
homes as brothers. While it had previously been no strange experience for Jews and Egyptians, Germans and Gauls, to meet one
another in Rome, one could now frequently see blond hair and blue
eyes in the marts and camps even of the East. When after the

6, 3) Suetonius, *Augustus,* XXII. They were open only during war.
And they had been closed but twice before in the 700 years since the founding
of Rome.

death of Cleopatra the services of her splendid body-guard of four hundred Gauls were no longer needed in Alexandria, Augustus generously made them over to Herod.[1) There were Germans in Jerusalem at the time of the birth of Christ. When Herod the Great died, his body was transported to its resting-place under the escort of a Thracian-German-Gallic guard.[2) During Christ's sojourn on earth, until the last Jewish war, the stalwart and burly figures of Germans were familiar sights in the streets of Jerusalem.[3)

8.

Originally the Romans were little more than conquering barbarians, who had small regard for civilization and culture. Already they had wiped out two ancient and in some respects superior civilizations, those of Etruria and Carthage, so that hardly a trace of them remained. The ancient languages and dialects of Italy, for instance, the Sabine, the Etruscan, and the Venetian, sank into oblivion. The language of the conqueror, though with some inevitable mixture or corruption, was adopted in Italy, Africa, Spain, and Gaul, and only in the mountains or among the peasants faint traces of the Punic, Celtic, or other idioms were preserved. It was, however, but a cold civilization which the conquered nations received from the children of Mars. And it is hard to conceive what a scourge Rome would have proved to the world had she merely

Domination of Greek Culture. continued in her victorious course without the tempering influence of superior civilization and culture. The shades of night would have descended upon the Roman world. But with the conquest of Greece untutored Mars came under the spell of cultured Pallas Athene.[1) Intellectually victorious Rome was herself subdued by the arts of Greece. The immortal writers of classical Greece, Homer, Sophocles, Herodotus, Aristotle, and others, still the bogy of the college student and the admiration of his teacher, were soon made the favorite objects of Roman study and imitation. Of course, these elegant pastimes were not suffered to interfere with the more serious business of the *pax Romana* and the policies of imperial rule. Nevertheless the contact was of the greatest importance. It marked the end of a pure, independent Latin civili-

7, 1) Heinrich Graetz, *History of the Jews*, II, 103. Josephus, *Wars*, I, XX, 3.
2) Josephus, *Antiquities*, XVII, VIII, 3; *Wars*, I, XXXII, 9.
3) Josephus, *Wars*, II, XVI, 4.
8, 1) Gibbon, *Rome*, I, 46.

zation — if there ever had been any — and the beginning of a culture known as the Greco-Roman civilization. Latin poets and historians might complain that captured Hellas led captive her captor,[2] but it was a good thing that it happened. For thus Christ was ushered into a civilized and Greek-speaking world.[3]

9.

While it must be admitted that Roman protection and the adoption of Greek culture were of the greatest importance, it must be pointed out that this factor has been wrongly represented as a *praeparatio evangelica.* Socrates, Plato, Aristotle, the eclecticism of Greek thought, and Stoic philosophy cannot be called school-masters leading men to Christ.

Must Not be Regarded as a Praeparatio Evangelica. For, after all, Greek civilization, in spite of some beautiful aspects, was pagan, degenerate, and corrupt. Its true character was quickly recognized, even in Rome. The simplicity, frugality, and morality of an earlier day were replaced by Oriental extravagance, luxury, and vice. Along with the many helpful elements of culture which the Romans had received from the East, they also received the germs of moral and social disease. And "to learn Greek is to learn knavery" became a proverb in Rome.[1]

10.

In its far-reaching consequences, however, one of the results of the Greco-Roman civilization was to be of the greatest importance. Though not Greek civilization as such, yet the world-wide spread and dominating influence of the Greek language was a most valuable aid to the cause of Christ's kingdom. As a result of the Macedonian conquests not only Greek thought and culture pervaded the entire East, but also the Greek language was generally spoken by the people from Asia Minor to India. The Greek language had been previously known and spoken in the many Greek colonies of the Mediterranean Basin along with Latin and

The Greek Language Aids the Spread of the Gospel. everywhere except where forcibly and successfully suppressed; but now it had entered, and permanently established itself in, even the strangest surroundings. Who would have dreamed of finding flourishing

---

8,   2) *Graecia capta ferum victorem cepit.*
      3) S. Angus, in *Int. St. B. Encycl.,* under "Roman Empire and Christianity."
9,   1) Myers, *General History,* 178.

Greek cities in the land of Israel [1] and among the extraordinarily home-loving Palestinian Jews? Thus our Savior was intimately brought into contact with Greek and occasionally may have spoken it. Greek was even officially recognized by the Jews as a proper language for religious services. Their sacred writings, the Old Testament, had been translated into Greek. [2] Some of their books, not part of the canon, did not have to be translated, because they had been originally written in Greek. [3] The inscription on the wall of the outer Temple court in Jerusalem forbidding Gentiles to enter under pain of death was posted in Greek. [4]

11.

And when the Romans came upon the scene, they found the Greek language so widely known and so deeply rooted that they could not hope to suppress it. Indeed, they did not even try to do so. Merely asserting the dignity of the Latin tongue and employing it in the administration of civil and military affairs in their Eastern dominions, they were glad to accept the Greek language as a common means of communication. And so it came about, at first in the East, but gradually throughout the whole empire, that the language of Alexander became both the language of the gospels and the *lingua franca* of the Greco-Roman world. It was used to a much greater extent in the Roman Empire than Latin. [1] It was almost impossible in any province to find a Roman subject of liberal education ignorant of Greek. [2] No business man of consequence could afford

Greek Adopted as a World Language by the Romans.

to be a stranger to Greek. Due to an overestimate of Greek literature the only books read, studied, and imitated as to style — except Law, and that for good reasons — were Greek. So it was in Alexandria, in Jerusalem, in Antioch, in Rome, yes, even in Cadiz and Lyons. Alexander's ambitions of a world-conquest had in a way been fulfilled. His language was spoken from the many Alexandrias which had been founded, in Babylonia, in Africa, etc., to the statue of Alexander before which Julius Caesar had sighed in Spain. [3] It is true, his kingdom was shattered, having

10, 1) The Decapolis.   2) The Septuagint, LXX.
     3) The apocryphal books: Additions to Daniel and Esther, Second Maccabees, Wisdom of Solomon, and others.
     4) Deissmann, *Licht vom Osten*, 63.
11, 1) Deissmann, *Licht vom Osten*, 50.
     2) Gibbon, I, 47.   3) Suetonius, *Julius*, VII.

been largely swallowed up by Rome, but his language remained. His successors, the masters of Rome, themselves studied it and were able to use it. Julius Caesar did not say, *"Et tu, Brute?"* as usually reported, but his dying words were Greek.[4] Some of the famous sayings of Augustus were originally uttered in Greek.[5] Tiberius understood Greek.[6] Caligula could quote Homeric verses,[7] Nero, it seems, could compose imitations of them on the spot,[8] and Marcus Aurelius, though born in Rome, in 121 A. D., nevertheless wrote his philosophy in Greek.

12.

It was but natural that the early Christian Church was Greek. With its universal appeal it could hardly be anything else. The gospels were written in Greek. St. Paul writes an epistle to the capital city of a Latin empire — and is understood — in Greek. In fact, all the early Christian writings which appeared in what would

The Early Christian Church Was Greek. seem the Latin half of the empire, the *Epistles of Clement,* the *Shepherd* of Hermas, the *Apology* of Tatian, and others, were Greek. The Christian churches of the first three hundred years, East and West, their language, their confessions, their hymns, their liturgy,[1] and many vestiges and traditions were Greek. And Latin Christianity, when it did come, did not originate in Rome, but in Africa.[2] We find the very same thing in Gaul. Irenaeus, Bishop of Lyons, wrote in Greek. And the first Christians in what is now France were settled in Greek cities, which owned Marseilles as their parent.[3]

13.

The Greek language as an aid to the cause of Christ can hardly be overestimated. Without it the spread of Christianity would hardly have been possible. Latin never was popular in the East. As late as the third century A. D. Cornelius of Rome writes to Fabius of Antioch in Greek. When Cyprian, Bishop of Carthage, Northern Africa, also wrote to Fabius, but in Latin, Eusebius,

---

11, 4) *Ibid., LXXXII.*

5) More haste, less speed.   Better a safe commander than a bold. *Ibid., Augustus, XXV.*

6) *Ibid., Tiberius, XXI.*   7) *Ibid., Caligula, XXII.*

8) *Ibid., Nero, XXXVIII.* Tacitus, *Annales,* XV, 39.

12, 1) The *Kyrie Eleison* has survived to the present day.

2) Tertullian in Carthage. Milman, *Hist. of Lat. Christianity,* I, 55.

3) Founded by Greeks 600 B. C.

reporting it,[1] almost considered it an innovation. And as the West, centering around the Bishop of Rome, gradually became Latin, a separation took place. It was a separation of Latin and Greek, of East and West, in Church and empire. And it really was a loss to the world in more than one respect. Was it that

Separation of East and West.

a faithful ally had withdrawn? Is it not remarkable that after a thousand years, just before the Reformation, it was again the Greek language which was to usher in a revival of learning and incidentally to serve the cause of the Reformation, the dispelling of spiritual darkness and the dispensing of the saving light of "the everlasting Gospel through Luther"?

14.

Before modern discoveries in archeology proved beyond the possibility of doubt that New Testament Greek was really the Greek spoken, written, and understood throughout the first Christian century of the Roman empire, Biblical scholars were long at a loss and at loggerheads with one another as to its linguistic classification. But it is now clear [1] that the language of the gospels, while not on a par with literary Attic, is not by any means a sort of corrupt Jewish-Greek nor a distinctive creation of the Holy Ghost,[2] but that it was in all essential respects simply the Greek vernacular of the first century A. D. It was the *lingua franca* of the Greco-Roman Empire and the legacy of Alexander the Great, namely, a world-speech, with Attic as the base, but affected and

The Koine.

influenced by dialectal and provincial idioms. Just as the language used in these pages is not the English of Shakespeare or of Addison, but the language commonly used in the present-day English-speaking world, so the Greek of Paul and John does not compare unfavorably with the style of Greek authors of those days. For had they used a Greek of special creation or as corrupted by the Jews, how could they have been understood by readers of Greek descent? But as it was, the Lord

---

13, 1) *Eccl. Hist.*, VI, 43.

14, 1) From paypri, ostraca, and inscriptions. Ad. Deissmann, *Licht vom Osten,* 53 ff.

2) Cremer, in his *Biblico-Theological Lexicon of the N. T. Greek,* quoting Rothe. See also Ad. Deissmann, *Licht vom Osten,* 55: "*Streit der Puristen und Hebraisten. — Dass die Heilige Schrift allermindestens in das klassische Sprachgewand eines Demosthenes und Plato gekleidet sein muesse, das erschien vielen als selbstverstaendlich, und gegenteilige Behauptungen empfand man als ein Attentat auf den Heiligen Geist. Wir unsererseits stehen auf seiten derer, die den wilden Rosenstrauch nicht deshalb fuer unschoen halten, weil er keine gloire de Dijon traegt.*"

in His wisdom used the existing world-language as a means of preparing the world for the reception of the message of Christ. The *koine* was the language which Christ heard and probably also used at times, although Aramaic was His native tongue. There really exists an intimate linguistic bond therefore between all students of the Greek New Testament and their Master in the very words presented in the Greek of the gospels according to Matthew, Mark, Luke, and John.

15.

A cruel hand of destiny seems to have "sifted the house of Israel among all nations, like as corn is sifted in a sieve; yet shall not the least grain fall upon the earth";[1] and still this sifting of Israel among all nations is one of the marvels of divine purpose in preparing the advent of Christ. In addition to the above we may mention another circumstance that aided the spreading of Christianity. We read in the Old Testament that Shalmaneser, the king of Assyria, "took Samaria and carried Israel [the ten tribes] away

The Jewish Dispersion. into Assyria and placed them in Halah and in Habor, by the river of Gozan, and in the cities of the Medes."[2] Judah, about 125 years later, met with a like fate when Nebuchadnezzar, the king of Babylon, swooped down upon the southern kingdom and "carried away all Jerusalem, and all the princes, and all the mighty men of valor, even ten thousand captives, and all the craftsmen and smiths," so that only the poorest in the land remained.[3] Besides these there were other captivities. Ptolemy I of Egypt, who, after capturing Jerusalem 320 B. C., took many Jews with him to Egypt, added largely to the Jewish population of Alexandria.[4] Antiochus the Great of Syria, 223—187 B. C., removed 2,000 Jewish families, whose ancestors had elected to remain in Babylon when Cyrus, 538 B. C., permitted the Jews to return to the land of their fathers, from that city and settled them in Phrygia and Lydia.[5] And after his capture of Jerusalem, Pompey,[6] 63 B. C., carried off hundreds of Jews to be sold as slaves in Rome.

16.

There was, however, also a voluntary immigration of Jews, for the purpose of trade and commerce, into all the chief cities of the ancient world.[1] Nearly a million Jews are said to have settled

15, 1) Amos 9, 9.   2) 2 Kings 17, 6.
    3) 2 Kings 24, 14.   4) Josephus, *Ant.*, XII, 1.
    5) *Ibid.*, XII, 3, 4.   6) *Ibid.*, XIV, 4; *Wars*, I, 7.
16, 1) Already in the time of Jeremiah, and against the will of the prophet, Jer. 43, 4—7.

in Egypt alone.[2] For the sake of consolidating their possessions, the Diadochi, the successors of Alexander, attracted masses of Jewish settlers into their newly founded towns. Attractive offers were made, rights of citizenship and other privileges were granted.[3]

Voluntary Jewish Emigration. As a consequence the seed of Abraham was found in large numbers in every section of the Roman world; at the mouths of all principal rivers, the Nile, the Euphrates, the Tigris, and the Danube; in all the principal cities of the empire, Alexandria, Antioch, Damascus, Athens, Corinth, Thessalonica, and Rome; on the islands of the Mediterranean; from Babylonia to the south of France and Spain; and myriads in Parthia beyond the Roman Empire.[4] Thus even in ancient times the total numbers of the Jews in the Diaspora were not to be counted by the thousands, but by the millions.[5]

17.

When the Roman conquerors came upon the scene, they witnessed the strange spectacle of a scattered race and millions of potential disturbers of the peace within their borders. In the interest of the *pax Romana* they bestowed upon a despised population particular favors and protection. This was a wise move. At home the Jews were the greatest revolutionists, but abroad the staunchest loyalists and supporters of Rome.[1] The

Roman Protection of Jewish Settlers. loyalists and supporters of Rome.[1] The Roman senate at one time had a special circular letter written in their favor and sent it to all the kings of the East and to all the cities, islands, and provinces of the Mediterranean, where presumably a larger or smaller number of Jews was to be found.[2] Because they established religious colonies wherever they went and at the same time kept in touch with Jerusalem and the Temple, it is not at all surprising that on Pentecost Day Jews from every quarter of the Roman Empire could be addressed and a contact established for the message of the Gospel in the uttermost parts of the earth.[3]

16, 2) H. Graetz, *History of the Jews,* II, 201.

3) Schuerer, *History of the Jewish People in the Time of Christ,* II, II, 220.

4) Josephus, *Ant.,* XI, V, 2. Graetz, *ibid.,* II, 203.

5) Graetz, *ibid.,* II, 223.

17, 1) Suetonius, *Julius,* LIX.

2) 1 Macc. 15, 15 ff.

3) Acts 2, 9—12.

18.

Also in an economic and material respect the world was ripe
for the coming of Christ. It was but natural for commerce to
follow order and peace. Travel was safe by land and sea. The
pirates had been destroyed by Gnaeus Pompeius, and after the death
of Sextus Pompeius no hostile maritime forces remained. And as
to intercommunication by land, it was one of Rome's first concerns
in her policy of expansion to secure her conquests by means of
splendid military roads. Rome's road-building campaign, begun
in 312 B. C. with the construction of the Via Appia, was continued
until all parts of the empire were connected with one another by
well-kept highways issuing from the capital, passing through the
provinces, and terminating only at the frontiers.[1] Road-houses

**Roman Roads as a
Praeparatio Evangelica.**
were erected everywhere at a distance of only a few miles from
each other. Each of them was
constantly provided with horses, and by the help of relays it
was possible to cover a hundred miles in a single day.[2] In the
first century of the Christian era it was possible to travel, by
land or sea, through the length and breadth of the empire, from
Alexandria to Cadiz or from Jerusalem to York, with safety and
comfort, and all this also in the service of the Gospel, which five
centuries later would have been well-nigh impossible.[3] The
great system of well-constructed Roman highways and bridges,
which in some places have not to this day entirely yielded to the
devastating efforts of nearly two thousand years,[4] served not only
the legions and imperial escorts and made possible the carrying
out of the decree of Emperor Caesar Augustus that "all the world
should be taxed," but were of equal service in conveying the message
of the ambassadors of Christ to all parts of the then known world.

19.

But there was one thing that Rome could not offer its subjects.
It could give them a wonderful government, peace, protection, culture, commerce, a universal language, prosperity, good roads, and
material blessings, but it was not able to supply them with a religion
satisfying human needs. The religion which the original Romans

---

18, 1) Gibbon, *Rome*, I, 63.
    2) Suetonius, *Julius*, LVII; *Augustus*, XLIX.
    3) For an interesting itinerary from York to Jerusalem, 3,740 miles,
see Gibbon, *Rome*, I, 63, n. 85.
    4) See beautiful full-page photograph of Roman bridge over upper
Jordan River in *Int. Stand. Bible Encycl.*, IV, 2602.

practised was extremely simple. Even the usual idols of paganism were missing. The mysterious influences or forces of nature which were supposed to direct the visible phenomena of the physical world were considered the "powers"[1] whose favor was necessary to the

Negative "Preparation."

material prosperity of man. The objects around which this worship centered — not so much as objects of worship, but rather as symbols for the forces for which they stood — were the fireplace, the pantry,[2] the door,[3] the spear,[4] and others. Especially the spear, because, betraying their warlike proclivities, the Romans delighted to call themselves the children of Mars. And since their gods were not originally conceived as having human form, it was not necessary to carve out their likenesses or to cast them into a certain form; besides, they did not know how. A spear stuck into the ground represented Mars. But later when they came into contact with the Etruscans and Greeks, they discovered that their gods were all given a human form. And so Etruscan artists were called upon to aid them in giving a respectable appearance to their local gods.

20.

In her march of conquest, however, Rome was confronted with a serious problem. While it was a rather simple matter to impose the terms of Roman peace upon those who fell before her arms, she was at a loss as to what should be done with the gods of the newly conquered nations. Of course, her own gods must have been stronger; else how explain the victories? In some cases the defeated nations could be induced to forsake their inefficient protectors. But though the deities of the conquered nations could not withstand the mightier gods of the invading Romans, yet the existence of the defeated divinities was not denied.[1] But suppose the foreign divin-

Polytheism.

ities should unite and fight against the Roman gods? That would not be according to the policy of *"Divide et impera,"* and it would not be conducive to the expansion of Rome. And so, to solve a problem which might conceivably prove rather vexatious, both the conquered nations and their gods were admitted as members into the empire. The foreign gods were treated with marked respect and invited to transfer their

---

19,   1) *Numina,* not *dei.*

    2) *Lares et penates.* The hearth as symbolizing the family and home and the pantry, or cupboard, as symbolizing food and provisions.

    3) Janus, probably as a symbol of peace and safety.   4) Mars.

20,   1) H. H. Milman, *History of Christianity,* 22.

abode to hospitable Rome and to bestow their favors upon it. Their votaries were granted a license or privilege, and their worship was recognized as a fully accredited Roman religion.[2] This was done according to the principle of Roman religious liberty and toleration. The Christian persecution of a later day was a different matter and need not concern us here. All religions were considered by the people as equally true, by the philosophers as equally false, and by the rulers as equally useful.[3]

21.

However, not only gods, but also superstition, magic, sorcery, immorality, vice, and every form of corruption flourished under the Roman sun. Rome was a cesspool of everything infamous and

Bankruptcy of Paganism. abominable.[1] The religious life and morals of imperial Rome were hopelessly steeped in paganism and polytheism and were utterly corrupt. Every throne was occupied, the throne of power, art, law, and culture; also the thrones of vice and sin; but one throne was vacant, the throne which Christ was to fill.

22.

And was He expected? Owing to a few remarks made by secular writers concerning a belief prevalent that a deliverer was to come from the East, the claim is often made that Messianic expectations were universal in the Roman Empire. We are told that Rome was awaiting the coming of Christ. But these references — Suetonius,[1] Tacitus,[2] and Josephus [3] — related in connection with

20, 2) *Religio licita.* Among these was also the Jewish religion.

3) Gibbon, I, 34. Augustus rebuilt eighty-two heathen temples in Rome.

21, 1) Tacitus, *Annales*, XV, 45; Rom. 1, 25 ff.

22, 1) *Titus*, IV, at the time of the last Jewish war: "There had spread over all the Orient an old and established belief that it was fated at that time for men coming from Judea to rule the world. This prediction, referring to the emperor of Rome, as afterwards appeared from the event, the people of Judea took to themselves."

2) *Histories*, V, 13, also referring to the last Jewish war: "The greater part had a firm belief that it was contained in the old sacerdotal books that at this very time the East would prevail and that some that came out of Judea should obtain the empire of the world, which obscure oracle foretold Vespasian and Titus. But the generality of the common people, as usual, indulged in their own inclination."

3) *Wars*, VI, V, 4, likewise referring to the last Jewish war: "But what more than all else incited them [the Jews] to war was an ambiguous oracle, likewise found in their sacred Scriptures, to the effect that at that time one of their country would become ruler of the world. This they

the destruction of Jerusalem and interpreted as referring to Titus or Vespasian, can rather be adduced as an indirect historical proof that Christ had come than as an example of a wide-spread expecta-

Messianic Expectations. tion of a Messiah who was to come.[4] Two other references — the *Sibylline Oracles* [5] and the "Messianic" *Eclogue* of Vergil [6] — are too vague to merit any serious consideration. But for the sake of argument, supposing that they actually referred to Christ, they would not have proved the existence of a universal expectation in the Roman world. And while it is true that the hope of a coming Redeemer was never absent in the heart of believing Israelites and that many with whom those of them who lived in heathen countries came into contact may have received some glimmering of Israel's hope, the world at large was in ignorance of, and not consciously prepared for, the coming of Christ. Indeed, to a large extent the Jews themselves were ignorant [7] of the true nature of the promised kingdom and its King. The time, however, as we have seen, God's time, was ripe for the coming of Christ.

---

understood to mean some one of their own race, and many of their wise men went astray in their interpretation of it. The oracle, however, in reality signified the sovereignty of Vespasian, who was proclaimed emperor on Jewish soil." Thus Josephus proves that he knew of the true Messianic expectations of his people, but that he himself did not share them and was base enough to deny and betray them.

22, 4) John 1, 10.

5) III, 652—6. In its oldest part, 170 B. C., there occurs the brief prediction of a king whom God shall send from the sun, "who shall cause the whole earth to cease from wicked war, killing some and exacting faithful oaths from others." The general picture of Messianic times presented is generally admitted to have formed the basis of Vergil's dream of the Golden Age. See Edersheim, I, 172. 203.

6) This *Eclogue* (IV) of Vergil, 70—19 B. C., celebrates the birth of a child, though there was no agreement as to who this child was whose birth was to be coincident with the advent of a new era and who, after filling the other great offices of state, was to "rule with his father's virtues the world at peace." On account of this supposed prophecy of the coming Christ, Vergil became so popular in the Middle Ages as to be almost considered an unwitting instrument of the Holy Ghost.

7) Rom. 9, 32; 11, 25.

CHAPTER II.

THE STATE OF THE JEWS.

1.

The scepter had departed from Judah, but not yet completely. This did not happen definitely until the removal of Archelaus in 6 A. D.,[1] when Judea was turned into a Roman province and even the last slender thread of Maccabean connection was broken and

The Scepter of Judah. the Jews themselves volunteered the admission: "We have no king but Caesar."[2] But until the coming of Christ, according to divine promise,[3] the scepter continued with the descendants of Judah, at least nominally, or, which was equivalent, in the hands of the Levite high priests, who adhered to them. Let us briefly review the circumstances which brought about this state of affairs.

2.

The key to Israel's involved history lies in the geographical position of the country, in its relation to the surrounding nations. It is often called the Holy Land, because it was hallowed by the footsteps of our Savior. The Land of Israel it is still lovingly called in the Hebrew readers of the Jewish schools; but in our geographical text-books the name given it is Palestine. This is,

אֶרֶץ יִשְׂרָאֵל however, really a misnomer; for, etymologically denoting the territory of the Philistines, it is made to include an area which at times was claimed by the Hebrews, but was never settled by them, and to exclude the outlying sections really belonging to the *Erets Israel*, the Land of Israel.[1] However, in the proverbial expression "from Dan to Beersheba"[2] an indication of the normal north-to-south limits of the Land of Israel has been preserved. A small land, but 150 miles in length and 25—80 miles in breadth, with a total area of about 7,000 square miles, — not as large as Massachusetts or

---

1, 1) Or still later, when the destruction of Jerusalem brought final proof that the Savior had come.

2) John 18, 15.   3) Gen. 49, 10.

2, 1) The territory from the "River of Egypt" to the "entrance of Hamath," as promised by Moses in Num. 34, 5—8, and from the Lebanon to Tadmor, the Roman Palmyra, the city which Solomon "built in the desert," 2 Chron. 8, 4.

2) Judg. 20, 1.

New Jersey, — and yet in certain respects the very heart of the ancient world. The attention of the student of history is at once attracted by the immensely favorable strategic position of this little bit of Jewish soil. In depicting the world as a circle, with Jerusalem as its center, the medieval cartographer was undoubtedly actuated by theological motives; nevertheless his good judgment has been confirmed by history.[3] And we can but marvel at Divine Providence for choosing this particular tract of largely sandy and rocky soil as the abode of a people which was to receive the divine message throughout the Old Testament and as the actual scene of the revelation and physical manifestation of God's grace in the person and work of Christ.

3.

Between the twenty-fifth and thirty-fifth parallels northern latitude there lies a strip of territory in the Old World of fairly uniform type beginning at the Straits of Gibraltar, embracing both shores of the Mediterranean, and extending to the border of

In Its Geographical Relation. the great Asiatic mountain systems of the distant East. To-day most of this is barren, except on the north Mediterranean coast-line, and the lands are suited for cultivation only in great river valleys; but in earlier times, due, as it was thought,[1] to a northward shifting of moist westerly winds, it consisted of grassy steppes. Now, it happens that in this general belt the scene is laid of nearly all of what is known and recorded of ancient human history.

4.

In Western Asia this territory may be roughly divided into three great belts.[1]

First, a northern belt of mountains and high tablelands,[2] extending from the Eastern shores of the Persian Gulf through Persia and Kurdistan into Asia Minor. This formidable barrier prevented the cradle civilization from coming into contact with its

---

2, 3) Robinson, Hunkin, and Burkitt, *Palestine in General History*, p. 3.

3, 1) *Loc. cit.*

4, 1) See A. W. F. Blunt, *Israel in World History*, p. 9 ff.

2) Notice the remarkable boundary line of mountains and highlands between the present rulers of the world and the world rulers of the past. A high fence extends in an almost unbroken line: the Himalayas, Pamir, Hindu Kush, Elburz, Caucasus, the Kurdistan and Armenian Highlands; and in Europe: the Balkans, the Carpathians, the Alps, and the Pyrenees. W. R. Shepherd, *Historical Atlas*, pp. 2. 3.

unknown northern neighbors and at the same time served as a protection against the Scythians, Gog and Magog, and such barbarian dangers as might be lurking beyond. Only once in Old Testament times, during the reign of Josiah, was this barrier crossed,[3] and ancient civilization — Assyria, Babylon, Media, Israel, Egypt, and even Asia Minor and Greece — stood aghast at the spectacle of northern barbarians rushing down on the seats of luxury and power.[4]

Secondly, that vast belt of forbidding deserts along the twenty-fifth parallel, extending in ancient times, and still extending, from the Persian Gulf through Arabia and across the whole of Northern Africa to the Atlantic Coast.[5]

And thirdly, between these two another belt is placed, a large semicircle, with its open side to the south, on which was staged the whole of the world's ancient history. Because land suited for agriculture is found nearly all along this belt, at least grass and pasture during the rainy season, the term "Fertile Crescent" has

The Fertile Crescent.

been suggested as an appropriate designation and is now widely used.[6] In the shape of a crescent or an inverted U it can easily be traced from the valley of the Nile northward, then along the Mediterranean to Palestine, back of the Lebanon to the Euphrates, eastward to the Tigris, and then southward to the Persian Gulf. Babylon and Assyria occupy its eastern arm, Syria the crest, and Palestine and Egypt its western wing. Or starting from Ur in Chaldea, the itinerary of Abraham may be repeated to Babylon, Nineveh, Haran, Damascus, Dan, Jerusalem, Hebron, Beersheba, and Egypt.

4, 3) The Scythian invasion, 632 B. C. This marks the first of a long series of invasions: Parthians, Turks, Mongols, Goths, Vandals, and Huns, until the barbarians themselves took a hand in ruling the world.

4) Alluded to Zeph. 2, 4—6; Jer. 1, 14. See Dean Stanley, *History of the Jewish Church*, II, 432 ff. Breaking through the barriers of the Caucasus, the Scythians swept down like a swarm of locusts upon Media and Assyria, turned fruitful fields into deserts, and, pushing across Mesopotamia, ravaged Syria, crossed Palestine, and penetrated to the borders of Egypt, where they were bought off by Psammetichus I. For twenty-eight years they remained in Western Asia, but only one trace of their passage remained. The name of the old Canaanite city of Beth-shean, Judg. 1, 27, was changed into Scythopolis, that is, the city of the Scythians (one of the cities of the Decapolis). And as the result of the invasion Russia has won a name in the Hebrew and Greek texts of the Sacred Book. (Rosh, Ezek. 38, 2. 3 and 39, 1, is wrongly translated "chief prince" in the Authorized Version.)

5) The Syrian, Lybian, and Sahara deserts.

6) J. H. Breasted, *The Conquest of Civilization*, p. 117.

5.

On this general belt the Land of Israel occupied the key position and lay like a bridge or corridor for the trader as well as for the conqueror between Asia and Africa, with solid barriers on both sides. On the one side was the Mediterranean, an open road to Europe, but until the coming of the Romans the realm of the pirates and jealously guarded by the Phenicians, themselves securely barricaded by the Lebanon at their back.[1] And on the other side were the shores of a vast desert bay some five hundred miles across, not of water, but of the sweeping sands of the Arabian Desert. The strategic position of the Land of Israel is apparent to all. It was

The Bridge. the only open and firm ancient highway between Asia and Africa. And after the time of Alexander its importance only increased; for then it became a turntable for the whole then known world, the three continents Europe, Asia, and Africa. And finally, after Rome had completed its own crescent all the way around the Mediterranean Sea, is it just mere coincidence that these two crescents, the eastern and the western, should form a conjunction and meet in a letter X on Jewish soil? In a wonderful way, at the psychological moment and at the most suitable spot, Divine Providence directed all circumstances to the coming of Christ. Rome itself would not have provided a better place for the appearance of Christ. It was not even the best location for Rome. Three hundred years later, when it was too late, Constantine moved the capital of the Roman Empire to the East. And it is therefore no overstatement when the Land of Israel has been called the very center of the ancient world.[2]

6.

But Palestine's eminently favored geographical position also had grave disadvantages. The Land of Israel, itself lacking in size, agricultural wealth, natural resources, harbors, and other regular empire-builders' appendages, was fated to be the coveted prize of succeeding kingdoms rising on both arms of the Fertile Crescent. For Egypt, 120 miles away, it was highly desirable to dominate an area which might serve both as a buffer and a jumping-off place

---

5, 1) Both the cause of their prosperity and the source of their protection. They did not live on the international highway and so for the most part could afford to be "careless after the manner of the Sidonians," and were "quiet and secure," Judg. 18, 7.

2) Lewis Browne, *The Graphic Bible*, p. 21.

against Mesopotamia. And besides, there was the highly desirable Phenician timber of the Lebanon. And to the imperial aspirations of Babylonia and Assyria it was almost mandatory to be provided with an outpost against Egypt, to control a district which commanded the last section of the great trade routes between the Euphrates and the Nile, and to have access to the commerce

Coveted Prize of Empire-Builders.
deflected from the Orient by means of the Phenician cities on the Mediterranean coast. And so on both extremities of the Crescent the possession of Palestine was of vital importance for both commercial and military reasons. The march of empire in the end all hinged on business, and the only question was whether the military flag should precede and secure, or follow and protect, the caravan. Thus Palestine's favored position — a highroad of commerce or a vantage-ground of empire, the one contingent upon the other — meant that Israel was never left unmolested. In the gradual progress of human civilization it was, humanly speaking, as impossible for the indwellers of the Land of Promise to live at peace as it would be to enjoy still-fishing in the locks of Sault Sainte Marie. Israel enjoyed peace only when it was united and strong, — and that was not often and never long, — but at the first sign of weakening it had no more chance of avoiding being crushed than a tiny grain between two mill-stones, no matter which way it turned.[1] And this brings us back to our opening remark: The scepter had departed from Judah.

7.

Of course, Israel enjoyed a brief spell of political glory. During the times of David and Solomon it had won and held a considerable portion of the Fertile Crescent: from the River of Egypt to the Crossing of Euphrates.[1] Moreover, during the whole course of its checkered history true to divine promise the scepter did not

Israel's Moment of Political Greatness.
depart from Judah altogether. Israel departed from the Lord, it fell into discord, it became subject, it paid tribute, it returned to the Lord, it united, it revolted, it collected tribute, and in turn became subject again; but it always somehow succeeded, at least nominally, to manage its own affairs. In all the pages

6,   1) See Lewis Browne, *The Graphic Bible,* p. 66.

7,   1) From Elath, at the northern extremity of the Red Sea, to Tiphsah, at the Euphrates, an area of 60,000 square miles, as compared with the 7,000 square miles of the tribal possession. J. L. Hurlbut, *Bible Atlas,* p. 69.

of world history there are not to be found chapters of greater patriotism, bravery, loyalty, suffering, sacrifices, and more soul-stirring and heart-touching accounts of political martyrdom than are to be found in the pages of Judah's own historical tragedy.[2]

8.

But that is not the important consideration. It seems that Israel on the whole constantly misconstrued and deliberately misunderstood the true nature and character of the divinely promised Messianic kingdom. And thus it sadly overlooked its real, divinely appointed place and purpose in history. This purpose was not imperial glamor or political glory, a Jewish world-empire, but an infinitely greater honor and privilege, namely, to be the people from which the Savior was to come, to provide His earthly abode, to prepare His way, to set the stage, and to usher in His coming into this world. An Israelitish world-empire, continued Jewish national and political glory, would not have helped the cause of Christ. Had Christ appeared in the flesh in a firmly established, powerful Jewish state, Christianity, humanly speaking, might have

Israel's Own Mistaken Ambition. been essentially Jewish. Had He been born in Rome, Christianity might have been essentially Roman. But because He was born in a country such as Palestine was then and among a people such as the Jews were politically at that time, Christianity, again humanly speaking, could more easily become universal, in accordance with God's promise to Abraham: "In thee shall all families of the earth be blessed." [1] The Lord was not referring to a political empire, but to the universal spiritual Kingdom of Grace when He promised that a lineal descendant of David "shall build a house for My name, and I will stablish the throne of His kingdom forever." [2] This thought ought to reconcile us to the tragic course of Israel's history, while it is a puzzling problem to such students of history and a source of sorrow for such Jews as do not accept the Savior-King of promise. And this fact relieves us of the necessity of explaining in detail just what happened to the Jewish state, and how and why, except just to give a brief outline of Israel's history as a fitting introduction of the reader to the state of the Jews with reference to the life of Christ.

7, 2) Compare Josephus, *Wars*, VII, VII, 1; IX, 1.
8, 1) Gen. 12, 3.
   2) 2 Sam. 7, 13.

9.

Almost immediately after the death of Solomon, in 935 B. C., the empire which David had won and Solomon had elevated fell into disruption, never to be reunited. And for the next two hundred years the fragments into which it had broken are to be found either fighting for their place or for supremacy on the Palestinian Bridge.[1] Only once in the history of the divided kingdoms did it seem as though the political glory of David and Solomon would be restored. But that was due to the collapse of Syria and while Assyria was still asleep. Profiting by these circumstances, Jeroboam II of Israel,

The Divided Kingdom. a grand, but very wicked king, regained nearly all of Syria, made Judah tributary, restored the "coast of Israel, from the entering of Hamath unto the sea of the plain" (from Orontes to the Dead Sea), and gave the king of Judah a chance to take Elath (on the Red Sea) and to "spread his name abroad even to the entering of Egypt." [2] It was the Indian summer of Israel's history. Commerce increased, cities grew, and the people felt safe and secure. But this glory did not last. Outward splendor was accompanied by spiritual decay. It was the lull before the storm. In vain did the prophets

---

9, 1) 1. *The Kingdom of Israel,* or of the Ten Tribes. It secured allegiance of all the tribes east of the Jordan. Nineteen kings ruled over this kingdom, from Jeroboam I to Hoshea, representing several dynasties, with intervals of anarchy and frequent change, until its fall in 722 B. C. and the deportation of the ten tribes into Assyria. — 2. *The Kingdom of Judah,* including Judah, Benjamin, and the Levitical cities. The latter, thirteen in number, were all located in the tribes of Judah, Benjamin, and Simeon — a most remarkable arrangement, Judg. 21, 9—19. Perhaps also a portion of Simeon adhered to the Kingdom of Judah. This kingdom remained loyal to the house of David during all its history and was ruled by twenty-one kings, from Rehoboam to Zedekiah, until the Babylonian Captivity, 587 B. C. — 3. *The Kingdom of Syria,* north of Dan and Palestine proper, with Damascus as its capital. This kingdom, small at first, soon rose to power under Benhadad I and II, and at the height of its power, under Hazael, was the leading nation in Asia west of the Euphrates. In 732 B. C. it was subjugated by Assyria. — 4. *The Kingdom of Moab,* lying east of the Dead Sea, between the river Arnon and the brook Zered. It was usually subject to Israel, but at times it revolted and set up a government of its own. Eventually it also had to bow to Assyria and Babylonia. Later in history it was overrun by the Arabians, with whom the Moabites were afterwards confounded. Josephus, *Ant.,* XIII, XIII, 5. Machaerus, the scene of the tragic death of John the Baptist, was located in Moab. — 5. *The Kingdom of Edom,* south of the Dead Sea. It held about the same relation to Judah as Moab held to Israel. Its conquest opened to Solomon the ports of the Red Sea. But like all the fragments of Solomon's empire it also fell under the rule of Nebuchadnezzar. This country was to be a particular curse to Judah in the declining days of its history. As Idumea it was taken by Judas Maccabaeus in 165 B. C. (1 Macc. 4, 29); but it revenged itself upon its conquerors when the Idumean Herods finally succeeded in placing themselves on the Jewish throne. See Hurlbut, *Bible Atlas,* p. 78.

2) 2 Kings 14, 22—29; 2 Chron. 26, 2—8.

Hosea and Amos preach repentance and threaten punishment and captivity.[3] But on the other hand, Jonah, who had promised this last flare of prosperity, was sent down to Nineveh to preach repentance, against his will; and his word took effect.[4]

10.

The wild roar of strange beasts was soon to be heard in the Land of Israel, that is, the symbolic roaring of the winged, human-headed, and bearded bulls and lions of ancient Assyria. "They shall roar and lay hold of the prey and shall carry it away safe; and none shall deliver it."[1] In 745 B. C. a new king ascended the throne of Assyria, Tiglath-Pileser IV, who opened his reign with a whirlwind conquest of his neighbors. In three years his opponents were overawed, and then he began to rule the Crescent. In 738 B. C. both Syria and Israel were "giving" their annual "presents." "And Pul [Tiglath-Pileser], the king of Assyria, came against the land; and Menahem [king of Israel] gave Pul a thousand talents of silver that his hand might be with him to confirm the kingdom in his hand."[2] But in four years he had to return because a coalition had been formed to throw off the Assyrian yoke. In a short time the revolt was crushed. And in order to secure his conquest and to prevent future occurrences of this nature, a recent imperial invention was for the first time employed on a larger scale, namely, the policy of deporting rebellious conquered people.[3] Thousands

The Fall of Israel. of the inhabitants of the territory afterwards commonly called Galilee were carried into captivity. This territory, first to be depopulated, was afterwards first to see the Light.[4] The purpose of this method — though effective, yet cruel and also politically unwise, because it crippled tribute-bearing areas — was to break up local ties and to make the new settlers in their alien surroundings completely dependent upon the central government. Thus Israel was punished; but it did not humble itself and did not hearken to the Lord.[5] Tiglath-Pileser died, and Hoshea decided to rebel. Foolishly depending upon the support of Egypt, Hoshea failed to send the annual

---

9, 3) Hos. 14, 1. 2. 3; 9, 3; Amos 7, 8—11.

4) 2 Kings 14, 25; Jonah 1, 2; 3, 5.

10, 1) Is. 5, 29.   2) 2 Kings 15, 19.

3) A. W. F. Blunt, *Israel in World History,* p. 57.

4) 2 Kings 15, 29; Is. 9, 1. 2 — the promise. Matt. 4, 15. 16 — the fulfilment.

5) 2 Kings 17, 13—17.

present.[6] Egypt was anxious to have a buffer state between itself and Assyria and was ever ready to incite Israel to hopeless rebellion and to promise help, but never to supply it. Egypt, the "Rahab that sitteth still," was "a bruised reed, whereon, if a man lean, it will go into his hand and pierce it." [7] The new king of Assyria, Shalmaneser V, struck at once and hard. Three years Israel resisted. Shalmaneser was killed before Israel fell. This is an amazing testimony to the desperate resistance Israel offered. But Sargon, Shalmaneser's successor, succeeded in defeating the army of Israel. Hoshea was taken prisoner. In 722 B. C. the kingdom of Israel came to an end. "In the ninth year of Hoshea the king of Assyria took Samaria and carried Israel away into Assyria and placed them in Halah and in Habor, by the river of Gozan, and in the cities of the Medes." [8] Foreign colonists were imported and "placed in the cities of Samaria instead of the children of Israel; and they possessed Samaria and dwelt in the cities thereof." [9] These heathen colonists intermarried with such remnants of the ten tribes as had not been carried away into captivity, probably, as in the case of Judah later, "the poor of the land," which resulted in the planting of a mixed religion in the confines of the former Kingdom of Israel.[10] Ten tribes of Jacob thus faded out of history's picture. Judah was spared — for the present — and at a price.

11.

After the ten tribes had passed out of history, the Kingdom of Judah continued for more than a century, but most of the time as a subject nation to the "great king" of Assyria, to whom Ahaz and his successors annually sent their "presents," that is, until Nineveh itself was doomed. The Assyrian war lords were great conquerors, but did not know how to rule. The Scythian invasion definitely put an end to Assyria's Palestinian control.[1] And south

The Fall of Nineveh. of Assyria there was the more ancient Babylon, whose pride had never readily accepted the Assyrian rule. In July, 612 B. C., Cyaxares destroyed Nineveh with the help of the Medes, Babylonians, and Scythians, and so effectually that, two hundred years later, Xenophon, passing near its former site, did not even know that the ruins of that great city lay before him.[2] And in the

---

10, 6) 2 Kings 17, 3. 4. 7) King So of Egypt. Is. 36, 6; 30, 7.
8) 2 Kings 17, 6. 9) 2 Kings 17, 24.
10) See 2 Kings 17, 24—34. 41.
11, 1) Ca. 632—604 B. C. A. W. F. Blunt, *Israel in World History*, p. 77.
2) J. H. Breasted, *Conquest of Civilization*, 179. 405.

book of the prophet Nahum we hear the exulting shout that the terrible, bloody city of the East shall be laid low.[3] A new power, the later Babylonian Empire, was in the ascendent, in the lower arm of the ancient Crescent.

12.

But for the present this was Egypt's chance. And again Judah, alone on the Crossing, was like a tiny grain between two millstones, doomed to be crushed, no matter which way it turned.[1] First it fell into the hands of Egypt. It was during the reign of Josiah, the best king that Judah ever had, including even David and

The Egyptians. Solomon; for "like unto him there was no king before him that turned to the Lord with all his heart and with all his soul and with all his might." [2] "Notwithstanding the Lord turned not from the fierceness of His great wrath." The House of Judah was doomed. Bravely Josiah went out to meet Pharaoh-necho; but in the first skirmish he was killed, and his army was destroyed. The Egyptians swept northward as far as the Euphrates, exacted silver and gold as tribute, deposed a Jewish king and put another in his stead. However, the triumph of Egypt was of brief duration.

13.

Nebuchadnezzar is now introduced into history as the rod of God's anger to bring about that awful day of judgment which the prophets had foretold.[1] The Egyptians were soon driven back to the Nile, and the land of Judah had to recognize its new overlord. But after three years the foolhardy Jehoiakim [2] "forgot" the annual tribute, and then the trouble began. Jerusalem was taken, the

The Fall of Judah. Temple robbed of its treasure, and in order to make submission permanent, the Oriental invention of deportation was again employed. Jehoiachin,[3] the nobles, and thousands of captives were carried off, so that only the poorest of the land remained. The year 606 B. C. marks the beginning of the seventy years of the Babylonian Captivity.[4] But the Babylonian king had underestimated the inflexible patriotism of the Jews, a patriotism that inflamed them to desperate resistance. The foolish remnants listened to

11, 3) 2, 10—13; 3, 7 ff.
12, 1) Lewis Browne, *The Graphic Bible*, p. 66.   2) 2 Kings 23, 25.
13, 1) Jer. 34, 2. 3, etc.; Is. 10, 5.   2) 2 Kings 24, 1.
    3) Jehoiakim's successor.   4) Jer. 29, 10.

Egyptian and Syrian intriguers. The die, however, was cast, and Jerusalem's last hour had struck. Nebuchadnezzar returned and directed his battering-rams against the walls of Jerusalem; but only after a year and a half — this shows the desperate resistance — a breach was made. The city was then utterly destroyed. Zedekiah, the last kinglet, was captured and blinded, his sons were killed, sixty leading citizens put to death, about 25,000 of the inhabitants led into exile, and only the dregs of the land remained.[5] Thus the curtain descended upon the first act of Judah's historical tragedy. A man of fine character, named Gedaliah, appointed governor of Judah by Nebuchadnezzar, tried his best to give the remaining poor wretches a sort of government; but they rebelled against him and slew him. Dreading the certain consequences of this final revolt, a large portion of the remaining terrified element fled to Egypt, forcibly taking the old and protesting prophet Jeremiah with them.[6]

14.

Babylonia, however, was not long permitted to retain her ascendency on the Fertile Crescent. The center of gravity was gradually shifting to the Medes and Persians. A new sun had

Fall of Babylon. risen in the distant East, the hereditary king of Persia, Cyrus the Great. After heading a revolt against the Medes, he conquered Lydia, entered Babylon in 538 B. C., killed Belshazzar,[1] and soon established himself from the Indus to the Hellespont and from Armenia to the Nile as the new world monarch.

15.

In accordance with prophecy and in obedience to divine command[1] Cyrus gave the Jewish Babylonian exiles permission to return to the country of their fathers. In a short time thousands

The Return of the Exiles. of returning Judeans, or Jews, as they were now called, were again settled on their ancestral soil. This was a wise political move on the part of the Persian king. Not only did it restore a tribute-paying area, but with the settlement of a friendly colony of home-loving inhabitants on that most important sector it also decreased the danger of an Egyptian approach.

13, 5) 2 Kings 25; Jer. 39 and 52.
6) 2 Kings 25, 25. 26; Jer. 43, 7. Lewis Browne, *The Graphic Bible*, p. 71.   14,   1) Dan. 5, 28—31.
15, 1) Is. 44, 48; Jer. 25, 12; 29, 10; Ezra 1, 1. 2.

16.

The two centuries of Persian government — 536—332 B. C. — were a period of comparative rest for the returned Jewish exiles. While many did not return, still probably 50,000,[1] mostly from Judah and Benjamin,[2] were again gathered on Jewish soil. To these were added such as had fled to Egypt immediately before the final doom. The rebuilding of the Temple was at once begun. In 516 B. C. it was dedicated to the Lord. While the restored Temple could not compare with the Temple of Solomon, God's prophet held out this comforting promise that "the glory of this latter house shall be greater than of the former." [3] Christ was to preach in it. "In this place will I give peace, saith the Lord of hosts." With the return to Jerusalem of Ezra and an additional

Temple Rebuilt. group of exiles and with the rebuilding of the walls of the Holy City [4] by Nehemiah, a firmer hold on the famous Crossing was again made. The government itself lay virtually in the hands of the Levite priests, among whom the high priest, chosen from the descendants of Zadok,[5] was practically king. From now on the language spoken in Palestine was Aramaic, a Semitic language, which displaced the Hebrew and became the language of commerce and diplomacy of the entire Fertile Crescent, from the Nile to the Persian Gulf. Until displaced by the Greek as a universal language, it was the *lingua franca* of the Oriental world.[6] In the synagog, likewise originating with the Captivity, the Law was read in the Hebrew and interpreted in the Aramaic — the Targum. The Persian period finally marks the close of the long line of holy prophets from Moses to Malachi, who concluded the writings of the Old Testament with the promise of the forerunner of Christ.[7]

17.

On the whole, the Persian government was an excellent one. For proof of this we may point to the fact that it held together as long as it did. It was a precursor, as it were, of the Roman

16, 1) Ezra 2, 64. 65.
   2) The "lost" ten tribes have definitely passed out of history.
   3) Hag. 2, 9.
   4) 445 B. C. Called Holy City in Neh. 11, 1; also in Is. 48, 2; 52, 1.
   5) 1 Chron. 29, 22.
   6) J. H. Breasted, *Conquest of Civilization.* 164. 198.
   7) Mal. 3, 1.

Empire, the first government to establish a sort of imperial or-
ganization. The 120 satrapies into which it was divided were
generally peaceful and prosperous. There was little oppression.

The Fall of Persia.

Religious toleration was the universal
rule. But in the end it wore out. It
was an unnatural empire in that it was sprawled all across Asia,
its tentacles thrusting 'way into, but weakly connecting it with,
Africa and Europe.[1] The Persian Empire was a premature attempt
at something that was not successful until Rome gained world
dominion. Until then it lasted principally because there was no
power at hand to end it.[2] The Eastern world had worn out. The
world was waiting for a new master; and when he did come, the
Persian Empire collapsed like a house of cards.

18.

His name was Alexander. The center of gravity had suddenly
shifted from Asia and Africa to Europe. In the fateful year
333 B. C. Alexander of Macedon defeated the Persian army in the
Battle of Issus, and a year later he was already crossing the Palestinian bridge on his way to Egypt. After founding Alexandria,
he returned, descended the Fertile Crescent, and soon made himself
sole master of Western Asia as far as India. But this Alexander
was quite unlike the usual ancient empire-builders. His aim seems
to have been not so much the establishment of brutal power as
rather making the world safe for Greek civilization. And in this
he succeeded, although he died at the age of thirty-three.[1] His

Alexander the Great.

Greek colonies dotted all the then
known world. His immense con-
quests resulted in greater consequences for the Jews, both at home
and in the Diaspora, than those of any other non-Jew in history.[2]
He was generous to them and gave them a fair measure of liberty.[3]
But at the same time he located peaceful Greek settlements throughout Palestine.[4] The result was a growing familiarity in his Asiatic
dominions with all things Greek. The Greek language, Greek
thought, manners, culture, literature, and art, Greek civilization and
Greek games, were largely introduced; but also Greek vice and

17, 1) By way of Palestine and the Hellespont.

2) A. W. F. Blunt, *Israel in World History*, p. 96.

18, 1) 323 B. C.   2) Lewis Browne, *The Graphic Bible*, p. 80.

3) Josephus, *Ant.*, XI, VIII, 5.

4) Particularly in Samaria. Afterwards organized by Pompey into
the Decapolis. E. Schuerer, *The Jewish People*, II, I, 123.

corruption infiltrated into the body politic. The career of Alexander himself was brilliant, but brief. Yet in its effects his victorious Asiatic campaigns, coupled with the founding of his marvelous world monarchy, was vastly more important than he could foresee. On account of the resulting universal use of the Greek language it is almost impossible to overestimate [5] the magnitude of his bequest, as it were, to succeeding generations and peoples; for it made possible the promulgation of the Gospel throughout "the ends of the world." [6]

19.

The death of Alexander was followed by bitter strife among his ablest officers, the Diadochi, each of whom aimed at a dominant position in the empire which their great leader had left masterless. In the end the confusion of competing claimants, omitting minor contenders, was reduced to the Ptolemies in Egypt and the Seleucidae of Syria. [1] Between these two powers the Eastern world was

The Diadochi. again divided. And Palestine was again the battle-ground of both. But both powers, let us note, were, and continued to be, Greek kingdoms, — true, Greek with a difference, now called Hellenistic and thus distinguished from the pure Hellenic culture of Greece. [2] Both the Ptolemaic and the Seleucid courts were predominantly Hellenistic, and the monarchs of both lines aspired to be the champions of the new Hellenistic craze. And still, all this had to serve the cause of Christ. The two dynasties stood in the breach in protecting Hellenism against the possibilities of relapse into Orientalism, until Rome, already in the rising, was ready to take their place.

20.

For the first one hundred and twenty-five years of this period [1] the land of Judea was ruled by the high priests, but under the suzerainty of Egypt and with much confusion and bloodshed back

18, 5) *Int. St. B. Encycl.,* I, 93.

6) Πέρατα τῆς οἰκουμένης. Rom. 10, 18.

19, 1) The kingdom of the Ptolemies in Egypt was founded in 323 B. C. by Ptolemy I and continued for almost three centuries. In 30 B. C., the year which marks the death of Cleopatra, it was turned into a Roman province. The Syrian kingdom, founded by Seleucus Nicator, famous as the builder of cities, and by his successors subjected to harassing vicissitudes, came to an end in 63 B. C., when it was dissolved and its lands incorporated into the Roman Republic.

2) From Hellenist, a non-Greek who adopts the Greek language and Greek customs and manners.

20, 1) B. C. 321—198.

and forth across the Bridge. The most important event in this epoch was the translation of the Old Testament into the Greek language. This version, commonly called the Septuagint (LXX),

The Ptolemies and the Septuagint. owes its name to the story, now discredited, that it was the work of seventy-two translators who were deputed to Egypt to prepare a version of the Jewish Law for the royal library at Alexandria.[2] This story may be attributable to legends; but the translation itself is a fact and was of the greatest importance for the New Testament Church. This translation was adopted by the Greek-speaking Jews, was used by Paul and the apostles as a missionary agency, and was even regarded as inspired by some of the early Christian Fathers. As a true *preparatio evangelica* it was of the greatest service. Without it Hellenistic Judaism would have been as inconceivable as the Church of the Reformation without Luther's translation of the Bible.[3]

21.

At the beginning of the second century before Christ the kingdom of Syria grew more powerful and prepared to wrest the land of the Jews from Egypt. In a bloody battle Antiochus III

The Seleucidae. of Syria[1] drove back the Egyptians and formally annexed Palestine. Hellenism, which had been steadily seeping into Palestine, was now threatening to extinguish the Jewish religion altogether. The priesthood had become corrupt. Circumcision had ceased. Heathenish playhouses were erected in Jerusalem. And it seemed as if even reactionary Judea had been made safe for Greek civilization.[2]

22.

But one day there arose a king in Syria named Antiochus Epiphanes,[1] who spoiled everything. On the way home from a successful campaign against Egypt[2] he stopped in Jerusalem to

---

20, 2) The story is as follows: King Ptolemy II Philadelphus (283 to 247 B. C.) was induced by his librarian to have the laws of the Jews translated into Greek for his library. At his request the Jewish high priest Eleazar sent him seventy-two able men, six out of each tribe, who finished their task in seventy-two days. E. Schuerer, *Jewish People*, II, III, 159.
    3) *Ibid.*, 159.
21, 1) *Ibid.*, II, I, 59. B. C. 198. 1 Macc. 1, 10. The Syrian supremacy lasted from 198 to 166 B. C.   2) Schuerer, I, I, 203.
22, 1) *Ibid.*, I, I, 201. Meaning "the Evident God"; but also called Epimanes, "the Madman."   2) 169 B. C.

accelerate the already quickly advancing process of Hellenization by force. He looted the Temple, carried off the sacred vessels, killed many Jews, and ordered Judaism to cease. Just that! No more Sabbath, no more circumcision, no more clean and unclean

Antiochus Epiphanes and the Abomination of Desolation. food, and no more Holy Scripture. Henceforth swine's flesh was to be laid on the altar of sacrifice, and all their sacrifices were to be made either to Antiochus or to Zeus.[3] Disobedience was to be punished with death. According to the blind heathen Tacitus [4] he meant well with the Jews; he wanted to "improve the condition of this most detestable race." Many of the Jews obeyed man rather than God; yet not a few refused to forsake the Law and statutes of the Lord.[5] Starkest horror swept the land as the army of Antiochus began to put his orders into effect. There was looting and murder, wailing and shame, and greater trials than in any previous period of Jewish history. But then, like the breaking out of mad fire, the nation blazed into rebellion.[6]

23.

A pious priest named Mattathias ran his sword through one of the Syrian officers and started the first war for religious liberty in history.[1] This introduces us to the brief spell of glorious Jewish history, the Maccabean period, with its chief figures, the brave members of the Asmonean house.[2] Fleeing into the wilderness with his five sons, Mattathias gathered around himself a band of desperate zealots. Fierce warfare ensued, in which repeated losses were inflicted on the Syrian forces. Four great armies were sent against

The Maccabees. them, but Judas, who succeeded his father, defeated them all. Then came a lull in fighting. The Temple was cleansed of its swinish filth and rededicated to God.[3] Then war commenced again. The Syrian king sent army after army into Judea; and although Judas and

---

22, 3) 1 Macc. 1, 23—29.

4) *History*, V, 8.

5) The original Pharisees; the party of the 'Pious,' or Hasideans, 1 Macc. 2, 42.

6) See Lewis Browne, *The Graphic Bible*, 83.

23, 1) Mattathias of the house of Asmoneans and of the order of Joiarib (Jehoiarib). Josephus, *Ant.*, XII, VI, 1. 1 Chron. 24, 7. Lewis Browne, *The Graphic Bible*, 84.

2) 166—163 B. C. Maccabean, from Judas Maccabaeus, "the Hammerer," son of Mattathias.

3) On the 25th of Kisleu, 165 B. C. 1 Macc. 4, 52—59.

three of his four brothers were killed, the revolt could not be stamped out. Fighting for a most glorious principle, religious liberty, Judas and his followers withstood the onslaught of the best-equipped armies of the time, infantry, cavalry, and elephants, and although defeated at times, still won in the end.[4] After repeated reverses the Syrians gave up the attempt as hopeless and withdrew from Palestine forever.[5] At last, but also for the last time, Judea was again gloriously independent and free.

24.

But the triumph of the Maccabees was too complete. The war which at first had been waged for religious freedom only, ended, as we just said, with complete political independence. For centuries the Jews had had little occasion to indulge in political aspirations. But now, drunk with recent success, they again became king-minded. But there was a

Monarchic Aspirations.

little difficulty. Their present Asmonean leaders were of priestly rather than of royal stock. Moreover, as descendants of Jehoiarib [1] rather than of Zadok,[2] they were not even entitled to the high-priestly office,[3] which had become vacant by the recent murder of Onias. However, the national crisis overrode ceremonial scruples, and the high-priesthood passed over to Jehoiarib's Maccabean descendants.[4]

25.

But there was another, and it seemed a greater, difficulty. What about the royal dignity? What about the King who according to the divine promise had to be a son and heir of David? [1] A provisional solution of this difficulty was made in the combination of the royal and priestly office by making Simon, the sole survivor of Mattathias, both high priest *and* king. There was, however, a significant reservation, namely, that this arrangement

---

23, 4) In the battle at Beth-Zachariah 100,000 men, 20,000 riders, and 32 wine-crazed elephants were engaged. 1 Macc. 6, 30—48.

    5) 143 B. C.
24, 1) 1 Chron. 24, 7.

    2) 1 Kings 2, 35.   The office was hereditary. Only twice had the line been broken in Jewish history: when Eli superseded the elder house of Eleazar and when Zadok replaced Abiathar. Stanley, *Jewish Church*, III, 314.

    3) Schuerer, *Jewish People*, II, I, 223. 224.

    4) When Jonathan was made high priest, about 153 B. C. 1 Macc. 10, 18—21.
25, 1) 2 Sam. 7, 12 ff.

was to continue in full force "forever and ever," that is, his royal office was to be hereditary, "and *until* the coming of that faithful prophet." [2] In other words, Jewish royalty was to be held in trust

Jewish Royalty Held in Trust for the Coming Christ.

for Christ. But though the Asmonean rulers neither succeeded in holding, nor probably even intended to hold, Jewish royalty in trust for the coming Christ, — they did not even succeed in holding the sacerdotal dignity, — one valuable service they did perform, which was that they kept Judaism intact and preserved it against threatened Hellenistic dissolution.[3] For the present it seemed that bright Old Testament sunshine were flooding the land of Judah. Independence had been won by the force of victorious arms, a throne had been set up, and a king had been crowned and hailed by popular acclaim. Moreover, the Jewish position as an independent state was officially recognized by Egypt, Syria, Cyprus, yes, even by Sparta and Rome.[4] But, alas, this light was but the last bright, flickering rays of a foreboding sunset. For with Rome is introduced into Jewish history a name [5] which ever after must be associated with the political doom of the Jews.

26.

It was during the reign of Simon's successor, John Hyrcanus I,[1] that a beginning of the end was made, first of all by the conflict between the Sadducees and the Pharisees, whose names here for the first time enter into the arena of history.[2] As a power these two influential Jewish religious parties had their rise at the same

Pharisees and Sadducees.

time with the Maccabees, but properly the Maccabees belonged to neither of them. The zeal for the Law and for religious liberty at first gave them the support of the Pharisees.[3] But the Pharisees would not have a son of Levi ascend the throne of David, and they could not forgive Judas Maccabaeus for making an alliance with idolatrous Rome.[4] And, on the other hand, in the eyes of the Sadducees it was an act of usurpation that the upstart descendants of Jehoiarib should take away the high-priesthood from

---

25, 2) 1 Macc. 14, 41. See Deut. 18, 15. Schuerer, I, I, 264. 265. September, 141 B. C.
    3) Cf. Schuerer, I, 1, 3.
    4) 1 Macc. 15, 1; 12, 2; 14, 20; 15, 16.   5) Herod.
26, 1) B. C. 135—105.   2) *Ant.*, XIII, v, 9.
    3) Schuerer, I, I, 287. The Chasidim, 1 Macc. 2, 42; 3, 13.
    4) 1 Macc. 8, 1—29.

the time-honored sons of Zadok, to whose party they adhered or to whose supposed descendants they belonged. That is why they called themselves Zadokites, or Sadducees.[5] As Hellenized aristocrats they were willing, however, to set aside religious scruples as long as they could meddle with power. Their strong point was politics.[6] While the Pharisees enjoyed a popular following and represented the religious world, the Sadducees represented money and class, and it was but natural that the ruling powers, from the Asmonean to the Herodian-Roman period, should cater to them. Of course, at the same time they were careful not to ignore the power of the Pharisees as the leaders of the people. But the dissension of these two religious parties resulted in severe internecine struggle and shedding of blood.[7] And it was not good for the newly founded Jewish state.

27.

John Hyrcanus not only broke with the Pharisees, but became guilty of an offense which in its baneful consequences brought about the fall of his own house and added to the misery of the impending Jewish doom. This otherwise very able prince forgot that he owed his throne to the Maccabean struggle for religious liberty. In a quick campaign he built up a sizable kingdom, conquered the trans-Jordanic territory, added Samaria to his rule, defeated the unruly sons of Esau, the Idumeans, and — here is where he made his mistake — compelled them to accept circumcision and the same sort ot corrupted Jewish religion to which he adhered.[1] That was religious persecution. And in thus bringing the Herodians to the surface, he helped to end the Jewish rule. Little did Hyrcanus dream that with this enforced conversion he nursed the evil genius of the Maccabean house.

Enforced Idumean Conversion.

28.

What remains now of the Maccabean period is but the story of the death throes of this house — internecine strife, war, bloodshed, the Herods, and Rome. The seventh world-power, and the most terrible of all, was to enter into the tragic history of the Jews; after Egypt, Syria, Assyria, Babylonia, Persia, and Greece, Rome

---

26, 5) E. Schuerer, *Jewish People,* I, I, 287.

6) *Ibid.,* II, II, 42.

7) In the time of Alexander Jannaeus, a Sadducean prince (104—78 B. C.), 800 Pharisees were crucified in Jerusalem. This was the first appearance of the cross in the hills of Palestine. See Josephus, *Ant.,* XIII, 14, 2.

27, 1) Josephus, *Ant.,* XIII, IX, 1.

now appeared on the scene. It was in the year 63 B. C. That was the year in which Caesar Augustus was born. Pompey had just cleared the Mediterranean of the pirates and was bringing the *pax Romana* to Asia. Mithridates, the marvelous king of Pontus, had been defeated. The last remnant of the Syrian monarchy had been dissolved at Antioch. And then Pompey advanced to Damascus. It was but natural for him to turn to the bridge which connects Asia with Africa. Like every world-conqueror before him he wanted that little bit of vital territory, the key to the Orient and now the very center of the ancient world. Nor was it difficult to satisfy his desire. At Damascus he was met by a Jewish delegation extending to him an invitation to come.

The Coming of Rome.

29.

After the death of Queen Alexandra [1] her two sons quarreled over the tottering Maccabean throne. Hyrcanus II was the elder of the two and as such had the better claim; but he was weaker than his brother, enjoying, however, the support of the rich and powerful Idumean governor Antipater, [2] whose father had been appointed as the first native governor of Idumea. Aristobulus, the younger and abler, had the support of the priestly Sadducees. Both parties sent delegations to Pompey with presents and the request to intervene in their favor. [3] But there was also a third party, the Jewish people, led by the Pharisees. They were sick of the unending evils which the priest-kings had brought and were begging for a chance to get rid of royalty altogether. These three requests for intervention gave Pompey a perfect excuse to invade Palestine.

Pompey.

30.

Originally the intervention had been intended for Aristobulus; but through the machinations of scheming Antipater, Hyrcanus was favored. Aristobulus hereupon prepared for war. After a stubborn siege of three months Jerusalem was taken, but even then only because Pompey took advantage of a religious scruple and attacked the walls on a fast-day, [1] on which the Jews would not fight. With Jerusalem in his hands, Pompey proceeded at once to

29, 1) B. C. 78—69.
 2) Josephus, *Ant.*, XIV, I, 3. It was in accordance with his own ambitious schemes to have a weak overlord placed on the Judean throne.
 3) *Ant.*, XIV, III, 2.
30, 1) *Ibid.*, XIV, IV, 3.

put fear into the hearts of the Jews. 12,000 rebels were put to the sword. And then he investigated the Temple. He was curious to see the deity which this strange and stubborn people so zealously worshiped. He entered the Holy of Holies, — a mortal sin for all except the high priest, — drew the curtain aside, and received the

Jerusalem Taken in 63 B. C. greatest surprise of his life.[2] He found nothing. This was the first time that he had ever entered a temple where there was no image of a god. Pompey tried to settle Jewish affairs for the present by imprisoning Aristobulus and giving the conquered territory over to Hyrcanus, who was recognized as high priest and nominal ruler, but without the title of king. And then he returned to Rome for one of the grandest triumphs that Rome had ever seen.

31.

It was some time, however,[1] before the Jews submitted to their new Roman overlord. The sons of Aristobulus,[2] who had graced Pompey's Roman triumphal procession, escaped and started trouble. Civil war ensued, in which Antipater shrewdly kept himself in the background, making himself useful to the Romans in various ways,[3] while the wretched little land of Judea was crushed and torn by the talons of Rome. Finally events took a new turn. Pompey and Caesar were fighting for political supremacy. It was

Antipater. now that the scheming Antipater and his old friend, the high priest Hyrcanus, came forward and immediately attached themselves to Caesar's party. This man Antipater was a man of astounding astuteness. He had a keen perception, especially for shifting political winds. He clearly beheld two things: the unconquerable power of Rome and the pitiful weakness of the decadent Asmonean house. And out of these two factors he hoped to build a house of his own. As a result, when Caesar emerged as victor in the Roman civil war,[4] Antipater came in for a rich reward. He was appointed to no less a position than that of procurator of Judea, while Hyrcanus, the innocent dupe, received merely the high-priestly title.[5]

30, 2) *Ant.*, XIV, IV, 4.
31, 1) In fact, eighty years.
    2) Alexander and Antigonus.   3) Josephus, *Ant.,* XIV, VI, 2.
    4) By defeating Pompey at Pharsalus, August 9, 48 B. C.
    5) Caesar permitted him to choose the principality he desired and allowed him to select the title he wished to bear. Antipater, returning the compliment, left the decision to Caesar, and Caesar made him procurator of Judea, while Hyrcanus received honor, but no power. *Ibid.,* XIV, VIII, 5.

32.

The government of Judea had now passed over to the Herodians under Roman control. Antipater immediately proceeded to secure his power by appointing his sons Phasaelus and Herod governors of Jerusalem and Galilee, respectively. The latter, the young governor of Galilee, we now meet for the first time. Already at an early age he gave proof of the abilities which later placed him on the throne. Meanwhile, with the murder of Julius Caesar,[1] there occurred another change in the Roman world. At first Cassius became powerful in the East. Immediately Antipater and

The Last Maccabean Kinglet. Herod made themselves useful to him. But soon Antipater was killed.[2] Young Herod, however, avenging his father's death, was able to play the political game alone. When Brutus and Cassius were defeated,[3] the Roman dominions were divided between Mark Antony and Octavian. With one stroke the East fell into the hands of Antony. And so it was Herod's cue to fawn on him. He sent him nice presents and flattered him with pretty speeches, and in return was confirmed governor of Judea and Galilee, yet still under the nominal rule of doting Hyrcanus. But after a Parthian invasion soon afterwards Herod was left high and dry. The Parthians took his possessions, carried off Hyrcanus, slashed off his ears[4] in order to make him unfit for the high-priesthood, and set up Antigonus as the last of the Maccabean kings.[5]

33.

But Herod was not discouraged. It was not in the interest of the Romans to permit the Parthians to control the Palestinian bridge. Herod was soon appointed king of Judea; but he had to

Herod, 37 B. C. go and win his own recognition, his crown, and his kingdom.[1] And this is exactly what he set himself to do. In less than three years with the help of Roman soldiers, Samaritans, Idumeans, and hired troops he literally carved his way to the Jewish throne. The country was

---

32, 1) 44 B. C.   2) 43 B. C.   3) 42 B. C.

4) It was Antigonus who slashed off his ears. According to one report Antigonus himself bit off his uncle's ears with his teeth! Josephus, *Wars,* I, XIII, 9; *Ant.,* XIV, XIII, 10.

5) B. C. 40—37. *Ant.,* XIV, XIII, 10. See Lev. 21, 17—24. Antigonus was the last surviving son of Aristobulus. He with Hyrcanus were the last of the Maccabean princes, except Aristobulus III, young son of Alexander.

33, 1) *Ant.,* XIV, XIV, 4. 5.

taken, Jerusalem was stormed, and the mercy-imploring Antigonus was led to the block.[2]   However, in the hope of healing the breach which his success would only widen, but also for love, Herod married Mariamne, the granddaughter of Hyrcanus, to whom he had been previously engaged.   Thus the Maccabean kingdom had come to an end.   A despised and much-hated half-Jew had inherited the kingdom.[3]

34.

Herod was a born ruler.[1]   He was blessed with a powerful body, endowed with great mental gifts, was highly ambitious, and was untiring in his efforts to reach his goal.   His insatiable ambition was kindled already in tender youth, when an Essene seer saluted him as king of the Jews,[2] and this soon became his one aim in life.   With an equally cunning and scheming father preparing the way, all his later plans and plots, intrigues and crimes, were directed to this one end, to make himself king of the

Herod's Ambition.   Jews.   This ambition is the key to his whole career.   Difficulties that beset his path were but inducements to put forth added strength.   This unwearied striving continued to characterize him until his miserable death.   Only by a combination of cunning native shrewdness, unpitying cruelty for those who crossed his path and fell into his hands, and cringing servility before those whose favor it was necessary to obtain, was it possible for him to exist in the first few years of life-and-death struggle and then to attain to such greatness, though unenviable, as he reached.[3]

In the first period of his reign Herod had to contend with many powerful adversaries: the Jewish people under the leadership

---

33, 2) Sosius was the name of the Roman general sent by Antony to assist Herod.   From Sosius, Antigonus was hurried off in chains to Antony at Antioch.   A bribe from Herod to Antony sealed his fate.   *Ant.,* XIV, XVI, 4. Thus with Mattathias the Asmonean dynasty began, and with Antigonus, who was also called Mattathias, it came to an end.

3) According to Josephus, Herod was a descendant of an honorable Idumean family.   *Wars,* I, VI, 2.   Eusebius says that Herod was an Idumean on his father's side and an Arabian on that of his mother, and quoting Julius Africanus, he adds that he believed him to be descended from a Philistine slave.   Eusebius, *Eccl. Hist.,* I, VI.   See Schuerer, I, I, 314.   This explains the epithet "Edomite Slave."   On account of the enforced Idumean conversion he was also called "Half-Jew."   *Ant.,* XIV, XV, 2.   In the Talmud he is referred to as "the slave of King Jannaeus."   Stanley, *Jewish Church,* III, 361.

34, 1) Schuerer, I, I, 416 f.   2) *Ant.,* XV, X, 5.

3) The title "Great" was bestowed upon him by his Greek flatterers.

of the Pharisees, the wealthy nobility as represented by the Sadducees, the surviving members of the displaced Asmonean family,
and — Cleopatra.[4]

35.

I (37—25 B. C.).

Herod was well aware of the unconquerable strength of Rome.
His view was wide enough and his judgment sufficiently keen to
perceive that in order to maintain his position, he could gain nothing except through the favor of the Romans — at all costs. And
on the other hand, the Romans knew the value to them of Herod.
He was the one strong man in the East to hold the Palestinian

Herod's Reign. bridge, and the whole security of Rome in
the East depended upon his loyalty. So there
was mutual, albeit selfish, love between Herod and Rome. But
the Jewish people, wholly in the hands of the Pharisees, spat at the
very mention of his name [1] and submitted only with the deepest
aversion to the rule of the Idumean half-Jew and friend of the
Romans.[2] By the application of no torments could they be forced
to call him king. It was only by the utmost rigors that he was
able to secure for himself an obedience which at its best was only
a hypocritical submission. The more pliable of the population he
won over by the bestowal of honor and favors.

36.

Among the Sadducean nobles in Jerusalem there were numerous
adherents of Antigonus. Herod got rid of them at the outset by
executing forty-five of the most wealthy and prominent members.
And by confiscating their property he gained great wealth, which

Forty-Five Nobles Slain. he employed to secure the friend-
Aristobulus Drowned. ship of Antony.[1] Of the Asmonean family there were still
a number who stood in his way. First of all, there was his mother-
in-law Alexandra, Mariamne's mother, who pursued him with un-
remitting enmity. By appealing to, and even instigating, Antony
and Cleopatra, she forced Herod to appoint her son Aristobulus,
a stripling youth of seventeen years, to the office of high priest.
But shortly after his appointment Aristobulus was mysteriously
drowned.[2]

34, 4) Schuerer, I, I, 419 ff.
35, 1) *Wars*, I, 16, 4.   2) *Ant.*, XIV, XV, 2.
36, 1) *Wars*, I, XVIII, 4. *Ant.*, XV, I, 2. Schuerer, I, I, 420.
     2) *Ant.*, XV, III, 3.

37.

The fourth hostile power at the beginning of Herod's reign was the scheming queen of Egypt. On account of the influence

Cleopatra. she had on Antony, Herod was forced to give up to her valuable territory.[1] Cleopatra even tried to draw him into her net; but Herod was cunning enough not to surrender himself completely to her power.[2]

38.

And then there came another change in the Roman political world. Antony, Herod's patron and Cleopatra's lover, and Octavian were engaged in a death-struggle for Roman supremacy. Herod at first supported the cause of Antony; but just at the right time he turned over to the camp of the conquering Augustus and by a clever act gave him proof of his change of heart.[1] Before presenting himself, however, to his new master Augustus for con-

Battle of Actium, 31 B. C. firmation of his possessions,
Murder of Hyrcanus II. he secured himself against a possible "miscarriage of jus-

tice" by putting a rival to the throne, with better claims to it than he had, out of the way. This rival was none other than Hyrcanus II, the former high priest, a feeble and babbling memorial of a grand Asmonean past. The mere existence of an altogether harmless eighty-year-old man who more than he was entitled to the throne was to him sufficient reason for the bloody deed. Herod himself had invited him to return from his exile in Parthia in order to have him in his power.[2] And Hyrcanus, who had already lost his ears, was now to lose his life.[3]

39.

When Herod presented himself to Augustus at Rhodes in 30 B. C., he played his part skilfully. He boasted of his friend-

Again Confirmed by Augustus ship with Antony and
as King of the Jews. of the services which he had rendered *him* as a

proof how useful he might be to any one whose party he might join. And Augustus found it to his advantage to favor this crafty Idumean. In whatever else he may have been deficient, he

---

37, 1) Territory along the coast and an especially valuable district around Jericho.   2) *Ant.,* XV, IV, 1. 2.

38, 1) *Ant.,* XV, VI, 1.   2) *Ant.,* XV, II, 3.

     3) *Ant.,* XV, VI, 1—4. Schuerer, I, I, 428 f.

certainly did not lack ability. Augustus confirmed him in his royal rank and gave him not only Cleopatra's domains in Palestine, but other valuable possessions besides, practically all Palestine.[1] In proof of his gratitude Herod accompanied Augustus on his way home from Egypt as far as Antioch.[2] And again Herod was fully confirmed as the king of the Jews.

40.

But now Herod had trouble with his queen. According to all reports Mariamne was the noblest of women. Unlike her mother she never shared in the mean plots in the interest of the Asmonean house. When she charged Herod with the death of her kindred, she spoke to him boldly and frankly as to a husband, on whose affections, if he was left to himself, she knew she could rely.[1] But she failed to reckon with a real serpent, Herod's sister Salome, who managed to fabricate a plot according to which the queen was charged with, and convicted of, conspiring against Herod. Now, Herod was passionately in love with Mariamne, and undoubtedly she was innocent; but it was extremely dangerous even to be accused, let alone convicted, of such a crime. For was he not king of the Jews? And so Mari-

Mariamne, Alexandra, and Others Executed.

amne was led to execution, and with her Herod threw away a pearl of greater value than all that he had gained. For this rash deed he was afterwards sorry almost to despair.[2] Alexandra was the next to fall. This scheming woman had long deserved her fate far more than others when she paid the price of Maccabean striving against the Herodian rule.[3] And in order to rid himself of the hateful Asmoneans altogether, Herod had some distant relatives tracked down and killed who, it seems, had been preserved by his own Idumean brother-in-law Costobar for possible future use. It is a question whether they were guilty or not; at any rate, Costobar and his *protégés* paid the penalty which Herod had provided for conspiring against the king of the Jews.[4] At last Herod's mind was at rest. For the present none survived who could set up a claim to the Jewish throne.

39, 1) Schuerer, I, I, 428; *Ant.,* XV, VII, 3.
    2) End of 30 B. C. *Ant.,* XV, VII, 4.
40, 1) Stanley, *Jewish Church,* III, 376.
    2) End of 29 B. C. *Ant.,* XV, VII, 6.
    3) Some time in 28 B. C. *Ant.,* XV, VII, 8.
    4) *Ibid.*

41.

II (25—13 B. C.).

With the consolidation of his kingdom and with his subjects so thoroughly in his power that they could not revolt against him,

Glamor. Herod began a period of glamor in his reign the like of which had not been seen since the days of Solomon. His dominion was almost as large as Solomon's. And in order that it might pay tribute to his genius and gain glory for its builder, he began to embellish it with magnificent structures and strong fortifications, for which he made his subjects pay.[1]

42.

For the advancement of his people a theater, an amphitheater, and a hippodrome were reared in Jerusalem, besides hippodromes and playhouses in other cities, and for himself a royal palace was built, upon which marble and gold were lavished in profusion. Already during the time of Antony he had the citadel north of the Temple rebuilt and named Antonia in honor of his patron. In this fort the paraphernalia of the high priest were kept, without which he could not perform his duties and the retention of which controlled the office. "These vestments *Herod kept* in that

The Builder. place."[1] Many cities throughout the land were built under his direction. On the site of ancient Strato's Tower a new city with powerful breakwaters was built and named Caesarea.[2] At Jericho a fort was erected and named Cypros after his mother. Other places were founded and named after his brother and father. Old Samaria was reconstructed and renamed Sebaste[3] in honor of Caesar Augustus. Two forts were honored with his own name — Herodium. Two ancient strongholds were restored and fortified, Machaerus and Masada, the former the probable scene of John the Baptist's death, the latter one of the last strongholds in the last Jewish war. These fortresses, however, were erected not only to protect him from foreign foes, but also to keep his own subjects in check.[4]

41, 1) Schuerer, I, I, 432 ff.; *Ant.,* XVII, XI, 2.

42, 1) *Ant.,* XV, XI, 4.

    2) *Ant.,* XV, IX, 6.

    3) A Greek word corresponding to the Latin Augustus, venerable, august.

    4) *Wars,* II, VI, 2.

43.

Herod was a master builder in an age of builders. He even reached beyond his own boundaries to bring honor to his name — at Jewish expense —: at Ascalon, Damascus, Tyre, Sidon, Tripoli, Ptolemais, even at Athens and Lacedemonia.[1] But his most magnificent building operation was the restoration of the Temple at Jerusalem, which has been called "a monument of penitence."[2] The old Temple of Zerubbabel was no longer in harmony with its more beautiful surroundings. The neighborhood palaces quite

The Temple Rebuilt. eclipsed it in grandeur. And so Herod decided upon its complete restoration. The rebuilding[3] was begun in the eighteenth year of Herod, corresponding to B. C. 20—19, or A. U. C. 734—735.[4] After eighteen months of building, during which it is said to have rained only at night, so that the work of construction would not be interrupted, the Temple proper was dedicated.[5] Its beauty was proverbial: "He that has not seen Herod's building has not seen anything beautiful."[6] But Herod combined beauty with usefulness; for "there was an occult passage for the king, which led from Antonia to the inner Temple, at its eastern gate, over which he erected a tower in order to guard against any sedition that might be attempted by the people against their kings."[7]

44.

Yet in spite of all this the Jews never ceased to hate Herod; for they knew that vanity had prompted him to rebuild the Temple, not love to God. And they also knew that with the same money with which he had restored the Temple he also sponsored pagan exhibitions in which the life of men and animals were but little valued and erected temples also to heathen gods. To all appearances Herod took little interest in the Jewish religion. Though as king of the Jews he at times insisted upon the observance of ritualistic forms of Judaism,[1] as a Jewish humanist it was his ambition

---

43, 1) Gymnasia, walls, halls, porticoes, temples, market-places, theaters, aqueducts, baths, fountains, colonnades, playgrounds, and polished-marble street pavements. *Wars*, I, XXI, 11.　　2) Stanley, III, 384.

3) Not a new building. The Temple of Herod was regarded as identical with that of Zerubbabel.

4) *Ant.*, XV, XI, 1. For the date see Schuerer, I, I, 410.

5) *Ant.*, XV, XI, 7. But the building was carried on for the next eighty years, during the entire life of Christ, and was only completed in the time of Albinus (62—64 A. D.), a few years before its final destruction.

6) Schuerer I, I, 438. 7) *Ant.*, XV, XI, 7.

44, 1) *Ant.*, XVI, VII, 5.

to foster liberal arts and culture.   His architectural proclivities
served him an ill turn with the common people, who hated him
for imposing heavy taxes upon them to carry out his extravagant
building program.   Foreign glory and Roman friendship were distasteful to them because it was secured by oppression and accompanied by departure from the laws of the fathers.   The Sanhedrin,
the highest court of the nation, was stripped of all its powers, so

**The Much-Hated
Jewish Humanist.**
that doubts have been entertained as to its
very existence under Herod.[2]   High priests
were appointed and removed at will.   The
Sadducean nobles were tossed aside with ruthless violence because
of their Maccabean sympathies.   The legalistic Pharisees with their
popular following never could regard the government of a Roman
vassal king seated on David's throne as existing by right.   And so
in all quarters the "Edomite slave" was equally hated and despised.

45.

And still, in some respects Herod's government was beneficial
to the people.   He was the second man in the Roman Empire.[1]
Many of the buildings he erected served useful purposes.[2]   By his
strong hand, conditions were created by which trade was encouraged
and travelers protected.   Herod at times made attempts to win

Herod's Good Qualities.
the hearts of his subjects.[3]   In
a famine which spread over the
land he sought by all means to lend assistance, even by converting into money his table-plate.[4]   Of course, he was careful to
let the people know that the help came from him.   And by
keeping on the friendliest of terms with Rome at all times, he
secured the Jews of the dispersion against all oppression and
infringements on their rights.   For all this, however, he received
but little thanks.

46.

III (13—4 B. C.).

And now we come to the third period of Herod's reign.[1]
It is as bloody as the beginning.   The bright side is in the middle.
And again we notice that the unforgivable sin of the Jews against

44, 2) Klausner, *Jesus of Nazareth,* 151.   Schuerer, I, I, 445.
45, 1) *Wars,* I, 20, 4; *Ant.,* XV, 10, 3.   Stanley, III, 410.
    2) Schuerer, I, I, 448.
    3) By remitting taxes.   *Ant.,* XV, X, 4; XVI, II, 5.
    4) *Ant.,* XV, IX, 1. 2.
46, 1) Schuerer, I, I, 454 ff.

Herod was their failure to recognize him as king of the Jews. This period, B. C. 13—4, constitutes the period of domestic misery. Herod thought he had fully suppressed the Asmonean royal aspirations, never thinking of the fact that on the maternal side his own sons were of half-Asmonean blood. Herod had a numerous family. He had ten wives, which, Josephus said, was allowed (?) by the

Domestic Misery. Law.[2] This is a striking proof of his sensuality. His first wife was Doris, by whom he had one son, Antipater. Mariamne bore him five children, of whom only two, Aristobulus and Alexander, interest us here. Of the other eight wives only the Samaritan Malthace, mother of Archelaus and Antipas, and Cleopatra of Jerusalem, the mother of Philip, need now be mentioned.[3]

47.

About the year 23 B. C. Herod sent Aristobulus and Alexander to Rome to have them educated there. After their return, some years later, they married, according to custom, at an early age. By marriage they were brought into closer relation with the Idumean house, but still their pride would not let them forget their supposedly superior Maccabean blood. As a result there was continual jangling between the Asmonean and Idumean stepbrothers and -sisters. And here is where Antipater, the son of Doris, comes in. Herod himself preferred the sons of Mariamne and would not let the wranglings interfere with the love for these

Aristobulus, Alexander, and Three Hundred Adherents Put to Death. his sons. But Antipater, not in his father's good graces for a time, but later restored to favor, labored incessantly in true Herodian fashion to carve his way to the Jewish throne.[1] By calumniating his — probably guilty — stepbrothers, he finally inveigled his father into siding with him.[2] Plotting against his throne was the one sin which Herod could not forgive. And so he decided to accuse his sons before Augustus. The earnest, yet mild Augustus temporarily restored peace. But scarcely had the contending parties returned from Rome, when the old feud was renewed. Antipater, aided by the old serpent Salome, Herod's sister, revived old slanders, possibly to some extent founded on

---

46, 2) *Ant., XVII,* I, 2.

3) And Herod Philip of Mariamne II, the high priest's (Simon's) daughter. Herod Philip was the first husband of Herodias, Mark 6, 17.

47, 1) Schuerer, I, I, 457.   2) *Ant., XVI,* III, 3.

facts, and so finally Augustus authorized Herod to proceed against his sons as he thought best.[3] The sons were tried, convicted, and together with three hundred adherents were put to death.[4]

48.

Antipater was now all-powerful in court, but — overshot his mark. He could not await his father's death and conspired against him. This was reported to the king. Antipater, the heir to the

Antipater Put to Death. throne, had made himself guilty of the unpardonable sin.[1] And so he also was brought to trial, was convicted, and put in fetters. A report was made to the emperor;[2] and when the permission came from Augustus, he, too, was put to death. This happened just a few days before the death of Herod himself.

49.

This, then, is the key to Herod's whole career — he wanted to be king, and whoever else aspired to the Jewish throne was put to death by him. His insane ambition reached its most ghastly height

Key to Herod's Character. in "the slaughter of the innocents" at Bethlehem.[1] When this life of seemingly unceasing crime finally came to an end at Jericho in March 4 B. C., it was amid the rejoicing of his subjects. Unmourned and unwept he was carried to his grave.[2] The day of Herod's death was afterwards regarded as a day when fasting and public mourning were *not* allowed.[3]

50.

Thus ends the story of Herod the Great, of whom it is said that he stole his way to the throne like a fox, ruled like a tiger, and died like a dog.[1] He was a successful, but an extremely wicked

Herod's Place in History. Oriental despot. But God made even so wicked a king as Herod was serve His wonderful purpose. After Herod's death and the misrule of Archelaus the Jews had enough of kings, even expressing the desire to be ruled by Roman governors.[2] From Herod himself they could have learned what kind of king not to expect.

And now we are ready to take up the story of Christ.

47, 3) *Ant.*, XVI, 11, 1.   4) Probably 7 B. C. *Ibid.*, 2—8.
48, 1) *Ant.*, XVII, IV, 1. 2.   2) *Ant.*, XVII, V, 3—7.
49, 1) Matt. 2, 16.   2) *Ant.*, XVII, VIII, 1. 2.
   3) Edersheim, *Temple*, 176.
50, 1) J. Klausner, *Jesus of Nazareth*, 145.   2) *Wars*, II, VI.

CHAPTER III.

ON THE THRESHOLD OF THE NEW TESTAMENT.

Probably September, 748 A. U. C., or 6 B. C.,
to spring 749 A. U. C., or 5 B. C.

Luke 1, 5—25.   **1.**

The story of Christ begins with the story of His forerunner. In the days of King Herod there lived in the hill country of Judah

Zacharias, the Priest. a priest by the name of Zacharias and his wife Elisabeth, who was of the daughters of Aaron.[1] On account of his rural residence he was most likely treated with benevolent contempt by the high-brow, city-dwelling Zadokites;[2] but he was to be honored beyond all his fellows.

Luke 1, 5—25.   **2.**

After the conquest of Canaan the land was divided among the descendants of Jacob's twelve sons, except the tribe of Levi, which formed a priestly caste, without a separate possession, but was allotted certain cities throughout the tribes. These so-called Levitical cities were of two classes: those for the priests proper, or descendants of Aaron, thirteen in number, and all in the territory afterwards called Judea, and those for the Levites or sub-

The Twenty-Four Priestly Courses. ordinate priests, thirty-five in number, distributed among the other tribes. On account of the great number of priests, already in the time of David,[1] it was simply impossible for all to officiate at the same time. And in order to work out a plan according to which all could serve in regular rotation, the whole body of priests and Levites was divided into twenty-four families, or courses of service, each course being in service one week at a time, the change being made on the Sabbath, between the morning and the

---

1,   1) Luke 1, 39. The name of the city of Judah in which they lived is not given. Hebron has been suggested on account of Josh. 21, 11.

    2) Schuerer, II, I, 222—224; Edersheim, *Jesus*, I, 141.

2,   1) 8,580 Levites in the time of Moses, Num. 4, 48; 38,000 in the time of David, 1 Chron. 23, 3. And Josephus speaks of 20,000 priests, *Against Apion*, II, 8.

evening sacrifice.[2]) Likewise all the people were divided into twenty-four courses of service, so that there was always, besides the other worshipers, a representation of Israel at hand, which "stood by" while the sacrifices were offered.

Luke 1, 5—25.   3.

This institution of David and Solomon continued till the Captivity. But when, after the Captivity, only three, at the most four,[1]) of the original families returned, the remaining courses were artificially supplied from the returning number. Naturally the priesthood could now claim only continuity of, not identity with, those courses whose names they actually bore; and still, strange

The Course of Abia.   to say, it was afterwards considered a mark of great advantage to belong to the first of the twenty-four courses, the class of Jehoiarib, which had the honor of being the ancestors of the Maccabean family and the Asmonean princes.[2]) Now, Zacharias belonged to the eighth of these courses, the course of Abia. But we do not know from which priestly branch he was actually descended, whether from Zadok,[3]) from Eleazar, or from Ithamar.[4]) Nor does it matter. At any rate, being a descendant of one of these branches, he was a true priest of the sons of Aaron. And his wife Elisabeth, too, was of true priestly descent.

Luke 1, 5—25.   4.

At the time when this honorable priestly couple is introduced into history, they were both well stricken in years. Zacharias was probably about as old as Caesar Augustus. He was an upright and righteous man before the Lord and enjoyed the honor and

"Righteous before God."   respect of his community. Being a priest, he was entitled to his share of the many sources of income, and we can therefore suppose that he was living in comfortable circumstances.[1]) And besides, although well advanced in years, he was still sound in body and able to meet the physical requirements which were necessary for

---

2,   2) Schuerer, II, I, 273; *Ant.*, VII, XIV, 7. The act of the worship proper and the sacrifices were in the hands of the officiating priests. The Levites acted as assistants, Temple servants, guards, gate-keepers, singers, musicians, and the like. See also Edersheim, *Temple*, 63.
3,   1) Three families, the second, third, and sixteenth, in the order of 1 Chron. 24, 7 ff.; according to Ezra 2, 36 f. the children of Jedaiah, Immer, Pashur, and Harim.
       2) Josephus, *Life*, I; Edersheim, *Jesus*, I, 135; Schuerer, II, I, 222.
       3) Which is unlikely.   4) 1 Chron. 24, 2. 3.
4,   1) For the emoluments of the priesthood see Schuerer, II, I, 235—249.

the performance of his sacred office. An officiating priest had to be totally free from every sort of physical defect.[2] Blameless, honorable, healthy, in comfortable circumstances, still there was a shadow which like a dark cloud bore down on his declining years. "They had no child." This was a calamity from the Jewish point of view and for many a year must have been the burden of thoughts and prayers as well as a burden of reproach which Elisabeth always seemed to carry about with her.

Luke 1, 5—25. 　　　　　　5.

But a wonderful thing was to happen. It was at the beginning of October, 748 A. U. C., or 6 B. C. — At this point let us say something about the division of time. Our present era, called the Christian or the Dionysian Era, is computed from the supposed year of the birth of our Lord, that is, *anno Domini* or *ab incarnatione Domini.* It was introduced by the Roman abbot Dionysius Exiguus in 525 in preparing the Easter tables for that year. According to his calculations, which slowly won acceptance throughout the Christian world, the year 1 was supposed to correspond to the year 754 of the building of Rome, *ab urbe condita,* or A. U. C.

The Time. But it has been found that this was at least four years too late; for it has been ascertained with, we may say, almost absolute certainty that Herod died shortly before the Passover of 750 A. U. C. To obtain the years of Rome after Christ, we must add 753 to the number in question: Thus the year 30 A. D. would correspond to 783 A. U. C. If we would obtain the year of Rome before the birth of Christ, we must subtract the number in question from 754. Thus, if Herod died four years before the Christian Era, or 4 B. C., then, subtracting 4 from 754, we arrive at 750 A. U. C., which ought to have been the latest point for the beginning of the Dionysian Era.[1] — But let us accompany Zacharias to the Temple at Jerusalem, the work of reconstruction of which was still carried on.

Luke 1, 5—25. 　　　　　　6.

The Temple itself with its surrounding courts was reared on the heights of Mount Moriah. It was separated from the Upper City, Mount Zion, by a deep valley, the Valley of Tyropoeon, and

---

4, 2) Compare Lev. 21, 16—23. No fewer than 142 disqualifying bodily defects were counted. But at the same time a priest who for any reason was debarred from exercising the functions of his office was entitled to his share of the emoluments as belonging to the *ordo.* Schuerer, II, I, 214.
5, 1) See S. Andrews, p. 1.

connected with it by a wonderful bridge on arches, its usual approach. This bridge, now called the Royal Bridge, or Robinson's Arch, was 354 feet long, 50 feet broad, and no less than 225 feet above the valley below. From its heights the city spread out to the observer like a map. Immediately in front, that is, to the east, were seen the rows of Corinthian monoliths surrounding the outer courts of the Temple area, each 37½ feet high and overtopped by others, 100 feet high, and towering above them could be seen the

The Temple. Mount of Olives with its orchards and trees and separated from the Temple area itself by the Valley of Kedron, 400 feet below. To the left lay the Lower City and the Hill of Acra and in particular that mighty fortress, guarding and controlling the Temple, called the Tower of Antonia. To the rear Herod's beautiful palace and the Upper City fell into view. And to the right arose the Hill Ophel with its crowded and narrow streets and the priests' quarters. And a well-paved valley street was immediately below.[1] Striking indeed must have been the appearance of this sacred place — the lower courts, standing on its magnificent terraces; the inner courts on a higher level and surrounded by massive towers and gates; and within this the Temple itself with its white walls and golden roof crowning the view; and the whole scene soaring out of the depths of the dark glen which lay below. It must have been one of the most splendid architectural combinations in the ancient world.[2]

Luke 1, 5—25.   7.

The Temple plateau itself had been artificially leveled and enlarged at immense labor and cost. In order to gain room for all the Temple courts, the small surface of the hill was increased by building out from its sides successive platforms, supported by

The Court of the Gentiles. immense substructures of brick and stone, so that the whole hill is now honeycombed with artificial caves. The four principal entrances to the Temple area, all of them from the west,[1] led the visitor through the outer row of pillars into the large Court of the Gentiles, which surrounded the Temple proper on all sides. It was so named because it was the only part of the building in which foreigners were allowed. On two sides there was a covered

6,   1) See Hurlbut, *Bible Atlas*, 64.
         2) Stanley, *Jewish Church*, III, 389.
7,   1) The gate through which the scapegoat was led was to the east. Edersheim, *Temple*, 278.

corridor: Solomon's Porch on the east, where the Savior walked at the Feast of the Dedication,[2] and Herod's Royal Portico on the south. Seats were placed in these halls or porches around the Court of the Gentiles, and they must have been convenient places for friendly meetings or religious discussions.[3] Here Jesus, while still a child, was found disputing with the doctors. Here He afterwards so often taught the people. And here the first assemblies of Christians were held.[4] On the floor of this court there was a market for sacrificial meats with the tables of the money-changers, twice broken up by our Lord.[5]

Luke 1, 5—25.　　　　　　　**8.**

The Court of the Gentiles, the largest of the courts, three-fourths of a mile in circuit, surrounded the so-called Sacred Enclosure, or *Chel,* on all sides. This enclosure, embracing the Court

The Sacred Enclosure.

of the Women, the Court of Israel, and the Court of Priests, measured about 650 feet on the north and south and 300 feet on the east and west. No Gentile was allowed to enter this enclosure. There were signs erected at different places forbidding the entrance to Gentiles under penalty of death.[1] At one time Paul was arrested because it was asserted that he had led Greeks into the Sacred Enclosure.[2]

Luke 1, 5—25.　　　　　　　**9.**

Passing through one of the doors of the thick walls in the eastern half of the enclosure, the Jewish visitor — for none other were allowed to enter — now found himself in an open court about

---

7, 　2) John 10, 23.

　3) There was even supposed to have been a Temple synagog within the bounds of the sacred building, although Edersheim considers this "quite untenable." *Life and Times of Jesus,* I, 246; II, 742.

　4) Edersheim, *Temple,* 22.

　5) For a description of Herod's Temple see Schuerer, II, I, 280 ff.; Edersheim, *Temple,* 22 ff.; Hurlbut, *Bible Atlas,* 137 ff.

8, 　1) Josephus, *Wars,* VI, II, 4. Deissmann, *Licht vom Osten,* 63. A fragment of this wall with its inscription was found in Jerusalem in 1871. In the Slavonic version of Josephus there is an interesting addition concerning the Temple inscription and also incidentally concerning Jesus: "And in it there stood equal pillars, and upon them there were titles in Greek and Latin and Jewish characters, giving warning of the law of purification that no foreigner should enter within; for it was called the inner sanctuary, being approached by fourteen steps and the upper area being built in quadrangular form. And above these titles was hung a fourth title in the same characters, announcing that Jesus [the] King did not reign, [but was] crucified [by the Jews] because He prophesied the destruction of the city and the devastation of the Temple." Thackeray's edition of Josephus, Vol. III, 657.

　2) Acts 21, 28.

240 feet square and called the Court of the Women, or the Treasury. It was called Court of the Women not on account of its exclusive use by the women, but because this was as far as the women were allowed to go.[1] It was also called the Treasury on account of the thirteen chests, or trumpets, into which the worshipers deposited their Temple dues or free-will offerings. There

The Court of the Women. were four gates leading into this court, of which the eastern gate was called the Gate Beautiful. At this gate beggars were wont to sit.[2] The western gate, which led into the Court of Israel, was called the Gate of Nicanor, because, as some hold, the head of Nicanor, a Syrian enemy in the time of the Maccabees, had once been placed upon it.[3] Here in the Gate of Nicanor all that was ordered to be done before the Lord, presentation of purified women, cleansed lepers, and the like, took place. Under the floor of this court, and with an opening and a guard-room near the Gate Beautiful, there was a subterranean passage, leading from the Tower of Antonia, by which Herod and afterwards the Romans assured themselves of military control. By this passage Paul was at one time rescued from a Jewish mob.[4]

Luke 1, 5—25.   **10.**

Passing through the Gate of Nicanor and up fifteen steps, another court was entered, which was called the Court of Israel, or the Court of the Men. It occupied the western end of the Sacred Enclosure and was really a narrow corridor, which completely surrounded the next court, the Court of the Priests. This was the place where the men of Israel stood to view the sacrifices,

The Court of Israel. which, however, could be viewed also from the Court of the Women, only at a greater distance. Three gates led up to the Court of Israel from both the north and the south and the Gate of Nicanor from the east. This was as far as the Lord Jesus was allowed to go, because He was not of priestly stock. In the southeastern corner of this court there was a room called the Hall Gazith, in which the members of the Sanhedrin, seated in a semicircle on stone seats, usually assembled. Chambers were built into the walls and furnished for storehouses and living-rooms for the officiating priests and the Temple attendants.

9, 1) Josephus, *Apion*, II, 8. 2) Acts 3, 2.
  3) 1 Macc. 7, 47; 2 Macc. 15, 35. 4) Acts 21, 31. 32.

Luke 1, 5—25. **11.**

On a raised platform, a few steps higher and surrounding the Temple proper on three sides, east, north, and south, was the Court of the Priests. This court, about 275 feet long by 200 feet wide, was mainly occupied by the House of God, the Sanctuary, which stood in the western half of the Court of Israel and was itself divided into the Holy and Most Holy, or Holy of Holies. In front of the Temple proper and in the eastern section of the Court of the Priests stood the Great Altar, or Altar of Burnt Offerings, of unhewn stones and built upon the site which now lies under the Dome of the Rock. In its construction only unhewn stones were used, which no tool had ever touched.[1] Upon it every act

The Court of the Priests and the Great Altar. of sacrifice, with the exception of the burning of incense, had to be performed.[2] It was fully forty-eight feet square and fifteen feet high, diminishing in size towards the top, around which ran a circuit for the administering priests. A fire upon this altar was continually kept burning by night as well as by day. Between the altar and the porch of the Temple proper, towards the left, that is, to the south, there was at one time a large laver of brass, supported by twelve colossal lions, which was drained every evening and filled every morning by machinery, where the required washing of the priests could be made previous to their duties in the Sanctuary. Indeed, the water-supply as also a perfect sewer system into the Brook of Kedron was one of the Sanctuary's most wonderful arrangements. An aqueduct supplied the Temple with water from the hills about Hebron, from Bethlehem, from Etham, and from the Pools of Solomon at a distance of over forty miles.[3]

Luke 1, 5—25. **12.**

The Temple proper, or House of God, not a large and some-what dark, but a handsome edifice, including the projections of the porch, about 150 by 150 feet, occupied about one half of the

The Temple Proper. space in the Court of Priests. Its floor was eight feet above the level of the Court of Priests. In the front part, towards the east, a porch, or vestibule, extended across the Temple. It was built of

---

11, 1) Ex. 20, 25; 1 Macc. 4, 47.
   2) See Schuerer, II, I, 282 f.   3) Edersheim, *Temple,* 33 f.
   THE LIFE OF CHRIST.   5

marble, richly ornamented, was about 120 feet high, and consisted of several stories. Its roof was steep and was covered with golden spikes to keep birds from settling upon and defiling it.[1]

Luke 1, 5—25.   **13.**

Two-leaved doors with gold plating formed the entrance from the porch into the Holy Place. Above it hung the symbol of Israel, a gigantic vine of pure gold, each cluster the height of a man. In the Holy Place itself, about 30 by 60 feet, were found, to the

The Holy Place.   right, the golden Table of Showbread, on which twelve loaves were placed every Sabbath-day.[1]   To the left, that is, to the south, the Golden Lampstand, generally, but incorrectly, called the Golden Candle-stick, was placed. Its seven lamps, not candles, had to be kept constantly burning.[2]   And at its farther end, towards the west and near the entrance to the Holy of Holies, was the golden Altar of Incense. Upon this altar, also called the Inner Altar, incense was burned every morning and evening.

Luke 1, 5—25.   **14.**

Beyond the Holy Place, separated from it by a heavy curtain, or veil, which was rent from the top to the bottom at our Savior's death,[1] was the room called the Most Holy, or Holy of Holies. This room, the most sacred place, was a cube, each dimension being

The Holy of Holies.   thirty feet. It was empty, contain-ing only a large stone, upon which the high priest sprinkled the blood of the sacrifices on the Great Day of Atonement, and occupying the place where once the Ark of the Covenant, surmounted by the mercy-seat, had stood in Solomon's Temple. No one was allowed to enter it except the High Priest, and he but once a year, on that day. This is the sanctuary of sanctuaries which Pompey insisted upon entering, expecting to find some material object of worship — "and found nothing."

Luke 1, 5—25.   **15.**

Such was the beautiful Temple on which Herod, as a monu-ment of penitence for the murder of Mariamne,[1] had lavished

---

12, 1) Josephus, *Wars,* V, v, 6.
13, 1) Schuerer, II, I, 282.   2) See note in Schuerer, II, I, 281.
14, 1) Mark 15, 38.
15, 1) Stanley, *Jewish Church,* III, 384.

The Beauty of the Temple. marble, gold, and brass and for which he received no thanks. The Rabbis were never weary of praising its beauties, but not once did they mention Herod's name. That he had rebuilt it was passed over with absolute silence.[2] Of the great building not one stone has remained.

Luke 1, 5—25.   16.

Upon one October morning in the year 748 A. U. C., or 6 B. C., as we take it, there stood among those priests who had assembled in the Hall of Polished Stones, the Hall Gazith, for the distribution of lots, a priest upon whom the snows of at least sixty winters had fallen.[1] His course, the course of Abia, was on duty for the week and the house of his fathers for that particular day. During his week of duty he slept in a room in the

October 748 A. U. C.   inner court, and he had already before dawn submersed himself in a well-appointed subterranean bathroom in order to be Levitically clean.[2] Then he put on his official dress, which the priests wore only while on actual duty: short white linen breeches, a long white linen, close-fitting coat, a girdle of white linen (byssus), with embroidery work on it in scarlet, purple, and blue. And he had a kind of turban on his head, because priests were not permitted to present themselves before the Lord with uncovered head. Shoes are nowhere mentioned, and we can safely suppose that he had nothing on his feet.[3]

Luke 1, 5—25.   17.

In all, four lots were taken for the purpose of deciding how the various functions of the day were to be apportioned. The first lot decided who was to prepare the Great Altar, carry away the ashes, and carry the wood and lay it on the altar. Immediately

The First Lot.   after this lot was drawn and while it was still dark, with no light except a flickering blaze from the fire on the Great Altar, the designated priests washed their hands and feet in the Great Laver and set themselves to per-

---

15, 2) The first mention of Herod's name in connection with the rebuilding of the Temple occurs in the Babylonian Talmud, and then neither gratefully nor graciously. Edersheim, *Temple*, 36.

16, 1) Edersheim, I, 135.

2) Schuerer, II, I, 278; Edersheim, *Temple*, 122.

3) Schuerer, II, I, 276; *Ant.*, III, VII, 1—3. Ex. 28, 40—43; 39, 27—29; Ezek. 44, 17—19.

form their appointed tasks. And after they had performed their duties and again washed their hands and feet, they again presented themselves in the Hall of Polished Stones for a further drawing of lots.

Luke 1, 5—25.   **18.**

The second lot, taken while it was still dark, determined who was to kill the victim, prepare its body, and sprinkle the blood upon the altar, and who was to prepare the Altar of Incense, trim

The Second Lot. and replenish the lamps, and attend to various other duties. The next step was to go out and see whether there was as yet any sign of day. As soon as the gray dawn was breaking, the lamb was led forth from the lamb-house, the ninety-three [1] sacred utensils were brought from the utensil house, the lamb was watered out of a golden bowl, suspended from a ring on the north side of the altar, and its fore and hind feet were tied together.

Luke 1, 5—25.   **19.**

Immediately upon this there was heard the blast of a silver trumpet, which was a signal for the great gates leading into the Holy Place to be opened, for the Levites to be ready with the music and be prepared to perform their duties, and for the representatives of the people, the so-called stationary men, to present themselves to witness the morning sacrifice. The opening of the

The Slaying of the Lamb. gates was also the signal for the slaying of the sacrificial lamb. [1] While the lamb was slain and its blood sprinkled on the altar, the priests who had been chosen for that purpose entered the now open doors of the Holy Place to dress the Golden Lampstand and to prepare the Altar of Incense. After this had been done and the body of the victim had been prepared for the burnt offering, the priests again betook themselves to the Hall Gazith for the third drawing of lots.

18, 1) Schuerer, II, I, 293.

19, 1) According to Josephus the services of two hundred men were required every time the Temple gates were closed. The heavy brazen gate on the east side of the Temple proper required the service of twenty men. The creaking of the gates is said to have been heard as far as Jericho! *Contra Apionem*, II, 9. Schuerer, II, I, 267. In all, 240 Levites and 30 priests were on duty every night and 50 priests every day. Edersheim, I, 134, note; *Temple*, 119.

Luke 1, 5—25.   **20.**

The most solemn part of the service was now to begin, the determining by lot who was to offer the incense. The president of the course called upon all the assembled priests to join in the prescribed prayer and the repeating of the Shema, which might be called a sort of *credo,* or confession of faith: "Hear, O Israel, the

The Lot for the Burning of Incense. Lord, our God, is one Lord." [1] After this the lot was cast for the burning of incense, which was regarded as the most

solemn stage of the whole sacrificial act. No one might take part in this drawing of lots who already previously had been called upon to offer incense. Only once in a lifetime, after which he would be called rich and holy, should a priest receive this honor. [2] Now Zacharias, the aged priest from the hill country of Judea, was accorded this honor. But before taking up the story of Zacharias, let us finish the account of the service.

Luke 1, 5—25.   **21.**

The lot for the burning of incense was immediately followed by the fourth and last lot, by which it was to be ascertained whose

The Fourth Lot. duty it was to put the various parts of the slaughtered lamb on the fire of the

Altar of Burnt Sacrifice. Those upon whom no lot had fallen took off their official attire, hung it in the proper place, and were then at liberty to leave the Sanctuary.

Luke 1, 5—25.   **22.**

The incense-offering priest with two assistants, one of whom carried live coals from the fire of the Great Altar and the other the incense, which was composed of twelve kinds of sweet-smelling

The Burning of Incense. spices, [1] now entered the Holy Place, the Temple proper. As

they passed into the Holy Place, a signal was given at the sound of which all priests hastened from all parts to worship. The Levites occupied the places allotted to them for the playing of the string

---

20, 1) The *credo* was a collection of three passages: Deut. 4, 6—9; 11, 14—21; Num. 15, 37—42.   2) Edersheim, I, 134.

22, 1) Besides the three ingredients mentioned in Ex. 30, 34, stacte, onycha, and galbanum, there were added in Rabbinic times myrrh, cassia, spikenard, saffron, costus, mace, cinnamon, salt, and a herb which had the property of causing the smoke to ascend vertically. Thackeray, in note to Josephus, *Wars,* V, V; III, p. 266.

instruments and the singing of psalms, the chief of the stationary
men arranged his course at the Gate of Nicanor, and slowly the
incense-burning priest approached the altar.   One of the assistants
reverently placed the coals on the altar and then withdrew.   Another
arranged the incense and then withdrew.   The chief officiating
priest was then left alone to await the signal for the burning of
incense.   It was always a solemn moment.   Throughout the Temple
courts silence reigned, while within the Sanctuary itself the solitary
priest laid the incense upon the fire and thick clouds of sweet-
smelling odor rose up before the Lord.

Luke 1, 5—25.   **23.**

After the offering up of incense the officiating priest and his
assistants as well as those of the second lot who had prepared the
lamp and the Altar of Incense, proceeded to the steps in front of
the Sanctuary and solemnly pronounced the benediction.   In the
course of this blessing the so-called ineffable name of "Jehovah,"
which now among Jews is never spoken, was pronounced as it is
spelled, that is, Jehovah, not Lord or Adonai.[1]   At this point the
sacrificing of the burnt offering was begun.   Those parts of the
lamb that had been designated by the Lord to be burned were then

**The Burnt Offering
and the Benediction.**
laid upon the altar.[2]   Besides this
regular daily burnt offering, other
offerings, meat-offerings and drink-
offerings, were presented.   While the priest was bending forward
to pour out the appropriate drink-offering, a signal was given for
the musical part of the service to begin.   The twelve-voiced Levite
choir sang the psalm appointed for the day to the accompaniment
of the musical instruments.   At the blast of the silver trumpets the
people fell down and worshiped.   This ended the morning service.
The evening service was similar to the morning service.   The only
difference was that lots were drawn only for the burning of incense,
and instead of the burnt sacrifice's being offered after the burning
of incense the order was reversed.   Thus the daily burnt offering
was girt round, as it were, with the offering of incense.[3]

23,   1) Num. 6, 24—26. Edersheim, *Temple,* 141 f.   Schuerer, II, I, 296.

2) This was the public sacrifice.   But day by day numerous victims
were slaughtered and their flesh burned upon the altar, and at all the high
festivals so many sacrifices were offered that the officiating priests were kept
extremely busy.   Schuerer, II, I, 298.

3) See Schuerer, II, I, 290. 273—297. Edersheim, *Temple,* 121—144.

Luke 1, 5—25.   **24.**

And now let us return to Zacharias. Deep silence had fallen upon the worshipers as prayerfully they waited for the ascending clouds of sweet odors to fill the house of God. Zacharias paused until he saw the incense burning. Then he, too, bowing, would **A Celestial Visitor.** have reverently withdrawn had not his attention been arrested by a startling sight.[1] Was he dreaming? There on the right side of the Golden Altar[2] he clearly beheld an angelic form. One of those holy beings of God's invisible creation here assumed visible form, and it is evident why Zacharias was — and for that matter why any one in his place would have been — troubled with fear.

Luke 1, 5—25.   **25.**

But except for the fact of the sudden appearance of God's holy messenger to him, a sinful man, there was no reason for fear. "Fear not, Zacharias," the angel said, "for thy prayer is heard, and thy wife Elisabeth shall bear thee a son, and thou shalt call his name John." This does not mean that the birth of a son had at that moment been the particular burden of his prayer, for as the incensing priest he was serving in an official capacity. And the prayer referred to concerned the deepest desire of all true Israel, namely, the Messianic deliverance of the people: "Be graciously **John the Baptist Promised.** pleased, Jehovah, our God, with Thy people Israel and with their prayer. Appoint peace, goodness, and blessing, grace, mercy, and compassion, for us and for all Israel, Thy people." [1] "Oh, that the salvation of Israel were come out of Zion! When the Lord bringeth back the captivity of His people, Jacob shall rejoice, and Israel shall be glad." [2] This prayer had been heard. But the Lord had held in remembrance also the other prayer of Zacharias, that oft-repeated private prayer. And now as a sign of the advent of the Messiah in the near future the long-prayed-for, though now no longer expected son shall be born to serve as His forerunner. What honor and glory for the humble priest from the

---

24, 1) Edersheim, I, 138.

2) Which was the right side? From the standpoint of the angel, who probably made his appearance from the direction of the Holy of Holies, it was on the south side of the altar, between the altar and the lampstand; from that of Zacharias it was on the north side, between the altar and the Table of Showbread.

25, 1) Edersheim, *Temple,* 139. 140.   2) Ps. 14, 7.

hill country! There was a peculiar significance in the name John selected for the unborn child, referring to the *grace of God.*[3] The time for the gracious coming of Christ, whose forerunner John was to be, had finally arrived. And therefore many would rejoice at his birth. According to the word of the angel this child was to be "great in the sight of the Lord," a truly great man. Moreover, like Samson and Samuel of old he was to consecrate himself as a life-Nazirite unto the Lord.[4] He was to abstain from wine and strong drink; and the angel said he would be filled with the Holy Ghost, and that already before his birth. In the strength of God he would lay the ax to the root of the tree, bare the sin and corruption of the people, go to the root of the evil, the sinful heart, by preaching the Law of God as it should be preached and showing the wrath of the holy God upon all sinners. Like Samuel he would turn many of the children of Israel to the Lord, their God, and like Elijah [5] "turn the hearts of the fathers to the children and the disobedient to the wisdom of the just," by pointing those who, after hearing the curse of the Law, truly repented of their sins, to Him who alone can save them from their sins, so that, by the grace of God, they would return to the faith of their little children and thus become truly wise.[6] His real mission was to "make ready a people prepared for the Lord," willing, yea, eager to receive the Messiah.

Luke 1, 5—25.   **26.**

These words of the angel filled the soul of Zacharias with bewilderment and his heart with doubt. But it was inexcusable doubt. His demand of some visible sign by which to know "this" distinguished his doubt from the reaction of Abraham and Ma-

---

25, 3) John in Hebrew means "God is gracious."

   4) Samson, Judg. 13, 7; Samuel, 1 Sam. 1, 11. There were two kinds of Nazirite vows according to Num. 6, 2—8 and 30, 2, a positive and a negative vow, a *Neder* and an *Issar*. In the former "a man vowed a vow unto Jehovah" in which He consecrated unto God himself, some person, or a certain thing; in the latter he "swore an oath to bind his soul with a bond," that is, he renounced the use of certain things. The keeping of the vow of a life-Nazirite, or Nazirite from birth, entailed 1. complete abstinence from wine and the fruit of the vine; 2. keeping hair and beard unshorn; 3. guarding against touching a dead body; 4. refraining from eating Levitically unclean food. Only three life-Nazirites are mentioned in the Bible: Samson, Samuel, and John the Baptist. See Edersheim, *Temple*, 322 ff. Tradition adds James the Just. Eusebius, *H. E.*, II, 23. — Temporary Nazirites vowed to consecrate themselves to the Lord for a specified time. Num. 6, 1—21.

   5) 1 Kings 18, 37.
   6) Matt. 3, 1—6; 11, 10. 14; Mal. 3, 1.

noah,[1] with which the doubt of Zacharias has been compared, to somewhat similar announcements. But even a cursory reading of the passages conveys the impression of a marked difference. The doubt of Zacharias was, however, not to make the promises of God come to naught. He that asked for a sign received it. But before giving it, the angel, by way of justifying the penalty

The Doubt of Zacharias. which he had to announce, said, "I am Gabriel, that stand in the presence of God, and am sent to speak unto thee these glad tidings." [2] Gabriel means *Vir Dei*, or the Strength of God; [3] he was a special messenger sent by God to Zacharias for this particular purpose.

Luke 1, 5—25. **27.**

And now the sign. "Thou shalt be dumb and not able to speak until the day that these things shall be performed, because thou believest not my words, which shall be fulfilled in their season."

The Sign. Immediate dumbness was to be the sign, which, however, was not caused by a stroke of apoplexy or by terror, nor was a state of prolonged stupefaction,[1] but was a *miraculous* penalty for the reason that the "glad tidings" were not believed. In the course of a few minutes three miracles have been noted: the appearance of an angel, a prediction of an extraordinary event, and miraculous dumbness.

Luke 1, 5—25. **28.**

Considerable time had passed since the signal for the burning of incense had been given. The prayers of the people had been said. They were now waiting for the return of the priest to lead

The People without. in the priestly blessing which preceded the daily burnt offering and the psalm of praise. It was a rule with the priests to spend only a short time in the Sanctuary because otherwise the worshipers might fear that they had been slain by God for having become guilty of some wrong.[1] And so the unusually long delay of Zacharias in coming forth from the Holy Place caused the people to marvel.[2]

26, 1) Gen. 17, 17; Judg. 13, 17.

2) In Greek εὐαγγελίσασθαι. For the first time we meet with the beautiful word εὐαγγέλιον, that is, the Gospel.

3) Also met with in Dan. 8, 16; 9, 21.

27, 1) Since negative views are not testimonies, it will be unnecessary always to mention the holders of such views and to quote the respective titles and pages of their books.

28, 1) Meyer *in loco.* 2) Luke 1, 21.

When he finally did emerge and tried to speak, but could not, helplessly endeavoring by signs to indicate his inability to pronounce the Benediction, the awe-struck assembly knew that something uncommon had happened and that he had received a revelation or seen a vision in the Temple. After the first excitement had passed over, it is probable that by means of a written communication Zacharias gave an explanation.[3] Wondering, all disperse, priests and worshipers.

Luke 1, 5—25.   **29.**

The day's service over, another family took the place of the family to which Zacharias belonged. The week over, another course, the ninth, the course of Jeshuah,[1] was ready to relieve the course of Abia. The priests returned to their homes, some to Ophel, some to Jericho, while Zacharias, now "rich and noble" [2] on account of the lot which had made him an incense-offering priest, dumb, and yet happy, traced a silent homeward course to the hill country of Judea. Upon arrival at his home he communicated to the **Zacharias Returns Home.** aged and anxious Elisabeth the things which had come to pass.[3] God fulfilled the promise which He had given by His angel; and the more Zacharias meditated on all these things, the vision of the angel, the wonderful announcement, the punishment his doubting had brought upon him, and now the cheering pregnancy of his devoted wife, the more fully he must have realized that in truth the redemption of Israel was drawing nigh. And as for Elisabeth, we can suppose that she marveled and devoutly meditated on those things like her husband. Rejoicing in her heart, she was satisfied for the present that the Lord had looked upon her and taken away her reproach among men. And so the next five months passed by in deepest silence.

Luke 1, 26—38.   **30.**

From the hill country of Judea we now proceed to Galilee, to a town called Nazareth. Galilee, meaning "circuit" or "border," included a territory originally claimed, but never completely possessed, by the tribes of Naphtali, Zebulun, Issachar, and Asher.

28, 3) As suggested by Ebrard on account of Luke 1, 63. *Gospel History,* 164.

29, 1) 1 Chron. 24, 11.

2) Edersheim, I, 134.

3) From Luke 1, 60 we see that Zacharias, now dumb, in some way communicated to Elisabeth all that had happened to him in the Sanctuary.

Hence the name "Galilee of the Gentiles," [1] on account of its mixed population of Phenicians and Arabs and because in the time of our Lord the Greek language was currently spoken there. In the time of David this territory was united with his kingdom. For services rendered in the building of the Temple, Solomon gave Hiram, the king of Tyre, twenty cities in the land of Galilee. But it seems that Hiram was not quite satisfied; for when he came out to look at the cities, "they pleased him not. And he called them the land of Cabul to this day." [2] From that time on it seems always to have been the fate of Galilee to be despised. Following Jeroboam after the death of Solomon, it helped to form the Kingdom of Israel; but in the time of Tiglath-pileser it was the first to fall. Eleven years before the final doom of Israel thousands of the inhabitants of Galilee were carried captive to Assyria. [3] But

Galilee. this territory, first to fall, was also first to see the Light. [4] After the Babylonian Captivity it was largely settled by returning Jewish colonists, who, carefully avoiding the schismatic Samaritans, faithfully maintained religious fellowship with Jerusalem. But not belonging to Judea proper, its Jewish population was considered a part of the Jewish Diaspora. During the Maccabean uprising a closer contact was established with the mother country. One of the first acts of the Maccabee brothers, after the restoration of the worship in Jerusalem, was to defend their northern brethren against heathen persecution; Simon went to Galilee and Judas to Gilead. [5] But beyond bringing help to their brethren and transporting them safely to Jewish soil, properly so called, no attempt was made to subjugate the territory itself. This was not done until during the short reign of Aristobulus I, when a large portion of the northern territory, including Galilee, was conquered and made subject to the high priest at Jerusalem. [6] Thus Galilee was again politically embodied with the ancient Land of Israel, but still within its own boundaries and under foreign rule. For when the Romans left the weak Hyrcanus II as high priest and nominally as "ethnarch" of the Jews, — but with Antipater as the real power behind the throne, — Phasael was appointed

---

30, 1) Judg. 4, 2; Is. 9. 1; Matt. 4, 15; 1 Macc. 5, 15.

 2) 1 Kings 9, 12. 13. *Cabul*, according to Josephus, means "disgusting" or "what does not please." *Ant.*, VIII, V, 3.

 3) 735 B. C. 2 Kings 15, 29.

 4) Is. 9, 1. 2; Matt. 4, 13—16.

 5) 1 Macc. 5, 9—58.

 6) 105—104 B. C. See Schuerer, I, I, 294.

governor of Jerusalem and young Herod governor of Galilee. So it happened that Herod began his political career as governor of Galilee, which ended with the title King of the Jews.

Luke 1, 26—38. **31.**

In the course of time a nationalism and patriotism developed in Galilee as intense as that in Judea itself, notwithstanding the contempt with which the high-brow metropolitans of Jerusalem regarded the Galilean provincials. Their very speech, their amusing Galilean brogue, which was probably a confusion in the pronunciation of gutturals, was held in contempt.[1] Belittling proverbial sayings were hurled against them, such as "Out of Galilee ariseth no prophet." [2] But what about Deborah, Jonah, Elisha, and probably Hosea?

The Galileans.

Of their intense Jewish patriotism, of Galilean manhood and womanhood, there was no question, as witnessed by Josephus,[3] himself a Galilean governor at the outbreak of the last Jewish war.[4] The soil of Galilee was richer than that of Judea, and its inhabitants were more prosperous, according to a common saying: "If a person wishes to be rich, let him go North; if he wants to be wise, let him come South." [5] And still Galilee was to Judaism only the "Court of the Gentiles," while Judea was its "innermost Sanctuary." But, after all, some of the best Jewish families, if not as to position and influence, at least as to lineage and blood, had made Galilee, for instance, Nazareth, their home.

Luke 1, 26—38. **32.**

As to the etymology of Nazareth many conjectures have been offered; but on account of the quotation of St. Matthew "He shall be called a Nazarene" it is probably best to connect it with *netzer,*

31, 1) Matt. 26, 73.

2) John 7, 52.

3) *Wars,* III, III, 2; VII, 31.

4) Much is made by some writers — for instance, Emil Ludwig in *The Son of Man* and by those whom he has followed — of the carnal and political Messianic hopes and revolutionary tendencies of the Galilean zealots in explanation of the Galilean success and supposed purpose of the Lord's public ministry. But as we can see no particular connection of these thoughts — or facts — with the history of Christ's work, except probably to explain John 6, 66; 7, 3, and similar passages, we are giving them only this passing notice.

5) Quoted by Edersheim, I, 223. It is here in Galilee that Asher "dipped his foot in oil," Deut. 33, 24. The Rabbis themselves said that it was easier to rear a forest of olive-trees in Galilee than one child in Judea. Quoted by Edersheim, I, 224.

a branch or twig, conforming to the prophecy: "And there shall come forth a rod out of the stem of Jesse, and a Branch shall grow out of its roots." [1]   The town is not mentioned in Josephus and

Despised Nazareth.

in the Old Testament; but the New Testament Scriptures not only mention it, but give it due prominence.[2]   It was a small and secluded town of a few thousand inhabitants, despised at that, — "Can there any good thing come out of Nazareth?" [3] — which was to lend its inglorious name to the scornful title on the cross "Jesus of Nazareth," yet a title which the Lord Himself did not despise to use when He appeared to persecuting Saul [4] and by which His despised followers, or "Nazarenes," are still known in the Oriental world.

Luke 1, 26—38.   33.

But Nazareth was beautifully situated. Travelers tell us that the beauty of its surrounding must be seen to be appreciated. It lies on the western and northwestern slopes of a hollow among the hills of Lower Galilee, away from the main caravan route [1] and just north of the great Plain of Esdraelon, from which it is reached by a steep and rocky path. Still the quiet little town was no stagnant pool of rustic seclusion; for while its own immediate horizon was limited, from the summit of a near-by hill there is a splendid view. To the west are the low-lying hills stretching toward the Mediterranean Sea, whose blue waters turn to a silver sheen under the shining sun. Following the coast-line to the left, the eye is arrested by the only promontory on the Palestinian coast, the thickly wooded ridge of Carmel, where Elijah slew the prophets

---

32, 1) Matt. 2, 23; Is. 11, 1; Zech. 6, 12. Some derive Nazareth from *notser*, to guard or keep (Edersheim, I, 146), others from *nezer*, to separate, and Jerome says it means a flower: "Let us go to Nazareth and see the 'Flower of Galilee.'" (*Epistola*, XLVI, Ad Marcellam; quoted by Andrews, *Life of Our Lord*, 105.) But since Matt. 2, 23 is no direct quotation, it is also possible that a comparison was intended with the Messianic picture in Is. 53 on account of the low estimate in which Nazareth was held. But, as applied to Jesus, under no condition is it permissible, thus charging Matthew with confusion, to derive the term from *nazir* in the attempt to make a Nazirite out of Jesus, which is contrary to the promises and facts of the life of the Savior. See J. Klausner in his recent *Jesus of Nazareth*, 230.

2) Neither is it apparently mentioned by any Christian writer prior to Eusebius, in the fourth century, *H. E.*, I, VII. But after that it became one of the most famous of holy places.

3) John 1, 46. We can no longer trace the source of popular prejudice against it.   4) Acts 22, 8.

33, 1) See H. Guthe's *Bible Atlas*, 13. However, Edersheim (I, 147), Andrews (106), MacCoun (*The Holy Land*, II, 86), and others suppose the *Via Maris*, the ancient caravan route between Acco (Accho) and Damascus, to have passed through Nazareth.

of Baal.[2]   To the south there extends the great Plain of Esdraelon, framed in by the bare mountains of Samaria, with its vegetation and trees looking like a sea of green, bordered by yellow shores.[3]   The scene is crowned by the Hill of Moreh, or Little Hermon, with Nain clinging to its slopes, the battle-field of Gideon,[4] and Gilboa, where Saul was slain.[5]   To the east there first falls into view the rounded top of Mount Tabor, behind it the

Its Beautiful Setting.   deep Jordan valley, to the left the shining waters of the Sea of Galilee, and beyond it all in the distance the yellow horizon of the heights of Gilead and Bashan, plowed, as it were, into sandy furrows by the desert winds.   To the north the eye rests on Cana and many other little villages, glittering like white spots here and there in the bright sunlight.   Passing over romantic hills and glens and pausing for a moment on Safed, the supposed "city set upon a hill," [6] the view is bounded by far-off Mount Hermon with its crest of everlasting snow.[7]

Luke 1, 26—38.   **34.**

However, in spite of its seclusion and the fact that the Old Testament writers down to Josephus fail to mention it, we are not to suppose that it was a place of little importance and that its

Its Importance.   inhabitants were people of but little culture. On the contrary, there was a synagog at Nazareth.[1]   According to some writers it was a priest center, a gathering-place for priests, from where they "went up in company to Jerusalem" and the Temple.[2]   Indeed, if a rabbinic tradition is to be credited, it was the home of the eighteenth course of priests,

---

33, 2) 1 Kings 18, 19.

3) The Plain of Esdraelon, a Y-shaped region, 250 feet above sealevel, surrounded by mountains, is situated between Mounts Carmel, Tabor. Gilboa, and Hill Moreh.   More battles are said to have been fought on this plain than on any other field in the world, the latest being the battle between General Allenby and the Turks in 1917, which completed the British conquest of Palestine.   In the Old Testament it is called the Valley of Jezreel, from the city on its eastern end, its Greek name Esdraelon being a modification of Jezreel.   It is also called the Valley of Megiddo, from the city on its western edge.   Armageddon or Harmageddon (Rev. 16, 16) is the Greek for the Mountain of Megiddo.   (Hurlbut, *Bible Atlas,* 15.)

4) Judg. 7, 1.   5) 1 Sam. 28, 4.   6) Sephad, Matt. 5, 14.

7) Each writer on Palestine tries to paint a picture of the splendid panorama: J. Klausner, *Jesus of Nazareth,* 236; B. Weiss, *Life of Christ,* I, 211; S. J. Andrews, 107; Edersheim, I, 145; Farrar, I, 100; and others.

34, 1) Luke 4, 16.

2) Neubauer, *Sketches of Jewish Social Life;* quoted by Edersheim, I, 147, and Andrews, 106.

the course of Aphses.[3]   But what is more, at the time that we are taking up our story it was also the home of ex-royalty.   Two members of the house of David, a son and a daughter, and probably also their families, had made it their home.[4]   According to an ancient tradition, which merits small credence, there were other members of David's family living in the same territory.

Luke 1, 26—38.   35.

Fully five months after the conception of Elisabeth, that is, in the sixth month, and, as we take it, in the latter part of March, 749 A. U. C., or 5 B. C., the angel Gabriel was sent by God to a virgin in Nazareth who was espoused to Joseph[1] of the house of David and a carpenter by trade.   This time, however, the appearance was not in the solemn grandeur of God's Sanctuary, but in a humble private home.[2]   The name of the virgin was Mary. Whether or not the prevalence of this name in the New Testament was a tribute to the popularity of Mariamne, the murdered wife of Herod, we do not know.   It does not seem likely in the case of Mary, because Marys, or Miriams, are mentioned already in the Old Testament, for instance, the sister of Moses;[3] besides, she was a royal princess herself of the house of David.[4]   Of her age we

---

34, 3) 1 Chron. 24, 15.   Quoted by J. Klausner, a recent Jewish writer from Jerusalem, in his *Jesus of Nazareth*, 229.

4) We do not suppose that they made their home away from their ancestral seat in despised Galilee and in an obscure village in order not to arouse the jealousy of Herod.   Of this there is no proof.   It is rather to be explained as a sign of the fallen estate of that once royal house.   See Andrews, 66.

35, 1) According to one tradition, Joseph had been previously married to Melcha (or Escha or Salome), by whom he had two daughters and four sons, of whom the youngest was James the Less, "the Lord's brother."   His marriage to Mary is placed a year after his wife's death.   (*Cath. Encycl., sub* "Joseph," VIII, 505.)

2) The Greek Church affirms that the Annunciation took place at the village fountain, at present marked by the Church of the Annunciation. And the Latins believe that the angel found the virgin in a grotto, where a church has been erected, which, after that of the Holy Sepulcher, is said to be the most beautiful in Syria.   And Bengel thinks that the appearance was at evening.   Andrews, 68.

3) Ex. 15, 20.

4) While it is true that the grammatical construction of this particular passage, Luke 1, 27: "espoused to a man whose name was Joseph, of the house of David; and the virgin's name was Mary," favors the reference to Joseph only, there is no doubt about the Davidic descent of Mary, even if both genealogies are taken as those of Joseph.   Meyer, who claims that "the descent of Mary from David cannot at all be proved in the New Testament," should rather have said that the proof is too evident to be denied. Luke 1, 27 and 69 prove her Davidic descent beyond the shadow of a doubt. And besides, there are the inescapable inferences in Acts 2, 30;   Rom. 1, 3; 2 Tim. 2, 8;   Heb. 7, 14.

know nothing, but suppose that she was still quite young [5] when espoused to Joseph, whom tradition is disposed to introduce at a rather advanced and infirm age.[6]   But we must not forget that he was still alive twelve years later and paid his annual visit to the Temple.[7]   When or why these two persons of royal descent, including probably their immediate family, had left the ancestral home of Bethlehem in Judea and made Nazareth in Galilee their permanent residence, is impossible to state.   At the time of their entry into the story they had been recently engaged.[8]   It was probably a simple betrothal, not because Joseph was a carpenter, — since

Mary of the House of David.

among the Jews it was regarded as almost a religious duty for every boy to learn a trade, — but because they were poor.[9]   A promise was given in the presence of witnesses, a pledge was added, a small coin or coin's worth, a meal was enjoyed, the benediction was spoken over the statutory cup of wine, and a son and a daughter of David had become groom and bride.[10] From that moment Mary had become the betrothed wife of Joseph. Their relation was as sacred as if they had been already wedded. Any breach of this relation would be treated as adultery.   But before the actual marriage of Joseph and Mary took place a few months later,[11] a most remarkable thing was to happen, and both Mary and Joseph were to receive revelations which were to prove of the most momentous consequences for the history of mankind.

Luke 1, 26—38.   36.

A greeting from heaven was brought to Mary. "Hail, thou that art favored! The Lord is with thee; blessed art thou among women."   Naturally, the awe of the supernatural fell upon her.[1] But it was not so much the appearance of the mysterious stranger as the words of greeting, implying most distinctive blessings, that

---

35, 5) Andrews, 57.

6) Ephiphanius and the *Historia Iosephi* both give his age as eighty years. Andrews, 56.   7) Luke 2, 43.

8) Prolonged intervals between betrothal and marriage were deemed undesirable for many reasons. Geo. B. Eager, in *Int. St. Bible Encycl., sub* "Marriage," 1897.

9) Luke 2, 24.   10) Edersheim, I, 149.

11) Depending upon the order in which the action of Joseph is placed, Matt. 1, 24, before or after the three months' visit of Mary to Elisabeth, Luke 1, 56; most likely after. See Andrews, 68. Meyer, 244 (Ebrard, 172).
36, 1) Edersheim, I, 150.

disturbed the humble maiden. After a friendly "Fear not" the blessings, which are not awarded on account of merit, but are bestowed upon her as a special favor by the grace of God, are unfolded. She, a virgin, was to conceive and bear a son and call His name Jesus.[2] He would be great and would be called the Son of the Highest, and upon Him God would confer the title to the throne of His father David [3] and give Him *eternal* dominion. It is evident from this message of the angel that the long-awaited fulness of time had come and that the promised Messiah was now

The Annunciation. to appear on this sin-cursed earth, to be born of a virgin.[4] It is clear that Mary of the house of David was directly conscious as to *who* was meant. Not for a moment did she entertain any doubt as to the possibility and truth of the promise.[5] Only as to certain details did she volunteer an expression of inward perplexity: "How shall this be, seeing I know not a man?" It is true, she was espoused to Joseph of the royal line, but she was as yet not married to him, and besides, the promise of the angel was given to her without reference to her impending marriage to Joseph.[6] The angel had not spoken of a child of which Joseph was to be the father. Still the fulfilment of the promise of the incomprehensibly wonderful event is taken confidently for granted. And her humble inquiry for additional enlightenment is not at all a word of trembling doubt, the requirement of a sign on which to lean, but rather the request for guidance in obedient self-surrender.[7] To her who believed the angel pointed out a glorious path. That did not seem strange. Only that *she* was favored to walk in it seemed so.[8]

Luke 1, 26—38. **37.**

And now the angel comes to her aid with an explanation in words so tender and chaste, however little she may have understood their full meaning, which had really nothing strange about them,

---

36, 2) No interpretation of the name here as in Matt. 1, 21.

3) If Jesus is to be *her* son and David is called *His* father, then surely Christ's Davidic descent through Mary is granted at the outset. V, 69.

4) Is. 7, 14; 9, 6. 7; 2 Sam. 7, 12.

5) Compare Zacharias, Luke 1, 18.

6) Meyer *in loco.* Ebrard, 167.

7) Edersheim, I, 152. *"Inquirendo dixit, non desperando."* Augustine. "I know not a man" is not to be taken as a vow of perpetual virginity or a resolution to that effect. Meyer *in loco.*

8) Edersheim, I, 152.

except probably that *she* should be thus favored, namely, that it should be a miraculous conception. "The Holy Ghost shall come upon thee, and the power of the Highest shall overshadow thee; therefore also that Holy Thing which shall be born of thee shall be called the Son of God." [1)] This is the answer to Mary's per-

"Conceived by the Holy Ghost." plexity — how a mother and still a virgin? Because she would conceive by the power of the Holy Ghost, her virginity would

not be affected. And, moreover, the Holy Product of the Holy Agency not only shall be called, but will truly *be* the Son of God.[2)] Thus the divine mystery of the miraculous conception of the Son of God is most tenderly and decorously, yet most clearly, expressed.

Luke 1, 26—38.   38.

Mary did not ask for a sign. Yet unasked a sign was given to strengthen her faith and to confirm the words which had been spoken. The angel gives her an example of the omnipotence of God by telling her that her relative Elisabeth, notwithstanding her age and supposedly hopeless barrenness, has been with child for the past six months. It was not a case parallel to her own, but

The Sign. on account of her age nevertheless also beyond the ordinary course of nature and therefore likewise

a miracle wrought by the hand of God. Just how Mary, of the tribe of Judah and of the house of David, and Elisabeth, of the tribe of Levi and a daughter of Aaron, were related the Bible does not state;[1)] most likely, however, on the maternal side, as the priests were not compelled to marry within their own tribe. With the devotion of a childlike and firm faith Mary replied, "Behold the handmaid of the Lord; be it unto me according to thy word," [2)] whereupon the angel departed from her.

37, 1) V. 35.

2) *Expositor's Greek N. T. in loco.* — Justin. Meyer *in loco.*

38, 1) There are different traditions. According to the apocryphal Gospel of James (second century) the parents of Mary were Joachin and Anna. Joachim — Eliachim — Eli. The name of God Jahveh is substituted for Elohim — Eli. This agrees with the rabbinical tradition that Mary was the daughter of Eli. Anna, her mother, was supposed to have been of priestly stock. (*Cath. Encycl.*, sub "Virgin," XV, 464 E.) According to another (late) tradition Matthan had two daughters, Anna and Soba, and a son, Jacob. Anna was the mother of Mary and Soba the mother of Elisabeth. (Quoted by Andrews, 57; also in *Cath. Encycl.*, sub "Elisabeth," V, 387.) The source is also given: Nicephorus Callistus, quoting Hippolytus, *Hist. Eccl.*, II, III.

2) Luke 1, 38.

Luke 1, 39—45. **39.**

The information concerning Elisabeth was at the same time a direction. Without communicating with Joseph [1] or with any one else, which under the condition was natural, and trusting in the Lord for guidance in the whole matter, she immediately arose and hastened [2] to the hill country of Judea [3] to communicate and confide her deepest feelings to that kinswoman and friend who also was highly favored. The whole narrative implies that both

Visit of Mary to Elisabeth. Mary and Elisabeth, full of faith, quietly waited for God to reveal Himself what He had done. Upon the arrival of Mary in the house of Zacharias full confirmation was made of that which the angel had spoken concerning Elisabeth. And on the other hand, Elisabeth must have learned from her husband the destiny of her unborn child and the near advent of the Messiah. But she could not know either when or of whom He was to be born. [4] And now the mother of her Lord was standing before her! Immediately her own child, leaping in her womb, gave signs of life, and Elisabeth was filled with the Holy Ghost. [5]

Luke 1, 46—56. **40.**

Two mothers meet: the mother of the way-preparer and the mother of Him for whom he was to prepare the way. Elisabeth, filled with the Holy Ghost, expressed the homage which her unborn child offered to his Lord, while in her hymn Mary herself offered that homage to God. The words of her hymn were taken

---

39, 1) See Meyer, *Luke*, 249. 259.

2) Ἐν ταῖς ἡμέραις ταύταις, in these days, not in those days, ἐκείναις. (A. V. Bruce, *sub loco*.) This really seems the best view on the subject in opposition to Ebrard (172) and others, who would place Mary's visit with Elisabeth *after* her marriage to Joseph because "virgins were *never* allowed to travel." (Alone?) If any such law was in force at that time, — Rabbinical authorities are quoted, — then Mary may have journeyed with friends, under the protection of a servant, or with neighbors and friends going to the Passover. (Andrews, 69. Meyer, *Luke*, 244.) After her three-month visit it is said, v. 56, that she returned to her own house, which also seems to imply that she was not yet married.

3) This is also the arrangement in Tatian's *Diatessaron*, the earliest Life of Christ (ca. 150 A. D.). (Edition J. H. Hill, p. 44.)

4) Edersheim, I, 152.

5) Commentators discuss the connection between maternal excitement and the quickening of the child; but these and other details should be passed over in respectful silence. (Bruce *sub loco*.)

from the Old Testament;[1] but the music was of the New.[2] And
the key-note of all was the grace and favor of God — shown to
Abraham, to Israel, to Elisabeth, to her, the handmaid, to the
humble and poor, to all believers who rejoice in their Savior and
their God. Elisabeth praises Mary and her faith; but Mary gives
all glory to God.[3] Elisabeth replies to the greeting of Mary:
"Blessed art thou among women, and blessed is the fruit of thy

The Magnificat of Mary.   womb. And whence is this
                                            to me, that the mother of my
Lord should come to me? Blessed is she that believed; for there
shall be a performance of those things which were told her from
the Lord." And Mary answered: "My soul doth magnify the
Lord, and my spirit hath rejoiced in God, my Savior. For He hath
regarded the low estate of His handmaiden. . . . He that is mighty
hath done to me great things; and holy is His name. And His
mercy is on them that fear Him, from generation to generation.
He hath showed strength with His arm; He hath put down the
mighty from their seats and exalted them of low degree. He hath
holpen His servant Israel in remembrance of His mercy, as He
spake to our fathers, to Abraham, and to His seed forever." Thus
Mary, in a hymn which the Church has called the Magnificat, gives
expression to her exceeding gladness and to the cause of her joy.
Then she describes the new order in Christ's kingdom and sets it
all down as a deed of divine mercy and grace.[4]

Luke 1, 46—56.   **41.**

After a stay of about three months,[1] for which no details are
given, until the middle of June, 5 B. C., and before the birth of

The Return of Mary.   John the Baptist, Mary again re-
                                         turned to her own house.[2] Some
think that Mary stayed with Elisabeth and helped her until after

---

40, 1) 1 Sam. 1, 11; 2, 1—10; Ps. 103, 17; 107, 9; Is. 47, 8. 9; etc.

2) Edersheim, I, 153.

3) G. Stoeckhardt, *Biblische Geschichte,* 7.

4) The hymn naturally divides itself into four parts: 1. the singer's
joy, vv. 46—48 a; 2. the cause of gladness, vv. 48 b—50; 3. the new order
of the Gospel in Christ's kingdom, vv. 51—53; 4. the birth of Christ as
a deed of God's mercy and grace, vv. 54. 55.

41, 1) Luke 1, 56.

2) "She returned to her own house." This expression may imply
that she had not been taken to the house of Joseph. Andrews, 69.
Matt. 1, 24.

the birth and circumcision of John.[3])   But it seems best to have her return now in an arrangement which is permissible and by which she is screened from public view.

Luke 1, 57—80.   **42.**

Elisabeth's conception took place contrary to the common laws of nature, but now, after it had taken place, the time for her delivery arrived in the ordinary course of time.[1])   In the whole community it was an unexpected event.   When the near-by neighbors and more distant relatives heard that the Lord had magnified [2]) His grace upon her, — for by this birth, so long deferred and so contrary to all expectation, they clearly saw a proof of special divine compassion, — they came and cordially congratulated her.   On the eighth day, the divinely prescribed day for circumcision,[3]) a special gathering was arranged.   "They came to circumcise the child," namely, the relatives and friends and those who were invited for that purpose.   Since Zacharias and Elisabeth were most likely living in comfortable circumstances, they were able to prepare a little celebration for this highly exceptional event.   As it was, a day of circumcision in a Jewish family was always a day of domestic solemnity and joy, in which a son of Abraham was put under the yoke of God's holy law, with all the duties and privileges which this implied.[4])   With the circumcision itself there was also associated,

Birth and Circumcision of John.
according to ancient custom, the giving of the name.[5])   Ordinarily the head of the family made all arrangements; but in the house of Zacharias, it seems, the relatives and friends had matters pretty well in hand, including even such important details as selecting the name.   Without consulting Elisabeth in the matter and without attempting to communicate with the dumb-stricken Zacharias, they called [6]) the infant Zacharias after his father.   It ob-

---

41, 3) Weiss, I, 236.   Although the return of Mary is mentioned before the delivery of Elisabeth, the evangelist, they explain, wanted to finish the passage concerning Mary first before proceeding with the account of John's birth.   There is no reason, however, to assume a "historical anticipation" at this place.   Ylvisaker, 72.

42, 1) The traditional day for the nativity of John is June 24.   The discoveries of certain mythologists, according to which the Gospel-stories are supposed to have "astronomical correspondence," do not merit our attention.

2) Ἐμεγάλυνε.

3) Gen. 17, 13.   4) Edersheim, I, 157.

5) Gen. 21, 3. 4.   The naming of Isaac was connected with the circumcision on the eighth day.

6) Ἐκάλουν, the imperfect, attempted to call.

viously was, they thought, the proper thing to do. And what greater honor could be accorded Zacharias than to have his name so unexpectedly perpetuated by the birth of a son? But Elisabeth objected. "Not so; but he shall be called John." This was not merely the expression of a personal desire; it was a mother's decision, and it was final. Very likely Zacharias had communicated to her what the angel had told him regarding the name to be given his child.[7] And they said unto her: "There is none of thy kindred that is called by this name." Not as if the name of John had been unknown. It is true, there were certain well-known Johns of priestly line, the last of whom had been murdered by Herod about twenty-five years before;[8] but even that would have been considered too remote to suggest the selection of that name. And so in the difficulty, and perchance to have their proposed name confirmed, they decided to get into communication with Zacharias, who but for this incident would probably have been well-nigh forgotten by the happy gathering.

Luke 1, 57—80.   **43.**

All this while Zacharias had sat there as a deaf-and-dumb [1] witness, until Elisabeth interrupted the solemn proceeding at the point when in the benediction the name of the child was inserted.[2] And the appeal was made to Zacharias to name his son. Zacharias **"His Name Is John."** asked [3] for a writing-table, most likely a small tablet covered with wax. Upon this he inscribed the words "His name is John." [4] Thus, firmly and finally, he expressed himself in agreement with Elisabeth for a name foreign to the family, not, however, merely to assert his parental authority, but to indicate that he was obeying

---

42, 7) Older commentators, Origin and Ambrose, but also Meyer, supposed a divine revelation. But Ebrard, Weiss, Stoeckhardt, and others disagree with them.

8) John Hyrcanus II, 30 B. C.

43, 1) For this seems to be the implication of ἐνένευον, made signs to him (used only here in the New Testament), that he was stricken both deaf and dumb, although various suggestions have been made to evade the conclusion: Meyer and others, that only a sign was needed, Zacharias having heard all that was said, etc.

2) Edersheim, I, 158.

3) How did he ask? Likewise through a sign. For even if he was able to hear, as some think, he at least could not speak.

4) Luke 1, 63. "He wrote, saying." Ἔγραψε λέγων. While it is to be admitted that the explanation "He wrote and at the same time said" fits beautifully into the story, it seems that the speech of Zacharias did not return until v. 64 and that the word λέγων is used here in true Hebrew fashion — to the effect, he said by writing. Bruce *sub loco*.

a divine command. The assembled guests marveled at this strange way of giving assent to his wife, no doubt feeling that there must be something behind it all. But this was not the sole cause for their astonishment. For immediately Zacharias's mouth was opened and his tongue loosed, and he burst forth into rapturous praise of God. A dumb Zacharias, an unusual birth, a singular name, and the sudden recovery of speech — surely sufficient cause for a religious awe!

Luke 1, 57—80. **44.**

The last words of Zacharias in the Temple were words of unbelief and doubt, and now his first words were an expression of faith. He could not even utter the name of his child, and now he bursts into a lengthy praise of the name of God. The first evidence of his dumbness had been when his tongue refused to pronounce the benediction upon the assembled worshipers, and now, filled with the Holy Ghost, he spoke a message embodying sublime praise of God. Like the Magnificat of Mary his song, which is called the Benedictus on account of the opening word in the Latin version, begins in the Old Testament and ends in the New. The hymn itself [1] sees the fulfilment of the Messianic prayers said by the priests in the Temple before the lot was cast for incensing and by the people during incensing [2] and then speaks of the ministry and mission of John. "Blessed be the Lord God of Israel; for He hath visited and redeemed His people and hath raised up an horn of salvation for us in the house of His servant David." Thus it was promised in Paradise, then to Abraham, to David, through

The Benedictus. Moses and the prophets, [3] "that we, being delivered out of the hands of our enemies, might serve Him without fear, in holiness and righteousness before Him, all the days of our life." It is the fulfilment of the promise of salvation from sin by the coming Savior, for whom his child was to prepare the way. "And thou, child, shalt be called the prophet of the Highest; for thou shalt go before the face of the Lord to prepare His ways, to give knowledge of salvation unto His people by the remission of their sins, through the tender mercy of our God." By the virtue of this mercy "the Dayspring from on

---

44, 1) It is best divided into two parts: 1. Verses 68—75. A prayer of thanksgiving for the Messianic deliverance and blessing already accomplished. Notice the past tense. 2. Verses 76—79. Prophecies concerning John the Baptist. Notice the future tense.

2) Edersheim, I, 158.

3) Gen. 3, 15; 22, 16 ff.; Deut. 18, 15; 2 Sam. 23, 1 ff.; etc.

high hath visited us [4] to give light to them that sit in darkness and in the shadow of death." Thus the Benedictus of Zacharias, steeped in Old Testament language, is at the same time a commentary for the correct understanding of the Old Testament Messianic promises. Though thousands of Abraham's descendants, now groaning under Herod's yoke, might be tempted to entertain the false hope of being delivered from the yoke of a pagan ruler by the yearned-for Messiah, Zacharias here plainly told them what kind of Messiah to expect, namely, one who would gain for them and grant them remission of sins. That was the kind of salvation which the Messiah was to bring and the kind of Messiah whose way John was to prepare.

Luke 1, 57—80.   **45.**

Far and wide these marvelous tidings spread through the hill country of Judea. Awe fell upon the people. The long and dreary night had at last given place to day, and the light of hope had begun to fill their hearts. Reflecting upon the utterances of Zacharias, an uncommon future was rightly foretokened for the child. The question was asked, "What manner of child shall

The Youth of John. this be?" And there was good reason to expect great things of this child because "the hand of the Lord was with him." [1] Zacharias and Elisabeth now pass out of the picture; instead we learn that "the child grew and waxed strong in spirit and was in the deserts till the day of his showing unto Israel." [2] The desert which he loved was the foster-mother of him who was to be the stern preacher of repentance in the wilderness: "Repent ye; for the kingdom of heaven is at hand." [3] The Essenes were not far off, but there is no indication of contact, either inwardly or outwardly, with them. [4]

Matt. 1, 18—25.   **46.**

And now let us return to Nazareth. After her stay of about three months with Elisabeth, Mary had returned to her own home in Nazareth. [1] A number of months had passed since the Annun-

---

44, 4) Figurative designation of the Messiah. 'Ανατολή is taken by some as the Greek equivalent for branch in the Septuagint rendering of Jer. 23, 5; Zech. 3, 11; etc. But see Meyer *in loco.* Some texts have "shall visit us," future tense.
45, 1) Luke 1, 66.   2) V. 80.   3) Matt. 3, 2.
    4) *Expositor's Greek New Testament in loco.* See chapter XV, 3.
46, 1) Luke 1, 56.

ciation, and conscious as Mary was of what had brought about her condition, — others did not know, — still it must have been as if a sword had pierced her heart when her secret became known. She was found to be with child, and the fact of her pregnancy could no longer remain unknown. Naturally one of the first to find out was Joseph, to whom she was espoused and who had not yet taken her home.[2] There was a discovery and a surprise. And

The Perplexity of Joseph.

in order to forestall any unholy thoughts, the evangelist quickly inserts: "She was found with child *of the Holy Ghost.*" Of course, of this Joseph was ignorant. This belongs to the realm of revelation and faith. And therefore as the betrothed husband of Mary, with a husband's rights and responsibilities, and acting in a strictly legal manner, he could not overlook what appeared as adultery. On the other hand, however, still loving Mary and unwilling to expose her to public shame, he resolved to put her away privately. Of course, even this action, that is, a quiet canceling of the betrothal bond, was in opposition to the strict application of the Mosaic Law. The least [3] that the Law required in such a case [4] was a bill of divorcement, and that, as a public document, would have been opposed to the gentle expedient upon which he had resolved.[5]

Matt. 1, 18—25. 47.

While Joseph, at first in a strait betwixt two plans, finally resolved [1] on the course of abandoning Mary privately [2] and probably was painfully deliberating on even so harsh a measure, an angel appeared to him in a dream and delivered him from his perplexity. We need not enter into the question of dreams and visions, except to state that we are here dealing with a divine reve-

---

46, 2) How did Joseph find out? From "suspicious women," the so-called *pronubae,* through whom the bride and bridegroom before their marriage had to make their communication (Ebrard), or from Mary herself (Edersheim), or by observation? And did he, as "the first Ebionite" (denying the Virgin Birth), refuse to believe her (Lange, quoted in Meyer, *Luke,* 244)? We simply do not know.

    3) Deut. 22, 23 does not apply.

    4) According to Deut. 24, 1. This also applies to betrothed persons. See Meyer *in loco.*

    5) A dismissal by a letter of divorcement, but under arrangements providing for secrecy and handed her in the presence of two or three witnesses (Edersheim), is contrary to Joseph's intended λάθρα.

47, 1) Ἐβουλήθη, he made the resolution.

    2) Ἀπολύσαι αὐτήν, to put her away.

lation. "Joseph, thou son of David,[3] fear not to take unto thee Mary, thy wife." Before God she is already his lawfully wedded wife. He should not leave her. And an explanation is offered concerning her present condition. "For that which is conceived of

Joseph's Dream. her is of the Holy Ghost." Thus at once, briefly and definitely, the suspicion which had tormented Joseph was shown to be without foundation. "And she shall bring forth a son." But the angel is careful not to add "unto thee," as was done in the case of Zacharias,[4] as if Joseph were the physical father. And still Joseph is to take a real father's place, namely, in the naming of the child. "And thou shalt call His name JESUS." This is a command and a prediction. There is a singular significance connected with this name. "For He," emphatically,[5] He and none other, "shall save His people from their sins." Thus the angel. What a glorious prediction about a child whose approaching birth had filled him with such keen sorrow and toward whom he was privileged to occupy the relation of father! The still unborn child was to be the Messiah, the Christ, the Savior, who was to "save His people from their sins." [6]

Matt. 1, 18—25.   **48.**

In all this the evangelist sees a fulfilment of prophecy — not merely in the singular name nor in the mere fact of a miraculous virgin birth; but these matters were as links welded into a golden chain. "Now, all this was done that it might be fulfilled which

The Virgin Birth. was spoken of the Lord by the prophet, saying, Behold, a virgin shall be with child and shall bring forth a son." This is the fulfilment of the sign Isaiah had given Ahaz to confirm the promise he had made to him that Syria and Israel (Ephraim) should not prevail against Judah and "set up a king in the midst of it," namely, "Behold, a virgin shall conceive." [1] This promise was not forgotten, for

---

47, 3) The reason why the angel thus addressed Joseph was that he was to bring tidings of the coming of the Messiah. And the fact that he called him son of David confirms the view that the genealogy of Matthew is that of Joseph, while Luke, writing the account of the infancy of Jesus from the standpoint of Mary, was apparently supplied with the genealogy of her family in writing his gospel.

   4) Luke 1, 13.
   5) Αὐτὸς γάρ.
   6) "His people"; these first, but also the Gentiles, John 4, 22; Rom. 1, 16. "From their sins," ἀπὸ τῶν ἁμαρτιῶν, not merely "from sinning."
48, 1) Is. 7, 14.

here is that virgin of whom Isaiah spoke.[2]   And in passing it may be noted that the Hebrew word for virgin, as translated by the Septuagint into Greek and used by Matthew, is sufficient evidence of the admissibility of rendering the term used by Isaiah as a virgin in the strictest sense.[3]   "And they shall call His name Emmanuel; which, being interpreted, is God with us."   In this Child, God is to be with us in His loving-kindness and grace.

Matt. 1, 18—25.   49.

Joseph hesitated no more.   He understood and believed.   He rose from his sleep and did what the angel had bidden him.   This is indeed a characteristic of the silent saint, of whom in all the Scriptures not a word or phrase is recorded.   Silently he performed

"He Called His Name Jesus."   his duty.   And the highest duty towards Mary and the unborn Jesus demanded immediate marriage,[1] which would afford not only outward, but also moral protection to both.[2]   And so he "took unto him his wife and knew her not till she had brought forth her first-born son.   And he called His name JESUS."   Thus Joseph showed his faith.   The sole purpose of his marriage to Mary was now to legitimize the Child, the Messiah, whose advent was now at hand.[3]

48, 2) ʿΗ (emphatic) παρϑένος.

3) הָעַלְמָה.   Also here *the* virgin.

49, 1) There is no contradiction in the fact that Luke 2, 5 Mary is still called Joseph's betrothed wife.   This expression must be read in connection with Matthew.

2) Edersheim, I, 155.

3) Whatever view may be taken of the brothers and sisters of the Lord, whether they are regarded as the children of Joseph of a former marriage or as his children with Mary, or as the cousins of Jesus, an appeal cannot be made to this verse in support of the "perpetual virginity" of Mary. Really it does not matter.   The chief consideration is not, "What think ye of Mary?" but, "What think ye of Christ?"   See Meyer *in loco.*   Pieper, *Dogmatik,* II, 367 f.

CHAPTER IV.

THE BIRTH AND CHILDHOOD OF JESUS.

Probably December 25, 749 A. U. C., or 5 B. C., to 761 A. U. C., or 8 A. D.

Matt. 2, 1. Luke 2, 1—7. **1.**

From Jerusalem to the Judean hill country, to Nazareth, to Rome! It is remarkable how the course of ancient history is wrapped up in the destiny of Rome. Rome rises as Israel and other nations fall. The rising of the mighty power on the banks of the Tiber was sensed in the Eastern world, as evidenced by an ancient legend,[1] which makes the founding of Rome an instrument of divine wrath. After the marriage of Solomon to the daughter of **Rome.** Pharaoh[2] the angel Gabriel, according to the legend, descended into the sea and fixed a reed in it, around which a mud bank gathered and on which a forest sprang up. On this site imperial Rome was built. And the meaning of this legend is that, when Israel began to fall away from God, the punishment was prepared which culminated in the dominion of Rome. This agrees with history. But Rome was not only the instrument of wrath with respect to Israel, it was also in a way[3] an ally to the coming Christ. The periodic and universal enrolments inaugurated by Caesar Augustus, by the governance of God, ushered in the birth of Christ.

Matt. 2, 1. Luke 2, 1—7. **2.**

Julius Caesar had put an end to the Roman republic and made himself master of Rome; but it was Augustus who became the real founder of the empire. His dominion embraced the *orbis terrarum*, practically the whole of the then known world. And **The Decree of Caesar Augustus.** since it was to his interest to know both the strength and the weakness of the vast empire which he had consolidated as well as the strength of potential rebels and the dangers to the *pax Romana* which might be lurking in certain quarters, he inaugurated the system of periodic universal enrolments by issuing the decree that "all the world should be taxed," that is, registered, or en-

---

1,   1) Quoted by Edersheim, II, 751.
      2) 1 Kings 3, 1.
      3) See chapter I.

[92]

rolled.[1]   The ancient historical writers do not directly mention a general imperial census;[2] but it has now been established that Caesar Augustus laid down the principle of systematic, periodic enrolments, to take place every fourteen years, which lasted for over two hundred and fifty years, and that this first general enrolment was originally decreed for 8 B. C., when Cyrenius, or Quirinius, was for the first time governor of Syria.[3]

2,   1) Ἀπογράφεσθαι.   Notice the present tense, Luke 2, 1 and 3.   Not a single census, but the introduction of a new system.   But notice the change to the aorist in v. 5, ἀπογράψασθαι, to indicate one definite occasion.

2) The following material cannot be appealed to: 1. The *Breviarium Imperii*, a booklet of Augustus in his own handwriting, which contained accounts of the number of soldiers, taxes, imposts, and the like.   Tacitus, *Annales*, I, XI.   It concluded with the advice never to aim at an extension of empire.   It is also mentioned by Suetonius, *Augustus*, Cl, *Breviarium totius imperii*, to be cut upon bronze tablets and set up at the entrance to the mausoleum of Augustus.   The original of this inscription is lost, but the greater part of a copy inscribed in Greek and Latin on marble has been preserved at Ancyra, Asia Minor, and is known as the *Monumentum Ancyranum*.   (Wieseler, *Synopsis*, 79 ff.)   While it gives much information on the reign of Augustus, it does not mention the detail in question, a general census.   2. A passage of Dio Cassius, LIV, 35: "Augustus set on foot a census, to which he allowed his own private property to be submitted, just as if he were a private person, that he might avoid all possible cause of offense."   3. A few passages of a later (Christian) period, in words of Cassiodorus and others.   Cassiodorus, *Variarum*, III, 52: "The Augusti at various times wrote out a census of the *orbis Romanus terrarum*."   Isidorus, *Etymologiarum*, V, 36, which Schuerer calls a confused rigmarole: "An era inaugurated by Caesar Augustus, the first to institute a census and to write up the *orbem Romanum*."   (Isidorus was a Spanish encyclopedist and historian, ca. 560—636.)   Suidas (Greek lexicographer, tenth century), *Lexicon*, s. v. ἀπογραφή and Αὐγοῦστος: "Caesar Augustus conducted this first census, and twenty men of high character were appointed to carry it out in the provinces."   Not much stress, however, is laid on these passages, because it is supposed that they rest only upon the narrative of Luke. All of the above references may be found in Schuerer, I, II, 114 ff., and Wieseler, *Synopsis*, 68 ff.

3) Thanks to inscriptions (W. M. Ramsay, *Was Christ Born in Bethlehem?* chaps. VIII and XI) and to the papyri found in the rubbish piles and graves of ancient Egypt.   (*Ibid.*, chap. VII, p. 170.   Preface, p. X, and p. 148.)   The notice in Luke is a chronological tag for Syria, to which province Judea belonged.   Luke omits the story of the flight into Egypt, which a writer connected with Egypt would be most unlikely to do, which proves that Luke did not construct his story after the conditions in Egypt. *Ibid.*, p. 149. — The governorship of Quirinius formerly offered a real problem.   It was thought by many that Luke was mistaken or that he confused the decree of Augustus with the days of the taxing in 6 A. D., Acts 5, 37. Josephus, *Ant.*, XVII, 13; XVIII, 1, 6.   But since 1764 it has been known (the famous Quirinius stone discovered at Tivoli, Italy. Ramsay, *l. c.*, 227. Schuerer, I, I, 354) that Cyrenius was governor of Syria twice: 6—9 A. D. and at some previous time.   The problem, however, was when to place this earlier tenure of office without conflicting with Josephus and with other known facts of history.   The arrangement of Zumpt, Mommsen, and Schuerer (Andrews, 78), by which the first governorship of Quirinius was placed somewhere between 4—1 B. C., never quite satisfied the Christian student because it dated the term of office *after* the death of Herod, which does not agree with the account that Christ was born in the days of King

Matt. 2, 1. Luke 2, 1—7.　　**3.**

However, a consideration of the situation in Syria and Palestine about this time and of certain other facts [1] will show that the enrolment in Herod's kingdom was very likely postponed for several years. The will of Augustus was supreme in Judea when he willed it, and still the dominion of Herod enjoyed official Roman recognition, and it was to the interest of Rome to retain the good will and services of Herod to preserve order on the Palestinian bridge. And while it was Herod's policy to retain the good will of the Romans at all costs, it would certainly not be in keeping with his character to accept what would seem to him a degrading Roman imperial measure without some form of protest. For was he not a *rex socius* [2] and Augustus his friend? The prime requirement of his government was to maintain order and peace, and if he had endeavored to force upon his people anything Roman, insurrection would have been almost certain to follow, as it did come in 6 A. D., in "the days of the taxing." [3] Ever since the days of David's folly, when he said to Joab, "Go, number Israel and Judah," [4] his people were opposed to the numbering of persons, [5] and therefore, if a census was to be taken, at any rate it would have to be given a different name, and Jewish susceptibilities had to be taken into account. And besides, there were internal difficulties at the time. Ordinarily a census would presuppose a period of domestic peace,

Herod.　while just at that time Herod was involved in a war with his Arabian neighbor. Sylleus, the Arabian minister, who was in Rome, obtained the ear and confidence of Augustus and made him believe that Herod had made war upon his people on his own account, without Roman permission. This roused the ire of Augustus, and he wrote to Herod that, whereas

---

Herod. Nor was the proposed solution satisfactory that the census was begun by C. S. Saturninus, 9—6 B. C., continued by P. Q. Varus, 6—4 B. C., and concluded by Quirinius, 3—1 B. C. But the two inscriptions discovered by Ramsay make it evident that the first governorship of Quirinius can safely be placed between 11 and 8 B. C. For details see Ramsay, *l. c.,* chaps. VI—XI, and *The Bearing of Recent Discovery on the Trustworthiness of the New Testament,* chaps. XIX—XXI; Ad. Deissmann, *Licht vom Osten,* 4th ed., 4, 5, note 1; 231, note 10; A. T. Robertson, *Luke the Historian,* chap. IX.

3,　1) The last-named date was too early for the birth of Christ as compared with other chronological data.

　　2) Schuerer, I, I, 449.　　3) Acts 5, 37.　　4) 2 Sam. 24.

　　5) Wieseler, *Synopsis,* 87. See also Edersheim, *Temple,* 122. When in the counting of the assembled priests the lot was taken in the Temple, the priests held up their hands to be counted, considering it unlawful to count persons.

he had treated him hitherto as a friend, he would henceforth treat him as a subject.[6]   And therefore, when some time in 8 B. C. the decree of Augustus reached Jerusalem via Antioch,[7] we can well imagine Herod to have been in a plight — a census; the war with the Arabians; in disgrace with Augustus; and the prejudices of his Jewish subjects.   Naturally he could not accept this mark of servitude and degradation in rank without an effort to regain the emperor's favor.   His first attempt would be to stall for time. There was probably little difficulty [8] in obtaining leave from the next governor, Saturninus, who succeeded Quirinius ca. 7—6 B. C.,[9] to postpone the census until he had sent an embassy to Rome.   He had wielded great influence over Augustus, and he might become powerful again.   He could say with perfect truth that the census would endanger the peace.   Furthermore, according to Josephus his case was a good and strong one, and Sylleus was a calumniator.[10] An embassy was sent to Rome.   But it was not even given an audience and returned without having accomplished anything. After some time a second embassy was sent, headed by Nicolaus of Damascus, which in all probability was commissioned not to suggest exemption from enrolment, but to promise unconditional obedience in the matter.   And this embassy was successful.   Sylleus was condemned.   Augustus was reconciled to Herod.   He had even resolved to bestow the government of Arabia upon his reconciled friend; but upon second thought this resolution was not carried out, the determining factor being the age of Herod and his abominable relation to his sons.[11]   In respect to the census, however, Herod had to obey.

3,   6) Josephus, *Ant.*, XVI, 9, 3.   It seems that Herod was falsely accused.   It is uncertain when this letter was written.   Schuerer (I, I, 414) is inclined to date it 8 B. C., which is probably correct.

7) The chief city of Syria and third city of the empire.   Josephus, *War*, III, II, 4;   *Ant.*, XVII, V, 7: "palace of the Syrians."

8) Ramsay (*l. c.*, 182) suggests a bribe.

9) Tertullian (*Adv. Marc.*) says that Christ was born during the census taken by Saturninus.   But it seems that this date was set to bolster up Luke, which was unnecessary; besides, it is too early.   See Ramsay, *l. c.*, 155. Moreover, Tertullian contradicts himself; for in *Adv. Iud.*, 8, he gives 751 as the date of the birth of Christ.   See Wieseler, *Synopsis*, 99.   Robertson, *Harmony*, p. 262.   Also see Schuerer, I, I, 466.

10) Sylleus had a motive in casting aspersions on Herod before Augustus.   Herod had refused to give him permission to marry his sister Salome unless he submitted to circumcision and accepted Judaism, which he refused to do.   *Ant.*, XVI, IX, 1; VII, 5.

11) Augustus was probably even now thinking of reducing Judea to a Roman province, but not until after the death of Herod.

Matt. 2, 1. Luke 2, 1—7.   **4.**

The events just recited naturally consumed time, much more
time than similar transactions would occupy to-day. The year
8 B. C., when the copy of the decree arrived, is practically out of
consideration.[1]   Then came the negotiations, embassies, and the
final restoration of Herod to the favor of Augustus. A few years
may easily have passed in the mean while. But in the end Herod
had to obey. There is one thing, however, which he probably
gained: as a concession to his pride and to soothe the ever wakeful
jealousy and prejudices of his Jewish subjects, the enrolment was
given a tribal character; his subjects were called upon to repair

The Enrolment.   to their own ancestral cities for enrolment,
                      as if they were still living in the days of
David and Solomon. The marvelous success of Rome in the
administration of its provinces was due to its tolerant attitude
toward the prejudices of its subject population. With rare exceptions Rome humored the Jewish religious prejudices.[2]   Augustus
did not care what form the enrolment took as long as his orders
were obeyed. It may even be said that this form of Roman census
in Palestine was an advantage to Augustus. Judea had always
been a troublesome province to rule. Disturbances were always to
be apprehended. Now, this enrolment by tribes would mark off by
a clear line the true Jews — potential rebels — from the loyal
mongrel population of Palestine. All who claimed to be true Jews
were to report at the respective city of their tribe and family. The
census of the rest could be taken at their ordinary places of residence. There was thus an obvious advantage in knowing the exact
strength of potential rebels.[3]

Matt. 2, 1. Luke 2, 1—7.   **5.**

It was most likely the year 5 B. C., the last year of Herod's life,
that all arrangements were at last made in Judea for the carrying
out of the decree of Augustus that together with the other parts
of the world it should be registered, or enrolled. It is true, there
had been considerable delay, but Judea was always an exception.
This Pompey already had learned when for the first time he set
foot on Jewish soil. And as the census decree involved that every
one be personally presented to the officer for enumeration, it followed that the method of counting every person on a certain day

---

4,   1) Strictly speaking. the Syrian year, beginning in the spring of 8 B. C.
Ramsay, *l. c.,* 170.
     2) John 18, 28. 29.   3) Ramsay, *l. c.,* 188.

could not be employed. People might present themselves at their birthplace at any time during the year; but it is very likely that the last few weeks [1] of the year were most generally used.[2] "And all went to be taxed, every one into his own city," that is, as applied to Judea. Already in Egypt [3] and in other parts of the Roman **By Tribes.** Empire people had gone by households, and in Herod's kingdom the same thing was to be done, only by tribes, according to the Jewish method; and every one was to go into his own city. What power in the word of an emperor! What a stir, a regular *Voelkerwanderung*, in Palestine! What thought must not the term "own city" have aroused in those who were patriotically inclined! And which Jew was not a patriot at heart?

Matt. 2, 1. Luke 2, 1—7. **6.**

It almost seemed as if Old Testament times had come back. Of course, the proud and high-brow Zadokites would very likely stay right in Jerusalem.[1] The members of the once proud and now dispossessed Asmonean house, that is, if there were any left, could safely have a Maccabean family reunion at Modin.[2] And David's descendants would report at Bethlehem, the city of David. Really, they constituted some of the best blood in the land; but most of them were now living in humble circumstances. Still there was the famous Hillel, the supposed grandfather of Gamaliel [3] and reputed president of the Sanhedrin.[4] He is said to have **David's Descendants.** claimed descent from the house of David.[5] If this was true, and if this fact was not kept in the background on account of the Herodian surrounding, then it is likely that very distinguished company from Jerusalem made its appearance at Bethlehem. But most of the descendants of David very likely were of modest estate. Years later, in the time of Domitian, the combined wealth of David's

---

5, 1) Ramsay, *The Bearing of Recent Discovery on the New Testament,* 274. *Was Christ Born in Bethlehem?* 133. 134. 185. 222. 224.

2) If the census had to be completed according to the Roman year, then December 31 was the last day. But if an exception was made also in this particular, then the time was extended to about the 17th of April, the close of the Syrian year. After the Babylonian Exile, until the first century A. D., the Jewish year began with Nisan (April), but later — and this holds good to the present time — the ancient 7th of Tishri, in autumn, was revived for the beginning of the Jewish New Year.

3) Deissmann, *Licht vom Osten,* 231. Robertson, *Luke the Historian,* 126. 6, 1) Schuerer, II, I, 223. 1 Chron. 28, 22.

2) 1 Macc. 2, 1; 17, 70. 3) Acts 5, 34. Schuerer, II, I, 357.
4) 30 B. C. to 10 A. D. 5) Farrar, I, 9. Schuerer, II, I, 360.

heirs as represented by the members of the Lord's family did not amount to more than about eighteen hundred dollars,[6] and this not in silver, but as represented by thirty-nine acres of no doubt sandy Palestinian soil.[7] They belonged to the poor of the land. There were some obscure members of the family coming from Kochaba,[8] in Iturea, near Damascus.[9] There were others. And there was a carpenter from Nazareth in Galilee, with Mary, his espoused wife, who was great with child.

Matt. 2, 1. Luke 2, 1—7.   7.

Bethlehem! Not the Bethlehem of Zebulun,[1] seven miles northwest of Nazareth, but the Bethlehem of Judea, the Bethlehem-Ephratah, about six miles south of Jerusalem. There is where Rachel died.[2] A tomb has been erected to her memory just where the road to Bethlehem leaves the main highway to Hebron. There is where the rich farmer Boaz lived, who was one of the owners of the cornfields which gave to the city its name — the House of Bread. There is where he married Ruth, the lovely Moabite widow Ruth, who became the ancestress of David.[3] From the heights of her new home, 2,350 feet above the sea, through a break in the Eastern hills and across the heavy surface of the Sea of Judgment, she could even then view the mountains of her native land. South-

Bethlehem. ward the horizon was bounded by the highland wilderness and hill country of Judea, the home of John the Baptist. Passing it, the main highway wound its way to Hebron. To the north lay the valleys and hills which separated Bethlehem from Jerusalem, just concealing the Holy City. From that direction, leaving the highway at Rachel's Tomb, came the white-bearded priest Samuel with his cruse of oil to anoint David, at that time still a brown-eyed shepherd lad.[4] Thus Bethlehem became the home of kings. But still greater fame was promised it; for in the time of Hezekiah it was pointed out by the prophet Micah that Bethlehem should become the birthplace of Christ.[5] "But thou, Bethlehem-Ephratah, though thou be little among the thousands of Judah, yet out of thee shall He come forth unto Me that is to be Ruler in Israel." [6] And this promise was not discarded, for after the Exile one hundred and twenty-three Bethlehemites returned to reoccupy the ancestral site.[7]

6,   6) Nine thousand denarii.   7) Eusebius, III, XX.
      8) Eusebius, I, VII.   9) G. A. Smith, *Atlas,* C4, 18.
7,   1) Josh. 19, 10. 15.   2) Gen. 35, 19. 20.   3) Ruth 2, 4; 4, 17.
      4) 1 Sam. 16, 12.   5) The promise was known. John 7, 42.
      6) Micah 5, 2.   7) Ezra 2, 21.

Matt. 2, 1. Luke 2, 1—7. **8.**

It was very likely on a wintry day, not improbably December 25,[1] that Joseph[2] and Mary[2] arrived in Bethlehem as a result of the decree of Caesar Augustus. And it happened that with their arrival the days were accomplished for Mary to be delivered. Now, the first concern for Joseph in this pressing necessity was to find shelter and rest. But the little town of Bethlehem was **The Birth of Christ.** crowded with many other sons and daughters of David who had come from different quarters of Herod's kingdom to register their names. Not only were Joseph and Mary poor[4] and otherwise unable, by virtue of mere prominence, to secure desirable accommodation, but the very inn was filled, and the only available space was a sheltered place in the courtyard, where the cattle were stabled.[5]

8, 1) Of course, there is no certainty as to the date, December 25, but we see no reason why, without weighty arguments to the contrary, such a universally accepted traditional date should be discredited. While there are earlier references, it has been established that Pope Julius I (336—352) definitely fixed the celebration of Christmas for December 25. For a discussion on the matter as well as ancient references see *Encyclopedia Britannica* under "Christmas." Edersheim has an interesting Talmudic tradition which strengthens us in our supposition that December 25 is the true date. I, 187, note 3, a fast day (reasons not stated). The Eastern Church, which had previously favored January 6, gradually adopted the same date.

2) Whatever view may be taken as to the genealogies of Matthew and Luke with respect to Mary, even as regards her Davidic descent, there is every reason to suppose that Joseph, expecting the confinement of Mary, as a true son of David and in obedience to divine command, wanted the expected child of Mary entered in the public registers of Bethlehem as his legitimate son. Weiss, I, 252.

3) In reply to the objection that it was not necessary for Mary to accompany Joseph for the enrolment it may be said that in an Egyptian census, in the time of Commodus, twenty-seven persons were enumerated in one paper by a householder. Ramsay, *Was Christ Born in Bethlehem?* 146. See also p. 101. Deissmann, *Licht vom Osten,* 233. Ramsay, *Bearing of Recent Discovery,* etc., 273. Robertson, *Luke the Historian,* 125. 127. Robertson, *Harmony of the Gospels,* 266. Besides, Luke does not say that Mary had to go along.

4) See Luke 2, 24, which conclusively proves that Mary was not an heiress, with property in Bethlehem, which made necessary her personal appearance.

5) High authorities are inclined to regard a cave southeast of the town, now covered by a Latin convent, on the floor of which is seen the inscription *"Hic de virgine Maria Iesus Christus natus est,"* as the very place where the Virgin gave birth to Jesus. The evidence in its favor is given by Farrar, *Life of Christ,* I, 1 ff. See also Edersheim, I, 185; Andrews, 85; etc. *Contra,* Basil Matthews, *A Life of Jesus,* 3. On account of the shepherds, who hardly could have been expected to examine all the caves in the neighborhood, we believe it to be best to connect the birthplace with the inn and with the town of Bethlehem itself. At any rate, the Magi found the Child in a *house,* Matt. 2, 11.

"And she brought forth her first-born [6] son and wrapped Him in swaddling-clothes and laid Him in a manger, because there was no room for them in the inn." Thus in simple language the most important birth in human history is recorded. For the moment unnoticed and unheralded, like other momentous occasions in history, and yet all the previous history of Rome and Israel gathers about this manger. Caesar Augustus, though ruler of the whole civilized world, unconsciously brought it about that the Messiah, the Son of God, but also the son of David, born of the Virgin Mary, should be born in a "stable" at Bethlehem, though His mother's home was Nazareth. In fact, he opened the door.

Luke 2, 8—20.   9.

The world was still unaware of the birth of the Messiah, but the Lord was not. There were shepherds near Bethlehem, watching their flock that night. This is not in disagreement with the tradition that Christ was born in December. There were frequently dry seasons between December and February in Judea when the keeping of sheep in the open was possible.[1] Or the flocks were Temple-herds, destined for Temple-sacrifices, which, according to rabbinical references, lay out all the year round.[2] While the

The Shepherds. shepherds were thus bivouacking in the open, watching their herd, "heaven and earth seemed suddenly to mingle, and an angel of the Lord stood before their dazzled eyes." [3] Awe came upon them as the darkness was flooded with supernatural light, and they were sore afraid. But their fears were soon "hushed into calm and expectancy" when the angel began the first Christmas sermon with the words: "Fear not; for, behold, I bring you good tidings of great joy, which shall be to all people." The words which he then spoke were nothing less than the message that the long-promised Messiah and Savior of all nations had just been born in the city of David and that they might go and see Him and recognize Him by the humble circumstances attending His birth which the messenger of God had mentioned.[4]

8,   6) This term is used by Luke as a historian. It is not opposed to the view that Mary did not have other sons; but neither can it be used as an argument that she did. See Meyer *in loco* and on Matt. 1, 25.
9,   1) Andrews, 14.
     2) Edersheim, I, 186. 187.
     3) Edersheim, I, 187. 188.
     4) Luke 2, 12.

CODEX WASHINGTON. (W)

Now in Smithsonian Institution, Washington, D. C. Fourth century.
Luke 2, 1—12.

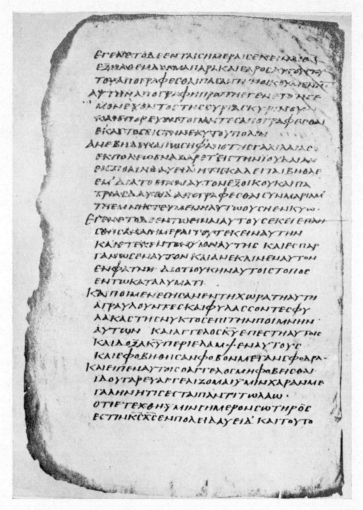

"For unto you is born this day in the city of David a Savior, which
is Christ the Lord." — *Luke 2, 11.*

ΟΤΙΕΤΕΧΘΗΥΜΙΝCΗΜΕΡΟΝCΩΤΗΡΟC

ὅτι ἐτέχθη ὑμῖν σήμερον σωτήρ, ὅς

ΕCΤΙΝΚCΧCΧΕΝΠΟΛΕΙΔΑΥΕΙΔ.

ἐστιν Κ(ύριο)ς Χ(ριστὸ)ς ἐν πόλει Δαυείδ.

(The last two lines.)

Luke 2, 8—20.   **10.**

It seems as if the celestial choir could hardly await the last words of this message; for suddenly there was with the announcing angel a multitude of the heavenly host, praising God and saying:

The Gloria in Excelsis. "Glory to God in the highest and on earth peace, good will toward men." [1)] In Isaiah's "rapt vision the Temple of heaven was opened," seraphim appeared and were heard crying one to another: "Holy, holy, holy, is the Lord of hosts; the whole earth is full of His glory." [2)] But never before had, and never afterwards did, the entire multitude of heavenly hosts become audible and visible to man.

Luke 2, 8 20.   **11.**

When the hymn was ended and the strains of the heavenly music had faded away, darkness returned, and the shepherds were left alone. But they remembered the message, and a sign had been given them by attending to which they could find the new-born Savior — the Babe was wrapped in swaddling-clothes and lying in a manger. Overcome with emotion, they said one to another: "Come, let us *now* [1)] go even unto Bethlehem and see this thing which is come to pass, which the Lord hath made known unto us." Quickly climbing the terraced heights, they soon found the holy

Adoration of the Shepherds. group: the virgin mother, Joseph, and — the Child lying in a manger. It all corresponded to the angelic announcement. What further passed we do not know. At least, they told what brought them there and what they had seen and heard. And this they published all around: in Bethlehem, in the field, probably also in near-by Jerusalem and in the Temple, whither they would bring their flocks. And all that heard wondered at the things which were told them by the shepherds. It seemed so sudden,

---

10, 1) The birth of Christ redounds to the glory of God. The "peace on earth" is not a chronological note, as taken by some writers, on account of the general civil peace existing at the time, but refers to the peace which the Lord has established in Christ. As regards "good will toward men" the variants are about equally divided between εὐδοκία and εὐδοκίας. We prefer to follow the *textus receptus* and to interpret: Not that the Lord has shown grace to men who are of good will, but that, regardless of their intentions towards Him, He has shown good will towards them.

2) Edersheim, 1, 188. Is. 6, 3.

11, 1) The particle δή occurs but a few times in the New Testament, but always with marked expressiveness. See *Expos. Greek N. T.* under Matt. 13, 23.

so strange. But what these humble men told, constituted the glad
tidings (news) which every Jewish ear tingled to hear and every
tongue was eager to repeat. If only no deception was practised
upon them! But Joseph knew. And Mary knew. And she kept
all these things and pondered them in her heart.

Luke 2, 21.   **12.**

Eight days pass, and the day of circumcision has arrived.
Nothing is said about a celebration, nor does this surprise us, in
spite of the fact that a lowly-born, yet royal son of David is "made
under the Law" and given a share in the ancient covenant which
God sealed unto Abraham.[1] Considering the divine origin and
mission of this Child, it may be mentioned that the rite in this case
also implied voluntary submission to the will of the Father and the
first shedding of blood "to redeem them that were under the
Law." [2] In connection with His circumcision, as was the custom,
the Child for the first time publicly received the name which Gabriel
by divine command had told both Joseph and Mary to give Him.[3]

The Circumcision and the Name JESUS.

Ordinarily there would have been
nothing significant in giving a child
this name. Jesus, meaning "Jeho-
vah is Salvation," was a name quite common among the Jews.
It had been the name of Joshua,[4] who led the children of Israel into
the Promised Land. There had been another great leader, the high
priest Joshua, or Jeshua,[5] who jointly with Zerubbabel brought
a band of former captives from Babylon to Jerusalem. And in the
New Testament we find one "Jesus, which is called Justus." [6] In
Josephus [7] no fewer than twelve persons of the same name are
mentioned besides those mentioned in Scripture. But here it acquired a significance infinitely more sacred as the human name of
the Son of God.[8] The Hebrew Messiah and the Greek Christ
were names which represented His office as anointed Prophet, Priest,
and King; but *Jesus of Nazareth* was the personal name, which
He bore when He emptied Himself of His glory [9] and became the
world-redeeming Son of Man. "Neither is there salvation in any
other; for there is none other name under heaven given among
men whereby we must be saved." [10]

12, 1) Gen. 17, 4 ff.; Lev. 12, 3.   2) Gal. 4, 5.
    3) Farrar, I, 19.   4) Called Jesus in Acts 7, 45.
    5) Ezra 2, 2; 3, 2; Zech. 3, 1.   6) Col. 4, 11.
    7) See Josephus in Index.   8) Farrar, I, 20.
    9) Phil. 2, 7.   10) Acts 4, 12.

Luke 2, 22—38. **13.**

Two other legal ordinances still remained to be observed, one affecting the Child and the other the mother. The first was to "present" the Infant Jesus to the Lord. Originally all the healthy, first-born sons of Israel were the special property of the Lord [1] and destined to do Temple-service. But after the separation of the Levites [2] for this particular duty the first-born among the other tribes were exempted; however, it was still necessary to present them to the Lord and to redeem them from this obligation with five shekels of silver.[3] This ransom could be paid to any priest; personal appearance in the Temple was therefore not necessary. But it was otherwise with another legal ordinance, the purification

The Presentation in the Temple.

of the mother.[4] After a number of weeks of seclusion [5] a gift of thanksgiving was offered. In the case of a male child forty days had to elapse. The payment was prescribed: a lamb of the first year for a burnt offering and a young pigeon or turtle-dove for a sin-offering. But if the parents were poor, a pair of young pigeons or turtle-doves would suffice, one for the burnt offering and the other for the sin-offering. Therefore, in obedience to divine command and, as we take it, in the beginning of February, 4 B. C., we find Joseph and Mary with the holy Child on their way to Jerusalem for a twofold purpose. The Lord of the Temple went up to the Temple of the Lord.[6] But of this there was no external or material evidence. While there was no discount in the redemption money, Joseph and Mary availed themselves of the privilege of making the permitted substitute offering for purification: the offering of the poor. Of the presentation and purification we have no further details, except that this visit to the Temple resulted in a double recognition of the infant Savior.

Luke 2, 22—38. **14.**

There was living in Jerusalem at that time Simeon, an aged and devout Israelite, of whom we have little — except legendary — knowledge. But the little that Scripture does say of him combines

---

13, 1) Ex. 13, 2.   2) Num. 3, 45; 8, 14.

3) Num. 3, 47; 18, 16. Five shekels ca. $3.00. Only those of non-Levitic descent had to be redeemed. This, therefore, Edersheim says (I, 194), disposes of the idea that Mary was of direct Aaronic or Levitic descent. The redemption money went to the priesthood.

4) Lev. 12, 6.   5) Seven plus thirty-three days. Lev. 12, 3. 4.

6) Bonaventura. Farrar, I, 21.

all the chief characteristics of Old Testament piety. He was just
in his relation to man, pious in his devotion to God, and, above all,
"waiting for the Consolation of Israel." [1]   The Holy Ghost was
upon him, and an answer to his greatest longing had been communicated to him, namely, "it was revealed unto him by the Holy
Ghost that he should not see death before he had seen the Lord's

Simeon.   Christ." [2]   We do not know the details. But tradition, interestingly enough, tells us that, while employing himself with Scripture, he stumbled at the words: "Behold,
a virgin shall conceive and bear a son." [3]   There was doubt in his
heart. And then the revelation was made that he himself should
live and take that virgin's son into his arms. [4]   Whatever historical
basis there may be for this tale, the fact is that God fulfilled His
word. By some inspired impulse Simeon entered the Temple just
when the "parents" [5] of Jesus brought in the Child to do for Him
what devolved upon them according to the Law. Simeon, immediately recognizing the Child, took Him into his arms and burst
into that glorious and inspired swan's song, the *Nunc Dimittis,*
which for nineteen centuries has been so dear to Christian hearts.

Luke 2, 22—38.   **15.**

After Simeon had seen the Infant Messiah, he was content
to be released from service and to depart in peace. His eyes had
actually seen the Salvation, so long prepared for a weary world.
He was the first prophet who could say that Christ *had* come. [1]
It was an old man's happy Christmas. His eyes had seen the true
Christmas light in its manifestation to all. Not only a beam to
shed the light of salvation upon God's chosen people and to reflect
glory upon the Jewish nation, [2] but a "Light to lighten the Gentiles." [3]   Except in its direct application, like in the Magnificat
and the Benedictus, there was really nothing new in the Nunc
Dimittis. It rested altogether on the Old Testament Messianic

---

14, 1) Legend gives Simeon an age of 113 years at the time and tries to
identify him with Simeon the father of Gamaliel I and son of Hillel, for
which, however, there is no historical basis. Farrar, I, 23 ff.

2) Χριστὸς Κυρίου. A beautiful expression. See Luke 9, 20.

3) Is. 7, 14.

4) *Expos. Greek N. T. in loco.* Farrar, I, 22 ff.

5) Γονεῖς. This expression, procreators, while not appropriate to the
bodily sonship of Jesus as applied to Joseph, has lost its etymological sig-
nification and is not at all a disavowal of the virgin birth of Christ.

15, 1) Bengel. Meyer *in loco.*

2) John 4, 22.   3) Is. 42, 6; 49, 6.

promises, correctly understood. Moreover, it was in accordance with the angelic revelations made to Zacharias and the Virgin Mary. But its unexpected voicing under the circumstances in the **The Nunc Dimittis.** sacred place, not by a priest, but by a devout Israelite, filled the hearts of Joseph and Mary with wonderment and silent awe. After blessing them and probably returning the Child to His mother's waiting arms, Simeon addressed himself in particular to the Virgin, whose marvelous relation to the Child he had recognized by illumination of the Holy Ghost. The blessing of privileged parenthood to this Child was undoubtedly great, but not unmixed with pain and sorrow; for this Child was to be a stone of stumbling [4] to all who would crash against Him, but also a solid Rock of Salvation [5] to all who would cling to Him in faith. "This Child is set for the fall and rising again of many in Israel and for a sign which shall be spoken against." The sword of deep personal sorrow would pierce the mother's heart, when the true inner nature of the opposition to the promised Bringer of salvation would be revealed and the hatred of the Jews would culminate in His crucifixion. Such, as regards Israel, was the history of Jesus, from His flight into Egypt until His death on the cross. And such, as regards natural man, has always been the history of the Gospel, which to them that perish is foolishness and a stumbling-block, but to those who believe in Him, a power of God unto salvation. [6]

Luke 2, 22—38. **16.**

And now another charming bit of the Old Testament projected into the New. There lived at this time in Jerusalem a pious and aged widow of whom just enough is known to make us anxious for more. She was a descendant of the "happy" [1] tribe of Asher, which occupied a region towards the Phenician seacoast and dipped its foot into the rich Galilean oil. [2] Curiously enough, the tribe of Asher, "acceptable to his brethren," "alone is celebrated in tradition for the beauty of its women and their fitness to be wedded to high priest or king." [3] It was now long vanished because it belonged to the ten tribes, which did not return from the exile. And the fact that Anna, the daughter of Phanuel, could still trace her ancestry back to a long-forgotten tribe is valuable proof for the

---

15, 4) Is. 8, 14.   5) Ps. 89, 26.
     6) Rom. 1, 16; 1 Cor. 1, 18. 23. 24.
16, 1) Gen. 30, 13.   2) Deut. 33, 24.   3) Edersheim, I, 200.

carefully preserved genealogical traditions in the time of Christ [4]
and seems to imply that hers was a family of distinction.[5]   While
ancient Asher sat still at the haven of the sea and "abode in his
breaches," [6] producing no prophet, raising no hero, and giving no
deliverer to the nation, still, as a belated contribution in the time of
Christ, it produced a *prophetess* to proclaim the advent of the
Messiah to all those who "looked for redemption at Jerusalem."
After a brief wedded life of seven years till now, when she was
eighty-four years old,[7] she departed not from the Temple [8] and

The Prophetess Anna.   devoted herself to praying and fast-
ing night and day.   The seemingly
hopeless extinction of her own tribe, the political state of the
land of Israel, — Herod, — the conditions of the Holy City, the
Hellenizing Sadducees, the externalizing Pharisees, all kindled in
her widowed heart as well as in those who were like-minded, an
earnest longing for the promised redemption.   And now, when the
Messiah *was* come, whom, being a prophetess, she recognized as
such, she joined Simeon in giving thanks unto the Lord and in
proclaiming to Jerusalem the advent of her Messiah and her King.

Matt. 2, 1—12.   17.

Shortly after the events just related Jerusalem was to experience a remarkable confirmation of this startling tale.   Star-guided
Magi came with the question: "Where is He that is born King of
the Jews?"   We might as well admit at the outset that we do
not know just who the Magi were and where they came from.   Even
their designation is obscured with ambiguity.   Originally the Magi
seem to have been members of a sacerdotal order, the Levites, as
it were, of the Median tribes.[1]   But in time the ethnic appellation
was transferred to a small, but learned section.   If Magism and
Chaldaism are practically the same, then Daniel was one of their
presidents in the time of Nebuchadnezzar.[2]   They were the learned

---

16, 4) See Herod's enrolment by tribes and the genealogies of Christ.
Farrar, I, 23.
    5) Edersheim, I, 200.   6) Judg. 5, 17.
    7) This seems to be the best interpretation of $\xi\omega\varsigma$, etc.   Otherwise her
age would be about 107.   Married, say, at sixteen, a widow at twenty-three,
and a widowhood of eighty-four years — in all 107 years.   See Meyer
in loco.
    8) This refers to the fervency of her service and does not mean that
she actually lived in the Temple.   "No one, least of all a woman, permanently resided in the Temple."   Edersheim, I, 200.
17, 1) According to Herodotus (I, 101), one of the six Median tribes.
    2) Dan. 2, 2. 48: "chief of the governors over all the wise men of
Babylon."

men and scientists of their day, who devoted themselves to the study of nature, medicine, mathematics, physics, astronomy, and the like, which studies, however, were not always untinged with superstition. The name Magi, at first a title of honor, gradually lost its better meaning. Among the Greeks and Romans it practically became the general designation of all who made pretensions to supernatural knowledge: magicians, interpreters of dreams, astrologers, necromancers, soothsayers, sorcerers, conjurers, false prophets, and all dealers in the black arts. In this lower sense we

The Magi. find the term used as applied to the Magus or Magian, the sorcerer, who opposed Paul on the island of Cyprus.[3] However, as to the Wise Men who sought Christ, we do not consider them astrologers, soothsayers, skilful dissemblers, medicine-men, or the like, nor do we hold that a delusion was used by Providence to guide them to the Light; for that would be ascribing to a pseudo-science a reality which it does not possess. At any rate, they were upright men, honorable in their vocation, and showed their wisdom in seeking Christ.

Matt. 2, 1—12. **18.**

We know neither their number nor the country whence they came: Arabia, Persia, Parthia, Babylonia, or even Egypt, all of which countries have been suggested.[1] The expression "from the East,"[2] as viewed from Palestine, is indefinite. They might have come from any of these countries and still have been Oriental Magi. But on account of the form of their question: "Where is He that is born King of the *Jews?*" we can safely suppose that they were heathen, the first-fruits among the Gentiles, as opposed to the suggestion that they were Jews living in the Diaspora. It is quite baseless to regard them as kings,[3] although this view was held already in ancient times.[4] As regards their number, there is

Legendary Embellishments. a double tradition. Some of the Fathers held[5] that there were twelve, but the common belief, arising probably from the triple gifts, is that there were three.[6] The Venerable Bede has even supplied them with names, family, and nationality, as it were, and

---

17, 3) Acts 13. 6. 8.
18, 1) See Meyer *in loco.*
2) Eastern lands, ἀπὸ ἀνατολῶν, Matt. 2, 1; 8, 11; 24, 27.
3) Which some have done on account of Ps. 68, 31; 72, 10; Is. 49, 7; 60, 3. 4) Tertullian, *Contra Marcionem.*
5) Augustine and Chrysostom. 6) Farrar, I, 27.

given us a description of their personal appearance. There was old Melchior of Asia, a descendant of Shem, a patriarch with a long white beard; Caspar, a dark-skinned youth of Africa, a strong and lusty son of Ham; and the European Balthasar, swarthy and in the prime of life. The skulls of these three worthy representatives of the three sons of Noah and the three periods of life, kings, if you will, each encircled with a crown of jeweled gold, are still exhibited among the relics in the Cathedral at Cologne.[7] Valueless as these fictions are for historical purposes, yet they have been rendered interesting on account of their influence on some of the most splendid productions of religious art.

Matt. 2, 1—12.   **19.**

And now let us return to the story. What brought these Magi to Jerusalem? "Where is He that is born King of the Jews? For we have seen His star." It is commonly supposed that general Messianic expectations pervaded the entire Orient at this time to the effect that a king should arise in Judea and gain dominion over the world.[1] But of this there is no historic evidence. The references in the Roman writers, most likely derived from Josephus

Messianic Expectations. and referred by him to the Flavian dynasty seventy years *after* the advent of Christ, can be adduced as an indirect proof of the historical verity of this story rather than as an evidence of Gentile Messianic expectations. And as regards the "splendid vaticination in the Fourth Eclogue of Vergil," regarded as among the "unconscious prophecies of heathendom,"[2] it is possibly based on the Sibylline Oracles, which were of Jewish authorship, dating probably from 160 B. C.[3] If a diffuse knowledge of the Messianic hope existed,[4] it must have been derived entirely from Jewish

---

18, 7) Farrar, I, 28.

19, 1) See chapter I, 22; Tacitus, *Hist.,* V, 13; Suetonius, *Vesp.,* 4; Josephus, *Wars,* VI, V, 4; and the famous Fourth Eclogue of Vergil, on account of which supposed Messianic prophecy Vergil gained such popularity in the Middle Ages as to be considered almost inspired.

2) Farrar, I, 29.   3) Schuerer, II, III, 277. Edersheim, I, 203.

4) Ramsay, with true historical instinct, thinks of the East struggling against the West (Rome) and believes that the Magi shared the Oriental interpretation of the Messiah as an Oriental delivery from European domination. That there was a struggling is a historic fact. "Mithridates received support from being champion of Asia against Europe. He had been destroyed." But that was only one stage of the struggle, and another deliverer was sought. — This may all be true, but it is a misconception of the Messianic promise and of Christ's mission and work. See W. S. Ramsay, *Bearing of Recent Discovery,* etc., 145.

sources and, we might add, probably was corrupted by carnal Jewish misinterpretation. This in reply to the common assumption of a general expectant Messianic attitude in the Eastern world. According to this view the Magi, as learned men and zealous partisans of the Orient against the Occident, *knew* of this expectation. And in particular as astrologers,[5] when they saw a rare planetary conjunction in the Jewish (?) sign of fishes, they immediately interpreted it as signalizing the advent of the promised Jewish deliverer and king. But even outside of the political considerations and misinterpreted Messianic expectations there is no satisfactory proof that at the time of the Lord's birth Judea was astrologically designated by the sign of the fishes.[6] The whole theory rests upon an altogether arbitrary and untenable supposition.

Matt. 2, 1—12.   **20.**

However, admitting for the present that the Jews connected the advent of Christ with the appearance of a star, — for which we have no historical proof till *after* the birth of Christ,[1] — there still remain some difficulties in connecting the narrative of the Magi with Balaam's prediction: "There shall come a Star out of Jacob, and a Scepter shall rise out of Israel." [2] This is not a prediction of a literal star, but a promise of the King.[3] Not a star to accompany the King, but the Star, the Scepter, and the King are one.[4]

Balaam's Prediction. The predicted star could hardly have been understood in this peculiar sense, except through a "decided astrological tendency." [5] And besides, while we admit that an argument from silence is always weak, it seems that, if Matthew had regarded Balaam's prophecy as actually referring to a star and the star of the Magi as a fulfilment of Old

---

19, 5) Dividing the zodiac into trigons, each of which denoted a particular country, while the sign of the fishes, Pisces, is supposed to have denoted Judea. Wieseler, 57.

6) The statement of the learned Rabbi Abarbanel, 1547 A. D., as to a much later belief, which makes Pisces the special constellation of the Israelites, is hardly sufficient. And still it is accepted by many. See Wieseler, 59. *Contra,* Andrews, 96; Meyer *in loco.*

20, 1) Bar Cochba, the pseudo-Messiah in the time of Hadrian, who called himself Son of a Star and caused a star to be stamped on his coinage. Wieseler, 55.

2) Num. 24, 17. The reference to Balaam has this in its favor, that he also came from the East, ἀπὸ ἀνατολῶν, Num. 23, 7, according to the LXX. But the silence of Matthew in *not* referring to this star as a fulfilment of prophecy is significant.

3) Even in the Targums it is interpreted in no other way.

4) B. Weiss, I, 266.   5) Wieseler, 58. Edersheim, I, 209.

Testament prophecy, he certainly would not, according to his well-
known custom,[6] have failed to express it. At any rate, even if
this promise of Balaam was remembered and understood as actually
indicating a star, this prophecy alone, without other revelation,
would hardly have been sufficient to set the Wise Men on
their way.

Matt. 2, 1—12.   **21.**

Now, it is to be admitted that, speaking astronomically and
without reference to controversy, a most remarkable conjunction of
planets[1] *did* take place in the constellation of Pisces, which occurs
only once in about 800 years, that of Jupiter and Saturn in 747
and, with Mars added, in 748 A. U. C. But a conjunction of
planets does not fit the case. At the outset there is no Scriptural
evidence that a planetary configuration can be drawn upon to indicate or foretell *anything*, much less the birth of Christ. To accept
it would be to encourage astrological superstition. And it does
not help us to suppose that in this instance delusion providentially
ended in truth.[2] According to Jewish tradition, knowledge is not

Planetary Conjunctions.   found with astrologers, and he
that learned even one thing from
a Magus deserved death.[3] The Scriptures are plain in their de-
nouncement of astrologers, star-gazers, and of those who use divi-
nation.[4] Moreover,[5] there were other conjunctions before and
after, and even a closer conjunction fifty-nine years before the birth
of Christ, which did *not* lead an investigating committee to Jerusalem. And finally, the planets never approached closer to each
other than twice the apparent diameter of the moon, so that they
could not have appeared as one star. It has been suggested[6] that
the observing Magi had weak eyes! But even if the planets stood
as one bright light in the southern sky over Bethlehem as the Wise
Men left Jerusalem, they would not a few hours later, when the
Magi arrived in the city of David, be standing "above the house
where the young Child was."

20, 6) 1, 23; 2, 6. 15. 23, etc.
21, 1) Edersheim, I, 212. Wieseler, 56 ff.
     2) The view of Farrar and others. I, 35.
     3) Edersheim, I, 210.
     4) Deut. 18, 9—12; Is. 47, 13. 14.
     5) As Professor Pritchard has pointed out in *Int. Standard Bible Encycl.*,
2, 849. Andrews, 9.
     6) By Ideler. Andrews, 9.

Matt. 2, 1—12. 22.

Neither can it have been a fixed star, because the degree of light of these heavenly bodies is constant, and their apparent movement with respect to one another is regular.[1] Nor can it have

New Stars and Comets. been a new star;[2] for since no previous knowledge of it existed, it could not have any astrological value. The same applies to comets.[3] Though popularly considered portents, yet as such, like unrelated planets, they cannot astrologically indicate events.[4] A satisfactory explanation based on the supposition that the Magi were astrologers cannot be made.

Matt. 2, 1—12. 23.

Fascinating as these theories may be in themselves and interesting to those who, while accepting the miraculous, are desirous of reducing it to the minimum, it seems necessary to admit the

A Miracle. occurrence of a miracle.[1] Nothing is gained by way of a natural explanation in the attempt to defend the evangelist or to fix the date of the Savior's birth. It is evident, however, that the whole story of the visit of the Magi places the Nativity not long before the slaughter of the infants and before the death of Herod, which at least still agrees with our view of February, 750 A. U. C.

Matt. 2, 1—12. 24.

Whatever the physical nature of the star of the Magi, whether it was one of the known or unknown heavenly bodies, whether previously existing, still existing, or not, or whether it was only a star-

---

22, 1) Andrews, 8.

2) The view of Kepler, Ebrard, and others, based on a brilliant periodical star of the first magnitude which appeared in connection with the conjunction of Jupiter and Saturn and the close of approximation of Mars in 1604. Ebrard, 178.

3) Chinese records preserve the appearance of one or two comets (Pingre) in 749 and 750 A. U. C. Wieseler combines the conjunction of planets in 747 and 748 with the appearance of a new star or comets in 749 and February, 750, and accounts for the difference of time by the setting out of the Magi after the first appearance, and followed by the second appearance after their departure from Jerusalem. Wieseler, 63.

4) Andrews, 8.

23, 1) The theory of planetary conjunctions, so popular a number of decades ago, has been quite generally given up, and conservative Biblical scholars are swinging away from this view. See A. T. Robertson, *Harmony of the Gospels*, 263. E. W. Maunder, "Star of the Magi," *Int. Stand. B. Encycl.*, 2, 848. Davis, *Dictionary of the Bible*, "Star," etc.

like supernatural light,[1] moving in the region of the terrene atmosphere,[2] its purpose was evidently to serve as a sign and as a guide. One verse more, and the evangelist could have explained all. But he does not bring that verse.[3]   And therefore, accepting the miraculous and without attempting further [4] explanation,

"Where Is He that is Born King of the Jews?" we hold that the Magi in their to us unknown Oriental native land and for some undisclosed reason of divine Providence had both a revelation [5] and an astral phenomenon, a sign, which betokened the birth of the Jewish Messiah King [6] and led them to make the inquiry: "Where is He that is born King of the Jews?"

Matt. 2, 1—12.   **25.**

The Magi are called "wise men," and they showed their wisdom by seeking Christ.[1]   Concerning the *fact* and the *time* [2] of the Savior's birth there is no question; "for we have seen His star in the East and are come to worship Him."   And they only asked about the *place* of His birth.[3]   They inquired in Jerusalem, not because they imagined that He must be born in the Jewish capital, but because they naturally expected there to obtain additional necessary and authentic information.   But to ask this question in Herodian Jerusalem was like setting fire to dry thorns.   For were not Herod's lifelong plans, intrigues, efforts, yes, many murders, wound up in the one aim to make himself and no one else king of the Jews? [4]   And had he not practically succeeded?   Of course, there was Rome, his late disfavor with Augustus, the enrolment, and the ideal of complete independence.   Still he was quite satisfied with existing arrangements.   And there was another matter.   There was the question of *birth*, a very difficult matter for a born Edomite

---

24, 1) A star, not by nature, but by appearance.   Chrysostom: Not φύσει, but ὄψει μόνον.   *Exp. Greek N. T. sub loco.*

2) The view of Augustine, some of the Fathers, Chemnitz, and others. Not one of the heavenly orbs, properly so called, but some extraordinary luminous starlike appearance.   Andrews, 10.

3) E. W. Maunder, *Int. St. B. Encycl., sub* "Star of the Magi."

4) The interesting legend of the Well.   *Ibid.*

5) Probably corresponding to Matt. 2, 12.

6) The usual assumption is that a tradition was kept alive based on a prophecy as to the coming of a star.

25, 1) Matthew Henry, commentary, *in loco.*

2) Ὁ τεχθείς, implying that the birth had already taken place.

3) Bengel and Meyer *in loco.*

4) See chapter II, 34 ff.

to improve. At one time he is said to have ordered all family records to be committed to the flames, since the foolish Israelite scruple about accurate genealogical records contributed nothing to his advantage.[5] And he encouraged the circulation of a flattering legend which credited him with descent from a noble Babylonian *Jew*.[6] But secretly he must have been goaded by the consciousness of ignoble extraction. And he must have felt guilty as a pretender to the Jewish throne. Therefore, when he heard of these tidings, the dread of possibilities must have crept over his

The Effect of the Inquiry upon Jerusalem.

frame.[7] "He was troubled and all Jerusalem with him." He had reigned long and with a heavy hand for thirty-seven years, and he liked it. He did not want himself nor his family to lose this power. The inhabitants of Jerusalem, on the other hand, had other reasons to be seized with fear. Those secretly opposed to the Idumean rule knew only too well the character of Herod and the consequences to any one who might, justly or unjustly, be suspected of sympathy with, and support of, any claimant to the royal throne. Still others, the Sadducean nobles, favored Herod, knowing that their interests coincided, and therefore were satisfied to have things remain as they were.[8]

Matt. 2, 1—12.　　　　　**26.**

Herod was resourceful and took measures he considered necessary to protect his throne. Whatever posterity may say of him, it cannot deny his uncanny ability and craftiness. He called together the high priests, past and present, the chairmen of the

"Bethlehem in the Land of Juda."

various sacerdotal orders, and the scribes, that is, the learned Rabbis,[1] and without committing himself, he put before them a theological problem: *Where* is Christ to be born? The answer was easy: According to prophecy[2] in the Judean Bethlehem, not in the Bethlehem of Zebulun. Then Herod called the Wise Men privately, and without revealing his real intentions to them, he questioned them about the precise time when the astral phenomenon had first attracted their attention. From his subsequent

---

25, 5) Eusebius, *H. E.*, I, VII.　　6) Josephus, *Ant.*, XIV, I, 3.

7) Edersheim, I, 204.　　8) Compare John 11, 47—50.

26, 1) Not necessarily the Sanhedrin, as shown by Meyer *in loco*, Edersheim, I, 215, etc., if indeed that body had anything more than a shadowy existence under Herod.

2) Micah 5, 2. Also according to common knowledge, John 7, 42.

course of action it seems that their answer was: more than one year before their arrival at Jerusalem.[3]   Then he directed them to Bethlehem, at the same time giving them instructions to report to him again, so that he also might "come and worship Him." Here we have a picture of Herod as he was during his entire reign.

Matt. 2, 1—12.   **27.**

As the Wise Men left Jerusalem [1] and looked up to the heavens,[2] to their surprise and joy the star which had attracted their attention in the East and which, it seems, had disappeared for a while, again appeared, moving from north to south, a most unusual course for a star,[3] and led them directly to the house [4] where the young Child was.   No details of the first meeting and greeting are given, except that they fell down and worshiped Him. At last they had found the object of their quest.   And then, as

The Adoration of the Magi.   true Orientals, they opened their treasures and presented their gifts: gold, frankincense, and myrrh.   Viewed by themselves, these gifts, except probably the gold as a tender aid to a poverty-stricken king,[5] seemed strangely inappropriate.   They were evidently intended as specimens of the product of their country.   But the Christian Church has from ancient times seen in these gifts a special significance: "gold, as to the King; frankincense, as to God; myrrh, as to a Savior destined to die";[6] or: gold for Shem, myrrh for Ham, and incense for Japheth;[7] or: myrrh for repentance, gold for faith, and incense for prayer.

26, 3) According to this view the first appearance of the star did not coincide with the exact moment of the birth of Christ, but rather with the Annunciation, or one might say, it took place at any time before the Nativity, not exceeding two years.   It is not stated that the Wise Men started immediately.   The distance, too, and the time the journey would consume must be taken into account.

27, 1) When?   In daytime?   At night?   We do not know.

2) Not into a well and in the water seeing the reflection of the star, as told in the Legend of the Well.   E. W. Maunder, *Int. St. B. Encycl.*, 2, 849.

3) "Really, in the view [?] of the evangelist, went before and stopped over the house." *Exp. Greek N. T. in loco.*

4) If the Christ-child was born in a cave, now at least He was found in a house.

5) It does not at all seem to us "a strange conceit" that the gold enabled the poor parents to make a hasty journey to Egypt. Meyer *in loco.*

6) *Exp. Greek N. T.*

7) Farrar, I, 36.

Matt. 2, 13—18.   **28.**

Danger threatened the Child. The Magi, however, were not to be the innocent instruments of Herod's murderous designs.[1] Warned by God in a dream, they did not return for their report to Herod, but departed into their own country another way. And Joseph also had a dream. He was directed by God to flee from Herod's dominion into near-by Egypt, the home of many Jews since the days of Alexander the Great; and although at one time it had been the house of bondage, still in Israel's history it had at many

Flight into Egypt. times served as a place of sheltering refuge. The reason given by the angel why Joseph should take the Christ-child to Egypt was: "For Herod will seek the young Child to destroy Him." Thus early the cross was placed aside the cradle of David's royal Son.[2] Of the flight into Egypt and its duration, which cannot have been long, Scripture gives us no particulars, except that it was a hasty departure by night and, according to instruction, extended until after the death of Herod. With the apocryphal legends, immortalized by the genius of Italian art, we are not concerned.[3] The Evangelist,[4] alluding only to the causes of the flight and the return, sees in it all a deeper significance, calling it the fulfilment of the words of Hosea: "Out of Egypt have I called My Son."[5]

Matt. 2, 13—18.   **29.**

When Herod saw that he was duped, from his point of view,[1] his jealous fury against a possible future rival knew no bounds. For once his crafty cunning had failed. Maddened with anger,

---

28, 1) Edersheim, I, 214.

2) Stoeckhardt, *B. Gesch.*, 7.

3) Tradition has it that Joseph traveled by way of Hebron, Gaza, and the desert, which, as the most direct way, is likely correct. The traditional place of refuge in Egypt is usually given as the village of Metariyeh, not far from Heliopolis, on the way to Cairo. See Meyer *in loco.* Andrews, 100. Farrar, I, 38.

4) Quoting directly from the Hebrew text and not from the LXX, which has τὰ τέκνα αὐτοῦ (the children of Israel).

5) Chap. 11, 1. Not a misunderstanding, but an antitype to the historical meaning of the words of Hosea, in order that the words of the prophet — not a prediction — might receive their Messianic fulfilment. In the flight of Jesus to Egypt a believing reader of the Old Testament cannot but see a correspondence to a type provided by God. See Meyer *in loco.*

29, 1) "Mocked," befooled. He no doubt regretted now that he had permitted the Wise Men to leave Jerusalem without even a guide to make sure that his crafty designs would be carried out.

he resolved upon even more cruel and truculent measures than he had at first intended — to kill all inhabitants of Bethlehem of a certain age to make sure of exterminating the supposed claimant to his throne. Incredible? Anything is credible of the man who murdered his own wife and killed his sons. He sent forth and slew all the children of Bethlehem and its environs, "from two years old and under, according to the time which he had diligently enquired of the Wise Men." He made his net wide. He kept the time learned from the Magi and added a liberal margin. This dreadful butchery of helpless innocent little children was wholesale murder, almost [2] unparalleled in the annals of history. Of their

The Massacre of the Innocents. number we know nothing; very likely there were only twenty or twenty-four, considering the probable population of Bethlehem.[3] But the deed was more than savagely atrocious nevertheless. We do not know how the decree was carried out. The most terrible deeds of tyrants such as Herod are sometimes hushed into oblivion. Josephus is silent. Probably he had a motive: his own opinion about nascent Christianity, not to say anything about Christ — in Rome.[4] "But the wild wail of the mothers thus cruelly robbed of their suckling infants could not be hushed." According to a vision of the prophet Jeremiah [5] the sympathizing tears of a typical mother of all Israel, Rachel, Jacob's beloved wife, who herself had died in the pains of childbirth and was buried on the way to Bethlehem [6] and whose tears had already flowed at Ramah [7] when the exiles were led into captivity in Babylon, again flowed for the misfortune of her children: "Rachel weeping for her children and would not be comforted because they are not." A sad tragedy, this merciless Massacre of the Innocents, but also an honor, since the Church has rightly regarded them as the protomartyrs,[8] or the first witnesses of Christ.[9]

29,   2) See, however, Suetonius, *Augustus*, XCIV, 3.   Farrar, I, 41.

3) Andrews, 101. Farrar, I, 41. Edersheim, I, 214. According to an extravagant legend the number was 14,000!

4) Andrews, 101. And still Rome knew about it, as reflected by the pun of Macrobius. In a confused narrative, which included Herod's son among the slain Syrian children, Augustus is quoted as commenting: "It is better to be Herod's swine (ὖν, *porcum*) than to be his son (υἱόν, *puerum*). Swine were safe before Herod, but not children! Macrobius lived about 400 A. D. Farrar, I, 44.

5) Jer. 31, 15.   6) Gen. 35, 19.   7) Jer. 40, 1.

8) Edersheim, I, 214. The flowers of martyrdom, or *flores martyrum*.

9) Stoeckhardt, 18. Edersheim, I, 214.

Matt. 2, 19—23. **30.**

The exile of the Holy Family in Egypt was probably of brief duration because the cup of Herod's misdeeds was full. After gaining the Jewish throne, the one ghost which haunted the whole later part of his life was the dread of a possible rival. And he could not lay that ghost. It had the habit of making its appearance in the midst of his most intimate surroundings. His eldest son, Antipater, had been nominated as the successor to the throne and had become all-powerful at court. But it seems that he overshot his mark. Not satisfied with clearing his own way to the throne

The Plotting of Antipater. by instigating the murder of his half-brothers Alexander and Aristobulus,[1] he grew impatient because of the long reign of his father. He complained that he was growing old himself, and when the kingdom would come to him, it would afford him no pleasure.[2] Indeed, it seems that he contrived to hasten Herod's end in connection with the mysterious poisoning of Pheroras, Herod's brother. Herod heard about it. He was told that the potion supplied by Antipater — now in Rome — and administered to his brother was actually intended for him. Under all sorts of pretenses Antipater was recalled for the purpose of being put to trial at home. Immediately upon his return unsuspecting Antipater was arrested and tried before Varus, the governor of Syria. On the strength of manifest proofs he was convicted, and a report of the matter was made to Emperor Augustus.[3]

Matt. 2, 19—23. **31.**

But there was something else that made the future look very gloomy for him. A most loathsome and dreadful disease, phthiriasis,[1] had fastened itself on his body, in plain words an excessive multiplication of lice and worms in his body. Josephus speaks of a slow-burning fire and a worm-producing putrefaction in the secretory organs.[2] As soon as the news spread that his disease was incurable, two Rabbis stirred up the people to tear down the golden eagles from the Temple gates. But they rejoiced too soon. Herod was still strong enough to pass sentences of death and to carry them out. The ring-leaders were burned alive. That very

---

30, 1) See chapter II, 47. 48. Briefly reviewed here for the purpose of connecting the events before us.

2) *Ant.,* XVII, IV, 1.   3) *Ant.,* XVII, V, 3. 7.

31, 1) Farrar, I, 47.   2) *Ant.,* XVII, VI, 5.

night there was an eclipse of the moon.[3] By the advice of physicians Herod was carried to the soothing waters of Callirhoe, east
of the Jordan; but death was rapidly approaching. The baths were
in vain, and the old king was carried to Jericho. He was fully
cognizant of the fact that death would soon claim him; but there
were still a few things which increased the torments of his putrefy-
ing body. When a king dies, there ought to be public mourning.

Herod's Disease. But Herod had reason to believe that only
tears of rejoicing would be shed at his
grave, and so he decided to provide such mourning as would befit
his death. He ordered all the noblest of the land of Israel to
assemble in the Hippodrome at Jericho. When they were all
seated there, he shut them up and gave orders to his sister Salome
to kill them all at the first news of his death. Thus he thought
he would provide for himself the honor of a memorable
mourning. — Another worry on Herod's mind was Antipater, who
had made himself guilty of the unpardonable sin. But five days
before his death his terrible pains were momentarily lightened by
some joyful news: the permission from Rome to act as father or
king — to banish his son or to put him to death, as he pleased.[4]
When he heard this, he felt somewhat better; but when the pains
suddenly returned, he forgot his thoughts of revenge and wanted
to turn a knife against himself. Woeful lamentation echoed
through the palace and reached the ears of fettered Antipater, who
thought that his father was already dead, and he already pictured
himself as ascending the throne. But he rejoiced too soon. Herod
was informed of this. In a fresh outburst of rage he ordered that
his son be killed without delay and forthwith and ignobly buried.[5]

Matt. 2, 19—23.   32.

Five days later the terror of Judea himself expired,[1] thirty-
seven years since his appointment as king of Judea and thirty-four
years since his conquest of Jerusalem and the execution of Antigonus, the last of the Maccabean rulers. Salome did not carry out
Herod's instructions with regard to his provision for a memorable
national mourning. The date of the death of Herod and of the
release of the imprisoned Jewish nobles from the Hippodrome was

31, 3) The only one mentioned by Josephus and important for its
chronological value. March 13, 750 A. U. C.
    4) *Ant.,* XVII, VII, 1.   5) *Ant.,* XVII, VII.
32, 1) A few days before the Passover 750 A. U. C., which fell on the
12th of April.

remembered by the Jews as a day of national rejoicing. Henceforth it was a day on which fasting and mourning were not allowed.[2] The royal corpse, with a crown on his head and a scepter in his hand, was placed on a splendid bier, covered with purple, and was carried by Thracian, German, and Galatian guards to its resting-place in the Herodium, a fortress which Herod had built

The Death of Herod. not far from the place where Christ was born. This concludes the story of a highly successful villain, a private man who became a king, and, though encompassed by ten thousand dangers, escaped them all and continued in power to a ripe old age.[3] According to the provisions of his thrice-altered will Archelaus was to receive Judea, Idumea, Samaria, and the crown; Antipas, the Herod of the gospels, was appointed tetrarch of Galilee and Philip tetrarch of the territories east of the Jordan.[4] Even in death the sly old fox showed his cunning, as seen from another provision of his will. For he bequeathed ten millions of coined money [5] to his friend Caesar Augustus and exceedingly fine and costly garments to Her Imperial Highness Julia, the empress (better known as Livia). It need therefore scarcely be said that the will was confirmed and that, for the present at least, his rule passed on to his descendants.[6] But less than a century later the whole race of Herod had been swept away.

Matt. 2, 19—23.   **33.**

It must have been after the death and burial of Herod and before the tidings of the actual accession of the cruel and suspicious Archelaus reached Joseph in Egypt that the Holy Family returned [1] to the beloved *Eretz Israel* (land of Israel).[2] An angel of the Lord appeared to Joseph in a dream, saying: "Arise and take the young Child and His mother and go into the land of Israel; for they are dead which sought the young Child's life." But to whom

---

32, 2) At least according to Edersheim, I, 219; Temple, 176. For comments on this tradition see also Schuerer, I, I, 467.

3) *Ant.,* XVII, VIII, 1.

4) Batanea, Trachonitis, and Auranitis. Luke 3, 1.

5) Drachmae. About $2,000,000.

6) After the complications connected with the death of Herod the kingdom was divided as indicated. Of the four quarters of the kingdom Archelaus received two, with the title ethnarch, which was to be exchanged for the title of king should he prove worthy of it. *Ant.,* XVII, XI, 4. Antipas and Philip received each a fourth of the kingdom with the corresponding title tetrarch.

33, 1) Not fled, but returned.

2) Ἦλθεν εἰς γῆν Ἰσραήλ.

does "they" refer? We do not know. Probably the plural form [3)]
is used as if in studious avoidance of Herod's dreaded name.[4)]
Or it expresses a general idea, although only a single person is
meant.[5)] It seems that Joseph at first intended to return to Beth-

Return to Nazareth.   lehem, the home of his fathers and
                          now made memorable by the birth of
Jesus. As a carpenter his trade would have easily supplied the
modest wants of his household there. But when, on reaching
Palestine, he heard that the mean and contemptible [6)] Archelaus
reigned,[7)] he did not know what to do. But by another divine
counsel given in a dream he was directed to turn aside into the
parts of Galilee [8)] and again made Nazareth in Galilee his home.
It is true, another son of Herod ruled in Galilee, the equally un-
scrupulous and immoral Antipas. But since he was at the same
time more good-natured and indifferent, the life of the Holy Family
under his dominion was secure, especially in consideration of the
storms which were soon to break out in the South. In all this,
however, the inspired evangelist sees a prophetic significance; he
states the return of the Christ-child to Galilee and His living in
the lowly and despised Nazareth to be a fulfilment of divine
prophecy: "He shall be called a Nazarene." [9)]

33, 3) *Oί ζητοῦντες.*

4) *Exp. Greek N. T. in loco.*

5) Something like the word of the Lord to Moses: "Go, return into
Egypt, for all the men are dead which sought thy life," Ex. 4, 19, although
it was *Pharaoh* from whom Moses fled. *Exp. Greek N. T. in loco.*

6) Archelaus is charged with having had merry meetings the same night
in which his father died, with shedding tears in the daytime and making mirth
at night for having succeeded him on the Jewish throne. *Ant.,* XVII, IX, 5.
He was afraid he would not be deemed Herod's true son; but he soon led
the nation to recognize his true Herodian descent. As a specimen of his future
virtues and as an example of his good rule, Josephus scornfully remarks that
he caused three thousand of his own countrymen to be killed at the Passover
gathering in the Temple a few days after Herod's death. *Ant.,* XVII, XI, 2.

7) *Βασιλεύει.* The word can also be used of another rule than that of
a *king* (to rule, *regnare;* Meyer *in loco*). But Archelaus actually *did* reign as
king for a short time until he came to Rome for confirmation of his royal title.
Augustus permitted him only the title of ethnarch until he would make himself worthy of the assumptions and trappings of royalty. *Ant.,* XVII, IX, 5. 6.
Josephus calls him king, chap. IX, 2. Farrar says (I, 50) it is remarkable
how near the evangelists often seem to be to an inaccuracy, while a closer inspection shows them to be, in these very points, minutely accurate.

8) Probably he chose a route along the coast, avoiding Judea altogether.

9) But of which prophecy? Of all pertinent prophecies, Is. 11, 1;
53, 2. 3; Zech. 6, 12, etc., it is probably best to derive the term Nazareth
from *netzer,* branch, a lowly and despised branch. Probably *we* should not
have seen the prophetic correspondence before the fulfilment; but "the
prophecies are the music; the key is the history, the fulfilment." *Exp. Greek
N. T. in loco.*

Luke 2, 39. 40.   **34.**

Of the child-life of Jesus we have only the notice [1] that He grew and developed like any other normal child, mentally and physically, and that, dear to God, He was the particular object of His paternal care. "The Child grew and waxed strong in spirit, filled with wisdom; and the grace of God was upon Him." [2] We can safely ignore the legendary embellishments. [3] The simple statement of St. Luke tells us more than all the pretended omniscience of the apocryphal gospels with their silly legends about the omnipotence and miraculous prowess shown by the Infant Jesus. — Twelve years pass by in sacred silence, that is, as we reckon it, from the spring of 4 B. C. to the spring of 8 A. D., or 750 to 761 A. U. C. Politically a great change had taken place in the land of Israel. Beyond all doubt and undisguised, yes, even by request, the scepter had actually departed from Judah. The weak and wicked rule of Archelaus lasted only nine years. Already at the beginning of his reign, shortly after the death of Herod, a Jewish delegation appeared before Augustus protesting against the imperial confirmation of Herod's will and petitioning him to deliver them altogether from a royal form of government and to add Judea to the province of Syria. [4] A most remarkable request and a significant commentary

Child-Life in Nazareth.
The Removal of Archelaus.

on that first request, made to Samuel in far-back Old Testament times: "Now make us a king to judge us like all the nations." [5] But at the time, and for reasons of his own, [6] Augustus saw fit to deny the request and to confirm the will of Herod. A few days afterwards he appointed Archelaus, not indeed king of the whole country,

---

34, 1) Of St. Luke (2, 40), who, omitting the flight into Egypt and the slaughter of the innocents altogether, passes from Bethlehem and the presentation immediately to Nazareth. But there is no contradiction. We must bear in mind the respective purpose of the two evangelistic accounts: of Luke (from the standpoint of Mary), to explain how Jesus, whose home was Nazareth, was born in Bethlehem; of Matthew, to show how it came about that Jesus, who was born in Bethlehem, lived in Nazareth.

2) Luke 2, 40.

3) As found in the *Proto-Evangelium,* the *Pseudo-Matthew,* and the *Arabic Gospel.* See *The Lost Books of the Bible.*

4) At the same time that Archelaus sailed to Rome to have Herod's testament confirmed. *Ant., XVII,* XI, 2.

5) 1 Sam. 8, 5.

6) The defense of Nicolaus of Damascus, the old friend of Herod, his own friendship for Herod, or that clause in Herod's will about the ten millions of coined money?

but ethnarch of one half of it, with the promise of the royal title
if he would deserve it.[7] The delegation returned, and Archelaus —
minus the coveted royal title and with a reduced income [8] — entered
his ethnarchy. But on account of his rough, tyrannical rule and
the scandal caused by his unlawful marriage the delegation,[9] nine
years later, returned to Augustus. This time the emperor was in
a receptive mood. The charges were serious, and Caesar was
angered. Thinking it beyond his imperial dignity to write to
Archelaus, he sent the Jewish ambassador to Jerusalem to tell his
master, Come. Archelaus came. And when he had come, Augustus
made short work of him. He took away his government and
banished him to Vienne, a city in Gaul. And he also took away
his money.[10] The portion over which Archelaus had ruled was
united to the Roman province Syria, as had already been desired
by a large Jewish party at the time of Herod's death. P. S. Quirinius, who once before the birth of Christ had been governor of
Syria, was appointed to a second term of office and sent to effect
the change.[11] The new arrangement of things, although brought
about by Jewish request and no doubt entered into with good
intentions on both sides, was nevertheless not completed without
violent convulsions.

Luke 2, 39. 40.   35.

It was again time for the Roman census. But Herod was
dead, and this time there was no delay nor Jewish disguise.
Quirinius was charged with carrying the census out along strictly
Roman lines, that is, a valuation of property in behoof of taxation.
This time there was no concession to Jewish prejudices. A measure

The Revolt of Judas.
of this kind, unpopular in any case
among the Jews [1] and now the
symbol of undisguised foreign rule just commencing, agitated the
populace and brought about rioting and revolt. There arose "Judas
of Galilee [2] in the days of the taxing and drew away much people

---

34, 7) *Ant.*, XVII, XI, 4.

8) A part of the regular income was confiscated for the imperial treasury
by the order of Augustus.

9) Fifty ambassadors, supported by the more than 8,000 Jews living in
Rome. *Ant.*, XVII, XI, 1.

10) *Ant.*, XVII, XIII, 2.

11) *Ant.*, XVII, XIII, 5.

35, 1) Ever since David's folly, 2 Sam. 24, 1.

2) Founder of the party of the Zealots. Acts 5, 37. *Ant.*, XVIII, I, 1.

after him." This insurrection was effectually crushed by Coponius, who was appointed procurator of Judea and endowed with supreme power, the power of life and death, and sent out by Augustus to accompany Quirinius, the governor of Syria.[3]

Luke 2, 39. 40.   **36.**

We do not know how the census of 6 A. D. affected the territory of Antipas, but it seems that, while there were troublous times in the South, the home of Jesus was not affected by the storm.

Silence in Galilee. The childhood of Jesus was most probably passed in calm and peace, under the reign of an easy-going, pleasure-seeking, and characterless prince, who entirely lacked his father's ability and strength of will, but who seems at least to have inherited the art of winning, and for many years holding, the favors of powerful Rome.[1]

Luke 2, 41—50.   **37.**

It was in the spring of 8 A. D., or 761 A. U. C., as we reckon it, after order had again been restored in Judea, that the silence of the gospels with regard to the life of Jesus is broken with the account of His first visit to the Paschal Feast in Jerusalem. According to the strict application of the Mosaic Law all the male

Passover. Israelites were required to present themselves in the Sanctuary for the three chief Jewish festivals: Passover, Pentecost, and Tabernacles.[1] But it seems that because of the national dispersion this rule could not be strictly observed, especially not by those living at a great distance from Jerusalem. However, if at all possible, every law-abiding Jew would try to make a journey to Jerusalem at least once a year, preferably at Passover, for the purpose of appearing before the Lord. This accounts for the almost incredible number of annual Passover pilgrims.[2]

35, 3) *Wars,* II, VIII, 1. This is the commonly accepted view, that of Ramsay and others. But recently Dr. W. Lodder, after an examination of Josephus (*Die Schaetzung des Quirinius bei Flavius Josephus. Eine Untersuchung: Hat sich Flavius Josephus in der Datierung der bekannten Schaetzung* [Luke 2, 2] *geirrt?* 1930), is inclined to identify the taxing of the Acts with the first enrolment and the rioting of Judas as immediately following the death of Herod.

36, 1) And when he did lose them in *39* A. D., it was on account of his wife, the ambitious and envious Herodias. *Ant.,* XVIII, VII, 2.

37, 1) Ex. 23, 17; Deut. 16, 16.

2) An innumerable multitude of people. *Wars,* II, I, 3. In a report made to Nero, who was anxious to learn the defensive strength of the city, it is stated that no fewer than 256,500 lambs were slaughtered for the

Of the obligation of women to make this journey there is no mention; but it seems that Mary, being a very pious woman, made this journey annually.[3]   As regards children, up to a certain age a Jewish boy was called *katon,* "little," but from his thirteenth year,[4] which age, however, was often anticipated by one year or more, he would be called *gadol,* "big."   Henceforth he would begin to wear the *tefillin,* or phylacteries.[5]   At this age he was presented by his father at the local synagog and called a *Ben ha Thorah,* "son of the Law."   Now he was bound to a full observance of the Law, and by Rabbinical injunction and national custom he was obliged to learn a trade.

Luke 2, 41—50.   **38.**

It was in accordance with these customs that the parents[1] of our Lord made their annual Passover journey and, joining their friends and neighbors in a company, took the twelve-year-old Jesus with them.   Nazareth is over sixty miles from Jerusalem.   We do not know by which road they traveled, but in spite of the evident hostility of the Samaritans we suppose that the traditional and more direct and also the safer route through Shechem was taken.[2]   The profane plumage of the Roman eagles was overshadowing the Holy City, but it was still the Jerusalem of which David sang[3] and for which the exiles yearned,[4] and towering above

The Journey to Jerusalem. its walls still glittered the great Temple with its gilded roofs and marble colonnades.   Who shall fathom the unspeakable emotion with which the Boy Jesus, nearing the city, gazed on that memorable and never-to-be-forgotten scene?   It was His first visit to the Holy City and His first appearance in the halls of the Temple.   At the time of the Passover Feast,[5] Quirinius was, as has been stated, governor of Syria, Coponius was the first Roman proc-

Paschal Feast.   If we count no fewer than ten participants for each Paschal meal, whereas there were sometimes as many as twenty, we arrive at a figure of over two and a half million worshipers, exclusive of foreigners and those who were ceremonially unclean.   *Wars,* VI, IX, 3.   Farrar, I, 72.

37,   3) Meyer *in loco.*

4) Schuerer, II, II, 52.   See also Farrar.

5) Matt. 23, 5.   Square capsules, covered with leather, containing on small scrolls of fine parchment the following Bible-passages: Ex. 13, 1—10. 11—16; Deut. 6, 4—9; 11, 13—21.   Schuerer, II, II, 113.

38,   1) Γονεῖς.   See chapter IV, 14.

2) Farrar, I, 70 ff.

3) Pss. 48 and 122.   4) Ps. 137.

5) Which in 8 A. D. began on April 8.   Andrews, 108.   Farrar, I, 70.

urator of Judea, and Annas, that wily diplomat, whom the then youthful Jesus was to meet later under other circumstances, was ruling the Temple.[6]   Living at Jerusalem at the time were probably also the great Hillel, the eminent jurist, mild, and now white with the snows of well-nigh one hundred years, whom the Jews reverenced almost as a second Moses, and his great rival, the stern Shammai, the two founders of opposing Jewish schools.[7]

Luke 2, 41—50.   39.

Of the Passover Festival itself as observed by the Holy Family and a group of Galilean friends, the selection and slaying of the paschal lamb, the sprinkling of the blood upon the altar, the meal itself,[1] and the Days of Unleavened Bread,[2] there is no record. We are only told that, when the days were fulfilled and all the legal ordinances had been observed and the vast multitudes were returning to their homes, the Child Jesus tarried behind, and His parents[3] knew it not.   This was, however, not a case of careless negligence, but on account of some circumstance unknown to us they were confident that the missing Boy could be found in the

Jesus Missing on the Return Journey.

caravan made up of Galilean relatives and friends.   A day elapsed before the parents discovered the loss. This probably happened as they arrived at the place which had been designated by the caravan as the evening rendezvous.[4]   On the next day — we can well imagine their anguish and concern — they returned to Jerusalem.   And still no trace at the temporary dwelling-place or camp where they had made their stay during the days of the feast.   Not until the third day did they find Him, strangely enough, in the place where they had least thought of searching for Him, "in the Temple, sitting in the midst of the doctors, both hearing them and asking them questions."   This was not in a synagog which some suppose to have been located in the Temple area, but most likely in one of the halls where such popular discourses were held.[5]

38, 6) John 18, 13. Schuerer, II, I, 198.

7) Schuerer, II, I, 359 ff. Edersheim, I, 239.

39, 1) Ten to twenty in a group.

2) Edersheim, *Temple,* 189 ff.

3) Some texts have "Joseph and Mary"; other texts "parents," as in v. 41.   The change was probably made for dogmatic reasons.

4) Tradition says at El Bireh, north of Jerusalem. Andrews, 109.

5) Edersheim, I, 246.

Luke 2, 41—50.   **40.**

We do not know the particular subject of the discourse, but it needs no proof that on this occasion [1] Jesus was not taking the part of a teacher, but, like a truly developing child, was humbly seeking to learn, at the same time giving evidence of His deep interest and His remarkable intelligence by fitting replies. There was no forwardness in His behavior, which would have been entirely foreign to Him "who knew no sin" and contrary to His bringing up.[2] And still, all that heard Him were astonished at His marvelous understanding and wisdom and at His discerning answers. And when the parents saw Him, they were amazed. The daily contact with this silent, obedient Child may have blunted the memory of His wonderful origin.[3] When they found Him in this

Found in His Father's House. austere presence and so occupied, they were utterly surprised. Mary spoke, venturing to address Him in language of tender reproach: "Son, why hast Thou thus dealt with us? Behold, Thy father and I have sought Thee sorrowing." To this mildly chiding expostulation Jesus replied — His first recorded utterance —: "How is it that ye sought Me? Wist ye not that I must be about My Father's business?" "This divinely natural and sublimely noble reply, showing the half-vexed astonishment which it expresses that they should so little understand Him, the perfect dignity which it combines, allowing no interference with His divinely appointed mission, is all in accordance with His person and His work." [4] Mary referred Him to His "father"; but in His reply Jesus reminded them that He was sent to this earth to do the business of His Father in heaven.[5] In the "Wist ye not?" He delicately recalled to them the fading memory of all they *did* know. And in the "I must" He lays down the law by which He must walk to the day of His death upon the cross.

40, 1) As the *Arabic Gospel* of Jesus' infancy depicts it. Farrar, I, 74.

2) Anything like forwardness in boys was peculiarly distasteful to the Jews (Farrar, I, 75), as, for instance, the almost incredible immodesty of Josephus: "While I was still a mere boy, about fourteen years old, I won universal applause for my love of letters, insomuch that the chief priests and the leading men of the city used constantly to come to me for precise information on some particular in our ordinances." (!) *Life,* 2.

3) Farrar, I, 77.

4) Farrar, I, 78. 79.

5) Notice the new term for God in Luke. Chap. 2, 29: δέσποτα, Lord, All-highest, Sovereign; here: Father.

Luke 2, 51. 52.   **41.**

"And they understood not the saying which He spake unto them." "A strange commentary on the first recorded utterance of the youthful Savior, spoken to those nearest and dearest to Him." But Mary remembered. She kept all these sayings in her heart.[1] "And they understood not the saying." Strange, but mournfully

Return to Nazareth. prophetic of what became so manifest throughout His ministry: "He came unto His own, and His own received Him not."[2] And yet, though conscious of His divine origin, and though one ray of hidden glory had flashed forth, in dutiful and willing obedience "He went down with them and came to Nazareth and was subject unto them." And again the gospel lets fall the veil upon this youthful life. The child became a youth, and the youth a man, which life, truly human and yet without sin, the evangelist sums up in the words: "And Jesus increased in wisdom and stature and in favor with God and man."

Luke 2, 51. 52.   **42.**

Eighteen years of deep silence in Nazareth and also general silence in Galilee, Judea, and Rome. For this obscure period in the life of Jesus we have no direct knowledge and must satisfy ourselves with what can be inferred with more or less certainty from a few incidental references in the Scriptural account. Because of His humble circumstances it is not likely that this royal Son of the house of David enjoyed any special education and training, none but that received from His mother and father[1] and in the local synagog,[2] and such knowledge as He may have naturally acquired through His cosmopolitan Galilean surroundings and in the process of normal development.[3] His language was undoubtedly the commonly spoken Aramaic;[4] but He also knew Hebrew, for some of His Scriptural quotations refer directly to the Hebrew original.[5] He was able to read;[6] for in His disputes with the

---

41, 1) Luke 2, 19. 51. See Farrar, VI.

2) John 1, 11. See Farrar, *ibid.*

42, 1) 2 Tim. 1, 5; 3, 15; Deut. 6, 6. 7.

2) Edersheim, I, 231.   3) Luke 2, 40. 52.

4) A Semitic form of speech related to the Hebrew, but differing from it in vocalization and in a number of grammatical forms. Schuerer, II, I, 8 ff. See Mark 15, 34. Farrar.

5) Mark 12, 29. 30; Luke 22, 37; Matt. 27, 46.

6) Matt. 5, 18; Luke 16, 17; John 7, 15. See Farrar, VII, for this section.

Pharisees and Sadducees He could, by appealing directly to Scripture, meet them on their own ground with the challenge, so often repeated: "Have ye not read?"[7]   And it seems that He could write.[8]   He also no doubt understood conversational Greek; for whenever He spoke to those who used that language, the Roman centurion,[9] the Syrophenician woman,[10] "the Greeks who would see Jesus,"[11] and with Pilate, no mention is made of an interpreter.[12]   Whether He showed extensive familiarity with Latin we cannot say.   A number of Latin words occur in His teaching.[13] And on one occasion He referred to an inscription on a Roman coin.[14]   The use of these languages, however, does not at all pre-

Education.   suppose a special training, but is easily accounted for in the life of a Galilean Jewish boy in a surrounding Greco-Roman world.[15]   And if this Boy received any special school education, which is doubtful, at any rate we assume that it must have ceased soon after His first paschal visit to Jerusalem.   For now He was humbly engaged in learning His father's trade.   For almost a score of years there was nothing that distinguished Him from any other youth of Nazareth, as far as the eye of man could see; He was a plain carpenter[16] and a carpenter's son.[17]   A hundred years later, according to Justin Martyr, there were still shown some plows and yokes that were said to have been made by Joseph and Jesus.[18]

Luke 2, 51. 52.   **43.**

Of the members constituting the intimate household of the Holy Family in Nazareth we have no record.   But it seems that besides Joseph and Mary and the Boy Jesus there were other children, boys and girls, in Joseph's house.   They appear afterwards as the Lord's brethren, but we do not know who they were.   The

---

42, 7) Matt. 22, 31, etc.

8) On one occasion He wrote in the sand, John 8, 6. Farrar, I, 90. But it is to be admitted that this writing may have been merely a tracing of symbolic figures.   Compare also the alleged correspondence of Christ with Abgarus, King of Edessa, related by Eusebius, I, 13.

9) Matt. 8, 5.   10) Matt. 15, 22.

11) John 12, 21. Farrar.   12) Weiss, I, 283.

13) For instance, modius, Matt. 5, 15; quadrans, Matt. 5, 26; legio, Matt. 26, 53.

14) Matt. 22, 19.

15) In many of our American cities there are numerous persons who can easliy carry on a conversation in a number of different languages: Polish, Slovak, Russian, Yiddish, German, and English.

16) Mark 6, 3.   17) Matt. 13, 55.

18) J. Klausner, 233.   Andrews, 110.

gospels give us the names of James, Joses, Judas, and Simon,[1] while the *History of Joseph* supplies the names of Anna and Lydia.[2] But we do not know whether they were children of Joseph by a former marriage,[3] whether they were cousins, the children of a deceased brother, Alphaeus, or Clopas,[4] and now legally adopted by Joseph,[5] or whether they were actually the children of Joseph and Mary.[6] And it really does not matter. Our exegetical conscience does not compel us to accept the literal sense of the term *brother* because the same evangelist also refers to Jesus as the carpenter's *son,*[7] while expressly stating in another passage that He was not his son.[8] Much can be said for and against each view. For instance, if Joseph had any children before the legally adopted Jesus, what about the status of Jesus as the rightful heir to the throne of David in the eyes of His followers? If they were cousins of Jesus, how is it that they are always called brothers and sisters and not cousins or kinsmen?[9] If they were the nephews of Joseph, how is it that they are invariably found in the company of Mary?[10]

The Lord's Brethren. Or were their mothers likewise sisters?[11] And if they were so devoted to Mary, or if they were actually her own children,[12] how is it that their opposition to Jesus[13] was apparently also extended to Mary, since the Lord entrusted the care of His mother to John?[14] And if they were not actually the children of Joseph and Mary, what about the "knew her not *until*" and "brought forth her *first-born son*"?[15] And finally, if they were actually the sons of Joseph

---

43, 1) Mark 6, 3; Matt. 13, 55: "And His sisters, are they not all with us?"

2) Possibly children of Joseph by his first wife. Andrews, 118.

3) The Epiphanian Theory.

4) According to an early tradition the same person. (Chrysostom.) Matt. 10, 3. Married to Mary, sister to Mary? Stoeckhardt, *Bibl. Gesch.*, p. 33. Luke 6, 15; Mark 15, 40; Matt. 27, 56; John 19, 25.

5) The Hieronymian Theory.

6) The Helvidian Theory. (All three theories named after their original or at least chief advocate.)

7) Matt. 13, 55.   8) Matt. 1, 20.

9) Ἀδελφοί and not ἀνεψιοί or συγγενεῖς?

10) John 2, 12; Matt. 12, 46; Mark 3, 31; Luke 8, 19.

11) See *Cath. Encycl. sub loco.*   12) The Helvidian Theory.

13) John 7, 5. This was not really unbelief, but only "relative" unbelief, shared also by His chosen Twelve. Matt. 17, 17. 20. (F. Pieper.)

14) John 19, 27.

15) Matt. 1, 25; Luke 2, 1. These terms, however, prove nothing as to what did or did not happen afterwards.

THE CHRONOLOGICAL AND HISTORICAL SETTING.

The calculation of our Christian Era was made by the Roman abbot Dionysius Exiguus. In preparing the Easter tables for the year 525 A.D., he counted the years from the birth of Christ. But due to a miscalculation the year of the Lord's birth was erroneously made to correspond with the year 754 of the building of Rome. This date is at least four years too late, because Herod died shortly before the Passover of 750 A.U.C., as has been astronomically ascertained. And Christ was born before Herod died. The following table is given as an aid in placing the events in their proper historical and chronological order.

	743	744	745	746	747	748	749	750	751	752	753	754	755	756	757	758	759	760
A.U.C.	743	744	745	746	747	748	749	750	751	752	753	754	755	756	757	758	759	760
B.C.	11	10	9	8	7	6	5	4	3	2	1	—	—	—	—	—	—	—
A.D.	—	—	—	—	—	—	—	—	—	—	—	1	2	3	4	5	6	7
Age of Jesus. Born 749 A.U.C.	—	—	—	—	—	—	—	1	2	3	4	5	6	7	8	9	10	11
Roman Emperor Augustus. B.C. 30—A.D. 14	—	—	—	—	—	—	—	—	—	—	—	—	—	—	—	—	—	—
Enrolments, beginning 9—8 B.C. (In fourteen-year periods)	—	—	—	1	—	—	—	—	—	—	—	—	—	—	—	—	2	—

(Acts 5, 37)

Jewish Rulers:—

Herod 37—4 B.C. Died March, 750 A.U.C.

{ Archelaus, Judea. Deposed 6 A.D.
Philip, Iturea. 4 B.C.—34 A.D.
Antipas, Galilee. 4 B.C.—39 A.D.

Governors of Syria:—

P. S. Quirinius	11—8 B.C.	First term
C. S. Saturninus	7—6 B.C.	
P. Q. Varus	6—2 B.C.	
C. Caesar	B.C. 1—4 A.D.	
L. V. Saturninus	4—5 A.D.	
P. S. Quirinius	6—10 A.D.	Second term

and Mary, what about the doctrine of the perpetual virginity: *"Semper mansisse virginem, dogma est fidei"?* And so forth. Without going farther into this vexed question [16] and with the admission of our own inability to determine the precise relation between Jesus and these "brethren and sisters," we can at least safely assume, whatever theory we may be inclined to accept, that the relation must have been a most close and intimate one, exercising a certain influence upon the human development of the youthful Jesus. And if, to state our own view, we are inclined to accept the view of Hegesippus [17] that they were the children of Joseph's brother Alphaeus and another Mary, it is not on account of any dogmatic interest in the perpetual virginity of Mary, but only our preference in a matter in which the Scriptures have not definitely spoken and tradition disagrees.[18] To the members of that family in Nazareth — now numbering six or seven children, boys and girls — we might also add two more cousins in Capernaum as belonging to the family circle, namely, James and John, the sons of Zebedee and Salome, the sister of Mary.[19] In this circle Jesus grew up. We lose sight of Joseph and suppose that he must have died some time during these silent years.

Luke 2, 51. 52.   **44.**

What happened in Rome while Israel was waiting? A little more than a year after Jesus' Passover journey sad news reached Rome from Germany. Quintilius Varus, the same Varus who was governor of Syria at the time of Herod's death, had been ignominiously defeated by Arminius in the Teutoburger Wald. This was the second of the only two severe defeats, both in Germany, which Augustus suffered in the forty-one years of his reign. For months he expressed his grief by letting his beard and hair grow and repeating, "Quintilius Varus, give me back my legions." [1] This was in 9 A. D. In 12 A. D. a son of the Empress Livia Drusilla

---

43, 16) See Andrews, 111 f.; Farrar, I, 95 f.; Weiss, I, 281 f.; Pieper, *Dogmatik*, II, 368 f.; *Int. Stand. B. Encycl.*, 518 f.; etc.

17) Quoted by Eusebius, III, XI; IV, XXII.

18) See Pieper, *Dogmatik*, II, 368 f.

19) Delicately alluded to, but unnamed, in John 19, 25 as compared with Matt. 27, 56 and Mark 15, 40. (Four women at the cross?) If Salome was a sister of Mary, it does not surprise us that her sons were at first disciples of the Baptist, whose mother and the Virgin were related (Luke 1, 36), and that Jesus entrusted His mother to John, who consequently would be her nephew. See Farrar, I, 99.

44, 1) Suetonius, *Augustus*, 23.

by a former marriage, Tiberius Claudius Nero, and now his own
adopted son and heir, was made "colleague in empire." [2]   On
August 19, 14 A. D., Augustus died and was promptly deified,
and the reins of government passed on to Tiberius.   In the
mean while as well as later there was little change in Judea outside

**Conditions in the
Roman World.**

the succession of procurators and high
priests. Of the latter a few names are
of interest, Ananos, or Hannas, the son
of Seth, who was himself high priest from 6 to 15 A. D. and after
a short interval was followed by his son Eleasar, 16—17 A. D., and
by his son-in-law Joseph, called Caiaphas, somewhere between
18 and 36 A. D. [3]   Hannas and Caiaphas are the two ecclesiastical
rulers who appear as the "high priests" in the New Testament,
although there was only one high priest, Caiaphas, actually holding
office, however, with Hannas as the real power behind the throne. [4]
There were also a number of procurators following Coponius, of
whom, however, with the exception of the last, little is known:
Marcus Ambivius, probably 9—12 A. D.; Annius Rufus, probably
12—15 A. D.; Valerius Gratus, 15—26 A. D., and Pontius Pilate,
26—36 A. D. [5]   The longer period during which the latter two
held office was due to the consideration of Tiberius for the
provinces; for he held that governors acted like flies upon the
body of a wounded animal; if once they were gorged, they would
become more modest in their exactions. [6]   And in Galilee, which
witnessed the luxurious, dissipated life and the Herodian building
operations of the tetrarch Antipas, there was hardly any change
at all.

44,   2) Suetonius, *Augustus*, 97, and *Tiberius*, 21.   Tacitus, *Ann.*, I, 3.
       3) Schuerer, II, I, 198. 199.
       4) Luke 3, 2; John 18, 13—24; Acts 4, 6.
       5) Schuerer, I, II, 81.
       6) *Ant.*, XVIII, VI, 5.

CHAPTER V.

THE PERIOD OF JOHN.

Late summer 26 A. D., or 779 A. U. C., to the beginning of 27 A. D.

A. U. C.	779	780	781	782	783
A. D.	26	27	28	29	30
Age of Jesus	30	31	32	33	34
Passovers		I	II	III	IV

1.

Matt. 3, 1. Mark 1, 1. Luke 3, 1. 2.

In the fifteenth year of the reign of Emperor Tiberius the entire nation of Israel was aroused by a powerful movement such as it had not experienced since the great days of the Maccabees. A great prophet had arisen on the banks of the Jordan. Twelve years had passed since the death of Caesar Augustus [1] and fourteen years since the coregency of his colleague and successor.[2] It was now in the fifteenth year of the reign of Tiberius Caesar and, as we take it, in the late summer of 779 A. U. C., or 26 A. D., that the call came to John, the son of Zacharias, in the wilderness, to be followed shortly afterwards by the beginning of Christ's public ministry, when both Christ and His forerunner were about thirty years of age. Of his previous life since his circumcision, when he received the name John, nothing is known except that he "was in the deserts till the day of his showing unto Israel." [3] The Essenes, being desert-dwellers, were near by, but there is no Scriptural evidence that John, similarly to Josephus, who speaks of his three-year discipleship with Banus in the desert,[4] had any inward or outward contact with them.[5] Nor is there any significance in

---

1,   1) August 19, 767 A. U. C., or 14 A. D. Suetonius, *Augustus,* 100.

2) Which began at the close of 764 or in the beginning of 765 A. U. C. Tacitus, *Annales,* I, 3. 7. Suetonius, *Augustus,* 97, and *Tiberius,* 20. 21. 12 A. D.

3) Luke 1, 80.   4) Josephus, *Life,* 2.

5) The Essenes were an obscure ascetic Jewish order of men of monastic and communistic tendencies, numbering about 4,000 members at the time of Christ. Their favorite dwelling-place was in the desert of Engedi on the Dead Sea, although they had "houses" in various cities of Palestine, notably in Jerusalem, where indeed one of the city gates was named after them. Their repeated lustrations were symbolic of inward purity, prompted by the desire to live a life of Levitical purity, being extremists in this respect. They were people of puritanical tendencies and peculiar customs. Since they were always dressed in white and their vestments were made of fine linen, they would

[133]

the fact that he began his public career at the age of thirty because the Levites began their service at that time.[6]   While he was by birth entitled to the priesthood, it is mere conjecture, in the absence of Scriptural proof, to assume that the priests entered upon their duties at the same age as the Levites.   The Rabbinical tradition states that a priest was duly qualified as soon as the first signs of manhood appeared, although there was no installation until the candidate had reached the age of twenty.[7]   And besides, there is no evidence that John assumed the priesthood at all.   It is rather as a prophet that he is introduced in the Gospel account.   And the divine call to this office was not bound by age, rule, custom, or tradition.   It is therefore all the more interesting to notice that in

The Exact Time.   Luke's account of John's ministry this prophet is introduced with the same historical accuracy as, for instance, the prophet Jeremiah.[8]   There are exactly six historical references to define the date of John's ministry with respect to the reigning Roman emperor and the civil and ecclesiastical rulers within the confines of ancient Palestine. The first, which has already been considered, refers to the fifteenth year of Emperor Tiberius, that is, 26 A. D.   Pontius Pilate was ruler of Judea.   This well-known Roman governor was appointed in the end of 778 or in the beginning of 779 A. U. C. and held office until he was recalled in 789.[9]   Herod Antipas, who had obtained his tetrarchy after the death of his father in 750 A. U. C., was still in the possession of the governorship of Galilee, which he held for forty-two years, until he was finally deposed in the autumn of 792 A. U. C.[10]   His own half-brother Philip, son of Herod the Great and Mariamne II, daughter of Simon the High Priest, was tetrarch of Iturea and the territories east of the Sea of Galilee, Batanea, Trachonitis, Auranitis, Gaulanitis, and Panias.[11]   He seems to have been the best of the Herodian princes, enjoying Roman favor from the time of his appointment in 750 A. U. C. to the time of his death in 786.[12]   A certain non-Jewish prince,

---

not have presented themselves in raiments of camel's hair, nor would they have eaten locusts like John the Baptist, as they abstained from all animal food.   Like the Sadducees they denied the resurrection of the body and other fundamental doctrines of Scripture and therefore were outside the pale of the Church of God.   *Ant.*, XVIII, I, 5;   *Wars*, II, VIII, 2—13.   Schuerer, II, II, 190—218.   Edersheim, I, 324—335.   264 and note.

1,   6) According to Num. 4, 3, etc.   7) Schuerer, II, I, 215.

        8) Jer. 1, 1—3.   Or Ezekiel, chap. 1, 1—3.

        9) Josephus, *Ant.*, XVIII, IV, 2.   26—36 A. D.

        10) 4 B. C. to 39 A. D.   11) Schuerer, I, II, 10.

        12) 4 B. C. to 33 A. D.   *Ant.*, XVIII, IV, 6.

Lysanias of Abilene, occupied the outlying territory between the Lebanon ranges near Damascus. This notice is relevant because this territory belonged to the Land of Israel in ancient times and because subsequently, nearer to the day of the evangelist, it formed a part of the territory assigned by Caligula to his favorite Herod Agrippa I, A. D. 37.[13] Although long doubted, this notice of Luke is now by competent scholars acknowledged as historically correct. It has been shown that Lysanias ruled over this region as a contemporary of Antipas and Philip (not to be confounded with the Lysanias who had ruled over it sixty years before).[14] Of the ecclesiastical rulers Annas and Caiaphas, that notorious pair, divided the honors, if not the functions, of a sacred office which they disgraced.[15] Of course, there could be but one actual high priest, and that position was held by Caiaphas. But Annas,[16] as the influential former high priest, father-in-law of Caiaphas, and the real power behind the throne, was also given this title.[17]

2.

Matt. 3, 2—6. Mark 1, 2—6. Luke 3, 3—6.

This, then, was the political and ecclesiastical situation when the word of God came to John in that wild range of uncultivated wilderness, stretching forth from Jericho to the fords of the Jordan and southward to the shores of the Dead Sea, to prepare the way for Christ by "preaching the baptism of repentance for the remission of sins." Thus his aged father, in agreement with what the angel Gabriel had told him, apostrophized on the day of John's circumcision: "Thou shalt go before the face of the Lord to prepare His ways."[1] And thus it was written in the combined promise of Isaiah and Malachi: "Behold, I send My messenger before Thy face, who shall prepare Thy way. The voice of one crying in the wilderness, Make ye ready the way of the Lord."[2] This is an announcement of the coming Lord and the identification of John as the herald to prepare His way. Preparation for the reception

---

1, 13) *Exp. Greek N. T. in loco.*
14) Schuerer, I, II, 338. Meyer *in loco.*
15) Farrar, I, 111.
16) Appointed by Quirinius and holding office from 6 to 15 A. D.
17) Caiaphas, ca. 18—36 A. D. Schuerer, II, I, 198. 199. Compare also John 18, 13—24; Acts 4, 6; Matt. 26, 3. 57; John 11, 49.
2, 1) Luke 1, 76.
2) Mal. 3, 1; Is. 40, 3. Mark mentions Isaiah only. This is not an error, however, but rather an indication that he had the quotation from Isaiah chiefly in mind.

of the coming King and admission into His kingdom was by repentance. "Every valley shall be filled, and every mountain and hill shall be made low." This is figurative language for the direct admonition: "Repent ye, for the kingdom of heaven is at hand."

The Appearance of John.

While the nature of this kingdom was probably wholly different from that expected by his hearers, John makes it quite clear that he was not preaching the hoped-for deliverance from foreign oppressors, but the kingdom of heaven, the redemption of all mankind from sin and life everlasting through the Messiah. This kingdom, now approaching, although spiritual, yet quite real notwithstanding, would not bring about glorious material changes. Admission into it required sincere repentance, a complete change of heart. Of this believing Israel was not unaware. So close was repentance connected in their thoughts with the advent of the Messiah that it was said in one of the Rabbinical traditions: "If Israel repented but one day, the Son of David would immediately come." [3] With his call to repentance as the proper preparation for the reception of the Messiah, John's own personal habits, his dress and food, were in striking harmony. Like Elijah, the prophet of judgment to the Northern Kingdom,[4] he was dressed in hairy garments. He was clothed with camel's hair and had a leathern girdle about his loins. This coarse Bedouin tunic emphasized the profound earnestness of his call to repentance. All in the man was real and true. He preached with his voice, with his dress, and with his food. His food was such as the desert supplied, roasted locusts, still the food of the poor in the East,[5] and wild honey, either such as he found in the clefts of the rocks or as flowed from a hole in lightning-riven trees.[6]

3.

Matt. 3, 2—6. Mark 1, 2—6. Luke 3, 3—6.

In addition to his call to repentance a new rite, Baptism, accompanied his word. It was this rite which gave him his name the Baptist.[1] The baptisms which he performed are not to be

2,   3) Edersheim, I, 272.

4) 2 Kings 1, 8.

5) Lev. 11, 22. *Exp. Greek N. T.*, Matthew *in loco.*

6) Opinion is divided between bee honey and tree honey, *i. e.,* honey made by wild bees in trees or holes in the rocks or a liquid exuding from palms and fig-trees. See Meyer, *Matthew, in loco.*

3,   1) Matt. 3, 1. Ἰωάννης ὁ βαπτιστής. Well known by this epithet and referred to under that designation by Josephus, *Ant.,* XVIII, v, 2.

confounded with the Levitical purifications and proselyte baptisms,[2] which perhaps did not even exist at that time.[3] While it is of no particular present-day interest or practical value to discuss what degree of difference, if any, or similarity existed between it and the Sacrament of Baptism instituted by Christ, it is clear that his

His Baptism. Baptism was a divine institution, as he said himself: "He that sent me to baptize with water."[4] It was not merely an initiatory ceremony, but an actual and effectual means of grace, bestowing upon those who received it upon sincere repentance, forgiveness of sins.[5] Christ Himself acknowledged its effectiveness and referred to it as a means by which the Holy Spirit wrought regeneration: "Except a man be born of water and of the Spirit, he cannot enter into the kingdom of God."[6]

4.

Matt. 3, 2—6. Mark 1, 2—6. Luke 3, 3—6.

In a short time John made himself felt as a power in the midst of his people. It soon became widely rumored that a prophet had arisen whose burning words it was worth while to hear. Here was

The Aroused Jewish Population. a man, talking about Judgment and the Kingdom, who by his expressions recalled Isaiah and by his life Elijah. It was probably in a Sabbatic year, beginning in the autumn of 779 A. U. C.,[1] when the people could rest from agriculture, business, and other labor. The news spread from the wilderness to the surrounding country, and the movement soon reached colossal dimensions. In widening circles it embraced Judea and even affected disdainful Jerusalem.

5.

Matt. 3, 7—10. Luke 3, 7—14.

Among those coming to John's baptism were also the self-glorifying professors of Jewish orthodoxy, the Pharisees, the strict exponents of piety and external righteousness, according to law

---

3, 2) Edersheim (*Life and Times of Jesus,* Appendix XII) states that among the Jews, proselytes of righteousness (such as adopted Judaism in its entirety) were obliged to accept, besides Circumcision, the initial rite of a certain baptism, which, however, "only implied a new relation to God and to Israel" and was not divinely commanded. Also see Schuerer, II, II, 319 ff.

3) *Exp. Greek N. T.,* under Matt. 3, 1.

4) John 1, 33. Cf. Luke 3, 2. 3.

5) Mark 1, 4; Luke 3, 3. Cf. Pieper, *Dogmatik,* III, 338.

6) John 3, 5.

4, 1) As Wieseler thinks, *Synopsis,* 186; Andrews, 145; Edersheim, I, 278; and others.

and statute. But also the liberal element made its appearance, that is, the exclusive and wealthy Sadducees, mostly men of affairs and largely belonging to the sacerdotal class. They came "to" [1] John's baptism, not because they were truly repentant,[2] nor because they were exactly opposed to his baptism and resolved to put down the movement; they came either as curious and interested witnesses — for, after all, they also shared with the common people the false Messianic hope — of a strange phenomenon or probably with the intention of submitting themselves, at least externally, to John's baptism as an act of preparation for the proper reception of the Messiah. But John had no words of welcome for them. "Ye offspring of vipers, who warned you to flee from the wrath to come?" To their well-known insincerity and deception they owed this harsh greeting.[3] In their minds they had connected judgment with the Messianic advent only as applied to the Roman oppressors; but now a warning of general wrath is sounded, and individual and universal repentance is demanded. Inde-

A Specimen of John's Preaching. pendently of their own personal faith and obedience to God's commandments they had considered their mere physical descent from Abraham as entitling them to seats of honor in the kingdom of heaven. But John tells them: "I say unto you that God is able of these stones to raise up children unto Abraham. Therefore every tree which bringeth not forth good fruit is hewn down and cast into the fire." This stinging rebuke, directed against the leaders of the Jewish people, instilled fear in others. The multitudes asked, "What shall we do?" A simple answer was given them. While John himself ate locusts and garbed himself in hairy garments, he did not require others to do the same. He did not tell his hearers to quit their honest calling, but only to change their way of living. Simple justice, mercy, and charity were imposed upon all. "He that hath two coats, let him impart to him that hath none." To the inquiring publicans, the deeply hated tax-collectors, he replied: "Exact no more than that which is appointed you." Soldiers also came to him; but John did not ask them to give up their calling. We do not know who they were, whether they were Jews, Romans, Thracians, or Germans. Neither is there any evidence that there was any war in progress in that region at that time.[4] Most

---

5, 1) Ἐπί. Matt. 3, 7.

2) Luke 7, 30.   3) Matt. 16, 1, etc.

4) The war Herod waged against Aretas was later.

likely they were soldiers in some way connected with the Roman provincial government. John told them not to do violence to any man, not to exact anything wrongfully, and to be content with their wages.

6.

Matt. 3, 11. 12. Mark 1, 7. 8. Luke 3, 15—18.
John 1, 15—18.

In addition to these simple precepts,. John had another and a stranger message to deliver. While the people mused in their hearts whether or not he himself were Christ, he made the statement that he would claim no authority for himself save as the divinely commissioned forerunner of Another. "I indeed baptize

Announcement of the Coming Christ.

you with water; but One mightier than I cometh, the latchet of whose shoes I am not worthy to unloose; He shall baptize you with the Holy Ghost and with fire; whose fan is in His hand; and He will thoroughly purge His floor and will gather the wheat into His garner; but the chaff He will burn with fire unquenchable." It was a useful evangelic ministry, but it was cut short, as St. Luke notes at this point, when John was cast into prison.[1]

6,　1) Luke 3, 19. 20.　(See chapter XV.)

CHAPTER VI.

THE BEGINNING OF CHRIST'S PUBLIC MINISTRY.

Early winter 27 A. D., or 780 A. U. C.

CONTEMPORANEOUS MINISTRY OF JESUS AND JOHN.

1.

Matt. 3, 13—17. Mark 1, 9—11. Luke 3, 21—22.
(John 1, 32—34.)

A few months have passed. It is probably the early winter of the year 780 A. U. C.[1] It seems that John, whose ministry began in the Wilderness of Judea,[2] in the neighborhood of the Dead Sea, had gradually ascended the El Ghor, the Jordan Valley, and had now reached the most northern point of his activity. For a long time the "Bethabara beyond the Jordan," [3] or rather the "Bethany beyond the Jordan," to distinguish it from the Bethany near the Mount of Olives,[4] was traditionally placed east of Jericho;[5] but it is now quite generally agreed that it was located at Arbarah, a ford of the Jordan above Beth-shean, and near the Sea of Galilee.[6] Here he baptized. This was about twenty miles from Nazareth. But long before he reached that spot, tidings of his words and deeds must have penetrated the silent carpenter shop in the Galilean hills.[7] Jesus knew John and his mission, and also that the time for the beginning of His own public ministry had come. But, although Jesus and John were distantly related on their maternal side, we have no evidence that the cousins were otherwise acquainted with each other and that John knew Jesus. Twice John emphatically declares: "I knew Him not." [8] Though he knew that the Messiah had appeared in the flesh, he had not met Him personally. When he saw Jesus for the first time, there was

---

1, 1) This agrees with the tradition that our Lord was baptized on the 6th or 10th of January. Edersheim, I, 278, n. 4. Andrews, I, 31.

2) Matt. 3, 1; Mark 1, 4; Luke 3, 2. 3) John 1, 28.

4) See Meyer sub John 1, 28. *Exp. Greek N. T.* A. T. Robertson, *Studies in the Text of the N. T.*, 34. 73.

5) Beth-nimrah, on a small stream east of the Jordan.

6) Hurlbut, *Bible Atlas*, 99. George Adam Smith, *Atlas*, 20.

7) The apocryphal Gospel to the Hebrews says that Jesus was urged to the baptism of John by His mother and brethren. Klausner, 251. But cf. Matt. 3, 15, from which we see that our Lord came to John of His own accord and why He desired to be baptized by him.

8) John 1, 31. 33.

something in His look, something in His bearing, something in the sinless beauty of His ways, which at once overawed and captivated him, and when therefore Jesus came to be baptized of him, he

The Baptism of Jesus.

would have hindered Him and said: "I have need to be baptized of Thee, and comest Thou to me?" It was his mission to baptize sinners with the baptism of repentance; but he knew that Jesus was the Holy One of God. But Jesus answered — the second recorded utterance since His boyhood visit to the Temple and the first word recorded since His entrance upon His public ministry: "Suffer it now; for thus it becometh Us to fulfil all righteousness." In saying this, Jesus admitted that, as far as obtaining remission of sins was concerned, He did not need to be baptized; however, because, as Luther aptly says, he had taken the place of all sinners and must fulfil the entire Law for them, John should "suffer it *now*." With His baptism Jesus began His Messianic work. Thus He became Jesus, the Savior of mankind. Upon hearing Jesus' answer, John "suffered Him," baptizing Him in the Jordan. Of the mode of the baptism no details are given. Immediately after the baptism of Jesus, and while He stood praying, John beheld that wonderful sign which had been promised to him to make him absolutely sure that this was indeed He that was to come: "Upon whom thou shalt see the Spirit descending and remaining on Him, the same is He which baptizeth with the Holy Ghost." There occurred a most exceptional manifestation of the Triune God. The incarnate Son of God was standing on the banks of Jordan. The heavens were opened, actually rent asunder,[9] and the Holy Spirit descended in the form of a dove. And a voice from heaven was heard and understood by those who stood by, especially by Jesus and by John, as saying: "Thou art My beloved Son, in whom I am well pleased." [10] Now John was divinely certain that here was God's own Anointed, the Messiah, the Christ, anointed with the Holy Ghost and with power [11] and now duly invested with His Messianic office by the Father Himself. Luke adds the chronological note which we have already previously observed that Jesus, when He began to teach, was about thirty years of age.[12]

1,   9) Compare Ezek. 1, 1; Acts 7, 56; Rev. 4, 1; Is. 64, 1.

    10) Compare Luke 9, 35; John 12, 28.

    11) Ps. 45, 7; Acts 10, 38.

    12) If Jesus was born in December, 749 A. U. C., and was baptized in January, 780, He was a few weeks over thirty years old. Here follows the genealogy of Jesus in the order of Luke, Luke 3, 23—38, commonly taken to give the line of descent through Mary.

2.

Matt. 4, 1—11. Mark 1, 12. 13. Luke 4, 1—13.

From the banks of the Jordan to the wilds of the desert. From the smiling sunshine of opened heavens to the assaults of the Evil One.[1] Immediately after His baptism Jesus was led by the Spirit into the wilderness to be tempted of the devil. Thus in the evan-

The Temptation. gelic account the fact, the impulse, and the purpose of this retirement are at once briefly and simply stated. In the solitude of the desert He sought communion with His Father and in fervent prayer besought Him to strengthen Him for the superhuman task that was awaiting Him, a task the performance of which was necessary for the deliverance of mankind from the power of the devil.[2] The struggle was real, the account of it no allegory, its outcome the ignominious defeat of the hellish Foe.

3.

Matt. 4, 1—11. Mark 1, 12. 13. Luke 4, 1—13.

As to the question whether Jesus, because of His absolute sinlessness, *could* be tempted to sin, that is, whether or not He was abstractly *capable* of committing a sin, — the question as to the peccability or impeccability of His human nature, and whether His sinlessness sprang from a *peccare non posse* or a *posse non peccare* (inability to sin or an ability not to sin, like Adam [1]), — the impeccability of Jesus must be maintained according to Scripture.[2] Since the human nature of Christ had personal existence only in the Son of God, it was as little possible for Jesus, as the Son of God, really to sin as this is possible for God.[3] Jesus, "being *full*

The Impeccability of Jesus. of the Holy Ghost," [4] was led by the Spirit into the wilderness. But considering the evident futility of the Satanic assault, was His great conflict, then, merely a deceptive phantasmagoria? [5] Was not, then, His temptation the semblance of a battle against the simulacrum of a foe? By no means. A battle can be a real battle even if there is no doubt as to the outcome.

2,   1) Edersheim, I, 291.

2) Heb. 2, 14. 15; 1 John 3, 8.

3,   1) Farrar, I, 123. Edersheim, I, 298. "Capable of not sinning, but not incapable of sinning."

2) Is. 53, 9; Luke 1, 35; John 8, 46; 2 Cor. 5, 21; 1 Pet. 1, 19; etc.

3) Pieper, *Dogmatik*, II, 79 ff.

4) Luke 4, 1.   5) Farrar, I, 123.

It was in the interest of Satan to strain every effort to frustrate his own predicted ultimate defeat.[6]   And since the same Satan whom Holy Writ pictures as exceedingly cunning is also shown to be at the same time so stupid and blind as to defeat his own ends, to the glory of God, it may properly be stated that he hoped he might gain the mastery over this Jesus whom he saw in the likeness of sinful flesh.

4.

Matt. 4, 1—11. Mark 1, 12. 13. Luke 4, 1—13.

No definite place is given where the Temptation took place. It was in the wilderness, most likely not so very far from the place of John's baptism and among the wild beasts.[1]   The latter are not mentioned to hint at the danger in which our Savior was, but rather to indicate the uninhabited nature of that region. Food

The Time and Place. and supplies were not considered, and hunger was necessarily a part of His experience. A tradition, but no older than the Crusades, fixes the scene at a mountain to the south of Jericho, which from this circumstance has received the name of Quarantana.[2]   But the scene may also be laid beyond Jordan, in the hills of Moab, where the Lord vouchsafed to Moses a view of the Promised Land.[3]   Forty days of fasting,[4] of solitude, and of various temptations,[5] probably in January and February, 780 A. U. C., covered the period. Three particular temptations are mentioned.

5.

Matt. 4, 1—11. Mark 1, 12. 13. Luke 4, 1—13.

The whole time had been one of moral and spiritual tension. Soldiers on battle-fields fight through battles unconscious of wounds and exhaustion; but when the enthusiasm is spent, nature asserts itself. Jesus was weary with the contest, alone in the desert, and faint with hunger. The moment was favorable for the satanic temptations recorded by the evangelists. It was probably in the hours of the early morning. Let us suppose that in the dim light

---

3,   6) Gen. 3, 15.

4,   1) Mark 1, 13.

2) Andrews, 155.   F. L. Anderson, in *Int. St. B. Encycl.* under "Temptation," calls it a good guess.

3) Edersheim, I, 300, n. 2, and others.

4) Absolute, if the words of Luke "He did eat nothing" are to be taken in the strictest literal sense.

5) Luke 4, 2.

of the dawn the stones of the desert assumed the form of little loaves of bread.[1] Satan, the Tempter, appeared to Jesus, in which disguise we do not know, and said: "If Thou be the Son of God, command that these stones be made bread." Now, Satan is not omniscient. But, no doubt, he had been a witness of the incident of the opened heaven on the banks of Jordan and had heard the voice calling Jesus the Son of God. This was, of course, interesting to one who for over four thousand years, since the fall of Adam, as a strong man armed, had kept his palace and enjoyed the fruits of his original victory.[2] As an attack his assault upon Jesus was in true satanic form. Simulating compassion with the hungry Jesus, he repeated his tactics of pretended friendship successfully employed in the case of Eve.[3] Likewise he injected the

The First Temptation. element of doubt: "*If* Thou be the Son of God." However, granting this divine Sonship for the present, he asks Jesus to "command that these stones be made bread." Since the heavenly Father evidently failed to provide for His beloved Son, he incited Jesus to rebellious thoughts and invited Him to help Himself by virtue of the miraculous powers bestowed upon Him. Jesus does not deny His hunger nor His ability to carry out the suggestion. In fact, it would not have been impossible or wrong for Jesus to relieve His need in the manner suggested by Satan; but under these circumstances — "led by the Spirit into the wilderness to be tempted of the devil" — and at the direction of Satan, His action would have indicated despair of God, disobedience to His Father's will, and failure to trust in His divine providence, and He would have done the will of God's inveterate enemy. This He could and would not do, neither as the Holy One of God nor as man's Substitute in this combat with the Prince of Darkness. On the contrary, He pointed the Tempter to Scripture: "It is written," and repelled the temptation by quoting a passage of Deuteronomy (from the Septuagint): "Man shall not live by bread alone, but by every word that proceedeth out of the mouth of God." [4] God, He said, can preserve man's life without bread. His Father had sustained Him without food of any kind for forty days, and therefore He would commend also the future to Him.[5]

5,   1) *Lapides Iudaici.* Farrar, I, 129.
     2) Luke 11, 21.   3) Gen. 3, 1.
     4) Deut. 8, 3.   5) Stoeckhardt, *Bibl. Gesch.,* 26.

6.

Matt. 4, 1—11. Mark 1, 12. 13. Luke 4, 1—13.

Satan tried again. Jesus next [1] permitted Himself to be bodily transported to Jerusalem, the Holy City,[2] and to be let down on the pinnacle of the Temple, probably at the southeastern angle of the Temple cloisters, "whence the view of the Kidron was to the stupendous depth of over 450 feet." [3] If we may venture a guess as to the time, we should say that it was probably at the hour of the morning sacrifice.[4] The vanishing dawn broke into the morning light, the Temple gates were slowly opened, and the blast of the silver trumpets summoned Israel to begin a new day by appearing before the Lord. Jesus had just proved His trust in God. And now Satan tried to tempt Him to an apparently greater trust, which, however, had Jesus yielded, would have been sheerest fanaticism and wicked presumption. "If Thou be the Son of God," — Satan very shrewdly observed that Jesus had not replied to these words, already used in the first temptation, and so he attacked Him again, — then "cast Thyself down." Surely no harm can come from that! Not if He is God's beloved Son and if He confidently trusts in God! And as Jesus surveys the scene, the dizzy heights of the columns, the wall of the Temple, and then the dark depths of Kidron, Satan quotes a passage of Scripture to

The Second Temptation. encourage Him to attempt the leap. Yes, Satan turns Rabbi and quotes, rather misquotes, the words of a psalm: "He shall give His angels charge concerning thee; and in their hands they shall bear thee up lest at any time thou dash thy foot against a stone." [5] But what about the omission of the words "to keep thee *in all thy ways*"? This was not a lapse of memory, but was intentional. Surely God protects His children, in the lions' den, in the fiery furnace, by a miracle if need be; but in this case it would have been most wicked presumption and desperate recklessness thus

---

6,   1) This seems to be the order, following Matthew: *"Then* the devil,'' etc., v. 5. Luke transposes the second and third temptations, but does not state a definite order of sequence.

2) Already called holy at the time of Isaiah (48, 2) and Nehemiah (11, 1) and by the Arabians still called El Kuds, that is, the Holy City. Compare Matt. 27, 53.

3) Edersheim, I, 303, n. 2, 450 feet. Josephus, *Ant.*, XV, XI, 5. F. L. Anderson: 326 feet above the bottom of the Kidron valley. *Int. St. B. Encycl.*, 2,943.

4) Edersheim, I, 304.

5) Ps. 91, 11. 12.

to put Divine Providence to test. However, as some think, there may also have been another consideration which prompted Satan to venture this temptation. The sudden appearance of Jesus among a gaping multitude below might easily have gained for Him popular recognition as the Messiah; for according to popular belief the Messiah would appear suddenly and in a marvelous manner.[6] However, repelling the temptation to gain for Himself easy recognition by way of spectacular demonstration and also disregarding the suggestion to thrust Himself needlessly into reckless perils, Jesus replies by quoting another Scripture-passage: "It is written again, Thou shalt not tempt the Lord, thy God." [7] True, God will protect His children; but they have no right to claim His miraculous intervention to keep them from harm if they actually court danger. They have no right to challenge His power to the proof.[8]

7.

Matt. 4, 1—11. Mark 1, 12. 13. Luke 4, 1—13.

The scene changes. By a supernatural mode of transportation the Lord is placed on the top of a high mountain. We do not know its exact geographical location. In the bright morning light, let us suppose, the devil dazzles the carpenter's son from Nazareth, just now entering upon His Messianic office, with something of the worldly glory and brazenly attempts to fill Him with unhallowed personal ambition. He points out the enticing prospects of a universal Messianic kingdom and claims the power and authority of disposing of it at will. The world in all its beauty and glory,

The Third Temptation. with all its treasures and the immense power their bestowal includes, is unveiled to Him. To His left lie Africa and Egypt. In the sandy regions back of Him are the kingdoms of the Arabian Desert. To His right the snowy crest of distant Hermon points the way to Damascus and to the mighty empires which once flourished between the Tigris and Euphrates. In front of Him His view falls upon His beloved Land of Israel, Judea, Samaria, and Galilee, once the kingdom of David and Solomon, but now in the grasp of a foreign oppressor. Beyond it stretch forth the shiny waters of the Mediterranean Sea, on the northern shores of which the glory of Greece and the power of Rome beckon Him. Dazzling

---

6,   6) Stalker, 44. *Contra,* Weiss, I, 346.
      7) Deut. 6, 16.
      8) Farrar, I, 134.

prospects! "All these things will I give Thee if Thou wilt fall down and worship me." Not only is Satan very liberal with Another's possession, — "The silver is Mine, and the gold is Mine, saith the Lord of hosts," [1] — but he also blasphemously makes a bid for divine honor. There is only one answer therefore to this preposterous request: "Get thee hence, Satan; for it is written, Thou shalt worship the Lord, thy God, and Him only shalt thou serve." Begone! the Savior shouts, manifesting at this point a ray of the divine glory that was His even in the state of humiliation. Yet He condescends to support this peremptory dismissal of Satan with an appeal to Scripture: "For it is written." For the third time He refers the infernal spirit to the Book of Deuteronomy,[2] which seems to have been one of His favorite books. The Tempter is foiled. He departs from Him, yet only for a season, postponing his return to a more convenient season and probably presenting his temptations in a different manner, hoping in his blindness to have better success at some other time.[3] — Now the angels of heaven came and ministered unto Jesus [4] in reply to the insinuation of Satan that God the Father did not treat Him as though He were His beloved Son. Since there were no human witnesses to the temptation, the story must have been related by Jesus Himself, and by inspiration of the Holy Spirit it was afterwards included in the gospel account.

John 1, 19—28.   **8.**

And now let us return to the banks of the Jordan. At the end of this forty-day period of Christ's temptation in the wilderness, in fact, a day previous [1] to His return, John the Baptist received an official visit. A number of Pharisees and Sadducees had already made their appearance among the multitudes coming to his baptism. In promptly calling them to repentance, John employed no ambiguous language.[2] Of course, they returned to Jerusalem with their report. But the scattering multitudes had also published their version. They mused in their hearts whether haply

---

7,   1) Hag. 2, 9.   2) Deut. 6, 13.

3) Luke. Historically there is no record that Jesus was later tempted again in like manner. There were other temptations, clearly satanic, but in these Satan was indirectly engaged, e. g., John 8, 40 ff.; 13, 2. 27; Matt. 16, 23. See Meyer under Luke 4, 13.

4) Though we may assume that they brought Him food, their chief ministration no doubt consisted in comforting Him after the fiery trial He had endured.

8,   1) John 1, 29.   2) Matt. 3, 7 ff.

he were the Christ.[3]   And this needed investigation.   According to a Rabbinic tradition the Sanhedrin was under a special obligation to prevent the appearing of false prophets.[4]   Hence a special deputation of priests and attending Levites, but with strong pharisaic tendencies,[5] was dispatched with the commission to find out

A Delegation to John.   what it was all about.   We remember that John's father was a priest, but since he lived in the country, he did not belong to the ruling sacerdotal class.   And what little the aristocratic Sadducees had seen of John's work and heard of his preaching must have convinced them "that his views and aims," his calling the people to repentance as a proper preparing of the way for the Messiah, "lay entirely beyond their horizon." [6]

John 1, 19—28.   9.

The scene is placed at "Bethany beyond Jordan," [1] now quite generally conceded to have been located at Abarah, an obscure ford or ferry above Beth-shean, near the Sea of Galilee.   As we shall see, there was a wedding at Cana in the following week.   And now, assuming that the bride of this wed-

Time and Place.   ding was a maiden and that in accordance with "uniform custom" [2] her wedding took place on a Wednesday, by counting back, we arrive at a Thursday for the day on which the committee of the Sanhedrin [3] called on John.[4]   The interview was rather laconic: formal in inquiry with little time wasted for polite sentiment, as we would naturally expect from a somewhat suspicious investigating committee, and straightforward in reply, in harmony with the character of John.

John 1, 19—28.   **10.**

The interview began with the question, "Who art thou?"   Not, What is your name or the date of your birth? — for John's questioners were evidently supplied with these data, — but, Who are you?   What personage do you claim to be? — with the implied

---

8,   3) Luke 3, 15.

4) Andrews, 155, n. 1.   Schuerer, II, I, 186.   Dods, in *Exp. Greek N. T., in loco.*

5) Vv. 24 f.   6) Edersheim, I, 310.

9,   1) See critical commentaries *sub* John 1, 28.

2) Edersheim, I, 344 f.   Andrews, 161.   3) John 1, 19.

4) Thursday the interview.   Friday "the next day," v. 29.   Saturday "again the next day," v. 35.   Sunday "the day following," v. 43.   Monday. Tuesday.   Wednesday "the third day," the marriage at Cana, 2, 1.

reference to possibly Messianic claims. "And he confessed and denied not; but confessed, I am not the Christ." The answer of John seems to indicate that his questioners had hinted at the possibility of his being the Messiah. This, in view of his popularity, was no small temptation. But the manner in which he replied to

"Who Art Thou?" the question brought out the earnestness, almost horror, with which he disclaimed the ascription to himself of Messianic honors.[1] If not Christ Himself, the next possibility was that he was His forerunner. "What then? Art thou Elias?" This was in reference to the prophecy of Malachi: "Behold, I will send you Elijah the prophet before the coming of the great and dreadful day of the Lord."[2] Now, John actually was the forerunner of the Messiah. He was that promised Elias. Christ Himself paid him that tribute: "Elias is come already."[3] But he was not Elias in the sense in which they had put the question; for they expected a physical return of that prophet before the coming of the Lord. And therefore he could not admit the suggested identity without misleading them. "And he said, I am not."

John 1, 19—28.   **11.**

Another possibility presented itself: "Art thou that prophet?" "And he answered, No." This question was also based upon a misunderstanding. Many Jews were expecting a special prophet to terminate the prophetic era and to usher in the Messianic reign,[1]

The Witness of John. whereas the particular prophet promised by Moses: "The Lord, thy God, will raise up unto thee a Prophet from the midst of thee like unto me,"[2] referred to Christ Himself. And so it was also generally understood.[3] And therefore, since John was neither that anticipated special prophet, according to the understanding of some, nor the prophet[4] in the promise of Moses, he could only answer, "No."

John 1, 19—28.   **12.**

But now their stock of leading questions was exhausted. Not Christ, not Elias, not the anticipated intermediary prophet, was John the Baptist; in fact, no prophet at all in their sense and according to their expectations. Thoroughly disappointed and

---

10, 1) Dods *sub loco.*   2) Mal. 4, 5.   3) Matt. 17, 12.
11, 1) Dods, in *Exp. Greek N. T.* Schuerer, II, II, 157.
    2) Deut. 18, 15.   3) 1 Macc. 14, 41; Acts 3, 22.
    4) Ὁ προφήτης.

baffled by the plain and austere wilderness preacher, they requested him to give an account of himself. "Who art thou? that we may give an answer to them that sent us." In his reply John applied

"I Am the Voice of One Crying in the Wilderness." to himself the prophecy of Isaiah: "I am the voice of one crying in the wilderness, Make straight the way of the Lord." [1)] By appropriating this prophecy to himself, John identified himself as the immediate precursor of the Lord.

John 1, 19—28. **13.**

But this answer did not satisfy his questioners. If he was not the Christ, nor Elias, nor "that prophet," nor any kind of prophet, — since he claimed to be only a voice, a mere noise, in a pathless, barren waste, — "Why baptizest thou, then?" If he disclaimed for himself the office and honor of a prophet, why assume its rights and privileges? If he was no prophet, why did he act like one? In attacking his baptism, they probably referred to certain peculiar symbolic actions and habits. At one time Jeremiah walked about with a wooden yoke dangling from his shoulders as a sign that Judah would have its neck put under the yoke of the king of Babylon. [1)] For three years Isaiah went naked and barefoot, "that is, with only his tunic, or shirtlike garment," to symbolize that the king of Assyria would lead the Egyptians prisoners, old and young, naked and barefoot. [2)] Other examples might be mentioned. These and other prophetic peculiarities the people in Old Testament times were accustomed to as attending the sacred office. But if John was no real prophet, what, then, was the idea of his wilderness life, his hairy garments, the leathern girdle, his peculiar food, wild honey and roasted grasshoppers? In particular, what about this novel rite, the baptism of repentance unto remission of sins? But now John, claiming no particular honor and distinction for himself on account of his baptism with water as

"Why Baptizest Thou, then?" a divinely appointed preparation for the immediate advent of the Messiah, delivered a blow: "I baptize with water; but there standeth One among you *whom ye know not.*" There is the trouble. Not only did they not know that He had come, which would excuse them, but they did not even care to know whether or not He had made His appearance. They, the investigating

---

12, 1) Is. 40, 3.　　　**13,** 1) Jer. 27, 2. 8.　　　2) Is. 20, 2—4.

committee, were on the lookout for false prophets, but missing the Prophet of all prophets, the Messiah! What they ought to have done was to form a Messianic reception committee. But they were evidently not interested in a preparation for the advent of the Messiah such as the Baptist demanded — humiliation and repentance and humble craving for the forgiveness of sins. Finally, in true humility and abasing himself in all sincerity, John made a beautiful confession of Christ: "He it is who, coming after me, is preferred before me, whose shoe's latchet I am not worthy to unloose."

Thus the interview ended. What effect the testimony of John had upon the investigating committee we are not told. Most likely they were not very much pleased with it. However, what he had replied to their questions gave them no sufficient grounds for citing him before the Sanhedrin. At any rate, when he later did lose his life because of his courageous testimony, it was not the Sanhedrin that caused his death, but some one else. And besides, although the Sanhedrin in a certain sense exercised jurisdiction over every Jewish community in the world, it was only within the limits of Judea proper that it exercised any *direct* authority.[3] Even if there had been cause for action, John, beyond the Jordan, had no reason to fear anything.

John 1, 29—34.   **14.**

On the following day Jesus again made His appearance on the banks of the Jordan. The motives which brought Him back to the scene of His baptism must remain in the indefiniteness in which Scripture has left it.[1] So far as we know, there was no interview then or afterwards between Jesus and John; just a meeting in the distance, as it were. Jesus approached John, came towards him,[2] but not directly to him; and yet He was close enough to him to be pointed out by him. Although it seems that Jesus had nothing to say to John, John had something wonderful to say about Jesus. Pointing out the approaching Jesus to those who were about him, he uttered these remarkable words: "Behold the Lamb of God, which taketh away the sin of the world." This was a reference to Isaiah's picture of the suffering Messiah[3] and an unmistakable testimony of Jesus as the Savior of the world. In the Old Testament lambs were sacrificed daily and on all festival days for the

---

13, 3) Schuerer, II, I, 185.   But compare Acts 9, 2.
14, 1) Edersheim, I, 344.
    2) Πρὸς αὐτόν.   3) Is. 53, 7.

atonement of the sins of the people as types of the supreme and perfect sacrifice to be brought by Him on whom the Lord would lay "the iniquity of us all." Therefore in John's designation of Jesus as the Lamb of God which taketh away the sin of the world

"Behold the Lamb of God!" there was already a forecast of Good Friday, of His suffering and death on the cross. Whether the details of Christ's suffering and death — outside of the fact of the slaughter of the innocent Lamb as depicted by Isaiah — had been especially revealed to John is only a matter of conjecture. But he was fully assured that Jesus was the Savior of the world; for he continued: "This is He of whom I said," namely, to the delegates from Jerusalem, "After me cometh a Man which is preferred before me; for He was before me." And he explained *how* he knew that Jesus was the Redeemer promised since the Fall. Without any personal knowledge at first of Him whom he was to introduce to Israel as the Messiah he had gone about his mission of preparing the way for Him, preaching repentance and baptizing with water. But then he had received a divine revelation, a sign, now fulfilled: "Upon whom thou shalt see the Spirit descending and remaining on Him, the same is He which baptizeth with the Holy Ghost. And I saw and bare record that this is the Son of God." To whom these words were spoken we do not know, but most likely they were uttered in the hearing of John the Evangelist, in whose gospel this account is given, who had himself been a disciple of John, but who, on hearing this beautiful testimony, became a disciple of Jesus.

John 1, 35—42.   **15.**

Again on the morrow and, as we picture it to ourselves,[1] on a Sabbath-day, John the Baptist was standing with two of his disciples as Jesus walked by. He fixed upon Him an earnest and intense gaze[2] and said, "Behold the Lamb of God!" The two disciples of John had already been impressed with this statement and its explanation as made by their master on the previous day; but now that they heard it again, they immediately left John and followed Jesus. A loss for John, it is true; but it was in accordance with his mission — to prepare the way for Christ. As they followed Jesus in modest silence, He turned and asked, "What

---

15,   1) Following Edersheim, I, 345.

2) Farrar, I, 144. Ἐμβλέψας. Mark 14, 67; Luke 22, 61. The Lord looked upon Peter, ἐνέβλεψε.

seek ye?" [3] This was a master question, penetrating their inmost souls. It is evident that they were seeking Him, but the form of the question compelled them to consider carefully the object of their search and to examine the motive which prompted them to forsake John and follow Him. Their reply was simple and plainly evidenced their sincerity of purpose. "Rabbi," that is, Master, or Teacher, they said, addressing Jesus with a title of honor and respect, suggesting that they desire to become His pupils, "where dwellest Thou?" which, in effect, meant, We are seeking Thee.

The First Disciples. This frank and sincere expression of their desire was met with a kind and generous response, "Come and see." Where Jesus was at that moment we do not know. Most likely it was at a modest and temporary dwelling-place in the neighborhood of where John was preaching and baptizing, probably some sort of tent or booth, [4] which served as the only shelter to the hundreds who had come to the baptism of John. They came and saw where Jesus dwelt, stayed with Him that day, and probably slept there that night; and before their first visit was over, they were fully satisfied that they had been in the presence of the promised Messiah. It was an unforgettable experience, this first hour of their personal communion with Jesus, remembered by John the Evangelist even in his old age, when he wrote his gospel, as having been the tenth hour of the day. "It was about the tenth hour." But what is meant by the tenth hour? The most learned commentators have bitten out their teeth in the attempt to answer the question how the evangelist calculated his hours. [5] We suppose that John employed the Jewish mode of reckoning time, from sunrise to sunset, [6] as marked off on the sun-dial, [7] except in the one instance at the trial of Jesus before Pilate, [8] in which, following strict Roman computation, he employed the language of the court. Therefore, according to our view this memorable first meeting with Jesus took place at the tenth hour of the civil day, that is, at four o'clock in the afternoon. [9]

15, 3) Farrar, I, 144.   4) Farrar, I, 145.

5) Lenski, *Eisenach Gospel Selections*, 241.   6) John 11, 9.

7) Cf. Dods *sub loco*.   8) John 19, 14.

9) Thus: John 1, 39 the "tenth hour" is equal to our 4 P. M.; 4, 6, "sixth hour," 12 noon; 4, 52, "seventh hour," 1 P. M.; 11, 9, "twelve hours," one day, from the rising to the setting of the sun; but 19, 14, "sixth hour," 6 A. M. (compare 18, 28: "It was early"). For 4 P. M., Jewish reckoning, see Farrar, I, 146; Weiss, I, 365; Dods and Meyer *sub loco;* etc.; for 10 A. M., Roman reckoning, Andrews, 159; Robertson, *Harmony*, 286; Wieseler, *Syn.*, 376; Ebrard, 210; Edersheim, I, 346; etc. The various methods of reconciling the statements are well given by Andrews, 159 ff. 545 ff.

John 1, 35—42.   **16.**

One of the two who heard John the Baptist speak and followed Jesus was Andrew.[1)] The name of the other is not mentioned in the gospel; but we are left to infer that it was the evangelist John himself. Since tradition states that he died at the end of the century, he must have been a youth of seventeen or eighteen years when he first met Jesus.[2)] His exquisite and consistent reticence concerning himself[3)] is one of the char-

Andrew and John. acteristics of his gospel. While he has praise for others, he only faintly alludes to himself. Andrew is the one to receive the honor of becoming the first disciple of Christ. We don't know much about him. He was a fisherman from Bethsaida, near the Sea of Galilee, which was the original home also of Peter.[4)] His father's name was John, or Jonah.[5)] Presumably he was no longer living at the time of this story. He had an elder brother by the name of Simon, who was to play an important part in the Gospel history and whom Andrew, as we shall presently learn, was instrumental in leading to Christ.

John 1, 35—42.   **17.**

"He," Andrew, "first findeth his own brother Simon" — the word "findeth" shows that he had been looking for him — and led him to Christ. "We [he and John] have found the Messias, which is, being interpreted, the Christ." That was his great eureka.[1)] "And he brought him to Jesus." That is the greatest service which one

Peter. brother can render another. Thus Andrew is praised for his missionary zeal, and Peter is introduced. In company with his younger brother Andrew and with James and John and their father Zebedee, Simon Peter was engaged in the fisherman's trade, with headquarters at Capernaum, where he owned a home.[2)] Originally he hailed from Bethsaida. If, as tradition states, he was about seventy-five years old at the time of his martyrdom in 67 A.D., he must have been already thirty-five years old at this

---

16, 1) The name is of Greek origin, Ἀνδρέας, manly; but it was in use among the Jews. Lightfoot, quoted by Farrar, I, 152, n. 1. It also occurs in the Jerusalem Talmud. Klausner, 260, n. 4.

2) Weiss, I, 367.

3) Extended to the members of his family, his brother James, and his mother Salome. The third of the women named by Mark, Salome, 15, 40, is the sister of Mary, the mother of Jesus, in John 19, 25. Weiss, 366 and n. 1.

4) Mark 1, 44.   5) John 1, 42; Matt. 16, 17.

17, 1) Εὑρήκαμεν τὸν Μεσσίαν. See Farrar, I, 147.

2) Luke 5, 10. Mark 1, 29.

important period of his life.[3] Andrew presented him to Jesus, who fixed His royal gaze upon him and read his inmost thoughts. At a glance He saw in that simple fisherman a fiery nature, impulsive enthusiasm, potential service of a high character to be rendered His kingdom, but also a great weakness — inconsistency.[4] At once He accepted him as His disciple with the greeting: "Thou art Simon, the son of Jona; thou shalt be called Cephas, which is, by interpretation, A stone." And history shows that Christ was not mistaken. By divine grace weak Peter became a rock. Upon the solid rock of his confession the Church of Christ is built. "And the gates of hell shall not prevail against it." [5]

John 1, 35—42.   18.

Andrew was *first* to bring *his* brother, but unassuming, contemplating John was not altogether to be outdone. He likewise had a brother, who, too, was probably near at hand. Andrew "first findeth his own brother." [1] Now, John, in his usual delicate reserve, does not say it directly, but something is clearly implied; namely, he also went out and found *his* brother — afterwards in the company of Jesus — and led him to Christ. Thus **James.** at the very beginning of His ministry two pairs of brothers, Andrew and Peter, John and James, were brought into contact with Christ. And it seems that this latter pair, James and John, were His own cousins. Their father Zebedee, the husband of Salome, was a prosperous fisherman, with hired servants [2] and connections as far as Jerusalem. For only so can we explain that afterwards John had connections, probably only through servants, with the high priest's house.[3] According to tradition their mother, Salome, was a sister of Mary, the mother of Jesus.[4]

John 1, 43—51.   19.

Another disciple was added, the fifth, to the list of future apostles,[1] who at first were occasional companions of Jesus and then became His constant attendants, until He solemnly chose

---

17, 3) *Int. St. B. Encycl.*, 2349.
    4) Farrar, I, 147.   5) Matt. 16, 16. 18.
18, 1) Πρῶτος. See Meyer *in loco.*
    2) Mark 1, 19. 20.   3) John 18, 15. Weiss, I, 366.
    4) Matt. 27, 56; John 19, 25. It quite answers to John's method not to refer to his own mother directly; for in speaking of himself, he never tells us his name and never even mentions his brother. Weiss, I, 366, n. 1.
19, 1) We notice that in all the four lists Philip takes fifth place: Mark 3, 16 f.; Matt. 10, 2 f.; Luke 6, 14 f.; Acts 1, 13 f.

them as His apostles and expressly designated them as such. Sabbath was over. On the next day, Sunday, Jesus intended to go forth again into Galilee, when He found Philip, who was of Bethsaida, Peter's native town. With Andrew and Simon he also

Philip. very likely had come to John's baptism and was now on the way back to his home. Of all the apostles he is the only one who had a typically Greek name,[2] being named perhaps after the tetrarch Philip;[3] for the custom of naming children after celebrities was as common then as it is now. If so, he must at this time have been below thirty. Possibly his Greek name suggests familiarity with the surrounding Greek-speaking population. At any rate, he was singled out by the Greeks who in the last week of Christ's life wished to see the Lord.[4] At his first meeting with Jesus a simple "Follow Me" made him a disciple. We are not told what Philip answered, but his hearty assent is fully implied by all that follows.

John 1, 43—51.   **20.**

Jesus found Philip, and Philip found Nathanael. Eager to communicate his rich discovery, Philip sought out his friend and jubilantly said to him, "We have found Him of whom Moses in the Law, and the prophets, did write," that is, the promised Messiah, namely, "Jesus of Nazareth, the son of Joseph." The last-named details Philip must have learned in his conversation with Jesus or from the newly accepted disciples. Nathanael, however, was not so easily convinced. He was from Cana,[1] only a few miles from Nazareth, but he had not heard about Jesus, the son of the carpenter Joseph of Nazareth, before; at least he had not been told that He was the Messiah. And now he found it hard to believe that despised Nazareth[2] could produce the Messiah. He therefore said to Philip, "Can there any good thing come out of Nazareth?" Philip, however, did not try to argue with him. He made a very wise reply, one that recalls the words of Jesus to

---

19,   2) Lover of horses. See note on Andrew, Section 16.

3) To whose territory Bethsaida belonged. But we are not so sure. There are some who suppose there were two Bethsaidas, on account of John 12, 21: "Philip, which was of Bethsaida of *Galilee.*" If Galilee is here used in the strict political sense as applied to this particular period of history, then there must have been two Bethsaidas, "houses of fishing," the Julias Bethsaida of the tetrarch Philip in lower Gaulanitis and another Bethsaida in Galilee, presumably near Capernaum, on the Sea of Galilee. See Dods *sub loco. Int. St. B. Encycl.,* sub "Bethsaida."

4) John 12, 21.

20, 1) John 21, 2.   2) See chapter III, 32.

Andrew and John, "Come and see." — Now, who was this Nathanael? His name, Nathanael, Theodore, gift of God, gives us no clue. In the list of apostles he does not appear at all, but is usually identified with Bartholomew, the sixth in the list.[3] This name, however, is merely a designation, a patronymic: Bar-Tolmai, that is, the son of Tolmai.[4] According to a legend of his later martyrdom he was sewed in a sack and cast into the sea.[5] And that is about all we know of him. From the words of Jesus we learn that he was a man without duplicity, thoroughly sincere, and probably was well versed in Scripture. His initial prejudice was soon removed. When Jesus first saw him, He remarked, "Behold an Israelite indeed in whom is no guile!" This was praise indeed,

Nathanael.   and more. It was a revelation, a hint, and the suggestion of some secret knowledge of something that Nathanael thought nobody else possessed. Of course, like every true Israelite he shared the waiting for Israel's salvation.[6] And if at first, by asking questions and making objections, — probably secretly hoping that the news *were* true, — he did not immediately recognize and acknowledge Jesus as the promised Messiah, what wrong was there in that? However, it seems that already by His opening words, "Behold an Israelite indeed in whom is no guile!" Jesus wrought in him the conviction that He was truly what Philip had called Him. Nathanael already half submitted when he asked, "Whence knowest Thou me?" Not only did Nathanael seem to have had no previous knowledge of Jesus, but he also had been of the opinion that Jesus had had no knowledge of him. But by asking now, "Whence knowest Thou me?" he virtually admitted that Jesus *did* know him, indeed, had a very intimate knowledge of him. And Jesus now gave him a manifest proof of this by the following answer, which was a testimony of His divine omniscience: "Before that Philip called thee, when thou wast under the fig-tree, I saw thee." There must have been some secret in connection with the fig-tree referred to by Jesus. Some think that Nathanael had been praying for the coming of the Messiah.[7] At any rate, Jesus' words thoroughly convinced him. He confessed: "Rabbi, Thou art the Son of God; Thou art

---

20, 3) Matt. 10, 2 f.; Mark 3, 16 f.; Luke 6, 14 f. Only in Acts 1, 13 f. he is given seventh place.

4) Farrar, I, 152.

5) See articles in Bible dictionaries.

6) Gen. 49, 18.

7) Weiss, I, 375; Farrar, I, 156; and others.

the King of Israel," to which Jesus replied: "Because I said unto thee, I saw thee under the fig-tree, believest thou? Thou shalt see greater things than these. . . . Verily, verily,[8] I say unto you, Hereafter ye shall see heaven open and the angels of God ascending and descending upon the Son of Man." What Jacob beheld in his dream was realized in Christ.[9] Not only once, but doubtless on many future occasions did he and his companions see this promise fulfilled; *i. e.*, with the eyes of faith they saw the heaven open and the angels of God ascending and descending upon the Son of Man. By calling Himself the "Son of Man" Jesus wished to indicate that He is the Messiah, true God and true man. This is the first time that He used it in speaking of Himself.[10]

John 2, 1—11.   **21.**

Three days afterwards [1] there was a wedding in Cana of Galilee, to which Jesus and His newly won disciples were invited. If we assume that the bride was a maiden, we arrive at a Wednesday.[2] It was a few weeks before the Passover of 27 A. D. that Jesus returned from the banks of the Jordan, after an absence of about two months, probably stopping first at Nazareth, where He

The Marriage at Cana. heard about the wedding at Cana and received the invitation, and then proceeding to join His mother and the members of His family, who were already there. While Cana was the home of Nathanael-Bartholomew,[3] there is no evidence that he had anything to do with the marriage.[4] Other details are equally uncertain. All conjecture as to the identity of the bridal pair is idle, although it is not improbable, because of the prominent position accorded her there, that it was the wedding of one of Mary's or Joseph's nephews

---

20, 8) Ἀμήν, ἀμήν. Used in this form twenty-five times in John (always single in the synoptic gospels) and well rendered "verily, verily." Christ Himself is the faithful and true Witness and called Amen in Rev. 3, 14. See Meyer and Dods *sub loco.*

9) Gen. 28, 10 ff.

10) Books have been written on Jesus' own designation of Himself as the Son of Man. For a true interpretation of it see Peter's answer to Christ's question: "Whom do men say that I, the Son of Man, am?" Matt. 16, 13. 15 f., an answer which the Lord approved of. Dan. 7, 13. 14. See Pieper, *Dogmatik,* II, 74 f. Kretzmann, *Pop. Com.,* I, 47.

21, 1) Counting from 1, 43. The Greeks reckoned thus: σήμερον αὔριον, τῇ τρίτῃ ἡμέρα — to-day, to-morrow, the day after to-morrow. Luke 13, 32.

2) Edersheim, I, 344 f.; *Jewish Social Life,* 151 ff.

3) John 21, 2.

4) Possibly, according to a legend, as paranymph, whose duty it was to escort the bride. See Farrar, I, 162.

or nieces. Joseph is no longer mentioned, probably because he was already dead. We need not go into details about the ceremonies or proceedings connected with a Jewish marriage in New Testament times, except to point out that the marriage customs prevailing in Galilee are said to have been pure and simple.[5] There was probably a procession to the house of the bridegroom on the eve of the marriage, the prescribed washing of hands, the signing of a formal legal instrument, and a simple benediction, which was followed by a liberal marriage-feast. It was for this joyous occasion that preparations were made in Cana of Galilee; but, strangely, we are not able to fix definitely the location of this little town. A number of different sites have been proposed;[6] however, the Kefr Kennah, accepted by the Greek and Latin churches, in the proximity of Nazareth and on the direct road to Lake Gennesaret, has the most probabilities in its favor.

John 2, 1—11.   **22.**

As we pass through the court of a festively adorned house in Cana, we notice six large stone water-pots, arranged after the manner of the Jews for purification, for the washing of the feet, the hands, before and after eating, and also of the vessels used. They contained two or three firkins apiece, that is, if a firkin was equivalent to a Hebrew bath, eighteen or twenty-seven gallons each.[1] As we enter the lofty dining-room, brilliantly lighted with lamps and candles, the guests are seen disposed around tables or seated on chairs. The feast proceeds. Oriental hospitality demands a sufficient supply of food and drink for the requirements of the invited guests. But at some point of the entertainment the wine suddenly gave out. This unexpected failure may have arisen from the accession of Jesus and His disciples to the number of expected guests, for whom, although they were invited, no provision had

---

21, 5) Edersheim, I, 355.

6) Cana, "Place of Reeds." The name of a stream on the borders of Ephraim and Manasseh, Josh. 16, 8 (Kanah). A city in Asher, Josh. 19, 28. Cana of Galilee is mentioned also by Josephus — *Life,* 16; *Wars,* I, XVII, 5 — to distinguish it from Cana in Coelesyria, *Ant.,* XV. V. 1. Khirbet Kana, or Kana el Jelil, about eight miles northeast of Nazareth. The Kana of the Crusaders, about eight miles south of Tyre. Ain Kana, about one and a half miles from Nazareth, on the way to Tiberias. And Kefr Kennah, on the same road, about four miles from Nazareth. However, there are no reeds in the neighborhood of the last-named town, and the double n is hard to explain. See *Int. St. B. Encycl. sub loco.* Andrews, 163 f.

22, 1) Liquid measure: 1 log, ca. 1 pint; 4 logs = 1 kab, ca. 2 quarts; 3 kabs = 1 hin, ca. 1½ gallons; 6 hins = 1 bath, ca. 9 gallons. *Int. Stand. B. Encycl. sub* "Weights and Measures."

originally been made. Most likely they were invited when they
appeared. Or was it the poverty of the bridal pair? At any rate,
the watchful eye of Mary quickly observed the imminent embarrass-
ment and communicated the fact to Jesus: "They have no wine."
This remark was evidently a pointed one, and its import was not

"They Have No Wine."

misunderstood. Mary did not
want the family of the bride-
groom to be disgraced. Now, if any one ought to have known
who Jesus really was, it was Mary. Probably she was not aware
of it at the moment, but consciously or unconsciously she was calling upon Jesus to exercise His Messianic power in the supply of
a need which His and His disciples' presence at the wedding had
possibly occasioned. At any rate, her words contained an indirect
appeal for help. And from the reply of Jesus it would indeed seem
that Mary had suggested, and Jesus actually intended, a miraculous
intervention for the benefit of the wedding guests, but in His own
manner and at His own appointed time. Jesus said to her,
"Woman, what have I to do with thee? Mine hour is not yet
come." In Greek the term *woman* is not one of disrespect.[2] Jesus
does not call Mary "mother"; for in this matter, the matter of
performing miracles and manifesting His power, the two, mother
and Son, stand on different grounds. "What have I to do with
thee?" The performance of miracles belongs to His office. In this
matter He brooks no interference, neither from His disciples nor
from His brother or mother.[3] He, too, had seen the lack of wine.
He was probably even now waiting for an opportunity to grant aid
in His own way and His own time. But "Mine hour is not
yet come."

John 2, 1—11.   **23.**

Mary was gently checked. She did not understand — and still
she understood. The reply of Jesus was not altogether a refusal. In
the little words "not yet" she beheld a distinct ray of hope; for she
said to the servants: "Whatsoever He saith unto you, do it." We
have already noticed the water-pots near the entrance of the house.
Probably the water-supply was nearly exhausted when Christ gave
the strange command "Fill the water-pots with water." Water was
specified in view of what was to follow. In their overgreat zeal
the servants filled the vessels to the brim. This is probably stated
for the purpose of pointing out the large quantity as well as to

---

22, 2) Compare John 19, 26 and Luke 13, 12. Dods *sub loco.*
    3) Matt. 12, 46—50.

exclude the possibility of some one's adding anything to the water. But why go into apologetic details? The miracle which follows is either a miracle, or it is not. And we are going either to accept or to reject the simple account. No argument is likely to convince the skeptic, and no amount of rationalizing is going to make a miracle more comprehensible.[1] And so we shall attempt neither, but rather make it our purpose to tell the story. "And He saith unto them, Draw out now and bear unto the governor of the feast." The

Water Changed into Wine.

servants were ordered to draw out the contents of the large water-pots, to put them into smaller vessels, and to carry these to the guest who according to the custom of the time had been elected "governor of the feast." [2] We might call him a butler or head waiter, whose duty it was to arrange the table and to taste the food and wine.[3] "And they bare it." But in the mean while a most remarkable thing had happened. A situation which had threatened to become very embarrassing had been quickly relieved; for what the servants poured in as water flowed out as wine. The ruler of the feast did not know what had taken place. When he tasted the water which had become wine and did not know whence it had been procured, impartially judging it as wine among wines, he mirthfully remarked to the bridegroom that in offering the good wine last, he had deviated from the rule observed at banquets. Commonly the best wine was offered first, and when the sense of taste had been somewhat dulled and the wedding guests could no longer appreciate a choice product, an inferior vintage was offered. But we need not suppose that the remark was intended to imply that the guests were well-nigh intoxicated. It merely establishes the superb quality of Christ's wedding-gift. Here was a miracle and not a mesmeric trick. The wine was real, and it was of the very best.

John 2, 1—11.　　　**24.**

Abruptly the story closes. This is divine reticence in contrast to our shallow talkativeness.[1] What the bridegroom said, the company thought, and Mary felt we can only surmise. But the narrator, St. John, tells us, what the synoptics, who begin their

---

23, 1) Accelerated process of nature, the powers of water magnetized into those of wine, the supernatural exaltation of the guests, and the like. Meyer *sub loco.* Farrar, I, 168 ff.

　　2) The ἀρχιτρίκλινος.　　3) Dods *sub loco.*

24, 1) Edersheim, I, 362.

account with the later Galilean ministry, have not recorded, namely, that "this beginning of miracles did Jesus in Cana of Galilee and manifested forth His glory." "This beginning of miracles" — these words are not to be construed as if the evangelist did not consider certain previous incidents as miraculous, for instance, the remark-

The Manifestation of His Glory.
able insight Jesus showed in the choice of His disciples; but what he wished to state was that here we have the beginning of those marvelous works, viewed as signs [2] or object-lessons of Him whose very existence, "God manifest in the flesh," [3] was the greatest miracle of all. — "And His disciples believed on Him." By this miracle He strengthened His disciples' faith in Him as the Messiah, which had been kindled a few days previously,[4] and manifested His glory, in particular proving Himself as the Lord of nature, God Omnipotent, and the benevolent Friend of man. By His presence at a humble wedding the incarnate Son of God sanctified the holy estate of matrimony. In the beginning of His public ministry, with much work awaiting Him, He still found time to attend the marriage of a country couple and to exercise His sovereign transforming power to relieve their perplexity.

John 2, 12.   **25.**

Shortly after this, Jesus went down to Capernaum with His mother, His brethren, and His disciples. Whether or not He first returned to Nazareth after the wedding and then proceeded to Capernaum the evangelist does not state. From Cana the distance would have been about sixteen and from Nazareth about twenty miles. His sisters are not mentioned, probably for the reason that they were already married and returned to Nazareth or else remained behind. Later we find them living at Nazareth.[1] The occasion of the departure of the family of Jesus from Nazareth is not mentioned. It seems, however, that the visit of Jesus Himself would first of all be to the closely related family of Zebedee, whose sons, James and John, had now joined Him as disciples with Andrew and Simon, in order to draw tighter their mutual bond.[2] It was only a brief visit. Later Capernaum was to be His permanent home; but this brief visit was remembered by the evangelist and

---

24, 2) Σημεῖα.   3) 1 Tim. 3, 16.   4) John 1, 37 ff.
25, 1) Mark 6, 3.

2) Not yet as apostles. First as occasional companions, then as constant attendants, and finally as chosen apostles.

was made memorable as the first visit of God's Chosen One in his fisherman's home. The little party actually went down [3] from the higher lands about Nazareth and Cana to the lower levels of the

Brief Visit at Capernaum. the lakeside, 680 feet below the Mediterranean Sea. We are not able to determine the exact location of Capernaum, [4] whether on the site of the present Tell Hum, nearly two and a half miles southwest of the mouth of the upper Jordan, or Khan Minyeh, fully two and a half miles farther southwest along the shore. On account of recent archeological discoveries it seems that the former has the better claim. [5] At that time Capernaum was a city of considerable importance, the residence of a royal officer, a custom-station, [6] occupied by a detachment of Roman soldiers, located on or near a great trade route from Damascus to the Mediterranean Sea and Egypt, with a flourishing fish-trade, its own synagog, and so forth. But whichever of the two was the site over which stood Peter's home, which was also the home of Christ, [7] both are now desolate. [8] "And thou, Capernaum, which art exalted unto heaven, shalt be brought down to hell; for if the mighty works which have been done in thee had been done in Sodom, it would have remained until this day." [9] This was Capernaum, the home of Jesus and the scene of many of His mighty works, where even now a few unrecorded mighty deeds may have been performed. [10] No long stay was made at this time, probably a few days at the end of February and beginning of March, 27 A. D., because the Jewish Passover was at hand.

25, 3) Κατέβη.

4) Capernaum, not mentioned in Scripture outside of the gospels. Twice mentioned in Josephus: *Life,* 72; *Wars,* III, X, 6. The meaning of the name is doubtful.

5) At Khan Minyeh Prof. R. A. A. Macalister found nothing older than the Arabian period, while at Tell Hum pottery of the Roman period abounds, exactly the period of the glory of Capernaum. *Int. St. B. Encycl. sub loco.*

6) Matt. 9, 9; John 4, 46; etc.   7) Matt. 8, 14.

8) Farrar, I, 182.   9) Matt. 11, 23; Luke 10, 15.

10) On account of Luke 4, 23. Unless reference is there made to John 4, 46—54.

CHAPTER VII.

THE EARLY JUDEAN MINISTRY.

Passover, 27 A. D., to winter, 28 A. D.

A. U. C.	779	780	781	782	783
A. D.	26	27	28	29	30
Age of Jesus	30	31	32	33	34
Passovers		I	II	III	IV

John 2, 13—25.   **1.**

In the nature of things it is in most instances quite impossible to be absolutely certain that our dating of Biblical events is correct; but if our computations are tenable, and if John began his ministry in the late summer of 779 A. U. C., or 26 A. D.,[1] and if Jesus was baptized in the early winter following,[2] then the first Passover of Christ's public ministry must have taken place in the spring of 27 A. D.[3] Preparations for the festival had indeed been in process for a number of weeks before. There was the necessary domestic preparation for those making the pilgrimage. Bridges and roads

The Jews' Passover. were put in repair. The sepulchers were whitewashed to prevent an accidental pollution of the pilgrims.[4] The whole land was in a state of preparation. The roads were filled with pilgrims. As many as two and a half million worshipers were gathered at Jerusalem from all parts of the Jewish world.[5] And among the Galilean pilgrims from Capernaum was Jesus of Nazareth with His little band of disciples.[6] The time had come for Him to present Himself to the nation as the promised Messiah. Of the journey itself and the particular route — probably along the Jordan valley to Jericho and then to Jerusalem — no details are given, except the notice that He

---

1,   1) Chapter V, 1.   2) Chapter VI, 1.

3) Andrews, 169. April 11—17. Also Prof. O. Gerhardt, *Stern des Messias,* 124. Weiss (I, 318. 391), assuming a two years' ministry, places this Passover in 28 A. D. A number of writers, Wieseler, Farrar, and others, place the baptism of Jesus in the summer of 27 A. D. and accordingly the first Passover in the spring of 28 A. D. But it seems improbable that nine or ten months should have elapsed between John's first appearance and the baptism of Jesus. Then another eight or nine months must be accounted for between the baptism and the first Passover. The only reason for this dating seems to be the forty-six years of John 2, 20. Compare Section 3 in this chapter. See Edersheim, I, 367, note.

4) See Meyer sub Matt. 23, 27. Edersheim, I, 367.

5) See chapter IV, 37.   6) V. 17; 3, 22.

"went up" to Jerusalem,[7] an expression literally accurate; for coming from Galilee one ascends from 680 feet below sea-level near the Lake of Gennesaret to 2,500 feet above the Mediterranean Sea, the altitude of Jerusalem.

John 2, 13—25.   **2.**

On reaching Jerusalem, the Lord of the Temple presented Himself at the Temple of the Lord.[1] But what He saw in the Court of the Gentiles did not at all please Him. He again noticed the disorder which doubtlessly had vexed Him on earlier occasions. It is true, the gospels mention only one previous visit, but we may well take it for granted that there had been others. The majestic Temple, rising above the surrounding courts, included in its area an extensive southern space, into which the magnificent outer gates opened directly, the Court of the Gentiles. Gentiles might walk there, but not beyond a stone railing, the Soreg, which menaced with death any non-Jew who would penetrate beyond.[2] In this space a Temple market had long ago been established, contrary to the sole purpose which according to the will of the Lord His **The Temple Market.** Temple was to serve — to be a "house of prayer" and the habitation where all His wondrous works should be proclaimed[3] and the Messiah-typifying sacrifices be offered. Now one of the courts had become a mart of trade where all that was needed for the sacrifices was offered for sale and where the money-changers exchanged — at a premium of not less than five per cent.[4] — the image-bearing foreign currency for the lawful Temple coin. Usually the foreign coins were also defiled with heathen symbols and inscriptions. And when it is remembered that, besides Palestinian silver and copper coin, Persian, Tyrian, Syrian, Egyptian, Grecian, and Roman money circulated in the country besides the foreign coin brought directly by the pilgrims from the Diaspora, it will be understood that both the work and the profit must have been enormous. All Jews and proselytes, women, slaves, and minors excepted, had to pay the annual Temple-tribute of half a shekel in statutory coin,[5] equal to about 30 cents in our money. This brought an immense revenue into the Temple-treasury, and for

---

1,   7) Ἀνέβη.

2,   1) St. Bonaventura. Farrar, I, 21.

     2) See chapter III, 8.   3) Is. 56, 7; Ps. 26, 7. 8.

     4) Edersheim, I, 368. Farrar, I, 185.

     5) Ex. 30, 11—16. Schuerer, II, I, 250.

every exchange a premium was charged. And besides, there was a great deal to be bought at the Temple-bazaars for the feast, for the sacrifices, for purification, for the purchase of which, of course, the right money was needed and for the exchange of which fresh charges were made. There stood the cattle-dealers with their animals for sacrifice, oxen, heifers, and lambs. Beside their cages sat the sellers of doves, offering to the poor worshipers what they needed for sacrifice. Oil, wine, and incense, the accessories of sacrifice, were kept ready within the booths. Of course, all this was convenient for the sacrificers, but the booths and stalls should have been outside of the Temple area. Besides, the prices charged were often exorbitant. The revenue realized by the regular Temple-tribute was immense, and the vast accumulation of illegally acquired wealth as realized by the Temple bankers and traders must have been simply enormous. No wonder that,[6] despite many previous spoliations, Crassus could carry away from the Temple-treasury ten thousand talents in gold.[7] And what became of the profit of the money-changers, and who were the real owners of the Temple market? Most likely Annas and the members of his high-priestly family.[8] — But to return. There was the disputing at the tables and the chaffering beside the live stock. Loud noises disturbed the worship, while usury and deceit desecrated the Sanctuary. Every finer religious feeling must have revolted against this state of things.

John 2, 13—25.   3.

To Jesus the Temple market constituted an intolerable abuse. Stooping down, He made a scourge of ropes made of rushes.[1] We need not suppose that He actually used it. This whip was probably designed as an emblem of His power. And then, in order to cleanse the sacred court of its worst pollutions, He drove out the oxen, sheep, and cattle and those that sold them. Then, going to the tables of the money-changers, He overthrew them with their carefully arranged piles of heterogeneous coin. To the sellers of doves He issued the command: "Take these things hence; make not Mine Father's house a house of merchandise." In His word

---

2,   6) In 54—53 B. C.

7) 2,000 talents in pure gold, 8,000 talents in other articles of value. 1 gold talent $30,750 (?). *Int. St. B. Encycl.* See Bible dictionaries. Edersheim (I, 369) estimates this immense amount at only two and a half million sterling, 54—53 B. C. Josephus, *Ant.,* XIV, VII, 1.

8) Edersheim, I, 371.

3,   1) *Flagellum.* Not of rushes, but of ropes made of rushes, φραγέλλιον ἐκ σχοινίων. Dods *sub loco.*

and action His Messiahship was clearly implied. He does not merely say "your Father," or "our Father," but "My Father's house." [2] — This, then, was Christ's first public act in Jerusalem: the first cleansing of the Temple. There was another at the close of His ministry. Of course, ordinarily a Jewish religious enthusiast would have had no actual right to interfere. That was the duty of the Temple police, assigned to it by the supreme ecclesiastical court. But this body had failed in its duty, and in a most particular sense Jesus was now about His Father's business. [3] In spite of the fact that the Messianic import of the cleansing was not recognized, all true friends of the Law saw the righteousness of the action. But in this cleansing of the Temple the disciples of Jesus saw the fulfilment of a prophetic utterance in a Messianic psalm: "The zeal of Thine house hath eaten Me up." [4]

Cleansing the Temple. The Jewish authorities, however, saw in the act and word of Jesus only unauthorized interference and unwarranted assumption of authority. It was quite characteristic of them to ask for a sign. "What sign showest Thou unto us, seeing that Thou doest these things?" This is not the last time that such questions will be asked. Jesus gave the enigmatic answer: "Destroy this temple, and in three days I will raise it up." In reply to their challenge He referred them to the greatest Messianic sign. The Jews misunderstood, but did not forget the words. Later on, during His final trial, they based on them their false charge. [5] Christ spoke of the temple of His body, as the evangelist observes. But the Jews thought that He was thinking of the still unfinished Herodian Temple, which was not fully completed until the time of Herod Agrippa II, in 63 A. D. [6] "Then said the Jews, Forty and six years was this temple in building, and wilt Thou rear it up in three days?" These words serve us as a chronological tag. The rebuilding of the Temple was begun in Kisleu (Chisleu), November-December, in the eighteenth year of the reign of Herod, corresponding to 20—19 B. C., or A. U. C. 734—735. In Jewish reckoning the uncompleted year was counted as a year. Thus forty-five full years would be completed by the autumn of 779 A. U. C., or 26 A. D. And the forty-sixth year would be regarded as running

---

3, 2) Dods *sub loco.*
    3) Luke 2, 49.
    4) Ps. 69, 9.
    5) Matt. 26, 61.
    6) Josephus, *Ant.,* XX, IX, 7.

at the Passover of 780 A. U. C., or 27 A. D.[7]　In the words of Jesus we also have His first prediction of His death and resurrection, as remembered by His disciples after He was risen from the dead.

John 2, 13—25.　　　　　**4.**

During this stay of Jesus in Jerusalem for the Passover a number of miracles were performed by Him of which we have no particular account. "Many believed in His name when they

Miracles in Jerusalem. saw the miracles which He did." But this faith was only a milk-faith, as Luther calls it,[1] which fed on signs and required miracles for its sustenance. It was a faith which was not genuine and did not reach down to the heart. And Jesus, who is a Discerner of men and looks into the heart, would not commit Himself to such followers or enter into any intimate relation with them such as He did, for instance, with His newly won Galilean friends.

John 3, 1—21.　　　　　**5.**

The reformatory act of Jesus in the Temple naturally aroused the enmity of the ecclesiastical powers. There was as yet no hostile step, but a bitter feud had begun, of which the sequel could not be doubtful. Nevertheless even among the Jewish authorities an early follower was found, a Pharisee, a rich man, a ruler, Nicodemus, a member of the Sanhedrin.[1]　A certain Bonai, surnamed

Nicodemus. Nakdimon, appears in the Talmud as one of the richest and most distinguished citizens of Jerusalem, whose daughter, after inheriting immense wealth, was reduced to abject poverty. But it seems that this legendary Nakdimon is not the Nicodemus of the Gospel.[2]　There is also a tradition in the Gospel of Nicodemus and in other apocryphal works, according to which, after giving a testimony in favor of Christ before Pilate, Nicodemus was divested of his office and banished by the hostile Jews, that he was baptized by Sts. Peter and John, and that his remains were found in a common grave beside those of Gamaliel and

---

3,　　7) See chapter II, 43. Schuerer, I, I, 410. The calculation which placed this Passover in 28 A. D., rests on an oversight. The writers who make this mistake forget that a fresh year had begun in autumn, at any rate at the Passover. If a Jew had calculated the time at the Passover in 781, he would not have said "forty-six," but "forty-seven," "years was this Temple in building." Edersheim, I, 375. Robertson, *Harmony*, 265.

4,　　1) Stoeckhardt, *B. G.*, 35.

5,　　1) John 7, 50; 19, 39.

　　　2) Dods *sub loco.* Edersheim, I, 381, n. 1.

St. Stephen.[3)] But our only authentic information of this interesting Rabbi is derived from the few scattered notices in the Gospel
of St. John.[4)] He came to Jesus by night. His secret visit was
probably because he feared he would be exposed to the ridicule and
hatred of his fellows, or because he thought himself too eminent
a person to compromise his dignity by making this visit in public.[5)]
Be that as it may, — he came. There was something about this
young Galilean Prophet that attracted him. There was a desire in
his soul, though he was "a master of Israel," to become more closely
acquainted with the doctrine of this Teacher come from God.
Possibly he had previously heard, and seriously meditated on, the
message of John the Baptist: "Repent ye; for the kingdom of
heaven is at hand," [6)] and was now conceiving it to be possible that
the recent deeds of Jesus were signs of the Kingdom.

John 3, 1—21.   **6.**

We do not know where the meeting took place. But since
John was the reporter and also perhaps a witness of the interview
and seems to have had a house in Jerusalem,[1)] it is probable that
the conversation took place in his house and in his presence. It was
on an evening in spring. A whispering breeze gently disturbs the
evening air.[2)] The city rests. But Nicodemus, a noble member of
the Sanhedrin, has something on his mind. He repairs to Jesus
for direction on a most delicate point of Jewish or Christian theology — the King and admission into the Kingdom. Or we might
state it in an unexpressed "What must I do in order to enter the
Messiah's kingdom?" [3)] Nicodemus was an unexpected and uncommon nightly visitor. But as Jesus was not intimidated by the
questioning Jewish authorities [4)] nor deceived by the "milk-faith"

"Thou Art a Teacher Come from God." of acclaiming multitudes,[5)] so He
was not now flattered into eager
politeness by the possibility of gain-
ing a convert from the Great Council of the Jews. There is neither
undue deference nor, on the other hand, an air of superiority. An
atmosphere of calm and earnest dignity prevailed. Probably not
every word of the interview has been recorded; what the Holy
Spirit has inspired the evangelist to write is an outline, the gist, of

---

5,   3) C. M. Kerr, in *Int. St. B. Encycl.*, sub "Nicodemus."
     4) John 3, 1—21; 7, 50—52; 19, 39—42.
     5) Farrar, I, 197.   6) Matt. 3, 2.
6,   1) See John 19, 27.   2) V. 8.
     3) Meyer *sub loco.*   4) John 2, 18.   5) John 2, 24.

an extended conversation, which, however, gives us all that is necessary to know. We can almost imagine the scene beside a flickering lamp. Nicodemus began: "Rabbi, we [6] know that Thou art a teacher come from God; for no man can do these miracles that Thou doest except God be with him." Thus by way of introduction he paid a fine tribute to Jesus. He thought well of Him, but not well enough. He regarded Him as a teacher, but not as the Savior. In speaking of Him as a miracle-working divine prophet, he probably thought he had made a great confession; but he had not yet so much as entered the porticoes of true knowledge. [7] He was still ignorant of the way to salvation.

John 3, 1—21.   **7.**

Without in the least responding to the words of esteem directed to Him, Jesus in His answer — if not to the *words*, then at least to the *question in the heart* of Nicodemus — replies: "Verily, verily, I say unto thee, Except a man be born again, [1] he cannot see the kingdom of God." He tells him point blank that the righteousness of works, upon which he, as a Pharisee, builds his hope of heaven, cannot avail before the just and holy God because no man is able to fulfil His Law. If he desires to enter the Kingdom, he must experience a radical change of **"Except a Man be Born Again."** heart and will; he must become an entirely new creature; a spiritual rebirth must take place. What He answers him corresponds to the message of the Baptist and to His own words: "The time is fulfilled, and the kingdom of God is at hand; repent ye and believe the Gospel." [2] Nicodemus could not understand. He thought Christ was referring to a physical rebirth. "How can a man be born when he is old? Can he enter the second time into his mother's womb and be born?" Jesus replied: "Except a man be born of water [3] and of the Spirit, he cannot enter into the kingdom of God. That which is born of the flesh is flesh, and that which is born of the Spirit is spirit." This rebirth is the spiritual regeneration most marvelously

---

6,   6) The plural form seems to include other members of the ruling class upon whom the ministry of Jesus in Jerusalem had made a favorable impression.

   7) Chrysostom, quoted by Meyer.

7,   1) Ἄνωθεν, from above or again? The latter; Nicodemus himself so understands it.

   2) Mark 1, 15.

   3) Notice that Christ recognized the effectiveness of the baptism of John.

brought about by the Holy Ghost in Word and Sacrament. It is necessary for every man on account of his sinful nature, original sin, inherited from our first parents; for "that which is born of the flesh is flesh." Only in those regenerated by the Spirit a new God-pleasing life is possible. An expression of confusion registers itself on the face of Nicodemus as he listens to these bewildering words. But hark! did he hear the brief rushing of the night breeze as it rose and fell? [4] He heard its sound, but he knew neither whence it came nor whither it went. So was every one that was born of the Spirit. "Marvel not that I said unto thee, Ye must be born again. The wind bloweth where it listeth, and thou hearest the sound thereof, but canst not tell whence it cometh and whither it goeth. So is every one that is born of the Spirit." Even as, for example, the wind, the thunder, the human soul, are invisible, though their existence and operation are evident, so also the effects of regeneration are apparent, but the process of regeneration, the manner in which the spiritual rebirth is brought about, is incomprehensible to human reason.

John 3, 1—21. **8.**

To the bewildered mind of Nicodemus this explanation does not explain. He asks, "How can these things be?" He had been of the opinion that the mere fact of his physical Jewish birth entitled him to admission into the kingdom of heaven, and now he hears: Not birth, but rebirth. As a teacher of Israel he was **"How can These Things Be?"** supposed to lead others on the way to salvation, and now he learns that he must be shown that way himself. And then this reference to the mysterious working of the Spirit. Question after question arises in his heart, "How can these things be?" Jesus replies, "Art thou a master of Israel and knowest not these things?" These words are not to be taken as reproachful irony, but rather as an expression of sincere sadness over this sorrowful state of ignorance. If the teacher is so obtuse, how great must be the dullness of those whom he teaches! [1]

7, 4) Farrar, I, 199.

8, 1) Dods *sub loco.* From the expression ὁ διδάσκαλος τοῦ Ἰσραήλ, Farrar has argued (I, 199) that Nicodemus was the third member of the Sanhedrin: 1. Nasi-president (king); 2. Ab-beth-din, vice-president (father of the house of judgment; presiding judge); 3. Chakam (wise man). But it seems that the designation "teacher" refers to Nicodemus as an individual, an acknowledged teacher of the people. Meyer *sub loco.* Of this term in an official sense Schuerer knows nothing. II, I, 184.

John 3, 1—21.   **9.**

The dialog ceases. But Jesus does not leave Nicodemus in a state of bewilderment. His nightly visitor's searching questions stirred Him into offering him a fuller explanation of heavenly things. Coordinating His teaching with that of the prophets, John the Baptist, and all divinely appointed messengers of the truth, He continues: "Verily, verily, I say unto thee, We speak that we do know and testify that we have seen; and ye receive not our witness." This is a sad complaint. The spiritual regeneration, while a wonderful work of God, yet is an earthly thing in this respect, that it takes place on earth, in the hearts of men. But "if I have told you earthly things and ye believe not, how shall ye believe if I tell you of heavenly things?" That is, if questions are asked concerning such matters as to a certain extent are open to human observation, at least in their effect, what if Christ will touch upon things wholly in the unseen? [1] And this He now does — "unto the Jews a stumbling-block, unto the Greeks foolishness, but unto them which are called the power of God and the wisdom of God." [2] He speaks of the mysteries concerning His own person and of the gracious counsel and purposes of God. To this category belong, as He shows, especially the Messianic mysteries, the divine decrees for the redemption and salvation of man. No

"Whosoever Believeth in Him." one but He can reveal these things. For "no man hath ascended up to heaven but He that came down from heaven, even the Son of Man, which is in heaven." He came down from heaven being true God from eternity together with the Father and the Holy Ghost, and still is in heaven, also according to His human nature and in His present state of humiliation. [3] Without controversy great is this mystery: God was manifest in the flesh; and the purpose of His incarnation is stated in the following: "And as Moses lifted up a serpent in the wilderness, even so must the Son of Man be lifted up," — thus early Christ makes an enigmatic allusion to His redeeming death by crucifixion, [4] — "that

---

9,   1) Wisdom of Sol. 9, 13—19. *Pop. Com.*, N. T., I, 422.

2) 1 Cor. 1, 23.

3) Probably because the words "which is in heaven" were not understood, they were omitted in certain ancient texts.

4) This He did because of the paramount importance of His suffering and death as the ransom paid for mankind's redemption. In the case of Nicodemus this enigmatic germ then sown bore fruit at the foot of the cross, John 19, 39. Meyer *in loco.*

CODEX VATICANUS. (B)

Now in the Vatican Library. Fourth century. John 2, 16—3,17.

"For God so loved the world that He gave His only-begotten Son."
John 3, 16.

ΟΥΤΩΣΓΑΡΗ   οὕτως γὰρ ἠ-
ΓΑΠΗΣΕΝΟΘΣΤΟΝΚΟΣΜΝ   γάπησεν ὁ θ(εὸ)ς τὸν κόσμ(ο)ν,
ΩΣΤΕΤΟΝΥΙΟΝΤΟΝΜΟ   ὥστε τὸν υἱὸν τὸν μο-
ΝΟΓΕΝΗΕΔΩΚΕΝ   νογενῆ ἔδωκεν.

(Beginning at the tenth line from the bottom, third column.)

whosoever believeth in Him should not perish, but have eternal
life." And, continuing, Christ utters those wonderful words, the
kernel of the Gospel: [5] "For God so loved the world that He gave
His only-begotten Son, that whosoever believeth in Him should
not perish, but have everlasting life." Jesus is the universal, the
only Savior of all mankind. He that believes on Him will not be
condemned; but he that believes not is condemned already. He
already has hell on his neck. [6] But, alas! men prefer sin and
destruction to the Savior, the Light of life, of their salvation; they
love darkness rather than light. This they show in their every-day
life. "For every one that doeth evil hateth the light, neither cometh
to the light, lest his deeds should be reproved. But he that doeth
truth," accepts Christ, "cometh to the light that his deeds may be
made manifest, that they are wrought in God."

John 3, 1—21.　　　　**10.**

But did not Christ contradict Himself? First He said:
"Except a man be born again, he cannot see the kingdom of God,"
and then He says: "He that believeth not is condemned already."
How do these statements agree? There is no contradiction in these

A Question. two statements. He that is born of the Spirit
believes in Christ. And he that believes is reborn
and shows his faith in a new, a Christian, life. — Thus the interview with Nicodemus came to an end. He came seeking and left
believing. At least, when he appears again, there is evidence that
the Spirit of God had moved his heart. [1] Born again? How can
these things be? But why ask? Even in his own heart these things
had actually taken place.

John 3, 22—24.　　　　**11.**

After the interview with Nicodemus, Jesus and His disciples
left the capital city for the rural section of the Judean country.
The location is not given, but most likely He traveled in a north-
easterly direction, towards the banks of the Jordan. We now hear
that Jesus baptized. But whereas John baptized with his own
hand, while it seems that his disciples did not administer Baptism,

---

9,　5) The words are Christ's and a continuation of His address to Nicodemus, to verse 21, and not, as some have thought, an explanatory meditation of the evangelist. The latter view is an assumption justified neither by
anything in the text nor by the use of the word μονογενής, although nowhere
else used by Christ. See Meyer *sub loco*.

6) Luther, quoted by Meyer *sub loco*.

10,　1) John 7, 50—52.

Jesus Himself did not baptize,[1] but delegated the baptism with water to His disciples. Thus Jesus rendered the act of baptism independent of His own personal presence and so provided for the maintenance of it in His Church after His departure.[2] We do not know how long Jesus continued His ministry here, but His must have been a prolonged stay,[3] covering, as we suppose, the period from May to December, 27 A. D., or 780 A. U. C.[4]

The Parallel Ministry of Jesus and John. In this same period John, after transferring the scene of his ministry from Bethany to the west side of the Jordan, was similarly engaged. But why did John continue to baptize? Was it because Jesus had not yet come forth, as John mistakenly thought He should? Or was it because John was not convinced of the Messiahship of Jesus? Or must the parallel ministry be looked upon as a splitting asunder of the Messianic movement?[5] Certainly not. The work and mission of John, to which his administration of Holy Baptism belonged, was of God[6] and had not yet been terminated by Him. While we do not know the exact location of our Lord's baptismal activity, the scene of John's ministry at that time is given as "Aenon, near to Salim, because there was much water there," a site that has not been definitely identified, though a number of localities have been proposed.[7] The tradition which places it a few miles south of Bethshean, Scythopolis, has this in its favor, that it was on this side of the Jordan[8] and that it locates the scene of John's last public labors close to the seat of Herod Antipas, into whose power he was soon to be delivered.[9]

11, 1) 4, 2.

2) Godet, quoted by Dods *sub loco.*

3) On account of v. 26, "All men come to Him," which seems to imply a considerable period of time.

4) On account of 4, 35. The saying will be considered *in loco.*

5) See Meyer *in loco.*

6) Luke 20, 4.

7) 1. On the *southern* border of Judea. Evidently out of the question. 2. Near Shechem. In the very heart of Samaria? Hardly possible. 3. Eight miles south of Scythopolis, in the corner, bordering on Samaria, Galilee, Decapolis, and Perea. Not far off are seven copious fountains, which might well be called Aenon, place of springs. And there is reason to believe that this district did not belong to Samaria, but was included in the Decapolis. W. Ewing, in *Int. St. B. Encycl.,* sub "Salim." Consult also Guthe's *Bible Atlas.*

8) On account of v. 26, where Bethany is spoken of as beyond the Jordan.

9) Edersheim, I, 393.

John 3, 25—36. **12.**

During this period — and probably in consequence of the relative proximity of the two baptizing activities — there arose a discussion between John's disciples and the Jews [1] about purification. Most likely the argument was about the relative importance of the two baptisms, the relation of one to the other, and the like. The questioning, it seems, was begun by the disciples of John,[2] who possibly challenged some Jew for desiring to be baptized by Jesus. In their zeal for their master they brought tidings to John of which he seems not to have been aware, indirectly complaining of what to them seemed interference with his work and something approaching presumption on the part of Jesus.[3] "Rabbi, He that was with thee beyond Jordan, to whom thou barest witness, behold, the same baptizeth, and all men come to Him." The significant suppression of the name of Jesus reveals a jealous irritation.[4] The complaint of John's disciples was that Jesus, who had gone forth from the fellowship of the Baptist and, as they thought, owed His standing to John's favorable testimony, now arose in competition with him and put him in the shade. John, however, made a noble reply to this complaint, in which his inherent greatness shone forth. "A man can receive nothing except it be given him from above." That is, all success, including that of the preacher of God's Word, comes from above. And in his case, had he not himself testified

John's Loyalty to Jesus. in their hearing: "I am not the Christ, but am sent before Him"? The success of Jesus should not be to them an occasion for complaint, but rather a source of joy. It is to the bridegroom, and to him alone, to whom the bride belongs. Now, he was not the Bridegroom, but the Bridegroom's friend,[5] and even now he was greatly gladdened by the Bridegroom's voice, an unmistakable evidence that the moment for the marriage had arrived. "He must increase, but I must decrease." The setting of his sun was the signal of the rising of One infinitely brighter. The end of his mission marked the beginning of Another's. While he was indeed a prophet, yet his words were only "of the earth," while Jesus, "that cometh from heaven, is above all." His disciples complainingly said of Jesus: "All men come to Him." If it only were

---

12, 1) Some texts have "a Jew." 2) They are mentioned first.
3) Edersheim, I, 391. 4) Farrar, I, 203.
5) The παρανύμφιος, who was employed to arrange the marriage. For marriage customs and festivities see Edersheim, I, 353 ff.

true! His complaint was that the number was much too small. "No man receiveth His testimony." And still there were some that believed. "The Father loveth the Son and hath given all things into His hand. He that believeth on the Son hath everlasting life; and he that believeth not the Son shall not see life, but the wrath of God abideth on him." A wonderful tribute to Christ. "He must increase, but I must decrease." What a depth of unselfish, humble loyalty! It was spoken from the bottom of his heart, because it was for the very thing of which his disciples complained that he had waited and worked. Now that it had come, he was content. It was all in order. — Moses disrobed Aaron,[6] but this Aaron of the New Testament unrobed himself ere he lay down to die.[7] "Verily, among men that are born of women there hath not risen a greater than John the Baptist."[8]

John 4, 1—3.   **13.**

"When therefore the Lord[1] knew how the Pharisees had heard that Jesus made and baptized more disciples than John,[2] He left Judea and departed again into Galilee." Here we have the facts: first, that Jesus made more disciples than John, which led the forerunner's disciples to complain; secondly, that this was known to the Pharisees, who evidently watched both Jesus and John; and thirdly, that Jesus, well aware that this was known to them,[3] left Judea. But are these all the facts, or were there other reasons why Jesus ceased to baptize and why He left Judea? The question is of some importance for chronological considerations. In the attempt to make this passage agree with the notice of the arrest and imprisonment of John[4] the answer usually given is that John was arrested at this time probably through the instrumentality of the Pharisees; that Jesus, fearing a similar fate, retired through Samaria to Galilee, beyond the jurisdiction of the Sanhedrin; and that this return to Galilee was followed by the beginning of His great Galilean ministry. But this does not agree with our present

---

12, 6) Num. 20, 28.

7) Edersheim, I, 392.   8) Matt. 11, 11.

13, 1) Notice the expression ὁ Κύριος. Compare 6, 23; Luke 7, 13, etc. Evidently the evangelist, writing later, unconsciously departs from contemporary speech and speaks for himself as a believer.

2) See No. 11.

3) Namely, in consequence of the concourse of people who flocked to Him.

4) Matt. 4, 12; Mark 1, 14; Luke 4, 14; 3, 19. 20. See Meyer under John 4, 1—3, n. 1.

text, which leaves us under the impression that John's work was still in progress. It is true that Jesus did not begin His own great Galilean ministry until John had run his course; but it seems improbable that the arrest of John took place at this time. There is no evidence that the Pharisees were instrumental in delivering

Departure for Galilee.

John over to Herod.[5] Jesus did not leave Judea because He was concerned about His own personal safety, but rather because He did not want to place Himself in competition with His friend and forerunner John. His greater success was offensive to the Pharisees; but that it led them to any overt act at this time is nowhere indicated. This retirement was clearly prompted by the motive to avoid any hindrance which His own baptismal activity might through misrepresentation place in the way of John. And therefore, as long as His divinely commissioned forerunner was still able, both in word and deed, to bear witness to Him as the Messiah, He chose to seek retirement and await the issue. And there are other considerations which cause us to believe that the imprisonment of John and the beginning of the Galilean labors did not take place at this time. The calling, or rather the recalling, of the disciples at Capernaum, as related by the synoptists, presupposes a period of retirement.[6] During Jesus' baptismal activity in Judea His disciples were His helpers; but after the return of their Master to Galilee they seem to have returned to their old calling, not to be recalled until He had begun His labors at Capernaum. That, by the way, is probably the reason why this period of the life of Christ is passed over in silence by the synoptists, while it was the purpose of John to fill this gap. Therefore, if it is now about December in 27 A. D., we place the imprisonment of John and the beginning of Christ's great Galilean ministry immediately after the unnamed feast, the Passover of 28 A. D.[7] — We now proceed with our story.

13, 5) This explanation is based upon the attempt to make John 4, 1—3 agree with Matt. 4, 12 and parallels.

6) Without this period of retirement the calling of the disciples in Matt. 4, 18—22; Mark 1, 16—20; and Luke 5, 1—11, or rather the recalling of the disciples as compared with John 1, 35—51, is hard to explain in the arrangement of most modern gospel harmonies: A. T. Robertson, Nos. 34—41; J. P. Cadman, Nos. 28—32; J. A. Broadus, Nos. 23—27; Stevens and Burton, Nos. 24—38; J. H. Kerr, Nos. 27—33.

7) In other words, the events of John 4 and 5 — the Samaritan ministry, the healing of the ruler's son, and the unnamed feast — are to be inserted before Matt. 4, 12 and parallels. In deciding upon this chronological order, we are following Wieseler, Andrews, and Stoeckhardt and no less a historical authority than Eusebius in his *Hist. Eccl.*, III, 24. For a full discussion see Wieseler, *Syn.*, 147 ff., and Andrews, 179 ff. 188. 215.

John 4, 4.   **14.**

"And He must needs go through Samaria." If we place the scene of this ministry in Northern Judea, that was the natural thing for Him to do. And if we may credit the report of Josephus,[1] the road through Samaria was generally taken by the Galilean pilgrims on their way to the capital, especially if they were in a hurry,[2] while on the other hand the traveling Judeans[3] seem chiefly to have made a detour through Perea in order to avoid the hostile and Levitically impure Samaritans. We need not enter into all the details of Samaritan history. We remember that after the fall of the Northern Kingdom[4] and the carrying away of the ten tribes the wasted and depopulated districts of this territory were repeopled with heathen colonists from the Babylonian dominion. There was thus formed a mixed people with a mixed

Samaria. religion. While the name Samaria and Samaritans still clung to the territory,[5] the principal settlers, "men of Cuth,"[6] contributed the name Cutheans, by which the Jews afterwards persistently designated the Samaritans.[7] This was intended as a term of reproach to mark them as a foreign race and to repudiate all connections between them and the Jews. A number of idols were naturally introduced by the imported colonists;[8] but as these heathen people gradually intermingled with the remnants of the Israelitish population, the worship of Jehovah was generally accepted. However, with exceptions. They strongly believed in the unity of God. They most strictly and zealously observed what of Biblical Law they still retained.[9] They observed the Sabbath and practised circumcision. They held to the doctrine of angels and devils, and it is doubtful whether they shared the Sadducean denial of the resurrection.[10] Of the Old Testament writings only the five books of Moses, the Pentateuch, were accepted

---

14, 1) *Ant.,* XX, VI, 1.

2) The distance from Galilee to Jerusalem could be covered in three days.

3) Jews living in Judea. Edersheim, I, 394.

4) Chapter II, 10.

5) From the city built by Omri as the capital of the Kingdom of Israel, 1 Kings 16, 24. It was destroyed by John Hyrcanus ca. 109 B. C., rebuilt by Herod, and named Sebaste in honor of Augustus.

6) 2 Kings 17, 30.   7) Edersheim, I, 395.

8) 2 Kings 17, 29 ff.   9) Unencumbered by pharisaic tradition.

10) As asserted by the Rabbis and, following them, by the Fathers. Edersheim, I, 402.

as canonical.[11]) They, too, hoped for the Messiah, expecting Him, however, to be an ethico-religious reformer, a prophet,[12]) not a king in the nationalistic, Jewish sense. When, after the return of the Jews from the Babylonian Captivity, Ezra and Nehemiah insisted upon a strict separation between them and the faithful Jews, they erected a rival temple on Mount Gerizim, above Shechem. A violent and constant hostility resulted, which was modified only on occasions. When the Jews were in the ascendency and it suited their purposes, the Samaritans would call themselves Jews, at least descendants of Jacob and Joseph through Manasseh and Ephraim; but when the Jews were in adversity, then they would claim to be of the stock of the Medes and Persians.[13]) In the troublous times of enforced Hellenization under Antiochus Epiphanes, when the Temple in Jerusalem was desecrated, sacrifices of swine were commanded, and Judaism was ordered to cease,[14]) the Samaritans escaped a similar fate by repudiating all connection with Israel and dedicating their temple to Jupiter. In the last Jewish struggle with Rome the Samaritans remained neutral. Since the time of Herod, Samaria had been a province of the Jewish kingdom, passing on to Archelaus and, after his deposition, to the Roman procurator. In the days of our Lord it was, the same as Judea, ruled by Pontius Pilate; but although under one administration, there was no love lost between the Jews and the Samaritans. When Jewish pilgrims passed through Samaria, scoffing was not lacking, nor were malicious deeds of violence wanting. The Jews, on the other hand, treated the Samaritans with every mark of supreme contempt. They excluded them entirely from their fellowship. They accused them of falsehood, folly, and irreligion, and this in the most offensive terms of assumed superiority and self-righteous, pharisaic bigotry.[15]) The expression "Thou art a Samaritan and hast a devil," [16]) which they hurled at Jesus shows in what egregiously low esteem the Jews held the Samaritans.

John 4, 5—9. **15.**

It was without this racial prejudice that Jesus, entering Samaria in December, 27 A. D., came to rest at Jacob's Well, just out of Sychar, near the estate which Jacob had bequeathed to his favorite

14, 11) They asserted that their roll of the Pentateuch was the only authentic copy.

12) On the ground of a passage from the Thorah, Deut. 18, 15.

13) Farrar, I, 210, n. 1. *Ant.,* IX, XIV, 3; XI, VIII, 6; XII, V, 5.

14) 169 B. C. See chapter II, 22.

15) Edersheim, I, 399. 16) John 8, 48.

son and where Joseph himself had commanded his bones to be buried.[1] There is now quite general agreement that this well[2] is located at the fork of an old Roman road, with Joseph's tomb and Sychar (El Askar) to the right (northeast), Shechem (Nablus) to the left (northwest); and just off the road to the south the giant bulk of "this mountain,"[3] Gerizim, overshadows the rear.[4] It was, as we take it, at the hour of noon, "about the sixth hour," that Jesus, "being weary with His journey, sat thus on the well."[5] The disciples had gone away into near-by Sychar to purchase food, Samaritan food, which curiously enough, was de-

At Jacob's Well. clared lawful in the time of Christ.[6] While Jesus rested there alone, — unless John, the recorder of this event, was with Him, — and waited for His disciples to return, "there cometh a woman of Samaria[7] to draw water." Jesus said unto her, "Give Me to drink." Every one who has traveled in the hospitable East knows with what ready response a request of this nature is usually met.[8] But here was a delicate situation. Even had Jesus not spoken, it seems that from His dress or appearance the woman had already recognized in Him the Jew. And His speech, His pronunciation and enunciation, would beyond doubt have revealed His nationality.[9] She well knew how haughtily the Jews generally looked down upon her despised race. It was a certain satisfaction to her to notice that thirst had forced a member of that proud race to make a request

---

15, 1) Farrar, I, 206. Gen. 33, 19; 50, 24 f.; Josh. 24, 32.

2) Of all the special localities of our Lord's life in Palestine this is almost the only one well-nigh undisputed.

3) V. 20.

4) See "Sychar" and "Jacob's Well" in *Int. St. B. Encycl.*

5) We suppose that John used the ordinary Jewish reckoning of time throughout except in 19, 14, where he quoted the time in the language of the Roman court. See chapter VI, 16. It could hardly have been six o'clock in the morning. While noon was not the hour for general resort to the well, the fact that the woman at the well was alone and held so long a private conversation uninterrupted, seems to favor our assumption. Also, Jesus apparently had no intention of halting here for the night, as He would have had, had it been evening. Andrews, 186. Dods *sub loco*.

6) Edersheim, I, 402.

7) That is, a Samaritan woman, not a woman of the city of Samaria, which was two miles distant from the well.

8) Farrar, I, 208.

9) The difference in pronunciation concerned chiefly the vowel sounds. Among the consonants, the letter s, for instance, was sometimes pronounced s and sometimes sh by the Hebrews; but the Samaritans always pronounced it sh. Edersheim, I, 409, n. 3.

which, as she thought, would ordinarily not have been made. "How is it that Thou, being a Jew, askest drink of me, which am a woman of Samaria?" "For the Jews," adds the evangelist, "have no dealings with the Samaritans."

John 4, 10—15.   **16.**

As to the woman, this meeting was unsought and accidental, and still it was providential in the truest sense of the word; for our omniscient Savior knew that He would meet her, and He was seeking to save her soul. Gently He turned the request and the reply to the Samaritan woman's spiritual welfare. The woman was utterly unconscious of standing on the threshold of the greatest possibilities.[1] Jesus told her that, if she had known the gift of God and Him who was making the request, she would have asked Him to give her living water. This gift of God is the Messiah and the living water His salvation. But the woman did not understand. She pointed to the well, a hundred feet deep.[2] And still she must have been impressed, for she now addressed her Jewish stranger with a title of respect: "Sir,[3] Thou hast nothing to draw with, and the well[4] is deep; from whence hast Thou that living water?" Or was He probably thinking of other and better water, that is, living and running spring water, which He

Living Water. could procure independently of the well? But then, even so, why should that water be better than that which she could draw for herself, consecrated by the memories of the patriarchs, and which had sufficed for the ancient fathers, for their household and cattle? "Art Thou better than our father Jacob, which gave us the well and drank thereof himself and his children and his cattle?" Jesus did not expect the woman to understand. His purpose was to attract and then to fix her attention. He was not deterred by the hard literalism of her reply, which, on the contrary, He seized upon to bring home to her that He was speaking of living water in a figurative sense.[5] Certainly, His water was better in quality than that of the patriarch's well,

---

16,   1) Dods *sub loco.*

2) The diameter of the traditional well is about seven feet, its present depth about 75 feet. Much rubbish has fallen into it. In ancient times it must have been much deeper. *Int. St. B. Encycl. sub loco.* Andrews, 185.

3) Κύριε.

4) Both terms, πηγή, v. 6, and φρέαρ, v. 11, are used, the former meaning the spring of the well of water, the latter the dug and built pit, or well.

5) Farrar, I, 210.

better than all earthly things. "Whosoever drinketh of this water shall thirst again; but whosoever drinketh of the water that I shall give him shall never thirst; but the water that I shall give him shall be in him a well of water springing up into everlasting life." But even this explanation suggested nothing to the woman. While a desire had been awakened in her, she was still thinking of the laborious drudgery and tiresome daily journey to the well. If she could only do away with that! "Sir, give me this water that I thirst not, neither come hither to draw."

John 4, 16—26.   17.

Jesus changes the subject. He strikes out on a different avenue in His approach to the woman's heart. The woman's material interests, as revealed in her reply, indicate that as yet she feels no spiritual need. There was only one way to open that understanding, and that was to awaken in her a sense of guilt. "Go, call thy husband and come hither." The woman answers, "I have no husband." Jesus replies, "Thou hast well said, I have no husband; for thou hast had five husbands;[1] and he whom thou now hast is not thy husband." Why, is He acquainted with her past life? He is. Here we have the same proof of divine omniscience which He revealed in His talk with Nathanael.[2] He knew that she had been married five times, but that the man with whom she was now living was not her husband, but only her paramour. He certainly knew about her past[3] and now reminded her of her life of sin and shame. The woman did not dare to deny the imputation, but was forced to acknowledge that Jesus was right. "Sir, I perceive that Thou art a prophet." But she did not yet recognize in Jesus *that* Prophet. Neither was she ready to ask, What must I do to be saved? In truly feminine artfulness, partly defending herself by assuming the offensive and beclouding the issue, partly exposing herself, yet not completely confiding in the newly discovered prophet, she challenged Jesus with a standing problem of the Samaritan religion.[4] It was a question which divided the Jews and the Samaritans and struck at the heart of their respective national and religious interests. If this question was answered to her satisfaction, then she could also tell whether He was of a truth

---

17, 1) Not ἄνδρα, but ἄνδρας; not man, but men; not husband, but husbands.

2) John 1, 48.   3) V. 29.   4) Dods *sub loco.*

a prophet or whether the supernatural knowledge just displayed was only a trick. In the latter case she would have permitted herself falsely to confide in Him as a prophet. "Our fathers worshiped in this mountain; and ye say that in Jerusalem is the place where men ought to worship." In His reply the Lord showed marvelous

God Is a Spirit. wisdom and both tender human insight and consideration. As to the proper place for worship the Jews were undoubtedly right. Jerusalem was the place which the Lord had chosen. As compared with the hybrid and defective Samaritan worship, the worship of the Jews was pure and true.[5] Even if inwardly they had betrayed their solemn trust, outwardly they still *had* Moses and the prophets. The Messiah was of the seed of David, and salvation was of the Jews, from which race it was to pass on to all. But before and after entering into the merely formal and physical phase of the controversy, Jesus pours out to the woman a taste of the living water. The hour shall come, yea, has already come, when "ye shall neither in this mountain nor yet at Jerusalem worship the Father." "The hour cometh, and now is, when the true worshipers shall worship the Father in spirit and in truth." It is not a question of the *where* of *worship,* but of the *whom* and *how.* "God is a spirit; and they that worship Him must worship Him in spirit and in truth." His presence is not confined to a temple built by the hand of man, nor are those who worship Him bound to mere forms, ceremonies, rituals, symbols, and sacrifices. This is a picture in miniature of the New Testament Christian Church, which is not bound to a certain place of worship and its prescribed ceremonies. The true children of God, the believers in Christ, need not observe such and such outward forms; it is all a matter of a truly believing heart. — The woman was deeply touched and moved. Her heart was directed to Messianic thoughts. In her heart a longing was awakened for the Messiah. She shared with her people the Samaritan conception of the promised Messiah. "I know that Messias cometh, which is called Christ; when He is come, He will tell us all things." As opposed to the Jewish imperial Messianic expectations the Samaritans saw in the expected Christ chiefly a Teacher and a Guide. With a sigh she referred the final solution of this and other difficult problems to Him. And now Jesus opens wide the floodgates of living water: "I that speak unto thee am He."

17, 5) Farrar, I, 212.

John 4, 27—30.   **18.**

In the mean while the disciples had returned. They were astonished at finding their Master in conversation with a Samaritan woman. To talk with a strange, particularly a Samaritan, woman was supposed to be against the dignity of a Jewish Rabbi.[1] But they were gradually learning that Jesus was at times wont to do strange things for reasons which were not always clearly evident. Awe of Him, however, prevented them from making any inquiries as to

The Woman Speaks to Her Samaritan Friends.

the motive or as to the subject-matter of the exceptional conversation which they had just interrupted. At the arrival of the disciples the woman withdrew. Only conscious of the new well-spring which had risen in her heart, she forgot all about her water-bearing errand. She left her water-pot at the well, hastened to the city, announced her great discovery, and called upon her townspeople to seek with her the prophet whom she ventured to describe as the Messiah: "Come, see a man which told me all things that ever I did; is not this the Christ?" This, on the part of the woman, was skilful leading without seeming to lead.[2] The curiosity of the townsfolk was aroused, and a number of them immediately set out on a mission of seeking Christ.

John 4, 31—38.   **19.**

The disciples now urged Jesus to eat of the food which they had brought from the city. But the soul of Jesus was otherwise engaged. At the moment He felt no need for bodily food. "I have meat to eat that ye know not of." There was food and satisfaction for Him in things of which the disciples were not aware. The

Discourse on the Fields White Already to Harvest.

disciples did not understand. No one could be seen who had given Him food. But Jesus explained: "My meat is to do the will of Him that sent Me." And, looking up, He saw the Samaritan townsfolk approaching through the fresh green of the springing grain. This, in line with His thoughts about the newly won Samaritan woman, probably suggested a notable discourse on the harvest-fields. The seed had been sown in November. Now in December, a month later, the fields were already fresh and green.[1] "Say not ye,

18, 1) Rabbinical authorities, quoted by Dods *sub loco;* Farrar, I, 214; etc.
    2) Dods *sub loco.*
19, 1) On the chronological value of this passage see Wieseler, 194 ff.; Meyer *sub loco;* Andrews, 182 ff.

There are yet four months, and then cometh harvest?" That is, the 16th day of Nisan, on which day harvesting legally commenced by the offering of the first sheaf.[2] "Behold, I say unto you, Lift up your eyes and look on the fields; for they are white already to harvest." The disciples saw only the green fields of springing corn. But in the approaching Samaritans the prophetic eye of Jesus saw a harvest-field.[3] There were the real first-fruits of a promising mission-harvest. In this field there was a sowing and a reaping unto life everlasting. "One soweth, and another reapeth"; but both he that sows and he that reaps should rejoice together. Jesus, the Sower, had just sown the seed. But already there was a harvest, not only in the Samaritan woman, but in the friends whom the woman was bringing to Christ. For the disciples there would also be a harvest, even in Samaria, and unto the ends of the earth. "I sent [4] you to reap that whereon ye bestowed no labor; other men labored, and ye are entered into their labors."

John 4, 39—42.   20.

It was as Jesus had said, "The fields are white already to harvest." The newly won Samaritan woman missionary had done good work. "Many of the Samaritans of that city believed on Him for the saying of the woman." And the personal intercourse with Jesus convinced many more. "And many more believed because of His own Word." As a result of the first interview with the Stranger at Jacob's Well an invitation was extended to Jesus by

Reception by the Samaritans. the Samaritans to tarry with them. He accepted the invitation, abode with them two days, and established faith in Him as the Messiah by His Word, which among them apparently did not need the aid of signs and wonders. The final result of this visit is summed up in an expression by the believing Sycharites to the first Samaritan missionary for Christ: "Now we believe, not because of thy saying; for we have heard Him ourselves and know that this is indeed the Christ, the Savior of the world." To suppose that the time was too short for this confession and that the latter part of this expression was put into the mouth of the Samaritans by the evangelist John is to deny the power of Christ's Word and to suppose that for two whole days Jesus did not disclose to them that He was indeed the Savior of the world.[1]

19, 2) Lev. 23, 10 ff.; Deut. 16, 9.   3) See Acts 8, 5.

4) Past tense. Not prophetic; with their calling as disciples their mission was already involved. See Meyer *in loco.*

20, 1) Meyer and Dods *sub loco.*

John 4, 43—45.   **21.**

After a stay of two days with the friendly Samaritans, Jesus returned to Galilee. His absence had extended over eight months, since the Passover in spring, shortly after His first miracle in Cana. We remember the reason for His departure from Judea at this time,[1] namely, the fact that more people were flocking to Him than to John, while in the counsel of God, John was to continue for a while yet to prepare the way for Him.[2] Nothing is said about the imprisonment of John at this time, nor about the instrumentality of the Pharisees in procuring his arrest, nor about the threatened collision of the Jewish authorities with Jesus on this account, nor about the resulting fear and flight of Jesus.[3] These are all deductions based upon gratuitous assumptions. No doubt He withdrew to Galilee to seek retirement for Himself and to await

Return to Galilee. such time as He would see fit to begin His own great ministry in earnest. In Galilee He would *not* be likely to be too highly honored on account of the prejudices connected with His humble origin and the familiarity created by the knowledge of His home surroundings; *"for* Jesus Himself testified,*"* either now or previously,[4] *"*that a prophet hath no honor in his own country.*"* Nor was He mistaken. In the beginning of His great Galilean ministry His first public appearance in Nazareth was promptly followed by His first rejection.[5] Neither was He deceived by this first gleam of transient reception.[6] *"*Then, when He was come into Galilee, the Galileans received Him, having seen all the things that He did at Jerusalem at the feast; for they also went unto the feast.*"* They *"*received*"* Him. The evangelist is very careful in His statement. The reception of the Galileans, based only upon signs and wonders, was not true, genuine faith such as was that of the Samaritans, which was grounded upon His saving Word.[7]

21, 1) No. 13.   2) John 4, 1—3.
    3) The various views of commentators.
    4) And afterwards, Luke 4, 24; Matt. 13, 57; Mark 6, 4.
    5) Luke 4, 22—30.   6) Compare John 2, 23—25.
    7) Compare v. 48 with v. 41. After considerable study of this most "perplexing passage" (Meyer) of John the above is the interpretation which we finally have decided upon to offer. The trouble is in the little word "for" in v. 44 and in the last two words of the same verse, "own country." A number of different explanations have been advanced for the particle "for," none of which, however, fully satisfy. In bringing the "for" into direct connection with v. 43 (as we must), compared with vv. 1—3, we approximate the view of Dods, with the exception of the "threatened collision with the Pharisees" in vv. 1—3. And as to the "own country" of Jesus,

John 4, 46. 47.   **22.**

Whether or not Jesus, on His return to Galilee, made a short stopover at Nazareth, just off the main caravan road, for many years His former home and probably even now the home of His sisters,[1] is not stated or even intimated in any of the four gospels. Most likely He continued His journey, at least as far as Cana, with Capernaum, the home of Simon and John and, it seems, the present home of His mother and His brethren,[2] as a possible objective. On His way there He was met by an officer of King Herod's court. Cana was the home of Nathanael, and it was here, we remember, that Jesus performed His first miracle, about nine months previously. We do not know the name of the royal officer nor the nature of his office, but because a Joanna, wife of Chuza, Herod's steward, afterwards appears as a follower of Jesus,[3] and because in consequence of the miracle here wrought this courtier believed

The Nobleman's Son. and all his house, it has been rather reasonably conjectured that it was none other than Chuza himself.[4] An urgent need prompted him to leave the bedside of his dying son at Capernaum and to walk the sixteen miles of hard traveling up the steep Way of the Sea across the hills to Cana to make an earnest appeal to Jesus, whose fame had preceded Him to Galilee and of whose arrival there he had heard. "When he heard that Jesus was come out of Judea into Galilee, he went unto Him and besought Him that He would come down and heal his son; for he was at the point of death." Outside of the general designation "fever" the nature of the sickness is not described. We need not assume that in his appeal for help this officer was actuated by his belief in Jesus as the Messiah.[5] Most likely despairing of a cure through other means already employed, he resolved to appeal to the new Galilean prophet. He believed that Jesus was able to heal his son, but he considered the personal presence of Jesus necessary to effect the cure. "And besought Him that He would come," sixteen miles, "and heal his son." Being a person of high standing, he did not hesitate to make the request.

---

a number of homes are proposed: Judea as opposed to Galilee in general, or *vice versa*, or Nazareth and Capernaum in particular as opposed to Galilee in general.

22, 1) Mark 6, 3. Chapter VI, 25. Farrar, I, 233.

2) John 2, 12. But Weiss, I, 378; II, 44, and Andrews, 189, think that the family of Jesus now resided at Cana.

3) Luke 8, 3.   4) Farrar, I, 231.   5) Edersheim, I, 424.

John 4, 48. 49.   23.

Jesus replied: "Except ye see signs and wonders, ye will not believe." It was not the purpose of Jesus to set Himself up as a miracle-monger, to gain fame for His healing powers, but through the miracles which He performed He desired to attest His doctrine and the truth that He was indeed that Prophet who was to come. Even without miracles His divine Word should have been believed.

"Except Ye See Signs and Wonders." But the courtier was in no mood for spiritual discussion. He thought only of his sick child. It was already one o'clock,[1] and Capernaum was sixteen miles away. "Sir, come down ere my child die." His confidence in the Lord's ability to help was still unshaken, that is, under the condition that He would personally appear at the bedside of his son, and as long as there was still life in him. Notice the little word "ere" in v. 49. Would it be too late after his son had passed away? Would the faith of the tormented father then have been put to too great a test?

John 4, 50—54.   24.

But Jesus knew what He was doing. After checking the request, which appears to have had little root in spiritual conviction, and rebuking the spirit which demanded signs as the ground of faith, He still showed that the nobleman's confidence was not misplaced. He was actually the benevolent physician for whom He was taken — and more. "Go thy way; thy son liveth." It is not necessary for Me to go along with thee. "Thy son liveth"; that is, he is cured and no longer at the point of death. "And the man believed the word that Jesus had spoken unto him, and he went his way." That was faith based upon the Word, as it should be, and not merely upon a miracle. And it was faith unmixed with

"Thy Son Liveth." doubt. "He went his way," believing, rejoicing, although he could not yet see that Jesus had kept His word. Believing and trusting, he did not even hurry. "He that believeth shall not make haste." [1] He could have reached Capernaum that night, but, calmed by faith in the promise, he slept at some point along the way. The next morning his servants met him with the joyful news. To his inquiry as to the time when the improvement had been accomplished, they

---

23, 1) The common reckoning of time. See No. 15. Chapter VI, 16.
24, 1) Is. 28, 16.

replied, "Yesterday at the seventh hour," that is, at 1 P. M., "the fever left him." "So the father knew that it was at the same hour in the which Jesus said unto him, Thy son liveth. And himself believed and his whole house." Notice the remarkable progress his faith had made. From a mere belief in the healing power of Jesus to faith in His Word, and then to absolute faith in Him as the Messiah, with a blessed effect upon the members of his house. Thus for a second time Jesus performed a miracle immediately upon His return from Judea to Galilee.[2]

24, 2) John 2, 11. If there were any unrecorded miracles during the brief stay at Capernaum, John 2, 12 as compared with Luke 4, 23, then the above is the correct understanding. But since the "whatsoever we have heard done in Capernaum" might possibly (though hardly) refer to this particular miracle performed at Cana from a distance, the understanding might also be: the second Galilean miracle. Weiss (II, 45) thinks that this miracle is the same as that narrated Matt. 8, 5—13; but the differences are so evident that his view hardly deserves serious consideration.

CHAPTER VIII.

THE UNNAMED FEAST.

THE IMPRISONMENT OF JOHN, 28 A. D.

A. U. C.	779	780	781	782	783
A. D.	26	27	28	29	30
Age of Jesus	30	31	32	33	34
Passovers		I	II	III	IV

John 5, 1.   **1.**

Following the return of Jesus from His early Judean ministry in December, 27 A. D., our Lord seems to have lived in retirement until He again went up to Jerusalem to attend a feast of the Jews in the following spring. Neither do we hear of the disciples until **The Connection.** the Synoptists take up the account. In St. John they do not appear again until at the feeding of the five thousand.[1] It seems that after the return of their Master through Samaria to Galilee they were permitted to return to their families and their accustomed labors, not to be recalled[2] until the beginning of the great Galilean ministry in spring. Possibly there was one exception: John, the beloved disciple, who, as a probable witness, brings the account of the story we are about to relate.

John 5, 1.   **2.**

"After this there was a feast of the Jews; and Jesus went up to Jerusalem." [1] We would indeed welcome a definite proof that this festival was the Passover; for then we would have a chrono-

---

1,   1) John 6, 3.

2) This may explain the intervening silence in the Synoptists' account as also the supplementary character of the Gospel of St. John.

2,   1) Because in 6, 4 a Passover is mentioned as still approaching, Keppler, Meyer, Wieseler, and others, have argued that reference is here made to a festival between the December of Christ's return and the Passover of 28 A. D., deciding upon Purim, the Feast of Lots, celebrated in March in commemoration of the national delivery from the bloody designs of Haman, Esther 9, 21. But the Passover of John 6, 4, which Jesus most likely did *not* attend, may just as well have been the Passover of 29 A. D. While the annual Passover was a festival which Jesus would *naturally* attend unless prevented by open hostility (none as yet appeared), Purim was more of a secular or patriotic holiday, accompanied with hilarity, feasting, and the exchange of gifts. Edersheim, placing Jesus' return from Judea in the middle of May and inclined to identify the unnamed feast with either the Ingathering of Wood or the Feast of Trumpets (August and September), "can scarcely conceive our

logical tag for determining the length of Christ's ministry. But it seems that the evangelist's inclusion of this notice was not prompted by chronological considerations. From a reference to a Jewish festival, which explains the presence of Jesus in Jerusalem, the evangelist proceeds to the account of a miracle, which, in turn,

"A Feast of the Jews." is introduced by the information that "there is at Jerusalem" [2] a well-known pool, called Bethesda in Hebrew, rather Aramaic, and enclosed within five arches, or porches, presumably near the Sheep Gate, at the northeastern corner of the city.

John 5, 2—13. **3.**

Various interpretations are offered for the term which, contrary to his usual practise,[1] John himself has left indefinite. No doubt the name Bethesda was designative, and we are quite willing to accept the common explanation Beth Chisda, that is, House of

Bethesda. Mercy; for this it was about to become. According to the Authorized Version its location is given "by the Sheep *Market*" and in the Revised Version by the Sheep Gate;[2] but even here the term employed to describe its more precise location has in part been supplied by the translators. All that we know from the Greek is that it was a pool provided with a pentagon of covered porticoes, or porches, at a site in or near Jerusalem which

---

Lord going up to a feast observed with such boisterous merriment as Purim was, while the season of the year in which it falls would scarcely tally with the statement that a great multitude of sick people were laid down in the porches of Bethesda." (I, 460; II, 768.) The question cannot be definitely decided. Nearly all the Jewish festivals have been mentioned as being the unnamed Feast of John 5, 1; but the opinions are chiefly divided between Purim and Passover. Fortunately, for the understanding of the passage it matters little which festival one believes it to have been. In our choice of the Passover in 28 A. D. we are unconscious of a "most glaring arbitrariness in placing a *spatium vacuum* of a year between it and 6, 1—4" (Meyer, who argues for Purim) because we remember that, whether the interval was a month or a year, John's apparent purpose in writing his gospel was not to present a complete outline, but to supplement the Synoptists' accounts of the life of Christ. There is no need of entering deeper into the discussion. For a more detailed examination of the problem see Andrews, 189 ff.; Meyer *sub loco;* and Robertson, *Harmony,* 267 ff.

2, 2) John's gospel may or may not have been written before the destruction of Jerusalem, to either of which conceptions the use of the present tense ἔστι is not opposed. What John represents is that the bath was still existing at his time. Compare his use of ἦν in 11, 18: "Bethany *was* nigh"; 18, 1: "where *was* a garden" (Gethsemane); 19, 41: "there *was* a garden" (at Golgotha).

3, 1) Compare 19, 13. 17.
   2) Neh. 3, 1. 32; 12, 39.

had something to do with sheep. The Sheep Gate, St. Stephen's
Gate (?), has been suggested through which the sheep destined for
sacrifices were led into the city;   likewise a market in which sacrificial sheep were sold; also a pool by the sheep-pool in which the
sheep used for sacrifice were washed.[3]   Of the several sites proposed — all in the same general vicinity — the traditional pool
recently rediscovered a little northwest of the Church of St. Anne
seems to have the greatest probabilities in its favor, although it is
impossible to speak on this matter with authority.[4]   All of this,
however, is of subordinate importance compared with the marvelous
facts of the narrative itself.[5]

John 5, 2—13.   **4.**

In the five porches surrounding the pool a great multitude of
impotent folk, blind, halt, and withered, lay in anxious hope of
a miraculous cure. They were waiting for the moving of the water.
Bethesda was most likely an intermittent pool, with periodic
bubbling and gushing of waters, which is still the character of
a number of Palestinian springs.[1]   At the first moment of bubbling
it possessed the highest degree of healing quality for the first person
who could scramble into it to profit by immersion. "For an angel
went down at a certain season into the pool and troubled the water;

**The Troubling
of the Water.**
whosoever then first, after the troubling of
the water, stepped in was made whole of
whatsoever disease he had."   We know that
the Lord can and does employ angels as His ministering spirits
in the service of mankind sent forth to carry out His commands.[2]
It is not stated that the angel was visible. A startling fact is here
related, wholly unlike anything related in any other part of
Scripture. However, we know that the evil angels afflict man with
all kinds of sicknesses and maladies; on the other hand, the holy
angels give suffering mankind various remedies which tend to
restore their health.[3]   In this case the angel of God "troubled
the water," *i. e.*, caused it to bubble up; not every day, but only
"at a certain season," whenever the Lord sent him to that pool for
this purpose.

3,   3) See Meyer and Dods *sub loco.*
      4) Andrews, 200.
      5) Edersheim, I, 463.
4,   1) Farrar, I, 372.
      2) Heb. 1, 14.
      3) Stoeckhardt, *B. G.,* 46.

John 5, 2—13.   **5.**

We are introduced to a man who had been helplessly infirm for thirty-eight years, possibly due to youthful excesses.[1] For many years he had haunted the porticoes of this health-giving pool. Friends had carried him there; but when the favorable moments of periodic troubling of the waters occurred, others more fortunate and less feeble had always managed to struggle in before him. The result was a life of hopeless despair. Thus Jesus found him with cheerless imbecility written over his face. He looked on him with heartfelt pity. According to His omniscience He knew how long the poor man had suffered.[2] He resolved to help him whom no one had helped before. "Wilt thou be · made whole?" But why ask that question? Certainly, he would be

"Wilt Thou be Made Whole?" delivered. But it was not a question of will and desire, but of opportunity.[3] Hopelessly he describes his discouraging condition: "Sir, I have no man, when the water is troubled, to put me into the pool; but while I am coming, another steppeth down before me." His thoughts were far from help as regards this unknown Stranger, and he was still futilely trusting in man. If only I had a *man* to help me! But Jesus had resolved upon a speedier and more effectual aid. "Rise, take up thy bed, and walk." With the Lord it was not a question of opportunity or of human aid. He *gave* what He commanded, and He commanded what He would. "And immediately the man was made whole and took up his bed and walked." For a moment the sick man hardly realized what had happened to him. He did not even know who had spoken the words. In glad amazement he looked around to thank his unknown Benefactor. But the crowd was large, and Jesus, anxious to escape noisy excitement, quietly "swam out"[4] of observation.

John 5, 2—13.   **6.**

But it was on a Sabbath-day! In spite of the marvelous cure many scrupulous and jealous eyes were upon this happy bed-bearing and freshly discharged member of the House of Mercy. Immediately he was rebuked by the members of the Sanhedrin:[1] "It is

---

5,   1) V. 14.   2) V. 6.

    3) *Pop. Com.*, 434. Dods *sub loco.*   4) Ἐξένευσεν, v. 13.

6,   1) The particular Jews are quite regularly so named by John because of their hostility to Jesus, vv. 15. 18. See also John 6, 41. 52 (in Galilee). Chapter XVI, 10.

the Sabbath-day; it is not lawful for thee to carry thy bed." They did not see the cure, but only, as they thought, a flagrant violation of the Law. Had not a man during the sojourning in the wilderness been stoned to death for carrying sticks on a Sabbath-day? [2] Did not the prophet Jeremiah say: "Take heed to yourselves and bear no burden on a Sabbath-day"? [3] It is true. But this was not marketing or trading or carrying burdens for personal interests and gain. [4] This was not a case of desecrating the Sabbath, but of honoring God for the cure which had been marvelously wrought

"It Is the Sabbath-Day."

and a sign or a witness to that effect, even if the impotent man was as yet ignorant of the fact that he had been cured by Christ. The man had not violated the Law of God, the basic principle of which is love; [5] he had merely acted contrary to Rabbinic traditions, according to which, *e. g.*, a nailed shoe might not be worn on a Sabbath because it was a burden, and one man might carry a loaf of bread, but two men must not carry it between them, and so forth, to the utmost limit of tyrannous absurdity. [6] Sensing a higher Law than that of the Sabbath, the healed man replied: "He that made me whole, the same said unto me, Take up thy bed and walk." This simple statement was followed by an angry reply, "What man is that," not that made thee whole, but "who said unto thee," gave the wicked command, "Take up thy bed and walk"? But so little apparently was the person of Jesus generally known in the suburbs of Jerusalem that neither the healed man himself nor any of the witnesses of the miracle could make the requested identification.

John 5, 14—47.   7.

The scene changes. Not long afterwards Jesus found the formerly impotent man in the Temple, whither he had evidently gone to thank God for his recovery. Improving the opportunity, Jesus admonished him not to bring upon himself a return of the infirmity by a relapse into former sinful excesses: "Sin no more lest a worse thing come unto thee." Jesus was interested not only in the welfare of his body, but also, and particularly, in the welfare of his immortal soul. He endeavored through His miracle to bring the man to repentance, in which, we assume, He was successful.

6,   2) Num. 15, 32—36.
3) Jer. 17, 21. Farrar, I, 375.   4) Compare Neh. 13, 15 ff.
5) Rom. 13, 10.   6) Farrar, I, 376.

No other conversation is recorded. But on this occasion the healed man learned, either directly or indirectly, who it was to whom he owed bodily health, gratitude, and obedience. The man now left his Benefactor and told "the Jews" that it was Jesus who had made

The Sanhedrin Informed.

him whole. But why must a special report be made to the ecclesiastical powers? Was it gratitude, the desire to gain recognition for Jesus among the members of the ruling class? Or was it a defiance of the constituted authorities? Or was it even, as has been suggested,[1] base ingratitude in seeking self-protection at the expense of another? Hardly. It was but natural for him to go to the Jews. He had been accused of Sabbath-breaking. And now, being in a position to supply the name of Him who had made him whole and, as he thought, to furnish a sufficiently complete vindication of the authority in obedience to which he had been charged with breaking the Law, he answered the question they had put to him, no doubt desiring to intimate at the same time that He who had the power to perform so great a miracle had a right to give him the command that He did and that, having obeyed such an authority, he ought to be acquitted of the charge of having broken the Sabbath.

John 5, 14—47.   8.

But the consequences of this report were immediate and momentous. For the first time Jesus was brought into direct conflict with the Jewish authorities, and this changed the entire tenor of His remaining life. Untouched by the evidence of tender compassion, unmoved by the display of truly miraculous powers, the Jewish inquisitors were at once up in arms against Him with their favorite piece of legalism.[1] "Therefore did the Jews persecute Jesus and sought to slay Him, because He had done these things on a Sabbath-day." A bitter conflict was commenced, which was not terminated until the death of Jesus on the cross. And not even

Beginning of Conflict with Jewish Authorities.

then. In defending His action, Jesus made the statement: "My Father worketh hitherto, and I work." As a result the Jews sought all the more to kill Him, "because He not only had broken the Sabbath, but said also that God was His Father, making Himself equal with God." Their inference was very correct. But to their horrified ears the words

---

7, 1) By Farrar, I, 378.   8, 1) Farrar, I, 378.

sounded like blasphemy. — Now follows an extensive and powerful discourse of Christ concerning Himself. Whether the words were spoken publicly in the Temple or in retirement before some committee of the Sanhedrin, we do not know. At any rate, the great Rabbis who had brought Jesus into their presence in order to warn Him were implacably infuriated because Jesus was warning *them.* They thought they could overawe Him; but they trembled and gnashed their teeth, though they dared not act, as Jesus overawed *them* by assuming the awe-inspiring dignity of the Son of God.

John 5, 14—47.   **9.**

In reply to the charge of Sabbath-breaking Jesus had pointed them to the example of His heavenly Father. The work of the Father was not terminated on the seventh day of Creation, but continued to the present hour. "My Father worketh hitherto, and I work." Jesus asserted that He was the Son of God, not in the sense in which other men may be called the sons of God, but in a sense which predicated equality with God. The accusers of Jesus understood this implication. But far from denying or hiding this equality with the Father in order to placate the Jewish authorities, Jesus insisted upon it in a powerful discourse, which explained His relation to the heavenly Father. There is perfect equality and agreement between the Son and the Father. "The Son can do nothing of Himself but what He seeth the Father do." And the Father takes a loving interest in the Son.[1] The same divine works and honor are equally shared between them. For instance, as the Father quickens, even so does the Son. It does not matter much what kind of quickening is meant. "The Son quickeneth whom He will," even though a person has lain as long and has been as incapable of helping himself as the impotent man, indeed, even though he be dead, spiritually or physically. In addition, the Father

Testimony of Jesus Concerning Himself.

has committed all Judgment to the Son because He is the only Mediator between God and men. It might seem incredible to them that the apportioning to men their eternal destiny should be assigned to the Son. But so it is. This supreme prerogative is given with the purpose "that all men should honor the Son even as they honor the Father." In denouncing Him for breaking the Sabbath, the Jews were really committing the great sin of dishonoring the Father. And by rejecting His Word, which

9,   1) Matt. 3, 17.

has the power to give them eternal life, they were shutting the gates of heaven against themselves. "Verily, verily, I say unto you, He that heareth My Word and believeth on Him that sent Me hath everlasting life and shall not come into condemnation." Even now He had given evidence of the power of His word by granting health to the impotent man and quickening him to a new spiritual life through it. Neither is this power confined to the care of this impotent man or merely to the spiritual sphere. "The hour is coming, and now is, when the dead shall hear the voice of the Son of God; and they that hear shall live." Yes, "the hour is coming in the which all that are in the graves shall hear His voice and shall come forth." On the Last Day the believers shall be raised to the resurrection of life and the unbelievers unto the resurrection of damnation. Spiritual quickening, raising the dead, and final Judgment are the works committed by the Father to the Son.

John 5, 14—47. 10.

Affidavits and certificates are not necessary for these truths, because these are statements made by One who is Himself Life and Truth. But since, according to human standards, the Speaker is making statements concerning Himself which, considering their nature, require verification, an appeal to a number of witnesses is made. The Jewish authorities are reminded of the delegation they sent to John. "Ye sent unto John, and he bare witness unto the truth." Whatever report this committee had made of the interview with John, it is a fact that John had given this testimony of Jesus: "There standeth One among you whom ye know not; He it is." [1] "He must increase, but I must decrease." [2] These words had been fulfilled, for it seems that John had now been imprisoned. "He was [3] a burning and a shining light; and ye were willing for a season to rejoice in his light." But they were not willing to heed his call to repentance. Another witness appears in the Father, rather in "the works which the Father hath given Me to finish. The same works that I do bear witness of Me that the Father hath sent Me. And the Father Himself, which hath sent Me, hath borne witness of Me," namely, in the sacred writings of the Old Testament. But that is the complete perversity of unbe-

---

10, 1) John 1, 26. 27.   2) John 3, 30.

3) The ἦν naturally refers to something in the past, but it does not, as some think (Dods *sub loco*), necessarily refer to the death of John, which did not occur until later.

lief: [4]) searching the Christ-containing Scriptures and still not finding Christ. And that is exactly what happened to them in spite of
the fact that they occupied themselves so much with the Scriptures.
They searched them, even counting the very letters; for in them
they imagined they had eternal life. Theoretically this was true,
but practically it was not the case because they did not find Christ.
Ye "search the Scriptures; for in them ye think ye have eternal
life; and they are they which testify of Me." A close study of
them reveals to us many testimonies to Christ as the Messiah; even
the books of Moses, another witness of whom they boasted, but

**Christ's Appeal
to Witnesses.**
whom they did not understand. "There is
one that accuseth you, even Moses, in whom
ye trust. For had ye believed Moses, ye
would have believed Me; for he wrote of Me." [5]) But since they
evidently had already rejected the true meaning of the Messianic
promises in the written words, how would they now believe the
spoken word to which they were listening with rage? This dispute
marked the commencement of the rupture of Jesus with the Jewish
authorities. Horrified at what seemed to them the pinnacle of
blasphemy, it was to be on their part a struggle unto death with
their Messiah, who had come to give them life. The hour of
conflict, however, had not yet arrived. At this point the evangelist
John interrupts his account of the life of Jesus, not to take it up
again until the feeding of the five thousand.

11.

Matt. 4, 12. Mark 1, 14. (Luke 3, 19. 20) 4, 14.

It was probably in the early spring of 28 A. D. and shortly
before the events just related that John the Baptist was cast into
prison. When we last met him in December of the previous year,
he was still engaged at Aenon, near Salim, in his work of preparing the way of the Lord.[1]) At that time a question had arisen
between his disciples and the Jews about purifying, which caused
the former to complain to their master that Jesus was making
more disciples than John. At the news of this, and out of consideration for His friend and forerunner, Jesus went into retirement until such time as the work of the forerunner would be
finished, when His own public ministry would begin in earnest.

10, 4) Meyer *sub loco.*
     5) Gen. 3, 15; 12, 3; 18, 18; 22, 18; 49, 10; Deut. 18, 15. 18.
11, 1) John 3, 23. 24. Chapter VII, 11. 12.

This time had now arrived. The public testimony of the forerunner was forcefully and suddenly checked. It seems that John had brought the message of repentance from Aenon northward into Galilee or across the Jordan into Perea. The last scene of his public ministry was in the neighborhood of both. At any rate, he brought his message of repentance and preparation for the coming Kingdom too close to the ears of Herod Antipas, to whom Galilee and Perea belonged. John was very outspoken in his language. Not only did

The Imprisonment of John.

he preach repentance in general, but he mentioned particular sins. And especially did he incur the hatred of Herodias, the former wife of Philip, now illegally married to her brother-in-law and uncle Herod Antipas. But in the eyes of the Galilean rulers the pet sins of the Herodian family, adultery, marriage irregularities, and other dark deeds, were not a matter for a coarse wilderness preacher to criticize or discuss. And what about this talk of the Kingdom? Had Herodias not severed her marriage bond with Philip [2] in her ambition [3] to make Antipas king of the Jews? Whereupon "Herod the tetrarch, being reproved by him for Herodias, his brother Philip's wife, and for all the evils which Herod had done, added yet this above all, that he shut up John in prison." In addition, Josephus suggests that Herod "feared lest the great influence John had over the people might put it into his power and inclination to raise a rebellion." [4] But if fear of a rebellion was an additional motive with Herod to imprison John the Baptist, he altogether misunderstood the work and mission of this great preacher. The place of imprisonment is given [5] as Machaerus, a castle east of the Dead Sea. This removal of John from the scene of activity served Jesus as a suggestion from His heavenly Father to enter to the full extent upon His Messianic career. [6]

11, 2) At one time named as successor of Herod the Great, but then dropped in his will and apparently living as private man of means in Rome. Josephus, *Ant.,* XVII, III, 2; XVIII, V, 1. *Wars,* I, XXX, 7.

3) *Wars,* II, IX, 6.   4) *Ant.,* XVIII, V, 2.

5) By Josephus.   6) Stoeckhardt, 51.

CHAPTER IX.

THE BEGINNING OF THE GREAT GALILEAN MINISTRY.

OPENING EVENTS.

Probably end of April, A. D. 28.

1.

Matt. 4, 17. Mark 1, 14. 15. Luke 4, 14. 15.

The imprisonment of John marked a great turning-point in the life of Jesus.[1] With the removal of the forerunner the time had arrived for Jesus to identify Himself as that Prophet who was to come. This He had already done when He proclaimed Himself in Jerusalem as the Son of the Father. But the leaders of the Jews had not received Him. They accused Him of Sabbath-breaking, charged Him with blasphemy, and contemplated taking His life. The introductory labors of the Baptist and His own work had been unavailing towards gaining their hearts, so that they would have accepted and proclaimed Him as the Messiah. David's city

A Great Turning-Point. was no safe place for David's Son. The house of His heavenly Father contained no auditorium for the saving message of His Son. And since in Judea the influence of a now hostile Sanhedrin was supreme, there was little likelihood of His winning recognition among the Judeans at the present time. But the rejection in Jerusalem was not regarded as final. If they, the leaders, would not recognize Him as what He truly was, He would present Himself to the nation at large. If He could not gain His people via Jerusalem, He would gain His Jerusalem via the people. Thus a great ministry was begun in and around the still predominantly Jewish[2] Galilee, where the Sanhedrin had no civil jurisdiction[3] and Herod Antipas was not likely to interfere.[4] Thus the early Judean ministry had come to a close.

1, 1) Andrews, 209 ff.

2) In spite of the many Phenician, Arabian, Syrian, and Greek inhabitants. Schuerer, I, I, 192; Andrews, 214.

3) Schuerer, II, I, 185. The Sanhedrin had no judicial jurisdiction over Jesus so long as He remained in Galilee. In a certain sense, no doubt, it exercised such jurisdiction over every Jewish community in the world and in that sense over Galilee as well. But it was only within the limits of Judea proper that it exercised any *direct* authority. However, compare Acts 9, 2.

4) In spite of the fact that he caused the arrest of John. Indeed, we know that for a considerable time he took no notice at all of the Lord and

2.

Matt. 4, 17. Mark 1, 14. 15. Luke 4, 14. 15.

The general character of the message of Jesus was the same as that of John: "Repent; for the kingdom of heaven is at hand." But there is an additional note sounded in the word "believe," which settles the nature of the Kingdom: "Repent ye

The Galilean Ministry Begun.

and believe the Gospel." However, while John, in keeping with his character, sought his listeners in the wilderness, Jesus, besides carrying on an open-air ministry, sought His hearers also "in the synagogs, being glorified of all." And as to His success: "There went out a fame of Him through all the region round about." But at first, at the very outset, a very bitter rejection awaited Him.

Luke 4, 16—30.   3.

According to the sequence of events which to us seems to be the correct one,[1] the Sabbath controversy in Jerusalem was followed by the Sabbath rejection at Nazareth, possibly even on the following Sabbath. It must have been with mingled feelings that Jesus "came to Nazareth, where He had been brought up." Great changes had occurred since He had left it in the early winter months a year before.[2] This is the town where He had lived with His mother and His foster-father since the days of His early child-

At Nazareth.

hood.[3] Here, no doubt, He had helped bury His foster-father Joseph, the husband of Mary and faithful guardian of His tender youth. Here He had received His training, learned His trade, and formed His associations, "increasing in wisdom and stature and in favor with God and man." [4] Here He had waited in silence to take up the work upon which He had now fully entered. This town He would honor in His first visit within its walls as the great Galilean Prophet. It was on a Sabbath-day. He entered the synagog, as was His custom

---

His work; and if he heard of Him, he regarded Him as one of the Rabbis, who was gathering disciples around Him and believed His work to be without political significance. Not till after the Baptist's death did he desire to see Him; and thus the Lord, unmolested by the authorities, could visit all parts of the province and teach openly in all places. Andrews, 214.

3, 1) Some harmonists make this visit parallel with Matt. 13. 53—58 and Mark 6. 1—6, which apparently, however, happened later. While there are points of similarity, the points of difference are more numerous and more plainly marked. For discussion see Andrews, 218; Meyer *sub loco;* Meyer sub Matt. 13, 53; and Wieseler, 258.

2) Chapter VI, 1.   3) Chapter IV, 43.   4) Luke 2, 52.

since His childhood days. Sabbath after Sabbath He had occupied His usual place and listened to the Word of God read and expounded there; but now — since the opening of His public ministry — He Himself preached the Gospel of God.

Luke 4, 16—30.   **4.**

Although the synagogs were popularly traced back to patriarchal times, it is quite generally supposed that these institutions of Jewish worship and instruction [1] originated during, or in consequence of, the Babylonian Captivity. We can easily understand how the need of places and opportunities for common worship on Sabbath and feast-days must have been keenly felt in those trying times.[2] After the return to Jerusalem the institution was transplanted to Palestine and at the same time regarded as all the more necessary for the perpetuation of Judaism on foreign soil. In the scattered Jewish communities those ignorant of Hebrew would not only gather for prayer, but would also have the assigned Scripture-lessons read and paraphrased to them.[3] In the course of time a confession of faith, prayers, and sermons or addresses were added. Thus the regular synagog services were gradually introduced, first
Synagogs. on Sabbaths and holidays and then on ordinary days, at the same time as, and in a sort of internal correspondence with, the worship at the Temple. The services on the market days, Mondays and Thursdays, were special, these being the days when the country people usually came to town. As a rule, every community would build its own synagog. These houses of worship, erected by popular subscription or private munificence, were built of local stone or, in wealthier communities, of white marble, simply porticoed rectangular halls, of which the projecting extremity usually pointed towards Jerusalem.[4] The furnishing was simple. Seats were arranged for the men and likewise for the women, who, however, shrouded in their long veils, were seated behind a lattice or in a gallery. At one end there was a painted ark, or chest, which contained the rolls of Sacred Scripture. In front of this, facing the congregation, the chief seats were placed for the ten or more men of leisure, the leaders of the

---

4,   1) For a more detailed discussion see Schuerer, II, II, 58 ff.; *Int. St. B. Encycl. sub loco;* Edersheim, I, 431 ff.; Farrar, I, 222 ff.

2) Edersheim, I, 432.

3) Targum, targuming. The Scripture read in Hebrew and repeated in the vernacular, the Aramaic.

4) Edersheim, I, 434. Not towards the east, *i. e.,* the consecrated direction of Mohammedan worship.

synagog. Preeminent among them was the seat of the presiding elder, or chief of the synagog. On one side there was an elevation, or platform, on which there was a lectern, or desk, from which the Law was read. Clergy, properly speaking, there were none; for the office of priests and Levites for the Temple-worship in Jerusalem was altogether different. There were, however, a number of officials. Besides the elders, who constituted the local tribunal, there was the presiding elder, or ruler, whose duty it was to keep order and to appoint at each meeting the reader or expounder of the Law and the Prophets; the servant, or Chazzan, the custodian of the Sacred Rolls and a sort of elementary school-teacher, who was to act also as janitor and to wield the scourge when punishment was inflicted; and the reader, or *delegate of the congregation*, appointed at each meeting by the ruler, whose duty it was to read and explain the Scriptures and to lead in prayer. Usually a scribe was appointed to this office. He had to be a man of good character. There was also the interpreter, or Targumist, the Methurge man, whose duty it was to render the Hebrew reading of the Scriptures immediately into the vernacular. And since this had to be done without written sketch [5] and on the spot, even without previous preparation, the person serving in this capacity would have to be a man of some learning. And finally there were the almoners, who collected for the poor.[6] A public worship presupposes a congregation. A synagog must be erected only at a place where there were ten Batlanim, or men of leisure, who could devote their time and services to the worship and the local administration. Tradition had it that the number ten was chosen because God said to Abraham that, if ten righteous had been found in Sodom and Gomorrah, these doomed cities would not have been destroyed.[7]

Luke 4, 16—30.   5.

The services in the synagogs were in some respect somewhat like our own. After the recitation of "Hear ye," or the Shema,[1] a confession of faith in the unity of God, and the prayers, in which Adonai was substituted for the unspeakable name Jehovah,[2] the

---

4,   5) This would popularly have been considered authoritative. Only the Hebrew original could be regarded as final.

6) The collecting had to be done by at least two and the distributing by at least three.

7) Edersheim, I, 433 f.

5,   1) Deut. 6, 4—9; 11, 13—21; Num. 15, 37—41.

2) Only in the Temple the name of God was pronounced as written. Schuerer, II, II, 82, n. 143.

liturgical part was concluded with a benediction.[3] If a priestly descendant of Aaron was present, the blessing was pronounced by him; if not, by the leader of the devotion. After this the Chazzan, or servant, stepped to the painted ark, or chest, and brought out the Megillah, or Sacred Roll, for the assigned readings from the Law, Parashah, and the Prophets, Haphtarah.[4] Since

The Service. the original Hebrew was no longer generally understood, the Targumist, or interpreter, stood by the side of the Maphtir, or reader, and translated the reading into the vernacular verse by verse, except in the section of the Prophets, which was rendered into Aramaic after three verses of reading. Since the Targum was not considered inspired, the interpreter might paraphrase freely for the better popular understanding. Only the substance of the text had to be correctly given. This may help us in a measure to understand the popular mode of the Old Testament quotations in the Septuagint and in the New Testament writings. This reading was immediately followed by an address or sermon, delivered by the appointed reader, that is, where a scribe or Rabbi capable of giving such instruction, or a distinguished stranger, was present.[5]

Luke 4, 16—30.   **6.**

On this particular Sabbath there was a distinguished Rabbi in the synagog of Nazareth. In recognition of His reputation Jesus was requested to perform the honorable function of Maphtir, or reader.[1] When He ascended the Bima, or platform, and stood up at the Luach, or lectern, "for to read," the Chazzan, or clerk, drew aside the silk curtain and brought forth the Megillah, which contained the Haphtarah of the day. Our Lord unrolled the volume and found the well-known passage in Isaiah 61.[2] The congregation stood as He read: "The Spirit of the Lord is upon Me, because He hath anointed Me to preach the Gospel to the

---

5, 3) Edersheim, I, 442.

 4) The Pentateuch was divided into 154 pericopes, so that the whole Law could be read in regular order in the course of three years. There was also a lectionary for the prophetical books.

 5) Edersheim, I, 445.

6, 1) Called also *Sheliach Tsibbur,* or delegate of the congregation.

 2) Farrar, I, 222. From this passage it has been argued that the Sabbath was on the Great Day of Atonement, because in later times Is. 61 was the lesson to be read on that day. But Edersheim and Meyer both contend that the modern lectionaries from the Prophets did not exist in the times of Jesus. Edersheim, I, 444. 452, n. 2; Meyer *sub loco,* n. 1.

poor. He hath sent Me to heal the broken-hearted, to preach deliverance to the captives and recovering of the sight to the blind, to set at liberty them that are bruised, to preach the acceptable year of the Lord." This is a free reproduction of the Septuagint, which freely reproduces the original Hebrew. It was probably first read in Hebrew, thereupon targumed into Aramaic, and then preached

"The Acceptable Year of the Lord." on by Jesus.[3] Stopping short before the stern phrase "and the day of vengeance of our God" the last words He read to His listeners were the gracious words "the acceptable year of the Lord." [4] Curiously enough this phrase has led a number of the Fathers to argue that our Lord's ministry lasted but a single year.[5] After the reading the Lord rolled up the Megillah, handed it back to the Chazzan, and, as was customary among the Jews, sat down on the Kisse, or chair, to deliver His sermon.[6]

Luke 4, 16—30.   7.

Whether the selection of this text was by choice or, as some think, part of the ordinary lesson of the day, the Spirit of the Lord was indeed upon Jesus in prompting Him to make it the basis of His first recorded Messianic sermon. It struck the keynote of His whole prophetic ministry. In breathless silence all eyes were upon Him as He made the astounding disclosure: "This day is this scripture fulfilled in your ears." There was no doubt as to the Messianic character of the text. But the people of Nazareth were taken by surprise at the announcement that the very voice of Him of whom the prophet prophesied had entered into their ears. From the very beginning of His ministry Jesus had the clear and certain consciousness that He was the Messiah. How clearly this passage gives the lie to the supposed gradual development

"This Day is This Scripture Fulfilled in Your Ears." of Messianic consciousness on the part of Jesus! We can imagine the awful thrill which passed through the hearts of His hearers as Jesus identified Himself with the subject of the prophecy: "He hath anointed ME to preach the Gospel to the poor." At any rate, before the reaction set in, there was one point in which they were all agreed: that they were marvelous words of grace which proceeded out of

---

6,   3) Dods *sub loco.*   4) Farrar, I, 223.
       5) See Meyer *sub loco.*   Farrar, I, 223, n. 2.
       6) Meyer *sub loco.*

His mouth.[1)]   At first held spellbound, they gradually began to realize the full meaning of the words.   Breathless silence and devout attention gave way to the after-sermon hum.   Since it was customary among the Jews to remain absolutely silent during the synagog discourse and then to give vent to their feelings in full, it was not long before Jesus became sensible of rebellious murmurs.[2)] What is that?   The Messiah?   "Is not this Joseph's son?"   Did we not know Him all this time as the carpenter's son?   What business has He to teach?   Whence could He know letters, having never learned? [3)]   In small-town jealousy, voices of disparagement were raised against the success of a distinguished native son.

Luke 4, 16—30.   8.

Jesus was aware of the change of feelings, but He did not deny the fact of His Messiahship in order to placate His listeners.[1)] The slur on His humble origin He passed by.   Other men of yet humbler origin had become distinguished.   Amos, "no prophet, neither a prophet's son," was taken from his flocks with the summons: "Go, prophesy unto My people Israel." [2)]   No doubt the Nazarenes would next demand visible proof of His being the Anointed of God.   They had *heard* the claim.   But now He should let them *see*.   Let Him *do* here in His own country — indeed, here all the more because it was His own country — "whatsoever we have heard done in Capernaum." [3)]   Does not charity begin at home?   And what about the proverb "Physician, heal thyself"? If Thou desirest to be a helper of others, the poor, blind, brokenhearted, and bruised, then why not begin at home, or first help Thyself from the lack of consideration and esteem which attaches

"No Prophet is Accepted in His Own Country." itself to Thee? [4)]   In reply to these objections in their hearts, and all but on their lips, Jesus points to the truth of another proverb as applied to His own sad experience: "No prophet is accepted in his own country." And then He shows them that, unless they accept Him in faith, the mere fact of compatriotism establishes no particular claim. "Miracles are not limited to geographical relation." [5)]   This is

---

7,   1) Words about the grace of God in the Pauline sense, whereby the prophecy was fulfilled.   Dods *sub loco.*
       2) Farrar, I, 224.   3) John 7, 15.
8,   1) Compare chapter VIII, 9.   2) Amos 7, 14. 15.   Farrar, I, 226.
       3) This reference implies an antecedent ministry there.   See chapter VI, 25.   John 2, 12 ("not many days").
       4) Meyer *sub loco.*   5) Farrar, I, 226.

clearly seen from two well-known instances in which not Jews, but Gentiles were most particularly favored in the ministry of Elijah and Elisha. "Many widows were in Israel in the days of Elias when the heaven was shut up three years and six months,[6] when great famine was throughout all the land; but unto none of them was Elias sent save unto Sarepta, a city of Sidon, unto a woman that was a widow. And many lepers were in Israel in the time of Eliseus, the prophet; and none of them was cleansed, saving Naaman, the Syrian." The Nazarenes were not slow in grasping the reference. A ministry which smacks of universalism! What is that? Pagans, Gentiles, not to mention the inhabitants of Capernaum, are better than we? There was but one answer, Away with Him!

Luke 4, 16—30. 9.

Nathanael was almost right: "Can there any good thing come out of Nazareth?"[1] The Nazarenes were filled with fury. They rose and thrust Him out of the synagog, out of the city, and led Him to the "eyebrow" of the hill on which the city was originally built, for the purpose of casting Him headlong over the cliff.[2]

Rejected by the Nazarenes. And all this on the Sabbath! But His hour was not yet come. Overawing His infuriated townsmen with His majesty, He passed through the midst of them and went His way. Certainly a sad parting from the town of His youth. Did He cast a longing glance at the humble home in which He had played and toiled and waited? Such questions are natural, but they are left unanswered.[3] Resting probably in the neighborhood until the Sabbath was spent, He pursued His downward[4] journey to Capernaum, which was henceforth to be His Galilean home.

8, 6) Three and a half years in accordance with Jas. 5, 17 and universal Jewish tradition is the exact time as compared with the round number, three years, in 1 Kings 17, 1; 18, 1.

9, 1) John 1, 46.

2) It is said that the ancient city stood higher on the slope than the modern. The Mount of Precipitation, a conspicuous object from the Plain of Esdraelon, which for many years has been pointed out as the place where the attempt was made on the Lord's life, lies some two miles from the village. Its distance from the village is sufficient proof that it cannot have been the real scene of the event. The cliff which travelers have generally fixed upon as best answering the narrative lies just back of the Maronite church and is some thirty or forty feet in height. Andrews, 221.

3) Farrar, I, 227.

4) The altitude of Nazareth is given as 1,602 feet above sea-level and Capernaum as 682 feet below the level of the Mediterranean Sea. In twenty miles a difference of over 2,200 feet.

10.

Matt. 4, 13—16. Luke 4, 31. 32.

Friendly Capernaum on the sunlit shores of the Galilean Sea. Our Lord had been there before. For a brief spell after the marriage of Cana He had made it His residence with His mother and brethren.[1] His own town had cast Him out; but here devoted friends and believing disciples would welcome Him. Either here or in the immediate vicinity were the homes of Simon and Andrew, and James and John, who, it seems, had returned to their accustomed labors after the return of their Master through Samaria to Galilee.[2] Soon they were to become His constant attendants and chosen apostles. Capernaum was probably already the home of Mary and His brethren,[3] while it seems that His sisters were married at Nazareth.[4] In this city He would preach on the Sabbaths in the synagog which the good centurion[5] had built and of which Jairus was one of the rulers.[6] Here was also the home of the now

A New Home at Capernaum. believing royal officer, whose son the word of Jesus spoken at a distance had restored to life.[7] And thus in Capernaum, as far as the Son of Man had a place to lay His head, He was among friends. Added to this, Capernaum and its vicinity, situated on the Sea of Galilee, with the great trade routes to Egypt and Syria, to Jerusalem and Damascus, passing through or by it, gave Him such facilities of intercourse with men as He could not have had in the more secluded Nazareth.[8] Finally, the removal of Jesus to Capernaum was in fulfilment of a prophecy. "The land of Zabulon and the land of Nephthalim by the way of the sea, beyond Jordan, Galilee of the Gentiles, the people which sat in darkness saw great

---

10, 1) Until Passover. John 2, 12. Chapter VI, 25.

2) Chapter VIII, 1.

3) Compare Andrews, 164. 239; Wieseler, 155 and n. 5. Chapter VII, 21. It cannot of course be stated with certainty. (Weiss thinks that the family of Jesus resided in Cana. I, 378; II, 44.) The reason of the "continued there not many days" in John 2, 12 is explained by v. 13: "The Jews' Passover was at hand." And even if Mary had returned to Nazareth, the "dreadful insult which Jesus had received would alone have been sufficient to influence the family of Jesus to leave the place, even if the other members did not directly share in the odium and persecution which His Word had caused." Farrar, I, 234. Alford: "The change of abode seems to have included the whole family, except the sisters, who may have been married at Nazareth." Greswell: "The incident respecting the tribute-money established that Jesus was a legal inhabitant of Capernaum." Quoted in Andrews, 240.

4) On account of Mark 6, 3. "Are not His sisters here with us?"

5) Luke 7, 5.   6) Mark 5, 22.

7) John 4, 40.   8) Andrews, 239.

light, and to them which sat in the region and shadow of death light is sprung up." [9]   These regions, first to be depopulated at the time of the fall of Israel,[10] were the first to see the Light.   The bright sunshine of Messianic summer now flooded Galilee of the Gentiles.   This must have been of peculiar interest to St. Matthew, the writer of the first gospel.   Seated at the receipt of custom,[11] he had no doubt often seen Jesus pass by and heard His words, until he himself heard and gladly obeyed the gracious summons, "Follow Me!" [12]

11.

Matt. 4, 18—22. Mark 1, 16—20. (Luke 5, 1—11.) [1]

The first notice we have of our Lord after His rejection at Nazareth brings Him before us as standing on the shores of the Galilean Sea, surrounded by people who were eager to hear the Word of God.   His growing reputation as a prophet, joined to what happened in Nazareth, would have provided Him with an audience in whatever village He entered, especially in the populated regions of the Sea of Galilee.   How long an interval had elapsed since He left Nazareth we do not know.   Most likely it was on the Friday in the week following His rejection at Nazareth, before the Sabbath of His first synagog appearance in Capernaum.[2] Approaching the lake, He again met His former disciples, Simon,

---

10, 9) Is. 9, 1. 2.   The quotation in Matt. 4, 15. 16 freely follows the original, with glances at the Septuagint.   Dods *sub loco.*

10) 2 Kings 15, 29.   Chapter II, 10.

11) Matt. 9, 9.   12) Edersheim, I, 458.

11, 1) The parentheses indicate that the passage has been taken out of its own true order.   Except in cases in which there is no chronological sequence involved, we for the first time are leaving the natural order of the individual gospels.   And until the account of the death of John the Baptist there will be other transpositions, especially in Matthew, whose Gospel, it seems, was in part based on topical rather than a strictly chronological arrangement.   In spite of the ingenious arrangement of some older harmonists, for instance, A. Osiander, 1537, and E. D. Hauber, 1740, they cannot be avoided. For the purpose of constructing a harmony which leaves each gospel in its own undisturbed sequence the present author made the same attempt, but after a concentrated effort, in which neither thought, labor, nor paper was spared, he was forced to give it up.   In the present instance, although there are still a number of harmonists who do *not* consider the above passages parallel, it seems to us that on account of the unexpected nature of the miracle, as evidenced in the reaction of Peter, Luke himself does not insist upon an order which places this miracle *after* the miraculous healing of Peter's mother-in-law. Weiss thinks that in the sudden introduction of the sons of Zebedee in verse 10 Luke himself seems to indicate that what is related in the story is coeval with what is recorded Matt. 4, 18—22 and Mark 1, 16—20.   I, 56, n. 1.

2) Mark 1, 21.   Weiss, II, 59.

Andrew, James,[3] and John, who, it seems, had left their Master after His journey through Samaria and returned to their fishing trade. The sea swarms with fish, and in the Lord's day its waters were covered with boats. A flourishing fish-trade was carried on with Jerusalem, where one of the gates was called the Fish Gate.[4] The Rabbis were veritable *connoisseurs* of fish,[5] and it seems that Zebedee, the father of James and John, was a prosperous fisherman, with connections in Jerusalem; for later we learn, if our interpreta-

The Recall of the Four Fishermen. tion of the respective passage is correct, that John was known in the high priest's palace.[6] Very likely Andrew and Simon had formed a partnership with them in a prosperous fish business and had their own boats and nets as well as hired servants. But this time they had not been successful. It had probably been a stormy night.[7] At least their toil had brought them no fish. Two of them, Simon and Andrew, were now washing and mending their nets. At a short distance, James and John, seated in their boat with their hired servants and Zebedee, their father, were similarly engaged. Thus Jesus found them. Very likely they were unconscious of His presence and surely unaware of the fact that the time had come for them to be recalled — and this time permanently — into His service. As He addressed Himself to them, the multitude that had followed Him gathered around. Beckoning Peter, Jesus stepped into his boat and requested him to pull out a little from the land. "Seated in this pleasant pulpit and safe from unseemly pressure, Jesus taught the multitudes as the little boat rocked on the blue ripples, sparkling in the sun."[8] We need not ask what He spoke. It would be words of Life, of their need, and of the beauty and glory of the Kingdom which was "at hand." When the sermon was over, Jesus made preparation to carry out what He had in mind.

12.

Matt. 4, 18—22. Mark 1, 16—20. (Luke 5, 1—11.)

"Now, when He had left speaking, He said unto Simon, Launch out into the deep and let down your nets for a draught." In the ears of an experienced fisherman certainly a strange com-

---

11, 3) This is the first time that we meet with James, although it is generally accepted that He was with his brother John at Bethany beyond the Jordan. John 1, 40 f. Chapter VI, 18.

4) Neh. 3, 3.

5) Edersheim, I, 473.   6) John 18, 15. Weiss, I, 366.

7) Edersheim, I, 472.   8) Farrar, I, 242.

mand. Success was doubly improbable both as to time and place; for fish were caught at night and near the shore.[1]   But when the Lord bids us let down our nets, there *must* be fish.   Peter, however, was filled with gloom.   "Master,[2] we have toiled all the night and have taken nothing."   Still, discarding his initial objection and speaking as the captain, he replies: "Nevertheless, at Thy word I will let down the net."   This obedience was rewarded.   Instantly a vast number of fishes crowded into the net.   A busy scene followed as the instinct of work first prevailed.[3]   "And they beckoned unto their partners which were in the other ship that they should help them.   And they came and filled both the ships, so that they began to sink."   When Simon Peter [4] now realized the greatness of the miracle, he thought only of his own unworthiness and of the presence of Jesus with him in the boat.   "He fell down at Jesus' knees, saying, Depart from me; for I am a sinful man, O Lord."   Not that he really wanted the Lord to depart or to dismiss him from His presence; but he was overcome by the sense of his own unworthiness and sin.   These passionate words are really a humble prayer, requesting the Lord to receive him and to stay.   Also the companions of Peter were overcome.   It was a miracle which only experienced and hardened fishermen could fully appreciate.   It was a real miracle.   Yet it was also a symbolic miracle and performed by Jesus for a definite purpose. "Fear not!"   "Come ye after Me."   "Follow Me, and I will make you fishers of men."   It was not at all a strange command.   Neither Peter and Andrew nor the sons of Zebedee could have misunderstood the call or even regarded it as strange.   They had heard it before.   But now the call for *permanent* discipleship had come. And there was only one answer — they forsook all, the boats, nets, hired servants, the fish,[5] Zebedee, and the members of their families and followed Him.

The Miraculous Draught of Fishes.

12,   1) Bruce sub Luke 5, 5.

2) The Greek word ἐπιστάτα is used instead of the usual Hebrew Rabbi. Occurs only in Luke.   Peter does not yet address Jesus as his Teacher.   Meyer in Luke 5, 5.

3) Farrar, I, 243.

4) The name Peter is here introduced for the first time without explanation, presumably to mark the great crisis in his history.   Dods *sub loco.*

5) But possibly the phrase "when they had brought their ships to land" also includes the disposal of the fish.

13.

Mark 1, 21—28. Luke 4, 33—37.

Followed by His first four permanent disciples, Jesus proceeded to near-by Capernaum, which was henceforth to provide Him with an earthly home.[1] This must have been a memorable occasion for the four Galilean friends and a day of which especially Peter loved to speak frequently and fully to Mark, the disciple and "interpreter of Peter, who wrote down accurately whatsoever he remembered of the things said or done by Christ." [2] Though originally from Bethsaida,[3] it seems that Andrew and Peter now owned a house and lived with their households [4] at Capernaum. Although Jesus had been in Capernaum before,[5] this is the first time after the beginning of His great Galilean ministry that He publicly appeared in Simon's town. He was probably even now

In the Synagog at Capernaum.

honoring Peter's house with His personal presence. On the next morning He presented Himself at the local synagog, again to serve in the capacity of Maphtir, or reader, as He had previously done at Nazareth. The Sabbath services in the synagog usually began at nine in the morning and lasted until noon,[6] after which the worshipers would gather in the house of some friend for a festive meal.[7] We do not know the subject of this particular Sabbath discourse. But we are told that the Lord astonished His listeners; for He taught them as having authority and not as the scribes, who as the *homines literati* of the day, teachers and lawyers, were usually appointed to serve as the lecturers in the synagog.[8] There was no appeal to

---

13, 1) When Jesus told a scribe who wanted to follow Him that He had "not where to lay His head" (Matt. 8, 20), He meant to say that He had no home of His own.

2) Eusebius, III, XXXIX, 15.

3) John 1, 44.

4) Mark 1, 29.

5) Chapter VI, 25. John 2, 12.

6) "The sixth hour, at which it is our custom on the Sabbath to take our midday meal." Josephus, *Life*, 54.

7) Luke 14, 1—3.

8) The scribes (*Sopherim*, lawyers, or Scripturists) date as a distinct body from the period of Ezra, himself a scribe. Their functions were to copy, read, explain, defend, and preserve the Law. In their zeal to protect the Law they invented the "fences" which under the title "Words of the Scribes" formed the nucleus of the "tradition of the elders," or oral law, as distinguished from the written Law, any transgression of which was declared to be more heinous than the transgression of the words of the Bible itself. Originally the priests and Levites were the teachers and guardians of the Law, Lev.

human authority, neither did He resort to subtle logical distinctions, legal niceties, witticisms, or clever sayings.[9] Clear and limpid words flowed from the spring, which was itself life and truth.

14.

Mark 1, 21—28. Luke 4, 31—37.

But suddenly the service was interrupted by the obscene cries and blasphemous ravings of an unhappy wretch who had a spirit of an unclean devil. "Away![1] What have we to do with Thee,[2]

A Demoniac. Thou Jesus of Nazareth? Art Thou come to destroy us? I know[3] Thee who Thou art, the Holy One of God." A testimony for Jesus by a demoniac. — But what is a demoniac? Whatever difficulty the term may offer, every reader of the New Testament cannot but form a definite idea of what a demoniac is. Scripture itself throws enough light upon the subject.

10, 11; Deut. 33, 10; 2 Chron. 15, 3. Gradually, however, this was changed, especially during the Exile and after, when no longer primarily the Temple-worship, but the Law served to keep a largely dispersed people united. The higher the Law rose in the estimation of the people, the more did its professional study and explanation become an independent calling. It was the Law of God, in which every member of the nation, and not only the priests had an individual interest. Hence, *non-priestly Israelites* more and more occupied themselves with its scientific study. The professional occupation of these real Rabbis and masters of Israel may be summed up as follows: 1. The theoretic development of the Law. What was clearly binding in principle was mechanically developed by continuous methodical labor into endless subtle casuistic details. And the more the credit of the scribes increased, the more did *their theory become valid Law.* 2. The teaching of the Law, that is, the written Law, as delivered by Moses, as well as their own gratuitous oral embellishments. The ambition of every scribe was to create popular professional acquaintance with the Law and to "bring up many scholars." 3. The passing of sentence in the courts of justice. In Jewish communities any one might be appointed judge through the confidence of his fellow-citizens. But since confidence is usually placed in proportion to the knowledge and ability displayed, it was but natural that scribes were usually appointed to the office of judges. The same held true with regard to delivering the lectures in the synagogs. Though this was open to all, the choice usually fell upon a local scribe. 4. Guardians and preservers of the written text of Scripture. Although as a class the scribes at the time of Christ were His implacable enemies, we owe them — rather, their successors of a later period — a great debt because of their extremely conscientious labors for the unadulterated preservation of the *sacred text.* See Schuerer, II, I, 312—328; Farrar, I, 265.

13, 9) For synagog sermons see Edersheim, I, 443 ff.

14, 1) Ἔα, ha! — a cry of horror.

2) Τί ἡμῖν καὶ σοί; What is there in common between us? John 2, 4.

3) The diseased man speaks for the demon in him and the demon for the entire infernal host, as having all the same interest, Mark 1, 24. Dods *sub loco.*

15.

Mark 1, 21—28. Luke 4, 31—37.

In diverging for a brief discussion of demoniacal possession, we may state at the outset that all kinds of ancient superstitions, beliefs, and irrational fears were prevalent in the days of Christ. Educated men of the time, Jews and Gentiles, were not free from it, neither the postapostolic Christians nor the Fathers of the Church, and we may add, neither are the people of our own day and age. Mysterious occurrences were promptly ascribed to supernatural forces. And strange maladies, psychical and physical disorders, were attributed to the invasion of spirits, or demons, the dispossession of whom by means of magic, incantation, and exorcism was frequently attempted. In order to gain reputation among the superstitious for their pretended arts the professional Jewish exorcists credited the invention of their spells to Solomon. In apostolic times [1] and in the Middle Ages the name of Jesus was used in the adjuration of wicked practitioners, who pretended to effect a cure of a particular spell, and is so used to-day. Wide-spread belief in the power of omens, signs, charms, and the like, based on **Ancient Superstitions.** fear and credulity, also as applied to possession and dispossession of demons, had taken root in the popular mind. Little information on those views and practises has reached us. Jesus at one time pointed to exorcism engaged in by some Jews when, in defense of His own real power over actual demons, He argued *ex concessis:* "If I by Beelzebub cast out devils, by whom do your children cast them out?" [2] They used the name of God, and with their activities the Pharisees found no fault. An example of superstitious exorcism is given by Josephus: "I have seen a certain man, whose name was Eleazar, releasing demons in the presence of Vespasian, Titus, their officers, and army. His method was to draw the demon out through the nostril by a ring and a particular root. And then, in proof of the cure, he placed a basin of water a little way off and bade the demon overturn it." [3] Now, the evangelists were simple men, yet to what scorn would they have been subjected, and how their credulity would have been ridiculed, if they had related the story of an exorcism such as *this!* However, they did not. Their account, told in simple language, does not deal with superstitions, but with facts. And we can rest assured that they did not share the erroneous opinions of their age.

15, 1) Acts 19, 13.   2) Matt. 12, 27.
    3) *Ant.*, VIII, II, 5. *Wars*, VII, VI, 3.

16.

Mark 1, 21—28. Luke 4, 31—37.

But did Jesus perhaps *accommodate* Himself to the popular conceptions of the day? It has been said that like a good physician He *seemed to agree* with the popular notion and to enter into the fancy of the afflicted patient in order the more easily to effect a cure.[1] But outside of the fact that this view would transform all cases of possession into hallucinations, this method of treatment would not have been honest. If this "canon of accommodation" were true, then Jesus — by the same argument — might have possessed advance information in other matters, and all His miracles [2]

Demoniacal Possession as Viewed by Jesus.

might have been performed by applying until then or even to this day undiscovered natural forces. Then the inspired gospel narratives might be transformed into a series of historically untrustworthy legends. No! Far from accommodating Himself to a supposed popular prejudice, Jesus regarded His own cures of demon possession as direct conquests of Satan and his powers. In sending out His disciples, He did not equip them with supposed might against non-existing, fictitious devils, but He gave them real power against unclean spirits, power *to cast them out,* and to heal all manner of sickness and disease. He said: *"Cast out devils!* Freely ye have received, freely give." [3] When the Seventy returned and reported of their success, He made this very fact, the expulsion of devils, a matter of thanksgiving to God.[4]

17.

Mark 1, 21—28. Luke 4, 31—37.

Because the inhabitation of an unclean spirit in some cases affected the possessed person physically, producing ordinary diseases, it has been thought that the Jews accounted for the mental and physical diseases and for the visible effects on both body and mind of such persons by the fact that through a service of sin they had enslaved themselves to Satan. However, as we have pointed out, this view would deny the fact of diabolical possession in an attempt to explain the phenomenon as due to the popular ignorance of natural causes. And what was the character of this remarkable phenomenon? The answer is as simple as the statement of the

---

16, 1) Edersheim, I, 480.   2) As is actually claimed by some writers.
3) Matt. 10, 1. 8.   4) Luke 10, 17—20.

gospels. Without apparent reason or cause the victims appear as
"demonized," as "having a demon, or spirit," who is called "evil"
or "unclean." This, of course, correctly presupposes the existence
of a personal devil together with a host of evil spirits. While it
is to be admitted that a mass of superstition is popularly associated

The Demonized State. with the notion "devil," it cannot be denied that Scripture plainly teaches the existence and manifestation of Satan and innumerable evil spirits,[1] and from the gospels we see that they were at times divinely permitted to take bodily possession of men, so that for a longer or shorter period of time the demonized person was no longer himself. In this demonized state, sometimes accompanied with physical suffering, the afflicted person was in the power of the evil spirit, who tormented him, robbed him of his senses, turned him into a raving maniac, and made him utter indecencies and even blasphemies. The irresponsible sufferer may or may not have previously led an exceptionally sinful life. Really, we know very little about the character of the maladies that were conjoined with demoniacal possession. In the Gadarene maniac we have a case of violent madness.[2] Another one of the sufferers was only dumb.[3] The deaf-and-dumb demoniac boy in the region of Caesarea Philippi was an epileptic and raving maniac.[4] The sick daughter of the Syrophenician woman was "grievously vexed with a devil," [5] while the Capernaum demoniac was writhing with pain.[6]

18.

Mark 1, 21—28. Luke 4, 31—37.

Whether or not there are still cases of diabolical possession is hard to decide. However, as little as the possible occurrence of present-day miracles can be denied, just so little the possibility of demoniacal possession. But it would be difficult to establish a particular case. In the writer's opinion they have practically ceased as such, at least in Christian countries.[1] And still, physicians admit, and family members sometimes sadly experience, cases where

---

17, 1) Gen. 3, 1 (cp. Rev. 12, 9) ; Job 2; Matt. 4, 1 ff.; 1 Pet. 5, 8;
Jas. 4, 7; Jude 6; etc., etc.
2) Mark 5 2—5.   3) Matt. 9, 32.   4) Mark 9, 14—29.
5) Matt. 15, 21—28; Mark 7, 24—30.   6) Matt. 17, 14—21.
18, 1) What is called demon possession is familiar to-day in Asia, Africa,
and the Malay Archipelago, where such "demons" are frequently "cast out,"
for instance, by Christian Chinese and others. Basil Matthews, *Life of
Jesus*, 504.

sickness, in particular mental diseases and nervous disorders, produces phenomena in a patient almost unbelievable: gigantic strength in an emaciated body; the senses, eyesight and hearing, so sharpened as to be most uncanny; the mental faculties so keen as to be almost supernatural; and ravings so fierce as to be almost diabolical. There are still many phenomena "in heaven and earth" of which even our enlightened philosophy has no adequate conception.[2]

Present-Day Occurrences? However, in the time and land of Jesus the appearance of demoniacs must have been quite prevalent. And for this there was a very good reason. Because the Son of God came into the world for the purpose of destroying the works of the devil, we can well understand a corresponding period of developed enmity in the satanic Kingdom of Darkness. Knowing that Jesus Christ assumed human nature for the purpose of taking our infirmities,[3] but, above all, of bearing our sins and saving our souls,[4] we can also well understand that the Prince of Darkness in the days of Christ in accentuated measure sought to injure and destroy men by sending out his evil spirits to possess them bodily and to rob them of their salvation. Add to this the *time* of the coming of Christ.[5] It was a time when the ancient world to a peculiarly large extent seemed to have been abandoned by all the forces of health and vitality and therefore to have fallen more deeply into sin and under the powers of darkness.[6] — We are now ready to proceed with our story.

19.

Mark 1, 21—28. Luke 4, 31—37.

In one respect all demoniacs in the gospels were alike: they all owned the power of Jesus. The Jewish nation, upon the whole, still remained in ignorance as to the identity of Jesus. But ever since the opening of the heavens at the banks of the Jordan and the temptation in the wilderness the devils knew — and trembled.[1] But if Jesus checked the nation's revolutionary hopes by discouraging direct testimony as to His Messiahship,[2] He least of all

---

18,　2) Edersheim, I, 483.　　　3) Matt. 8, 17.

　　4) Is. 53, 5; 1 Pet. 2, 24.　　5) See chapter I.

　　6) So long as the usual definition for demoniac is given as a person who is *supposed* to be under the influence of a demon, it is clear why most of the articles under this subject are not satisfactory. For a positive discussion see Weiss, I, 76—88; Edersheim, I, 479—484; and the few sentences in Pieper, *Christl. Dogmatik*, I, 615.

19,　1) Jas. 2, 19.　　　2) Mark 1, 44.

desired a satanic testimony as to His origin and office.[3]   Whatever the motive of the Prince of Darkness was, it was bound to be satanic.   "And Jesus rebuked him, saying, Hold thy peace"; literally, "Be thou muzzled," "and come out of him."   The ring and magical root of certain Jewish exorcists was not required.   Jesus' word sufficed.   One wild paroxysm, and the poor sufferer was free from demoniacal possession; one final fit, and he was perfectly healed.[4]   Stupor and astonishment fell upon the assembly in the synagog.   Questioning remarks passed from one to another.   What is this?   What new, powerful teaching is this?   He commandeth even the unclean spirits, and they obey Him!   There was no question as to the miraculous powers displayed.   Neither was there this time any questioning as to Christ's doing this on the Sabbath-day.   As a result the fame of Jesus spread along the lake north and south, back into the hill country, and into all the regions of Galilee roundabout.

"Hold Thy Peace and Come out of Him."

20.

(Matt. 8, 14. 15.)[1]   *Mark 1, 29—31.   Luke 4, 38. 39.*

From the synagog we follow the Savior and His four called

19,   3) Luke 4, 41.

4) Edersheim, I, 485.

20,   1) Transposed.   See remarks on previous transposition, No. 11. — This is the first time that we are leaving the natural order of Matthew.   And not without good reason.   In comparing Matthew with Mark and Luke, it seems that the events of the first gospel up to the death of John the Baptist are not related in strict chronological sequence, but are given in topical order for didactic purposes.   With all due respect to the learning and labor of the keenest minds we are convinced that the problem of the chronological sequence of the various events of the life of Jesus, in particular those now under consideration, cannot be solved by criticism nor in a mathematical or mechanical way.   1. *Criticism*.   The "synoptic problem."   According to this theory an original and now lost written or oral source (commonly called Q for *Quelle* [source] or *Logia* [oral tradition], upon the basis of which the first gospel, for instance, Matthew or Mark, was written) is presupposed.   Using the material at hand, editing, revising, changing, or supplying, the other gospels followed.   Each of the three synoptic gospels was in turn placed first in order. But of late Mark is enjoying the greatest favor.   In the words of Robertson: "It is plain as a pikestaff that both our Matthew and Luke *used* practically all of Mark and followed his general order of events."   (*Harmony*, 255.) There is truth in the statement with respect to the *order* of Mark.   But in accepting the *principle*, questions naturally arise, and conclusions follow. Without entering into the controversy, we merely wish to state that we cannot accept any theory which exalts any one gospel at the expense of another, as all are equally inspired.   The more we study the matter, the more we are convinced that the evangelists wrote *independently* of one another and that in finding the true order of the respective events, a) the natural order of the individual gospels must be followed, but b) unless it is expressly stated, a considera-

disciples into Peter's wedded home.[2]   But no festive Sabbath meal, as was the Jewish custom,[3] awaited Him there.   A sudden and severe fever had stricken down Simon's mother-in-law, who lived

The Healing of Peter's Mother-in-Law.

with him.   Again the Lord was in the presence of suffering and pain.   However, a mere notice of the afflicted family to Him who had just rebuked Satan sufficed. "And He rebuked the fever."   Standing over her, "He touched her hand, and the fever left her."   "Immediately she arose and ministered unto them."[4]   She was now able and willing to serve.

21.

(Matt. 8, 16. 17.)[1]   *Mark 1, 32—34.   Luke 4, 40. 41.*

While they were still sitting at meat, the daylight faded.   The Sabbath had come to an end.   The report of the wonderful occurrence in the synagog had been whispered from door to door.   The people, no longer restrained by the rule of rest, brought all manner of sick and possessed and themselves began to flock to Simon's house.   At last the whole town was gathered at his door.   What

---

tion of the purpose for which the events are grouped or of the circumstances in which they are introduced is permitted.   We agree with Prof. M. B. Riddle: "The writer may be pardoned for alluding to his own experience in connection with this point [origin and relation of the synoptic gospels].   In the exegetical labors of some years he found himself accepting the theory that the three Synoptists wrote independently of one another.   Afterwards, when the task of editing Dr. Robinson's Greek *Harmony* compelled him to compare again and again every word of each account, the evidence of independence seemed to him to be overwhelming."   (In the introductory essay to *St. Augustine's Harmony of the Gospels. Nicene and Post-Nicene Fathers,* Vol. VI. 68, n. 1.) — 2. A *mathematical* solution was attempted by Dr. J. H. A. Ebrard in his *Gospel History.*   In sharing the view that the employment of earlier gospels was "unnecessary, even impossible," p. 555, he attempted a solution in a mathematical way.   After a detailed examination of the data relative to sequence in the individual gospels and the connecting formulas, whether "immediate, mediate, loose, or general concluding," the various events were ingeniously arranged in lettered chains ("syndesms" — G. S. D. T., etc.) and intervening numbered links, — but with unsatisfactory result.   Notice the permutations in the following passages, which are supposed to be in immediate parallel sequence: —

Matt. 4, 18—22, followed by 12, 22—50, followed by 8, 18—22
Mark 1, 16—20, followed by 3, 23—35, followed by 4, 35—40
Luke 5, 1—11, followed by 11, 14—28, followed by 8, 22—25
(See Ebrard, pp. 59 ff. 135 ff. 234 ff.)

3. Neither can a solution be found in a *mechanical* way.   For a study of the synoptic problem the student is referred to the *Introductions* of Th. Zahn and B. Weiss.

20,   2) 1 Cor. 9, 5.

3) Edersheim, I, 485.   Josephus, *Life,* 54.

4) Or "Him," according to some MSS. of Matthew.

21,   1) Transposed, but in order.

a strange scene! The limpid waters of the Galilean Sea; the last flush of sunset gilding the ascending western hills;[2] a motley crowd casting curious glances at Simon's door. But for many it was a door of longing hope. Parents, children, husbands, wives,

In the Evening Many Others are Healed.

brought, led, and carried their beloved sick. A peaceful scene of faith and hope. But also a scene of suffering humanity. Suddenly the evening stillness was disturbed by the wild shrieks of demoniacs. Satanic testimonies to the presence of the Son of God were heard: "Thou art Christ, the Son of God." But the Lord would have none of that. Rebuking the evil spirits, He suffered them not to speak and commanded them to leave their afflicted victims. And He "healed all that were sick that it might be fulfilled which was spoken by Esaias the prophet, saying, Himself took our infirmities and bare our sicknesses."[3] How well the ideas are associated: sin and sickness, healing and the Savior! Thus the healing ministry of Jesus is placed into the proper light. And thus on the Sabbath eve we see the initial fulfilment of the hope to which the God-directed hand of the prophet had pointed.[4]

21, 2) Farrar, I, 238.   3) Is. 53, 4.   4) Edersheim, I, 488.

CHAPTER X.

FROM THE FIRST GALILEAN CIRCUIT
TO THE CHOICE OF THE TWELVE.

Probably spring, 28 A. D.

1.

Mark 1, 35—38. Luke 4, 42. 43.

A modern book must have divisions and parts. Thus we begin a new chapter, although there are no mechanical divisions in the life of Christ. An examination of our Lord's ministry, however, seems to point to a number of stages distinctly marked. The first is the period immediately following His baptism and extending from the first Passover [1] to the unnamed feast, when the impotent man was healed, and embracing a little over one year. It extended from the first calling of His disciples, the first miracle, and the first cleansing of the Temple to the attempt of the Jews to kill Him, a year later, because He declared Himself equal with God.[2]

Divisions in the Lord's Ministry. During this time His labors were chiefly confined to Judea.[3] Near the close of this period we have placed the imprisonment of John. The second stage is the period following His return to Galilee immediately after the Feast of the Passover. It embraces the whole duration of His Great Galilean Ministry, or about a year and six months,[4] and may be divided into the period preceding and following the death of John. The third stage begins with His final departure from Galilee and ends with the death on the cross. This period embraces about five or six months. The first part of the second stage of our Lord's ministry, the Great Galilean Ministry before the death of John, is before us now. For the sake of giving the crowded events a place in our minds we have grouped them under the heads of Galilean circuits, with intervening chapters for the Sermon on the Mount and the Parables by the Sea.

1,   1) John 2, 13.
      2) John 5, 16. 18.   Spring, 27 A. D., to spring, 28 A. D.
      3) The Early Judean Ministry.
      4) April, 28 A. D., to November, 29 A. D.

2.

Mark 1, 35—38. Luke 4, 42. 43.

The closing events of the last chapter present Jesus as a much-sought healing Guest in Peter's home. The short evening hours passed, devoted by Jesus to the healing of the sick. The night was spent in Peter's house. Day had not yet dawned, however, when Jesus quit the dwelling and withdrew to a near-by desert place to be alone with His Father in heaven. Again and again during His public ministry we shall find the Lord seeking retirement for the purpose of prayer.[1] There was probably also an additional reason for this particular retirement. He had healed many the evening before. He knew that, as the news was carried from door to door, many others who had not been healed would scarcely await the dawn in their search of aid. It was, however, not His purpose to establish a clinic at Capernaum. Now, this seems to have been what the people at Capernaum expected. While He was engaged in prayer, throngs of petitioners were storming Peter's door. They

Retirement to a Solitary Place. impelled him to seek after Jesus and to return with Him at once. Peter and his companions set out to search for their

Master; and when they found Him, they endeavored to induce Him to return with them and to keep Him from doing what He seemed inclined to do, to leave Capernaum for the present with some of the sick still unhealed. "All men seek for Thee," they said. But to escape the multitudes was one reason why He had left Capernaum. It was not His object to become the center of a miracle-admiring population. The purpose of His miracles was to gain the hearts for the good tidings of the Kingdom. And besides, His blessings were not to be confined to Capernaum. There were Dalmanutha, Magdala, Chorazin, Bethsaida, and other towns and villages near at hand. "Let us go," He said, "into the next towns that I may preach there also. For therefor came I forth," that is, from Capernaum. "I must preach the kingdom of God to other cities also; for therefor am I sent." Whether or not Jesus yielded to the anxiety of the waiting multitude or whether He instantly carried out[2] His intention Mark and Luke do not expressly state. At any rate, a Galilean preaching and healing circuit was now begun.

2,   1) Luke 6, 12; Matt. 14, 22; Luke 5, 16; 9, 28; Mark 14, 32.
   2) As seems likely on account of the "again" in Mark 2, 1.

3.

Matt. 4, 23—25. Mark 1, 39. Luke 4, 44.

The general character of the Galilean preaching tour in which
Jesus now engaged is given as preaching, teaching, and healing.
Galilee at this time was extremely populous.[1]   Jesus was assured
of an audience wherever He went.   The joy which He brought to
some afflicted sufferer would give Him a chance to announce the
good tidings of the kingdom of heaven to the gathering attracted
by His miracles.   This was an open-air ministry.   But especially

**"And Jesus Went
about All Galilee."**
did He desire to bring His message
also to the congregations assembled in
the synagog.   His activities were not
those of a political agitator; His purpose was to announce the
coming of the heavenly kingdom.   And subordinate to this ministry of preaching and teaching was His ministry of healing.   Those
afflicted with fever, the blind, palsied, epileptics, demoniacs, and
lunatics [2] — whose seizures followed upon the phases of the
moon — were brought to Him, and He healed them all.   Naturally,
the report spread.   His fame spread through Galilee and then
through Syria, to which Roman province Galilee and the whole
of Palestine belonged.   Multitudes were attracted from all quarters:
Galilee, Decapolis, Jerusalem, Judea, and Perea beyond the Jordan.[3]

4.

(Matt. 8, 2—4.) [1] *Mark 1, 40—45. Luke 5, 12—15.*

It was on this journey that Jesus was approached by one who
was smitten with a loathsome and terrible disease — leprosy.[2]   Even

---

3,   1) Josephus, *Wars*, III, III, 2.   2) Σεληνιαζομένους.
   3) Here follows the miraculous draught of fishes in the order of Luke,
Luke 5, 1—11. See chapter IX, 11.
4,   1) See previous notes on transpositions, chapter IX, 11. 21. 22. The
healing of the leper cannot have taken place after the Sermon on the Mount, —
for "great multitudes followed Him" then, Matt. 8, 1, — but privately, which
is evident from the command of silence given the healed leper, v. 4, — although
he nevertheless "began to publish it much and to blaze abroad the matter,"
Mark 1, 45. That this healing is not placed chronologically by Matthew
appears also from the whole arrangement of chapters 8, 9, and 11, successive
miracles recorded after 8, 2 without regard to the exact order of time — from
here to the parables.
   2) Some writers believe that the disease called λέπρα by the Greeks and
the plague of Lev. 13 — zara'ath — are not identical. The disease mentioned in Scripture seems to have been curable, whereas the leprosy of the
Greeks — Elephantiasis Graecorum — was not, except in the early stages.
The former is now usually identified with psoriasis, dry tetter, a non-
contagious, irritating skin disease in which white scales form on the body

to-day the name of this dreadful scourge of the Eastern world strikes terror into our hearts. Egypt is called its cradle, but it also appeared in Assyria, Babylonia, India, and China two and three thousand years ago. The father of Medicine, Hippocrates,[3] calls it the Phenician disease, and Galen names it elephantiasis.[4] In the Old Testament it first appears as a sign given by God to Moses,[5] but shortly afterwards the sister of Moses, Miriam, was stricken with it.[6] In the Mosaic Law definite rules for its recognition, the preliminary quarantine period, and ceremonial methods of cleansing

Leprosy.   are given.[7] The Alexandrian conquerors returned with the disease to Eastern Europe. The Romans contracted it from the Greeks. Pompey carried it into Italy. The Mohammedans brought it into new areas. Pilgrims from the Holy Land introduced it into England. And the returning crusaders brought it into other parts of Europe. Thus in the course of time this dreadful disease made itself felt all over the civilized world.[8] According to Herodotus the ancient Persians exiled the lepers. The Chinese burned them alive. But segregation was employed at an early date. This was the custom of the Egyptians, the Jews, and also the practise of the afflicted European nations. In the beginning of the thirteenth century there were two thousand leper houses in France and nineteen thousand in Europe, excluding those of Russia and Sweden. Modern methods have checked the disease, but it is estimated that there are still three million lepers in the world to-day, most of them in China and India.[9]

5.

(Matt. 8, 2—4.) Mark 1, 40—45. Luke 5, 12—15.

We are told that the dreadful scourge itself is really a skin disease;[1] however, not a superficial, but a deep-seated malady. Its

---

("a leper white as snow"). These scales spread till they become the size of a quarter or half dollar, by which time they fall from the central part of the circle, leaving it red. Perhaps the Hebrew term *zara'ath* was generic, and elephantiasis and psoriasis were two of its species. See Basil Matthews, *Life of Jesus*, p. 504. Davis, *Dictionary of the Bible*, sub "Leprosy."

4,   3) 460—357 B. C.   4) 130—200 A. D.

5) Ex. 6, 4.   A punitive miracle.

6) Num. 12, 13.   7) Lev. 13 and 14.

8) With an exception. There have been cases, but there has never been an invasion of the New World by this dreaded disease.

9) See articles on leprosy in *Int. St. B. Encycl.*; Davis, *Dictionary of the Bible; New Int. Encycl.*; and *Encycl. Brit.* Edersheim, I, 491 ff. Weiss, II. 163 ff.

5,   1) Now included among the parasitic diseases. The cause is believed to be an infection by the *bacillus leprae*, a specific microbe discovered in 1871.

essential character is described as a great multiplication of cells resembling the granulation cells of lupus and syphilis in the tissues affected, which become infiltrated and thickened, with degeneration and destruction of the normal elements. The invasion is usually slow and intermittent. White shining spots are seen, appearing to be deeper than the skin. Red or coppery patches appear on face, hands, feet, or on other parts of the body. Lumpy excrescences arise, at first pink, but changing to brown. The skin of the face **Its Character.** and the mucous membranes [2] of the nose and throat are thickened, producing a distorted appearance and impeding the breathing and impairing the voice. The eyebrows drop off, and the eye tissues undergo degenerative changes. The ears and the nose become thickened and enlarged. As the disease progresses, the knotty surface breaks down in ulcerating sores. The nails of the fingers may become hard and clawed. Portions of the extremities, including whole fingers and toes, die and drop off. The gums are absorbed, and the teeth disappear. The nose, the eyes, the tongue, and the palate are gradually consumed. Slowly and surely the malady progresses. Living death seizes upon one organ after another, until, perhaps after the lapse of years, the patient is carried off, death being often hastened by some intervening disease.

6.

(Matt. 8, 2—4.) Mark 1, 40—45. Luke 5, 12—15.

Among the Jews those afflicted with leprosy were shunned by their fellow-men not only because of the loathsomeness of their disease, but also because they were in a special manner regarded as ceremonially unclean. There was not only the danger of contagion, but mere contact with a leper defiled whoever touched him. While the cure of other diseases was called healing, that of leprosy, if there was any, is usually called cleansing. A leper was considered an outcast, socially and morally, although it is not possible to determine precisely to what extent the unfortunate sufferers were ex- **"Unclean, Unclean!"** cluded from the intercourse with other men. A place was set aside for them in the synagogs, and the strictest precautionary measures were taken.[1] The leper was obliged to avoid the towns and to go about with torn garments, bared head, and covered chin. The

---

5, 2) The lining of the cavities leading to the exterior of the human body.
6, 1) Edersheim, I, 493.

only care he received was from such as were similarly afflicted. As
he passed by, wrapped in a mourner's garb, as it were, he was
required to cry, "Unclean, unclean!" [2] thus proclaiming that his
was both a living and a moral death.[3] Special treatment there was
none. If he recovered from the disease, he was obliged to submit
to an extended priestly inspection and to prolonged ceremonial
purifications. And not till after the presentation of the legal
offering was he pronounced clean.

7.

(Matt. 8, 2—4.) Mark 1, 40—45. Luke 5, 12—15.

While Jesus was in a certain city [1] a man "full of leprosy"
came to Him, threw himself down before Him, and besought Him
in the ground tone of all true Christian prayer: "Lord, if Thou
wilt, Thou canst make me clean." That was faith in the power of
Jesus and absolute committal to Him in his helpless and, generally
speaking, hopeless state. The Lord was moved with compassion.

"Be Thou Clean!" There was not a moment's hesitation
on the part of Jesus. "Prompt as an
echo" [2] came the reply: "I will; be thou clean." [3] Almighty
Power spoke. Stretching forth His hand, the Lord touched the
leper. There was no shrinking from the loathsome disease. And
as soon as Jesus had uttered those words, the leper was cleansed.
"The touching hand of Jesus was not defiled by the leper's body,
but the leper's body was cleansed by Jesus' touch. Thus Jesus
touched our sinful nature and yet Himself remained without the
touch of sin." [4]

8.

(Matt. 8, 2—4.) Mark 1, 40—45. Luke 5, 12—15.

"And He straitly charged Him and forthwith sent him away."
Almost vehemently the Lord dismissed him from His presence with
a twofold charge: to keep silence and to obtain the legal priestly
certificate of his cleansing. The latter command was most likely
given for the purpose of establishing the proof of the miracle, out
of consideration for the sufferer, whose social rehabilitation might
otherwise be frustrated, and especially in obedience to the Levitico-

---

6,   2) Lev. 13, 45.   3) Edersheim, I, 491.
7,   1) Weiss (II, 164) thinks that it was in a synagog, on account of
Mark 1, 39. 43: "cast him out." But ἐξέβαλεν may also refer to the city
or to a crowd. See Bruce *sub loco.*
     2) Farrar, I, 275.
     3) Θέλω, καθαρίσθητι.   4) Farrar, I, 275.

ceremonial ordinance.[1]   According to the Mosaic Law any one who claimed to be cured of the plague had to submit to a rigid priestly inspection for the purpose of obtaining the legal certificate

"Show Thyself to the Priest."

that he was actually clean.   In many cases the person suspected of having contracted the malady was not afflicted with true leprosy, in which case a cleansing could be announced by the priest after fourteen days.   But a true leper usually remained a leper.[2] However, if the priestly inspection proved favorable, an offering was both permitted[3] and required, after which the former leper was again admitted to the society of his family and friends.   This command of Jesus clearly shows that it was His desire to fulfil all righteousness,[4] even to submit to the ordinances of the Ceremonial Law.   There was to be no just cause of complaint against Him nor against the person whom He had helped.   "Go thy way, show thyself to the priest,[5] and offer the gift that Moses commanded, for a testimony unto them," namely, as evidence and testimony to the people that thou hast been healed.[6]

9.

(Matt. 8, 2—4.)   Mark 1, 40—45.   Luke 5, 12—15.

"And He charged him to tell no man."   But why this command of silence?   We can only guess at the answer.   Was it that the healed man should "silently reflect upon the wonderful work of God"?[1]   Was it to "avoid the excitement and tumult of the already overexcited multitudes of Galilee"?[2]   Or was it, as seems

"See Thou Tell No Man."

most likely, the desire to discourage any publicity which might lead to a false conception of His Messianic work, of the purpose for which He had come into the world?[3]   It seems that the leper complied with that part of the Lord's direction which concerned his purification and social rehabilitation, but in respect to the command of silence he used his own mistaken judgment.   "But

---

8,   1) Lev. 13, 49 ff.;   14, 2—32.

2) A cure through human agency was never contemplated by the Jews. Edersheim, I, 492.   Josephus speaks of the possibility of a cure in answer to prayer.   *Ant.,* III, XI, 3.   Compare also 2 Kings 5, 7.

3) Only clean persons were allowed to offer sacrifices. Lev. 14, 10.

4) Matt. 3, 15;   5, 17.

5) Not necessarily in Jerusalem, but to the priest in the province whose business it was to attend to this duty.   Bruce, sub Luke 5, 14.

6) Meyer, sub Matt. 8, 4.   9, 1) Stoeckhardt, *B. G.,* 106.

2) Farrar, I, 277.   3) Compare IX, 20.

he went out and began to publish it much and to blaze abroad the matter." [4]   The result was that the Lord's work was retarded on account of the man's well-meant disobedience. It is true, great multitudes flocked to Jesus. However, their purpose was not so much to hear the Word of God [5] as "to hear" about the great Miracle-worker and to secure healing for themselves. But this was not the popularity which the Lord desired. In order to counteract this unwanted publicity, He made Himself inaccessible for the time being by avoiding the open cities and retiring to desert places for the purpose of solitude and prayer.[6]   And still they came to Him from every quarter.

10.

(Matt. 9, 2—8.) [1]   *Mark 2, 1—12.* [2]   *Luke 5, 17—26.*

We know neither the extent nor the route of our Lord's first Galilean circuit.[3]   Returning quietly to Capernaum "after some days," [4] it was noised abroad that He was at home, presumably in Peter's house.[5]   Soon a crowd gathered in ever-growing numbers,

Returning to Capernaum. filling the house and the surrounding courtyard and occupying every foot of available space without and within. Peter's house was packed to the door.[6]   Among those gathered were believing disciples, friendly neighbors, and curious strangers, generally sympathetic, but also Pharisees and doctors of the Law from Galilee, Judea, and Jerusalem, who, it seems, had come for

9,   4) Τὸν λόγον, the report of the healing word.

5) Luke 5, 1.

6) It is interesting to note that Luke constantly refers to the prayers of Jesus: 3, 21; 5, 16; 6. 12; 8, 18; 9, 28; 11, 1; 23, 34; 23, 46.

10, 1) Transposed. Chronologically this section, Matt. 9, 2—17, including the call of Matthew, and 12, 1—21, belong before the Sermon on the Mount.

2) The presence of Pharisees and scribes from Jerusalem, the charge of blasphemy, the word to the paralytic 'Arise, take up thy bed, and walk' (cf. John 5, 8), and the reference of Jesus to the authority given Him by the Father (cf. John 5, 27) convince us that this miracle took place *after* the encounter at the unknown feast rather than as shown in the usual chronological arrangement, by which John 5 is placed immediately before the plucking of grain on a Sabbath-day, Mark 2, 23—28 and parallels.

3) Probably a few weeks in the early summer of 28 A. D.

4) Δι' ἡμερῶν.

5) The preferred reading is εἰς οἶκον, at home. Bruce sub Mark 2, 1.

6) If the house was, as we suppose, Peter's home, it must have been one of the better dwellings of the middle class, since it contained, besides a large family-room for friends and guests, accommodations for Peter and his wife, for Peter's mother-in-law, and for Jesus as the honored Guest. Edersheim, I, 502.

a purpose. Following the encounter in Jerusalem at the unknown feast, it appears that representatives had been sent for the purpose of watching, opposing, and, if possible, entrapping Jesus. And so, we might say, there was a gathering in Peter's home "like the gathering of Israel on Mount Carmel to witness the issue as between Elijah and the priests of Baal." [7]   As always, the power of the Lord went with Jesus to heal. But the first thing He did was to preach.

11.

(Matt. 9, 2—8.) Mark 2, 1—12. Luke 5, 17—26.

While Jesus was busily engaged in preaching "the Word," [1] a remarkable thing happened. Four men approached, bearing a paralytic on his pallet. Of course, this was not strange. Of late it had become too common a scene to see sick carried to Jesus to attract special attention. But with the house packed to the doors and no one apparently willing to leave his place, access to Jesus was simply impossible. What was to be done? The four men were absolutely determined and probably solemnly pledged to bring their patient to Jesus. We do not know who the sufferer was. He was "sick of the palsy." [2]   The disease is characterized by extreme loss of the power of motion resultant from some affection either of the motor centers of the brain or of the spinal cord. It is always

The Man Sick with the Palsy. serious, usually intractable, and generally sudden in its onset. [3]   Though the Lord addressed him affectionately as "son," this was not necessarily a proof that he was young. [4]   And though He prefaced the cure by declaring to him the forgiveness of sins, we need not infer from this that the disease was the result of a wicked life, although it may have been. It seemed as if it were impossible to have the sufferer brought into the presence of Jesus. But necessity is the mother of invention. When the four men saw that they could not approach Jesus by clearing a path for themselves through the crowd, they made their way to the roof of the house, perhaps by an outer staircase. [5]   There they removed the tiles and through an opening let down their burden exactly in

---

10, 7) Edersheim, I, 501.

11, 1) The Word *κατ' ἐξοχήν*, the Gospel. The phrase reminds us of the Apostolic Church. Bruce sub Mark 2, 2.

2) *Παραλυτικός.*   3) 1 Macc. 9, 55 ff.

4) *Τέκνον*, child, affectionately. Mark 10, 24; Luke 16, 25. Meyer sub Matt. 9, 2.

5) Matt. 24, 17. Or over the flat roofs of the adjoining houses. "The road of the roofs." Edersheim, I, 503.

front of the place where Jesus was. We can imagine the surprise
of the assembly within as Jesus' discourse was interrupted by a disturbance overhead and a pallet was slowly lowered, on which a paralytic lay, silent, with "fevered face and glistening eyes upturned
to Jesus." [6]

12.

(Matt. 9, 2—8.) Mark 2, 1—12. Luke 5, 17—26.

Many sick had been brought to Jesus. But such a display of
purposeful energy, unhesitating boldness, and unyielding determination of a heroic faith had never been witnessed before. And it
was faith, at least a firm belief in the almighty healing power of
Jesus, both on the part of the sufferer and of his friends, but probably also a faith in Jesus as the promised Messiah of God. Jesus
saw, and Jesus spoke. "And Jesus, seeing their faith,[1] said unto
the sick of the palsy, Son, be of good cheer; thy sins be forgiven
thee." Certainly a strange greeting to one the primary intention

"Thy Sins be Forgiven Thee." of whose strange coming had been prompted
by a different motive. But whether or not
the man had brought on his suffering by
a previous licentious life, it was the purpose of Jesus to set the temporal and the spiritual into proper relation. The first and greatest
need of every man, whether sick or healthy, is the gracious forgiveness of sins. And regardless of the degree of his knowledge
and faith in Jesus as the Messiah, the sufferer was no doubt
a repentant Israelite, who acknowledged himself a sinner, felt the
need of forgiveness, and as such was beyond "the coarse Judaic
standpoint, which viewed suffering itself as an expiation of sin." [2]
As a kind Physician, Jesus inspires confidence at the outset with
a tender, cheering word: "Son, be of good cheer." And then He
deals first with the disease of the soul: "Thy sins be forgiven thee."

13.

(Matt. 9, 2—8.) Mark 2, 1—12. Luke 5, 17—26.

And now the scribes [1] played their part. The sufferer's approach to Jesus had been accomplished only by the employment of
most unusual means; but it seems that the scribes and the Pharisees
were early on the spot and in a position to hear and see Jesus
distinctly. While many others were standing, they had even found

---

11, 6) Edersheim, I, 503.
12, 1) Πίστιν αὐτῶν. We see no reason why the faith of the sick man
should not be included in the αὐτῶν.
    2) Edersheim, I, 504.
13, 1) Chapter IX, 13.

comfortable seats[2] and were now in sullen silence carrying on a dialog[3] in their hearts: "Why does this man thus speak? He blasphemeth. Who can forgive sins but One, even God?"[4] From their point of view they were right. But Jesus was God, which truth, however, they were not ready to accept. Immediately Jesus gave a proof of His divinity.

"Who can Forgive Sins but God Only?" The reasoning of their hearts was known to Him. It is true, He was a man, in every respect except sin like all other men, but also the "Son of Man" in the emphatic and well-understood sense,[5] the promised Messiah and Mediator between God and men. When He perceived in His spirit that they so reasoned within themselves, He said to them: "Wherefore think ye evil in your hearts? For whether is easier to say, Thy sins be forgiven thee, or to say, Arise and walk?" As regards the mere words, both were manifestly alike easy. "And they were both equally difficult if spoken with any result." If the mere utterance constituted blasphemy and pretense, the effective utterance demonstrated divine authority and power. "There was this difference, however, that in the command of healing the authorization could be seen and criticized accordingly. The latter proved the former."[6]

14.

(Matt. 9, 2—8.) Mark 2, 1—12. Luke 5, 17—26.

"Whether is easier?" If Jesus could by one word of His divine power heal this man, who was hopelessly palsied, would it not have to be admitted that He has power on earth to forgive sins? "The unanswerable question was received with the silence of an invincible obstinacy."[1] But in order to prove that the declaration of forgiveness was no pretense and

"Arise, Take Up Thy Bed, and Walk." "that the Son of Man hath power on earth to forgive sins," He turned once more to the paralytic and said to him: "Arise, take up thy bed, and walk." "At once power was restored to the palsied limbs and peace to the troubled soul."[2] The man was healed, spiritually and physically. He arose, took up his pallet, opened a passage through the crowd, and went to his house, glorifying God.

13, 2) Καθήμενοι.

3) Διαλογιζόμενοι.   4) Revised Version.

5) The term *Son of Man* occurs here for the first time in Mark. Cf. Dan. 7, 13. 14. Pieper, *Dogmatik*, II, 74. 75. Cp. John 1, 51; Matt. 8, 20. Chapter VI, 20.

6) Weiss, II, 233.   14, 1) Farrar, I, 346.   2) Farrar, I, 346.

Said, done. Who could now, in the face of this ocular proof, persist in the charge of blasphemy against Jesus? The effect the miracle had upon the scribes and the Pharisees is not recorded. Very likely their "evil" thoughts remained unchanged.[3] The multitude dispersed, glorifying God. Exclamations of astonishment were heard, intermingled with expressions of amazement and fear. "We never saw it on this fashion." "We have seen strange[4] things to-day."

15.

(Matt. 9, 9.)[1] *Mark 2, 13. 14. Luke 5, 27. 28.*

And now comes a memorable day for the evangelist St. Matthew. Shortly after the healing of the paralytic Jesus seems to have departed to His near-by favorite shore. As usual, He was soon surrounded by an ever-increasing multitude. At or near Capernaum there was a receipt of customs. Passing by the place, after having

At the Custom-House near Capernaum.

taught the people, He beheld a publican, or customs official, sitting at the place of toll, to whom He extended the call, "Follow Me." We are quite safe in supposing a previous acquaintance and friendship. But the time had now come for Jesus to include him among the number of constant companions. However, before directing our attention to this new disciple of Jesus, this is probably the place to say something about the office of a publican and the reputation of that class of officials to which Matthew up to this time had belonged.

16.

(Matt. 9, 9.) Mark 2, 13. 14. Luke 5, 27. 28.

The scepter had indeed departed from Judah, and the Jews were made to feel the weight of the tribute-taking hand of a foreign ruler, although the Roman government as such could not be called

---

14, 3) Cp. Matt. 9, 11; Mark 3, 6.

4) Paradoxes, παράδοξα, Luke 5, 26. The only place in the New Testament where this word occurs.

15, 1) Transposed. If Levi is the same as Matthew and to be identified with the evangelist St. Matthew, of which there is hardly any doubt, then it seems that the writer of the first gospel does not insist upon placing his call *after* the Sermon on the Mount, which he himself has reported at length. The feast spoken of Matt. 9, 10 ff. may have been given later, before the healing of Jairus's daughter, Mark 5, 22; Luke 8, 41, on account of the words "while He spake these things," Matt. 9, 18, but is here related in order to gather in a group all that concerned Levi-Matthew personally. Or the call of Matthew may have occurred earlier, according to the arrangement of many gospel harmonies, *e. g.,* that of Tatian (A. D. 170), who, however, seems to have considered Levi and Matthew as two different persons. Compare Hill's edition of Tatian's *Diatessaron,* 7, 9 and 5, 25.

particularly rapacious in this respect. Indeed, a change had been made regarding the financial administration of the provinces since the days of the republic. In the imperial era the direct taxes, ground, income, and poll-taxes, were no longer sold or farmed out to the highest bidders, that is, the revenues of a particular district or province were not leased to the so-called *publicani* for a fixed period or sum, but were now collected by the procurators or ruling princes in their regular routine of official duty.[1] Indeed, it seems that in order to check the rapacity of the provincial rulers, the territorial princes were provided with a fixed annual salary in the days of Caesar Augustus.[2] And lest they be still tempted to take advantage of their position, Tiberius, the emperor at the time, introduced the policy of leaving them at their posts as long as possible, hoping that, after having gorged themselves at the beginning, they would become more moderate in their exactions.[3] But while the Roman government in general adopted a mild policy with respect to provincial administration, the actual governing hand was often cruel and harsh. The taxes were heavy. And what has just been said applies only to the direct taxes. In spite of all leniency and consideration in many matters, — no tribute in sabbatical years,[4] — the fact could not be disguised that a proud nation, which felt itself called upon to govern the world, found itself paying tribute to Caesar.[5]

Taxes.

17.

(Matt. 9, 9.) Mark 2, 13. 14. Luke 5, 27. 28.

It seems that the aversion to paying taxes is ingrained in human nature. But the Jewish hatred of Roman taxes was directed especially against one source of revenue, the customs, and against the officials who collected them. This tax, which was still farmed out, was collected at various places and levied not only upon exports and imports, but upon all goods in the hands of merchants passing through the country. Its collectors were the familiar publicans of the New Testament. The name[1] was extended from the Roman farmer-general of an entire province to his subordinate local officials. Sufficient cause for their unpopularity in New Testament times is not far to seek. Customs officials are always unpopular. The man

---

16, 1) Schuerer, I, II, 68.
    2) Schuerer, I, II, 7. Josephus, *Ant.,* XVII, XI, 4. 5. The salary of Herod Antipas — 200 talents — was ca. $400,000!
    3) *Ant.,* XVIII, VI, 5. Schuerer, I, II, 82. See chapter IV, 44.
    4) *Ant.,* XIV, X, 5.   5) Schuerer, I, II, 79.
17, 1) *Publicanus,* τελώνης.

who opens boxes and bundles for the purpose of appraising their value and is on the lookout for mostly non-existing hidden pearls is at best a tolerated evil. Among the Jews all circumstances combined to send the publican beyond the social pale. He was the very embodiment of antinationalism. He represented, and at a very sore spot brought the individual into contact with, the hated power of Rome. The tax was looked upon not only as a civil imposition, but as a religious wrong, and its payment was considered by many even a sin, an act of disloyalty to God. If the tax-gatherer was

Customs.   a Jew, as many of them were, he was a renegade in the eyes of his fellows. Since he had to pay for his concession, he had to be a man of some wealth. It was in his interest to make a sound financial investment. If the sum of the fixed revenue exceeded the expected amount, it was his gain. If, however, he failed to collect the specified amount, he had to bear the loss. The tariff rates were vague and indefinite, which permitted him to protect his investment with a liberal margin. In collecting the dues, he was always under the suspicion of extortion, and in many instances he actually *was* an extortioner. Where publicans are mentioned in the New Testament, they are usually associated with "sinners." The story is told of the death of a publican and of a very pious man. The publican, at his burial, received all honor from his townsmen, while the pious man was carried to his grave unmourned. This anomaly was explained in this way, that the pious man had committed one sin, while the publican had done one good deed. Later, however, the fate of the two men was satisfactorily adjusted. The pious man was seen walking beside the heavenly water-brooks, while the publican was burning in hell.[2] This illustrates the low esteem in which the publicans were popularly held. On the other hand, examples could also be given of contrivances and ways for defrauding the revenue.[3] There were three principal stations in Palestine for the collecting of customs: Caesarea, Jericho, and Capernaum.[4]

18.

(Matt. 9, 9.) Mark 2, 13. 14. Luke 5, 27. 28.

We are now ready to make the acquaintance of one of the publicans at Capernaum. Whether he was the principal customs collector of the Capernaum district or one of his subordinates we

---

17, 2) Edersheim, I, 517.

3) Walking-sticks with a secret place for pearls. Schuerer, I, II, 71.

4) Josephus, *Wars*, II, XIV, 4.

do not know. From the fact that he was seated at the place of toll it has been argued [1] that he was a "small Mokhes, or *douanier,*" that is, a subordinate official and publican of the worst kind, who had secured a concession for himself in the hope of making profit on his own account. Capernaum itself was ideally located, and for that reason probably chosen, for a customs station. Touching the lake in the neighborhood was the great road of Eastern commerce, which led from Damascus and beyond to the harbors of the west. The lake itself and the caravan route around the shores would serve in transferring goods to and from the Arabian interior. Diverging from the Way to the Sea there was a choice of roads southwards to Jerusalem and Egypt.[2] At the juncture of these roads, customs stations would be located, with the tax-collectors sitting at the place of toll. Levi was the name of one of them, the son of an otherwise unknown Alphaeus, not to be identified with the father of James the Less and of Jude.[3] But it seems that in conformity with Jewish custom on the occasion of a decisive change of life he re-

Levi-Matthew.   ceived or adopted a name indicative of his entry into the discipleship of Jesus. Very fittingly Levi the publican called himself Matthew, that is, Theodore, or the Gift of God.[4] Or the name may have been changed by Jesus,[5] perhaps partly to "obliterate the painful reminiscences of his former disreputable calling." — In this case we note the touching humility with which in the list of the apostles he alone among the evangelists gives to himself the dishonorable title of "Matthew the Publican." [6] That the former publican Levi is to be identified with the Apostle Matthew and that he wrote the first of the four gospels is universally accepted in the Christian Church.[7] He must have heard and seen Jesus frequently as He taught by the seaside. He may have witnessed the call of the first disciples. His calling would make him acquainted with the fishermen and ship-owners of Capernaum. Long before the eventful day which forever decided his future life he had probably in his heart become a disciple of Jesus. But on account of his social standing, being a despised

---

18, 1) By Edersheim, I, 517.   2) G. A. Smith, *Bible Atlas,* 20.

3) Matt. 10, 3; Mark 3, 18. A confusion that actually arose in very early times, the consequence of which was that in some manuscripts we find the reading James (instead of Levi), Mark 2, 14. See Meyer *in loco.*

4) Meyer, *Introduction to Matthew,* 1. The λεγόμενον in Matt. 9, 9 seems to imply a change of name.

5) Cf. John 1, 42.   6) Matt. 10, 3. Farrar, I, 248, n. 1.

7) See Eusebius, 24, 5; 39, 4. Bruce's and Meyer's *Introd. to Matthew,* etc.

publican, he did not dare to hope for personal recognition, far less
for a call to discipleship. He was mistaken. When Jesus fixed
His look of love upon him, which pierced the inmost depths of his
soul, and said to him, "Follow Me," the summons needed not
a moment's consideration. "His past was swallowed up in a heaven
of bliss." He said not a word, but rose, forsook all, and followed Him.[8]

19.

(Matt. 9, 10—13.) Mark 2, 15—17. Luke 5, 29—32.

From the progress of the story a return to near-by [1] Capernaum is inferred. Matthew's first act as a disciple of Jesus was
to prepare a great feast in honor of His new Master. The
invited guests, besides Jesus and His disciples, included a multitude
of those who in the pharisaic vocabulary were classified as "publicans and sinners." But disregarding this for the present, we take
it that Matthew was a man of some wealth and, at least in the circle
in which he moved, also of some social standing and the owner
of a large house or roomy court, spacious enough to accommodate

Matthew's Feast. a large number of guests. As publican
he would be acquainted with the repre-
sentatives of the Roman government, with whom he very likely was
able to converse in Greek. His acquaintance may have included
some of the officers of Herod's court. And he would be known
to the traders and business men of Capernaum. His feast was
a farewell feast, as some take it, and given for the purpose of
affording such people an opportunity to hear the Gospel of the
Kingdom and to meet Jesus as were contemptuously designated
sinners and because of some offense against the traditions were
excluded from the synagog. To sit at meat with such guests was
in full accord with the mission of Jesus, but in the eyes of the
"orthodox" it was a scandalous affair.

20.

(Matt. 9, 10—13.) Mark 2, 15—17. Luke 5, 29—32.

When some members of the pharisaic party "saw it," namely,
when they beheld Jesus at Matthew's festive board, they became
indignant that one who passed for a Rabbi should have so little

---

18, 8) Edersheim, I, 519.
19, 1) We do not know where to place Matthew's booth because we are
not certain of the location of Capernaum. Chapter VI, 25. If Capernaum
is to be located at Khan Minyeh, then the intersection of the trade routes
would be to the north; if at Tell Hum, to the south of Capernaum. See
G. A. Smith, *Atlas,* 20.

consideration for the honor of the learned profession and that He
who "pretended to be a preacher of virtue did not hesitate to con-
taminate Himself by the society of such disreputable company." [1]
But how could they see Him? Were they present themselves?
Most likely not, at least not as invited guests. At such occasions,
however, there is no privacy in the East. [2] In exercising their func-

"Publicans and Sinners." tions as guardians of the Law,
they may, in passing by, have
looked in; for otherwise "their presence as invited guests would
have involved them in the same blame which they were now casting
upon the Lord." [3] Under the circumstances none of them dared
to reproach Jesus directly; they contented themselves for the time
being with making spiteful observations to His disciples: "Why
eateth your Master with publicans and sinners?" In putting this
question to the disciples rather than to Jesus, the critics showed
a certain amount of cowardly cunning. The disciples were but
"initial learners." The question was one which concerned acknowledged Jewish propriety. "Had they been able to shake the confidence of the disciples in their new Master, they would at the same
time have seriously injured the cause of Christ." [4]

21.

(Matt. 9, 10—13.) Mark 2, 15—17. Luke 5, 29—32.

As soon as Jesus heard of it, He took the faultfinding and
"murmuring respectabilities" to task. [1] In defending His own conduct, He quotes a proverb, implying at the same time a criticism of
their own self-righteous attitude. "They that be whole need not
a physician, but they that are sick." This is true in the spiritual
as well as in the physical sense. "I came not to call the righteous,

Jesus' Self-Defense. but sinners, to repentance." Not as if
there were actually any "righteous,"
but the trouble with the Pharisees was that they considered themselves whole and righteous. They felt no need of a Savior from
sin. A miserable delusion. They were sinners as well as others,
howbeit self-righteous sinners, blind to their real condition, while
those whom they called "publicans and sinners" were conscious
of their sin. In their self-righteousness they would now combine
against Jesus, not on account of any sinful act of His, but on

---

20, 1) Weiss, II, 25.   2) *Exp. Greek N. T.,* 498.
     3) Farrar, I, 348.   4) Edersheim, I, 519.
21, 1) Farrar, I, 348.

account of His association with sinners. Applying "a rabbinic formula, so often used when superficial speciousness of knowledge is directed to further thought and study," Jesus bade them "go and learn what that meaneth, I will have mercy and not sacrifice." [2] Mercy goes before sacrifice. Love is the fulfilling of the Law. Outward formalism, mere Levitical piety, and dead orthodoxy are an abomination to the Lord. In the number of sin-sick and salvation-needing souls they had forgotten to include themselves. Had it never occurred to their scandalized minds, "overlaid with a crust of mere Levitism, that the love which condescends to mingle with sinners in the effort to win their hearts is more pleasing to God than a century of accumulated fasting, a hecatomb of rams, or a river of oil"? [3]

22.

(Matt. 9, 14. 15.) Mark 2, 18—20. Luke 5, 33—35.

Not only was the association of Jesus with publicans and sinners offensive to the pharisaic mind, but the feast itself seems to have been in conflict with current opinion and practise. Instead of a fast a feast. The feast of the converted Levi-Matthew in honor of Jesus probably took place on one of the two days appointed for weekly fasts.[1] Another reason for complaint. By this time John the Baptist "lay in the dreary misery of a Machaerus dungeon." [2] Misunderstanding the austere manner of their master and imitating it in a false manner, a number of John's disciples had not followed his suggestion to leave him and follow Jesus, but had associated themselves with the Pharisees, who above all wanted to regulate the piety of Jesus by their own. A number of men of both parties approached Jesus with a question concerning the strict observance of prayers,[3] fasting, and days, regarding which they and the party of Jesus were apparently at variance. "Why do we and the Pharisees fast oft, but Thy disciples fast not?" The attack was cunning. If the

Fasting.

21, 2) Edersheim, I, 520. Hos. 6, 6 (Septuagint).

3) Farrar, I, 349.

22, 1) Edersheim, I, 662. On account of Mark 2, 18: "were fasting" (R. V.). These days were Mondays and Thursdays; for Moses was supposed to have gone up the Mount for the second tables of the Law on the fifth day of the week and to have returned on a Monday. Farrar, I, 349, n. 3. Only one day of fasting was divinely appointed for the entire year, the Day of Atonement, Lev. 16, 29; Num. 29, 7. But it appears that in the period of the Exile four annual fasts had sprung up, Zech. 8, 19; 7, 1—12, which in the time of Jesus had increased to two a week, Luke 18, 12.

2) Farrar, I, 349.   3) Luke 5, 33.

exact relation of Jesus and John was not known and accepted, it was at least a matter of common knowledge that John was highly respected by Jesus. The question drew from Jesus three of His first "parabolic impromptus." [4] In replying He both shielded His forerunner and gently answered His critics.

23.

(Matt. 9, 14. 15.) Mark 2, 18—20. Luke 5, 33—35.

The last recorded public testimony of John had pointed to Jesus as the Bridegroom.[1] His presence marks the marriage week. Even according to rabbinic law this was to be a time of unmixed festivity.[2] During the marriage week all mourning was to be suspended, and even the daily prescribed prayers were not obligatory then. Was it not, then, inconsistent to "make the children of the bridechamber fast while the bridegroom is with them"? Jesus is the Bridegroom. His disciples are the sons of the bridal feast,

The Sons of the Bridechamber. the best men at the wedding. The mere suggestion of the name of "sons of the bridechamber" explains all, paranymphs, companions of the bridegroom, who act for him and in his interest and bring the bride to him. How can they be sad? When the bridegroom is conducted by his friends into the bridal chamber, that is the time for perfect enjoyment. If it should happen, however, that the bridegroom be seized by sudden death in the midst of the marriage rejoicing, then indeed there would be a time for them to fast. And calmly looking "down at the deep abyss which yawned before Him," [3] although at the time it was not understood, Jesus again [4] alluded to the violent end which awaited Him: "But the days will come when the Bridegroom shall be taken away from them, and then shall they fast."

24.

(Matt. 9, 16.) Mark 2, 21. Luke 5, 36.

Just as Jesus emphasizes the fitness of things with respect to fasting in His apology for His disciples, so He also insists upon proper "congruity in religion." [1] "No man putteth a piece of new

---

22, 4) Bruce sub Matt. 9, 15.
23, 1) John 3, 29.   2) Edersheim, I, 663.   3) Farrar, I, 351.
    4) Compare John 2, 19; 3, 14. From the very first Jesus knew His death to be divinely appointed and did not only gradually attain to this knowledge, after experiencing such opposition as He did.
24, 1) Bruce sub Matt. 9, 16.

cloth unto an old garment; for that which is put in to fill it up taketh from the garment, and the rent is made worse." This happens when a piece of unfulled cloth [2] or a piece cut from a new **New Cloth.** garment [3] is taken to repair an old. [4] The process would only make matters worse. If shrunk, the new cloth would not accommodate itself to the fit of the dress. It would draw threads from the weak part and render worse the original rent. At best it would present a piebald appearance and make the patch all the more conspicuous. The point is that it is "bootless to mix heterogeneous things"; [5] indeed, worse than useless. The observance of fasting, prayers, and days in a self-righteous spirit does not agree with the doctrine of grace and therefore shuts out from the Kingdom.

25.

(Matt. 9, 17.) Mark 2, 22. Luke 5, 37—39.

The illustrations are beautiful, an association of ideas suggested by the introductory figure of a wedding-feast — the bridegroom, fasting, vesture, and wine. "Neither do men put new wine into old bottles," that is, skins used as bottles; "else the bottles break, and the wine runneth out, and the bottles perish. But they put new wine into new bottles, and both are preserved." Until thoroughly aged, new wine, still in its expansive strength, must be kept in fresh and elastic containers. Thus in a gentle manner Jesus gives His questioners more than they had asked for. All that He has said answers the question raised at Matthew's feast: "Why eateth your Master with publicans and sinners?" Mercy goes before **New Wine.** sacrifice. All service of the lips and sacrifice of the hands, all mere outward worship, self-righteous fastings, prayers, and observance of days, are an abomination to the Lord. The piety of the Pharisees, based on ultra-legalism, and the doctrine of Jesus will not agree. The heart must not be bound up in the old garments, the filthy rags, of its own righteousness. Neither can the new and sweet wine of the Gospel be contained in carnal hearts. The Gospel does not require form, but faith. However, and here is a sad feature, as evidenced by

---

24, 2) Matthew and Mark.   3) Luke.

4) For a critical discussion see *Exp. Greek N. T.* or Meyer. At any rate, the verbal variations of the Synoptists in recording this saying of our Lord present the strongest internal evidence against the theory of dependence on each other or on an earlier written source.

5) Bruce sub Matt. 9, 16.

the haggling Pharisees and the misunderstanding disciples of John: "No man also, having drunk old wine, straightway desireth new; for he saith, The old is better." They still loved the "old wine of legal piety and did not care for the new," [1] the Gospel proclaimed by the Lord. They found the old wine so good that they did not wish to taste any other and therefore disdained the new doctrine of salvation full and free in Christ Jesus.[2]

26.

(Matt. 12, 1—8.) [1] *Mark 2, 23—28. Luke 6, 1—5.*

According to the chronology which we have adopted it was now late spring or early summer of 28 A. D., or 781 A. U. C. We suppose that what is related here happened near Capernaum.[2] While passing through a field of wheat [3] on a Sabbath-day,[4] the

25, 1) Bruce sub Luke 5, 39.

2) At this point many harmonists insert John 5, 1—47, the unnamed feast. For a discussion of it see chapter VIII.

26, 1) A new transposition. Chronologically this section (Matt. 12, 1—21) must be placed before the Sermon on the Mount.

2) On account of the words "He entered *again* into the synagog" (Mark 3, 1), that is, the synagog already mentioned (1, 21), called "their synagog" in Matt. 12, 9, where the Pharisees who put a reproachful question to the disciples are spoken of as members of that synagog.

3) That is, we suppose it to have been wheat. For chronological reasons many, placing the event after the unnamed feast (Passover) of John 5, have supposed that it was barley. But barley, besides being the usual feed for horses, — though barley-bread was eaten by the poorer classes, also by Jesus and His disciples, John 6, 9 (Edersheim, I, 681), — is not so readily rubbed in the hands for immediate consumption. See Andrews, p. 259.

4) The mysterious δευτεροπρώτη, "second-first" of Luke, missing in some of the best MSS., has caused considerable discussion. Meyer and Bruce do not accept its authenticity, but we believe that the term is genuine. While it is true that it is used only in this one instance, it is so peculiar that it must not be regarded as an interpolation. Evidently it was chosen designedly by the evangelist to indicate something well understood by his readers. But we are not so sure of its meaning; yet even if we could discover the exact significance of this isolated expression, not much importance would attach to it because the time of the year is sufficiently marked by the fact that the grain was ripe. — Of the different explanations proposed we mention the following: 1. The first Sabbath in the second year of the seven-year sabbatical cycle. But if, as is generally supposed, the sabbatic year began in October, the "second-first" Sabbath would fall in autumn. 2. The first Sabbath after the second day of Passover, on which day the sheaves of the first-fruits of the field were offered to the Lord and from which day the following Sabbaths were reckoned until the day of Pentecost, the Feast of Weeks. This is quite commonly accepted, but we believe that this date is too early. 3. The first Sabbath of the second month. 4. A Sabbath following a "Sabbath," a New Moon, or some other festival. A very plausible explanation. Just like Sunday following the 4th of July. 5. A technical expression for the first Sabbath after the second of the chief annual festivals, that is, Pentecost. Of all the explanations the last two appeal to us most. In the latter view a first-first Sabbath would be the first Sabbath after Passover, a second-first the first after Pentecost. In like manner we count Sundays as

exact time of which cannot be determined, the disciples of Jesus, being hungry, began to pluck ears of the ripe wheat and to eat the kernels, after rubbing off the chaff with their hands. To spying Pharisees, who were ever on the outlook for offenses committed by some one, this action was a fortunate discovery. According to their statutes the disciples of Jesus entangled themselves in at least two sins. With a "contemptuous gesture towards them" [5] (the disciples) they approach our Lord with an angry question: "Behold,

Plucking Ears of Corn on a Sabbath.
why do they on the Sabbath-day that which is not lawful?" It seems that Jesus Himself was not

directly implicated. It also seems that the rabbinic rule of the Sabbath-day's journey, which was not to exceed two thousand cubits, was not transgressed.[6] Neither was their action looked upon as stealing, for the plucking of ears from the neighbor's wheat was not only sanctioned by custom, but permitted by Law.[7] But a far more heinous crime was discovered, which, technically speaking, rendered the offenders liable to death by stoning. The plucking and rubbing was done on a Sabbath. According to rabbinic interpretation these acts constituted reaping and threshing.[8] Of course, there was no wrong done, even from the standpoint of the strictest interpretation of the Jewish Law. But the Pharisees — always unable to penetrate to the principle of a thing and engrossing themselves in a maze of rules — so construed it and incidentally accused Jesus as an accomplice for permitting the assumed sacrilege.

27.

(Matt. 12, 1—8.) Mark 2, 23—28. Luke 6, 1—5.

Jesus defends the action of His disciples with unassailable arguments and then declares Himself to be the Lord of the Sabbath. The first argument was taken from a well-known incident of Bib-

---

the First Sunday after Epiphany, and the like. If we regard the second-first Sabbath as the first Sabbath after Pentecost, which in this year has been placed on the 19th of May, we can satisfactorily place the event about the end of the month. Stoeckhardt, who believes that it was a Sabbath follow-ing a New Moon holiday, says: *"Wir werden etwa in die Pfingstzeit ver-setzt."* *Bibl. Gesch.*, 84. For a discussion see Wieseler, *Synopsis*, 203 ff.; Andrews, 256 ff.; Bruce and Meyer *sub loco.*

26, 5) Farrar, I, 436.

6) A Sabbath-day's journey, Acts 1, 12, reckoned at 2,000 cubits, was the assumed distance from the tents of the children of Israel to the Tabernacle during their sojourn in the wilderness and the distance they had to keep from it while crossing the Jordan, Josh. 3, 4.

7) Deut. 23, 25.   8) Edersheim, II, 56.

lical history. When David fled before the wrath of Saul and was in need and hungry, he came to the Sanctuary of God at Nob, where Abiathar, most likely the assistant, with the distinct sanction of his father Ahimelech,[1] supplied him with showbread, "which was not lawful for him to eat, neither for them which were with him, but only for the priests." [2] "The case of David was apposite. It was a case of eating. It was an emergency." What constituted the particular emergency in the case of the disciples, which forced them to appease their hunger in the fields of grain, we do not know. — "It was probably also on a Sabbath.[3] It concerned not only David, but, as in the present instance, his followers." [4] Now, if David, their national hero and saint, had thus violated the letter of the Law [5] and had yet been held blameless on the plea of its having been a case of necessity,[6] why should the disciples be blamed for the harmless act of appeasing their hunger? — The second argument is taken from the discharge of priestly duties on the Sabbath-days. "For certainly to hew the wood for the burnt offer-

Jesus Defends His Disciples.

ing, to light the fires, to place hot, fresh-baked showbread on the table, to slay the victims, and to circumcise children on the eighth day, involved work for the servants of the Temple of the Lord. And if they were held blameless, should not the servants of the Lord of the Temple be excused?" [7] "But I say unto you that in this place is One greater than the Temple." [8] And recurring to the charge made at the feast given by Matthew of eating with publicans and sinners,[9] Jesus strikes at the principle: "If ye had known what this meaneth, I will have mercy and not sacrifice, ye would not have condemned the guiltless." Here Jesus defends His conduct of shielding the disciples by an appeal to the voice of prophecy.[10] The Pharisees as men of a thousand "rules

---

27, 1) 1 Sam. 22, 20. Josephus, *Ant.*, VI, 12. 6.

2) Lev. 22, 10.

3) 1 Sam. 21, 6, compared with Lev. 24, 8. 9.

4) Bruce sub Matt. 12, 3. From the Old Testament account we may probably have concluded that David was really alone and only pretended to have companions.

5) Lev. 24, 5—9.

6) According to the principle that danger to life (the life of an Israelite) superseded the Sabbath law. "It was argued that a man was to keep the commandments that he might live, — certainly not that by so doing he might die." Lev. 18, 5 was quoted. Edersheim, II, 57.

7) Farrar, I, 438.

8) According to the reading $\mu\varepsilon i\zeta\omega\nu$, Matt. 12, 6. A reference not to the work, but to the person of Jesus. Meyer sub Matt. 12, 6.

9) Matt. 9, 11. 13.   10) Hos. 6, 6.

were not accustomed to go back on principles"; [11] but love clearly is the fulfilling of the Law. [12] "Conflicting ceremonial laws must be overruled by higher considerations." [13]   With the sacrificing priests it was the Temple.   Here was One greater than the Temple. [14]   In the case of Abiathar or Ahimelech it was the love of a needy neighbor.   In the case of the disciples it was hunger that must be appeased.   Instead of spying, why did it not occur to them to offer food?   And as to the Sabbath rest, this applied only to the regular work of weekly labor.   Deeds of love and mercy were at all times permitted.

28.

(Matt. 12, 1—8.)   Mark 2, 23—28.   Luke 6, 1—5.

That this is the correct interpretation of the Sabbath law and that the great underlying principle of the Sabbath is only a means to an end, man's highest good, Jesus now states in a great word, preserved only in Mark: "The Sabbath was made for man and not man for the Sabbath." [1]   The Sabbath, as God intended it for the Jews, was to serve them as a day of rest, but His intention never had been to make them slaves of its observance and to bind them with fetters.   The Sabbath was given for their highest good. And as far as the whole question is concerned, Jesus points to Himself as being greater than the Temple and greater than the Sabbath.   The old injunctions concerning sacrifices, new moons, and Sabbaths were in force till He came.   They were "a shadow

The Lord of the Sabbath. of things to come; but the body is of Christ." [2]   This truth stands for all times.   Upon the believers in the New Testament the Third Commandment of the Decalog enjoins only this, that they gladly hear and learn the Word of God.   Whether the Pharisees understood it or not we do not know, but the fact is: "The Son of Man is Lord also of the Sabbath." [3]   One of the an-

---

27, 11) Bruce sub Matt. 12, 6.   12) Rom. 13, 10.

13) Bruce sub Matt. 12, 4.   14) Compare Matt. 12, 6.

28, 1) Bruce observes *in loco:* "For this saying alone and the parable of gradual growth (4, 26—29), his gospel was worth preserving."

2) Col. 2, 16. 17.

3) Concerning the term *Son of Man* see *supra,* 13, and chapter VI, 20. A designation of Jesus as the Messiah which occurs eighty-four times in the New Testament.   A mere "ideal" man is certainly not Lord of the Sabbath.   It evidently refers to His person as the Messiah: "True God, begotten of the Father from eternity, and also true man, born of the Virgin Mary, my Lord."   See also Kretzmann, *Popular Commentary,* 47. 48. — Dan. 7, 13.

cient manuscripts concludes this story with a remarkable addition.[4] It reads as follows: "On the same day, seeing one working on the Sabbath, He said to him, O man, if indeed thou knowest what thou doest, thou art blessed; but if thou knowest not, thou art accursed and a transgressor of the Law." The incident is curious. But no doubt the paragraph is an interpolation. At most it contains one of those so-called "unrecorded sayings" of our Lord.[5] However, it illustrates the spirit of our Lord's teaching as understood by St. Paul: "Whatsoever is not of faith is sin." [6]

29.

(Matt. 12, 9—14.) Mark 3, 1—6. Luke 6, 6—11.

The Pharisees were corrected, but not convinced. At the first opportunity they renewed their attack upon the Lord because of His alleged breaking of the Sabbath. This took place, as it would seem, the following Sabbath [1] in Capernaum.[2] According to the custom of His earlier life as a worshiper and since the beginning of His public ministry as a teacher, Jesus entered the synagog. Among those present in that Sabbath gathering was a man whose right hand was dry, or withered,[3] as a result of an accident or a disease. According to a legend he was a stone mason, maimed by an accident, who implored Jesus to restore the use of his working hand, that he might not be forced to beg.[4] The evangelists do not state whether or not the Pharisees were responsible for his

The Man with a Withered Hand. presence. At any rate, his presence and his condition were known, and it was their purpose to watch Jesus "whether He would heal him on the Sabbath-day that they might accuse Him." By this time Jesus had gravely offended them on a number of different points: He had assumed the right to forgive sins; He associated with publicans and sinners; He disregarded their tradi-

---

28, 4) Following Luke 6, 4 in Codex D (Bezae), now at the University Library, Cambridge.

5) Somewhat like Acts 20, 35, which, however, is recorded in a canonical book.

6) Rom. 14, 23. And Heb. 11, 6: "Without faith it is impossible to please Him."

29, 1) Luke 6, 6: ἐν ἑτέρῳ σαββάτῳ.

2) Πάλιν, Mark 3, 1. Inferred from the progress of the story. The synagog previously mentioned, Mark 1, 21: "synagog"; 2, 1: "Capernaum"; 2, 15: "Capernaum"; 3, 1: "synagog."

3) Ξηρά, possibly a familiar expression in Hebrew pathology.

4) Hebrew Gospel of Nazarenes and Ebionites. Farrar, I, 439.

tions of fasting; He was guilty of Sabbath infractions. And although He had fully justified His actions and ably defended His position, their hatred was intensified with each new defeat. If by reasoning with Him they did not succeed in gaining their end, they hoped to do so by prosecuting Him according to the Mosaic Law. In the end they could resort to violence. If it must be admitted according to their own statutes that emergencies and danger to life warranted a breach of the Sabbath observance,[5] surely here was a case of healing which could easily stand postponement till the morrow. In their eagerness to provoke the Lord they asked the question: "Is it lawful to heal on the Sabbath-days?"

30.

(Matt. 12, 9—14.) Mark 3, 1—6. Luke 6, 6—11.

Jesus did not leave His questioners long in doubt. First He requested the man with the withered hand to stand forth in their midst. Then He asked a counter-question: "Is it lawful to do good on the Sabbath-days or to do evil? to save life or to kill?" In agreement with the principle stated the week before, Christ taught that "the ethically good coincides with the humane."[1] Deeds of love and mercy are never limited to days. Then there is also the possibility of doing evil by omitting to do good.[2] At any time to neglect to do good which it is in one's power to do is to do evil, to sin. And not to save life when an opportunity to do so presents itself is to kill. Would it be a proper observance of God's holy-day to do evil, to kill? "But they held their peace." They could not answer such an argument. Here was an altogether different point of view, "the ethical instead of the purely legal view of rules," to which they had always been accustomed.[3] Neither were they anxious to "go and learn."[4] Their whole purpose was to find a transgression upon which they could successfully base

Jesus Defends His Healing on a Sabbath. a charge before the Sanhedrin or, if not, to turn the admiration of the people for Jesus into suspicion and to mark Him with the stigma of a Sabbath-breaker. In an appeal to their well-nigh dead feelings of humanity Jesus justified His action by citing a practise which

29, 5) Edersheim, II, 59.
30, 1) Bruce sub Mark 3, 4.   2) Jas. 4, 17.
        3) Bruce sub Mark 3, 4.   4) Matt. 9, 13.

they themselves followed: "What man [5] shall there be among you that shall have one sheep, and if it fall into a pit on the Sabbath-day, will he not lay hold on it and lift it out?" Their own Rabbis made provisions for such cases.[6] "How much, then, is a man better than a sheep?" The argument is unanswerable. "Wherefore it is lawful to do well on the Sabbath-days." Beneficent actions are never unseasonable. And looking upon His silent and sullen accusers in just anger, "being grieved for their hearts, He saith unto the man, Stretch forth thine hand. And he stretched it out; and his hand was restored whole as the other." Thus Jesus had not broken the Sabbath law, not even according to their strictest interpretation of it. Surely it was not wrong to speak a word! For neither by touch nor by remedy nor by outward application, merely by His word of power, had He healed the man. But the Pharisees, now filled with an insane rage, went out and took counsel with the Herodians how they might destroy Him.

31.

(Matt. 12, 9—14.) Mark 3, 1—6. Luke 6, 6—11.

This was the second direct plot against the life of Jesus, first in Jerusalem, at the unnamed feast,[1] and now in the Prophet's own home province, Galilee. This is the first time that the Herodians are mentioned. While both the Herodians and the Pharisees hated the Roman rule — and each other, the Herodians were those among the people who favored the pretensions of the Herodian family to kingly power. Just why the Herodians, **The Herodians.** a political party with Sadducean tendencies, should now combine with the Pharisees against Jesus is not clear. However, in a false understanding of the King and the Kingdom they would be naturally jealous and watchful of any one whom they supposed to put forth any Messianic claims. And because the Pharisees were angry with Jesus on religious grounds, yet unable to take any measures against Him without the assent of Herod, a union of the two parties for the destruction of Jesus was very easily effected.[2]

30, 5) Τίς ἄνθρωπος. One is tempted to put emphasis on *man*. "Humanity was what was lacking in pharisaic character." Bruce sub Matt. 12. 11.

6) They held it to be permissible to pull a sheep out of a pit if it was in danger of drowning. In less extreme cases planks could be put in and food furnished. Farrar, I, 440, n. 1. Out of hatred to Christians later Jewish law was made stricter. Bruce sub Matt. 12, 12.

31, 1) John 5, 18.   2) Andrews, 261.

32.

(Matt. 12, 15—21.) Mark 3, 7—12.

The enmity of the religious and the political leaders did not cause Jesus to lose popular favor. However, their constant attacks upon Him did make it desirable for Him to remove to some other place. Jointly with His disciples, who by this time were His constant companions and were soon to be appointed to permanent apostleship, He sought a retreat on the shores of the Galilean Sea. If the need should arise for another withdrawal, He could follow the shore or retire to a secluded place across the sea. But the opposition which had been aroused against Him on the one hand had on the other resulted in a popular prestige in a manner which no one had anticipated. His visit to the unnamed feast in early spring, followed by the opening of His Great Galilean Ministry, had caused His fame to spread in every part of the land. It has always been an Oriental characteristic to flock to a prophet or popular leader.[1] Multitudes flocked to Him from every part of the Palestinian soil. There were the people of near-by Galilee. Others came from the North and South, from the busy ports of Tyre and Sidon to the hills of sandy Idumea.[2] Even exclusive Judea and haughty Jerusalem were represented, in fact, the Land

Jesus Sought by Multitudes. of Israel from Dan to Beersheba, from Perea to the

Mediterranean Sea. It was a revival movement affecting the land. There was hardly a person of average intelligence in all Palestine who had not heard of the preaching and healing of this great Galilean Prophet. From all directions they came. So great was the onrush that Jesus had to take precautionary measures. His disciples were instructed to have a small boat in readiness at all times, so that He could at once withdraw from the press should necessity so demand. "For He had healed many, insomuch that they pressed upon Him for to touch Him, as many as had plagues." It seems that it was mainly the desire for miracles which had attracted the crowds. While His Savior sympathy went out to all those afflicted with plagues and scourges,[3] while He healed "them all," [4] even permitting some to be healed by the mere touch of His

32, 1) Mark 1, 5. The case of John the Baptist.

2) Mark 3, 8. Mentioned only here in the New Testament. The country of the Edomites, Hebron and the surrounding territory, belonging to Judea. Hurlbut, *Bible Atlas,* 94. 96.

3) Μάστιγας, Mark 3, 10.   4) Matt. 12, 16.

garments, yet that was not the chief purpose of His miracles. It was not His aim to set Himself up as a miracle-monger, but to be received by believing hearts as the Messiah and Son of God. That is why He "charged them," almost vehemently, not to "make Him known." [5] Neither did He want a confession as to His divine Sonship at the urge of demons. "And unclean spirits, when they saw Him, fell down before Him and cried, saying, Thou art the Son of God. And He straitly charged them that they should not make Him known." [6]

33.

(Matt. 12, 15—21.) Mark 3, 7—12.

But there was an acknowledgment which befitted His ministry, the sincere faith of those who accepted Him as the Savior and depended upon Him for help not only for the body, but also for the soul. Thus the prophecy of Isaiah was fulfilled.[1] The Messiah, the beloved Servant of God, had at His baptism received the Spirit of God without measure. His gentle Gospel shall be a light to lighten the Gentiles to the end of the earth. His spirit would not be the sensation-seeking self-advertisement of a demagog, but the gentle and sympathetic ministry of One who supplies strength to the "bruised reed" and fresh oil to the "smoking flax." By this ministry He will bring final victory over Satan's forces and human pride. "And in His name shall the Gentiles trust."

"In His Name shall the Gentiles Trust."

32, 5) *"Er wollte mit seinen Wundern keinen Rumor machen."* Stoeckhardt, *B. G.,* 85.

6) See chapter IX, 19. 21. Luke 4, 41; Mark 1, 34.

33, 1) Is. 42, 1—4. Freely quoted by Matthew from the Hebrew with side-glances at the Septuagint. Bruce *in loco.*

CHAPTER XI.

CHOOSING OF THE TWELVE AND THE SERMON ON THE MOUNT.

Probably spring or early summer, 28 A. D.

Mark 3, 13 a. Luke 6, 12.   **1.**

Events of far-reaching importance were soon to happen. As the work of the King was rapidly shaping itself and friends and enemies were either flocking to His banner or banding themselves together to plan His ruin, the time had come for Him to select, and attach to His person, a definite number of accredited ambassadors, — not simply friendly disciples, — who might be prepared to take an actual and authorized part in the work and to deliver to them as well as to the acclaiming multitudes a manifesto of His kingdom. With these things in mind, considering also the growing

A Night in Prayer. hostility of His enemies, it was probably after a brief return to Capernaum that He went out [1] one evening in the spring of 28 A. D. to some near-by height to spend a night in prayer.[2] How often did our Lord in the days of His flesh offer up prayers and supplications [3] to His Father to gather strength for the superhuman task He had undertaken to perform — the redemption of mankind! How eagerly He set aside long hours for communion with Him in conjunction with whom He had formed the adorable, loving decree to gain fallen man back for the abodes of bliss! And on the morning, as we shall hear anon, He wanted to choose those men who were to be His messengers unto the ends of the earth; for this most important work He asked for wisdom and guidance.

Mark 3, 13 a. Luke 6, 12.   **2.**

The scene of this elevated and lonely vigil is not known. But the hill which tradition has chosen, known as the Kurn (Horns of) Hattin, from its peculiar shape, "so strikingly coincides with the intimation of the gospel narrative as almost to force the inference." [1]

1,   1) Ἐξῆλθεν (Luke), propably suggesting Capernaum, as compared with Luke 7, 1: εἰσῆλθεν εἰς Καπερναούμ.

2) Compare Mark 1, 33 and various passages in Luke. Chapter X, 2.

3) Heb. 5, 7.

2,   1) Stanley, in Andrews, 269.

[250]

It lies about eight miles from Capernaum, off the road from Tiberias to Nazareth, at an elevation of 1,720 feet above the waters of the near-by Galilean Sea.[2] Its peculiar shape attracts the attention of travelers — a ridge about a quarter of a mile in length,

The Mount. running east and west, with a small cone, or horn, on each end. Thus with its two horns the hill closely resembles the form of an Oriental saddle.[3] It is called by the Latins the Mount of Beatitudes, and it overlooks the spot where the army of Crusaders, in 1187 A. D., made its last memorable stand and was almost utterly annihilated by the vengeful hosts of Saladin.[4]

3.

Mark 3, 13 b—19 a. Luke 6, 13—16.

Whether or not the disciples were with Jesus during His night of prayer we do not know. At any rate, they knew where He was to be found and through them probably also the multitudes who were soon to assemble. It was at dawn of day and before the crowd arrived that our Lord summoned into His immediate presence the disciples, who had gradually made their appearance, very likely by special appointment.[1] The time had come when out of the number of general followers He wished to make a final choice of those whom He designated apostles. They were to be His present helpers in proclaiming the kingdom of God and in calling their countrymen's attention to the fact that Jesus was the promised Messiah. They were commissioned to preach, and in confirmation of their testimony and their appointment they were empowered

The Choice of the Twelve. to heal and authorized to cast out devils. But, as the result showed, their work had its chief significance, not in their present witness and work, but in their future labors when they were instrumental in establishing the Church, "built upon the foundation of the apostles and prophets, Jesus Christ Himself being the chief

---

2,   2) Or 1,083 feet above the Mediterranean Sea.   G. A. Smith, *Bible Atlas,* 20.

3) Farrar, I, 250.

4) W. W. Smith, *Historical Geography of the Holy Land,* 10.   In presenting our preference we admit that there is no certainty in the matter. The tradition does not date farther back than the 12th or 13th century. Robinson contends that there are a dozen other mountains in the vicinity of the lake which would answer the purpose as well. Andrews, 269.   And Edersheim says that Kurn Hattin for many reasons is unsuitable. I, 524.

3,   1) Farrar, I, 250.

Corner-stone." [2])   It is doubtful, however, whether at this time they realized the significance.   They themselves above all needed to be thoroughly instructed as to the Lord's person and work.   Their qualification for the office consisted in their having been in the company of Jesus as witnesses from the time of the baptizing activities of John to the Lord's ascension.[3])   The selection of twelve men was probably made to comport with the number of tribes of Israel.[4]) By what formal act or process, if any, He ordained or "made" [5]) them apostles we do not know.   And now, without entering deeply into the many disputed points of names and relationship, let us take a look at the list.

4.

(Compare Matt. 10, 2—4.)   Mark 3, 13 b—19 a.
Luke 6, 13—16.   (Compare Acts 1, 13.)

It is interesting to compare the lists of the apostles as given by Matthew, Mark, Luke, and the Book of Acts.

The Twelve.

	Matthew	Mark	Luke	Acts
1.	Simon Peter	Simon Peter	Simon Peter	Peter
2.	Andrew, his brother	James, son of Zebedee	Andrew, his brother	James
3.	James, son of Zebedee	John, his brother	James	John
4.	John, his brother	Andrew	John	Andrew
5.	Philip	Philip	Philip	Philip
6.	Bartholomew	Bartholomew	Bartholomew	Thomas
7.	Thomas	Matthew	Matthew	Bartholomew
8.	Matthew, the publican	Thomas	Thomas	Matthew
9.	James, son of Alphaeus	James, son of Alphaeus	James, son of Alphaeus	James, son of Alphaeus
10.	Lebbaeus, called Thaddaeus	Thaddaeus	Simon, called Zelotes	Simon Zelotes
11.	Simon the Canaanite (Kananite)	Simon the Canaanite	Judas, brother of James	Judas, brother of James
12.	Judas Iscariot	Judas Iscariot	Judas Iscariot	

3,   2) Eph. 2,20.   3) Acts 1, 21. 22.
      4) Matt. 10, 6; 19, 28; Rev. 21, 12—14.
      5) Ἐποίησε.   Bruce sub Mark 3, 14.

5.

(Compare Matt. 10, 2—4.) Mark 3, 13b—19a.
Luke 6, 13—16. (Compare Acts 1, 13.)

First of all, leading the lists, is *Peter*, the eager, impulsive, faithful, loving, and then suddenly weak, unsteady, and staggering Simon Peter. His name is mentioned first, not as if the lists were arranged according to rank, — for Jesus reproved the apostles for disputing about that privilege,[1] — but according to the common rule of priority or seniority. In the apostolic circle the group of four fishermen who were first called naturally took precedence. And **1. Peter.** in that particular group it was Peter who took the lead. Most likely he was a little older than the rest, probably about thirty-nine by this time. By occupation he was a fisherman, originally an inhabitant of Bethsaida, on the Sea of Galilee, but subsequently living with his family at Capernaum.[2] We shall meet him again and again in the gospel history. There is a tradition that he died a martyr at Rome about 67 A. D., when about seventy-five years old. His Lord and Master predicted a violent death for him;[3] he is believed to have been crucified under Nero. It is said that at his own desire he was crucified head downward, feeling unworthy to die exactly like his Master.[4]

6.

(Compare Matt. 10, 2—4.) Mark 3, 13b—19a.
Luke 6, 13—16. (Compare Acts 1, 13.)

Strictly speaking, it was really the mission-minded *Andrew*, the brother of Peter, to whom the honor goes of being the first to be called into the intimate fellowship of Jesus. On learning of John the Baptist's powerful preaching of repentance, he left Bethsaida for the banks of the Jordan, there to become a disciple of the forerunner of Jesus. Upon the announcement that Jesus was "the Lamb of God" prophesied by Isaiah, he left John and followed Jesus.[1] This great eureka moved him to look for his brother **2. Andrew.** Simon and to say to him: "We have found the Messiah." Outside of the few references in the gospel narrative nothing trustworthy is recorded of his subsequent life. According to a tradition he suffered martyrdom in Greece by crucifixion on a cross shaped like the letter X, which therefore

---

5, 1) Mark 9, 33.   2) John 1, 40; Matt. 8, 14; Mark 1, 21. 30.
    3) John 21, 18. 19.   4) Eusebius, II, 25; III, 1.
6, 1) John 1, 36—42.

is called St. Andrew's Cross. It is also related that a ship bearing two supposed relics of him was wrecked in what is now called St. Andrew's Bay in Scotland. The mariners who reached the shore introduced the Gospel in that region. Thus Andrew became the patron saint of Scotland. His festival is kept by the Greek and Latin churches on November 30. In the Church of England it has become customary on that day to preach on the subject of missions.[2]

7.

(Compare Matt. 10, 2—4.) Mark 3, 13 b—19 a. Luke 6, 13—16. (Compare Acts 1, 13.)

Next in the list we have *James* and John, the sons of Zebedee and Salome, who, it seems, was the sister of Mary, the mother of Jesus.[1] Together with his sons, Zebedee carried on a flourishing fishing trade. He had boats and hired servants, and his connections may have extended to Jerusalem; in this way can it be explained how it was that John was known in the house of the high priest,[2] though probably only by the servants.[3] That he was a man of some wealth is also usually inferred from the fact that his wife was one of those women who ministered of their substance to Jesus.[4] As the Synoptists usually place the name of James

3. James.   before that of John, it is supposed that he was the elder of this pair of brothers. That James was also among the first of the disciples of Jesus is inferred from the words of the Evangelist John: "He *first* findeth his own brother Simon,"[5] the inference being that, after Andrew had found his brother Simon, John, who does not name himself, found his brother James. He and John received from Christ the surname Boanerges, sons of thunder, probably on account of their fiery disposition, which later caused them on one occasion to desire the punishment of the Samaritans by fire from heaven.[6] The few notices of James contained in the New Testament close with the account of his

---

6,   2) Davis, *Bible Dictionary.*

7,   1) See chapter IV, 43.

2) There is also a tradition which states that Zebedee was of the house of Levi. And Eusebius (III, XXXI, 3) quotes an *Epistle of Polycrates,* Bishop of Ephesus, to Victor, Bishop of Rome, in which it is claimed that John was a priest.

3) Mark 1, 20; John 18, 15. Weiss, I, 366. The Egyptian scholar Nonnus (about 400 A. D.), quoted by B. Matthews, 477, says: "And another young companion who, being well known to the famous high priest, through his trade as a fisherman, went after Christ," etc.

4) Matt. 27, 55. 56.   Chapter VI, 18.

5) John 1, 41.   6) Luke 9, 54.

death at the hands of Herod Agrippa I, who had him beheaded, probably 44 A. D.[7]   Thus he was the first of the apostles to seal his testimony with his blood and to drink of the cup of his Lord and Master.[8]

8.

(Compare Matt. 10, 2—4.) Mark 3, 13b—19a.
Luke 6, 13—16. (Compare Acts 1, 13.)

We now come to *John*, the disciple "whom Jesus loved." [1] At least we are convinced that it was this disciple who appears in the synoptic account as John, the son of Zebedee [2] and (as is supposed) Salome, was the brother of James, and is the author of the gospel that bears the name of John. From the synoptic gospels we gain the information that he became a disciple of Jesus, that together with Peter, James, and probably Andrew he belonged to the "inner circle," [3] and that he was continually with our Lord to the end.   And from the fourth gospel we gain additional intimate glimpses, confirming our belief that this gospel was written by him. This gospel supplies us with many incidents of our Lord's ministry in Judea which have been entirely omitted by the other evangelists. It was evidently written by an eye-witness for the purpose of supplementing the synoptic account. And incidentally also we learn certain facts about the writer — that he leaned upon

4. John. the Savior when He celebrated the last Passover with His disciples and instituted His Holy Supper,[4] that the grief-stricken mother of the Savior was conducted to his house,[5] and that he outstripped Peter in running to the Savior's grave on that memorable Easter morning.[6]   John's was a meditative and contemplative disposition, and he deeply absorbed the doctrine and spirit of his Master. On account of his shrinking disposition (he does not directly mention himself, his mother, or even his brother) and the tenderness and depth which his writings reveal, his character has often been misjudged. But far from being a mystic and pietist, such as he has been represented,[7] the theological heights to which he soared in his gospel, the intensity of his devotion and zeal, and

---

7,   7) Acts 12, 2.   8) Mark 10, 39.
8,   1) John 13, 23.

2) Zebedee was of the house of Levi and Salome of the house of Judah, according to apocryphal tradition.

3) Mark 5, 37; Luke 9, 28; Mark 9, 2; 14, 33; Matt. 26, 37; Mark 13, 3.

4) John 13, 25.   5) John 19, 27.

6) John 20, 4.   7) By Brandes in *Jesus: A Myth.*

the wonderful revelations recorded in the Apocalypse show that in him was "the spirit of the soaring eagle, which, rather than the dove, has been his immemorial symbol." [8]   If, according to a thoroughly credible tradition, John lived in Ephesus till toward the end of the century,[9] he must have been very youthful at the time of his call to the apostleship in 28 A. D.   Unlike most of his associates he is said to have died a natural death.   He reached an age of about a hundred years.

9.

(Compare Matt. 10, 2—4.)   Mark 3, 13 b—19 a.
Luke 6, 13—16.   (Compare Acts 1, 13.)

Matthew and Luke group the apostles in pairs, but it seems that they can be arranged also in groups of four, the second group beginning with *Philip.*   Along with his fellow-townsmen Andrew and Simon from Bethsaida he also had journeyed to Bethany to hear the teaching of John the Baptist and there had received the first call of Jesus.[1]   Like Andrew he, too, immediately won a fresh

5. Philip.   follower, Nathanael, for Christ.[2]   His was a Greek name, Philip, lover of horses, and it seems that he also possessed a knowledge of Greek;   for a few days before the final Passover we find him acting as spokesman for certain Greeks who sought an interview with Jesus.[3]   There is little probability that the tradition identifying him with the disciple who asked permission to go and bury his father is based on fact.[4]   With the notice of his presence in the upper chamber at Jerusalem [5] his name passes into confused ecclesiastical tradition.   According to one account he is said to have proclaimed the Gospel in Asia Minor, where he suffered death by crucifixion.[6]

10.

(Compare Matt. 10, 2—4.)   Mark 3, 13 b—19 a.
Luke 6, 13—16.   (Compare Acts 1, 13.)

Because the name of *Bartholomew* is closely associated with Philip in three of the lists of the apostles, this disciple is usually identified with Nathanael of Cana, whom we remember as the

---

8,   8) Farrar, I, 256.   9) Eusebius, V, 20. 24. Weiss, I, 92.
9,   1) John 1, 43. 44.   2) John 1, 45.   3) John 12, 20—22.
    4) Matt. 8, 21;   Luke 9, 59.   Clement of Alexandria, *Int. St. B. Encycl.,* 2368.
    5) Acts 1, 13.
    6) Kretzmann, *Pop. Com.,* I, 296.   Eusebius says, V, XXIV, 3, that he fell asleep in Hierapolis, that he had two aged virgin daughters, and another daughter, who was laid to rest at Ephesus.

disciple under the fig-tree, to whom our Lord paid the tribute: "Behold an Israelite indeed in whom is no guile." [1] If so, then Bartholomew is probably a patronymic, the apostle's full name being Nathanael Bartolmai, *i. e.*, the son of Tolmai. After the

6. Bartholomew. ascension of the Lord he is said to have gone on a missionary tour to India, then a very wide geographical designation, where he left behind him a copy of the Gospel of St. Matthew. [2] According to a legend he suffered martyrdom, being sewed in a sack and cast into the sea. Another account relates how he was flayed alive and then crucified with his head downward. In works of art he is generally represented with a large knife, the instrument of his martyrdom, or, as in Michelangelo's "Last Judgment," with his own skin hanging over his arm. The festival of St. Bartholomew is celebrated on the 24th of August.

11.

(Compare Matt. 10, 2—4.) Mark 3, 13b—19a. Luke 6, 13—16. (Compare Acts 1, 13.)

This completes the group of earlier disciples gained from the circle of John the Baptist. They were present with Jesus at the marriage of Cana and subsequently followed Him to Capernaum. [1] We have already made the acquaintance of *Matthew,* the next member of the apostolic band. Modest Matthew, we are inclined to say; for, though the commonly accepted author of the Gospel according to St. Matthew, he calls himself publican, referring to his former occupation, and he mentions his name as second in a pair of two, whereas Mark and Luke mention him first. It is

7. Matthew. practically beyond all doubt that he is that Levi, the son of an unknown Alphaeus, who sat at the place of toll near Capernaum and to whom the call of the Lord came "Follow Me." "And he arose and followed Him." [2] No other information is furnished of this very important apostle and evangelist until the notice of his appearance with the other apostles at Jerusalem. [3] According to an old tradition he is said to have written his gospel in Aramaic or Hebrew. [4] But both his own original Greek style and his evident purpose in writing his

---

10, 1) John 1, 47. Chapter VI, 20. 2) Eusebius, *H. E.,* V, 10.
11, 1) John 2, 12. 2) Mark 2, 13 f. and parallels. Chapter X, 18.
3) Acts 1, 13. 4) Eusebius, III, 39.

gospel for Greek-speaking Jews [5] as well as other considerations [6] speak against this view. [7] He is said to have been the first apostle of the Ethiopians, where according to some he died a natural death, while according to others he suffered martyrdom, nails being driven through his body. [8]

12.

(Compare Matt. 10, 2—4.) Mark 3, 13 b—19 a.
     Luke 6, 13—16. (Compare Acts 1, 13.)

Associated with Matthew is Didymus, [1] the Greek name for the Hebrew *Thomas,* or Twin. On account of his doubt or disbelief regarding the resurrection of Jesus the term "the doubting Thomas" has become proverbial. He is generally described as a fearless, upright man, but slow of apprehension. Still he was the first clearly to apprehend that the Master was going forward to certain death. [2] From the point of view of his own dark outlook the Lord's comforting farewell addresses missed their mark.

8. Thomas. Puzzled Thomas interrupted the Master with the question: "Lord, we know not whither Thou goest; and how can we know the way?" [3] Not that he was frightened, but he was frankly in the dark. Thomas was no coward. When the other disciples were in hiding, although he ought to have been with them, he was out. When the joyful news of the resurrection reached his ears, he would not believe except on the evidence of his senses. Yet in the end he made a glorious confession: "My Lord and my God." [4] He was sincere to the core, but very human. Tradition has it that he labored in Parthia and Persia. At a later period India is named as the place where he preached and suffered martyrdom. An elevation near Madras is called St. Thomas Mount. [5]

13.

(Compare Matt. 10, 2—4.) Mark 3, 13 b—19 a.
     Luke 6, 13—16. (Compare Acts 1, 13.)

The third group of four apostles each is headed in all the lists by *James, the son of Alphaeus.* He is also called James the Less, [1] either on account of his stature or in order to distinguish him from James, the brother of John. His father Alphaeus is not to be iden-

---

11, 5) Quotations from the Old Testament and translation of Hebrew words and phrases, chap. 1, 23; 27, 33. 46.
     6) Primitive Gospel and original source theories.
     7) Fuerbringer, *Einleitung in d. N. T.,* 23.
     8) Kretzmann, I, 296; Meyer, *Matthew,* p. 2.
12, 1) John 11, 16.   2) John 11, 16.   3) John 14, 5.
     4) John 20, 28.   5) Davis, *Bible Dictionary.*
13, 1) Mark 15, 40.

tified with the father of Matthew; for otherwise Matthew and this James would have been brothers, a view, it is true, which has also been held.[2] So many considerations enter into the discussion that we cannot hope to solve the problem. According to our view this Alphaeus, the father of James, was the brother of Joseph, was also

9. James the Less. called Clopas,[3] and was married to a certain Mary.[4] Since Alphaeus and Clopas are probably both Greek variations of the same Hebrew name, since Mary, the wife of Clopas, is mentioned among the women standing below the cross of Jesus and since she appears as the mother of James the Less and Joses,[5] it seems that the Apostle James the Less was the son of Mary and Alphaeus.[6] Thus he was a close relative of the Lord. We identify him as the head of the church in Jerusalem in the Apostolic Age,[7] as the James who is referred to by St. Paul as the "Lord's brother," [8] and as the "James, a servant of God and of the Lord Jesus Christ," in the General Epistle of James.[9] It seems that it was this James, "the Lord's brother," who was hurled from the pinnacle of the Temple and stoned in 62 A. D.[10]

14.

(Compare Matt. 10, 2—4.) Mark 3, 13 b—19 a.
   Luke 6, 13—16. (Compare Acts 1, 13.)

As with James, the son of Alphaeus, so we meet with a problem of relationship also respecting *Judas*, "not Iscariot," [1] the brother of James, also called *Thaddaeus* or *Lebbaeus*. In his case we have a multiplicity of names and a paucity of knowledge. Thaddaeus and Lebbaeus, both terms of endearment, are believed to mean the same thing, the hearty or beloved one.[2] Since the names of Thaddaeus and Judas occupy corresponding places in the apostolic roster, it is believed that they signify the same person. There is some

---

13, 2) Farrar, I, 251.

3) It is inferred that Κλωπᾶς and Ἀλφαῖος are two slightly varying forms of the same name: חִלְפִּי. See both Meyer and Dods sub John 19, 25.

4) John 19, 25; Mark 15, 40. Chapter IV, 3. Some think that this Mary was a sister of the mother of our Lord.

5) Mark 15, 40.   6) Weiss, II, 270.

7) Stoeckhardt, *B. G.*, 87. Acts 12, 17; 15, 13; 21, 18.

8) Gal. 1, 19; 2, 9. 12.

9) Jas. 1, 1. Kretzmann, I, 297. Fuerbringer, *Einleitung*, 94.

10) Eusebius, II, 23. Josephus, *Ant.*, XX, 9, 1.

14, 1) John 14, 22.

2) Robertson, *Harmony*, 273. Leb = heart, Hebrew. Thad = a mother's breast, Aramaic. Davis, *Bible Dictionary*. Fuerbringer, *Einleitung*, 99.

dispute as to whether "Jude of James" [3] is to be rendered son or brother of James. It seems that both renderings are permissible.[4] Yet the conception "son of James" would only complicate matters. They are complicated enough already. We believe that he was the brother of James and the author of the Epistle of Jude.[5] The traditions concerning this apostle are contradictory and confusing.

10. Thaddaeus. The general consensus, however, seems to be that he labored in Edéssa. His burial is placed in Beirut and in Egypt. Of more interest is the story which concerns his grandchildren, who were brought before the suspicious Emperor Domitian, who, like Herod, it seems, feared the descendants of David. After assuring himself of their royal descent, but hearing of the spiritual character of the Kingdom, and then inquiring about their thirty-nine acres of sandy Palestinian soil and noticing their calloused hands, he felt relieved.[6]

15.

(Compare Matt. 10, 2—4.)   Mark 3, 13b—19a.
Luke 6, 13—16.   (Compare Acts 1, 13.)

Of *Simon the Canaanite*, or *Zelotes*, still less is known. By some he is connected with Cana and identified with Nathanael of Cana.[1] By others he is considered a former member of the Rome-hating Zealots, headed by Judas of Galilee, who "in the days of the taxing" [2] bitterly opposed the threatening increase of taxation

11. Simon Zelotes. at the second census of Quirinius and would have hastened by the sword the fulfilment of the Messianic prophecies. And there is still another view, according to which he, as a third brother, joins James and Judas as sons of Alphaeus.[3] Eusebius refers to a Simon who succeeded James as bishop of Jerusalem and suffered martyrdom under Trajan at the age of one hundred and twenty years.[4] And Hegesippus, whom Eusebius professes to quote, calls this son Simon a son of Clopas and Clopas a brother of Joseph.

14, 3) ʼΙούδαν ʼΙακώβου, Luke 6, 16.

4) Meyer says sub Luke 12, 14: " 'The brother of James' is without foundation in exegesis." Edersheim (I, 522): "Less probably the son of James."

5) Jude 1.   6) Eusebius, III, 19. 20.

15, 1) On account of the term Canaanite, Καναγίτης or Καναῖος. Possibly a piece of information based on an independent, yet seemingly reliable source as referring to the name of a place (Cana?); or an interpretation of a Hebrew word, קַנְאָיֵי, for ζηλώτης, zealot. See Bruce or Meyer sub Matt. 10, 4.

2) Acts 5, 37.   3) Matt. 14, 55; Mark 6, 3.

4) Trajan, 98—117 A. D.   Eusebius, II, 11. 32; IV, 22.

16.

(Compare Matt. 10, 2—4.)   Mark 3, 13 b—19 a.
Luke 6, 13—16.   (Compare Acts 1, 13.)

It seems that all these apostles were Galileans. Only one, *Judas Iscariot*,[1] that is, the man from Kerioth, located "toward the coast of Edom southward," [2] seems to have been a native Judean.[3] His name invariably appears last, and always the fatal epithet clings to him "who also betrayed Him." He presents the dark problem in the apostolate. We have the express testimony that Jesus knew him from the beginning.[4] And yet He chose him.

12. Judas Iscariot. He did not take him for the purpose of proving him a traitor. That he afterwards became a traitor can no more be charged to Jesus than the denial of Peter, which Jesus also foreknew. It cannot be doubted that Judas was sincere when he entered the ranks of the apostles, and he must have possessed special qualities which made him desirable as a disciple. In choosing His apostles, Jesus considered the special gifts and qualities of the men whom He desired to associate with Him; and as everything else that He did, so also this was done in full agreement with the Father [5] and in order that the Scriptures might be fulfilled.[6] That is about all we can say in the matter.

17.

(Compare Matt. 10, 2—4.)   Mark 3, 13 b—19 a.
Luke 6, 13—16.   (Compare Acts 1, 13.)

This, then, is "the glorious company of apostles" [1] whom the Lord united into one band as He sat with them on the summit of Kurn Hattin. They were men of different ages, tribes, abilities, occupations, training, relationship, connections, character, and

"The Glorious Company." disposition. All were chosen for a purpose. "Henceforth there was to be no return to the fisher's boat or to the publican's booth. They had now definitely attached themselves to the leadership of a Master whose fortunes they were willing to share. If need be, they would be weary with Him under the burning sun or sleep, as He did, under the starry sky." [2] And now let us return to the story.

16, 1) Judas, the son of Simon Iscariot, John 6, 71; 13, 2.
2) Josh. 15, 21. 25.   Probably near Hebron.
3) Farrar, I, 254.   4) John 6, 64.
5) John 5, 19.   6) John 13, 18.
17, 1) Farrar, I, 252.   2) Farrar, I, 258.

18.

Matt. 5, 1. 2.[1]) Luke 6, 17—20 a.

While the Lord was choosing His apostles, a vast multitude began to gather. From the densely populated shores of the Sea of Galilee, from Judea and Jerusalem, even from the coasts, or borders, of Tyre and Sidon, people came to Him in vast numbers, hoping to be healed by Him [2]) and eager to hear His words. From the peak of the mount He descended to a flat space lower down the hill.[3]) We thus combine the account of Luke and Matthew, assuming the identity of both accounts.[4]) There is "no objection at all to the supposition that our Lord may have repeated parts of His teaching at different times and places and to different

The Gathering Multitudes.

audiences and that the discourse may have summarized the contents of other sermons delivered on the Galilean hills." [5]) But before the Savior began His great discourse, His heart went out in divine pity to those of His anxious hearers who approached Him with their physical ailments. He healed all who were afflicted with diseases or were vexed with unclean spirits. And when the whole audience was seated, the newly appointed group of twelve apostles, the larger circle of disciples, and the great multitude of people,[6]) He lifted up His eyes,[7]) opened His mouth, and delivered that memorable discourse ever since known as "the Sermon on the Mount." The words may have been chiefly directed to the disciples, but they were intended also for the multitudes within reach of His voice and, since the sermon has been recorded, for all who hear or read these words.

19.

Matt. 5, 3—12. Luke 6, 20 b—26.

The Sermon on the Mount is a long sermon with many parts, the longest single discourse recorded by any of the gospel-writers. As recorded by Matthew it may be the condensation of a still longer

---

18, 1) Here we have come back to the natural order of Matthew. The topical arrangement and apparent chronological inversion of events in his gospel appears, among other things, in his placing the call of the apostles, including his own call, after the Sermon on the Mount. See notes in chapter IX, 11. 21, and X, 4.

2) Compare Mark 3, 10.   3) Καταβὰς . . . ἐπὶ τόπου πεδινοῦ.

4) For a discussion see Andrews, 268—273; A. Tholuck, *Die Bergrede Christi, Einleitung,* 1 ff.

5) Farrar, I, 258, n. 2.

6) "The company of His disciples and a great multitude of people," Luke 6, 17.

7) V. 20.

address or the inclusion of parts of other addresses delivered also on other occasions.   It is not within the sphere of this work to present a detailed analysis, and therefore we shall merely attempt a brief review of what already is a masterpiece of brevity.   The Sermon on the Mount is essentially a proclamation of the Law, but not in the fiery manner of Sinai, where thunder, lightning, and the voice of the trumpet shook the hearts with terror and agitation.[1] Nor is it a new law and the abrogation of the old,[2] but the words which the Lord spoke at this time were addressed principally to such as were children of God through faith in Him, His disciples.[3]

Beatitudes and Woes.   Some have contended that the Sermon on the Mount was not original with Jesus, especially modern Jews, who are desirous of crediting their Rabbis with most of the words of wisdom spoken by our Lord.[4]   It is claimed that every item of our Lord's teaching can be paralleled in either the Old Testament, the Apocrypha, or in the Talmudic and Midrashic literature of the period near to the time of Jesus.[5]   But what is there to this claim?   The bright sayings of the Talmud are as a few grains of wheat in an almost "immeasurable rubbish-heap in which they are embedded." [6]   We need not be disturbed by the criticisms leveled against Him who taught with authority and not as the scribes.[7]   He began His sermon with the word "blessed" and with an octave [8] of Beatitudes. Just what the thought connection was for the introduction we do not know.   An expectant multitude of people was gathered around Jesus as around its Messiah and King.   According to the hope and wish of many, if not of most of them, the Messiah should break the heavy Roman yoke resting on their necks and establish an earthly kingdom with the pomp of victory and vengeance.   Probably in order to dispel this incorrect view of His person and His kingdom, the Lord immediately set forth in unmistakable terms to

---

19,   1) Ex. 19, 16.   2) Matt. 5, 17.   3) Matt. 5, 2.

4) Emil Ludwig, *Son of Man,* 130.   J. Klausner, *Jesus of Nazareth,* 384.

5) While it is admitted that the oral Rabbinical traditions are of ancient origin, it must be noted that they were not collected and edited until toward the end of the second century after Christ.   Schuerer, I, I, 129.

6) Farrar, I, 267, n. 1.   7) Matt. 7, 29.

8) At the first glance we would count eight, viewing verses 11 and 12 as an enlargement of 10.   The traditional number, however, is seven, verses 10—12 being regarded as a transition to a new topic.   In an attempt to establish an analogy with the Decalog ten have been counted.   Bruce sub Matt. 5, 3.

explain the principles of His kingdom, to expound its laws, and to exhibit its righteousness. While it is true that He is a blessing-bestowing King, the subjects of His kingdom should not hope to be covered with jewels and showered with manna. "Blessed," yes, blessed and happy, "are the *poor in spirit; for theirs is the kingdom of heaven.*" His royal blessings reverse the world's standard of blessings in similar matters. He calls His subjects blessed, happy,— why? 1) True, most of them have not much of this world's goods, nor do they set their affections on them; in addition, they do not boast of good works and saintly virtues, but rather deplore their spiritual poverty in the sight of God. However, seeking, and through faith in Christ being partakers of, the imperishable riches of the kingdom of God, they are truly to be accounted happy. 2) In this life they mourn and weep while the world rejoices, bearing a heavier load of ills and afflictions, as a rule, than "the ungodly, who prosper in the world," but particularly lamenting over their sins. However, they shall be comforted, already in this life; above all, however, in the life to come. 3) While with regard to earthly possessions as well as to honor before men they do not insist on what is due them, which men of the world consider the only proper course, much less are proud and arrogant, but are meek and submissive, they nevertheless "inherit the earth," receiving many temporal blessings from God and enjoying them in peace and contentment. 4) They lead a life of external, or civic, right-eousness on earth, endeavoring to shine as lights in this godless world, crucifying their flesh with the affections and lusts, which to those who are not of Christ seems foolish; however, in yonder life they will, by the grace of God, eat the fruit of their works and thus be filled. 5) They are merciful, that is, they have compassion with their needy and suffering fellow-men and therefore are rich in deeds of mercy, which are an outflow of a heart filled with love. Blessed are they; for their works of charity please the Lord, and on that Great Day He will graciously reward them for all the love and mercy shown by them in this life. 6) Though *in* this world, they are not *of* the world, cleansing themselves from all filthiness of the flesh and spirit, perfecting holiness in the fear of God. In consequence of this theirs is the joy of a good conscience during their sojourn here, and when they awake in the likeness of God, they will behold His face in righteousness. 7) Being justified by faith, they have peace with God, and they therefore desire to have peace with all men, as far as this is possible, and also use their best efforts in promoting peace among men. That proves them to be true children of the God of peace, and on Judgment Day He will acknowledge them to be such before all men. What great honor! 8) Because they confess Christ and follow after holiness and are not conformed to this world, the world hates them as it did their Savior and persecutes or at least ridicules their faith, reviles and abuses them, and tries to harm them. But what a glorious prospect opens up before them! "Theirs is the kingdom of heaven" with its unspeakable bliss — a glorious compensation for all that they suffered for Christ's sake. — "But woe unto you that are rich!" that is, "rich" in the same sense as above,[9] rich, filled up, satisfied in laughing self-righteousness; for then you have your consolation, the only consolation, in advance! And another woe, of particular interest to His newly appointed apostles, is added: "Woe unto you when all men shall speak well of you!" That is no recommendation, for the chances are that undue popular praises indicate a pastoral omission of fearless denunciation of sin.

Matt. 5, 13—16.   **20.**

However, the Lord continues, in the possession of true godliness of character His followers act as a salt of the earth and shine as a light of the world.[1] The purpose of salt is to give flavor to food and to preserve it against corruption. Now, if salt loses its virtue, "it is thenceforth good for nothing but to be cast out and to be trodden under foot of men."[2] Notice our Lord's apt illustra-

The Salt of the Earth and the Light of the World.

tions and concrete, forceful language. "Ye are the light of the world." The disciple function is now considered as illuminating. The very nature of light is to shine. Otherwise it is no light. And "a city that is set on a hill cannot be hid." No particular city is named, but lofty Safed, located on a prominent elevation and visible about twelve miles to the north, has been conjectured.[3] "Neither do men light a candle and put it under a bushel."[4] The meaning is

---

19, 9) The reference of Jesus is not exclusively or chiefly physical wealth.
20, 1) Notice the all-embracing "earth" and "world." And even if $\gamma\tilde{\eta}$ is to be restricted to the Jewish soil, you still have the universal $\varkappa\acute{o}\sigma\mu o\varsigma$.

2) See Mark 9, 50; Luke 14, 34. 35. The Lord often repeated His sayings.

3) Edersheim, I, 146. Meyer *in loco.*

4) Mark 4, 21; Luke 8, 16; 11, 33: $\mu\acute{o}\delta\iota o\varsigma$, a Latin word, *modius.* See chapter IV, 42.

obvious. And as applied to the high calling of His followers: "Even so [5] let your light shine before men that they may see your good [6] works and glorify your Father [7] which is in heaven." Of course, Jesus is the only true Light of the world.[8] But the disciples, who receive their illumination through Him and power to give light to others from Him, are cautioned against a "policy of obscuration, of hiding beliefs and convictions." The world observes keenly how they live, and they are to show that, as God has called them unto holiness, so they are truly "holy in all manner of conversation."

Matt. 5, 17—20.   **21.**

Good works had been urged. Jesus now explains to His listeners what really constitutes good works before the Law. But, first of all, He defines His own position with respect to the Mosaic Law. Although the teaching of His kingdom, the Gospel, is a doctrine radically different from the Law of Moses, it does not abrogate that Law. On the contrary, One that is greater than the Temple and the Law [1] solemnly [2] affirms that He did not come to destroy, but to fulfil, and that "till heaven and earth pass, one jot or one tittle [3] shall in no wise pass from the Law till all be fulfilled." [4] This being His own attitude toward the Law, Jesus takes a firm stand against those who transgress it. He who sets aside the least of its injunctions "shall be called the least," that is, shall not be received into His kingdom, shall be excluded from its glories.[5] And he that teaches the Law in its great purpose of preparing the heart for the Gospel shall receive the reward of faithfulness. A strong statement from

"I am Not Come to Destroy, but to Fulfil."

20, 5) Revised Version.

6) Καλὰ ἔργα. "Nice" works are good works.

7) Jesus had previously called God His Father, John 5, 17, but here, quite naturally and as a matter of course, He introduces God to His disciples as "your Father which is in heaven."

8) John 8, 12.

21, 1) Matt. 12, 6—8.

2) Ἀμήν, often used by Jesus. Used iteratively by John. See chapter VI, 20. John 1, 51.

3) Luke 16, 17. Ἰῶτα is the smallest letter in the Hebrew alphabet: י. And κεραία, horn, is a little projecting point or base line distinguishing certain letters from another, similar one: ר-ד, ב-כ. See Meyer sub Matt. 5, 18, n. 1.

4) The first "till" is a strong way of saying never. The second "till" implies the adequate fulfilment made by Christ.

5) The view of Luther and others. Moral zero — the Pharisees. See Meyer and Bruce *sub loco.*

One who had been accused by the scribes and Pharisees [6] of break-ing the Law. The trouble with these people was, as Jesus shows, that in setting aside the "moral for the ritual, the divine for the traditional," [7] making a show of their pretended piety before the multitude, but in their hearts departing from the Lord, they alto-gether missed the righteousness which they so ardently sought. Granting a reward for righteousness, theirs was in no wise right-eousness, and therefore they would receive no reward. Better righteousness was necessary. For "except your righteousness exceed the righteousness of the scribes and Pharisees, ye shall in no case enter into the kingdom of heaven." That there is a higher right-eousness in the fulfilling of the Law than that exhibited in the synagog Christ shows in a number of striking illustrations.

Matt. 5, 21—26. **22.**

Referring to the customary reading of the Law in the synagogs, Christ takes His first argument from the commandment "Thou shalt not kill." [1] But the addition of the penalty, [2] "Whosoever shall kill shall be in danger of the judgment," was restricted by the Rabbis to actual murder, whereby the commandment of God was made a mere external legal enactment. Striking at the root of the matter, Jesus explains that unrighteous anger, [3] anger directed not against the sin (holy wrath), but against one's neighbor, in-sulting language, [4] and "utter disregard for a fellow-man's position in the sight of God," [5] was in God's sight an offense equal to

"Thou Shalt Not Kill." murder and punishable by the fires of hell. [6] The obligation of this commandment does not merely include the avoidance of actual killing, but reconciliation and a forgiving heart. If in the very act of sacrifice the worshiper suddenly remembers an offense

---

21, 6) The scribes were the acknowledged teachers of the people, and the Pharisees were a sect, to which many of the scribes belonged. See chapter IX, 14.

7) Bruce sub Matt. 5, 20.

22, 1) Ex. 20, 13.

2) Gen. 9, 5. 6; Lev. 24, 17; Num. 35, 16 ff.

3) "Without cause," εἰκῆ, missing in many MSS. "But whether genuine or not, this word expresses the true sense. Eph. 4, 26." Farrar, I, 261, n. 1.

4) Ῥακά, empty head!

5) "Thou fool," μωρέ, expressing contempt for some one.

6) The fire of Hinnom, the valley where the refuse of Jerusalem was burned — a figure often used by Jesus in speaking of the punishment of hell-fire. Kretzmann, I, 27. Notice: "Judgment" = local court of seven; "Council" = the court of seventy, the Sanhedrin, the Supreme Council; "hell-fire" = the highest court.

against his brother, let him interrupt his worship, and first seek
forgiveness. Mercy before sacrifice. There will be plenty of time
for sacrifice later, "lest at any time the adversary deliver thee to
the judge and the judge deliver thee to the officer and thou be
cast into prison. Verily, I say unto thee, Thou shalt by no means
come out thence till thou hast paid the uttermost farthing." [7]
"The picture is that of a debtor on the way to court with his
creditor." If any one has insulted or provoked his brother by
demeanor or language and does not seek reconciliation before he or
his brother has reached the end of a possibly short span of life, the
Judge, on the Last Day, will condemn him to that prison from
which there is no escape in all eternity.

Matt. 5, 27—32.   **23.**

In like manner Jesus opened to His hearers the proper understanding of the commandment "Thou shalt not commit adultery."
According to Rabbinical interpretation, adultery meant only deliberate unfaithfulness of those joined together in wedlock. But
Jesus explains that already a lascivious look is a transgression of
the Sixth Commandment in the sight of God. The eye must
therefore be closely guarded. And not only the eye, but also the
hand and foot. Figuratively speaking, these members and all other
"Thou Shalt Not members of the body must be con-
Commit Adultery." trolled, if necessary, by an absolute and
painful severance, or amputation, as it
were, lest the whole body be condemned. [1] Spiritual plucking out
and cutting off is meant here, as Luther remarks; or as St. Paul
puts it, the members of our body must be mortified by our battling
against "uncleanness, inordinate affection, and evil concupiscence"
in our hearts. — Continuing His explanation of the commandment,
Jesus adds a word about divorce. Because of the hardness of
hearts Moses had, as a civil measure, permitted a husband to divorce
his wife if she "find no favor in his eyes." [2] In the eyes of God,
however, there is only one true cause for divorce, [3] and that is
adultery. "Whosoever shall put away his wife saving for the cause
of fornication causeth her to commit adultery." [4]

22, 7) Κοδράντης, a Latin word, *quadrans,* worth about 3/10 cents. See
chapter IV, 42.
23, 1) Mark 9, 43—47. Repeated Matt. 18, 8. 9.
    2) Matt. 19, 7. 8; Deut. 24, 1.
    3) Mentioned here. Another ground for divorce, mentioned by St. Paul,
is malicious desertion, 1 Cor. 7, 2. 9. 15; indeed, "desertion *is* in itself
divorce." (Fritz, *Pastoral Theology,* p. 181.)
    4) Matt. 19, 9; Mark 10, 11. 12; Luke 16, 18.

Matt. 5, 33—37. **24.**

Better righteousness than that of the Pharisees is necessary also with regard to the commandment "Thou shalt not forswear thyself, but shalt perform unto the Lord thine oaths." The words as heard in the synagogs are correctly given.[1] But it seems that the interpretation left much to be desired. Among the Jewish doctors there was much sophistical and also superstitious quibbling as to the degree of the oath, whether "the ineffable name" of Jehovah was used[2] or whether the oath taken was "by heaven,"

"Thou Shalt Not Forswear Thyself." "by the earth," "by Jerusalem," or "by the head" in an attempt to evade or diminish the obligatory powers of the pledge. As Christ points out, it all amounts to the same. In the end all such oaths involve reference to God. The Lord's command is "Swear not at all." Develop such a love of, and reputation for, truthfulness that there will be no need for oaths. Of course, in this world full of falsehood an affirmation must sometimes be fortified with a solemn oath, for instance, in court, "because of the untruth and consequent distrust prevailing in the world."[3] "But it comes of evil, the evil of untruthfulness. See that the evil be not in you."[4] For all general purposes a simple "Yea, yea; Nay, nay" should suffice among God's children.

Matt. 5, 38—42. **25.**

The next reference of Jesus is to the common law of retaliation as contained in the Levitical ordinance: "An eye for an eye and a tooth for a tooth."[1] This was a good rule for the judge, but should not be privately applied. A disciple of Jesus should be willing to suffer patiently, even wrongfully, and not seek revenge by returning evil for evil. "Whosoever shall smite thee on the right cheek, turn to him the other also. And if any man will sue thee at the law and take away thy coat, let him have thy cloak also.[2] And whosoever shall compel thee to go a mile," probably a soldier forcing you to carry his baggage,[3] "go with him twain."

24, 1) Lev. 19, 12; Num. 30, 2; Deut. 23, 21.   2) Deut. 6, 13.

3) *Exp. Greek N. T.*, p. 111.   4) Bruce *in loco.*

25, 1) Ex. 21, 24.   2) Luke 6, 29. 30.

3) Bruce *in loco. Μίλιον,* another word derived from the Latin (*milia*, plural of *mille*, meaning a thousand). The term signifies a thousand paces, equal to 1,618 English yards.

A strange doctrine! Does this mean that all outrages should henceforth go unchallenged? The meaning is that the followers of
Jesus, "so far as their own person is concerned, will wisely submit
to abuses and cheerfully render exacted service and even do more
than is asked rather than stubbornly resist the inevitable." [4] There
is a time to submit, but there is also a time to fight. Passive be-
Retaliation.   havior ceases when it comes into conflict with the
law of love. Naturally, a Christian's duties to his
family, community, or country may compel him to resist rather
than to submit to injustice and insult. But that is not the point
in the present consideration. Rather than harbor evil and vengeful
thoughts in the prosecution of his individual interests a Christian
should be ready to render assistance: "Give to him that asketh thee,
and from him that would borrow of thee turn not thou away." [5]

26.

Matt. 5, 43—48. Luke 6, 27—30; 32—36.

A final illustration of the righteousness of the Kingdom as
compared with the righteousness of the synagog is taken from the
general law of love: "Thou shalt love thy neighbor." But it seems
that the Rabbis had added: "and hate thine enemy." In the Old
Testament the whole verse reads: "Thou shalt not avenge [revenge
thyself] nor have any grudge against the children of thy people;
but thou shalt love thy neighbor as thyself: I am the Lord." [1]
In understanding "neighbor" to refer to an Israelite, it seems the
inference was made that it was permissible to hate a Gentile. For
did not God in many passages command Israel to destroy the
heathen nations? It was, however, forgotten that in these instances
Israel was merely the instrument of God's penal justice.[2] The
argument could therefore not stand, especially not in view of the
precept not to vex or oppress strangers.[3] For this reason the spirit
which at the time fostered an ever-increasing hostility towards the
Gentiles, or Goyim,[4] was altogether wrong. Whether it was a per-
Love of Enemies.   sonal or a national enemy or an enemy
of the true religion, Jesus insists that all
hatred is contrary to the Law of love and the spirit which He
was striving to foster. "But I say unto you, Love your enemies,
bless them that curse you, do good to them that hate you, and
pray for them which despitefully use you and persecute you."

---

25. 4) Kretzmann, I 30.   5) See also Luke 6, 30.
26, 1) Lev. 19, 18.   2) Kretzmann, I, 30.
     3) Ex. 22, 21.   4) *Int. St. B. Encycl.,* 1215.

Certainly a strange doctrine, contrary to natural, carnal urge and instinct. And it is to be applied at all times and in all places. Whatever means the enemy may devise, "love's ingenuity must find a way to overwhelm him with goodness." [5] This is sound practise, for which we have the example of our Father in heaven, "who maketh His sun to rise on the evil and on the good and sendeth rain on the just and on the unjust." And in following this practise, a Christian will not seek his own advantage or gain. "For if ye love them which love you, what reward have ye?" "And if ye do good to them which do good to you, what thank have ye? For sinners do even the same." Nay, since love is the fulfilling of the Law, it must also, and especially, be directed to an object which will put it to test and by which it will be established as love. For this a Christian has the example of his Master,[6] the command, the example, and the promised reward of the merciful Father in heaven.

Matt. 6, 1—4.   **27.**

A right interpretation of the Mosaic Law makes it clear that the law of the scribes fell far short of the standards of true righteousness. And now Jesus directs His attention to hypocritical pharisaic practise. Certainly real righteousness is unlike the osten-

Almsgiving.   tatious hypocrisy affected, for instance, by the Pharisees in their trumpet-sounding [1] almsgiving in the streets and synagogs. "Verily, I say unto you, They have their reward. But when thou doest alms, let not thy left hand know what thy right hand doeth." But this is not opposed to the command that the disciples should let their light shine before men.[2] The difference is in the motive: the glory of God or the self-glorification of man.

Matt. 6, 5—8.   **28.**

The same applies to the theatrical and public-attracting synagog or street-corner prayers. The practise of reducing prayers to a system is contrary to the very nature of prayers.[1] With the exception of the public invocation of a worshiping group, or congregation, this act of individual worship is peculiarly an affair of

---

26, 5) Kretzmann, I, 30.   6) Luke 23, 34.

27, 1) To be understood metaphorically. By the way, the word hypocrite is derived from the Greek ὑποκριτής, stage actor, and then dissimulator in an evil sense.   2) Matt. 5, 16.

28, 1) Methodizing, at stated hours and with self-devised forms. It began after the days of Ezra and grew in the Judaistic period. Thus the hour of required prayer might — by arrangement — overtake a man anywhere. Bruce *sub loco.*

strictest privacy between the supplicant and his Maker.   Therefore, "when thou prayest, enter into thy closet, and when thou hast shut thy door, pray to thy Father, which is in secret; and thy Father, which seeth in secret, shall reward thee openly."   Neither is there any merit in vain repetitions.   As if much speaking or

Prayer. iteration were needed to reach the divine ear! This was the Gentile practise and belief; with them a very flood of words or a repetition of phrases should suggest sincerity and practically weary the gods into complying with their request.[2] Babbling prayers are utterly absurd.   It is not so much what we say to God as what He can do for us.   We need not teach God what to give, but we should learn what we need.

Matt. 6, 9—15.   **29.**

In order to instruct His disciples as to their various needs and God's manifold gifts and also, incidentally, to give them a brief formula of a proper prayer, — not to be abused, — the Lord teaches them a prayer which, because coming from Him, has always been called *the Lord's Prayer*.[1]   As to its form, it matters little or nothing whether some of the phrases have their parallels in the Old Testament or in Rabbinic expressions.   Its beauty lies in this, that the Lord has gathered matchless pearls and arranged them into a chain of costless price.   It is usually divided into the introduction, the seven petitions, and the conclusion, or Doxology.   It begins with the words *"Our Father which art in heaven."*   The

The Lord's Prayer. disciples are invited to approach God "with confidence and ask Him as dear children ask their dear father."[2]   *"Hallowed be Thy name."* Since He whom Christ wants us to address in His prayer is the only true God, it follows that He is to be made the universal and the only object of worship and to be duly honored in faith and life, by what we teach and believe and by all our deeds and actions. *"Thy kingdom come."*   That was the prayer of all Jews.   But it all depends upon what kingdom is understood.   The kingdom of the Lord comes to those only who truly hallow the one truly divine name and accept Jesus as their King, and therefore our prayer must be that it may come also to those who do not as yet know, and believe in, the Savior-King.   *"Thy will be done in earth as it is in heaven."*   Since God is our Lord and Sovereign and the kingdom

---

28, 2) 1 Kings 18, 26; Acts 19, 34.
29, 1) See also Luke 11, 2—4. Chapter XXI, 11.
       2) Luther's Catechism.

which Christ preached is a Kingdom of Grace, it follows that both His holy and His good and gracious will is to be done. It is done perfectly by the angels in heaven, whose example we, God's children, should follow, obeying God in all things and under all circumstances, and that willingly and cheerfully. *"Give us this day our daily bread."* This includes temporal gifts, daily bread, humbly and confidently to be asked for, wisely and graciously given by our Father in heaven, and with a grateful and contented heart to be received by us.[3] *"And forgive us our debts, as we forgive our debtors."* [4] This petition refers to man's greatest spiritual need, the forgiveness of sins. Forgiveness is needed daily, yea, every minute, and it is graciously granted for the sake of Christ. And "the more conscious men are of their own sins and anxious for forgiveness, the more indulgent they should become of the shortcomings of others." [5] *"And lead us not into temptation."* Not as if God tempted any one to sin; but a Christian is to beseech God that, if according to His wisdom and will he be exposed to temptation, he may "finally overcome and obtain the victory." *"But deliver us from evil."* [6] All contingencies are provided for. As the sum of all, Christians ask to be delivered from every evil of body and soul, property and honor, and finally, when their last hour has come, graciously to be taken from this vale of tears into heaven.[7] *"For Thine is the kingdom and the power and the glory forever. Amen."* Thus with a glorious doxology and fervent amen this *breviarium Evangelii* [8] is closed.[9]

29, 3) Daily, ἐπιούσιον, only here and in Luke 11, 3. An apparently simple, yet puzzling term. A *Volkswort*, says Deissmann, *Licht vom Osten*, 61. It reminds us of the word ὁμοούσιος. Jerome, in Matt. 6, 11, translates: *supersubstantialis*, while in Luke 11 he renders the word by *quotidianus*. The problem is to account for an undoubtedly simple and at the time well-understood term. Whether it is qualitative, needful, or temporal, daily, depends upon whether it is derived from ἐπεῖναι or ἐπιέναι; however, as far as grammar, at least as far as interpretation, is concerned, the temporal interpretation has most in its favor. For discussion see Bruce and Meyer *sub loco*. Tholuck, *Bergrede Christi*, 407—426.

4) The old translation "trespasses" used in Lutheran churches is that employed in the translation of Luther's Catechism in the confessional writings.

5) V. 14. 15. Bruce *sub loco*.

6) Luther's Catechism. The Revised Version renders πονηροῦ "from the Evil One." "The Eastern mind naturally thinks in the concrete, but the Western mind naturally in the abstract. This change from the Authorized Version in the Revised Version is unfortunate." Bruce *sub loco*.

7) Luther's Catechism. 8) Tertullian.

9) The closing words of the Lord's Prayer are regarded by most modern critics as an ancient liturgical insertion. They are not included in the Vulgate, St. Jerome's officially adopted Latin version, and hence the omission in the

Matt. 6, 16—18.   **30.**

What has been said of show-making almsgiving and prayers
also applies to the deception of gloomy-faced fasting. Without
condemning fasting itself,[1] Jesus next attacks the pharisaic practise
which reduced an otherwise laudable custom to a show-making

Fasting.   system. It is the heart that should show sorrow and
humility, not the body or face. And much less should
an outward sign of repentance be made a parading act of self-
glorification. "Verily I say unto you, They have their reward."
Rather than present a haggard appearance the fasting penitent
should not neglect his usual daily washing and anointing in order
that men may not even know that he is fasting. "And thy Father,
which seeth in secret, shall reward thee openly."

Matt. 6, 19—21.   **31.**

Passing on, the Lord admonishes His disciples to single-hearted
devotion to God as opposed to worldly aims and anxieties. In
spite of their pretended piety the Pharisees were, after all, a greedy

Treasure-Hoarding.   and covetous lot. The disciples are
therefore warned not to hoard up trea-
sures upon earth, "where moth and rust doth corrupt and where
thieves break through and steal; but lay up for yourselves treasures
in heaven." [1] These heavenly treasures are the lasting spiritual
gifts offered to them in the Word of God's grace. And in seeking
them, their hearts become heavenly-minded. "For where your treasure is, there will your heart be also."

Matt. 6, 22. 23.   **32.**

On the other hand, if one seeks the treasures of this world,
there also his heart will be. And what covetousness leads to
Jesus explains in the parable of the Eye.[1] The eye is the lamp

---

Latin churches. They are not found in the three leading and most ancient
existing manuscripts of the Greek New Testament, and hence their omission
in some leading printed editions and also in the Revised English Version.
But on the other hand, the words appear in the *textus receptus*, the traditional
text, and upon it Luther's translation and also the King James Version are
based. Of the thousands of manuscripts of the Greek New Testament still
in existence the words are present in 99 out of 100 copies. Moreover, they
are present in Tatian's *Diatessaron*, a harmony of the four gospels, written
about 160 A. D., earlier than any of the present-day existing manuscripts
were made. We believe that the words are genuine. And we also believe
that St. Paul refers to them in 1 Tim. 6, 15. 16. See *Hom. Mag.*, 1919,
567 ff.
30, 1) See chapter X, 22.
31, 1) Compare Luke 12, 33. 34.   **32,** 1) Compare Luke 11, 34. 35.

of the body. If the eye is healthy,[2] it gives light for all bodily functions. But if it is diseased,[3] it fails to that extent in this service. So with the eye of the soul. If the light of the love of God is shed abroad in it, love of the neighbor will follow and manifest

The Parable of the Eye. itself in deeds of love and mercy, and the whole body will be full of light. But a soul in which this light is not found begrudges the needy its temporal and spiritual welfare, and then the whole body is in darkness. And therefore, if the light-giving eye itself be dark, how great is the darkness! [4]

Matt. 6, 24.   **33.**

Covetousness perverts the heart. In fact, it is idolatry. "No man can serve two masters; for either he will hate the one and love

God and Mammon. the other, or else he will hold to the one and despise the other." A new master is chosen, to whom attachment is made. A new god is set up, whose name is Mammon.[1] "Ye cannot serve God and Mammon." [2] It is impossible for a Christian to be faithful to God and make an idol out of wealth.

Matt. 6, 25—34.   **34.**

However, a person need not necessarily be rich to be a servant of Mammon. Consequently a warning against worries and cares follows. "Therefore I say unto you, Take no thought for your life what ye shall eat or what ye shall drink nor yet for your body what ye shall put on." [1] Trust in the Lord. "Behold the fowls of the air; for they sow not, neither do they reap nor gather into barns; yet your heavenly Father feedeth them. Are ye not much better than they?" Cares are needless and bootless. "Which of you by taking thought can add one cubit unto his stature?" [2]

32,   2) Ἁπλοῦς, "single," integer, sound.

    3) Πονηρός, evil.   4) Bruce *sub loco.*

33, 1) Riches personified. Μαμωνᾶς, Plutus, a Chaldee, Syriac, and Punic word. Bruce *sub loco.*

    2) See also Luke 16, 13.

34, 1) See also Luke 12, 22—31.

    2) Ἡλικία means both stature and age; πῆχυς means ell, six handbreadths, or 1½ feet. There is much difference of opinion as to whether Jesus referred to height of body or length of life. Most recent interpreters favor the latter. Ps. 39, 5; Job 14, 5. "Who would call adding a cubit to his height a small matter, the expression of Luke 12, 26?" Bruce *sub loco.* The adoption of either the one or the other view leaves the thought unchanged.

Or take the example of flowers. "Consider the lilies of the field.[3] How they grow! They toil not, neither do they spin." How affectionately the Lord speaks of flowers! "The lilies are viewed individually as living beings, almost as friends." [4] "Solomon in all his glory was not arrayed like one of these." "These are golden words of a Savior who had eyes for the beauties of nature. And now the lesson." "If God doth so clothe the grass in the field, which to-day is and to-morrow is cast into the oven,[5] shall He not

Counsels against Care.

much more clothe you, O ye of little faith?" The disciples of Jesus should therefore guard against the Gentile practise of distrust and sinful cares. "Your heavenly Father knoweth that ye have need of all these things." There is only one permissible care: "Seek ye first the kingdom of God and His righteousness." Then the little things of this earthly body and life will come as a matter of course. "Take therefore no thought for the morrow; for the morrow shall take thought for the things of itself. Sufficient unto the day is the evil thereof."

35.

Matt. 7, 1—5. Luke 6, 37—42.

Not only a pharisaic vice, but a common sin found in every-day life, is the sin of fault-finding, of criticizing or judging others. To this subject Jesus turns without apparent connection. In the practise of many a very cheap way of claiming moral superiority is to exalt themselves by disparaging others. But Jesus says: "Judge not that ye be not judged." This command does not refer to a certain kind of judging enjoined in Scripture, as that

"Judge Not, Condemn Not."

of an erring brother,[1] or of people in public office, but rather the sin of gratuitous condemning, outside the divinely authorized sphere. Besides its general injustice and its being committed in a spirit of self-satisfaction, it does nobody any good. Before any one attempts to censure others, he ought, first of all, to have a proper self-knowledge. "Can the blind lead the blind?"

34, 3) Κρίνα τοῦ ἀγροῦ. The *lilium Persicum,* Emperor's crown, or *Kaiserkrone,* according to some; the red anemone, growing luxuriantly under thorn-bushes, according to others. We don't know. All flowers as represented by the lily is probably the best view. "Jesus would have said the same thing of the primrose." The reference points to the season of spring when the flowers are in bloom. Bruce *sub loco.*

4) Bruce *sub loco.*

5) Hay was used to heat clay ovens. Meyer *sub loco.*

35, 1) Matt. 18, 15.

Very often he that sees the faults of others is blind to his own. "Why beholdest thou the mote [2] that is in thy brother's eye, but considerest not the beam [3] that is in thine own eye? First cast out the beam out of thine own eye, and thou shalt then see clearly to cast out the mote out of thy brother's eye."

Matt. 7, 6. 36.

A sort of corresponding reverse to uncharitable judging is to give holy things to the dogs and to cast pearls before the swine. A Christian's most holy things are the pearls of God's Word and

Casting Pearls Before Swine.

the Sacraments. To cast these before dogs and swine, that is, before people of whom it is known that nothing is sacred to them, is to expose that which is sacred to desecration. In the blasphemous attacks "some of the mud will spatter on him who lacked judgment, and the offender will be responsible for the desecration and therefore also guilty before God." [1]

Matt. 7, 7—11. 37.

The subject of prayer is taken up again. In the struggle for true righteousness prayer is necessary if any progress is to be made. "Ask" in all humility, "seek" with untiring application, and "knock" with earnestness and perseverance. [1] Every one will

Ask, Seek, Knock.

receive if he but comes as a child to his father. A parable explains this truth. "What man is there of you, whom if his son ask bread, will he give him a stone? Or if he ask a fish, will he give him a serpent?" [2] A loving father may be unable to comply with the request made to him, but he would not add mockery to inability. And the application: "If ye, then, being evil, [3] know how to give good gifts unto your children, how much more shall your Father in heaven give good things to them that ask Him!"

35, 2) Κάρφος, chaff.

3) Δοκός, wooden beam, joist.

36, 1) Kretzmann, I, 37.

37, 1) Kretzmann, I, 38. See Luke 11, 9—13.

2) Ὄφις, serpentlike fish found in the Sea of Galilee, three feet long, often caught in the nets, and of course thrown away like the dogfish in our waters. Bruce *sub loco*.

3) Πονηροί, a strong word, morally evil. "Such a mean spirit is considered unnatural even among men, from whom one might, according to the natural depravity of the hearts, possibly expect a behavior of that kind." Kretzmann, I, 38. Or "evil" as compared with God. Meyer *sub loco*.

38.

Matt. 7, 12. (Luke 6, 31.)[1]

And now a rule for all men and all times. It is generally known as *the Golden Rule*. Since it agrees with the fundamental requirements of the law of neighborly love, it sums up the Law and the Prophets. While coincidences of a more meager kind[2] might be advanced from apocryphal[3] sources, from Greek, Roman, and **The Golden Rule.** Oriental teachers, — something similar, but not quite like it, — the commandment as given by Jesus is revolutionary in the ethical experience of mankind.[4] "All things whatsoever ye would that men should do to you, do ye even so to them; for this is the Law and the Prophets." Probably this precept is more frequently quoted than any other divine rule of Christian conduct. However, it would be desirable that, rather than the usual appeal of "should do to you," there would be more compliance with "do ye to them." Then peace, love, and harmony would soon generally obtain in the world.

Matt. 7, 13. 14.   ## 39.

In conclusion, a few lessons of personal righteousness are driven home by powerful parables. Two ways are briefly sketched, leading from the present life to that beyond the grave. "Enter ye in at **The Narrow Way.** the strait gate; for wide is the gate, and broad is the way, that leadeth to destruction; and many there be which go in thereat."[1] The broad way is the way of sinful indulgence and unrestricted liberty; but it "leadeth to destruction." The narrow way is the way of the Kingdom as outlined by Christ, the way of righteousness, strait, narrow, contracted; but it "leadeth unto life. And few there be that find it."

40.

Matt. 7, 15—23. Luke 6, 43—45.

The way to life is easily missed. In fact, a warning must be posted against such as would deliberately misdirect travelers on their way to heaven. "Beware of false prophets, which come to you in

---

38, 1) Transposed.   2) Meyer *sub loco*.

3) Negative in Tobit 4, 15. "The negative confines us to the reign of justice, which is still far from the positive, which takes us into the region of generosity and grace and so embraces the Law and the Prophets." Bruce *sub loco*. Edersheim, II, 236.

4) James Stalker, in *The Ethics of Jesus; Int. St. B. Encycl.*, 1029.
39, 1) Compare Luke 13, 23.

sheep's clothing; but inwardly they are ravening wolves." Certainly a striking description of those soul-murderers who falsify God's Word and substitute for it their own "tongues and say, He saith." [1] Even as in the Old Testament they caused God's people to fall into error and in the time of Christ raised their voice of deception, so they are still doing their nefarious work to-day. Many of them are greedy for money and eager for power. Therefore "try the spirits whether they are of God." [2] The principle of testing them is "their fruits." "Do men gather grapes of thorns or figs of thistles?" "Wherefore by their fruits ye shall know them." And what are these fruits? Their professed loyalty, their apparent sincerity, and evident zeal?

Wolves in Sheep's Clothing.

No. "Not every one that saith unto Me, Lord, Lord, shall enter into the kingdom of heaven." They and their followers may display the greatest piety and religious fervor. Or are deeds of charity, even prophecy, the casting out of devils, healing, or some other wonderful works the fruits by which they are to be known? All these are no safe criterions. Fruits of this kind may be the deceptive sheep's clothing of which the Lord has spoken. Looking forward to a later day, when false prophets and "Gospel merchants" and their followers would deceive people in the name of Christ and to the day when they will be finally judged, Jesus says: "Many will say to Me in that Day, Lord, Lord, have we not prophesied in Thy name and in Thy name have cast out devils and in Thy name done many wonderful works? And I will profess unto them, I never knew you; depart from Me, ye that work iniquity." The fruits by which we are to recognize them as false prophets are their pernicious doctrines, which destroy the souls of men. Their false teachings make them, not murderers or thieves or tyrants, but — *false prophets.*[3]

41.

Matt. 7, 24—27. Luke 6, 46—49.

And now, in the form of a majestic parable, a grand *finale.* A proper hearing of Christ's words implies appropriate obedience to them.[1] He who heard and did these sayings is likened unto a wise man who built the house of his life upon the solid foundation of a living rock. "And the rain descended, and the floods

---

40, 1) Jer. 23, 31.   2) 1 John 4, 1.   3) Ψευδοπροφῆται.
41, 1) Jas. 1, 22.

came, and the winds blew and beat upon that house; and it fell not, for it was founded upon a rock." To "evangelic ears this eloquent description may, in the first instant, have a legal sound, but the doing which Christ had in mind is the opposite of pharisaic

The Two Builders. legalism." [2]   Not the builder's doing or obedience makes him firm, but the foundation upon which his house is erected. "On Christ, the solid Rock, I stand; All other ground is sinking sand." [3]   Storms and tempests will not blow down this house, and trials and temptations will not find the builder unprepared.   But the playhouse of life easily and quickly erected upon smooth sands of good-weather Christianity, of hearing and not doing, is inevitably destined to collapse before the onrushing surge.   "And every one that heareth these sayings of Mine and doeth them not shall be likened unto a foolish man, which built his house upon the sand; and the rain descended, and the floods came, and the winds blew and beat upon that house; and it fell, and great was the fall of it."

42.

Matt. 7, 28—8, 1.

The Sermon on the Mount left a profound impression upon the multitudes. "The people were astonished at His doctrine; for He taught them as one having authority and not as the scribes." [1]   Here was a teacher with a message of eternal truth. While the professional teachers "droned out their traditions and the injunctions of a Law which was in effect dead in their own

Teaching as One Having Authority. lives," [2] never as much as by a hair's breadth passing beyond the carefully watched boundary lines of commentary and precedent, here was authoritative preaching; it was the voice of Him who was both God and man in one person.   At the conclusion of the sermon the immense throng dispersed.   But there were still many, most likely those whose homes lay in the Plain of Gennesaret, who followed their descending Teacher — once more on His way to near-by Capernaum.

Here follows in the order of Matthew the healing of the leper.[3]

41,   2) Bruce *sub loco.*

3) Rev. Edward Mote in the hymn "My Hope is Built on Nothing Less."

42,   1) Mark 1, 22.   With regard to the scribes see chapter IX, 14.

2) Kretzmann, I, 41.   3) Matt. 8, 2—4.   See chapter X, 4.

43.

Matt. 8, 5—13. Mark 3, 19 b. Luke 7, 1—10.

Our Lord had scarcely arrived at His "home," in Peter's house, when He was approached by a delegation of Jewish elders, probably the leaders of the local synagog,[1] in the interest of a centurion whose faithful and beloved servant lay in the agony and peril of paralytic attack.[2] Most likely this captain of a hundred soldiers — whether Roman or not we do not know, but certainly of heathen descent — was a military officer of Herod Antipas [3] and probably stationed just out of Capernaum, on the Way to the Sea. From a glimpse which we get of his person and character we are not surprised that he appealed to Jesus for help. He was a worthy man, who loved Israel, a thing most rare in any Gentile, and reverenced Israel's God. This affection for God's people took visible form in the erection by him of a beautiful synagog at his own expense, the ruins of which, it is believed, can still be seen to-day.[4] Nor was the name of Jesus unknown to him. Capernaum was the headquarters of this new Galilean Prophet and the scene of many of His recent miracles as well as the home of a fellow-official

The Centurion's Servant. of the court of Herod, the *basilikos,* whose son Jesus had healed from a distance at Cana, about seven months before.[5] Quite consistent with his character were his scruples to make a direct and personal appeal to Jesus. The more highly he esteemed Jesus, the more he felt his own unworthiness, probably even foolishly entertaining scruples on account of his Gentile birth. Therefore the employment of Jewish friends to intercede in his behalf. Their willingness to plead the cause of a despised Gentile speaks well for them as well as for the centurion. Incidentally it also shows that not all the Jewish leaders had turned against Jesus, especially not in Galilee. Not only did these elders plead the cause of the centurion, but they pleaded it well. Immediately Jesus promised to grant the request. "I will come and heal him." We are led to

---

43, 1) Luke 7, 3: πρεσβυτέρους. Bruce thinks that the reference to the elders is probably to the elders of the city rather than to the rulers of the synagog. According to Schuerer, II, I, 150, in strictly Jewish communities the same men would be the elders of the community and the rulers of the synagog.

2) Παραλυτικός. See Matt. 9, 2. Probably inflammatory rheumatism. Andrews, 644. See chapter X, 11.

3) Andrews, 274.

4) Edersheim, 8, 434. Barton, *Archeology and the Bible,* 98.

5) See chapter VII, 21. John 4, 46—54.

infer that the house of the centurion was not in Capernaum itself, but rather in the neighborhood, probably on the road southward to the near-by Galilean capital Tiberias, recently rebuilt by Herod. But on the way other messengers arrested the approaching Lord with the request not to enter under the roof of an unworthy Gentile,[6] but to heal the suffering servant by a mere word of power.   An argument is advanced from the centurion's own military experience. Though a subordinate officer himself, "under authority," yet he had well-disciplined servants, ever ready to do his bidding.   "And I say unto one, Go, and he goeth; and to another, Come, and he cometh; and to my servant, Do this, and he doeth it."   How much more, then, could not Jesus, with the hosts of heaven at His command, send His "viewless messengers to do His will without undergoing all this personal labor"![7]   The Lord was struck by this remarkable faith.   What He expected in Israel He received from the Gentiles.   Turning to the multitude following Him, He stated the solemn truth that many of those called by the Rabbis "children of darkness"[8] would come from the East and West and recline with Abraham, Isaac, and Jacob at the tables of the Messianic banquet hall, but the "children of the Kingdom," or "the children of the banquet hall," themselves would be cast out into outer darkness, where there is weeping and gnashing of teeth.   "The imagery is Jewish, but the truth is universal and lasting."[9]   To stress the greatness of the miracle, the remark is added that the suffering servant — of whom no details are given — was "healed in the self-same hour," as was ascertained by the messengers at their return.

Here follow in the order of Matthew the healing of Peter's mother-in-law and in the evening the healing of many others.[10]

43, 6) Ἱκανός, "I am not worthy," not fit, Levitically or Judaistically speaking, and therefore not worthy spiritually, morally, religiously.   Edersheim, I, 548.

7) Farrar, I, 281.

8) Edersheim, I, 550.

9) Bruce sub Matt. 8, 12.

10) Matt. 8, 14—17.   See chapter IX, 20. 21.

CODEX ALEXANDRINUS. (A)

Now in the British Museum. Fifth century. Luke 6, 42—7, 16.

"Young man, I say unto thee, Arise. And he that was dead sat up."
Luke 7, 14. 15.

ΝΕΑΝΙCΚΕCΟΙΛΕΓΩ	Νεανίσκε, σοὶ λέγω,
ΕΓΕΡΘΗΤΙΚΑΙΑΝΕΚΑΘΕΙCΕΝ	ἐγέρθητι. Καὶ ἀνεκάθισεν
ΟΝΕΚΡΟC	ὁ νεκρός.

(Fifth line from bottom, second column.)

CHAPTER XII.

A SECOND PREACHING TOUR, INCLUDING THE PARABLES BY THE SEA:

Probably summer and autumn, 28 A. D.

1.

Luke 7, 11—17.

After a brief stay in Capernaum, in fact, the very next day,[1] we find Jesus on a twenty-five-mile journey to a city in Southern Galilee, on the slopes of Jebel el Duhy, or Little Hermon. The name Nain — or Nein, which it still retains — means Green Pastures or Vale of Beauty, and its situation, commanding an extensive view of the Plain of Esdraelon and the northern hills, justifies its flattering title.[2] It is a long journey, but we are told that Orientals walk rapidly and start early in the morning, so that the town may have been reached some time in the afternoon.[3] Traveling with

The Raising of the Widow's Son at Nain. Jesus were His disciples and an adoring and rejoicing crowd. As the glad procession was climbing to the gates of the city, it was met by another — and sad — procession issuing forth to bury a dead youth outside of the walls. It was an exceptionally sad funeral, since the young man was an only son and his mother was a widow. We can picture to ourselves the mournful scene: the flute-players and the mourning women; the simple bier, that is, an ordinary open wooden frame, on which the body was carried to the grave; the lonely widow, accompanied by her relatives, neighbors, and a host of sympathizing friends. "And when the Lord saw her," — this is the first time that the Evangelist Luke uses this title,[4] — "He had compassion on her and said unto her, Weep not." This was not only a pious phrase, but what Jesus thought Jesus wrought. Of course, the grief-stricken widow could not yet fully comprehend what Jesus meant, especially when He "came and touched the bier." It was a moment of breathless

---

1, 1) Ἐν τῇ ἑξῆς (ἡμέρᾳ, understood). Farrar, I, 284, n. 1.

2) Farrar, I, 284. 3) Andrews, 277.

4) Ὁ Κύριος, the heavenly Christ and Lord of the Church. Bruce *sub loco.*

expectation. "And they that bare him stood still." Here was one who unconcernedly disregarded the greatest of all defilements, that of contact with the dead.[5] But His was a touch which rendered clean and removed that which made the ceremonial ordinances necessary.[6] Immediately the heart-thrilling and life-giving utterance was heard: "Young man, I say unto thee, Arise." But would this word pierce "the more than midnight darkness of the world beyond the grave"?[7] It did. It was a word of sovereign command. The supposedly impossible happened. Life itself again pulsated through the lifeless body. "And he that was dead sat up and began to speak." Truly, the days of Elijah and Elisha had returned.[8] Yes, far greater days had come. The miracle was not the result of earnest supplication and much wrestling in prayer, but here was the Source of Life, personally restoring a dead person to life. "And He delivered him unto his mother." The miracle could have but one effect: "And there came a fear upon all." The manifestation of the almighty power which had just been witnessed moved many to glorify God — at least for the moment — and to admit that a great prophet had risen up and that God had visited His people. There was no doubt about the miracle because its reality was undeniably evident. Here was a living and walking witness who could testify to the truth that Jesus was the Lord. Many years later an apologist of the early Christian Church, Quadratus, whom Eusebius called an *auditor apostolorum,* a pupil of the apostles, could point out to the Roman Emperor Hadrian: "The works of our Savior were always present, for they were genuine: those that were healed and those that were raised from the dead, who were seen not only when they were healed and when they were raised, but were also always present; and not merely while the Savior was on earth, but also after His death they were alive for quite a while, so that some of them have lived even to our day."[9] The rumor of the astounding miracle performed by the Lord spread to Judea and to all the region round about, to the North, South, East, and West, and also penetrated the prison-walls at Machaerus, where John the Baptist lay imprisoned.

1,   5) Edersheim, I, 557.

     6) See Matt. 8, 3.   Chapter X, 7.   Num. 19, 11 ff.

     7) Farrar, I, 286.

     8) 1 Kings 17, 21;   2 Kings 4, 35.

     9) Eusebius, *H. E.,* IV, 3.

2.

(Matt. 11, 2—6.)[1] *Luke 7, 18—23.*

By this time John the Baptist had spent a number of months in prison.[2] When the report of our Lord's wonderful ministry reached him, he sent two of his disciples who still clung to him to Jesus with the question, "Art Thou He that should come, or do we look for another?" Not that there was any doubt in the mind of him who had said, "Behold the Lamb of God, which taketh away the sin of the world," [3] and who had already released some of his best disciples to Jesus. But some of his disciples refused to give up their allegiance to him. They could not distinguish between essentials and non-essentials and felt that the austere habits of John belonged to the substance of a truly moral life. A number of them were even now allying themselves with the Pharisees,[4] and others, still adhering to him, would probably be tempted to perpetuate their allegiance to him by organizing a sect of Johannites instead of following Christ and becoming Christians.[5] True to his God-given mission, which was to direct the people to Christ as the Redeemer, John improved this favorable opportunity by

The Message from John the Baptist. sending two of his disciples to Jesus with a definitely worded question. What he himself failed to do by testimony and direction he hoped Jesus would accomplish by attraction and Messianic identification. The moment was auspicious; for just then Jesus was performing miracles. The proof of His Messiahship was before their very eyes. In His answer Jesus definitely identified Himself as the Messiah by an appeal to prophecy: The blind see, the lame walk, the lepers are cleansed, the deaf hear, and — for no doubt they had heard of the miracles at Nain — the dead are raised up; and the poor have the Gospel preached to them.[6] Let them draw their own conclusions from this prophetic summary of what the Messiah would do. In its form the reply was directed to John, "Tell John," but in its appeal to his disciples, especially the final remark: "Blessed is he whosoever shall not be offended in Me." [7] This is a word of warning directed especially

---

2, 1) Transposed.

2) Since the early spring of 28 A. D. See chapter VIII, 11. He seems to have enjoyed a measure of freedom and intercourse with his disciples even during his confinement.

3) John 1, 29.   4) Matt. 9, 14.   Chapter X, 22.

5) Luther, quoted by Kretzmann, I, 61.   6) Is. 35, 5. 6; 61, 1.

7) Notice the "Me." By changing a general to a personal statement, Jesus plainly identifies Himself with the promised Christ.

to the two messengers. Some of the disciples of John were not satisfied with the manner in which Jesus and His disciples were conducting themselves as to fasting, washing of hands, and other Levitical regulations.[8] "If any one is so carried away with a false asceticism as to want to curtail the liberty of the New Testament and for that reason is offended at Jesus, he has only himself to blame for the consequences." [9]

3.

(Matt. 11, 7—15.) Luke 7, 24—28.

No sooner had the messengers of John departed than Jesus delivered that memorable eulogy over His friend and forerunner, not in the spirit of idle flattery nor for the purpose of restoring his supposedly endangered authority,[1] but to convince the people, especially their leaders, of their inconsistency in accepting John as a divinely appointed prophet, but rejecting Him to whom he had always pointed. "What went ye out into the wilderness for to see? A reed shaken with the wind?" A public-pleasing demagog? A well-fed and -clothed, man-serving court preacher? A prophet? "Yea, I say unto you, and much more than a prophet. This is he of whom it is written, Behold, I send My messenger before Thy face which shall prepare Thy way before Thee." [2] Not only of all Old Testament prophets, but also of all Old Testament people, indeed, of all "that are born of women," he was the greatest. There was no one in Old Testament times that approached him in the capacity of rendering such direct, such way-preparing service to the kingdom of God. Other prophets

Encomium of the Baptist. had pointed from the dim distance, but he stood on the threshold. And yet, as compared with the children of the Kingdom, even he, John, remained a child of the Old Testament. He introduced, but did not fully see and enjoy, the day of Jesus Christ. His career closed before Jesus entered into His glory. In this respect therefore it is true: "He that is least in the Kingdom is greater than he." Until the day of John the children of God were kept under the Law, the schoolmaster;[3] but since John the Gospel ruled. As a result many who by Pharisaic legislation had previously been ruled out of the Kingdom, the publicans, the sinners, and heathen coming to sincere repentance, were now, as it were, storm-

---

2,   8) Luke 5, 33.   9) Kretzmann, I, 303.
3,   1) On account of his embassy to Christ, John 1, 19—25.
      2) Mal. 3, 1.   3) Gal. 3, 23. 24.

ing the kingdom of heaven, taking it by force.[4] In one prophecy
the herald of the Messiah is also called Elijah.[5] This prophecy
does not refer to a return of Elijah in person, but, correctly understood, John was this Elijah, sent to make ready the hearts of men
for the acceptance of the Messiah. In fact, the correct understanding of the whole matter is this: The purpose and the person
of the herald, the nature of the preparation, the nature of the
King and the Kingdom, required intelligent attention and believing
hearts. "He that hath ears to hear, let him hear." [6]

4.

(*Matt. 11, 16—19.*) *Luke 7, 29—35.*

In spite of his greatness, John did not receive the general
recognition which he deserved. While many among the common
herd, the publicans and sinners, acknowledged the prophetic legit-
imacy and power of his office and thus "justified," or endorsed,
God in sending him as a herald of the Messiah-King, the accredited
leaders and teachers "rejected the counsel of God against themselves, being not baptized of him." Not only, however, did they
take offense at his message of repentance, but they were also
greatly displeased with his austere ways and manner of living,
which so biased them against him that they declared him to be
possessed of a demon.[1] But their attitude toward Jesus was not
a whit better notwithstanding the fact that, in contrast to John
the Baptist, His demeanor and address were such as to draw the

"Wisdom Justified of All Her Children." masses to Him, and His mode of
living did not differ from that of
other people. These leaders were
men of peculiar whims and fancies, whom no one could please.
They were like capricious children, whom no game suits which
their playmates propose. "We have piped unto you, and ye have
not danced; we have mourned to you, and ye have not wept."
When some want to play at marriage, others want to play at funeral.
John, because of his abstemiousness and rigorous life, was a madman; Jesus, because He ate and drank as did other men, was called
"a gluttonous man and a wine-bibber, a friend of publicans and

---

3, 4) Matt. 11, 12.

5) Mal. 4, 5. 6. Without any authority from the Hebrew the LXX
here reads Ἐλίαν τὸν Θεσβίτην.

6) A proverbial form of speech often used by Jesus after an important
utterance, here for the first time.

4, 1) When and where this was said has not been recorded by any of the
evangelists.

sinners." "But," said Jesus, "wisdom is justified of all her children." John and Jesus taught the true heavenly wisdom, and there were, by the grace of God, always some who were thankful for this wisdom unto salvation, for instance, the disciples of Jesus, "the publicans and the harlots," [2] and others, who realized that they were sick and therefore needed a physician, a physician for their souls, Jesus.[3]

(Matt. 11, 20—24.) [1]   **5.**

The Lord is kind and gracious; but woe unto them that reject His grace! It was during the time of this portion of His Galilean ministry, it seems,[2] that Jesus delivered His famous woes over the cities that had been so highly favored. The land of Zebulun and Naphtali had seen a glorious light;[3] its inhabitants had been filled with astonishment; they had praised the manifest glory of God; they had flocked to the Great Prophet arisen in their midst; they had eagerly sought and received His help for their bodily needs; *but* — they did not repent. There was Chorazin, otherwise unmentioned, a town near the northwestern shore of the Sea of Galilee, where mighty unrecorded works of Jesus had been performed. If these same works had been performed in the heathen cities of Tyre and Sidon, rarely visited by the prophets of old, these

"Woe unto Thee, Chorazin!" cities would have repented in sackcloth and ashes. And there was Bethsaida, on the northern shore of the lake, in whose streets Andrew, Philip, and Peter had played in their boyhood days, likewise the scene of many unrecorded works of Christ. "It shall be more tolerable for Tyre and Sidon at the Day of Judgment than for you." And especially Capernaum, which had been honored more than any other city on Jewish soil. Bethlehem was justly honored as the town of the Savior's birth. Nazareth received the privilege of sheltering Him in the days of His childhood and youth. But Capernaum, the scene of His greatest activity and His headquarters and home during the greater part of His public ministry, had been "exalted unto heaven." However, had it

---

4,   2) Matt. 21, 32.   3) Matt. 9, 12. 13.

5,   1) Compare also Luke 10, 13—16.

2) In Luke's arrangement the woes are placed in the time when the Lord sent out the Seventy, in which connection, at the final withdrawal of Jesus from Galilee, they are also perfectly in order. Useless difficulties in the historical arrangement can be avoided by remembering that Jesus found need and occasion to repeat many of His sayings. Andrews, 280. Kretzmann, I, 64.

3) Matt. 4, 15.

repented? The greater the opportunity, the greater the responsibility. "If the mighty works which have been done in thee had been done in Sodom, it would have remained until this day. But I say unto you, That it shall be more tolerable for the land of Sodom in the Day of Judgment than for thee." Such is the curse. And these words are no idle threat; for it is a terrible thing to despise God's visitation of grace.

(Matt. 11, 25—27.) [1]   **6.**

On the other hand, the Lord be thanked that some did see the light. Probably these were not always found among the wise and intelligent generally, the scribes and Pharisees, who deemed

"Revealed unto Babes." themselves the custodians and dispensers of true wisdom, but among the novices and babes, unversed in scholastic wisdom, such as the fishermen disciples, yes, publicans, harlots, and sinners. This came about by the gracious will of the Father, and in perfect accord with it Jesus was at particular pains to reveal the way of salvation to this despised class of people; and He thanked the Father for having given success to His preaching. [2]

(Matt. 11, 28—30.)   **7.**

Now He extends a gracious invitation to all who feel the burden of their sin and yearn to be relieved of it to seek refuge with Him. "Come unto Me, all ye that labor and are heavy laden, and I will give you rest." These wonderful words of universal

"Come unto Me, grace should receive individual appli-
All Ye that Labor." cation. If offered to all, then also to you personally. Accept Christ in childlike faith as your Lord and Savior. In Rabbinical imagery [1] and Old Testament words [2] New Testament Gospel truths are expressed. "For My yoke is easy, and My burden is light." Notwithstanding the strait gate, the narrow way, and the cross that is to be imposed, all believers in Christ will find true rest for their souls in Him who has taken the burden of their sins from their shoulders and put them upon His own.

6,   1) Compare also Luke 10, 21. 22.

2) On this and the following, this perfect pearl of the sayings of Jesus in Matthew, one of "Johannean" splendor, see Meyer in Matt. 11, 22 ff.

7,   1) "Take My yoke and learn from Me" expresses the relation of master and pupil.

2) Jer. 6, 16.

Luke 7, 36—50.   **8.**

"Come unto Me, all ye that labor and are heavy laden, and I will give you rest." It was soon seen that these infinitely tender and inviting words could be put to a practical test. While the Lord was in an unknown city in this period of His Galilean ministry, He received and accepted an invitation into a Pharisee's house. Some think that it was at Nain, but it seems that some time must be allowed for the report to John the Baptist and the embassy of His disciples. And on account of the progress of the story others think that it was at Magdala, on the western shore of the Sea of Galilee. This is on account of the popular identification of the unknown sinner with Mary Magdalene. But we are not so sure of that. Neither do we know the particular cause or object of the invitation. But since there was not yet an open rupture with the pharisaic party, and in order that there might be no excuse for saying that Jesus ate with publicans and sinners and avoided the Pharisees, there was no reason for a refusal of the invitation. Of one thing, however, there is no doubt, namely, that the inviting host, whose name was the common Simon, but who otherwise is unknown,[1] was a Pharisee both by party affiliation and character. In a few lines the term "Pharisee" is repeated four times by the evangelist, almost, as it were, by intention. While Jesus outwardly enjoyed the hospitality of a Pharisee, it seems that the ordinary attentions which would have been paid to an honored guest were purposely omitted. "There was no water for the weary and dusty feet, no kiss of welcome upon the cheek, no perfume for the hair, nothing but a somewhat ungracious admission to a vacant seat, and the distant courtesies, so managed that the Guest might feel He was receiving, and not conferring, an honor." [2] In order that the mats, or carpets, which were hallowed by domestic prayer, might not be rendered unclean by the pollution of the street, the entering guest took off his sandals and left them at the door. After the customary ablutions and anointing with oil he then assumed a recumbent posture in the banquet-room, with his left elbow resting on the table, his body reclined upon a couch, and his feet turned in the direction of the wall.[3]

An Invitation to the House of Simon the Pharisee.

8,   1) It is futile to make the attempt to identify Simon the Pharisee with Simon the leper and the unknown sinner who anointed Jesus with Mary of Bethany, who anointed Him during Passion week. Matt. 26, 6—13; John 12, 2—8; Mark 14, 3—9. See Meyer *in loco.* Robertson, *Harmony,* 187.
    2) Farrar, I, 297.   3) Edersheim, I, 564.

Luke 7, 36—50. 9.

The story which follows is perhaps a "history more fit to be wept over than to be commented upon." [1] While Jesus was supping in the Pharisee's house, a woman, probably known to the host and to some of the guests, who on account of her past unchaste life was called, and from the standpoint of public opinion still was, a sinner, entered the banquet-room. According to popular opinion, it was Mary Magdalene. Her very name has in all civilized languages become a byword for "accepted penitence and pardoned sin." [2] But we are going to follow the lead of St. Luke, who, as we take it, introduces Mary Magdalene as a new historical figure in the next section and then not as a woman of a previously unchaste life, but as one out of whom the Lord had cast out seven devils. [3] And that is quite a different matter. By the way, the inclusion of this touching story in the record of St. Luke along with the annunciation of Mary, the stories of the Infant Jesus, the women followers in the next section, the story of Mary and

The Anointing of Christ's Feet by a Sinful Woman.

Martha of Bethany, [4] and the like, has led some writers [5] to believe that among his sources Luke had some women reporters from the intimate circle of Jesus. In the present instance and for reasons of his own it seems that the evangelist concealed the identity of the fallen woman by covering her with a cloak of namelessness. She came to the house of the Pharisee with a purpose. Summoning up courage to intrude upon that respectable house and company, she made her way through the throng carrying with her an alabaster flask of perfume. She found the Object of her search, and as she stood behind Him and thought of what He had said and of what she had been, of His sinlessness and of her life of vice and shame, she began to weep. As it happened, tear drops fell upon His unsandaled feet. There was no napkin at hand, and bending down to hide her confusion and shame, she quickly wiped the tears away with the long tresses of her disheveled hair. Overcome by emotion and seeing that no resistance was offered her, she kissed those holy feet again and again and anointed them with her costly and

---

9, 1) St. Gregory, quoted by Edersheim, I, 563.

2) Farrar, I, 305. For a discussion see Andrews, 285, and Meyer *in loco.*

3) Luke 8, 3. 4) Luke 10, 38—42.

5) For instance, Basil Matthews, *A Life of Jesus,* 242. W. M. Ramsay, *Was Christ Born in Bethlehem?* 74.

fragrant nard. At the proper moment, according to her purpose, she probably had hoped to anoint His head, but because of the unexpected turn of events she had instead anointed His feet!

Luke 7, 36—50.   **10.**

Not a word had as yet been spoken in this silent drama. Thus the woman. Thus the non-repelling Jesus. A tense situation. But the scene could not have been more natural and more human even if it had been prearranged. And also the Pharisee played his part true to form. First of all, in some way acquainted with the woman and her history, he had looked on with icy dislike and disapproval. A self-righteous and impenitent saint. The heart-breaking scene of sincere penitence left him unmoved. If this man, he thought, had been a prophet, and not simply ignorant like any other man, and if He had known who and what sort of woman had imposed upon Him her defiling touch, He would immediately have repulsed her with contempt and indignation, as he himself would have done. But Jesus *was* a Prophet, and in a fuller sense than Simon had imagined. Replying to the thought concealed in his heart and to the contempt probably written on his face, Jesus addressed Himself to Simon with the words: "Simon, I have somewhat to say unto thee." "Master" (or "Teacher"), "say on," — politeness demanding the title, — was his constrained reply.

"Thy Sins are Forgiven. Thy Faith hath Saved Thee; Go in Peace." Thereupon the parable of the Two Debtors and One Creditor. One of the two debtors owed five hundred denarii, about eighty-five dollars, and the other fifty, about eight dollars and a half. Both were unable to pay. And the creditor forgave them both. "Tell Me therefore, which of them will love him most?" Thrown off his guard, Simon had no suspicion of personal reference. Rather indifferent to the whole matter, he answered: "I suppose that he to whom he forgave most." In agreement with Jewish theology, so much for so much, that would be the natural conclusion. Then let it apply in the present case. Though Simon, like David in Nathan's parable,[1] was slow in making the application, perhaps the penitent sinner, with the quick intuition of a contrite woman's heart, had grasped the point. For the first time Jesus turned to her directly and also asked Simon to notice her whom he had so despised. Probably at her entry he had not even

---

10, 1) 2 Sam. 12, 1—4.

given her the attention of a condescending glance. But Jesus sharply contrasts her behavior with his. As regards Jesus, Simon had not even observed the courtesies commonly extended to invited guests. "I entered into thine house, thou gavest Me no water for My feet; but she hath washed My feet with tears and wiped them with the hairs of her head. Thou gavest Me no kiss; but this woman, since the time I came in, hath not ceased to kiss My feet. My head with oil thou didst not anoint; but this woman hath anointed My feet with ointment. Wherefore I say unto thee, Her sins, which are many, are forgiven; for she loved much. But to whom little is forgiven, the same loveth little." Now, these words are no premium on sin. As applied to Simon, there was with him no consciousness of sin; he believed to have no particular need of forgiveness, and therefore there was no expression of love. Though knowing of the woman's great sin, Simon did not believe her to be penitent. As applied to the woman, her forgiveness was not the result of her love, but coming to Jesus, as she did, with a truly contrite and believing heart, seeking and receiving forgiveness, her love was the result of her forgiveness. And giving her the assurance that this was actually the case, Jesus said: "Thy sins are forgiven." In surprised silence these words were heard. But frowning faces clearly expressed the familiar "Who can forgive sins but God only?" [2] Concerned, however, only with the penitent sinner, Jesus uttered the peace-bestowing and rest-giving words: "Thy faith hath saved thee; go in peace."

Luke 8, 1—3.   **11.**

The evangelists do not present, nor do they intend to present, a complete life of Christ. Here a glimpse, probably an incident related with fullest details, and then a gap or a summary of unrecorded events; here the exact time and strict chronological sequence, and then only a loose chronological connection. Thus we continue our narrative with the notice of our Lord's itinerant preaching ministry through Galilee, this

With the Twelve and a Number of Women Followers on a Tour through Galilee.

time in the company of the Twelve, properly so called, and a number of loving, grateful women followers whom He attached to His person by healing deeds of love. Among these three are especially named. The first is Mary Magdalene, of Magdala, a Sabbath's journey from Tiberias, who had received special benefits for body

10,   2) Mark 2, 7.

and soul from Jesus. From her seven devils had been cast out. She is not, we believe, the unknown sinner whose history ends with the previous section, but a new historical figure, whom we shall meet again during Passion week at Jerusalem.[1] The second is Joanna, the wife or widow of Herod's steward Chuza, probably the court official whose son Jesus had healed by the word spoken at Cana.[2] Lastly Susanna, otherwise unknown. The names of the others have not been inscribed on the pages of the sacred records; but their names are recorded in the Book of Life.[3] Being women of some means, they ministered unto Jesus of their substance, thus returning love for love and illustrating the rule of Christ's kingdom: Much forgiven, much love.

Mark 3, 19 b—21.   **12.**

We are again in Capernaum.[1] It is remarkable how much of what is connected with our Lord's life and ministry centers about this thriving fishing town on the shores of the Galilean Sea. No sooner had the news spread than the multitudes were at hand,

The Friends Concerned about Jesus.

so that the party of Jesus "could not so much as eat bread." The Savior was imposed upon by cure-seeking crowds to the extent that His friends[2] feared that the constant strain and His own all-consuming zeal[3] would seriously injure His health. They considered it their duty to rush to His rescue and take Him into their hands, because in their opinion He was in a state of excitement bordering on insanity; "for they said, He is beside Himself."

13.

(Matt. 12, 22—37.)[1]   Mark 3, 22—30.[2]

The opinion expressed by well-meaning, but mistaken friends was certainly not flattering to Jesus. But it was as nothing compared with what was said by the scribes and Pharisees. When an

---

11,   1) Matt. 27, 56. 61.

2) John 4, 46—54. See chapter VII, 21. Luke 23, 55; 24, 10.

3) Edersheim, I, 573.

12,   1) Now they come back to the house, εἰς οἶκον, home, namely, in Capernaum, as in 2, 1, to which also the subsequent πάλιν points back. Meyer *in loco.*

2) Those "with Him," *sui,* relatives coming from Nazareth or the outer circle of disciples. Bruce *sub loco.*

3) John 2, 17.

13,   1) Transposed.

2) Compare also Luke 11, 14—36, which brings the repetition of a similar blasphemous accusation uttered against the Lord in Judea.

unfortunate victim of demoniacal possession, stricken dumb and blind, was healed by Jesus and the amazed multitude was almost convinced that Jesus must be the Son of David in the sense of Old Testament Scripture, certain scribes and Pharisees from Jerusalem declared that the devils that had possessed that man had been cast out by Beelzebub, the prince of the devils. We remember that

"He Hath Beelzebub." after the raising of the widow's son at Nain reports concerning Jesus had gone out to Judea and roundabout.[3] As the result a delegation had come from John's prison at Machaerus.[4] And now the reaction from Jerusalem.[5] With regard to the cures of demoniacs the theory was advanced that these deeds were performed with the help of Beelzebul, the prince of the devils. The name of this patron idol of Ekron, a city of the Philistines,[6] was really Beelzebub, the god of flies; but probably in order to show their contempt for this heathenish god, the Israelites had perverted his name to Beelzebul, the Lord of dung.[7] It was a blasphemous accusation to assert that Christ cast out devils by the help of Satan. But whether they were conscious of it or not, what they said was an involuntary admission that He *cast out demons.*

14.

(Matt. 12, 22—37.) Mark 3, 22—30.

To this charge Jesus replied that it would be utterly absurd to suppose that Satan would be so foolish as they made him out to be. That would be against his own best interests. "How can Satan cast out Satan? And if a kingdom be divided against itself, that kingdom cannot stand." For the purpose of furthering his own purposes Satan must certainly be given credit for more sense; for Satan casting out Satan would mean self-stultification.[1] It is evident that Satan, as a strong man, would not yield unless overcome by some one endowed with superior strength. It is not

The Defense of Jesus. a matter of an alliance with Satan or a sort of satanic incarnation, but the overpowering of Satan by the Spirit of God and of taking possession of "his goods," that is, of releasing human souls previously held by him in bondage. Moreover, it was a well-known

---

13, 3) Luke 7, 17.   4) Matt. 11, 2 ff.
   5) Enough time had elapsed since the event recorded Luke 7, 11—17.
   6) 2 Kings 1, 2. 3. 16.
   7) *Int. St. B. Encycl.,* sub "Beelzebub."
14, 1) Bruce sub Matt. 12, 26.

fact that with pharisaic sanction a certain kind of exorcism was practised among the Jews by which under the name of Jehovah the attempt was made on their part and by their disciples to cast out devils. Without entering into the merit or the effectiveness of the practise itself, Jesus raises an argument *ad hominem:* [2] "If I by Beelzebub cast out devils, by whom do your children cast them out? Therefore they shall be your judges." In criticizing they would thus be silenced, judged, and condemned by their own practise.

15.

(Matt. 12, 22—37.) Mark 3, 22—30.

If not by the help of the devil, and if fraud and deception were not practised, then there could be only this alternative — by the power and Spirit of God. And the accusation just made against Jesus was really a sin against the Spirit of God, inasmuch as by discrediting and rejecting Jesus in the face of all evidence and better conviction they deliberately and blasphemously rejected the work of the Spirit of God. If in their judgment the Pharisees would have been mistaken only in theory, they would have been guilty of an offense against the Son of Man, a less heinous sin by comparison; but they wilfully hardened their hearts against the gracious operation of the Holy Ghost. "Verily I say unto you,

The Sin against the Holy Ghost. All sins shall be forgiven unto the sons of men and blasphemies wherewithsoever they shall blaspheme; but he that shall blaspheme against the Holy Ghost hath never forgiveness, but is in danger of eternal damnation, — because they said, He hath an unclean spirit." [1] For all sins there is forgiveness; but the final rejection of the only saving grace of God in Christ, the "malicious and persistent resistance against the converting and sanctifying work of the Holy Ghost" in and through the Gospel, is the rejection of the only possibility of forgiveness, the rejection of forgiveness itself. And that in the last analysis is the sin against the Holy Ghost. And in the Sermon on the Mount, Jesus points to the fruit of His critics and to the evidence of their own conduct, which all goes to show that they were dangerously near, if not already fatally affected with, this terrible hardening of their hearts. [2]

14, 2) Bruce *sub loco.*
15, 1) The sin is unpardonable not on account of its greatness, but on account of its nature. Compare Matt. 12, 31. 32. Chapter XXI, 18.
2) See article in Kretzmann, *Popular Commentary,* I, 179. Matt. 12, 33—37 compared with Luke 6, 43—45.

(Matt. 12, 38—45.)[1]   **16.**

These were strong words, especially since they were spoken in the hearing of the great teachers from Jerusalem, who in all probability had been sent by the Sanhedrin to pay close attention to every word Christ would utter. That He assumed such royal and judicial authority was resented by them, and a sign from heaven was immediately demanded of Him with which to substantiate this claim. The implication of course was that the sign they had just seen was insufficient. But their request was declined. It came from such as were guilty of spiritual adultery, having by their rejection of Jesus as the true Messiah become unfaithful to God, their Husband.[2] The sign given to them would be the death and resurrection of Jesus as typified in the history of Jonas.[3] "For as Jonas was three days and three nights in the whale's belly, so shall the Son of Man be three days and three nights in the heart of the earth." A veiled reference is made to Christ's death and resur-

The Sign of the Prophet Jonas. rection. They would put Him to death; "but He would rise again to their confusion, if not to their conversion."[4] By the way, the Lord accepted the story of Jonah. And the reference to this prophet leads to another thought. The people of Nineveh repented, — "and, behold, a Greater than Jonas is here." After her return from her visit to Solomon the queen of Sheba brought true wisdom to her country, —[5] "and, behold, a Greater than Solomon is here." But this wicked generation is like a demoniac from whom evil spirits had been cast out, who therefore could have been rid of the Evil One forever, but who, rather than enjoy his being permanently released from him, actually prepares for the evil spirit's return to him. The homesick spirit, roaming in a far-off desolate waste, is welcome to take possession again of him from whom he had been cast out, and he says, "I will return into my house from whence I came out." "And when he is come, he findeth it empty, swept, and garnished. Then goeth he and taketh with himself seven other spirits more wicked than himself, and they enter in and dwell there; and the last state of that man is worse than the

---

16, 1) Compare Luke 11, 29—32.

2) Is. 23, 17; Jer. 31, 32.

3) Jonah 1, 17. "The expression means little more than the νυχθήμερον of 2 Cor. 11, 25. Compare 1 Sam. 30, 12. 13; 2 Chron. 10, 5. 12." The popular method of computation by which parts of a day were counted as whole days. Meyer *in loco.* Farrar, I, 461, n.

4) Bruce *sub loco.*   5) 1 Kings 10, 1—10.

first." This is the sin of sins, the damnable final, fatal self-surrender to Satan, resulting from the rejection of Christ. "The end is damnation, yes, twofold damnation, by nature and by choice." [6]

17.

(Matt. 12, 46—50.) Mark 3, 31—35. (Luke 8, 19—21.) [1]

The discourse was broken at this point by a sudden interruption. News had reached the family of Jesus, His mother and His brethren, [2] of the dense throngs surrounding His person, of the strange and threatening words uttered by Him, and probably also of the presence of the spying delegation from Jerusalem. Alarm seized them, and they felt it their duty to save Jesus from Himself; but they had some difficulty in reaching Him on account of the crowds. They were standing without. And it was not for **Interfering Kinsmen.** the purpose of attracting attention to themselves that they sent word to Jesus: "Behold, Thy mother and Thy brethren stand without, desiring to speak with Thee." But Jesus would not tolerate any interference. "Alas, had they not yet learned what it is to enter? It was in their place to stand without." [3] However, without denying the rights of relationship "nor condemning them, but placing His Father first," [4] He looked around, His eye sweeping the whole circle of His audience, and stretching forth His hand towards His disciples, He said: "Behold My mother and My brethren! For whosoever shall do the will of My Father which is in heaven, the same is My brother and sister and mother."

18.

(Matt. 13, 1—3 a.) Mark 4, 1—3 a. Luke 8, 4.

On the same late summer or autumn day of 28 A. D. we find our Savior leaving the house where He was staying in Capernaum on His way to the near-by shores of the Sea of Galilee. This, by the way, was to be one of the busiest days of which we have any knowledge in the life of our Lord, from the time when He was besieged by the multitudes upon His return to Capernaum until late in the same day, when He rested His weary head in the rocking bed of a storm-tossed ship on the Sea of Galilee. As the multi-

---

16, 6) Kretzmann, I, 70.

17, 1) Luke's placing of this incident after the parables by the sea is evidently topical. Bruce *sub loco.*

2) Evidently none of those of His brethren, if indeed there were such, who now belonged to the apostolic band. See chapter IV, 43; XI, 12 ff.

3) Farrar, I, 462.   4) Edersheim, I, 577. Luke 2, 49.

tudes gathered, He seated Himself in a boat in preparation for a lengthy discourse, while His hearers stood upon the beach. Thus He began what is known as the great group of Parables by the Sea.[1] Without going into details, just an introductory word about parables. They are a method of speech used by many other teachers, but especially developed by Jesus, in which moral or religious truths are illustrated from the analogy of human experience.

Parables. They were used by Jesus in every period of His public ministry. But there came a time, it seems, when a larger and a special place was given to parables in His ministry. In His public ministry there seems to be a ratio of parabolic speech to the popular opposition against His work. When it became increasingly evident that the great bulk of the Jewish people, especially the leaders, would not accept Him as the promised Messiah and continued tenaciously to cling to their carnal Messianic ideas and ideals, Christ ceased largely to direct Himself to them and confined His instructions chiefly to His disciples and special friends, to whom He addressed Himself in parables. By these means spiritual truths, clothed in images, were shielded from public attack. The purpose of parables was both to reveal and to conceal. Two reasons for parabolic speech are given. One is that the Scriptures might be fulfilled.[2] The other reason was the policy of our Lord not to cast pearls before the swine. The time had come to instruct His followers, who were to carry on His work after His departure; but, as Jesus Himself indicates, the truth should be hidden from those who would only hear it without repenting of their sins.[3] In the presence of obdurate enemies, who were only watching to employ His words against Him, the truth was to be cautiously uttered, and for the fickle multitudes, who would have refused to accept His words if they had perceived their full import, they should be carefully veiled. On the other hand, with but a very gentle hint at what He meant to teach, a simple-minded follower of Christ would nevertheless readily understand figurative illustrations of spiritual truths such as would be absolute enigmas to the most educated doctors and scribes, trained in the Law,[4] the Word of God, but impervious to its saving truths.

18, 1) There are two other groups. One in Luke only, chapters 14—16; another group during the last week in Jerusalem, Matt. 21, 22, 24, 25, and parallels.

2) Matt. 13, 14. 34. 35. According to his custom, Matthew points this out.

3) This He does in His answer to the question, "Why speakest Thou unto them in parables?" Matt. 13, 10.

4) Andrews, 293. G. H. Schodde, sub "Parable," in *Int. St. B. Encycl.*

19.

(Matt. 13, 3b—9.) Mark 4, 3b—9. Luke 8, 5—8.

Like a number of other parables the first one of the nine is taken from agricultural life. "Behold," Jesus said, "a sower went out to sow his seed." And as he sowed it, some fell on the foot-paths in the field, where it was either trodden under foot or the birds of the heaven came and devoured it. Other fell upon shallow ground, with rock near the surface, hard-pan, where it

1. The Sower. made a lively start, but because of the lack of deep soil and of moisture and on account of the burning sun was quickly killed. Some fell among the thorn-infested soil, and when, in competition, the thorn seeds or roots grew up and choked it, it yielded no fruit. Other seed, however, fell into soft, clean, and good ground, where it grew and yielded fruit, wholly satisfactorily, some thirtyfold, some sixtyfold, and some a hundredfold — thirtyfold, good; sixtyfold, better; a hundredfold, best. And giving His listeners an invitation to think of the hidden meaning or rather a hint that there was a hidden meaning, Jesus said: "He that hath ears to hear, let him hear."

20.

(Matt. 13, 10—17.) Mark 4, 10—12. Luke 8, 9. 10.

There must have been a short pause. During the brief interval, in which the boat was probably withdrawn a little from the shore, so that they might be strictly alone,[1] the Twelve and other disciples asked Jesus about His method of teaching in parables and requested Him to give them an explanation of this particular parable. There was an answer for both questions. As to His parabolic method: "Unto you it is given to know the mystery of the kingdom of God, but unto those that are without all these things are done in parables." These words are to be understood in the light of the terrible warning against the sin of blasphemy against the Holy Spirit, spoken by Christ on the same day.[2] Since they who asked the question are believing disciples and as such are not offended at His doctrine, the "mysteries" of the Kingdom are no longer mysteries to them because the doctrines have been revealed to them.[3] Christianity has no secret doctrines; for what has been

---

20, 1) Mark 4, 10.
    2) Mark 3, 28—30; Matt. 12, 31—37; 13, 1.
    3) Kretzmann, 182. *Int. St. B. Encycl.* sub "Mystery," 2105.

publicly proclaimed is no longer a secret. As believing disciples this knowledge has been given *them,* but to others "all these things are done in parables, that,[4] seeing, they may see and not perceive, and hearing, they may hear and not understand, lest at any time they should be converted and their sins should be forgiven them." This does not refer to a decree of God by which some people are predestined unto eternal condemnation. There is no such terrible decree. Nor does it mean that Christ employed the

The Reason for the Parables. parabolic method in part on account of the increased opposition, to blind the people. This is rather one of those notable passages in which it is pointed out, as a solemn warning, what deliberate rejection and self-hardening leads to. Thus the same sweet Gospel which is to believers a savor of life unto life becomes to unbelievers a savor of death unto death.[5] A terrible judgment of God will befall those who harden their hearts against the Gospel of mercy, whose purpose is to save souls. This judgment upon Israel, as Jesus points out,[6] began in the days of Isaiah and was now fulfilled. "But blessed are your eyes, for they see, and your ears, for they hear." [7] Judgment for rejectors, but blessings for believers.

21.

(Matt. 13, 18—23.) Mark 4, 13—20. Luke 8, 11—15.

And now the explanation of the parable. "The seed is the Word of God." Now, when one hears the Word of the Kingdom, preached either by Christ or by His ministers and does not "take it in," [1] "then cometh the Wicked One and catcheth away that which was sown in his heart." This is the seed that was sown

The Explanation. by the wayside. That which is sown in the rocky places is that sown in shallow and emotional hearts. The ready acceptance of the Gospel by such hearers is sometimes almost embarrassing. But they have no root. And in times of tribulation, adversity, and persecution they fall away. That which fell among the thorns are they who, having heard the Word, promise well indeed; but the cares of the world, the deceitfulness of riches, and the lusts of other things choke the

---

20, 4) Ἵνα in Mark 4, 12 and Luke 8, 10; ὅτι in Matt. 13, 13. See *Int. St. B. Encycl.,* 2244.

5) 2 Cor. 2, 15. 16; 1 Cor. 1, 18.

6) If we regard the quotation from Is. 6, 9. 10 as words of Christ and not of Matthew.

7) Compare Luke 10, 23. 24.

21, 1) Συνιέντος, Matt. 13, 19.

Word, so that it brings no fruit. Thus with some of the unfruitful hearers it is a case of lack of interest at the outset. With others it is a case of want of steadfastness. With still others there is a deplorable absence of real sincerity. Only those of another class, by the grace of God, present soil ready for a crop of fruit that is well-pleasing to the Lord. They are those who receive the Word into fine, good hearts, "having heard the Word, keep it and bring forth fruit with patience." With them the heart was properly plowed and prepared by the Law. After they have heard and accepted the Gospel, they bring forth God-pleasing fruit in accordance with the gifts received and opportunities offered them in their individual lives.

22.

Mark 4, 21—25. Luke 8, 16—18.

Sometimes a speaker tells one story to illustrate another. Christ's purpose in telling the parable of the Sower was to show His hearers that, after hearing the Word, they must yield God-pleasing fruit. It was the disciples' privilege to receive a special explanation of the parable. In giving them the requested explanation, Jesus admonished them to make the proper use of this special instruction. "No man, when he hath lighted a candle, covereth it with a vessel or putteth it under a bed, but setteth it on a candle-

The Proper Use of the Explanation. stick."[1] The Lord often repeated His sayings. "Take heed therefore *how* ye hear; for whosoever hath, to him shall be given; and whosoever hath not, from him shall be taken even that which he seemeth [thinketh] to have." To him who has Christian knowledge the Lord gives an additional store of it. But if one is indifferent about growing in knowledge and manifesting his faith in life, then even that little which he foolishly believes to have will be taken from him. Privileged possession entails increased responsibility. And even as in other matters the rule applies "With what measure ye mete it shall be measured to you," so also in this case the reward of prayerful attention to the Word is an increase of saving knowledge.

23.

Mark 4, 26—29.

Even in the case of the fourth class of hearers the yielding of fruit is a gradual process, demanding time. This the Lord sets forth in a beautiful parable, peculiar to the Gospel according to

---

22, 1) Matt. 5, 15; Luke 11, 33; Matt. 25, 29; Luke 19, 26; etc.

St. Mark: The kingdom of God is as if a man should cast seed into the ground and then sleep night and day, with nothing in particular to do beyond patiently waiting for the result of what he

2. The Seed Growing of Itself.

has already done. For what else is there for him to do?[1] Should he worry about the outcome? Should he go out into the wheat-fields and disturb the roots or forcibly stretch the plants in a harmful attempt to hasten the crop? "For the earth bringeth forth fruit of herself; first the blade, then the ear, after that the full corn in the ear." It is not until the fruit is ripe that he "putteth in the sickle because the harvest is come." Thus it is also in spiritual matters. Worrying about results is foolish and useless. The power of God is in the Word, and He has promised that it shall not return to Him void.[2]

(Matt. 13, 24—30.)   24.

By this time, it seems, Jesus again directed His attention to the assembled multitudes.[1] The present parable is also taken from agricultural life. But while the parable of the Sower describes disappointing past experiences, the parable of the Tares is prophetic of a future state of things. The kingdom of heaven is likened unto a man who sowed good seed into his field. But, as afterwards became evident, while the man slept, his enemy came with a certain malignant seed, a degenerate form of wheat, whose stalks and spikes closely resemble the true grain,[2] and maliciously sowed it into the ground. Not until the crop began to mature, was the spiteful trick discovered. The surprised farm laborers suggested to the householder to have them go and pull it out. But the

3. The Tares.

householder, who knew the reason for the presence of the tares and also knew that an uprooting at this time would be harmful to the wheat, arranged for a different course of action: "Let both grow together until the harvest; and in the time of harvest I will say to the reapers, Gather ye together first the tares and bind them in bundles to burn them; but gather the wheat into my barn." This parable,

---

23, 1) Many Western wheat-growers practically do nothing but eat and sleep between seed-time and harvest.

    2) Is. 55, 10. 11.

24, 1) "Another parable put He forth unto them," αὐτοῖς, to the multitudes. Compare verses 3, 10, and 34. Meyer *sub loco.*

    2) Ζιζάνια, bastard wheat, darnel, common in Palestine.

which Jesus Himself explains,[3] illustrates the truth that in the visible Kingdom, or Church, the bad, hypocrites, are mingled with the good, the true believers. Forceful means for an attempted elimination of the wicked, heretics, and false Christians are not to be employed. This of course does not deny to the visible Church the right of discipline by way of individual excommunication or restoration. But even so, a visible church consisting only of saints cannot be established. And to attempt a separation to that effect of believers and unbelievers is not a thing with which man is competent to deal, but which must be left in the hands of the Judge. "They who to-day are tares may to-morrow be grain."[4]

25.

(Matt. 13, 31. 32.) Mark 4, 30—32.[1]

Sore disappointments, extended waitings, fiendish opposition to the Kingdom — and still marvelous growth. This the Lord sets forth in the parable of the Mustard-seed. "Whereunto shall we liken the kingdom of God, or with what comparison shall we compare it?" The Word "fruitful only in a few, and in them only after a time, what is the best emblem for this state of things?"[2] "The kingdom of heaven is like to a grain of mustard-seed." Among the Rabbis the phrase "like a grain of mustard-seed" was a common expression for anything very minute.[3] A number

4. The Mustard-Seed. of varieties of the mustard-plant, all having very small seed and in a short time reaching a striking growth of treelike proportions, meets the requirements of the parable. "Which a man took and sowed in his field." This tiny seed is "less than all the seeds that be in the earth; but when it is sown, it groweth up and becometh greater than all herbs and shooteth out great branches, so that the fowls of the air may lodge under the shadow of it." Thus the preaching of the Gospel may be considered insignificant before men, but from it the Christian Church was born, a power that has changed the course of the world's history and is a source of true rest and peace for all nations under the sun.

24, 3) Verses 36—43.

  4) Augustine, quoted by Meyer *sub loco.*

25, 1) Compare also Luke 13, 18. 19. Chapter XXI, 31.

  2) Bruce *sub* Mark 4, 30.

  3) This explains our Lord's phrase "faith as a grain of mustard-seed," Matt. 17, 20; Luke 17, 6.

(Matt. 13, 33.)[1]   **26.**

A mere handful of disciples was gathered in the upper room at Jerusalem, and in a short time they and their followers went out and conquered the world.   And what brought about this remark-

5. The Leaven.   able change?   Clearly it was the hidden, silent, mysterious, and still all-pervading and transforming power of the Word.   That seems to be the point in the next parable, in which the Lord speaks of the leaven "which a woman took and hid in three measures of meal till the whole was leavened."

27.

(Matt. 13, 34. 35.)   Mark 4, 33. 34.

Thus Jesus, for reasons indicated above,[1] addressed the multitudes in parables.   And without parables He was not wont to speak to the people, not merely on that day, but at any time.   Privately He expounded the parables to His disciples that they "might under-

The Parabolic Method.   stand the better."[2]   A few of His interpretations have been recorded. As regards the various details of the parables, we must remember that all comparisons halt.   To attempt to interpret all the details, for instance, in the parable of the Leaven, that the woman took *three* measures of meal, and so forth, is both needless and fruitless. We know what is meant, and we must guard against going beyond the point of comparison.   And as regards the whole matter of parabolic teaching, the Evangelist Matthew points to a fulfilment of prophecy.[3]

(Matt. 13, 36—43.)   **28.**

After Jesus had spoken His fifth parable, He dismissed the multitude and "went into the house."[1]   Most likely it was His home in Capernaum.   The parable of the Tares must have made a deep impression upon His disciples; for they came to Him, saying: "Declare," explain, interpret,[2] "unto us the parable of the Tares of the Field."   Point for point the parable was thereupon explained by the Lord.   The wide world is the harvest-field of the Son of Man, who here represents Himself as the Lord of the Church.   With the good seed is represented — not the Word this

---

26,   1) Compare also Luke 13, 20. 21.   Chapter **XXI,** 31.
27,   1) § 18.   2) Bruce *sub loco.*
      3) Ps. 78, 2.   Meyer *sub loco.*
28,   1) The same house referred to in v. 1.
      2) Φράσον, here and 15, 15.

time,[3] but — the children of the Kingdom, while the tares are the seed and children of the devil. In the time of harvest, at the end of the world, the unbelief of the latter will become apparent, though during their lifetime they had skilfully hidden it behind a semblance of piety and hindered the development of the good grain. At the command of the Son of Man the reaping angels will then issue

Explanation of the Parable of the Tares. forth and gather out of His kingdom the offenders and "cast them into a furnace of fire; there shall be wailing and gnashing of teeth." But the righteous shall "shine forth as the sun in the kingdom of the Father." At this final harvest, and not before, a forceful sifting of believers and unbelievers is to take place. On the one hand, there is the outlook of everlasting bliss and a glorious reward; on the other, a terrible and eternal punishment. "Who hath ears to hear, let him hear."

(Matt. 13, 44.)   29.

As Christ next points out in two brief parables, the supreme value of the bliss of heaven and the promised gracious reward outweighs everything else, and the man who understands this will with pleasure part with all. "The kingdom of heaven is like unto treasure hid in a field, the which, when a man hath found, he hideth and for joy thereof goeth and selleth all that he hath and

6. The Hidden Treasure. buyeth that field." Jesus is here not concerned with the moral aspect of the act, if indeed this comes into consideration here at all. It is a story which has found its parallel often enough. A certain treasure which had been hidden in the ground was found by a man, who then, eager to secure the treasure, carefully covered it up again, sold his property, and bought this extremely valuable piece of ground. The salvation offered in the Gospel is such a find. While it cannot be earned or purchased, no sacrifice is too great to obtain possession of it and to retain it by the grace of God.[1]

(Matt. 13, 45. 46.)   30.

"Again, the kingdom of heaven is like unto a merchantman seeking goodly pearls; who, when he had found one pearl of great price, went and sold all that he had and bought it." A *"connoisseur* of valuables is completely taken by surprise." [1] A pearl merchant,

---

28, 3) Luke 8, 12.
29, 1) Luke 10, 42; Phil. 3, 8. 13.   30, 1) Bruce *sub loco.*

an expert in his line, finds a pearl of rare beauty and worth. Recognizing its value, he sells all that he has and buys this pearl of great

7. The Pearl of Great Price.

price. He strips himself of all his possessions and risks all in the one great venture of his life. So also the earnest seeker of the saving truth is completely taken by surprise when he finds the pearl and realizes the value of the treasure contained in the Gospel of Christ. Though he is a seeker, still the true treasure comes to him as a find. Nor is he able actually by purchase to gain its possession, but after "he has learned to know this priceless gift, he will gladly renounce all goods, joys, and delights of this world and consider all human wisdom and righteousness but loss in order to gain Christ." [2]

(Matt. 13, 47—50.)   **31.**

Christ's parables are taken from every-day life, and especially the parable of the Net offered a picture with which the disciples were very familiar. The kingdom of heaven is like a large net which is cast into the sea. In the great number of fish enclosed, good and bad, the value of the catch among fishermen is in the edible fish, the rest being carefully separated and thrown away. They are not really counted as belonging to the catch. Thus also

8. The Parable of the Net.

the kingdom of heaven as it appears here upon earth is such a net. The preaching of the Gospel results in an outward collection of such as are really members of the Kingdom as well as of such as merely have a semblance of membership. Upon earth the entire netful is drawn toward the shores of eternal life. But on the Last Day "the angels shall come forth and sever the wicked from the just and shall cast them into the furnace of fire; there shall be wailing and gnashing of teeth." As distinguished from the true believers in the kingdom of heaven, similar to the parable of the Tares, nominal Christians and hypocrites are depicted here.

(Matt. 13, 51—53.)   **32.**

In concluding this great series of parables, Jesus asked His disciples the question: "Have ye understood all these things?" As far as their understanding went, they unhesitatingly said they did. Pleased with this profession of understanding, which reflected favorably both upon the ability of the Teacher and the aptitude of the learners, the Lord gave them some additional in-

---

30, 2) Kretzmann, I, 76.

struction pertaining especially to their future work as teachers. "Therefore every scribe," in this case, every Christian teacher, "which is instructed unto the kingdom of heaven is like unto a man that is an householder, which bringeth forth out of his

9. The Householder.

treasure things new and old." Unlike the scribe, Rabbinical in spirit, who produces only "the old and stale, the disciple of the Kingdom, like the Master, is always fresh-minded and able to present the old Gospel in a new dress." [1]   And as he himself grows in knowledge, so he is able to aid also his hearers to increase therein. [2]

32,   1) Bruce *sub loco.*

2) Here follows in the order of Luke: "Jesus is called by His mother and brethren." Luke 8, 19—21.   See § 17: "Interfering Kinsmen."   Luke's placing of the incident after the parables by the sea is evidently topical.

CHAPTER XIII.

THE GADARENE JOURNEY.

Probably autumn, 28 A. D.

1.

Matt. 8, 18.[1] Mark 4, 35. Luke 8, 22.

A busy day in the life of Christ was coming to a close. We had almost forgotten that this was still the same day on which Jesus had returned to Capernaum after His second tour of Galilee.[2] It was probably in the forenoon that Jesus taught a dense throng of people, some of whom insulted and blasphemed Him, while **The Command to Cross Over to the Other Side.** others demanded a sign and His friends considered Him beside Himself, so that at length His mother and His brethren felt it their duty to interfere and to save Him from Himself, as it were.[3] In the afternoon He chose as His method of instruction a group of most remarkable parables, several of which He explained. And now, towards evening, tired and worn out, He entered a boat "as He was"[4] in order to escape the great multitudes about Him and gave His disciples the command to depart with Him to the other side.

2.

Matt. 8, 19—22. (Luke 9, 57—62.)[1]

But before Jesus could sail out into the lake, a remarkable interruption occurred. Three of His listeners, struck perhaps by

---

1, 1) A return to the natural order of Matthew. See note under next section.

2) Mark 3, 19. See chapter XII, 12.

3) See chapter XII, 17.

4) Mark 4, 36. Probably without food or other preparation for the trip across the lake.

2, 1) See also chapter XXI, 3. — The multitude from which Jesus escapes in Mark's narrative is that gathered on the shore in connection with the parable discourse. In agreement with Matthew and Luke this is followed by the crossing of the lake, the stilling of the tempest, and the Gadarene journey. From this it seems to follow that the whole section in Matt. 11, 2—30; 12, 22—50; and 13, 1—53 has been related out of its chronological order, and we therefore now return to Matt. 8, 18 ff. And the placing of the present incident in Luke seems to indicate a loose arrangement, though what is related here may have happened again, at a later time. See Farrar, I, 327; Stoeckhardt, 176.

"the power of His teaching or dazzled by the zenith of His popularity, desired, or thought that they desired, to attach themselves to His person as permanent disciples." [2] The first applicant was a scribe. If he already belonged to the outer circle of disciples,[3] the designation *scribe* seems to indicate that he was still attached to a party utterly opposed to the ways of Jesus. "Master, I will follow Thee whithersoever Thou goest." Have we here a "Saul among the prophets"? [4] Did the good man really think that he was able to follow Jesus in any way which he should choose or be

Three Applicants for Discipleship.
1. Inconsiderate Impulse.

obliged to go? In his enthusiasm he was evidently ignorant of the real cost of being a disciple of Jesus. Jesus did not turn him away, but very likely He chilled his enthusiasm by telling him: "The foxes have holes and the birds of the air have nests,[5] but the Son of Man [6] hath not where to lay His head." Now, Jesus was no pauper. The picture of His poverty must not be overdrawn. His wants and needs were always provided for. But according to His will and purpose He had no house or piece of land which He could call His own. In pointing to His personal poverty, He shows the manner in which His disciples are to follow Him. That indeed, as far as the enthusiastic scribe is concerned, was the decisive and necessary thing.

3.

Matt. 8, 19—22. (Luke 9, 57—62.)

The second applicant already was a partial disciple, but before complying with the request of Jesus to follow Him, he wished first to bury his father. Whether he wished to live at home till the death of his probably aged father or whether the father had just died, in which case the permission would have involved very little delay, or whether the burial included also the arranging of the family affairs and the distribution of the inheritance, we cannot say.[1] Neither have we any information as to the identity of

---

2,   2) Farrar, I, 327.

     3) As assumed by Meyer on account of the expressions εἷς γραμματεύς᾽ that is, *one* (disciple), a scribe, v. 19, and *another* disciple, v. 21.

     4) Bruce sub Matt. 8, 19.

     5) Κατασκηνώσεις, that is, roosts. For the birds do not live in nests.

     6) This term appears for the first time here in Matthew = the Messiah. Compare Acts 7, 55. 56. See chapter VI, 20.

3,   1) Farrar, I, 328, n. 1.

this or the other applicants.[2] The answer of Jesus is: "Follow Me and let the dead bury the dead." It seems that the word "dead" must be taken in a twofold sense: Let the spiritually dead bury the physically dead. According to another explanation the meaning is: "Let the dead be taken care of by those whose occupation

2. Conflicting Duties.

it is to inter the earthly remains."[3] At any rate, it is a hard answer; "but doubtless Jesus knew to whom He was speaking. The saying can be understood and justified." If there is a conflict of interests, even duties, in the service of Christ, there can be but one choice.[4] "And the saying can also be misunderstood and abused; but woe unto him who does so!"[5]

4.

Matt. 8, 19—22. (Luke 9, 57—62.)

A third aspirant for discipleship[1] likewise pleaded for delay. He first wanted to bid farewell to those at home in his house. Seemingly a small request,[2] but at the same time a dangerous thing. The thing has been tried often enough. Many times the influence of family, relatives, and friends has prevented new converts from coming under the full power and control of Jesus. Added to this, this man seems to have belonged to that type of men who always "want to do something else first in which they are personally inter-

3. A Divided Heart.

ested before addressing themselves to the main duty to which they have been called."[3] Jesus answers him: "No man having put his hand to the plow and looking back is fit for the kingdom of God." This saying has become proverbial for all time. In the service of the Kingdom there can be no divided mind. There must be firm intention and a steady eye. The ambition of all plowmen is to make a straight furrow. This skill, like the highest calling in the Kingdom, needs a forward-looking eye. "When the East calls,

---

3,   2) Judas Iscariot, Thomas, and Matthew, according to Lange. Assuredly those applicants for discipleship were none of the Twelve. Luke 6, 13 ff. See Meyer sub Luke 9, 57—60.

3) Kretzmann, I, 45.

4) Matt. 10, 35—39.

5) Bruce sub Matt. 8, 19—22.

4,   1) In making the incident in Luke parallel.

2) Something like Luther, who, upon entering the monastery at Erfurt, invited his friends for a farewell feast.

3) Bruce sub Luke 9, 61. 62.

thoughts must be turned from the fading West." [4)]   In the Lord's kingdom, as applied to the three aspirants, there must be no "inconsiderate impulse, no conflicting duties, and no divided mind." [5)]

5.

Matt. 8, 23—27. Mark 4, 36—41. Luke 8, 23—25.

After all these delays the trip across the lake finally could begin. The departure was hasty, for the disciples had taken Jesus into the ship "even as He was." But even now He was followed by others; for "there were also with Him other little ships." But these were probably soon scattered or frightened back on account of an approaching storm. At any rate, in His own boat [1)] and among His trusted disciples He could soon rest His head on a cushion, or pillow, in the steersman's seat. But this rest, so sorely needed, was soon violently disturbed. One of those fierce storms of which travelers tell us, "peculiar to that strange hollow in the earth's surface, swept down with sudden fury upon that little inland sea." [2)]   To understand the causes of these sudden and violent tempests, we must remember that the lake lies over six hundred feet below the level of the Mediterranean Sea, that "naked plateaus rise upward and backward to the snowy heights of distant Hermon, that the watercourses have cut deep ravines converging

"Lord, Save Us; We Perish!"

at the head of the lake, and that these gorges act like gigantic funnels to conduct the descending cold winds down the valley of the Upper Jordan against the surface of the lake." [3)]   At scarcely a moment's notice the air was filled with a whirlwind, and the smiling evening waters were whipped into a boiling sea. The wild waves rose and fell and tossed, lashed, and broke over, the ship, rapidly filling it with water, and threatened to hurl it into the deep. The danger was extreme. The violence of the tempest caused even the strong hearts of experienced and weather-beaten fishermen to quake with fear. But Jesus was asleep. With a cry of terror the imperiled disciples aroused their sleeping Master. "Lord, save us; we perish!" Just what they expected Jesus to do we do not know.

4,   4) St. Augustine, quoted by Farrar, I, 328.

5) Bruce sub Luke 9, 62.

5,   1) He was in *"the* ship" (Mark), the well-known boat of the sons of Jonas or of Zebedee, both of which were always at His disposal.

2) Farrar, I, 329.

3) Andrews, 294.

Hardly that which actually happened, since "great fear came over them as they had witnessed it." [4] At any rate, with cries of terror and excitement they implored Jesus' help.

6.

Matt. 8, 23—27. Mark 4, 36—41. Luke 8, 23—25.

Calmly Jesus awoke from His slumbers and addressed His disciples from the dripping stern: "Why are ye fearful, O ye of little faith?" And then, rising to His feet and standing in the dashing spray, the hurricane raging, and His garments and hair fluttering in the wind, He rebuked [1] the wind and the wild waters of the raging sea: "Peace, be still." The double imperative "Silence! Be muzzled!" [2] reveals an energy almost untranslatable. [3]

"Peace, Be Still." "And the wind ceased, and there was a great calm" — instantaneously. As in the calm starlight, a moment later, the disciples, still trembling and dripping, could gaze into the quiet waters, they were overcome by an awesome fear, which caused them to whisper to one another: "What manner of man is this?" It was a stupendous miracle. In almost the same words the event is related by three evangelists. "It was one of those miracles of power which cannot be explained away by existing laws." [4] Yes, "what manner of man is this that even the winds and the sea obey Him!" It is the God-man, "the manner of man, O Lord God." [5]

7.

Matt. 8, 28—9, 1. Mark 5, 1—21. Luke 8, 26—40.

The next morning [1] we find Jesus and His companions on the other side of the lake. But not even on the farther shore was He **In the Country of the Gadarenes.** to find seclusion and rest. No sooner had He reached that part of ancient Manasseh directly over against Galilee, now included in the tetrarchy of Philip and the confederacy of the Decapolis, but here properly called either the land of the Gerasenes or

---

5, 4) Edersheim, I, 601.

6, 1) Ἐπετίμησε, chided.

2) Σιώπα, πεφίμωσο (from φιμόω).

3) Farrar, I, 331. 4) Farrar, I, 331. 5) 2 Sam. 7, 19.

7, 1) Because the demoniac saw Jesus afar off, Mark 5, 6. Daytime as against the view (Edersheim, I, 606) that the arrival of Jesus from Capernaum after the stilling of the storm took place the same evening and that the healing of the demonized at Gerasa was a night scene.

Gergesenes (Gerasa or Gergesa), with reference to the local center, or the land of the Gadarenes (Gadara), with reference to the superior city,[2] than He was "met with such an exhibition of human fury and degradation as was even more startling than the rage of the troubled sea." [3]

7,   2) There has long been a controversy regarding both site and text. The identification of the site clears up the "discrepancy" of the text. It cannot have been the Greek city Gerasa, in the eastern extremity of Perea, in Gilead, about thirty-six miles from the Galilean Sea. It cannot have been Gadara, another city of the Decapolis, lying about seven miles southeast of Gennesaret, unless — which is likely — as the chief city in the region it lent its name to the district as that of the Gadarenes. The latter view explains the matter with respect to the reading "Gadarenes." And it seems that there was another Gerasa (Kersa, Chersa, Gersa, or Gergesa) to account for the readings "Gerasenes" or "Gergesenes." It has been said that we owe the introduction of "Gergesenes" into the text of Matthew to Origen. Farrar, I, 333, n. 1. But it seems that Origen was correct. We are satisfied with the explanation by which the "discrepancies" are cleared up as follows: 1. All three readings, Gerasenes, Gergesenes, and Gadarenes, are correct; the first two refer to the particular site or city and the third to the district to which the site belonged. 2. The discovery of a site nearly opposite the Plain of Gennesaret under various names: Kersa, Chersa, or Gersa, not to be confounded with the Gerasa of Gilead, completely accounts for the term "Gergesenes" and all the details of the miracle. Says Dr. Thomson, *Land and Book,* II, 25, quoted by Andrews, 298: "In this Gersa" (nearly opposite the Plain of Gennesaret, where Wady Semak enters the lake) "we have a position which fulfils every requirement of the narrative and with a name so near that in Matthew as to be in itself a strong corroboration of the truth of this identification. It is within a few rods of the shore, and an immense mountain rises directly above it, in which are ancient tombs, out of some of which the two men possessed of the devils may have issued to meet Jesus. The lake is so near the base of the mountain that the swine, rushing madly down it, could not stop, but would be hurried on unto the water and drowned. The place is one which our Lord would be likely to visit, having Capernaum in full view to the north [west] and Galilee 'over against it,' as Luke says it was (8, 26). The name, however, pronounced by Bedawin Arabs, is so similar to Gergesa that to all my inquiries for this place they invariably said that it was at Chersa, and they insisted that they were identical; and I agree with them in this opinion." Here Dr. Thomson found some ruins. "It was a small place, but the walls can be traced all around, and there seem to have been considerable suburbs." Likewise Colonel Wilson (*Recovery of Jerusalem,* 286) is quoted as follows: "On the left bank of Wady Semak, and at the point where the hills end and the plain stretches out toward the lake, are the ruins of Khersa-Gergesa. About a mile south of this the hills, which everywhere else on the eastern side are recessed from half to three quarters of a mile from the water's edge, approach within forty feet of it; they do not terminate abruptly, but there is a steep even slope, which we would identify with the 'steep place' down which the herd of swine ran violently into the sea and so were choked." — As regards the term *Gergesenes,* there must have been in point of fact something more than a conjecture of Origen in this verse; for it is found in eight uncials, most cursives and (among others) in the Coptic and Ethiopic versions. It is to be remembered that Matthew lived on the shore of the lake and was likely to know its minute topography. Farrar, I, 333, n. 1. See also *Exp. Greek N. T.,* I, 144; Barton, *Archeology and the Bible,* 214; Kretzmann, *Pop. Commentary,* I, 186; Ylvisaker, *Gospel,* 189.

    3) Farrar, I, 334.

8.

Matt. 8, 28—9, 1. Mark 5, 1—21. Luke 8, 26—40.

"There met Him two possessed with devils, coming out of the tombs, exceeding fierce, so that no man might pass that way." Thus Matthew. But Mark and Luke single out and describe one, probably as the more grievously afflicted and the spokesman of the two. Their fierceness, the unclean nature of their dwelling-places in the tombs, or limestone caves, the impossibility of their being controlled by others, their supernatural strength in rending chains and fetters, their suicidal frenzy in gashing and cutting themselves with stones, their solitude-disturbing yells and cries night and day, their tendency to bare themselves of every rag of clothing, are all vividly described. With irresistible force they were drawn to Jesus as He touched the shore. However, their first contact with Jesus was not

The Two Demoniacs. the occasion of a fresh outbreak of fury. As at other times, the demons knew Jesus, and His presence forced them to an identification concerning themselves and incidentally also to an acknowledgment of His superior power. Mingling their own personality with that of their possessed victims and sensing from Christ's manner and look that the sufferers were soon to be released, they entreated the Lord not to torment them before the time. In Jesus they recognized their final Judge, by whom they would of a certainty be eventually consigned to everlasting punishment. They addressed Him in the well-known Jewish formula: "What have we to do with Thee?" or rather, "What is there between us and Thee?"[1] "Jesus, Thou Son of God? Art Thou come hither to torment us before the time?" The apprehension of their defeat and ultimate punishment was based upon the fact that Jesus had said, rather, was about to say, "Come out of the man, thou unclean spirit."

9.

Matt. 8, 28—9, 1. Mark 5, 1—21. Luke 8, 26—40.

"Instead of insisting upon immediate release, Jesus adopts a roundabout way in dealing with the case."[1] He addresses one of the victims with the question: "What is thy name?" Still absorbed "in the hideous tyranny of a multitude of demons, under whose influence his own true personality was destroyed,"[2] the

---

8, 1) See John 2, 4. Edersheim, I, 610.
9, 1) Bruce *sub loco*. Mark.
  2) Farrar, I, 336.

unfortunate sufferer replies: "My name is Legion; for we are many." This designation, by this time naturalized into Greek and Aramean,[3] is used here not to determine an exact number of about six thousand soldiers, but to convey the idea of a multitude

"My Name Is Legion." of armed and strong warriors of evil, and incidentally it is also a tribute to the universal and well-organized power of imperial Rome. As the well-organized legions, everywhere seen and felt in the Roman world, so also they were well-organized; and there were many of them.

10.

Matt. 8, 28—9, 1. Mark 5, 1—21. Luke 8, 26—40.

And now we come to a difficult part of the story. The devils felt that their time for torturing these victims would soon be over. But if there was to be a dispossession, they begged Jesus not to banish them from a district which had been so favorable for their infernal purposes nor to precipitate them into the abyss "before the time." And if they must needs leave man, they begged to be permitted to enter at least swine. This is certainly a strange suggestion, but also truly devilish and cruel. Satan's one desire is to destroy the life which God has created. As a roaring lion he walketh about, seeking whom he may devour,[1] if not the soul, then the body of man; and if not the human body, then the dumb beast.[2] Now, at a distance, yet within view, there was a herd of about two thousand swine feeding on the hillside. Doubtless they were the property of some Gentile inhabitants, but they may have belonged to some apostatizing Jews in violation of the Law. With a laconic "Go!" Jesus gave them leave to enter into the swine.

The Demons Enter Swine. They were commanded to leave their victims and were not hindered from entering into the swine.[3] Thus in a self-staged infernal *finale* the devils wreaked their fiendishness, their mania for destroying God's creatures, on dumb brutes. "And when they were come out, they went into the herd of swine. And, behold, the whole herd of swine ran violently down a steep place into the sea and perished in the waters." But was not the request to enter the swine and then immediately to destroy their new habitation extremely stupid on the part of the devils? As we shall see, this act of the devils secured an extended continuance to them in that

---

9,　3) Bruce *sub loco.*
10,　1) 1 Pet. 5, 8.　　　2) Kretzmann, I, 187.　　　3) Bruce *sub loco.*

country and effected the removal of Jesus from that region. The
incident has exhausted the wit of the critic and apologist in
every age. Truly, the sufferers had been freed from their hellish
tormentors; but what about the property rights of others and the
loss of the swine? We answer: Is He not the Lord? Is God
unjust in sending earthquakes, floods, or deadly diseases among
men and cattle? [4] And are not two souls worth more than two
thousand swine? [5] Besides, the loss of the swine was a punishment
for the apostate or at least indifferent Jews and low-bred Gentiles
of the Decapolis, who loved their precious swine more than they
did the Lord.[6] The Jews, we know, were not allowed to have swine.

11.

Matt. 8, 28—9, 1. Mark 5, 1—21. Luke 8, 26—40.

In wild terror the swine-herders brought the news of the terrible catastrophe to Gerasa and the region round about. They
knew or felt that there must be some connection between the coming
of Jesus, the release of the demoniacs, and the headlong rush of
their herds into the sea. A multitude soon gathered, probably with
thoughts of revenge on whoever was guilty of the loss of the swine.
But the truth was soon learned. There sat the man who had been

The Sequel.   a terror to the country, clothed and in his right
       mind. A charitable hand had flung a robe over
his naked figure. There was the proof of the power of the mighty
Stranger who had thus visited their country. "And they were
afraid." They were awed by the presence of Him whose power
over the demons had been demonstrated beyond a doubt. Truly, it
was a remarkable cure. But there was also the matter of the swine!
While the cure could not be denied, had it not also caused
a calamity? Here was both a benefactor and a dangerous man!
"With disgraceful and urgent unanimity they request Jesus to leave
the coasts." [1] His presence might cause another cure and —
catastrophe.

12.

Matt. 8, 28—9, 1. Mark 5, 1—21. Luke 8, 26—40.

Jesus did not need much urging. Since the people of that
region were evidently little interested in the person of the Miracle-
worker and the purpose of His miracles, He left them. But while

---

10,   4) Ylvisaker, *Gospel*, 191.
      5) Rosenmueller, quoted in *Exp. Greek N. T.*, 146.
      6) Farrar, I, 341.
11,   1) Farrar, I, 341.

the multitudes had requested His departure, one of the healed demoniacs asked leave of Jesus to remain in His presence. The application was made just as Jesus was entering the boat. "Howbeit Jesus suffered him not." Nevertheless, while He refused his petition, He did not dispense with his services. He commissioned

"Tell How Great Things the Lord hath Done for Thee."

him as the first missionary, as it were, to the heathen of those parts. He commanded him to go to his home and friends and give them a full account of the great blessings of God which he had experienced and especially also of the mercy the Lord had bestowed upon him. This he did. "He began to publish in Decapolis how great things Jesus had done for him. And all men did marvel." Whether or not there was any other result the evangelists have not stated. At any rate, the population had the opportunity to hear about the great Prophet in whom according to the prophecy the Gentiles would trust.[1] In the mean while Jesus had returned to Capernaum.[2]

13.

Matt. 9, 18—26. Mark 5, 22—43. Luke 8, 41—56.

No doubt the friends of Jesus in Capernaum who had witnessed His sudden departure the evening before as well as the furious tempest while He was crossing the lake were by this time concerned about His safety and that of His companions. When therefore He returned safe and sound, "the people gladly received Him; for they were all waiting for Him." As the tidings of His return rapidly spread, the usual multitude gathered, including two supplicants, to whom no help but that of Jesus could be of possible avail. One of them was an elder in the local synagog,

---

12, 1) Matt. 12, 21.

   2) *Here follows in the order of Matthew:* —

The paralytic healed	9, 2—8	All in order, but
Matthew called	9—13	transposed as com-
The question about fasting and John's		pared with Mark
disciples	14. 15	and Luke. See
A parable: New wine and new bottles	16. 17	chapter X, 12 ff.

There are some difficulties as to the proper sequence of events on account of the words "while He yet spake" in Matt. 9, 18, which seems to compel a connection with v. 17. However, since Matthew is not chronological in this part of his gospel, it is best to follow the order of Mark and Luke, but to bear in mind that the feast previously referred to and probably there related to bring together everything that concerns Levi-Matthew personally, may have taken place at this time. See chapter X, 15. Compare James Orr in *Int. St. B. Encycl.*, 1641. 1646.

Jairus by name. It is not altogether improbable that on a previous occasion this Jairus belonged to a delegation sent to Jesus in behalf of the centurion's servant who was at the point of death, although the words used are not quite the same.[1]) At any rate, as one of the synagog rulers of Capernaum he had witnessed the words and deeds of Jesus. He had seen and heard others appeal to Jesus, and this time he was in need himself. Casting himself at the feet of Jesus, he told Him that his twelve-year-old daughter, his "little

Jairus. daughter," his "only daughter," was dying; yes, a few moments later, after hearing the last report, he had to say that she was "even now dead." [2]) Still, even now, if He would but come and lay His hand on her, she would live. But if his daughter was seriously ill, why did he not apply for help yesterday? Why wait? Only in the hour of supreme need did he resort to Jesus. There was faith, but there was also need to perfect such faith. The merciful Savior was not deaf to the heart-broken father's cry. He at once set out to go to Capernaum, followed not only by His disciples, but by a dense and thronging crowd, anxious to witness a scene.

14.

Matt. 9, 18—26. Mark 5, 22—43. Luke 8, 41—56.

At this point an interlude occurred. While Jesus was on the way to the ruler's house, He was prayerfully touched by an afflicted woman who secretly hoped, as it were, "to steal from Jesus a blessing for which she longed." [1]) According to a legend it was Veronica,[2]) a woman from Caesarea Philippi, at the foot of Mount Hermon. In commemoration of her cure by Jesus she is said to have erected a statue of Jesus in bronze, in which she is represented in the act of touching the robe of Christ. This alleged statue of Jesus, the earliest, by the way, of which we seem to have any record, was seen by Eusebius, who tells the story. It was destroyed by Julian the Apostate.[3]) For twelve years she had suffered from

---

13, 1) Farrar, I, 353. Luke 7, 3. See chapter XI, 43, πρεσβυτέρους, but here ἀρχών. In strictly Jewish communities the same men would be officers of the city and of the synagog. Schuerer, II, I, 150.

2) The passage has created work for the harmonist, because Mark and Luke say "dying" and Matthew says "dead." The latter was actually the case when the final report came, Mark 5, 35. For the sake of brevity, it seems, Matthew contracts the whole narrative into the briefest possible summary.

14, 1) Farrar, I, 355.

2) That is, *vera icon* (εἰκών), "true image."

3) Eusebius, *H. E.,* VII, 18. Sozomenus, *H. E.,* V, 21. Farrar, I, 356, n. 2.

a distressing malady, an issue of blood, peculiar to her sex, which was not only extremely afflicting, but, since it rendered her Levitically unclean,[4] made her unfit for all usual relationships of life. She had spent all her living on physicians in search of a cure and found none; if anything, her condition had grown worse. As a last desperate recourse she determined to gain relief "from the Great Physician without money and without price." [5] Having heard the things concerning Jesus, she came in the crowd behind and quietly and quickly touched the fringe of His garment. — Just a word

The Woman with the Issue of Blood.

about the clothes of Jesus. Not the inner garment, "without seam, woven from the top throughout," [6] is meant, but the outer garment, the mantle,[7] upon which were fastened fringes, or tassels, in accordance with the Law.[8] "For she said, If I may touch but His clothes, I shall be made whole." According to her secret hope the least possible degree of contact was enough to insure a cure. This was faith. "But it was also mingled with superstition and cunning" because she hoped to gain a cure by touch, notwithstanding the touch by one in her state was forbidden.[9] Immediately there was a turn for the better. "And straightway the fountain of her blood was dried up, and she felt in her body that she was healed of that plague."

15.

Matt. 9, 18—26. Mark 5, 22—43. Luke 8, 41—56.

The incident was unnoticed by others, but not by Jesus. He knew and felt, and He instantly complied with the woman's unspoken request. In the throng many had touched Jesus, but only one had touched Him in faith. Perceiving that healing power had gone forth from Him, He turned about and asked: "Who touched My clothes?" Not as if He did not know, or as if He were giving vent to Rabbinical anger because the touch of an unclean woman had polluted Him. "His touch had cleansed her, not her touch did pollute Him." [1] The purpose of the question was that the faith of the woman should be revealed. Of course, the disciples could not know. They had not noticed any wilful jolting,

---

14, 4) Lev. 15, 25.   5) Farrar, I, 354.
    6) The χιτών, John 19, 23.
    7) Ἱμάτιον.
    8) Num. 15, 38—41; Deut. 22, 12.   Edersheim, I, 624.
    9) Bruce sub Mark 5, 28.   Cf. Lev. 15, 19—27.
15, 1) Farrar, I, 356.

and in view of the crowd the question seemed strange. Peter was almost impatient with his Master, which is evident from his reply: "Thou seest the multitude thronging Thee, and sayest Thou, Who touched Me?" But Jesus, His eyes still sweeping over the many faces, insisted that there was a difference between the accidental touching of curiosity and the intentional touching of faith. Naturally the woman was an interested witness of the dialog.

"Who Touched Me?" Seeing that neither she nor her action could any longer be hid, she came forward with fear and trembling, "fell down before Him, told Him all the truth." This included the cause of it all, her purpose, and the cure. Probably she feared the anger of Jesus because she had exposed Him to her defiling touch.[2] Still her faith was now fully revealed and Christ's purpose in putting the question achieved. In all kindness Jesus dismissed her with the assurance: "Daughter, be of good cheer; thy faith hath made thee whole; go in peace."

16.

Matt. 9, 18—26. Mark 5, 22—43. Luke 8, 41—56.

In consequence of this delay the urgent need of Jairus was well-nigh forgotten. But this was wholly in line with the plans of Jesus. At this point the report was brought to Jairus that his daughter had really died, and the suggestion was added: "Trouble not the Master." All help was now too late. However, Jesus, overhearing, but not heeding, the message, calmly continued on His way to the house of Jairus, addressing to him the memorable words: "Fear not; only believe." Upon His arrival at the house He found it already occupied by the customary company of wailing women and

"Talitha, Cumi." flute-players, the former weeping, howling, beating their breasts, and tearing hair, according to contract, the latter striking up mournful dirges — a veritable mockery of true sorrow and in weird contrast with the awful silence of death. "Mourning like everything else had been reduced to a system. At least two flute-players and one mourning woman at the burial of a wife, for instance, was incumbent on the poorest man." [1] The whole procedure was repulsive to Jesus. "Why make ye this ado and weep?" Moreover, "the damsel is not dead, but sleepeth." But they "laughed Him to scorn." Ejecting them all from the house, the crowd as well as the paid

---

15, 2) Lev. 15, 19.
16, 1) Bruce sub Matt. 9, 23. Farrar, I, 357. Ylvisaker, 205.

mourners, except the father and the mother of the departed maiden and three disciples, Peter, James, and John, of whom we here read for the first time that they were specially favored by their Master,[2] He grasped the cold little hand and uttered the life-giving words: "Talitha, cumi; which is, being interpreted, Damsel, I say unto thee, arise." "Jesus may have been bilingual and expressed Himself in Greek or in Syriac, as the occasion demanded. On a pathetic occasion like this He would naturally express Himself in the mother tongue of the sorrowing mother and father."[3] "And straightway the damsel arose and walked." Amazement seized the parents; but Jesus calmly directed them to give her something to eat. And if again Jesus added His customary warning that they should not speak of what had just happened, it was evidently His intention that they should not so much peddle His miracle as rather reflect upon it in silent faith and spread His doctrine. He would have nothing of that fanatical and extravagant enthusiasm which made of Him a mere miracle-monger and often disturbed the progress of faith. While Jesus often forbade miracle-spreading reports, He never forbade the spreading of His doctrine, which had the power to kindle faith. But in this case as well as in others the injunction was of no avail.

Matt. 9, 27—31.   **17.**

On His return from the home of Jairus, Jesus was for the first time publicly addressed with a familiar Messianic appellation. Two blind men uttered the cry: "Thou Son of David, have mercy on us." Now, Jesus was the Son of David. As such, in certain quarters, He was intimately known and believingly acknowledged. But it seems that at this time it was not welcome to Him to be thus pub-

Two Blind Men. licly invoked.[1] False Messianic expectations would have been nourished. An incorrect understanding of the title might have led to a popular uprising in His favor against the Roman government. The title must therefore be correctly understood and a test made of the faith of those who applied to Him for help. The blind men were permitted to follow Him to His house. Then He turned upon them with the question: "Believe ye that I am able to do this?" A prompt

---

16, 2) Special witnesses of His "greatest exaltation and most abject humiliation." Ylvisaker, 205. Compare the Transfiguration and the suffering in Gethsemane, Mark 5, 37; 14, 33.

3) Bruce sub Mark 5, 41.

17, 1) Bruce sub Matt. 9, 27.

"Yea, Lord" was the reply. The confession revealed both their confidence in the almighty power of Jesus as well as their faith in Him as their Messiah and merciful Lord. Without further hesitation Jesus touched their eyes and gave them their sight. The purpose of the touching probably was to impress upon them that the healing came from Him. Again there was a command of silence, most sternly given this time.[2] Probably the fear of a movement by which the people would be aroused to rebellion against Rome imposed the silence. But the command was disregarded, and therefore the publicity was an act of disobedience, and it cannot be excused by assuming that these men believed it was only the modesty of Jesus that had prompted the command.

Matt. 9, 32—34.   18.

Hardly had the two blind men been healed when a dumb person was brought into the presence of Jesus. In this case the dumbness was not due to a physical cause, but an evil spirit had blunted the faculty of speech. No sooner was the devil cast out than the dumb was able to speak. Again the crowd that was present

A Dumb Demoniac.   was filled with wonder, to which they gave expression by saying, "It was never so seen in Israel." Such miracles, signs, and wonders! It had gradually entered into the consciousness of the people that it was the promised Messiah who was blessing them with His presence among them. "The multitudes marveled; *but* the Pharisees *said:*[1] "He casteth out devils through the prince of the devils." In this case the blasphemous accusation was purposely ignored by our Lord.

17, 2) Ἐνεβριμήσατο, v. 30.
18, 1) Bruce *sub loco.*

CHAPTER XIV.

A THIRD PREACHING TOUR,
INCLUDING THE MISSION OF THE TWELVE.

Probably early in 29 A. D.
January to March, 782 A. U. C.

1.

(Matt. 13, 54—58).[1] *Mark 6, 1—6.*

After the crowded events related in the last chapter we picture to ourselves a period of solitude and rest for our Savior. Probably at Capernaum. Henceforth His beloved city ceases to be the center of His activities; it will be visited only occasionally. According to our chronology we have reached the winter months of 28 to 29 A. D. The time is fixed by the death of John the Baptist, which is placed during the time of the next circuit and the mission of the Twelve in the spring of 29 A. D. Already the public ministry of Jesus was

The Last Visit to Nazareth. drawing to its close, at least as far as some sections of the land of Israel were concerned. For the last time Jesus of Nazareth was to visit the city of Nazareth, again to be rejected as at the beginning of His great Galilean ministry, about eight or nine months before.[2] There is no sufficient occasion to identify this visit with that described by Luke. The time and the details are quite different. It is perfectly natural that Jesus should give the Nazarenes another opportunity to hear His teaching.[3] But what surprises us is what Jesus marveled at: the unbelief of His townsmen, which lay at the bottom of their estimate and treatment of a "native son."[4]

1,   1) Transposed. In the order of events we follow Mark rather than Luke. Matthew relates this visit to Nazareth immediately after the parables by the sea. Chronologically, however, the departure in Matt. 13, 53 was not to Nazareth, but across the sea to Gergesa, Mark 4, 35. We must therefore place the Gadarene journey, the healing of the demoniacs, the raising of Jairus's daughter, the healing of the woman with the issue of blood, of the two blind men, and of the dumb possessed with an evil spirit between Matt. 13, 53 and 54. This brings us to the last visit Jesus made at Nazareth. And taking up the broken thread in Matt. 9, 35, we have returned to the synoptic order. (Next section.)

   2) Luke 4, 16—30.
   3) Robertson, *Harmony*, 77.
   4) Mark 6, 6.

2.

(Matt. 13, 54—58.) Mark 6, 1—6.

When Jesus arrived at Nazareth in the company of His disciples, it was but natural for Him to make His Sabbath appearance in the local synagog. And on account of His fame it was also quite natural that an invitation to teach was extended to Him as a visiting Rabbi. Even if His address on that particular morning was of a nature to provoke astonishment, we are surprised at the reaction to His teaching. Regardless of the fact that He happened to be a townsman, if He was a prophet, the extraordinary was quite naturally to be expected. The comments were many and varied. "Whence hath this man this wisdom and these mighty works?" The answer is of course, From God. And both the particular words and deeds argue for His Messiahship. But the "Is Not This the Carpenter's Son?" Nazarenes were unwilling to concede this distinction to a "native son." "Is not this the carpenter's son? [1] Is not His mother called Mary and His brethren James and Joses, and Simon, and Judas? [2] And His sisters, [3] are they not all with us?" [4] "And they were offended at Him." Jesus could only refer to the common proverb that "a prophet is not without honor save in his own country and in His own house." [5] Therefore, outside of a few minor works of healing, performed upon those who *did* accept Him in faith, Jesus "could there do no mighty works" on account of the general unbelief. Unbelief shuts out man from the blessings God had intended for him. Neither was it fitting that Jesus should benefit these people against their will. But the attitude of His townsmen caused Him to wonder. He had not expected this insusceptibility among His neighbors. Their reasoning against His Messiahship based upon residence and previous acquaintance was most unreasonable.

2,   1) See chapter IV, 43; XI, 10.

2) Chapter IV, 43.

3) Unknown. The *History of Joseph* supplies the names of Anna and Lydia. And the Coptic apocryphal gospels mention Lysia and (or) Lydia. Rendel Harris, *The Twelve Apostles*, 50.

4) Compare John 2, 12. Chapter VI, 25. Luke 4, 31. Chapter IX, 10. It seems that the "sisters" of Jesus, now mentioned as residing at Nazareth, probably married, did not accompany Him and His "brethren" to Capernaum.

5) Compare Luke 4, 24. A repetition of John 4, 44, with a changed reference and in a different connection. This brings to our mind a Logion of Jesus as found in the Oxyrhynchus Papyri: "A physician does not work cures on them that know him." *Int. St. B. Encycl.*, III, 1911.

Matt. 9, 35. Mark 6, 6b.   3.

After His rejection at Nazareth, Jesus again assumed the role of an itinerant preacher, visiting Galilean cities and vil-

A Brief Itinerancy. lages, teaching in the synagog on the Sabbath, "preaching the Gospel of the Kingdom, and healing every sickness and every disease among the people."

Matt. 9, 36—38.   4.

This itinerant preaching brought our Lord into the most intimate touch with the people, giving Him an insight into their moral and religious condition. Two pictures suggested themselves to His mind: a neglected flock of sheep and a harvest going to waste for lack of reapers. Both imply not only a pitiful plight of the people, but a blameworthy neglect of duty on the part of their

"Pray Ye the Lord of the Harvest." religious guides.[1] As usual, where Jesus was, the crowds gathered. And when He saw the multitudes, He was moved with compassion because they were "as sheep having no shepherd."[2] A shepherdless flock, what a pitiful sight! — unprotected, distressed, and scattered, "footsore and fleece-torn."[3] Then a new figure flashes into the Lord's mind, not only reflecting His divine sympathy, but showing His ardent desire to help these poor people spiritually. "The harvest, truly, is plenteous, but the laborers are few. Pray ye therefore the Lord of the harvest that He will send forth laborers into His harvest."[4]

5.

Matt. 10, 1—4. Mark 6, 7. Luke 9, 1.

Immediately the Savior decides upon a special mission for His twelve apostles. Of course, "they will be but poor substitutes for Him, but they had already received some training and had imbibed

The Mission of the Twelve. somewhat of His spirit of love."[1] He called them unto Himself for the purpose of sending them forth to preach the kingdom of God and to perform works of mercy in His name. Out of consideration for their initial timidity and for the pur-

4,   1) Bruce *sub loco.*
    2) The image used again Mark 6, 34.
    3) Bruce *sub loco.*
    4) The saying is repeated in connection with the sending out of the Seventy, Luke 10, 2.
5,   1) Bruce sub Matt. 10, 1.

pose of giving them moral backing He sent them out two by two. In order that they might prove their divine calling, He equipped them with power — probably for the first confined only to this mission — "against unclean spirits, to cast them out, and to heal all manner of sickness and all manner of disease." [2] We have already become acquainted with the individual members of the apostolic band,[3] but the Evangelist Matthew finds here a convenient place in his account for giving the names of the Twelve, to whom a number of special instructions are given.

6.

Matt. 10, 5—15. Mark 6, 8—11. Luke 9, 2—5.

Some day the Gospel would be brought to all, but during the period of this mission the apostles should not go "into the way of the Gentiles" nor enter "into any city of the Samaritans.[1] But go rather to the lost sheep of the house of Israel." And wherever they would go, they should above all *preach,* namely, that "the kingdom of heaven is at hand." And that their message might bear weight, they should back up their preaching with such signs as would be accepted as proofs of their divine mission. "Heal the sick, cleanse the lepers, cast out devils," yes, even "raise the dead." [2] However, this power was not to be for hire nor to be sold for money. "Freely ye have received, freely give." As regards provisions for

Their Instructions.   the journey, they should take nothing along, no bread, no wallet, no money, neither two coats, nor shoes; and if they had no staff, they should not procure one.[3] "For the workman is worthy of his meat." Upon entering a village, they should establish a center of activity and carefully inquire into the moral worthiness of a probable host. Having found a favorable prospect, they should enter his house with the time-honored and much-valued blessing, "Peace be unto you." If the house sheltered children of peace, then this blessing would be effective. If not, then "let your peace return to you";

5,   2) Up to this time it has not been mentioned that the Twelve wrought any miracles, nor is it recorded that they did so after they rejoined the Lord. However, even then the power was not absolutely withdrawn; the exercising of it depended upon their faith. Matt. 21, 19. 20. Andrews, 312.

3) Chapter XI, 4 ff.

6,   1) On account of this injunction it is likely that Judea was not reached.

2) This clause is well attested in the best MSS. But it is unlikely that the apostles used this power before Christ Himself rose from the dead. Bruce sub Matt. 10, 8. Kretzmann, I, 55.

3) From a comparison of the three evangelists we infer this to be the meaning of this injunction. Farrar, I, 363, n. 2.

then they were to shake the dust off their feet in witness of the fact that they had spoken faithfully, and thus symbolically clear themselves of all responsibility for the wrath of God which would come upon the haters of the Word of God. "Verily I say unto you, It shall be more tolerable for the land of Sodom and Gomorrah [4] in the Day of Judgment than for that city."

Matt. 10, 16—23.   7.

It seems that the Evangelist Matthew, "guided, as usual, by the unity of subject, has collected into one focus the scattered rays of instruction," [1] delivered perhaps on several occasions. [2] Some of the expressions, while applicable to the present apostolic mission, have general reference to experiences which as yet lay in the future. But that need not disturb us. What applies to the apostles in particular might apply also to disciples of Christ in general. It is a great honor to be a follower of Jesus. But there are also perils of discipleship; persecutions are predicted. Although the disciples were sent forth on an errand of peace, they and their followers would not always be peacefully received. "Behold, I send you forth as sheep in the midst of wolves." The situation calls for diplomacy both blameless and prudent. "Be ye therefore wise as serpents and

Persecutions Predicted.   harmless as doves." "The question is not whether or not serpents and doves are in themselves exceptionally cunning or particularly harmless, but what they represent in Scripture" and in the popular mind. [3] Neither have we here a license for Christians to practise the duplicity of serpents; for that would be out of harmony with the proverbial sincerity of the dove. It may be difficult in practical life to combine the sagacity of a serpent with the simplicity of a dove; but these are traits which every believer must cultivate. Enemies will be found on every hand. Generally speaking, the natural mind will be found to be inimical toward the Gospel. Therefore "beware of men. They will deliver you up to the councils [4] and will scourge you in their synagogs." [5] Even the civil

---

6,   4) Incidentally this is a proof of the one-time existence of the doomed cities as well as of the resurrection of the wicked.

7,   1) Farrar, I, 367.

2) Compare Luke 10, 2—12; 12, 2—9; 21, 12—19; Mark 13, 9—13.

3) Gen. 3, 1; Hos. 7, 11. Ylvisaker, 317.

4) Plural. Not the Sanhedrin, but the local courts.

5) Acts 22, 19; 26, 11.

courts, provincial rulers, and Herodian princes may be called upon to pronounce judgment upon the followers of Christ. The outlook is not pleasant, but many opportunities will thus be presented to witness for the cause of Christ. However, in the critical hour they need not trouble themselves as to manner or matter of word or thought. "For it shall be given you in that same hour what ye shall speak." [6] Theirs it was boldly to confess; God's, to make a wise apology. "The grandest utterances in defense of Christianity have sometimes been made by the simplest minds." [7] Gold is tested in the trial of fire. And some of the trials are fiery indeed, especially when the enmity against the Gospel makes itself felt among those who are otherwise bound together by the strongest ties of love. "And the brother shall deliver up the brother to death and the father the child." But even in spite of this most painful opposition a disciple of Christ must persevere. "He that endureth to the end shall be saved." Discipleship might end in martyrdom. But this does not mean that the disciples should rush headlong to such a death. "When they persecute you in this city, flee ye into another." Thus persecution might serve the spreading of the Gospel. And as to persecution and opposition, there is also judgment in the end. Now Jesus makes a solemn declaration: "Ye shall not have gone over the cities of Israel till the Son of Man be come." We must feel our way as to the thought connection and meaning of some of the sayings of Jesus. Evidently the second coming, unto Judgment, is not meant directly. It seems to us that we have here a veiled reference to the destruction of Jerusalem, namely, a "coming of the Son of Man," not in the understanding of the Jews and according to their wish, but in judgment upon their city and state in vindication of the Kingship which Israel had disowned.[8]

Matt. 10, 24—31.[1]   **8.**

But also encouragement is offered. There is a source of consolation in the companionship of suffering with the Master. "The disciple is not above his master nor the servant above his lord." And if the enemies have gone so far as to call "the Master of the house Beelzebub," [2] how can they of the household expect less?

7, 6) Chapter XXI, 18.

   7) Bruce *sub loco*.

   8) The view of Edersheim, I, 646, and Ylvisaker, 319.

8, 1) Compare Luke 12, 2—9. Chapter XXI, 18.

   2) Mark 3, 22.

Reference might here be made to the time when the vilest epithets were heaped upon the Christians, such as "atheists" and "worshipers of the ass's head"; and when they were reputed to have perpetrated the most scandalous crimes, Thyestean banquets, Oedipean incest, nightly orgies, child murder, and the like,[3] and when they were said to be given to "abominable and atrocious superstition" and to be guilty of "hatred of the human race." [4] But "fear them not," the Lord encouraged them; "for there is nothing covered that shall not be revealed and [nothing] hid that shall not be known." If they were to be

Encouragement Offered.

of any use as apostles and missionaries, it would be but natural for them to achieve publicity, some of which would bring upon them the hatred and hostility of men. Nevertheless, "what I tell you in darkness, that speak ye in light; and what ye hear in the ear, that preach ye upon the housetops." Fearless testimony should not be silenced on account of threatened persecution. And the proper antidote for the fear of man is the fear of God. "A mighty Fortress is our God." "Fear not them which kill the body, but are not able to kill the soul; but rather fear Him which is able to destroy both body and soul in hell." And as to earthly persecutors, why fear at all? Are you not in the hands of the heavenly Father? "Are not two sparrows sold for a farthing?" [5] We are surprised that they had any value at all. "And one of them shall not fall on the ground" — a beautiful expression — "without your Father." "But the very hairs of your head are all numbered." Not as if they had been counted once for all, but that "one hair cannot go a-missing unobserved." [6]

Matt. 10, 32—39.[1]   9.

This, then, is encouraging. However, not only is encouragement offered, but also a steadfast defense of the truth is demanded of every follower of Christ. "Whosoever therefore shall confess Me before men, him will I confess also before My Father which is in heaven. But whosoever shall deny Me before men, him will I also deny before My Father which is in heaven." And what will be the result of such brave and uncompromising Christian confession? Cannot the Gospel of forgiveness and the new religion of peace propagate itself quietly and peacefully? The question is

---

8,   3) *Int. St. B. Encycl.,* 2604.   4) Tacitus, *Ann.,* XV, 44. 45.
   5) Ἀσσάριον, an as, a brass coin equal to about one cent.
   6) Bruce *sub loco.*   9,   1) Compare Luke 12, 8. 9.

CODEX SINAITICUS. (ℵ)

Now in London. Fourth century. Matt. 10, 17—11, 5.

"Whosoever therefore shall confess Me before men, him will I confess also before My Father which is in heaven." — *Matt. 10, 32.*

ΟΥΝΟϹΤΙϹΟΜΟΛΟ	οὖν ὅστις ὁμολο-
ΓΗϹΙΕΝΕΜΟΙΕΜ	γήσ(ε)ι ἐν ἐμοὶ ἔμ-
ΠΡΟϹΘΕΝΤΩΝΑΝΩΝ	προσθεν τῶν ἀν(θρώπ)ων,
ΟΜΟΛΟΓΗϹΩΚΑ	ὁμολογήσω κἀ-
ΓΩΕΝΑΥΤΩΕΜΠΡο	γὼ ἐν αὐτῷ ἔμπρο-
ϹΘΕΝΤΟΥΠΡϹΜΟΥ	σθεν τοῦ π(ατ)ρ(ό)ς μου
ΤΟΥΕΝΟΥΡΑΝΟΙϹ	τοῦ ἐν οὐρανοῖς.

(First seven lines, third column.)

answered decidedly in the negative. "Think not that I am come to send peace on earth; I came not to send peace, but a sword." A surprising statement. Of course, the purpose of Christ's coming

Loyalty Demanded. was to bring peace. "Peace on earth" the angels proclaimed. But to a great extent the opposite was the result. Not as though Christ or His Gospel were to blame; but it was due to carnal enmity, which found its expression in the hatred against Christ and the persecutions which followed the introduction of the Gospel. And "there is no more bitter hatred and strife than that due to religious difference. It estranges relatives, disrupts families, and causes lasting enmities between the closest of friends." [2] "And a man's foes shall be they of his own household." "He that loveth father or mother more than Me is not worthy of Me; and he that loveth son or daughter more than Me is not worthy of Me." Not as if filial or parental love were prohibited, but Christ must be loved more than father and mother or son and daughter. And in the event of a family disruption for the sake of Christ the ensuing hatred must be willingly endured. Thus a Christian must take up his cross. [3] But there is also a reward for loyalty unto death. "He that loseth his life for My sake shall find it."

Matt. 10, 40—42. **10.**

In a concluding reminder Jesus points out to His apostles that in the mission on which He was sending them they are His duly accredited and commissioned representatives and messengers. Whatever happens to them happens to Him. The treatment accorded the messenger reverts to his master. "He that receiveth you

The Proper Attitude to the Ministers of Christ. receiveth Me, and he that receiveth Me receiveth Him that sent Me." Any kindness or courtesy extended to a true prophet, in this case to a minister or disciple of Jesus because he is His disciple, and if it were only a refreshing cup of water, will be regarded and remembered by the Savior as having been done unto Him. It is in His disciples that Jesus, as well as the Father who sent Him, would be loved and honored. And he that thus esteems and treats them, "verily, I say unto you, he shall in no wise lose his reward."

9, 2) Kretzmann, I, 59.

3) This is not necessarily an allusion to the death of Jesus by crucifixion. The Roman custom condemning a doomed criminal to carry his cross was known. Bruce *sub loco.*

11.

Matt. 11, 1. Mark 6, 12. 13. Luke 9, 6.

After Jesus had finished this discourse, He continued His labors in the usual manner, while the disciples set out two by two

The Departure of Jesus and the Disciples.

on their preliminary missionary tour. The burden of their message was repentance in order that the call of the Gospel might find ready acceptance. They cast out demons and healed the sick "everywhere," thus establishing their authority by miracles and signs. That they used oil in some instances,[1] does not detract from the supernatural character of their works of healing.[2] [3]

11, 1) Mark 6, 13.

2) Ylvisaker (*The Gospels*, 322) thinks that the procedure, being not directly enjoined by Jesus, was employed of their own accord. The passage has nothing to do with the *unctio extrema*.

3) Here follows in the order of Matthew: —

The message from John the Baptist	11, 2—19.	See chapter XII,	2—4.
Woes upon the cities of opportunity	20—30.	See chapter XII,	5—7.
The disciples plucking grain	12, 1— 8.	See chapter X,	26—28.
The man with a withered hand ...	9—14.	See chapter X,	29—31.
Jesus teaches and heals by the Sea of Galilee	15—21.	See chapter X,	32. 33.
Jesus defends Himself against a blasphemous accusation	22—37.	See chapter XII,	13—15.
Scribes and Pharisees demand a sign	38—45.	See chapter XII,	16.
Jesus is sought by His mother and His brethren	46—50.	See chapter XII,	17.
The parables by the sea	13, 1—53.	See chapter XII,	18—32.
The last visit at Nazareth	54—58.	See chapter XIV,	1. 2.

With the exception of a few details the account of the death of John the Baptist marks the end of the transpositions. Henceforth, to the end of the combined account, the fourfold gospel unfolds itself in a truly remarkable parallel account.

CHAPTER XV.

THE DEATH OF JOHN THE BAPTIST.

Machaerus. Probably latter part of March or the beginning of April,
782 A. U. C., or 29 A. D.

1.

Matt. 14, 1. 2. Mark 6, 14—16. Luke 9, 7—9.

The scene changes. It is now about the latter part of March
or the beginning of April, shortly before the Passover of 29 A. D.[1]
The spreading fame of Jesus had reached the ears of the tetrarch
Antipas, whose dominions embraced, in the north, Galilee, west of
the Jordan and the Lake of Galilee; in the south, Perea, east of
the Jordan. Like his father he was a builder and had a number
of strongholds and royal palaces: Sepphoris, which he made his
metropolis, and Tiberias in Galilee,[2] Julias, or Livias, opposite
Jericho,[3] and Machaerus opposite the Dead Sea, in Perea. But
because it was not until "at that time" that "Herod the Tetrarch
heard of the fame of Jesus," [4] we suppose that during the nine or
ten months of Christ's great Galilean ministry Herod must have

Herod's Superstitious Fears. resided in Perea, most likely
in Machaerus, that fortress
on the Arabian frontier which at the time must have required his
particular attention and which is mentioned by Josephus [5] as the
place of the Baptist's imprisonment and death. It is quite possible
that Antipas fled from the scene of his crime soon after the death
of John and returned to his own Tiberias on the Galilean Sea.
At any rate, when King Herod [6] — the title was freely applied to
all Eastern rulers — heard of the ministry of Jesus, he was immediately reminded of his infamous act. Was it possible, could there
be two such remarkable men in the same land and period? Because
of a wrong understanding of the prophecy of Malachi [7] some
believed Jesus to be *Elias Redivivus,* with extraordinary power and
mission. According to others He was one of the prophets of old,
who had risen from the dead, or at least like one of them. But
according to Herod himself, with a murder on his conscience and

---

1,   1) Schuerer, I, II, 32.   John 6, 4.
      2) Schuerer, II, I, 136 f. 143 f.; I, II, 19 f.
      3) Schuerer, *ibid.,* 141.   4) Matt. 14, 1.
      5) *Ant.,* XVIII, v, 2.
      6) Mark, writing for the Roman world.   7) Chap. 4, 5.

"the Baptist on his brain": [8] "This is John the Baptist; he is risen from the dead; and therefore mighty works do show forth themselves in Him." But it was just this superstitious fear on the part of Herod with respect to the fame of Jesus which caused the Synoptists to relate *post factum* how the "Heaven-enkindled and shining lamp of John the Baptist was suddenly quenched in blood." [9]

2.

Matt. 14, 3—12. Mark 6, 17—29. (Luke 3, 19. 20.)

When we last heard of John the Baptist, he was already in prison. The report of our Lord's wonderful ministry was the occasion of two of his disciples' being sent to Jesus with the question: "Art Thou He that should come, or do we look for another?" [1] which, in turn, led Jesus to that memorable encomium on His friend and forerunner. [2] It seems that the imprisonment of John was not devoid of a measure of freedom, intercourse with his friends and disciples, and communication with the outside. John had been too direct in his testimony. Because he had reproved

"It Is Not Lawful for Thee to Have Her."

Herod for his illicit marriage to the wife of his brother, "Herod himself had sent forth and laid hold upon John and bound him in prison for Herodias's sake, his brother Philip's wife; for he had married her. For John had said unto Herod, It is not lawful for thee to have thy brother's wife." [3] A subject's open declaration of the unlawfulness of a Herodian ruler's marriage as both incestuous and adulterous, was certainly carrying the call of repentance a little too far, especially, as in this case, when the king was called to account because of pet Herodian family sins. And especially did John incur the hatred of Herod's new wife, his former sister-in-law Herodias, the wife and niece of Philip, now illegally married to him who was both her brother-in-law and her half-uncle, Herod Antipas.

3.

Matt. 14, 3—12. Mark 6, 17—29. (Luke 3, 19. 20.)

There may also have been a political aspect, as mentioned by Josephus, [1] which led to the imprisonment of John. While the interesting passage does not give us the real motive, as supplied by

---

1,   8) Bruce sub Matt. 14, 1.   9) Farrar, I, 384.

2,   1) Summer, 28 A. D. Chapter XII, 2.

      2) Matt. 11, 2—15; Luke 7, 18—28.

      3) Lev. 18, 16; 20, 21.   3,   1) *Ant.,* XVIII, 5.

the evangelists, who let us look behind the scene, as it were,[2] it at least demonstrates that we are dealing with history in presenting the external and public aspects of the imprisonment and death of the forerunner of Christ. "John was a good man, who bade the Jews first cultivate virtue by justice towards each other and piety towards God and so to come to baptism; for immersion,[3] he said, would only appear acceptable to God if practised, not as an expia-

The Political Aspect.

tion for specific offenses, but for the purification of the body, when the soul had already been thoroughly cleansed by righteousness. Now, when all men listened to his words with the greatest delight and flocked to him, Herod feared that the powerful influence which he exercised over men's minds — for they seemed ready for any action which he advised — might lead to some form of revolt. He therefore decided to put him to death before any revolution arose through him. To forestall events appeared far better policy than a belated repentance when plunged in the turmoil of an insurrection. And so, because of Herod's suspicions, John was sent as a prisoner to Machaerus, the fortress already mentioned, and there put to death. The Jews supposed that the destruction of Herod's army was the penalty expressly inflicted upon him of God to avenge John." Herodias is not mentioned. The last sentence refers to the war which followed with Aretas. We agree with the interpretation of Josephus as an outsider and with his ascription of fear to Herod as an additional motive why he imprisoned John, but not as though John had been a revolutionary. It is true that Herod did fear the multitude, "because they counted him as a prophet." [4] According to the evangelists' statements Herod had John imprisoned because his marriage had been declared unlawful. And Josephus does not only call that marriage unlawful, but he tells us

---

3, 2) Writing later, Matthew, as one of the Twelve, was both a reporter and a witness to the reports. It is possible that Luke received some of his information from the family of Chuza, the steward of Herod, whose wife, Joanna, followed Jesus (Luke 8, 3; chapter XII, 11), as well as from a certain Manaen, "the foster-brother of the tetrarch," who appears as a leader in the church of Antioch, Acts 13, 1. The same applies to Mark, Acts 12, 25. But the assumption which makes this Manaen an Essene and a son of the Essene Manaen, who foretold the future dignity of Herod the Great, as told by Josephus, *Ant.*, XV, X, 5, and then to connect John the Baptist with the Essenes, is absolutely without historical foundation. See chapter III, 45, and Farrar, I, 394.

3) The translation of H. St. J. Thackeray is used (*Selections from Josephus*, 80. 81). The Greek terms used by Josephus are βαπτισμός and βάπτισις.

4) Matt. 14, 5.

how it came about.[5]   But, on the other hand, in view of John's influence with the multitude a rebellion would be an eventuality which a suspicious and power-loving member of the Herodian family would not fail to consider.

4.

Matt. 14, 3—12. Mark 6, 17—29. (Luke 3, 19. 20.)

We remember Herod Antipas as the son of Herod the Great by Malthace, the Samaritan. He had received the tetrarchy of Galilee after the death of his father. The name of king is applied to him by courtesy only; for by the grace of the Romans his domain extended merely over Galilee and Perea, east and west of the Jordan, with Samaria separating him from the now Roman

Herod Antipas. province of Syria, to which Judea belonged, with Pontius Pilate as governor. He had been married to the daughter of King Aretas of Arabia, but while on a visit in Rome, he lodged with his half-brother Herod Philip, the son of Mariamne II, the daughter of Simon the High Priest, enjoyed his hospitality, estranged his wife, and made the agreement with her that on his return he would repudiate the daughter of Aretas and wed her. But his wife heard of the plot and fled to her father. The adulterous marriage with Herodias followed.

5.

Matt. 14, 3—12. Mark 6, 17—29. (Luke 3, 19. 20.)

It has been thought that the gospel-writers were hopelessly confused, and so we must again set ourselves the task of entangling some of the already much-entangled Herodian family relation. Let us start with Philip. Who was he? Josephus tells us [1] that he was the son of Herod the Great by his wife Mariamne II, the daughter of Simon the High Priest. He is not to be confounded with the

Herod Philip. Philip the son of Cleopatra of Jerusalem, who appears as the tetrarch of East Jordan. At one time it seemed that this Herod Philip would have succeeded as the sole heir to his father's dominion, but because his mother plotted against her husband, the old tyrant again altered his will — he had done so before [2] — and left Philip with great wealth, but reduced him to a private person, apparently living at Rome. He was married to Herodias, really his (half-) niece; for she was

---

3,   5) *Ant.,* **XVIII,** 5, 1.
5,   1) *Wars,* I, 28, 4.   2) *Wars,* I, 30, 7, towards the end.

the granddaughter of the ill-fated Maccabean princess Mariamne I, the wife whom Herod had put to death, and the daughter of Aristobulus, one of the sons whom Herod had also put to death. Together — we are talking about Herod Philip and Herodias, uncle and niece — they had a daughter, Salome, now full grown.[3] We repeat that this Herod Philip is not the Philip of Iturea, mentioned by Luke.[4] This Philip, who seems to have been the best of the Herods, later appears as the *husband* of Salome, his (half-) niece, and in this respect was running true to Herodian form. Here is a puzzle for the curious: Through the marriage of Salome to Philip the Tetrarch, Herodias, who at first had been his *niece,* through her second marriage to Antipas became his *sister-in-law* and finally, through the marriage of Salome, *a mother-in-law* to Philip!

6.

Matt. 14, 3—12. Mark 6, 17—29. (Luke 3, 19. 20.)

Now, this much-related Herodias of the much-entangled Herodian family had a special grudge against John the Baptist. "She had a quarrel against him and would have killed him"; literally, according to the Greek, she had it "in for him."[1] "But she could not; for Herod feared John." But why this murderous hatred? Because John had condemned her adulterous marriage. But there may have been other reasons. She had first been married to a private person of great wealth. But being married to a private person little suited this highly ambitious woman. The intrigue with her brother-in-law, the tetrarch, was not at all out of harmony with her character, as depicted to us by history. Antipas, her uncle, through her marriage with (Herod) Philip had become her brother-in-law, and now he was her husband. But Antipas did not have a drop of Jewish blood in his veins,[2] while she, through her grandmother Mariamne I, was a Maccabean princess, albeit of priestly stock and not of the house of David.[3] And as such — like her grandfather — she certainly had no use for John, who as the forerunner preached the advent of *the King of the Jews.* She could not deny the deep-rooted Herodian suspicions, and it was and remained her ambition that her new husband should be the king of the Jews. "She proved to be the curse and ruin of Antipas. First came the murder of John the Baptist. Then

Herodias.

5, 3) *Ant.,* XVIII, 5, 4.   4) Chap. 3, 1.
6, 1) Ἐνεῖχεν.   2) The Herods were Idumeans.
   3) The Maccabees traced their ancestry to Jehoiarib, 1 Macc. 2, 1; 1 Chron. 24, 7.

came a war with Aretas on account of the daughter whom Herod Antipas had discarded, in which Herod was worsted." [4] Josephus brings this defeat directly into connection with the death of John the Baptist. And finally the wild ambitions of Herodias directed Antipas to Rome to solicit the title of king conferred upon her own brother Agrippa I.[5] She failed in her schemes for Antipas, who lost even his own possessions to Agrippa and was banished to Lyons and died in Spain, "whither his wife had followed him." [6] — But we are a little ahead of our story.

7.

Matt. 14, 3—12. Mark 6, 17—29. (Luke 3, 19. 20.)

"And would have killed him, but she could not; for Herod feared John, knowing that he was a just man and an holy, and observed him; and when he heard him, he did many things, and heard him gladly." But there was *"one* thing which Herod would not do, and that was to give up his guilty love and to dismiss the imperious woman who ruled his life after she had ruined his peace." [1] The feeble, vacillating Herod was between two fires,

The Attitude of Herod. the people on the one hand, who esteemed John as a prophet and who, as Herod at first feared, might start a revolution, and Herodias on the other hand, who grimly demanded John's death. To these we may add the little fire which was still burning in his heart. After Herod had put John safely behind strong walls at Machaerus, he no longer had any reason to entertain political fears. He heard John often, even gladly, although this fearless preacher had many unpleasant things to say, which caused him to think twice or thrice, and even kept him from committing further deeds of violence. But, oh! the "concentrated venom," the smoldering fire, in that revengeful woman's breast! [2]

8.

Matt. 14, 3—12. Mark 6, 17—29. (Luke 3, 19. 20.)

"And when a convenient day was come" — not for Herod nor for John, but for Herodias. It was most likely early spring again, just before the Passover, and the "convenient day" was either the tetrarch's birthday, as seems most likely, or, as some think, his accession anniversary, which also, according to an old custom, was

---

6, 4) Edersheim, I, 673.   5) 37 A. D.
    6) *Ant.,* XVIII, 7. *Wars,* II, 9.
7, 1) Farrar, I, 388.   2) Farrar, I, 389.

kept by the Herods as a festival.[1]   In any event it was a fit time for a "Herodian Belshazzar feast." [2]   It is evening, and the castle is lit up. Lords, courtiers, generals, and Galilean nobles are the invited guests. The merriment is at its height. "The king has nothing new to offer his excited guests, no food, no drink, no fresh

The "Convenient Day."
excitement, and so let other pleasures begin!" [3]   In comes Salome! Josephus supplies her name. She is a princess herself, a daughter of that once noble Asmonean or Maccabean house,[4] soon to become the wife of the Tetrarch Philip of Iturea and after his death and a childless marriage the wife of Aristobulus, king of Chalcis, and, as it seems, the mother of a king.[5]

9.

Matt. 14, 3—12. Mark 6, 17—29. (Luke 3, 19. 20.)

The entrance of Salome is made in the midst of sensual and half-intoxicated guests. She "danced and pleased Herod and them that sat with him." In the delirium of his drunken approval, like the well-known Xerxes, or Ahasuerus,[1] the king said to the damsel: "Ask of me whatsoever thou wilt, and I will give it thee, unto the half of my kingdom. And he sware unto her." The girl, being trained and educated to seek the Herodian interests at

"The Head of John the Baptist!"
all costs, hastened to her mother. "What shall I ask?" This was the moment Herodias had been waiting for; for to her revenge was sweeter than wealth or pride. She did not suggest robes, or jewels, or palaces, or whatever might please a maiden's heart. Quick as a flash the answer "hisses out": [2] "The head of John the Baptist!" And in order to make sure: "Give me here," that is, now on the spot, "John the Baptist's head *in a charger*," that is, on a dish, or platter. Silence chilled the assembly, and our story draws to a close. In the dance we have an example of the shameless Herodian orgies. In the oath we have an example of "maudlin

---

8,   1) *Ant.,* XV, XI, 6. See Meyer or Bruce sub Matt. 14, 6.
   2) Edersheim, I, 672.
   3) Edersheim, I, 672.
   4) *Ant.,* XVIII, v, 6.
   5) Schuerer, I, II, 342. 343. Farrar, I, 390. The Herodian princesses were famed for their beauty. Legend makes Salome die a retributive death in consequence of a fall on the ice. Edersheim, I, 673. Farrar, I, 394. The tradition is mentioned by Jerome and Nicephorus.
9,   1) Esther 5, 3. Farrar, I, 391.
   2) Farrar, I, 392.

amorous generosity." [3]   In the request we have an example of an
inborn and deep-rooted sanguinary spirit.   On the part of Herodias
we have the vengefulness and determination of a Jezebel to rid
herself of a hated person.   And even Salome is no better.   Her
impudent and pert manner in saying the gruesome words almost
outdoes her mother.   "And she came in straightway with haste unto
the king and asked, saying, I will that thou give me by and by
[instantly] in a charger the head of John the Baptist."   The
tetrarch was plunged into grief by this request.   "Fear, policy,
remorse, superstition, and whatever spark of better feeling still
remained unquenched under the dense white ashes of a heart
consumed by evil passions, made him shrink in disgust from this
sudden execution." [4]   He was sorry.   "Yet for his oath's sake
and for their sakes which sat with him he would not reject her."
It was an oath which should not have been made and, after it had
been made, should not have been kept.   Herod wavers.   But
a despicable pride and fear of man prevails over his better impulses.
Only for a moment he battles with indecision, and then the order
is given.   The guardsman leaves the hall and enters the dungeon.
"No time is given for preparation nor needed." [5]   In a few minutes
it is all over.   The ax falls.   "The head of the noblest of prophets
was shorn away," [6] and Herodias received her "ghastly dish." [7]   But
even this feature is not overdrawn.   In the same chapter in which
Josephus relates the marriage of Herodias to Herod and the war
with Aretas, in which he had the support of Tiberius, the order
was given by the Roman emperor to Vitellius, the president of Syria,
"either to take him [Aretas] alive and bring him in bonds or to
kill him and send him [Tiberius] his head." [8]

10.

Matt. 14, 3—12.   Mark 6, 17—29.   (Luke 3, 19. 20.)

Thus a "ruler's adulterous union was cemented with a prophet's
blood." [1]   When the disciples of John heard of it, "they came and
took up the body and buried it; and went and told Jesus."   What

---

9,   3) Bruce sub Mark 6, 23.
     4) Farrar, I, 393.   5) Edersheim, I, 674.
     6) Farrar, I, 393. Ἀπεκεφάλισε, a very expressive word.
     7) Edersheim, I, 674.
     8) Other examples: Cicero's head and hands were sent to Rome and
nailed to the rostra after Fulvia, wife of Antony, had thrust a hairpin
through his tongue.   The execution of Paulina Lollia and the examination
of her head by the raging Agrippina, the mother of Nero.
10,   1) Farrar, I, 387.

a depth of pathos and a wealth of suggestion in the three words "and told Jesus"! The dark deed was done. The shining light

"And Went and Told Jesus." was snuffed out.[2] The spreading news may have reached the Twelve, who were still happily engaged in their primary missionary endeavor. "And the apostles gathered themselves together unto Jesus and told Him all things, both what they had done and what they had taught." [3]

10, 2) To the omniscient Jesus the fate of His forerunner was prophetic of His own. Compare Mark 9, 12. 13.

3) Mark 6, 30.

CHAPTER XVI.

THE PERIOD OF RETIREMENTS AND SPECIAL TRAINING OF THE TWELVE.

THE FIRST RETIREMENT.

In Districts around Galilee.
Probably early spring 29 A. D.

A. U. C.	779	780	781	782	783
A. D.	26	27	28	29	30
Age of Jesus	30	31	32	33	34
Passovers		I	II	III	IV

1.

Matt. 14, 13. Mark 6, 30—33. Luke 9, 10.
John 6, 1. 2.[1]

Both the imprisonment and the death of John the Baptist form important turning-points in the life of Jesus. The imprisonment of John is followed by the Great Galilean Ministry of Jesus.[2] And the death of John introduces a period of retirement and gradual withdrawal of Jesus from public labors and special devotion to the instruction of the Twelve, which finally terminates in His last journey to Jerusalem and His death on the cross. — The last year of the life of Jesus had come. Outwardly, it would seem,

Retirement to Bethsaida Julias. Jesus was at the height of His popularity; but it did not rest upon the recognition of His true mission. He was forced into a position in which He must either accommodate Himself to the false popular Messianic expectations and begin the struggle for political freedom or meet the reaction which this refusal must inevitably bring. From this time therefore Jesus begins to act as in view of His approaching death. When the "dread intelligence of His forerunner's sad death reached Him,"[3] presumably at Capernaum, and the returning Twelve reported on their first missionary endeavors, He suggested a brief period of repose, such as

---

1, 1) See chapter VIII. An interval of one year, assuming that the unnamed Feast in John 5 was the Passover of 28 A. D. The following incident of the feeding of the five thousand is mentioned by all four evangelists. Since the time is given as near a Passover (John), which also agrees with the "grass" in the account of Matthew, Mark, and John, we have here an important chronological notice.

2) Chapter IX.   3) Farrar, I, 399.

was not possible for them to enjoy at Capernaum. "Come ye yourselves apart in a desert place and rest a while; for there were many coming and going, and they had no leisure so much as to eat." In the words of the inspired Preacher: "To every thing there is a season and a time to every purpose under the heaven," [4] also for a brief and well-earned pastoral vacation. Jesus was deeply moved by the news of the death of His forerunner, and He felt the need of solitude and rest. While we notice (here and later) that He did withdraw Himself from the territory of Herod, His departure was not through fear of personal violence; for on the very next day He returned to Capernaum.[5] It is rather an attempt to escape the crowds, which in their excitement might look to Jesus as the avenger of John, create a disturbance for Herod, and cause a disastrous crisis in the ministry of Jesus.[6] As St. John notes, it was near the Passover season, when all the roads and villages were filled with pilgrims. And therefore, instead of keeping Himself in the public eye and joining the pilgrims on their journey to Jerusalem,[7] when His presence would almost certainly have led to a false Messianic demonstration, He took the Twelve down to the beach [8] for the purpose of quietly setting out on an excursion to a place of seclusion and rest.[9] But He did not succeed in His purpose. At the northeastern corner of the lake, a little beyond the point where the Jordan makes its entry into it, there was a second "Fish House," or Bethsaida,[10] not the Bethsaida of Galilee,[11] near Capernaum, which was the home of Philip and his friends Andrew and

---

1,　4) Eccl. 3, 1.

5) John 6, 22. 24.

6) Kretzmann, I, 79. Christ's time had not yet come. The following year He would present Himself to the nation as the promised King.

7) We assume that this was a Passover which Jesus did not attend. The Passover week was late in that year, April 17—24. Wieseler, *Synopsis*, 434.

8) The Sea of Galilee here also called by John (6, 1) the Sea of Tiberias.

9) If, as seems probable, the discourse of John 6, 26—59 was on a Sabbath ("in the synagog, as He taught in Capernaum"), v. 59, then it is possible to fix the days of these events with a certain degree of probability: Thursday: The Crossing of the lake and the Feeding of the Five Thousand. Friday: The Reception at Gennesaret. Saturday: The Sermon on the Bread of Life. See Edersheim, II, 4; also Andrews, 330, who thinks that it was on a Sabbath, but points out that the synagog was used for teaching also on other days (Mondays and Thursdays).

10) Same root as in Sidon.

11) John 12, 21.

Peter,[12] but a near-by eastern namesake in the territory of Philip, tetrarch of Iturea, recently enlarged and rebuilt and for the sake of distinguishing it from the other Bethsaida called Bethsaida Julias, in honor of the beautiful, but dissolute daughter of Caesar Augustus.   To the south was a secluded and uninhabited little plain of rich silt soil, now covered with the green grass of early spring.   This fact is especially noted because this is about the only time of the year when this region is covered with grass.   Around the northeastern edge of the delta the land rises to the hills.[13] To this uncultivated, "desert" [14] place the little vessel steered its course with its "freight of weary and saddened hearts." [15]   But secret as the departure had been, it had not passed unobserved, nor did it remain unknown.   As the vessel slowly glided over the waters towards its goal, the people "ran afoot thither out of all cities and outwent them."   As a result there was already a throng at the landing-place when the prow of the vessel touched the sandy shore.   The quiet rest which Jesus had planned was spoiled.   The sad feature of it was that it was not a Savior-seeking, but a miracle-seeking crowd.   But even so, when Jesus came out and saw so many people, the vision of Ezekiel flashed into His mind.[16]   He was "moved with compassion toward them because they were as sheep not having a shepherd."   And though "they followed Him because they saw His miracles which He did on them that were diseased," Jesus lost no time in preaching to them "many things," especially of the true nature of the "kingdom of God."   And, in addition, "He healed them that had need of healing."

2.

Matt. 14, 14—21. Mark 6, 34—44. Luke 9, 11—17.
    John 6, 4—13.

We picture to ourselves the scene as follows.   After ministering to the multitudes at the shore of the lake immediately upon His landing, Jesus "went up into a mountain, and there He sat with His disciples."   Thus He tried to accomplish to some extent the purpose for which He had come.   A few hours passed by.[1]   Already the vast Safed heights to the northwest threw their gigantic shades

---

1,   12) Chapter VI, 19.   John 1, 44;   Mark 6, 45.
       13) B. Matthew, 248.
       14) Lonely and deserted.
       15) Farrar, I, 400.
       16) Ezek. 34, 1—15; also Num. 27, 17.
2,   1) Matt. 14, 15, early evening (afternoon) ; v. 23, the second or later evening.   See Edersheim I, 681.

across the landscape. The day began to wear away. Looking up, Jesus saw that the people to whom He had ministered after His landing had not dispersed, but that a still greater multitude was ascending the hill. We remember that "the Passover, a feast of the Jews, was nigh," and that the roads were filled with travelers. Approaching pilgrims most likely inquired into the reason of the unexpected gathering in a "desert place." They soon learned that Jesus was on the near-by hill. And once more the Savior was besieged by a multitude, which had been augmented by newcomers, with darkness creeping on. He lifted up His eyes and said unto Philip: "Whence [2] shall we buy bread that these may eat?" The question had a purpose. "And this He said to prove him; for He Himself knew what He would do." Undoubtedly Jesus intended to arouse

"Whence shall We Buy Bread that These may Eat?"

loving concern for the people in the hearts of the disciples. After a brief Oriental twilight the wandering crowds would suddenly find themselves hungry and in the dark. And the reason for addressing Philip is probably to be found in the character of this disciple, who, it seems, was a matter-of-fact person [3] and more inclined to demand visible evidence than to rely on unseen resources. [4] While this conversation was going on, the disciples began to grow uneasy and to whisper to one another. Moving up from where they sat, they said to Jesus: "This is a desert place, and the time is now past; send the multitudes away that they may go into the villages and buy themselves victuals." But to this suggestion Jesus replied: "They need not depart; give ye them to eat." Their response was: "Shall we go and buy two hundred pennyworth of bread and give them to eat?" But quick-figuring Philip swiftly pointed out the impossibility of supplying the need. "Two hundred pennyworth [5] of bread," that is, about forty dollars, — which was probably the approximate amount which their common treasury was known to contain at the time, — he said, "is not sufficient for them that every

---

2,   2) Πόθεν may mean either "from which village?" or "from what pecuniary resources?"

3) John 14, 8.

4) Cyril, quoted by Dods, sub John 6, 5.

5) Δηνάριον, denarius. A Roman silver coin, 25 of which made an *aureus*, the standard gold coin of the empire in the time of Augustus, which was equal in value to about $5.25. Hence the value of the denarius would be about 20 cents, which was the ordinary daily wage of a laborer or soldier. *Int. St. B. Encycl. sub loco.*

one of them may take a little." [6)]   This settled the matter as far
as financial resources were concerned.   But were there any provisions on hand?   "How many loaves have ye?   Go and see."   Thus
the possible charge of fraud in the subsequent miracle is forestalled
at the outset.   Andrew volunteered the information about a little
boy [7)] with five barley-loaves and two fishes.   "But this he said in
a despairing way and, as it were, to show the utter helplessness of
the suggestion which occurred to him." [8)]

3.

Matt. 14, 15—21.   Mark 6, 35—44.   Luke 9, 12—17.
John 6, 4—13.

But there was at least still a little supply.   And the reply of
Andrew suggested the action of Jesus.   "And Jesus said, Make
the men sit down."   Swiftly the disciples, puzzled, but obedient,
arranged the multitudes in groups of hundred and of fifty on the
thick green grass.   And then, standing in the midst of those who
would forever after remember Him as Teacher, Healer, and Host,
He took the loaves and fishes, raised His eyes to heaven, gave
thanks and blessed the loaves, broke them into small pieces, and
began to distribute them as well as the fishes to the disciples and
they to the multitudes, as much as

The Feeding of the Five Thousand.

every one desired. [1)]   "It was a humble,
but a complete and sufficient and to
hungry wayfarers a most delicious meal." [2)]   Out of His abundance
the Lord supplied in unlimited measure what was needed for the
maintenance of life.   And when all were amply satisfied, He gave
His disciples a proof of the extent and reality of the miracle as well
as a lesson that wastefulness, even after His miraculous power had
supplied such wonderful plenty, is not in accordance with His will.
"Infinite resources" nevertheless do "not justify waste." [3)]   But

---

2,   6) If one denarius would feed ten persons and 200 would provide
a day's ration for 2,000, then upon this basis 200 denarii would supply
4,000 with a most meager ration, a $\beta\rho\alpha\chi\acute{u}$ $\tau\iota$.

7) Who the "one ($\H{\epsilon}\nu$) little boy" was, whether a lad of their own
company guarding the boat or a shepherd boy of the neighborhood with his
food in his pouch, we do not know.   The $\H{\epsilon}\nu$ brings out the meagerness of
the supply.

8) Farrar, I, 401.

3,   1) "As much as they would."   Luther's translation, "As much as *He*
would," rests upon an unsupported reading in Erasmus.   Meyer sub John
6, 11. $\textquoteleft O\psi\acute{a}\rho\iota o\nu$ for fish in John is whatever is eaten with bread as a side-
dish, hence preeminently fish.   Dods *sub loco.*

2) Farrar, I, 402.   3) Kretzmann, I, 440.

rather "gather up the fragments that remain that nothing may be lost." The arrangement by fifties and hundreds easily showed that about five thousand men, besides women and children,[4] had been fed, and yet twelve large baskets [5] of fragments were gathered.[6]

4.

Matt. 14, 22. 23.   Mark 6, 45. 46.   Luke.[1]   John 6, 14. 15.

The effect of this miracle upon the minds of those present was overwhelming.   Surely here was a Messiah after their own heart! They began to whisper to one another that this must undoubtedly be "that Prophet that should come into the world" [2] and "the beginning of that reign of earthly abundance which in their carnal desires and in a false interpretation of Messianic promises they

The Attempt to Make Jesus King. thought the prophets had foretold." [3]   So great was their enthusiasm that they proposed among themselves to take Him by force, if necessary, and make Him a king.   What a king who could effect cures, supply food, and provide prosperity for all! With Him at their head, endowed with the power of the eternal God, which He had just displayed, He could lead them on, rid them of the detestable Herods, and conquer Rome.   Sweet dreams of the Golden Age and the Reign of God.   Thus the

---

3,   4) Probably there were not many in that lonely spot.

5) Κόφινος, a large wicker-basket, our "coffin" or "coffer."   In ancient times it always identified the Jew, who on account of special food regulations would, in traveling in non-Jewish communities, always carry his basket with provisions for a day or two.   Dods sub John 6, 12.   B. Matthew, 248.

6) It has been suggested that the number twelve is accounted for by the individual disciples.   But why, with nothing in them, they should be carrying baskets does not appear.

4,   1) Luke 9, between verses 17 and 18. — At this point occurs "the great gap" in the narrative of Luke as compared with Matthew and Mark, all of Matt. 14, 22 to 16, 12 and of Mark 6, 45 to 8, 27 being omitted: from the feeding of the five thousand to Peter's wonderful confession at Caesarea Philippi.   Various explanations are offered: accidental loss due to some unknown casualty; loss of a portion of original manuscript; mistake of the eye (of the writer in following Mark?), passing from the second feeding as if it were the first; etc.   See Bruce and Meyer *sub loco.*   All unsatisfactory.   These and other explanations imply that the omission was unintentional and that Luke's gospel is not complete in its present form, for which theory there is no proof.   A close examination will show that, as far as Luke is concerned, there is no omission at all.   It was the purpose of Jesus to retire, v. 10.   But it was some time before He could be alone, v. 18.   The fact that Luke does not relate intervening events certainly proves a great stumbling-block to the theory of his dependence on Mark.   The proponents of the dependence theory are usually quite silent at this point.

2) Deut. 18, 15.   3) Dods sub John 6, 14.

effect of the miracle just performed was to confirm them in their false Messianic hope. Here was the time for instant action. Jesus Himself was not deceived by this "brief blaze of a falsely founded popularity." [4]   He was aware of the danger of mob passion and instantly made His decision. First of all, and for their own good, the disciples, who were only too prone to share the popular conception, had to be removed. He ordered them, well-nigh compelled them, to go down to the beach and sail in the direction of Capernaum or the western Bethsaida.[5]   Aside from leaving their Master in the midst of this outburst of unprecedented popularity there may also have been the fear of crossing the lake alone in the night on account of a former experience,[6] especially, as again seemed likely, in view of an approaching storm. But "straightway Jesus constrained His disciples to get into a ship," with the promise, it seems, to meet them on some point along the shore later on.[7]   The disciples departed. And now, gradually and gently, Jesus proceeded to dismiss the crowd. In the gathering dusk all but the most persistent had streamed away. That some lingered we infer from the incidents of the following day.[8]   But leaving them, Jesus "went up into a mountain apart to pray. And when the evening was come,[9] He was there alone." Again a decisive hour had come. Once before He had spent the solitudes of a night in lonely prayer. That was the night before He made His choice of associates or apostles for the proclamation of the Kingdom He was about to establish.[10]   Far different were His feelings on this night when He ascended the rocky heights. The Passover was nigh. The events of the next Passover unfolded themselves before His eyes. John the Baptist had been foully killed. The public was enraged. Now the attempt to make Him king. Of a truth He *was* a King! In due time He would present Himself to the nation as Israel's true promised King. But this present attempt was an acclaim which He had to refuse.

4,   4) Farrar, I, 405.

5) This brings Mark 6, 45 (western Bethsaida) into agreement with Luke 9, 10 (eastern Bethsaida) and John 6, 17 ("unto Capernaum," in the immediate vicinity of western Bethsaida).

6) Matt. 8, 24.

7) On account of John 6, 17.

8) John 6, 22. 24. When they saw Jesus retire into the mountain, they probably hoped to renew their efforts to make Him king on His reappearance the following day.

9) Matt. 14, 23. Compare 14, 15. A later hour.

10) Luke 6, 12. 13.

5.

Matt. 14, 24—33. Mark 6, 47—52. John 6, 16—21.

Hours pass, and a storm begins to sweep down the barren hills. It is in the fourth watch of the night, that is, between three and six in the morning,[1] as the disciples, hugging the shore, rowed furiously in the teeth of a gale. After eight hours of hard labor they had not rowed more than about twenty-five or thirty furlongs,[2] a little more than one half of the distance, "and Jesus was not [3] come to them." While they were distressed with toiling at the oars and were tossed up and down on the perilous sea, there was not, as they probably had hoped,[4] any sign or signal of Jesus. But with the surface of the sea like a boiling caldron and in the face

Jesus Walking upon the Sea. of contrary winds it would have been impossible for the disciples to make a landing. They were experienced fishermen, well acquainted with the dangerous moods of this hill-bound, yet deep-lying [5] inland sea, and we can imagine their alarm over the plight in which they suddenly found themselves.[6] But "man's extremity is God's opportunity." [7] Jesus was neither ignorant of, nor indifferent to, the plight of His disciples. It was He who had directed them into the boat. From the mountain He had perceived their distress. Even now He was probably on the road running along the shore. But leaving the road, He turned down to the surf, walked out to the sea, and, contrary to the laws of nature, was *"walking on the sea."* [8] When the disciples saw a gleam in the darkness and

---

5, 1) In ancient days the Jews divided the night into three watches, Judg. 7, 19, but later the Roman division of four watches between 6 P. M. and 6 A. M. was generally adopted.

2) Stadium, a Greek measure equal to about 600 feet. Between eight and nine to a mile. Josephus says that the lake is about forty furlongs wide. *Wars*, III, X, 7. Thus the disciples had covered about three miles, or a little more than half of the destined course.

3) John 6, 17. Or "not yet" (οὔπω).

4) At some appointed rendezvous. Andrews, 327.

5) 682 feet below sea-level. Cold air always rushes *downwards*.

6) "My experience in this region enables me to sympathize with the disciples in their long night's contest with the wind. The wind howled down every way from the northeast and east, with such fury that no efforts of rowers could have brought a boat to shore at any point along the coast." Thomson, quoted by Andrews, 327 f. According to the view of Farrar, Godet, and others it was the intention of Jesus to join the disciples somewhere along the northwestern coast between Capernaum and the eastern and western Bethsaida, and now the disciples were driven *away* from the shores. At any rate, the winds were "contrary."

7) Farrar, I, 406, n. 3.

8) Περιπατῶν ἐπὶ τῆς θαλάσσης. Not "on the land above the sea-level" or "along the shore line" or "by the sea," but *on the water*.

a figure of one who to them looked like Jesus, — though they could not believe that it was He, — treading upon the waves of the sea,[9] calmly walking as if He meant to pass them by, they cried out in terror and rushed to the conclusion: A phantasm, a ghost! If they would have recalled the crossing to Decapolis,[10] they would, it seems, immediately have connected the Stiller of the tempest with this Traveler on the sea. But here we learn that even in its repetition and familiarity the miraculous strikes renewed terror into the sinful heart. It was only when Jesus spoke to them that their fear was removed. Above the roar of the raging sea and through the darkness of a storm-tossed night came the well-known, the calming and cheering voice: "It is I; be not afraid."

6.

Matt. 14, 24—34. Mark 6, 47—52. John 6, 16—21.

With their terrors stilled and Jesus' identity established, the disciples were ready to take Jesus into the boat. But in His impetuous joy Peter could not wait for his Master's approach. "Lord, if it be Thou, bid me come unto Thee on the water."[1] The request was foolhardy and presumptuous, but true to the character of Peter. With a gracious nod the Lord bade him, "Come!" And Peter actually left the boat and walked on the water.[2] "But when he saw the wind," that is, the effect of the wind in a boisterous wave, he was afraid. "He walked on the water, but feared the wind."[3] It is one thing to view the storm

Peter Walking upon the Water. from the deck of a ship and another to see it when one is in the midst of the waves. Then he began to sink and cried out, "Lord, save me!" When his faith failed for walking, he forgot how to swim.[4] Immediately Jesus stretched forth His hand and caught the struggling disciple with the gentle rebuke: "O thou of little faith, wherefore didst thou doubt?" The yearning love of Peter was satisfied and his overconfidence rebuked. At that moment, too, the storm was instantly stilled. And so, the One dry and the other dripping, they climbed into the boat.[5]

5,   9) Job 9, 8.   10) Matt. 8, 26.
6,   1) Ἐπὶ τὰ ὕδατα.
    2) Περιεπάτησεν ἐπὶ τὰ ὕδατα.
    3) Bruce sub Matt. 14, 30.
    4) Peter could swim. John 21, 7.
    5) There is no contradiction in John 6, 21. "They were willing" and of course did "receive Him into the boat." Farrar, I, 407.

After a night of distressing toil the alarmed disciples were somewhat composed, but the effect of the miracle which they had just witnessed still left them in a maze. The significance of the miracle of the loaves had not yet entered their heart.[6]   And now, a few hours later, in rapid succession, three other miracles, Jesus and Peter walking on the water and the stilling of the storm, were added to their experience. No wonder "they were sore amazed in themselves beyond measure and wondered." Despite doubting and a faltering faith they could not but realize that they were face to face with Divine Omnipotence, which caused them to fall down at the feet of Jesus with Nathanael's former confession on their lips: "Of a truth Thou art the Son of God."[7] Amid the rippling waves of a calmed sea and in the gentle light of an increasing Passover moon the Captain of the elements and the Possessor of all power in heaven and earth[8] as well as His puzzled, but joyful crew quickly reached land and moored their boat on their familiar shores.

7.

Matt. 14, 34—36. Mark 6, 53—56.

It seems that the landing was not made at Capernaum, but just a little to the south, towards Magdala, in the district called the Plain of Gennesaret.[1] No sooner, however, was Jesus on the beach than He was recognized. Rapidly the report spread that He was back from Bethsaida Julias.

Reception at Gennesaret.

Soon the usual crowds came streaming down the rocky paths from the rear and from the side up and down the shores, from Magdala, Capernaum, Chorazin, and all the villages and towns, to be healed. Patients everywhere, some walking, others borne by sympathizing friends and deposited at His feet in streets and market-places.[2] So great was the patients' faith in Him and so great also His power that, if they only touched the fringe of His robe, they were healed.[3]

6,   6) Mark 6, 52.   7) John 1, 49.   8) Matt. 28, 18.

7,   1) "Princely Gardens." Not a city, but a district, which may also have included Capernaum and the western Bethsaida, about four miles long and two miles wide. Josephus calls it "the ambition of nature," with grapes and figs hanging on the branches ten months of the year. The boundaries are given as thirty furlongs long and twenty in breadth. *Wars,* III, X, 8. In recent times an attempt has been made to restore its fertility, which "rewards the toil of the husbandman with all its ancient generosity." W. Ewing, in *Int. St. B. Encycl., sub loco.*

2) These verses at the same time may also sum up the Galilean ministry as a whole.

3) Mark 3, 10.

John 6, 22—59.   8.

What happened in the mean while to those "hot-headed nationalists" [1] who, we remember,[2] remained all night on the plain at Bethsaida Julias in the hope of linking up with Jesus when He descended from His retreat in the hills? When dawn was come, they were bewildered at His non-appearance. They had seen Him dismiss His disciples in the evening dusk. They had perhaps seen glimpses of Him as He climbed the hill. They had also noticed

Revolutionists Seeking Jesus.

that the wind was contrary and that no boat had left the shore except the one which the apostles had entered. Still, when morning dawned, there was no trace of Jesus, neither on the hill nor on the plain. Meanwhile a number of boats from Tiberias [3] had arrived "nigh unto the place where they did eat bread," perhaps driven to the shore by the same gale which had retarded the opposite course of the disciples on the night before.[4] These they hired. Going in quest of Jesus, they set off from the northern shore and then going south, at last found Him teaching, on a Sabbath-day,[5] it seems, in the synagog at Capernaum.

John 6, 22—59.   9.

Here they met Jesus with "Rabbi, when camest Thou hither?" This was an expression of natural surprise. "At the same time the *when* includes the *how*." [1] To them the whole matter was a mystery. In His answer Jesus did not refer to His walking on water, which in no way concerned them, but His reply was directed to the attitude of those who sought Him with a carnal heart. The fact of the matter was that the miraculous feeding had missed its purpose and that they sought Him not for what He was, their Savior, but for what they wanted Him to be, a bread king, now that they had eaten the loaves and enjoyed a good meal. Thus

---

8,   1) B. Matthew, 259.

2) Paragraph 4.

3) A city about six miles south of Capernaum, on the western shore. It had recently been rebuilt by Herod the tetrarch and named by him after the reigning Roman emperor Tiberius Caesar. Josephus, *Ant.*, XVIII, II, 3; *Wars*, II, IX, 1. Later it served as the capital of Galilee. After the destruction of Jerusalem it became the virtual metropolis of the Jewish nation.

4) The phrase is introduced parenthetically. Here we have an incidental confirmation of the truth that a gale had been blowing the night before. Dods sub John 6, 23.

5) See paragraph 1. Edersheim, II, 4.

9,   1) Kretzmann, I, 442.

He disapproved of their following Him, which had as its object mere physical satisfaction. Their efforts should be directed to a higher cause. "Labor not for the meat which perisheth, but for

"Ye Seek Me because Ye did Eat of the Loaves and were Filled."

the meat which endureth unto everlasting life, which the Son of Man shall give unto you; for Him that God the Father sealed," that is, confirmed and authenticated by great miracles [2] as the Messiah and therefore as the Giver of nourishment for life everlasting. Some at least of the crowd were impressed with these words of the Lord. They were anxious to labor for this meat and asked: "What shall we do that we might work the works of God?" Jesus answered: "This is the work of God, that ye believe on Him whom He hath sent." But since He was referring to Himself, they demanded that "He produce His credentials." It seems that to them the miracles of the loaves [3] did not prove His Messiahship. What miracle would He do which would convince them of this and enable them to become believers in Him? Now, for instance, there was Moses. For forty years he fed a whole nation in the desert. "Our fathers did eat manna in the desert," [4] which the psalmist called bread from heaven. [5] Again they betrayed their desire to have a leader who would above all feed their bodies.

John 6, 22—59.   **10.**

But at once Jesus "leads His listeners to loftier regions than those of historical connection." [1] Jesus points out to them with a solemn asseveration [2] that it was not Moses who gave the bread in the wilderness, but God. Only in poetic expression the manna was true bread from heaven. But here the heavenly Father is even now offering them the Bread of God "which cometh down from heaven and giveth life unto the world." However, with their mind still attached to earthly things, they ask: "Give us this bread." [3] Jesus explains: "I am the Bread of Life; he that cometh to

---

9,   2) John 10, 38.   3) Ylvisaker, 338.
     4) Ex. 16, 4.   5) Ps. 78, 24.

10, 1) Farrar, I, 413; or of false Messianic hopes. According to the legends of their nation the Messiah was to crown and enrich them; He was to banquet them on pomegranates from Eden, serve them with red wine, and feed them upon the flesh of Behemoth and Leviathan and of the great bird Bar Juchne. Farrar, I, 412.

     2) "Verily, verily." John repeats the "verily." See also verses 47 and 53.

     3) Compare this with what the woman of Samaria said, John 4, 15.

Me shall never hunger, and he that believeth on Me shall never thirst. . . . Him that cometh to Me I will in no wise cast out." Then He gives an outline of His Savior-mission, from His doing of the Father's will in coming into the world to His resurrection and His coming again unto Judgment on the Last Day. But there were only bewildered faces and objecting hearts. Quickly abandoning the objective argument, they became personal. How could He say that He had come down from heaven? "Is not this Jesus,[4]

The Sermon on the Bread of Life.

the son of Joseph, whose father and mother we know?" [5] Ignoring the personal reference, Jesus tells them to stop muttering and complaining. Nevertheless it is true that He is the Heaven-sent Way and Life. No man cometh to the Father except by the Son.[6] And "no man can come to Me except the Father, which hath sent Me, draw him." Coming to Christ is being drawn to Him by the Father. — Certainly "your fathers did eat manna in the wilderness." But what happened? They died. But here is the Bread that comes down from heaven. It is received by faith. "Verily, verily, I say unto you, He that believeth on Me hath everlasting life. I am the Bread of Life"; or, speaking metaphorically: "If any man eat of this Bread, he shall live forever. And the bread that I will give is My flesh, which I will give for the life of the world." He will give His body as a sacrifice for the salvation of the world. — At this point the Jews [7] broke out in angry debate. What does He mean? "How can this man give us his flesh to eat?" Of course, Jesus did not refer to physical eating, but to receiving Him, and partaking of Him and of His work, in faith. Thus He is the Bread of Life. And "except ye eat the flesh of the Son of Man and drink His blood, ye have no life in you." Not as the fathers ate manna and died; but "He that eateth of this Bread shall live forever."

10, 4) It was by this name that the "Rabbi," v. 25, was popularly known.

5) In the popular sense. Jesus passed by His miraculous birth lest by removing one stumbling-block He interpose another. (Euthymius, quoted by Dods *sub loco.*) "Whose father and mother *we* know" — Galileans. This seems to confirm our arrangement as compared with others in linking up the Sermon on the Bread of Life immediately with the miraculous feeding and the following, Matt. 14, 36; Mark 6, 56. The dispute with the Pharisees and scribes from *Jerusalem,* Judeans, will be treated in the next section.

6) See v. 65 and John 14, 6.

7) Not in the usual sense of John, as referring to the Jerusalem party, but with the same hostile implication in the use of the term. See Dods sub John 1, 19 and chapter VIII, 6.

John 6, 60—71.   **11.**

This, then, is in very brief outline the discourse on the Bread of Life, the famous and probably the final sermon delivered by Christ in the synagog of Capernaum. But in its effect it was very disappointing. It was puzzling even to the larger circle of friends and followers.[1] "Many therefore of His disciples when they had heard this, said, This is a hard saying; who can hear it?" The expression "eating His flesh and drinking His blood" was on their minds. They did not understand, nor would they believe. That is why the saying was hard to them. Now, Jesus was not referring to

"This Is a Hard Saying." the Holy Supper, not yet instituted, but to spiritual eating and drinking in faith.[2] Were the disciples of Jesus offended? Was the language of their Master too mysterious? Let them be patient. They will find it easier to believe that He came down from heaven when they see Him return to heaven. What then? Will they be more scandalized? Then they will be convinced that He is God. And as to "eating and drinking His flesh and blood," He Himself explains: "It is the Spirit that quickeneth; the flesh profiteth nothing. The *words* that I speak unto you, they are spirit, and they are life." Of course, these things are matters of faith. The sad part of it was, which Jesus knew, that there were some of the larger group of disciples who would not believe, yes, and that there was one among the Twelve who would even betray Him.

John 6, 60—71.   **12.**

In sheer disgust large numbers of those who had so ardently followed Jesus across the upper Jordan, had waited for Him through the hours of the night, and then had sailed back to find Him at Capernaum, turned away. They left Him forever. It was not that they could not understand. Now they understood very

"Will Ye Also Go Away?" well that Jesus was not what they wanted Him to be or at least did not declare Himself to that effect. It was the loaves of a political king that they wanted rather than the bread of everlasting life. Thus the Galilean campaign to make Jesus king collapsed because He would not meet the popular Messianic expectations. Turning sadly to the Twelve, Jesus asked them, "Will ye also go away?" It was a test. Ever ready and on the alert, Simon Peter

---

11, 1) The "disciples" as distinct from the Twelve.
     2) See Kretzmann, I, 447: "The Flesh of the Son of Man."

acts as spokesman for the Twelve: "Lord, to whom shall we go?" There is none other, none to whom we might apply. "Thou hast the words of eternal life. And we believe and are sure [1] that Thou art that Christ, the Son of the living God." It was a wonderful confession; and it was the confession not only of Peter, but it is the confession of every believer in Christ. At that moment, however, the heart of Jesus was saddened. At the very moment when a wonderful confession of His deity is given, we also have a truly human touch of the Son of God. So many of His disciples had turned away. And there was disloyalty even among the chosen Twelve. "Have not I chosen you twelve, and one of you is a devil?" Strong words and true. Yet tender. For, though uttering the warning, the identity of the betrayer was not revealed. But using the knowledge brought by subsequent events, the evangelist explains that Jesus spoke of Judas, the son of Simon Iscariot,[2] "being one of the Twelve."

13.

Matt. 15, 1—20. Mark 7, 1—23.

A delegation of lakeside Pharisees arrives in Jerusalem. They make a report to the Sanhedrin. It concerns the widely known and, in their minds, overpopular Galilean Prophet. The matter must be investigated. While the Jerusalem authorities could not make any arrests in Galilee, and while Jesus was safe as long as He stayed out of Judea, yet their power and influence was great throughout the Jewish land.[1] It was their special duty to safeguard Jewish religion and morals, to be on the lookout for the Messiah, and to pass on any prophetic and Messianic claims.[2] Thus we picture it to ourselves. At any rate, a group of "wise-looking and bearded scribes and Pharisees from Jerusalem" [3] makes

---

12, 1) We should like to think that there is a significance in the words 1) "we believe" and 2) "we know." Compare Augustine: *"Credimus ut intelligamus."* Dods sub John 6, 69. And surely, first we must accept with a believing heart, and then comes the better understanding. There are many truths which are first believed and then understood. But it seems from 1 John 4, 16 ("We have known and believed") that we cannot here press the order. Compare also John 10, 38.

2) Iscariot (Hebrew *Ish Kerioth*) = "the man of Kerioth." Kerioth was in the tribe of Judah. Josh. 15, 25.

13, 1) Schuerer, II, I, 185.

2) See Dods sub John 1, 19. "The judgment of the case of a false prophet is especially named in the Mishna as belonging to the Council of the Seventy-one." (Watkins.)

3) B. Matthew, 256.

another [4] appearance on the Galilean shore. It was probably shortly after the Passover of 29 A. D.[5] and while Jesus was still at Capernaum, before His journey to the north and west. They had been here once before. That was after the raising of the widow's son at Nain.[6] At that time the miracles of Jesus, in particular the dispossession of demoniacs, were accounted for as the work of Satan, whose special representative — almost incarnation — they said He was.[7] This time, besides the great miracle of the feeding and its effect on the popular mind, another matter, an act of unheard-of impiety, needed their careful investigation. It concerned the indifference of Jesus to the sacred traditions of the elders, particularly with respect to eating with unwashed hands. An example of it was before their own eyes when they actually caught some of the disciples defiling themselves by eating bread with unclean hands.[8] And probably that was the real offense [9] to them in that recent occurrence across the upper Jordan, not the miraculous feeding nor the outburst of natural enthusiasm, but the failure of the host to supply water or to insist upon the prescribed ceremonial ablutions. At any rate, this prophet must be watched, the public warned, and His growing influence, if possible, counteracted. With a "swelling sense of self-importance at the justice of their reproach" [10] they came to Jesus with the question: "Why do Thy disciples transgress the tradition [11] of the elders? For they wash not their hands when they eat bread."

Scribes and Pharisees from Jerusalem.

14.

Matt. 15, 1—20. Mark 7, 1—23.

At some time after the days of Ezra many additions had been made to the Old Testament canonical writings. These were called the traditions of the elders and were regarded by late Jews as equally authoritative as the Old Testament itself. These included: the oral laws of Moses, supposed to have been given by the great lawgiver in addition to the written laws; the decisions of various judges, which had become precedents in judicial cases; and the interpreta-

---

13, 4) Compare chapter XII, 13. Mark 3, 22.
  5) They would hardly leave Jerusalem until after the Passover.
  6) Luke 7, 17.   7) Mark 3, 22.
  8) "With common hands," κοιναῖς χερσί.
  9) As Edersheim suggests, II, 8.
  10) Farrar, I, 443.
  11) Παράδοσις. Founded on Deut. 4, 14; 17, 10.

tions of great teachers, which were regarded with the same reverence as the Old Testament Scriptures.[1]   In the time of Jesus these traditions had grown into a maze of laws and ordinances touching

Eating with Unwashed Hands.

every phase of Jewish life and conduct. As to the prescribed ablutions, especially before partaking of food, not only the Pharisees, but "all the Jews, except they wash their hands oft,[2] they eat not."   Now, to wash the hands as well as the food that came from the market, the cups and containers, were rules that were based on ordinary cleanliness and sound ideas of good health. But the tradition of the elders had exaggerated this practise to such an extent that to eat without washing was likened to the lowest kind of vice.[3]   While the law of Levitical purification was in the background,[4] the fear of defilement had even extended to precise washings[5] of cups, pots,[6] or vessels of wood,[7] utensils of brass, and of tables.[8]   And in the face of these ordinances the disciples dared to eat with unwashed hands!

15.

Matt. 15, 1—20. Mark 7, 1—23.

The attack was clever.   Either Jesus must defend what they asserted to be a sin, or the disciples must change their ways.   While ostensibly the disciples were accused, Jesus Himself was meant. If He would rise in their defense, as He naturally would, they could accuse Him of contempt of sacred institutions.   And if He would correct them, His standing as prophet would be discredited, and their own battle would be won.   But Jesus was not "overawed by the attacks of His sanctimonious critics." [1]   In effect He replies: Let your charge stand for the present; but here is a more serious matter: Suppose that in some instances time-honored traditions are disregarded for the sake of the commands of God, what about *you*

14,   1) See *Int. St. B. Encycl.* sub "Tradition."

2) Πυγμῇ, with the fist, that is, diligently, or to prevent the soiling of one hand with the palm of the other. Edersheim, II, 11.

3) It was contended that to eat with unwashed hands was just as sinful as to commit adultery. Ylvisaker. *Gospels,* 354.

4) Lev. 15, 11.   5) Βαπτισμούς.

6) Ξεστῶν, sextus or sextarius (containing about 1½ pints), another one of Mark's Latinisms.   (Compare 6, 37, δηναρίων, denarii.)   Here used without reference to contents.

7) Defiled earthen vessels would have to be broken, not washed, Lev. 15, 12.

8) Couches for meals, *triclinia.*

15, 1) Farrar, I, 445.

who deliberately set aside the commandments of God for the sake of your miserable traditions? [2] For God [3] said: "Honor thy father and mother; and, He that curseth father or mother, let him die the death." [4] But your gloss is that instead of giving to father or mother, a man may simply, in the form of a vow, give or designate the sum needed or intended for their support to the sacred treasury or for religious purposes and then, by pronouncing the

The Reply of Jesus. magic word "It is Corban, that is to say, a gift," [5] be exempted from further obligation and the burden of support. By this and other like evasions of duties [6] the divine Word was made void because of human traditions. To such play-acting,[7] obliterations of divine injunctions, the prophecy of Isaiah [8] might well be applied: "This people draweth nigh unto Me with their mouth and honoreth Me with their lips, but their heart is far from Me. But in vain they do worship Me, teaching for doctrines the commandments of men."

16.

Matt. 15, 1—20. Mark 7, 1—23.

By this time a multitude had gathered in the background which was very much interested in the discussion, because the people had been "trained to look up to the Pharisees as little gods." [1] Inviting

---

15, 2) The order in Mark 7, 9—13 is inverted as compared with Matt. 15, 3—6.

3) Moses in Mark. Which amounts to the same since Moses wrote by inspiration of God.

4) Ex. 20, 12; Deut. 5, 16; Ex. 21, 17; Lev. 21, 9.

5) $\Delta \tilde{\omega} \varrho o \nu$, קָרְבָּן, Lev. 1, 2; 2. 1; 3, 1. To say this word, however rashly and inconsiderately, involved a vow, and some of the Rabbis had expressly taught that this vow superseded the necessity of obedience to the Fourth Commandment. Farrar, I, 445. Edersheim, II, 18.

6) Mark 7, 13.

7) $^{\prime} Y \pi o \varkappa \varrho \iota \tau a i$, Matt. 6, 2. 5. 16; 7, 5. Here, it seems, for the first time applied directly to the Pharisees. To describe the character of the Pharisees, Epiphanius (*Haeres.*, XVI, 34) invented a very forcible expression, $\dot{\varepsilon} \vartheta \varepsilon \lambda o \pi \varepsilon \varrho \iota \sigma \sigma o \vartheta \varrho \eta \sigma \varkappa \varepsilon i a$, that is, voluntary, excessive, external service. An example of their hypocrisy: According to their self-imposed obligation a Sabbath-day's journey must not exceed 2,000 yards. Now, it was their custom to meet for banquets on a Sabbath. But suppose the distance was greater than 2,000 yards? Here is how they got around the difficulty: On the evening before the Sabbath they deposited some food at a distance of 2,000 yards. This created a fictitious home. From this fictitious home they would go 2,000 yards farther to the place of meeting. And in order to make sure, they could put door-posts and lintels at the end of various streets, so that all intervening space might be regarded as one large house! Farrar, II, 472.

8) Is. 29, 13. 16, 1) Farrar, I, 448.

them to step closer, Jesus said: "Hearken unto Me, every one of you, and understand: There is nothing from without a man that, entering into him, can defile him; but the things which come out of him, those are they that defile the man. If any man have ears

A Puzzling Parable. to hear, let him hear." [2] At the first glance there seems to be no connection, but the point is that in their external ceremonialism the Pharisees had altogether overlooked the real point at issue. As long as they considered true morality a symposium of outward acts, they had not touched the spirit of the Law.

17.

Matt. 15, 1—20. Mark 7, 1—23.

The people were dismissed. And Jesus returned to His home at Capernaum. Here the disciples were not slow to inform Him of the indignation which His words had caused. At the same time Peter confessed the ignorance of the Twelve, including his own, as to the meaning of the concluding parable. With reference to the indignation of His enemies Jesus expressed His indifference. Don't worry about the Pharisees! "Every plant which My Father hath not planted shall be rooted up. Let them alone." They are hope-

The Parable Explained. less. "They be leaders of the blind. And if the blind lead the blind, both shall fall into the ditch." [1] As to His parable, however, Jesus expressed His surprise at their ignorance. "Are ye also yet without understanding?" Do ye not grasp that what is swallowed into the stomach is afterwards cast out from the body? But the things which proceed out of the mouth come from the heart. It is they that defile man. "For out of the heart proceed evil thoughts, murders, adulteries, fornications, thefts, false witness, blasphemies," and other sins. "These are the things which defile a man; but to eat with unwashen hands defileth not a man."

16, 2) The last phrase is omitted in some ancient manuscripts. A proverbial form of speech and a common rabbinical expression. See chapter XII, 3.
17, 1) Luke 6, 39.

CHAPTER XVII.

THE SECOND AND THIRD RETIREMENTS.

In the Region of Tyre and Sidon and in the Decapolis.
Probably spring and early summer 29 A. D.

John 7, 1.   **1.**

After the counter-charge of Jesus that because of their tradition the holy Law of God itself was transgressed there was no
doubt as to the report which the incensed delegation of scribes and
Pharisees would render in Jerusalem. It was only too clear that
Jesus had become indifferent to the pharisaic institutions. From
their own observation and according to reliable testimony charges
of disregard of fasting,[1] Sabbath infringements,[2] disreputable
association,[3] affiliation with the devil,[4] insurrectionary tendencies,[5]
and the "monstrous impiety" [6] of eating with unwashed hands [7]
could be lodged against Him. But as long as Jesus stayed in
Galilee, He was safe from actual arrest. For while the influence
of the Sanhedrin was great, its judicial power did not extend to

Reason of Retirements. the tetrarchy of Herod Antipas.[8]
And therefore "after these things
Jesus walked in Galilee; for He would not walk in Jewry because
the Jews sought to kill Him." Not that He feared for His life,
but the time was not yet ripe for Him to present Himself in the
national capital as the promised Messiah and to expose Himself
to the hostility of the judicial authorities. But occasion arose for
Him to depart even from Galilee; not, however, because since the
death of John the Baptist He feared Herod and because the people
would make Him king. His departure into the tetrarchy of Philip
had not been through fear of Herod. If Herod really wished
to arrest Him, he could easily have done so, because on the very
next day He returned, landing in Gennesaret, and thence, attended
by crowds, went to Capernaum, where He taught publicly in the
synagog. And even later, during the Perean ministry, He was in
Herod's jurisdiction and was not molested.[9] Nor, as some suppose,
did He now leave Galilee because He feared the local Pharisees;

1,   1) Mark 2, 18.   2) Mark 2, 24.   3) Luke 7, 39; 15, 2.
4) Mark 3, 22.   5) John 6, 15.   6) Bruce sub Matt. 15, 2.
7) Mark 7, 2.   8) Schuerer, II, I, 157. 185.
9) The passage Luke 13, 31 will be examined later.

for these had no power to harm Him; they could do nothing beyond annoying Him and disaffecting those who had until then followed Him by threats of excommunication. The reason of His withdrawal from Galilee was threefold: to find seclusion and rest, to escape for a time the popular attention paid Him, and to devote Himself to the instruction of His disciples.

2.

Matt. 15, 21—28.   Mark 7, 24—30.

According to our chronology it was the spring of 29 A. D.[1] when Jesus and His disciples turned their backs on the lake in a journey into [2] the parts of Tyre and Sidon.[3]   Thus the region is called on account of the two chief cities, separated by about twenty-five miles of Mediterranean shore.   From more than six hundred feet below sea-level the travelers mounted the winding and rocky paths of the western hills, until nearly two thousand feet above the Mediterranean Sea they felt the spring breezes whipping their tunics about their knees.   Before them in the distance they

Phenicia.   beheld the wide expanse of the great Western Sea.
And below them, from Mount Carmel to the left, for about one hundred and fifty miles to the north, stretched out the long, tawny coast of ancient Phenicia.   Here dwelt the proud descendants of that portion of the original population of the land of Canaan [4] which Israel never was able fully to subdue.   In their long history these pirating seafarers and outstanding traders of the ancient world, securely barricaded behind the sheltering ranges of the Lebanon,[5] were for the most part proudly independent; at different periods, however, they had been subject to the ancient Assyrian, Babylonian, and Persian powers.   But after their stubborn resistance to Alexander and the period of the Seleucids of Syria they eventually passed — like the Punic kingdom of Africa, which they had founded — into the all-embracing power of Rome.   While originally Semitic, in the time of Christ their language became

---

2,   1) About the time of the Passover week, April 17—24.   Wieseler, *Synopsis,* 434.

2) *Εἰς,* towards or into.

3) Opinion is much divided.   Since there was no reason why He should not enter heathen territory on account of ceremonial defilement, — compare, for instance, the ministry in Samaria and in the practically heathenish Decapolis, — we are inclined to the view that εἰς should be rendered "into." This especially on account of the reading of notable manuscripts in Mark 7, 31.   "He went out from the borders of Tyre and came *through* Sidon unto the Sea of Galilee."

4) Gen. 10, 15.   5) See chapter II, 5.   Judg. 18, 7.

largely Greek, as testified by inscriptions and coins.[6] We remember that it was a Phenician king, Hiram of Tyre, who contributed to Solomon skilled labor and cedar- and fir-trees for the building of the house of God;[7] likewise, that it was a Phenician widow at Zarephath (Sarepta) who fed Elijah the Tishbite;[8] but also that it was a Phenician princess, the wicked Jezebel, who introduced the worship of Baal and Astarte into Hebrew life and contributed to the downfall of Ahab.[9] The Phenicians were daring seamen. They were the first who ventured to push out of sight of land in their voyages and sail through the Pillars of Hercules into the unknown sea. They were the founders of a number of colonies, the most famous of which was Carthage, on the northern coast of Africa, for a long time the persistent rival of Rome, by which it was finally crushed. Popular history books credit them with a number of great inventions: glass; the famous and precious Tyrian purple dye obtained from a shellfish, which finally became a synonym for royalty; the practical application of astronomy in navigation, which enabled them to sail from the Scilly Isles in Britain to the western coast of Africa; and the merit of bringing that invaluable aid of all knowledge, the alphabet, to the Western world, if not even of inventing it.[10]

3.

Matt. 15, 21—28. Mark 7, 24—30.

It was for the purpose of seclusion and rest that Jesus went to Phenicia. But even in this Gentile country, although the little company of wayfarers concealed themselves in a house, His presence became known. A woman whose daughter was being tormented by an evil spirit came to Him, fell down at His feet, and said: "Have mercy on me, O Lord, Thou Son of David;[1] my daughter

---

2, 6) H. Porter, in *Int. St. B. Encycl.,* 2351 sub "Phoenicia."

7) 1 Kings 5, 18. After the building of the Temple, Solomon gave Hiram twenty cities in the northern part of Galilee to recompense him for the skilled labor and the building material furnished him. When Hiram came out to view the cities, "they pleased him not," and he called them "the land of Cabul to this day," that is, displeasing or dirty, 1 Kings 9, 11. 13. This section was mostly inhabited by Gentiles and for that reason was called "Galilee of the nations," Is. 9, 1, an appellation extended later on to the whole province; for after the ten tribes had been led into the Assyrian Captivity, the majority of the inhabitants of Galilee were heathen until about 150 B. C., when Galilee became thoroughly Jewish.

8) 1 Kings 17, 9.   9) 1 Kings 16, 31.

10) Formerly generally so held.

3, 1) How did she know this? Compare Mark 3, 8; Luke 6, 17. People from Tyre and Sidon were among those who listened to Jesus and witnessed His miracles. The title was used (and heard) in Matt. 9, 27 and 12, 23.

is grievously vexed with a devil." By language this woman was a Greek; by birth a Canaanite, a heathen; by allegiance a Roman subject, a Syrophenician, of Syria, as distinguished from a Phenician of Carthage; and by faith a first-fruit of that harvest which was to spring up in Phenicia, in Greece, in Carthage, and in Rome.[2] Jesus understood the woman, "but He answered her not a word." Certainly a most strange behavior. This role of "indif-

The Syrophenician Woman. ference must have cost Him an effort." [3] Even among

the disciples it created surprise. When at last they were annoyed at her persistent pleading, they asked Jesus to aid her and "send her away, for she crieth after us"; she keeps on crying and weeping behind us, so importunate is she. But even this intercession was of no avail. Addressing His disciples, but probably speaking loud enough for the woman to understand Him, He said: "I am not sent but to the lost sheep of the house of Israel." Thus the Lord had instructed His disciples on their first missionary venture: "Go ye not into the way of the Gentiles, and into any city of the Samaritans enter ye not." [4] In His state of humiliation His prophetic actitvity should be limited to Israel according to the flesh. After He would be exalted, He would draw *all* men to Himself.[5] There is therefore no untruth in the statement. Of course, there were exceptions, for instance, the woman of Samaria [6] and the centurion of Capernaum.[7] But how unkind, even unfeeling the words sounded in the woman's ears!

4.

Matt. 15, 21—28. Mark 7, 24—30.

And what was the effect of this seemingly ungracious refusal? Did she who had so confidently sought Him out with a grief-torn heart now leave Him in a boiling rage? No. She thought of the agony and paroxysms of her tortured child. She now "came and worshiped Him, saying, Lord, help me." She was not interested in any herd-dividing classification of sheep as to which did and which did not belong to the house of Israel. She was only interested in one thing: "Lord, help me." And it was now the Lord's turn to decide the issue. Would He be coldly indifferent to that heart-touching appeal? Should it really be said that He had been

---

3, 　2) Farrar, I, 474.　　　3) Bruce sub Matt. 15, 23.
　　4) Matt. 10, 5. 6.　　　5) John 12, 32.
　　6) John 4, 7 ff.　　　7) Matt. 8, 1—13.

sought in vain? He replied to her earnest entreaty, but it seemed that He added insult to disdain. "Let the children first be filled; for it is not meet to take the children's bread and to cast it unto the dogs." So He called her a dog! But the word is not as harsh as it sounds; for the expression used by the Lord [1] refers to canine household pets rather than to the dogs on the street.[2] The illustration was probably taken from the room where the gathering was assembled. Even then a child was possibly surreptitiously tossing a morsel to the household pet. The answer might have chilled her soul, but in the allusion she quickly finds an object to which her heart might cling. "Yes, Lord," she agrees. For [3] "the dogs under the table eat of the children's crumbs." [4] Yes, I am a Gentile dog. So be it.

"It Is Not Meet to Cast the Children's Bread to Dogs."

But in many households, dogs are part of the family, in which the children indeed come first, but immediately after the children — the dog. If at the Lord's table she may not enjoy the position of children, she would be permitted to share at least the portion given to dogs. The Lord is conquered. The successful struggling of this unhoused Gentile sheep brings to mind the wrestling of Jacob with God: "I will not let Thee go except Thou bless me." [5] Not one moment longer did the Lord now prolong the agony of her suspense.[6] "O woman," He exclaimed, "great is thy faith; be it unto thee even as thou wilt." What a contrast between the native "traditionalism" which He had just experienced in the house of Israel and this "simple faith on pagan soil"! [7] "And her daughter was made whole from that very hour."

Matt. 15, 29. Mark 7, 31. 5.

Again Jesus moved out on the trail, and we regret that we have no fuller details of this northern trip. As we picture it to ourselves, for twenty-five miles He followed the road along the sea-washed shore, crossing the Leontes and passing through Sarepta, where Elijah was entertained by the widow,[1] with the hills that rise to ever greater heights until they reach the Lebanon on the

---

4, 1) Κυνάρια. 2) Bruce sub Matt. 15, 26.
3) Γάρ — not dissent, but eager assent. Stronger than "yet."
4) Ψιχία, the smallest crumbs, illustrating her humility.
5) Gen. 32, 26.
6) Farrar, I, 476. 7) Bruce sub Matt. 15, 28.
5, 1) 1 Kings 17, 9.

right and the Mediterranean to the left, until He reached the bustling port of Sidon, famous throughout the Roman Empire for its exquisite glass and its purple dye. And then, turning to the right,[2] He probably returned by passing over the Lebanon ranges,

Retirement to Decapolis. crossing the upper waters of the stripling Jordan, and then going southward through the territory of Philip, until He once more reached the Galilean Sea, but this time on its eastern or south-eastern shore. This we infer from the notice of His crossing over to Dalmanutha[3] or Magdala[4] and from there back to Bethsaida Julias to the other, or eastern, side.[5] It was this country which He had previously visited during the Gadarene journey, after the Parables by the Sea.[6] The general designation which clung to this country was the Decapolis, or the Ten Cities; but the name is a somewhat loose geographical term and refers to a number of urban communities, all except one on the eastern side of the Jordan, which after the conquest of Alexander became predominantly Greek. Wedged in between the tetrarchies of Philip and Antipas, this league of cities formed an independent political combination under the governor of Syria.[7]

6.

Matt. 15, 30. 31. Mark 7, 32—37.

The return from what seems to have been the longest single journey in the Lord's public ministry had been from the rear. This journey took Him out of the confines of the ancient Eretz Israel,[1] which He had not left since the flight into Egypt shortly after His birth. We know nothing of this journey except the story of the Syrophenician woman; but we are undoubtedly not far from right when we say that He employed the time in instructing the apostles for their future work. And we know nothing of His whereabouts in the Decapolis after His return; but we suppose that He so-

---

5, 2) See critical note on Mark 7, 31 in *Exp. Greek N. T.:* "Came through Sidon unto the Sea of Galilee."

3) Mark 8, 10.   4) Or Magadan, Matt. 15, 39.

5) Mark 8, 13. 22.   6) See chapter XIII.

7) The historians do not entirely agree on the names of the Ten Cities. We shall give them here as follows: 1) Scythopolis (Bethshean), the only one west of the Jordan (chapter VII, 11); 2) Gadara; 3) Gerasa; 4) Canatha; 5) Abila; 6) Raphana; 7) Hippos; 8) Dion; 9) Pella; 10) Capitolias. To these may be added: 11) Philadelphia (Rabbath Ammon) and 12) Damascus.

6, 1) Chapter II, 1.

journed off shore in the rolling uplands,[2] east or southeast of the Galilean Sea. But while the evangelists have left us in the dark as to these details, the multitudes knew where He was to be found. Where Jesus was, even in the out-of-the-way and semi-pagan Decapolis, the fame of Jesus had already gone before. Crowds gathered and, showing their chief interest, brought their sick to Him. These He healed. Among them there was a deaf-mute, whose healing is minutely described. "They beseech Him to put His hand upon him," that is, to heal him, as symbolized by that universal gesture which illustrates the transmission, or conveyance,

"Ephphatha!" of blessing. Immediately Jesus took him aside from the multitude, perhaps to impress upon him the greatness of the blessing he was to receive. Then "He put His fingers into his ears," probably one finger in each of the afflicted organs. Then "He spit," that is, moistened His finger, and "touched his tongue," pointing out also that afflicted member and indicating the source of the blessing. He might have healed the man with one word, without these strange actions, but thus He made it plain to him that "all help must and will come from Him." [3] And prayerfully "looking up to heaven, He sighed" in deepest sympathy with the sufferer. At last He called out in His native Aramaic "Ephphatha!" that is, "Be opened!" Immediately the gates of the man's hearing were opened, and the fettering strings of his tongue were loosed. And since the purpose of Christ's healing was not to gain publicity as a miracle-monger, but to bring those benefited to faith in Him as the Savior, He charged the man and his friends to "tell no man." [4] But, as usual, this injunction was disregarded, and all hope for seclusion was now at an end. "The more He charged them, so much the more a great deal they published it." The result was that a great multitude followed Him to the summit of a hill, brought to Him their lame, blind, dumb, maimed, and many others, and laid them down at His feet; and He healed them all. Filled beyond measure with astonishment and admiration, the semipagan population of the Decapolis could not tear themselves from the beloved Jesus. Glorifying the God of Israel, they said: "He hath done all things well; He maketh both the deaf to hear and the dumb to speak."

6,   2) A site is suggested in the neighborhood of the ravine nearly opposite to Magdala, which is now called Wady Semak. Andrews, 337.

3) Ylvisaker, 360.

4) Compare chapter X, 9. 32. Luke 5, 14; Matt. 12, 16.

7.

Matt. 15, 32—38. Mark 8, 1—9.

Three hot summer-days had passed, and the multitude was still encamped around the sun-scorched hill.[1] Jesus had pity on them and told His disciples: "I have compassion on the multitude because they continue with Me now three days and have nothing to eat; and I will not send them away fasting lest they faint in the way." Jesus manifestly has the intention to perform a miracle again; but it would be presumptuous on the part of the disciples to suggest a repetition of the miraculous feeding at Bethsaida.[2] The reply is: "Whence should we have so much bread in the wilderness as to fill so great a multitude? . . . How many loaves have ye?" A hurried search brings the reply: "Seven and a few little fishes." Again, as at the feeding of the five thousand, the people are commanded to sit down, but this time on the bare ground.[3] Again there was a supply, small, but at any rate a supply. Again Jesus blessed and broke the loaves and fishes and presented them to the disciples for distribution. Again the miraculous multiplication of a small supply for the satisfaction of many. Again, and this time unbidden, the disciples gather up the remaining fragments. They filled seven large hampers[4] after four thousand, excluding women and children, had been filled. Quietly and orderly, not with that noisy exhibition of carnal excitement which marked the former miracle, a grateful and rejoicing multitude was peacefully dismissed.

The Feeding of the Four Thousand.

8.

Matt. 15, 39; 16, 1—4. Mark 8, 10—13.

Immediately afterwards Jesus entered into a boat with His disciples for a brief return to Galilee and landed some place on the Plain of Gennesaret contiguous both to Magdala, the home of

---

7,   1) There is no reference to lilies and flowers, as when He preached the Sermon on the Mount, and to the green grass, as at the feeding of the five thousand at Bethsaida.

    2) Matthew and Mark relate the feeding of both the five and the four thousand. The same evangelists report Jesus as referring to both incidents, Matt. 16, 9. 10; Mark 8, 19. 20. In the face of these data, how can any one speak of confusion in the claim that both feedings are the same? — not to mention the difference of time, place, number, details, and results.

    3) Ἐπὶ τὴν γῆν.

    4) Σπυρίδας this time, not small κόφινοι, as in the previous miracle, the same kind of basket in which St. Paul was let down the wall of Damascus, Acts 9, 25.

Mary Magdalene,[1] and an otherwise unknown Dalmanutha.[2] But barely had Jesus set forth on the shore when the Jewish leaders began to attack Him. As if on the lookout for His return, the local Pharisees came out, this time in conjunction with their traditional rivals and enemies, the Hellenistic Sadducees, with a demand for a sign from heaven.[3] Just what kind of sign they wanted, a meteor, thunder, a lurid light, the Messiah dropping down from heaven,[4] or something of that

The Sign of Jonas at Magdala or Dalmanutha.

sort, they probably did not know themselves, except that they were not yet satisfied with the credentials given Him by God the Father which attested His Messiahship. Hitherto the unbelieving and worldly-minded Sadducees had paid little attention to Jesus. Their *forte* was not religion and orthodoxy, but wealth and power. They were the Liberals of the day, who had rather "advanced" views concerning angels, devils, and the life after death. They contented themselves with material things, things pertaining to this life. In dealing with these they were successful. They represented the priestly and ruling classes and counted the high priests in Jerusalem as well as the Herodian rulers among their members.[5] As long as Jesus limited His teaching to strictly spiritual matters, they were not much interested. But the late movement, which had as its object to make Jesus king, and the report of His sermon on the Bread of Life, which had been so sadly misunderstood, seem to have made them suspicious of Jesus as well as concerned about their high-priestly rule and their own Herodian hero.[6] Since in

---

8, 1) Luke 8, 2.

2) "Coasts of Magdala," ὅρια Μαγδαλά (Matthew). "Parts of Dalmanutha," μέρη Δαλμανουθά (Mark). Some of the best manuscripts in Matthew have "borders of Magadan," which is considered by most authorities the better reading on the ground that early copyists, ignorant, just as we are, of the existence of Magadan, changed the name to the more familiar Magdala, found in our common texts. It is likely that both readings refer to the same place. Identification with Magdala is made probable by the frequent interchange of *l* for *n*, e. g., Nathan (Hebrew) for Nethel (Aramaic). See W. Ewing under "Magadan" in *Int. St. B. Encycl.*

3) Edersheim (II, 68) shows that the demand for a sign was in accordance with rabbinic thought and practise.

4) It seems that the devil had this same thought in mind in tempting Jesus to cast Himself from the Temple, Matt. 4, 6.

5) Schuerer, II, II, 29 f.

6) Herod was all the Messiah they cared for or believed in. Bruce sub Matt. 16, 1. Cf. the reference of Jesus to the "leaven of Herod" in Mark 8, 15 as compared with the "leaven of the Sadducees" in Matt. 16, 11. They were friendly disposed to the government, local and Roman in general, as well as to the ruling high-priestly party.

their minds Jesus threatened to disturb the Sadducean conception of the Messiah, who was already here, and, on the other hand, did not conform with the pharisaic ideal of a Messiah, who was still to come, they, although otherwise not on friendly terms with the Pharisees, now made common cause against Jesus. While the Sadducees doubted the ability of Jesus to produce the desired sign, the Pharisees, for reasons of their own, to discredit Him before the people, "shrewdly counted on His repeated refusal to their presumptuous and unspiritual demand." [7]   Again the request for a sign! It caused Jesus to sigh deeply in spirit. As if His miracles were not signs! In His reply He denounced them for their hypocrisy, being able to discern the face of the heavens, but being blind to the signs of the time. "When it is evening, ye say, It will be fair weather to-day, for the sky is red. And in the morning, It will be foul weather to-day, for the sky is red and lowering." But they were blind to the notable phenomena which characterized their day — John the Baptist, Jesus' appearance, and the many signs which indicated the fulness of time. If these signs did not suffice to prove that He was in truth the Prophet who was to come, the Messiah, then nothing else would. And Jesus did not mince words as He addressed the vile and wicked brood: "A wicked and adulterous generation seeketh after a sign; and there shall no sign be given unto it but the sign of the prophet Jonas." [8]   He refused to give them any other sign than the one which would only increase their hatred against Him — His resurrection from the dead. When this greatest of all signs after the type of the prophet Jonas would be set before them, they would harden their hearts. With this judgment sternly pronounced upon them, Jesus abruptly turned His back and departed. After a brief stay the great Galilean Prophet again left Galilee. Entering into a ship, He departed in the direction of Bethsaida,[9] to the "other," [10] the eastern, side.

8,   7) Farrar, II, 3.   John 2, 18;   6, 30;   Matt. 12, 38 f. and again Luke 11, 29.

    8) Matt. 12, 38 f.;   John 2, 18;   Luke 11, 29.

    9) Mark 8, 22.

    10) Mark 8, 13.   Matt. 16, 5.

CHAPTER XVIII.

THE FOURTH RETIREMENT, INCLUDING THE TRANSFIGURATION.

INTO THE TETRARCHY OF PHILIP.

Probably summer A. D. 29.

1.

Matt. 16, 5—12. Mark 8, 14—21.

The stay of Jesus in Galilee after His return from the Decapolis was of short duration. While He was sailing with a heavy heart and with His mind still filled with the rejection, which undoubtedly caused Him to seek another place of retirement, He warned His disciples: "Take heed, beware of the leaven of the Pharisees [1] and of the leaven of Herod." Probably for different reasons the two chief exponents of Jewish thought, the Pharisees with their extreme legalism and the Sadducees with their worldly interests, had just combined against Him, and He warned His

The Leaven of the Pharisees and of the Sadducean Herodians. disciples against the teachings of both: against the religion of the Pharisees, who in a hypocritical manner pretended to be strict in their mode of worship and yet transgressed the commandments of God, and against the religion of the Sadducees, who, rather boldly casting off the skin of pharisaic hypocrisy, had introduced the religion of the flesh. But, as usually was the case, the disciples were dense. Due to their sudden departure from Galilee they had altogether forgotten to take bread, "and they reasoned among themselves, saying, It is because we have taken no bread." In His reply Jesus complained about their little faith. [2] Strange; they were always thinking about bread, bread, and its provision instead of the Kingdom and its extension. And with such little excuse! Where were their eyes to see, their ears to hear, their minds to remember, and their hearts to understand? Even if His reference had been to physical bread, would there have been any cause for worry?

1, 1) Luke 12, 1. Chapter XXI, 18. — Matt.: "Beware of the leaven of the Pharisees and of the Sadducees." The worldly-minded Sadducees adhered to the party of Herod. The morally vile views entertained by him and accepted by those who adhered to him are "the leaven of Herod." See Meyer sub Mark 8, 15.

2) Ὀλιγόπιστοι. Compare Matt. 8, 26.

"When I brake the five loaves among the five thousand, how many basketfuls [3] of fragments took ye up? They say unto Him, Twelve. And when the seven among four thousand, how many basketfuls [4] of fragments took ye up? And they said, Seven." After this explanation it finally dawned on their minds that the Master was warning them not against the leaven of bread, but against the doctrine of the Pharisees and Sadducees.

Mark 8, 22—26.　　　　　**2.**

As we picture it to ourselves, the little vessel in which Jesus and His disciples had embarked, passed northward by the white marble synagog of Capernaum and the near-by Bethsaida, where Peter and Andrew had been reared, and past Chorazin, off-shore, the scene of many unrecorded miracles,[1] and then, following the curving shores to the east and crossing the inrushing waters of the Upper Jordan, they landed at Bethsaida Julias, in the territory of Philip, near the place where the first feeding of the multitudes had taken place. On their arrival a blind man was led to Jesus with the request that He would touch him and restore his sight.

The Blind Man at Bethsaida. It seems that the man had not been born blind because the shapes of persons and trees were still vaguely impressed upon his memory from the time when he still had the gift of sight. In His cure the Lord proceeded in a manner similar to that employed in the healing of the deaf-and-dumb man in the Decapolis.[2] In order to avoid a run made on Him for cures, He took him by the hand and led his stumbling feet out of town. Here He moistened his eyes with spittle, laid His hands upon him, and touched his eyes.[3] Then He asked him whether he could see anything. Not as if the Lord had to cure him by stages, but in order to impress upon him that his cure was absolutely dependent upon Him. The man, looking up, answered that he could "see men as trees, walking"; that is, in his distorted vision he saw something, people, who looked to him like trees, except that they were walking. Jesus thereupon touched his eyes again, and now his eyesight was completely restored. Thus the Lord shows that divine omnipotence may manifest itself in various ways. But in any event, whether the cure was gradual or instant, whether effected mediately or immediately, it must not

---

1,　3) Κοφίνους.　Compare Matt. 14, 20.
　　4) Σπυρίδας.　Compare Matt. 15, 38.
2,　1) Matt. 11, 21.　　　2) Mark 7, 32 f.　　　3) V. 25: "again."

lend itself to the creation of cheap sensation. — The Lord was going into retirement and did not wish to be disturbed. The cured man was therefore dismissed with the express command to proceed directly to his house, "neither to go into the town nor to tell it to any man in the town."

3.

Matt. 16, 13—20. Mark 8, 27—30. Luke 9, 19—21.[1]

From the deep-lying level of the Sea of Galilee, Jesus proceeded up north past the marshy shores of Lake Huleh, the ancient Waters of Merom, to the borders of Caesarea Philippi in Gaulonitis, the capital city of the tetrarch Philip. From nearly seven hundred feet below sea-level in thirty miles an ascent is made to three thousand feet above the Mediterranean Sea. It is in this region where one of the largest fountains in the world [2] is found, which, pouring down the valley as the river Leddan, forms one of the three or four sources of the Upper Jordan. In ancient times this matchless spot of natural beauty was colonized by the Sidonians under the name of Laish and served as a center of the worship of Baal, their Phenician god. However, after its conquest by the Danites [3] its

Caesarea Philippi. name was changed to Dan, and it formed the northern limit of the Land of Israel as remembered in the familiar phrase "from Dan to Beersheba." [4] It was here that Jeroboam set up an image and instituted the worship of the golden calf.[5] About three miles to the east, at the southeast base of Mount Hermon, there is another famous fountain where at the foot of a cliff a stream over thirty feet wide gushes out to form another source of the Jordan.[6] After the conquest of Alexander the mystery of this wonder of nature called out the worship of the Greeks. Here, they believed, was the abode of the god of nature and of his dancing and laughing nymphs. Thus a temple to the worship of Pan was erected, and a Greek inscription in one of the niches on the face of the cliff, "Pan and his nymphs inhabit this spot," can still be clearly seen.[7] On account of the worship of Pan, in spite of the subsequent history, the name of Banias still clings to it. When the Romans followed

---

3,   1) At this point Luke again joins the synoptic account.   See chapter XVI, 4.

2) W. W. Smith, *Students' Hist. Geography*, 33.

3) Judg. 18, 7. 29.   4) Judg. 20, 1; 1 Sam. 3, 20; etc.

5) 1 Kings 12, 28. 29.   6) B. Matthew, 281.

7) *Int. St. B. Encycl.*, I, 536.

the Greeks, this territory was given to Herod, by whom a temple was built on the ancient site and named Caesarea in honor of his patron, Emperor Caesar Augustus. After the death of Herod the district passed over to his son, the tetrarch Philip of Iturea. He made Caesarea the capital of Gaulonitis, and after rebuilding and beautifying the city, he added his own name and called it Caesarea Philippi to distinguish it from the Caesarea on the Mediterranean Sea.[8]

4.

Matt. 16, 13—20. Mark 8, 27—30. Luke 9, 19—21.

It was in this delightful district, however, as we suppose, without entering into the capital of Philip itself, that Jesus sought seclusion and repose.[1] While He was not blind to the beauties of nature, He had other, most serious, matters on His mind. These He had just laid before His heavenly Father in solitary prayer. Having concluded His prayer, He beckoned His disciples and asked them two questions on the answer to which depended the outcome of all His work. "Whom do men say that I, the Son of Man, am?" It was not for His sake, but for the sake of the disciples that the question was asked. Frankly the disciples reported the popular reaction. In spite of the bitter attack of the popular teachers, the Pharisees, and the rising opposition of the priestly rulers, the Sadducees, the public opinion upon the whole was favorable, though crude. It seems that Jesus did not fulfil the political expectations of the general public. They considered Him only the precursor of the Messiah, not the Messiah Himself. Echoing the opinion of the superstitious Herod, some held that He was John the Baptist Redivivus.[2] Some seemed to hear in His "mighty utterances the thunder-tones of a new Elijah."[3] Others believed Him to be the prophet Jeremiah, who had been resuscitated to bring back to God's people the lost Urim, the sacred fire, the vanished Ark, or something of that sort.[4] "Or one of the prophets." That was about as far as they cared to go. A prophet, but not *the* Prophet. They thought well of Him, but not well enough.

"Whom do Men Say that I Am?"

3, 8) Josephus, *Ant.*, XVIII, II, 1; *Wars*, II, IX, 1.

4, 1) "Into the *coasts* of Caesarea Philippi."

  2) Matt. 14, 2; Mark 6, 12.

  3) Farrar, II, 11. Mal. 4, 5.

  4) 2 Macc. 2, 1—12. On the legend see Edersheim, II, 79.

5.

Matt. 16, 13—20. Mark 8, 27—30. Luke 9, 19—21.

"But whom say ye that I am?" That was the real question which the Lord's initial inquiry was designed to introduce. Again,[1] and with the correct word at the proper time, Peter acts as spokesman of his associates: "Thou art the Christ, the Son of the living God." This was the only and the correct answer, a wonderful confession, freely and frankly made.[2] In His reply to Peter, Jesus expresses pleasure and joy. "He would have no one call Him Christ under a misapprehension, but He congratulated Peter in His right conception of what the title meant."[3] "Blessed art thou, Simon Bar-jona." In solemn address the use of Peter's full name comes spontaneously. But He places the credit for this blissful knowledge where it rightly belongs. "For flesh and blood hath not revealed it unto thee, but My Father which is in heaven."[4]

The Confession of Peter. After this explanation Jesus continues: "Thou art Peter,[5] and upon this rock[6] I will build My Church,[7] and the gates of hell shall not prevail against it." "The statement is made in all safety and has nothing to do with future perversions of this memorable text."[8] Jesus does not say that His Church is to be built on the person of Peter, but upon "this rock." "Peterlike faith admits into the kingdom of heaven."[9] Upon this confession the Church is built. And in recognition of this faith Christ confers upon Peter and upon *all*[10] that share this faith a special distinction: "I will give unto thee the keys of the kingdom of heaven; and whatsoever thou shalt bind on earth shall be bound in heaven; and whatsoever thou shalt loose on earth shall be loosed in heaven." The possession of keys is an evidence of power and authority both to admit and to exclude. Thus also in the public exercise of the Great Commission given the Church, in the preaching of the Gospel and in the administration of the Sacraments, there is an authorized and effective

5, 1) John 6, 69.

2) Compare previous confessions: John the Baptist, John 1, 29; Andrew, John 1, 41; Philip, John 1, 45; Nathanael, John 1, 49; the disciples, Matt. 14, 33; the disciples (Peter), John 6, 69.

3) Bruce sub Matt. 16, 20.   4) Compare 1 Cor. 12, 3.

5) Πέτρος.   6) Πέτρα.

7) Ἐκκλησία. The new Israel. Not an anachronism, as if borrowed by a later order of things and put back into the mouth of Jesus. Deut. 18, 16; 23, 2; Ps. 22, 25. Bruce sub Matt. 16, 17.

8) Farrar (II, 14), who here refers to a statement by Bengel.

9) Bruce sub Matt. 16, 18.   10) Matt. 18, 18.

bestowal of divine favor upon all who gratefully accept the proffered grace of God and a pronouncement of judgment upon all those who reject it. But these things are still in the future. The time had not yet come for Jesus to carry out His purpose with respect to the advancement of His Messianic kingdom. Serious implications might arise if the disciples should prematurely begin to call Him Christ and proclaim Him as the Messiah. And therefore, for the present, strict silence is imposed upon them.

6.

Matt. 16, 21—23. Mark 8, 31—33. Luke 9, 22.

It was still news to the disciples, but it was not news to their Master, that Christ must first suffer before He could enter into His glory.[1] A second, and this time unmistakable, announcement to this effect, to be followed by others in the course of time, is therefore made.[2] In order that the disciples would not only be free from false ideas about the Messiah, but also be able to guide

Christ Foretells His Death and Resurrection. others in a correct appraisal of His redemptive work, Jesus began to show them "that He must go unto Jerusalem, and suffer many things of the elders and chief priests and scribes,[3] and be killed, and be raised again the third day." There is no mistaking the Lord this time. An outline of the whole Passion-story is given, including place, persons, suffering, and death. While there is as yet no notice of the manner [4] of death, the resurrection on the third day is clearly foretold. The dark prophecy was understood, at least that part which spoke of

---

6,   1) Luke 24, 26.

2)

	Matthew	Mark	Luke	John
1.				2, 18—22
2.	16, 21—23	8, 31—33	9, 22	
3.	17, 22. 23	9, 31. 32	9, 43—45	
4.	20, 17—19	10, 32—34	18, 28—30	
5.	26, 1. 2	14, 1. 2	22, 1. 2	

Besides other references: John 3, 14; Matt. 9, 15; John 6, 51; Matt. 16, 4.

3) The three constituent parts of the Sanhedrin. 1. Chief priests, ἀρχιερεῖς. As a rule named first. Probably the presidents of the twenty-four classes of priests or members of the reigning high-priestly family. Mostly of the Sadducean nobility. 2. Scribes, γραμματεῖς, Jewish canonists, learned councilors, mostly pharisaic doctors, who represented the teaching profession. 3. Elders, πρεσβύτεροι. Non-professional members. Priests and laymen alike who did not belong to classes one and two. See Meyer sub Matt. 2, 4. Schuerer, II, I, 178. The latter are also called ἄρχοντες, Luke 23, 13; 24, 20.

4) Probably intimated in Matt. 16, 24.

Jerusalem, of suffering and death. But the tragic outcome is deemed decidedly improbable and unnecessary. Peter therefore presumes to take Jesus in hand: "Be it far from Thee,[5] Lord! This shall not be unto Thee." Thus Peter has turned prophet. A minute ago he was speaking under inspiration from heaven, but now under inspiration from another direction. However, he did not get far; he would have upset God's whole plan for the redemption of the world, including his own. He would place a stumbling-block[6] in the way of Christ. This was a temptation. His own beloved disciple had become a tool of Satan to defeat the purpose of His coming into the world. With a flash of sudden indignation the Lord administered to him a crushing rebuke: "Get thee behind Me, Satan."[7] Thou art an offense unto Me; for thou savorest not[8] the things that be of God, but those that be of men." Peter's views as to His Master's Messianic office were still decidedly carnal.

7.

Matt. 16, 24—28. Mark 8, 34—38 (9, 1). Luke 9, 23—27.

Certainly Peter meant well. But in His vehement protest against what he thought was the wrong course of Jesus to attain the goal of Messiahship he clearly revealed the faulty nature of his own Messianic ideal. This fault must be corrected in the followers of Jesus, in the Twelve, in Peter, in all. Even in His retirement there were always some people in the background.[1] These Jesus called into His presence and told them and His disciples that

Taking Up the Cross with Jesus. the Messianic kingdom which He was establishing did not consist in glory to its heralds and distinction to its chieftains. Rather, "if any man will come after Me, let him deny himself and take up his cross[2] and follow Me." He that aims only at the life in this world will lose the life in Christ. And he who will cheerfully give up everything in this life, if need be, for the sake of the Gospel and of Christ will find true and everlasting life in the Redeemer. For in the end, "what is a man profited if he shall gain the whole world and lose his own soul?" and thus forfeit eternal

---

6,   5) Ἵλεώς σοι. (God) have mercy on Thee, God forbid! A sort of expletive, like *Gott bewahre!* in German. Farrar, II, 19.

    6) Σκάνδαλον.   7) Matt. 4, 10.   8) Φρονεῖς, mindest.

7,   1) Mark 8, 34.

    2) Punishment by crucifixion was well known. An intimation of the cross of Jesus, but at the same time a common phrase to denote extreme torment and disgrace. Bruce sub Matt. 16, 24.

salvation? "Or what shall a man give in exchange for his soul?" What purchase-money may he substitute for his soul that he may have eternal life? There is none. And that this is not mere talk about the hope of eternal life as well as the terrible possibility of judgment, Jesus shows in His concluding remarks. Even as the Son of Man "must suffer many things and be killed," so shall there also be a coming of the Son of Man in glory, accompanied by angels. What if this adulterous and sinful generation which hears the Gospel, but is ashamed to confess it, should see, as it certainly will, the Son of Man turn on His rejecters as avenging Judge? But why think of the distant Judgment at the end of the world? A sign, a complete vindication, of His rejected claim is near at hand. "Verily, I say unto you that there be some of them that stand here which shall not taste death till they have seen the kingdom of God come with power." A manifestation of Christ's glory would be clearly seen by three at the transfiguration and by many after His resurrection, even as a prelude to His final Judgment, attesting the truth of His words, could be clearly seen, and undoubtedly was seen and remembered, by many at the capture of Jerusalem and the destruction of the Temple in 70 A. D.

8.

Matt. 17, 1—8. Mark 9, 2—8. Luke 9, 28—36a.

After six [1] days, about the events of which the records are silent, Jesus took the three disciples who belonged to the "inner circle" [2] "and went up into a [3] mountain to pray." The three apostles chosen were Peter, James, and John, the "man of rock" [4] and the two "sons of thunder." [5] They were to witness the Lord's greatest glory on earth as well as His deepest degradation in the Garden of Gethsemane. The name of the mountain is not recorded, and the ancient tradition which has caused the erection of three churches on Mount Tabor in Galilee in commemoration of the great epiphany is evidently wrong. [6] We are left under the

8,   1) Matthew and Mark have "six" days, and Luke has "about eight" days, most likely including the day of Peter's confession and the night of the transfiguration of Christ. Edersheim, II, 92.

2) Chapter XIII, 16.

3) To be more exact, "the" mountain, according to St. Luke, the one outstanding elevation in that particular region.

4) Farrar, II, 26.   5) Mark 3, 17.

6) At the time of the transfiguration the summit of Tabor was occupied. Afterwards it was fortified by Josephus. Schuerer, I, II, 215; Josephus, *Wars*, IV, I, 1. 8; Andrews, 358; and others.

impression that Jesus had not departed from the neighborhood of Caesarea Philippi,[7] and hence the mountain which He ascended with those three disciples must have been one of the slopes of the gigantic, snow-capped Mount Hermon,[8] whose "glittering mass, the only snow-clad mountain in the Holy Land, is visible as far south as the Dead Sea." [9] And if Mount Hermon furnished the scene, then it is one of the few summits directly to gain the Scriptural epithet of "the holy mount." [10] It was in an evening hour,[11] as we suppose, that the Lord singled out His companions for a vigil of meditation and prayer far above the misery and toil of the world and to prepare Himself for the approaching outcome in Jerusalem which He had just foretold. While their Master knelt and prayed, the disciples, it seems, slept, which after a long ascent, during which they had inhaled the strong mountain air, was but natural for

The Transfiguration. these men of simple habits.[12] Thus the first part of the celestial visitation was probably missed. It was most likely towards dawn that their Master, still praying, was transfigured, or transformed,[13] before their half-dazed eyes. No, it was no dream or deception, but a glorious reality, which, as Peter himself testified, caused them to become suddenly wide awake and eye-witnesses of the majesty of Jesus.[14] Through the form of a servant they beheld the glory of His divinity.[15] Their Master was still there, but "the fashion of His countenance was altered," yes, it "did shine as the sun." His whole figure was bathed in light; His raiment was glistening white, "so as no fuller [16] on earth can white them." Only the choicest words descriptive of dazzling brilliance and only the best possible comparisons can portray to us, though but imperfectly, the celestial luster. Nor was this all. "Behold, there appeared unto them Moses and Elias talking with Him." Both of these erstwhile

---

8, 7) Not until the day of which we read Mark 9, 30.

8) 9,200 feet high; 16 to 20 miles long from north to south.

9) Farrar II, 25.

10) 2 Pet. 1, 18. Indirectly, Mount Horeb, Ex. 3, 5, and the "holy hill of Zion," Ps. 2, 6. Farrar, II, 25.

11) According to His custom, Mark 6, 46; Luke 6, 12. Also Luke 9, 32, compared with v. 37.

12) Edersheim, II, 96.   13) Μετεμορφώθη.

14) 2 Pet. 1, 16—18.   15) Phil. 2, 6.

16) Γναφεύς, the fuller, who was usually also the dyer. Before the woven cloth could be properly dyed, it must be freed from the oily and gummy substances in the raw fiber. White clay, the ashes of certain desert plants, and other aids were used. Mark 2, 21. — Ἄγναφου, new, that is, unfulled, cloth.

prophets and now residents of heaven, whom they probably recognized by the nature of their conversation,[17] stood before them with glorified [18] bodies and were heard talking with Jesus. As their bodies had been preserved from decay, so the body of Jesus should not see corruption.[19] They had been zealous for the Lord and His Law, one as the lawgiver, the other as a fiery reformer; but neither of them had been able to stop the transgression. Now they were talking to Jesus of His decease [20] at Jerusalem and the redemption which He was to accomplish.

9.

Matt. 17, 1—8. Mark 9, 2—8. Luke 9, 28—36a.

The disciples were seized with nameless terror.[1] And still they were overjoyed with the vision which never before had fallen on the sight of mortal man. They had heard "Heaven's converse and had tasted angels' food." [2] Fain would they have held what now seemed to escape their grasp. Knowing not how otherwise to word it than by an expression of ecstatic longing for the continuance of what they had seen and heard and of their willing readiness to do their part, Peter volunteers: "Lord,[3] it is good for us to be here.[4] If Thou wilt, let us make [5] three tabernacles,[6] one for Thee, and one for Moses, and one for Elias." But why three booths of wattled boughs? One would have been better for the enjoyment which Peter had in mind. Evidently, "he wist not what to say." His sug-

"This Is My Beloved Son." gestion was well meant, but the whole scheme showed that it was not for Peter to "construct a universe for his personal satisfaction. He had to learn the meaning of Calvary no less than that of Mount Hermon." "Not in a cloud of glory or in a chariot of fire was Jesus to accomplish His work, but with His arms out-

---

8,   17) Edersheim, II, 97.

18) Jude 9; Deut. 34, 6; 2 Kings 2, 11. Stoeckhardt, 147.

19) Ps. 16, 10; Acts 2, 27 f.

20) Ἔκβασις, departure, exodus. His "outgoing," but also including His "incoming," resurrection and ascension.

9,   1) Mark 9, 6.   2) Edersheim, II, 97.

3) Matthew: Lord. Mark: Rabbi. Luke: Master or Teacher.

4) Καλόν ἐστιν ἡμᾶς ὧδε εἶναι. Not as if it had been Peter's intention to say that it was good for himself and for other disciples to be present on this occasion, — for then he would have used the expression καλόν ἐστιν ἡμῖν, — but the meaning is: It is fortunate that we are here, for we can attend to the erection of tabernacles. Ylvisaker, 411.

5) Some texts have: I will make.

6) Σκηνάς, tents, or booths, of branches, shrubs, etc.

stretched on a cross; not between Moses and Elias, but between two thieves who were crucified with Him on either side." [7]   No answer was awarded this pleasant dream.   But while he was yet speaking, a luminous cloud overshadowed them as a token of God's presence, and a voice from out of it repeated the message spoken at the baptism of Jesus: "This is My beloved Son, in whom I am well pleased." [8]   Thus there was a divine confirmation of the confession made by Peter a few days before that Jesus was indeed the Messiah, the Son of the living God.   But the manner and the circumstance of the divine revelation caused the disciples to "hide their faces in the grass." [9]   In the mean while the shining faces, the celestial figures, the dazzling robes, the luminous cloud, and the heavenly voices passed away.   Jesus, ever kind and gentle, stepped forward, touched His fear-struck disciples, and encouraged them with reassuring words.   "Arise and be not afraid."   And as, at first startled, they looked suddenly up and around, they saw no one save Jesus alone.

10.

Matt. 17, 9—13.   Mark 9, 9—13.   Luke 9, 36 b.

It was, as we suppose, "the early dawn of another summer's day" [1] that the Master and His intimate friends made a silent descent to join the disciples whom on the previous evening they had left in the valley beneath.   No doubt the hearts and minds of the three disciples were filled with the glory which they had witnessed. At last the silence was broken with the command of Jesus to "tell the vision [2] to no man until the Son of Man be risen again from the dead."   "Visions are for those only who are prepared for them." The other disciples were but partially fit for them.   "It boots not to relate them to those who are not fit to receive them." [3]   The three to whom this vision had been vouchsafed should ponder over it in the depth of their hearts.   To announce it to their fellow-disciples might only tend to awake "jealousy and their own self-satisfaction.   And besides, until the Resurrection it would add noth-

9,   7) Farrar, II, 29.

8) But here the words are added: "Hear ye Him," indicating that Jesus was indeed that Prophet who was to come.   Compare Matt. 3, 17; Deut. 18, 15; Ps. 2, 7; Is. 42, 1.

9) Farrar, II, 29.

10,   1) Edersheim, II, 102.   The Feast of Transfiguration was anciently celebrated on August 6.   Andrews, 359.

2) Ὅραμα, Matt. 17, 9.   This word is found only here in the gospels; in Acts, 7, 31, etc.

3) Bruce sub Matt. 17, 9.

ing to the faith of others and might only confuse their conception of what was to be Christ's work on earth." [4]   The disciples heeded the Master's command, although they could probably attach no

"Tell No Man."   meaning to His allusion.   It was only among themselves that they could ask each other "what the rising from the dead should mean."   So entire was their submission that they did not even dare to ask Jesus for enlightenment regarding this personal reference.   And there was another thing on their minds.   They had seen Elias; Elias had come.   Now, they knew that Jesus was indeed Christ, the Lord; but now Elias was also gone!   And "how say the scribes" "Elias must first come and restore all things?"   According to Jewish legends Elias was to bring back the pot of manna and the rod of Aaron which were placed before the Ark of Covenant, but which had disappeared in the destruction of the Temple of Solomon, settle quarrels, restore all things, and the like, in preparation for the Messiah.   And then the Messiah Himself "should suffer many things and be set at naught."   How does that agree?   Jesus replied that Elias should indeed first come and he truly had come, not, however, in harmony with their false views, but in accord with the word of the prophet Malachi.[5]   "And they have done unto him whatsoever they liked, as is written of him."   Suffering is the appointed lot of the faithful servants of God: Elijah at the hands of Jezebel, John at the hands of Herod, and Jesus, too, must suffer. "Likewise shall also the Son of Man suffer of them." [6]   The latter reference was still a dark mystery to them, but now they understood that Jesus spake to them of John the Baptist.

11.

Matt. 17, 14—18. Mark 9, 14—27. Luke 9, 37—43 a.

When Jesus and His three intimates rejoined the other disciples, He saw, even from a distance, that there was an unusual commotion.   An excited crowd, among them once more scribes, probably from a neighboring synagog, was gathered with a heartbroken and disappointed father and his unhealed son around the "diminished band." [1]   A deaf-mute and moon-struck boy, suffering

---

10,   4) Farrar, II, 31.

5) Mal. 3, 1;   4, 5;   Luke 1, 17;   Matt. 11, 10.

6) When John disclaimed his being Elias, John 1, 21, he only wished to state that he was not Elias of old come back in person, according to the popular superstition.   "Without any authority from the Hebrew the LXX renders Mal. 4, 5 Elijah the Tishbite." Farrar, II, 31.

11,   1) Farrar, II, 32.

from attacks of epilepsy, which were "supposed to become aggra-
vated with the phases of the moon," [2] as well as suffering severe
attacks of intermittent diabolical possession, was brought for
healing. In the absence of Jesus an appeal for help had been made
to the disciples, who, it appears, willingly attempted, but signally
failed, to heal the boy. As a result they were sharply questioned
by the scribes, who always were on the trail of Jesus and now no
doubt were at hand to taunt His disciples in their hour of weakness
and at the same time to cast insinuating aspersions upon the power
and authority of the absent Lord. [3] At that moment Jesus appeared. When the people saw Him, they greeted Him with joyful
surprise. [4] Most likely, as reflecting the popular mind, they were

The Demoniac whom the Disciples could Not Heal.

in sympathy with the harassed
disciples and now, sensing the
dramatic, confidently hoped
that the Master Himself would accomplish that which they had
failed to do. "What question ye with them?" Jesus sharply asked
of the scribes. But before the question could be answered, the
man who had given the occasion for all this came forward and
implored Jesus on his knees: "Lord, have mercy on my son!" The
description of the affliction of his son reveals a pitiful case. First
of all, the lad was deaf and dumb. Added to this there were the
symptoms of epilepsy, spasms, foaming at the mouth, grinding of
the teeth, suicidal mania, and a final stage of atrophy and motion-
less stupor. At times the attacks were worse than at other times,
which was popularly ascribed to the influence of the moon. But
on the whole — and here the father rightly diagnosed the affliction — it was a case of demoniacal possession. And then he told
how he had come in search of Jesus, but having found only the
nine disciples, he spake to them "that they should cast him out;
and they could not." Now "I have brought unto Thee my son,"
"my only child." [5] The whole scene grieved Jesus at heart.
"O faithless and perverse generation," He exclaimed, "how long
shall I suffer you?" This complaint included all "the malicious
scribes, the miracle-seeking multitude, and His own faltering

---

11, 2) Bruce sub Matt. 17, 15.   Matt. 4, 24: "lunatic."

3) Bruce sub Mark 9, 14.

4) Ἐξεϑαμβήϑησαν. The amazement of joyous surprise on account of
His appearance at the critical moment. See Meyer sub Mark 9, 15. The term
is used by Mark here, 14, 33, and 16, 5 in connections which demand a
strong expression.

5) Luke 9, 38.

disciples." [6] Not that He had grown weary of well-doing, but He was grieved because the leaders would not accept Him as the Prophet that He was, because the people regarded Him as a prophet such as they hoped He was, and because the disciples, although He had given them power over the devils,[7] yet had lacked the faith to exercise it. He then directed the father to bring his boy closer to Him. But no sooner had the lad's eyes fallen on Jesus than he was seized with another attack of violent convulsions, and the devil tore him grievously, so that "he fell on the ground and wallowed foaming." Jesus asked the father: "How long is it ago this came unto him?" The father answered: "Of a child. And ofttimes it hath cast him into the fire and into the waters to destroy him. But if Thou canst do anything, have compassion on us and help us." If Thou canst? An ugly word! The leper said: "Lord, if Thou wilt." [8] Jesus replied that it was not a question of His power, but of the father's faith. "If thou canst believe;[9] all things are possible to him that believeth." The unhappy father accepted the correction. Humbled, but not discouraged, he cried out with agony in his soul: "Lord, I believe; help Thou mine unbelief." These memorable words have been uttered by millions of souls since who are painfully conscious of the weakness of their faith and then beseech Him to strengthen it. That cry of the father could not remain unanswered. Meanwhile the crowd had become greatly excited and came running, no doubt eager to learn whether Jesus would succeed where His disciples had failed. Turning to the poor sufferer, Jesus "rebuked the foul spirit, saying unto him: Thou dumb and deaf spirit, I charge thee, come out of him and enter no more into him." [10] A wild cry and a final convulsion followed these words. And then the boy lay on the ground "as one dead," and many said, too, "He is dead." But Jesus took him by the hand and, amid the exclamations of amazement at the majesty of God on the part of the people, restored him completely cured to his father.

12.

Matt. 17, 19—21. Mark 9, 28. 29.

The incident was followed by the retirement of Jesus to a near-by house. The puzzled disciples asked: "Why could not we cast him out?" Frankly Jesus told them: "Because of your

---

11, 6) Farrar, II, 33.   7) Matt. 10, 8.   8) Matt. 8, 2.

9) "Believe" is omitted in some manuscripts.

10) Μηκέτι εἰσέλθῃς. Enter not again! "This was the essential point in a case of intermittent possession. The spirit went out at the end of each attack, but returned again." Bruce sub Mark 9, 25.

unbelief." [1] At their first missionary venture they had gone forth joyfully, preaching the Gospel, casting out devils, and healing everywhere.[2] But here they had been lacking in faith. And had Jesus not just told the father of the demoniac boy: "All things are possible to him that believeth"? [3] Of a certainty. With the most solemn assurance "Verily I say unto you" Jesus points out that faith like a grain of mustard-seed,[4] that is, sincere faith unmixed with doubt,[5] could even say "unto this mountain," towering Mount Hermon: "Remove hence to yonder place, and it shall remove;

"Faith as a Grain of Mustard-Seed." and nothing shall be impossible unto you." Mighty words, from which nothing by way of interpretation is to be detracted. Faith apprehends God and His immeasurable power. "All things are truly ours if Christ is ours." [6] And who is going to limit God's power with respect even to the greatest physical barriers? This does not mean that all believers should now proceed to try out their faith, as it were, in the performance of miracles. They have not that command. But the disciples did have the authority and power. Still they failed, and the Lord tells them the reason why. With reference to the case in hand He says: "Howbeit this kind," that is, the demon which possessed the youth, "goeth not out but by prayer and fasting." [7]

12, 1) Relative unbelief. Pieper, *Dogmatik*, II, 368. There is no particular need for toning the ἀπιστίαν in Matt. 17, 20 down to ὀλιγοπιστίαν.

2) Mark 6, 13; Luke 9, 6.

3) Matt. 17, 20; Phil. 4, 13.

4) Matt. 13, 31; Luke 17, 6.

5) Matt. 21, 21. There is no difference between saving faith and miracle-working faith. That salvation is apprehended by faith is itself the greatest of miracles. The power, however, is given to faith in the interest of the Gospel and not to presumption and must be used only for the purpose for which the Lord has granted it. Compare also 1 John 5, 14.

6) Edersheim, II, 109.

7) The whole verse of Matt. 17, 21 and "fasting" in Mark 9, 29 are omitted in the best uncials and, in consequence, also by Tischendorf, Nestle, *et al.*

CHAPTER XIX.

THE CLOSE OF THE GALILEAN MINISTRY.

A FEW DAYS IN GALILEE.

Avoiding, as far as possible, public attention.
Probably late summer 29 A. D.

Matt. 17, 22 a. Mark 9, 30. **1.**

Leaving His retreat in the utmost borders of the Land of Israel at Caesarea Philippi our Lord seems to have crossed over westward through the hills and valleys of Upper Galilee, avoiding public attention and the main thoroughfares, in a journey which would take Him once more, and, as **Returning to Galilee.** far as we know, for the last time, to Capernaum. That the purpose of this circuit was not public teaching is stated in the words: "And they departed thence and passed through Galilee; and He would not that any man should know it." The reason given is: "For He taught His disciples." His one purpose was to instruct the Twelve and especially to prepare them for the approaching crisis.

2.

Matt. 17, 22 b. 23. Mark 9, 31. 32. Luke 9, 43 b—45.

Here another, and we may call it a third, a clear and emphatic announcement of His death and resurrection is given.[1] This one truth should sink into the hearts and minds of His disciples, that the consummation of their Master's Messianic career would **Third Announcement of Death and Resurrection.** not be that kind of glory for which they so ardently hoped, but death and resurrection. They had heard that saying before. But they could make nothing of those mysterious words of doom, to be followed by a resurrection on the third day. They did not understand, and yet they were afraid to ask. They were exceedingly sorry and yet preferred to live on in the hope that their Master was under a spell of hallucination.

3.

Matt. 17, 24—27. Mark 9, 33 a.

Again, and for the last time, it seems, Jesus had returned to His familiar Capernaum. Upon arrival at His home He was usually besought by sufferers in need of help. This time He was

---

2,　1) Compare chapter XVIII, 6.

[386]

sought, though indirectly, by — tax-collectors. "From the Mount of Transfiguration to money demands which one is too poor to meet, what a descent!" [1) Ever since the giving of the Law every male in Israel from twenty years upwards, whether rich or poor, was required to contribute to the Temple-treasury an annual sum of one half-shekel [2) or an Attic double drachma,[3) that is, about thirty cents in our money. This tax yielded vast sums in the aggregate, about three hundred thousand dollars for every million contributors. The purpose of the contribution was the purchase of all public sacrifices, that is, of those which were offered in the name of the whole congregation of Israel, such as the regular morning and evening sacrifices.[4) Even after

The Temple Tribute. the destruction of the Temple, Vespasian ordered that this tribute be paid by the Jews wheresoever they were and be used for the temple of Jupiter Capitolinus in Rome.[5) The time for the payment was from the fifteenth to the twenty-fifth of Adar, before the Passover, about the month of March.[6) The usual mode of procedure was to have the whole of the contributions of one community gathered by local collectors and then sent to Jerusalem, where at the time of the Passover the payment was legally made. Quite naturally delinquency was followed by a visit from those whose duty it was to receive the shekels. Jesus and Peter had not yet paid the tax. Nothing is stated about the other disciples. There was no payment recorded in Capernaum. Neither had Jesus been in Jerusalem for the Passover in spring, having at the time probably been on the borders of Tyre and Sidon. There was only the one consideration: Did He probably, after the manner of some famous Rabbis, claim exemption for Himself? [7) At any rate, the local officers considered it their duty to inquire. They approached Peter, in whose house Jesus presumably dwelt, and asked him, not impolitely, "Doth not your Master pay tribute?" Without hesitation Peter replied, "Yes." To the best of his knowledge such was the custom of Jesus. Not as if the Redeemer of all

---

3, 1) Bruce *sub loco.*   2) Ex. 30, 11—15.

3) Δίδραχμα. The only place in the New Testament where we meet with this word. Frequent in the LXX for the Hebrew shekel.

4) Edersheim, II, 112. Schuerer, II, I, 250.

5) Josephus, *Wars*, VII, VI, 6.

6) The commentators explain a certain passage in the Mishna and the Talmud as implying that the Jews in Palestine had to pay the Temple-tribute at Passover, that those of the neighboring lands might bring it at the Feast of Weeks and those of remote countries, such as Babylon and Media, as late as the Feast of Tabernacles. Edersheim, II, 111.

7) Meyer sub Matt. 17, 24.

souls was to pay a ransom for His own soul;[8] but "He paid for what He did not owe and to save them which owed and could not pay," [9] as well as for reasons which will shortly appear.

4.

Matt. 17, 24—27. Mark 9, 33 a.

When Peter came into the house, there was no chance for him to explain or to inform his Master of the question which he had just been asked. Jesus "prevented" him [1] by addressing him first with "What thinkest thou, Simon? Of whom do the kings of the earth take custom,[2] or tribute,[3] of their own children or of strangers?" The purpose of the question might have baffled Peter, but on the face of it there was but one answer: "Of strangers." Certainly a king, if he is at all worthy of his name, would tax his subjects, and not the members of his household, for the maintenance of his palace. Jesus replied: "Then are the children free." As to Christ's payment of the Temple-tribute, had not Peter himself confessed: "Thou art that Christ, the Son of the living God"? [4]

"Of Whom do the Kings of the Earth Take Custom?" And the Temple in Jerusalem, was it not the house of God? Why, then, should the Son be taxed for His Father's house? And in the New Testament even Peter and all followers of Christ would be sons, though in a different sense, and as such could not be legally required to pay the Temple-tribute. And if payments are made, it should not be a matter of positive obligation, but of free and cheerful giving. But it is doubtful whether this principle on which Christ's refusal of paying Temple-tribute could be justly based would have been understood by the tax-collectors and others. And there was another consideration: the matter of giving offense. "Notwithstanding, lest we should offend them,[5] go thou to the sea and cast an hook [6] and take up the fish that first cometh up; and when thou hast opened his mouth, thou shalt find a piece of money; that

---

3,　8) Ex. 30, 12.　　9) Farrar, II, 44.

4,　1) Προέφϑασεν, anticipated him.

　　2) Τέλη, indirect taxes on wares.

　　3) Κῆνσον, census, direct taxes on persons. From the use by the evangelist of neither of these two terms, but of τὰ δίδραχμα it is clear that the tax demanded was the Temple-tribute rather than a Roman tax, as some have tried to make out.

　　4) John 6, 69.　　5) Σκανδαλίσωμεν.

　　6) Ἄγκιστρον, a fishhook, not a net. The only place in the gospels in which mention is made of fishing with a hook.

take and give unto them for Me and thee." [7]   The miracle is taken so absolutely for granted that its fulfilment is not even recorded.[8]   Peter went out with hook and line, drew up a fish, opened its mouth, and took out of it a coin, a stater,[9] exactly equivalent to two double drachmas, sufficient for himself and for his Master.

5.

Matt. 18, 1—5. Mark 9, 33 b—37. Luke 9, 46—48.

Already on the way from Caesarea Philippi to Capernaum the disciples had been disputing with one another as to who was to occupy the highest place in the temporal kingdom which they believed their Master was about to establish.   That He would soon reveal Himself as the Messiah of their hopes was a belief firmly rooted in their minds.   In anticipation of the approaching fulfilment of their carnal desire the ambitions of human nature began to assert themselves, and with it jealousy against those who, they feared, would be unduly preferred.   Perhaps it was the misunderstood address to Peter about the keys of the Kingdom or the fact that only three of the Twelve had been privileged to be with the Master on the Mount of Transfiguration, not to mention the

"Who Is the Greatest in the Kingdom?" most recent occurrence, the prominence given to Peter in the payment of the Temple-tribute.   It was not until His arrival in Capernaum that Jesus took His muttering disciples to task.   "What is it that ye disputed among yourselves by the way?"   But they "held their peace"; however their deep silence was in itself an eloquent confession of their sinful ambition.   They were ashamed to confess, and yet they were anxious to hear what Christ would say.   "Who [then] is the greatest," that is, among us,[1] "in the kingdom of heaven?"   In order to teach them that only those who are like little children, trustful, humble, unambitious, could enter the heavenly kingdom, Jesus called a little child, set it in the midst of them, folded it in His arms, and warned them: "Verily, I say unto you, Except ye be converted and become as little children, ye shall not enter into the kingdom of heaven."   The point of comparison is not sinless innocence, but ingenuousness and simple humility.   And how highly

---

4,   7) Ἀντὶ ἐμοῦ καὶ σοῦ, "instead of," because the money was redemption money.   "For Me and for thee," not "for us," because the money was paid differently for each.   Farrar, II, 45.

8) Kretzmann, *Pop. Com.,* I, 97.   9) Στατήρ.

5,   1) Luke 9, 46: "which of them."

the childlike spirit is valued in the judgment of God is revealed
in the words: "Whosoever therefore shall humble himself as a little.
child, the same is greatest in the kingdom of heaven." It is easy
to humble oneself in "self-disparaging words or by symbolic acts,
as when the Egyptian monks wore hoods like children's caps; but
to be, in childlike manner, humble in spirit is as great in the moral
world as it is rare." [2] The disciples of Christ are to be like children
in this world. Not as if children were not in need of regeneration;
but every disciple, as the result of regeneration by the Spirit, becomes a child, whether or not he is a child in years. And then,
as the Lord turned to the child, considering its age as well as its
faith, He made this statement: "Whoso shall receive one such
little child in My name receiveth Me." What a glorious promise
for kindness bestowed upon forsaken, fatherless, Christ-redeemed
little children for the sake of the Redeemer! "The legendary spirit,
which dearly loves certainty in detail, identified this particular child
with St. Ignatius, who later became the second bishop of Antioch
and died as a martyr. As if that would make the lesson more
valuable!" [3]

6.

Mark 9, 38—41. Luke 9, 49. 50.

At that moment the discourse of Jesus was interrupted by the
Apostle John, to whom the expression "in My name" seems to have
suggested an experience which he and certain other disciples had
had at a time when they were separated from Jesus. In their work
they had run across a man who was casting out devils. Ordinarily
these exorcists conjured with the name of Abraham or Solomon in

The Mistaken Zeal of John.

their attempt to expel demons. But this man was
no ordinary sorcerer, nor was he, like a Simon Magus [1] or one of
the seven sons of Sceva,[2] who would use the name of Jesus and still
remain unbelieving in their hearts. He actually cast out devils in
the name of Christ. However, since he did not outwardly join the
company of followers, John and those with him had forbidden
him. And now John wondered whether what they had done

5,   2) Bruce sub Matt. 18, 4.

3) Bruce sub Matt. 18, 2.   See also Ylvisaker, 421.   Eusebius, III,
22. 36.   For all we know, the little child may have been Peter's little son. —
We shall not see Matthew, Mark, and Luke together again in a threefold
account until the blessing of little children in Perea, six months later.
Chapter XXV, 12.

6,   1) Acts 8, 18 ff.   2) Acts 19, 13 ff.

was right. Jesus replied: "Forbid them not; for there is no man which shall do a miracle in My name that can lightly [3] speak evil of Me. For he that is not against us is on our part." This man was a believer and was so acknowledged by Christ, even if he did not reach the point of considering it his duty to join the fellowship of His followers. He was by no means a neutral, to whom the word would have applied: "He that is not with Me is against Me." [4] The important thing is not always to follow disciples, but to follow Christ. And the important thing among followers of Christ is not to strive for an honorable position, but to be willing to render the humblest service, and though it be as insignificant a thing as the giving of a cup of water for the sake of Christ. "For whosoever shall give you a cup of water to drink in My name because ye belong to Christ, verily, I say unto you, he shall not lose his reward." [5]

7.

Matt. 18, 6—14. Mark 9, 42—50.

And then, gently resuming His discourse at the point where it had been interrupted by John, Jesus warns His disciples against the awful guilt incurred by causing youthful believers to stumble

Warning against Giving Offense.
from the path of faith. What a sin to separate children from the salvation which Christ has come to bring! It were better for such a one to have one of those large millstones turned by an ass [1] hung about his neck and be cast into the sea. That would keep him down and prevent him from doing mischief to others. But however glaring the sin of offense may be, in a world which lies in wickedness it cannot be avoided. "But woe to that man by whom the offense cometh!"

8.

Matt. 18, 6—14. Mark 9, 42—50.

Then there is another thing: the temptation into which one is not led by others, but which comes from the members of one's own body. It is the duty of every Christian to keep the members

---

6, 3) *Ταχύ*, quickly. He will do it neither now nor later.

4) Matt. 12, 30.

5) Compare Matt. 10, 42. There is no reason to suppose that this verse, Mark 9, 41, has been taken over from, or introduced into, Matt. 10, 42. Jesus repeated some of His sayings, sometimes in a different connection and with different application. — Note that Jesus here calls Himself Christ.

7, 1) *Μύλος ὀνικός*. Not the small house-mill, which could be placed on a table and turned by hand. Bruce sub Matt. 18, 6.

of his own body under perfect control; for the end of him who yields to temptation and places his members in the service of sin will be the everlasting fires of hell,[1] where their worm will not die nor their fire be quenched.[2] The matter is so serious that the Lord repeats some of the warnings of the Sermon on the Mount.[3] "Wherefore, if thy hand or thy foot offend thee, cut them off and cast them from thee; it is better for thee to enter into life halt or maimed rather than, having two hands or two feet, to be cast

"If Thine Eye Offend Thee." into everlasting fire. And if thine eye offend thee, pluck it out and cast it from thee; it is better for thee to enter into life with one eye

rather than, having two eyes, to be cast into hell-fire." This does not mean that a person should mutilate himself, but that he should subdue his members in the service of Christ, so that they do not perform those things which the sinful heart desires. This may involve a sacrifice, a crucifying of the flesh with the affections and lusts.[4] But this crucifying of the flesh is necessary. For just as salt is sprinkled over every sacrifice [5] for its purification, so every soul must be salted with fire, if need be, of the most painful self-sacrifice. "Salt is good." [6] But let not the salt lose its savor nor this fire its purifying powers. "Have salt in yourselves and have peace one with another." Instead of permitting themselves to be led into sin, Christians, who are purified by the Word and the Spirit, should act as a salt in the world midst the surrounding corruption.

9.

Matt. 18, 6—14. Mark 9, 42—50.

Once more, probably with the child still nestling in His arms, Jesus reverts to the "little ones" and charges His disciples of all times: "Take heed that ye despise not these little ones," whose

Parable of the Lost Sheep. guardian angels do always behold the face of the Father in

heaven. The Son of Man, who is come to save that which is lost, takes particular interest also in children. It is His will that not one of them should perish. He is just like the man who has a hundred

---

8,   1) *Εἰς τὴν γέενναν τοῦ πυρός.* The fires of the Valley of Hinnom, near Jerusalem, where the refuse of the city was burned, were commonly taken as a type of the fires of hell.

2) Is. 66, 24.   3) Matt. 5, 29. 30.

4) Gal. 5, 24.   5) Lev. 2, 13.   6) Matt. 5, 13.

sheep [1] pasturing on a mountain meadow. He notices that one has gone astray. Leaving the ninety and nine, he climbs up to the mountain in search of the one that has gone astray. "And if so be that he find it, verily, I say unto you, he rejoiceth more of that sheep than of the ninety and nine which have not gone astray." The Lord Himself became a child at Bethlehem. And as great as is the sin which causes the loss of a lamb of Christ, so great is the joy in heaven at the gain of a youthful soul. It is the will of the Father in heaven that not one "of these little ones should perish."

Matt. 18, 15—20.   10.

The heavenly Father has but one will, the will to save. This includes all, young and old. It also includes those who have fallen into sin, but who by loving patience and hard work might be won back. "If thy brother shall trespass against thee," not necessarily a strictly personal offense, but an evident act against a certain word of God, then treat him as an erring brother and "go and tell him his fault between thee and him alone. If he shall hear thee, thou hast gained thy brother." This is the general rule. And only upon failure to gain him in this way a second step is to be taken, to wit: "Take with thee one or two more that in the mouth of two or three witnesses every word may be established." This is common sense. And as to the number of witnesses the procedure is the same as that prescribed in the Old Testament.[1] If the purpose of these

"If Thy Brother shall Trespass against Thee." admonitions is not achieved, the case will have to be continued. The purpose of these steps is to lead the brother — for as such he is still to be regarded — back to the right path. And only after the failure of the second measure is the offense to be made known to a larger circle of brethren. "And if he neglect to hear them, tell it unto the church," the congregation of which he is a member. But even here the purpose must be to gain the sinner. — As regards the word *church* [2] the New Testament Christian Church had not yet been established; but, while using the term in the sense of a Jewish community, Jesus looks forward to the time of the establishment of local Christian congregations. By the members of a Christian congregation its verdict in the matter will be regarded as the verdict of Christ Himself. If, therefore, the offender who is requested to appear

9,   1) Compare Luke 15, 4—7.
10,   1) Deut. 19, 15.   2) Ἐκκλησία.

before this body will "neglect to hear the church," he has deprived himself of the rights and privileges granted a Christian congregation and must henceforth be adjudged "an heathen man and a publican."

Matt. 18, 15—20.   **11.**

This act of solemn excommunication, administered in the spirit of love, with the sincerely hoped-for restoration of the fallen as its objective, is binding, provided of course that all has been done in accordance with the Word of God. "Verily, I say unto you, Whatsoever ye shall bind on earth shall be bound in heaven, and whatsoever ye shall loose on earth shall be loosed in heaven." This applies, whether the local congregation of disciples is large or **The Office of the Keys.** small. When such a community on the basis of Scripture has reached a full agreement in the matter referred to above, the sad duty of dealing with a fallen brother, or in any other matter pertaining to the preaching of the Word and the furtherance of the Kingdom, it has the sanction of the Lord of the Church; indeed, as touching anything, Jesus said, that an assembly of Christians may ask, "it shall be done for them of My Father which is in heaven." What tremendous power Jesus grants to His Church on earth, even to the smallest Christian congregation! "For where two or three are gathered together in My name," [1] that is, literally, to His name, to the honor of His name, "there am I [2] in the midst of them."

Matt. 18, 21—35.   **12.**

The subject of dealing with a fallen brother attracted the particular attention of Peter. For the second time in the course of this discourse Jesus had been interrupted.[1] The disciples were at least paying attention. It seemed to Peter that Jesus was stretching the matter of brotherly love a little too far. Suppose a brother had **"How Oft shall I Forgive My Brother?"** to be dealt with again and again? According to the Rabbinical rule forgiveness had to be extended three times.[2] But Peter was willing to raise it to seven times. "Lord, how oft shall my brother sin against me and I forgive him? Till seven times?" But Jesus answered: "Say

---

11, 1) Εἰς τὸ ἐμὸν ὄνομα.

2) Looking into the future — "am I." Christ's presence is certain even with reference to the future. Bruce *sub loco.*

12, 1) No. 6.   2) Bruce *sub loco.* Based on Amos 1, 6.

not until seven times, but, Until seventy times seven." That is a figurative term for always. Forgiveness is not a matter of pharisaic exactness, but love and forgiveness should always dwell in the Christian heart.

Matt. 18, 21—35. **13.**

This truth is illustrated in the parable of the Unmerciful Servant. After all, even if the disciples of Christ would comply with the apparently unreasonable requirement of forgiving a fallen brother exactly four hundred and ninety times, what is that compared with what has already been remitted to them by God? [1] Among the debtors of a certain indolent and trusting Oriental king there was one whom he had fully trusted, but who now owed him ten thousand talents, an immense sum, let us say, millions of dollars. [2] We don't know how much, since it is not stated whether the weight was of silver or of gold. Nor does it matter. The case was hopeless. In accordance with the power of an Oriental monarch over life and property of his subjects, this ruler commanded the servant "to be sold, and his wife, and children, and all that he had, and payment to be made." Thereupon the servant fell down at his

The Unmerciful Servant. feet and asked for mercy with a promise beyond his ability to keep: "And I will pay thee all." The king was moved by this pitiful plea. He set the servant free, canceled the debt, and forgave him all. Now comes the other side of the picture. The servant, happily restored to his master's favor, immediately afterwards seized a fellow-servant by the throat who was indebted to him and would not forgive him a miserable little debt of one hundred pence. [3] This was an insignificant sum as compared with the immense debt which had just been canceled for him. His fellow-servant now also fell down and besought him: "Have patience with me, and I will pay thee all." But "he would not." Turning from the debtor in heartless cruelty, he "cast him into prison till he should pay the debt." This merciless deed was reported to the king. Once more the servant was summoned into the royal presence. "And his lord was wroth." With words of severest condemnation he turned him over to the tormentors. And the lesson? "So likewise shall My heavenly Father do also unto you if ye from your hearts forgive not every one his brother their trespasses."

13, 1) Bruce *sub loco.*
  2) Ταλάντων. A silver talent = $2,050; a gold talent = $30,750.
  3) Δηνάρια. A denarion = 16 to 20 cents.

CHAPTER XX.

AT THE FEAST OF TABERNACLES IN JERUSALEM.

Probably 13th to 19th of October, 782 A. U. C., or 29 A. D.

John 7, 2—9.   **1.**

One year and a half had elapsed since the last visit of Jesus to Jerusalem. That is, if, as we assume, the Unnamed Feast [1] is to be taken as the Passover of the year 28 A. D. At that time already the Jews had sought to kill Him,[2] but the time had not yet come for Him to present Himself as the Lamb of God that taketh away the sins of the world. This visit was followed by the Great Galilean Ministry, the death of John the Baptist, the period of retirement, and the close of the Galilean and the northern ministries. "Now, the Jews' Feast of Tabernacles was at hand." This was the second of the great annual Jewish harvest-festivals [3] and the third of the three great annual pilgrimage feasts: Passover, Pentecost, and

The Feast of Tabernacles. Tabernacles, observed in memory of the dwelling of Israel in tents in the wilderness.[4] It was held from the fifteenth to the twenty-first day of the seventh month, Tishri, which corresponds to our month of October, and as the last annual feast of thanksgiving for the harvest gathered in it was celebrated with universal joy. Translated into the dates of our calendar, this festival has been calculated to have fallen between the thirteenth [5] and nineteenth day of October.[6] The eighth day of the feast was observed with particular solemnity as a holy day of convocation.[7] In order to recall the days of the desert wanderings, the pilgrims lived in branch-constructed booths, or tents, during the whole time of the feast. During the week all the twenty-four courses of priests

---

1,   1) John 5, 1.   2) John 5, 16.

    3) Following the Feast of Weeks, or Pentecost, the day of first-fruits.

    4) Σκηνοπηγία, the fixing of tents, or booths. Deut. 16, 16; Lev. 23, 34—42.

    5) Thursday to Thursday. Oswald Gerhardt, *Der Stern des Messias*, p. 125.

    6) Wednesday to Wednesday, 12th—19th of October. Wieseler, *Synopsis*, 435.

    7) Lev. 23, 36; John 7, 37.

were employed in turn. A special sacrifice of seventy bullocks for the seventy nations of the world[8] was made in a decreased daily scale.[9] And on each day the Temple trumpets sounded twenty-one times an inspiring and rejoicing blast.[10] The joy of the occasion was doubtless heightened by the fact that the feast followed five days after the both awful and comforting ceremonies of the Day of Atonement, on which a solemn expiation was made for the sins of all the people.[11]

John 7, 2—9.   2.

As all Galilee was active in the preparation which preceded the starting of the caravans to Jerusalem, the brethren of Jesus besought Him publicly to reveal Himself in the capital city as the King of Israel. We understand these brethren of Jesus to be those of the Lord's cousins, Joseph and Simon, who had not like James and Judas become apostles of the Lord.[1] They had a certain faith in the miracle-working power of Jesus. In the fact that all who were attached to Him would be found at Jerusalem they saw an opportunity for their Relative to advance His Messianic claims. Their advice was: "Show Thyself to the world." No one who seeks public recognition confines his activities to a hidden corner. Thus these brethren failed to "believe in Him." Not as if theirs

The Unbelieving Brethren. was the unbelief of active opposition, but a relative unbelief,[2] shared also by others in the circle of Jesus, who, looking forward to a political Messiahship, failed to see the purpose of Christ's coming into the world. But Jesus rejected their carnal proposal. The proper time for His full Messianic revelation had not yet arrived. In revealing their carnal hopes, they indicated that they were of the world and therefore unhated by the world. If such were their hopes, and if that was the character of their discipleship, then their journey to Jerusalem was perfectly safe as far as the opposing world was concerned. To the extent of their

---

1,   8) Probably based on the list in Gen. 10.

9) $13+12+11+10+9+8+7 = 70$. Num. 29, 14—32.

10) Notice the recurrence of the holy number seven, a symbol of completeness, and its multiples.

11) Farrar, II, 48. Observed on the 10th of Tishri, Lev. 16. By the way, if "afflict your souls," Lev. 16, 19; 23, 27; Num. 29, 7, means fasting, then this was the only fast day prescribed by the Law. Compare Acts 27, 9.

2,   1) Mark 6, 3. Chapter XI, 13 f.; IV, 43.

2) Pieper, *Christl. Dogmatik*, II, 368.

spiritual ignorance they were really unbelieving disciples of Jesus. However, the Lord tells them: "Go ye up unto the feast" and do your duty. "I go not up yet unto the feast," at any rate, not for the purpose which they had in mind, to make the display they believed He should make. Not until the following spring would He make His triumphal entry into Jerusalem, to be followed, not by the fulfilment of false Messianic hopes, but by the establishment of a spiritual kingdom through suffering and death. And so, leaving His puzzled brethren in ignorance as to His references and plans, He stayed behind in Galilee.

John 7, 10.   **3.**

But. when the brethren were gone, Jesus also started out on the journey to Jerusalem, "but, as it were, in secret," and not for the purpose which they had suggested. In all truthfulness the brethren of Jesus could say if asked about the coming of Jesus,

Jesus Goes Privately to Jerusalem. as they surely would be, that He did not come with them, and whether He was coming at all they did not know. The presence of Jesus, however, in Jerusalem was confidently expected by many. Hardly had the party from Capernaum made its arrival when there were inquiries from all sides, "Where is He?" Likewise, there was also much wrangling concerning Him. Some said He was a good man; others, that He was a deceiver. But neither side dared to declare itself openly until the authorities of the Church had spoken.

John 7, 11—53.   **4.**

Suddenly, in the midst of the feast, Jesus appeared in the Temple and taught.[1] Although His presence in Jerusalem had been expected, still this sudden appearance came as a surprise. "And the Jews marveled." Not as if Jesus wanted to create a sensation; for His purpose was simply to attend to the duties of His prophetic office. For a while the people listened in silence; but soon the old scruples recurred to them. "How knoweth this man letters [learning], having never learned?" Just as if only he could excel in learning who had received the prescribed course of

---

4,   1) Probably on a Sabbath, if, as Wieseler has calculated, the first day fell on a Wednesday, October 12, 782 A. U. C., or 29 A. D. *Synopsis,* 435. According to the table of Gerhardt it must have been a Sunday. *Stern des Messias,* pp. 125. 126. If we combine the two views, we may come to the conclusion that it was Saturday evening, when the Sabbath was over.

formal educational training! [2] What the scribes considered their prerogative, the interpretation of Scripture, Jesus excelled in without their training. Jesus understood the questioning glances and told them that His learning came from the heavenly Father. And he who would earnestly seek to do the will of God would readily see that what He taught, both Law and Gospel, was the truth and that therefore He was "of God," the Son of the Father. There are two kinds of religious teachers: such as seek their

The Appearance of Jesus at the Festival. own glory and those who seek the glory of Him whose ambassadors they are. And since it was plain that Jesus revealed the truth, and advanced the glory, of Him who had sent Him, they had no right to appear as the champions of the Law against Him; yet that is what they did. In opposing Him and His Gospel, they appealed to Moses and the Law; "yet none of you keepeth the Law." If you would seriously examine yourselves according to the Law, you would soon realize that you have transgressed it and therefore need a Savior; and then you would believe in Me and not "go about to kill Me."

John 7, 11—53. 5.

Now, this reference to the determination to kill Jesus, primarily a secret of the leaders, but in the end a general resolve, aroused the people. Indignantly they resented the insinuation: "Thou hast a devil; who goeth about to kill Thee?" In His reply to this blasphemy uttered against Him Jesus refused to be turned aside from His argument. He had no devil. Neither was He a "monomaniac, laboring under the hallucination that people wished to kill Him," [1] because He knew perfectly well that the opposition to Him had reached the murderous stage. [2] In opposing Him, they appealed to the Law, and yet they did not keep the Law. They even sinned against it at times through a wrong interpretation of it, for instance, by insisting on the strict observance of the

"Thou Hast a Devil!" letter of certain portions of it contrary to the spirit of it. A year and a half ago He had healed a man on a Sabbath-day, [3] at which, it is true, they still marveled, but at the same time were horrified because this work had been done on a Sabbath-day. [4] But there

---

4, 2) "To the Jews there was only one kind of learning, that of theology, and only one road to it, the schools of the Rabbis. Their major was true, but their minor false; and Jesus hastened to correct it." Edersheim, II, 151.
5, 1) Dods *sub loco*. 3) John 5, 5 ff.
2) John 5, 16. 4) John 5, 16.

was no reason for this. According to a rigorous conception of the Law the Sabbath law was regularly transgressed whenever the act of circumcision was performed on the Sabbath, and yet no one ever paused to give it a thought. Now, if without scruple they sacrificed one ordinance for the sake of another, if, for example, the law of circumcision superseded a certain restriction of the Sabbath commandment, why not admit exceptions in the supreme law of love and mercy? [5] And if it was right — for the purpose of ceremonial purity — to inflict a wound upon one member of the body, why, then, should it be wrong by one word to effect a cure of the whole body? Therefore "judge not according to the appearance," but by a sane judgment reach a righteous decision.

John 7, 11—53.   **6.**

These words made an impression upon the hearers. "Is not this He whom they seek to kill?" Can He possibly be the very Christ? The leaders may have changed their opinion. For, "lo, He speaketh boldly, and they say nothing unto Him." Still they found it difficult to believe that the authorities had relented or to accept the Speaker as the promised Messiah because He did not satisfy their Messianic requirements. In the first place, as to origin. The leaders had taught them that, "when Christ cometh, no man knoweth whence He is." According to the apocalyptic literature Christ was to appear suddenly "in the clouds or from the sun," [1] while there was nothing miraculous in the arrival of Jesus in their midst. "Howbeit we know this man whence He is," Jesus of

"They Sought to Take Him." Nazareth, the son of Mary and of the carpenter Joseph. — As these opinions were loudly discussed in the Temple, Jesus shouted into the babel of voices: "Ye both know Me, and ye know whence I am; and I am not come of Myself, but He that sent Me is true, whom ye know not." Jesus granted them the knowledge of His earthly origin. That was no secret. But even as to these matters their knowledge clearly was still deficient. They did not know that He was born at Bethlehem. [2] But that did not matter. Of far greater importance was the fact that they were not aware of His preexistence, that they did not truly know the Father, who had sent Him, that they were ignorant of the purpose of His coming

---

5,   5) Farrar, II, 54.
6,   1) Dods sub John 7, 27.   2) V. 42.

into the world, and the like. This frank statement of His divine origin they did not fail to grasp. But it made them furious. "Then they sought to take Him"; still, they did not dare to do so. They were held back by a power that lamed their hands, "because His hour was not yet come." And besides, even at that moment faith was wrought by the words of Christ. "Many of the people believed on Him." And immediately they were willing to defend their faith. They were quite satisfied to cast their lot with Jesus. Even if Christ should come later, they argued, He would not be able to perform greater miracles "than these which this Man hath done," which the rulers had tried to make the people believe. At least the reality of Christ's miracles was not denied.

John 7, 11—53.   **7.**

As many people were moved to accept the teaching of Jesus, the Pharisees were alarmed and persuaded the Sanhedrin to send out officers, most likely members of the Temple guard, for His arrest. But Jesus was not afraid, and there was no arrest. "Yet a little while am I with you," He continued in His testimony to the people; then His earthly work would be finished; "then I go unto Him that sent Me." Then, when it is too late, "ye shall seek Me" — probably just then the officers of the Sanhedrin were slinking behind the pillars — "and shall not find Me; and where I am, thither ye cannot come." This was an urgent invitation to

The Sanhedrin Takes Action. make use of the brief period of grace. At the final destruction of Jerusalem the Jews vainly clung with the hope of despair to the promise of their leaders that the Messiah would yet come to deliver them; but they did not see Him. "And ye shall desire to see one of the days of the Son of Man, and ye shall not see it." [1] However, not only was the Lord's warning unheeded, but it was deliberately misinterpreted. "Whither will He go that we shall not find Him?" What is He talking about? they asked and sneeringly conjectured that He intended to teach the Jews in the Diaspora and the Gentiles among whom they lived. It was a contemptuous remark. But that is exactly the course that the Gospel took. The children of the Kingdom who proudly declined the proffered grace were cast out, and the despised Gentiles were made to sit in the Kingdom. — Thus passed this memorable day.

7,   1) Luke 19, 42—44; 17, 22.

John 7, 11—53.   **8.**

It was on "the last day, that great day of the feast," that Jesus was once more in the Temple.[1] The feast itself lasted seven days,[2] and on the eighth day there was a holy convocation,[3] on which the people celebrated their entrance into the Holy Land. As their fathers abandoned their wilderness tents as soon as they

The Last Day of the Feast.

occupied the Promised Land, so the booths were torn down on the last day of the feast, the leaves shaken off the willow-boughs, the palm-branches waved against the altar, and everybody returned to his dwelling.[4] Another custom was that daily during the festival,[5] at the time of the morning sacrifice, a priest would fill a golden vessel with water at the Pool of Siloam [6] and together with the wine used for the sacrifice pour it on the altar

---

8, 1) Possibly on a Thursday. There is some difference of opinion as to whether this last day was the seventh or the eighth. Most commentators maintain that the eighth was the day when the great feast as a whole was brought to a termination. See Andrews, 345. If the calculations of Wieseler and Gerhardt are correct, both of whom make the 15th of Nisan, 30 A. D., correspond with April 7, a Friday, then this last day of the feast, the 22d of Tishri, was a Thursday, October 20 (Gerhardt), or a Wednesday, October 19 (Wieseler), which agrees with the view that the "midst of the feast," when Jesus arrived, was on a Sabbath. See Gerhardt, *Stern des Messias,* pp. 125. 126. Wieseler, *Synopsis,* 435.

2) Lev. 23, 34; Neh. 8, 18.   3) Num. 29, 35.

4) Edersheim, *Temple,* 244.

5) And also on the eighth day. Farrar, II, 56, and others.

6) Siloah, meaning "sent," or "conducted" (by means of an aqueduct). It was an ancient, deep-walled pool, less than a half mile south of the Temple area, where the Tyropeon and Kidron valleys meet. For many hundred years before the days of Jesus the waters had come through an ancient tunnel from the fountain of Gihon, now called the Virgin's Fount, outside the city wall, in the Kidron Valley, through more than a thousand feet of rock, till it issued on the other side of the hill, inside the city wall. There the water ran into the oblong Pool of Siloam, hewn in the rock. It is flowing to this day, the only spring, or living water, in Jerusalem. B. Matthew writes (*A Life of Jesus,* p. 298) that he "waded through the tunnel from end to end. It was cut by masons, who began with hammer and chisel, from both ends, as can clearly be seen and as described on a Hebrew inscription (the oldest Hebrew inscription in the world) cut in Phenician characters, discovered in the tunnel and now in the Constantinople Museum. After many windings, totaling over seventeen hundred feet, the masons met in the middle. The height of the tunnel varies from three to fourteen feet, but for a good part of the distance a man must stoop." See also article in *Int. St. B. Encycl.* by E. W. G. Masterman, who connects the work and the pool with Hezekiah. "And the rest of the acts of Hezekiah and all his might, and how he made a pool and a conduit and brought water into the city, are they not written in the Book of the Chronicles of the Kings of Judah?" 2 Kings 20, 20. For a facsimile of the Siloam inscription see *Int. St. B. Encycl.,* 3120. Professor Sayce's translation is included in the article "Siloam" by E. W. G. Masterman.

in commemoration of the water from the rock in the wilderness [7] and their entry into the land of springs and water.[8]   At the signal "Raise thy hand" [9] the water was poured out,[10] and the Great Hallel [11] was sung in the manner prescribed: "O give thanks unto the Lord, for He is good; because His mercy endureth forever." Besides the historical reference this ceremony of the pouring of the water was believed to have some bearing on the dispensation of rain, the annual amount of which was thought to be determined by God at that feast.   But its main and real application was the misunderstood future outpouring of the Holy Spirit in fulfilment of prophecy: "Therefore with joy shall ye draw water out of the wells of salvation." [12]   In their daily circuit around the altar the chanting priests thought of the ingathering of the heathen nations. But on the eighth day this procession was made seven times, and, remembering how the walls of Jericho crumpled and fell down at the seventh march of the people round about them,[13] they pictured to themselves how by the direct interposition of God the walls of heathenism would fall before them, all the nations would be converted to Judaism, and the land lie open for the people to enter and possess it.

John 7, 11—53.   9.

Whatever the significance of the various ceremonies, Jesus applied the prophecy of Isaiah to Himself.[1]   And as He had done to the woman at the well of Sychar,[2] so here, too, He pointed to

Christct the Water of Life.   Himself as the Water of Life.
"If any man thirst, let him come unto Me and drink." He is the only true fountain of living water; for in Him there is true, everlasting life.   Not only shall the spiritual thirst of the believer be quenched, but he shall be the source of good for others. "He that believeth on Me, as the Scrip-

---

8,   7) Ex. 17, 6.   8) Josh. 12, 8.

9) To show that it was actually poured out.

10) There was some dispute on this point as well as on others between the Pharisees and Sadducees, the latter holding that the pouring of water upon the altar was not an ordinance instituted by Moses.   To give expression to his views, the high priest Alexander Jannaeus, instead of pouring the water on the altar, poured it on the ground.   The Pharisees in their fury hurled at his head the citron fruits which they were carrying — Lev. 23, 40: "the fruit [A. V.: "boughs"] of the goodly trees" — in their left hands.   Alexander called his mercenaries to his aid, and a riot ensued, in which about 6,000 people were killed in the Temple.   Josephus, *Ant.,* XIII, XIII, 5. Schuerer, I, I, 300.

11) Pss. 113—118.   12) Is. 12, 3.   13) Josh. 6, 15 ff.
9,   1) Is. 12, 3.   2) John 4, 10 ff.

ture [3]) hath said, out of his belly [4]) shall flow rivers of living water." The believer's life will manifest itself in deeds of the Spirit for the benefit of others. And while the work of the Holy Spirit was effective in all ages, yet there would be a special manifestation of it, as the evangelist remarks, after the glorification of Christ in the gift of the Spirit at Pentecost. "But this spake He of the Spirit which they that believe on Him should receive; for the Holy Ghost was not yet given, because that Jesus was not yet glorified."

John 7, 11—53.   **10.**

The effect of these words was instantaneous; but it manifested itself in various ways. The vast assembly could not help being aroused to the truth that they were suddenly brought face to face with the fulfilment of prophecy. Some were ready to believe that Jesus was the great Prophet promised by Moses,[1]) whom, however, they did not identify with the Messiah.[2]) Others gained the conviction that He was the Christ Himself. Still others, believing

The Effect of the Sermon.
that Scripture was on their side, objected: "Shall Christ come out of Galilee?" And what about the promise that Christ was to be born of the seed of David and come out of "the town of Bethlehem, where David was?"[3]) While this appeal to Scripture was perfectly in order, it was founded on ignorance of the fact that these requirements had actually been met. And so there was "a division [of opinion] among the people because of Him." The words of Jesus even cast a spell over those who had been sent to take Him. They would have made the arrest, but an unseen force rendered their hands impotent and checked their desire.

John 7. 11—53.   **11.**

For four days the officers of the Sanhedrin had kept a close watch on Jesus, but in the end they had to return empty-handed. Their commission had kept them in the neighborhood of Jesus

---

9,   3) Is. 44, 3; 58, 11. No direct quotations. Christ alludes to passages in which the Spirit, whom God would send in the days of the Messiah, is compared to streams of water. Dods *sub loco.*

4) Ἐκ τῆς κοιλίας αὐτοῦ. As represented in the metaphor, these rivers take their rise from the water which has been drunk; so the effect referred to flows forth in an oral effusion. The divine grace and truth which a believer has received out of Christ's fulness into his inner life does not remain shut up within, but will communicate itself abundantly as a life-giving stream to others. Meyer sub John 7, 38.

10, 1) Deut. 18, 15.   2) Compare 1 Macc. 14, 41; John 1, 21; 6. 14.
3) Micah 5, 2; Is. 11, 1; Jer. 23, 5.

and in the hearing of His teaching, and His words had had a powerful effect upon them. When they returned to make their report
to the Sanhedrin, the reason for their failure was at once demanded.
"Why have ye not brought Him?" All they could answer was:
"Never man spake like this man." The Pharisees immediately
suspected that the officers had come under the influence of Jesus.

The Report of the Officers. "Are ye also deceived?"
They felt that their power
was slipping from their hands when even trusted underlings could
not be depended upon. This was altogether out of order. It was
theirs to act mechanically, to carry out the order, and to leave the
matter of responsibility to their superiors. What right did they
have to form an opinion of their own, especially if the opinion did
not coincide with that of their masters? "Have any of the rulers or
of the Pharisees believed on Him?" That ought to settle the
matter as far as the servants were concerned. As to the "miserable
mob, whose favorite Jesus had become," [1] "this people, who
knoweth not the Law, are cursed." [2] Pharisaic pride entertained
but unbounded scorn for the "unlettered mob." [3]

John 7, 11—53.   **12.**

This was too much for one member of the Sanhedrin, Nicodemus, the same man who had come to Jesus by night. [1] He
demanded to know whether it was in accordance with the Law,
of the keeping of which they were always boasting, to condemn
a man unheard and in ignorance as to the nature of his deeds.
Truth hurts. Since there was no reply to the "justice of the
principle, the fellow-members of the Sanhedrin fell back on
taunts." [2] "Art thou also of Galilee" and inclined to become a fol-

Nicodemus: "Doth Our Law Judge Any Man before It Hear Him?" lower of this Galilean? Galilee
is not the soil to produce prophets!
Don't expect a prophet, much less
the Messiah, to come from there!
"Search and look, for out of Galilee ariseth no prophet." But
their perverseness was equaled only by their denseness. What about
Jonah of Gath-hepher in Zebulun? [3] And there may have been

11, 1) Farrar, II, 59.

2) Ἐπικατάρατοι. Compare Gal. 3, 10. 13.

3) Edersheim, II, 162. The people of the soil, the *'Am ha Aretz.*

12, 1) John 3, 1 ff.   2) Farrar, II, 59.

3) 2 Kings 14, 25; Josh. 19, 13.

others.[4]   And what about Naphtali and Zebulun in Galilee of the Gentiles, which should see the great Light? [5]   "But there is no ignorance so deep as the ignorance that will not know nor a blindness so incurable as that which will not see." [6]   The meeting broke up in a deadlock. "And every man went unto his own house," the members of the Sanhedrin and the worshipers in the Temple, while Jesus, having no home of His own, went out to stay with some friends on the Mount of Olives.

John 8, 1—11.[1]   **13.**

From the home of Lazarus, where we imagine Jesus to have spent the night,[2] an early return to the Temple was made on the following morning. But while the Savior was about His Father's

---

12, 4) Farrar, II, 59.   Elijah, Hosea, Nahum? (Capernaum = Caper Nahum, according to some.)

5) Is. 9, 1. 2; Matt. 4, 15. 16.   6) Farrar, II, 60.

13, 1) Without going into the many details as to the genuineness of this famous disputed passage about the woman taken in adultery, John 8, 1—11, together with 7, 53, attention is called to the following: 1. This passage is not contained in some of the best and oldest manuscripts, A, B, W, and others. Neither is it found in about 70 of the ancient cursives. Nor is it commented upon by most of the Fathers. But the rejection of the passage may have been due to a false dogmatic bias, or it may have been regarded as dangerous in its tendencies. 2. It is found in some old and important uncials, for instance, in D (Codex Bezae), in more than 300 cursives, in some copies of the Itala, and in the Vulgate. Its authenticity was defended already in ancient times, especially by Augustine, whose subjective judgment was that the story was rejected on account of the fear that impunity to sin would be given to wives *(peccandi impunitatem dari mulieribus suis).* 3. It is to be admitted that from a literary standpoint its style does not agree with the usual style of John, rather resembling that of the Synoptists, so that by four cursives it was placed after Luke 21, 37. 38. But as to the place in the narrative there appear to be references to it in the discourses which immediately follow, John 8, 15. 17. 24. 46. 4. Even if it is to be admitted that the passage was not originally written by John, but incorporated by him from an earlier source, which has not been proved, it can hardly be doubted that it is, if not of Johannean, at least of apostolic origin and that it describes a real, truly human, and most remarkable incident in the life of our Lord. The mere fact of dogmatic bias against the passage and its rejection by many ancient editors best explain the many variations and resulting corruptions of a text against which they were prejudiced. 5. On the whole, there is no reason at all why this beautiful story should not be accepted as genuine. — For detailed critical treatment the interested student is referred to the remarks of Meyer, who rejects the text (at the head of chapter VIII in his commentary). But comparison should be made with the notes of the American editor, A. C. Kendrick, D. D., who accepts it as a true incident in the life of our Lord (at the end of the chapter). See also the notes of Farrar, II, 61. 62. In the more recent literature we have run across the following: A Sa'idic ostracon preserves the section, which is otherwise unattested in the ancient Sa'idic N. T. And while the famous Codex W (Washington), found in 1906 in Egypt, *usually* agrees with Codex D, which contains the passage, we are in this instance surprised at its omission.

2) Luke 10, 38; John 11, 18;   12, 1; Mark 11, 11; Matt. 21, 17, as compared with Luke 21, 37. 38.

business, His old enemies, the scribes and Pharisees,[3] were busy with the work of their father, the devil.[4] They brought to Him a woman taken in adultery. Instead of delivering her to the proper authorities, they make her the instrument of satisfying their hatred against Jesus, "subject her to the horror of odious publicity, and drag her fresh from the agony of detection into the sacred precincts of the Temple."[5] There they "set her in the midst" and say unto Jesus: "Master, this woman was taken in adultery, in the very act." A shameful charge, but what about the witnesses and the partner of the crime? Evidently they were not so much under the strain of moral indignation and anxious to prefer charges against the woman as interested in preferring charges against Jesus. "Now, Moses in the Law commanded us that such[6] should be stoned; but what sayest Thou?" From the Law cited by them[7] it would appear that the woman who had committed this sin was a betrothed virgin. But since death generally, whether by stoning or by strangulation,[8] was the punishment adjudged to adulteresses as well as to adulterers, the particular relation of this accused woman cannot definitely be inferred from the use of the term. And besides, the actual carrying out of these laws had long fallen into disuse. Be that, however, as it may; that was not the real point at issue, but rather: "This they said, tempting Him, that they might accuse Him." They knew that Jesus had been lenient, according to their judgment, with publicans and sinners. According to their idea He had deviated from the Law of Moses before. And now, would He acquit this woman and make Himself liable to a charge of heresy? In the face of such flagrant transgression would He openly disregard the "fiery Law"? Or would He belie His "customary compassion so as ruthlessly to condemn?" How could He get out of doing either one or the other? In any event it would either cost Him His popularity, or He would be accused before the Sanhedrin. And if He would order stoning,

The Woman Taken in Adultery.

13, 3) Compare Mark 9, 14; 8, 11; 7, 1. As a rule, the scribes were Pharisees. Some of them were members of the Sanhedrin. But we assume that the opponents in this instance were not members of that august body.

4) John 8, 44.

5) Farrar, II, 66. Edersheim, who rejects the passage (II, 163, n. 1): "Farrar has devoted to the illustration of this narrative some of his most pictorial pages."

6) Τὰς τοιαύτας — contemptuously.

7) Deut. 22, 24. 8) Lev. 20, 10; Deut. 22, 22.

then they could accuse Him before the governor of advocating sedition and mob violence. "What a chance a weak and erring woman had given them!" [9]

John 8, 1—11.   **14.**

Satan is never lacking in willing and able servants. But in order to convey to His enemies that He wanted nothing to do with this affair, "Jesus stooped down and with His fingers wrote on the ground." Whether the Savior wrote words or only traced some figures on the ground [1] as a symbol of indifference or distraction, we do not know. The punishment of adultery is a matter of the court. To involve Himself in the present instance He had no call. Therefore this action "as though He heard them not." [2] But impudently the accusers pressed for an answer. Straightening Himself up, Jesus gave them a reply which came to them like a fiery bolt from the very Law to which they had appealed. "He

"Let Him First Cast a Stone at Her." that is without sin among you, let him [3] first [4] cast a stone at her." This was a startling solution. It was not an abrogation of the divine Law. "Thou shalt not commit adultery" was, and still remained, in the Decalog. Neither was the Law in need of a new interpretation. In no wise was the sin of the woman excused. But the matter of dealing with the sinner, as Jesus' enemies requested, belonged to the civil law, with the operation of which Jesus did not purpose to meddle. Since, however, they had illegally, as individuals, brought her to Him and demanded of Him to act in an unofficial capacity, as a private person, and since He knew their self-righteousness and hypocrisy, "He transfers the whole case from the forum of law to that of conscience." [5] The scribes and Pharisees should grieve over their own iniquities rather than judge the sins of others. After telling them exactly what they were in need of hearing, Jesus again "stooped down and wrote on the ground." With burning cheeks, "being convicted by their own conscience," one by one, from the eldest to the youngest, the accusers slunk away. When Jesus once more raised His head, He

13, 9) Farrar, II, 68.
14, 1) Under the circumstances the natural thing. If He would actually have written words, these presumably would have been recorded.

   2) This explanatory addition in the Authorized Version is not in the *textus receptus,* which we have been following throughout.

   3) A command: βαλέτω.

   4) As the first and chief witness. Thus the Law: Deut. 17, 7.

   5) Farrar, II, 69.

saw that all the accusers had melted away. "And Jesus was left alone and the woman standing in the midst." She, too, might have gone, but the same force which had repelled the accusers kept her in the presence of Jesus. Her stay was a sign of repentance and no doubt she craved for forgiveness. Addressing her, Jesus asked: "Woman, where are those thine accusers? Hath no man condemned thee?" "No man, Lord," was all that her trembling lips could answer. And with the words "Neither do I condemn thee; go and sin no more," does "divine Mercy graciously dismiss Misery from His presence." [6]

John 8, 12—20. **15.**

Just where in the Temple the above incident occurred is not evident. Because of the reference to stoning some have thought that the words were spoken in the colonnades of an unfinished part of the Temple.[1] But Jesus might have said the words without a single stone's lying about.[2] Of the following discourse, however, really a series of noisy interruptions, we are told that it took place "in the Treasury, as He taught in the Temple."[3] It was also called the Court of the Women because this was as far as the women were allowed to go.[4] On account of the thirteen trumpet-shaped receptacles, or chests, for contributions it received the name of "The Treasury." Nightly during the Tabernacle week four large golden candelabra were lighted[5] to add to the joy of the

Jesus the Light of the World. feast. This brilliant illumination was perhaps a memorial of the pillar of fire[6] which led the children of Israel during their wilderness pilgrimage. But like the pouring out of water this brilliant light was also brought into connection with the time of the Messiah, when, it was hoped, all the Gentile nations would be led to the Jewish light. Ordinarily, in common houses, windows were made narrow without and wide within, so that the rays of the sun could pour in. But in Solomon's Temple the windows were made narrow within and wide without, "because the light issuing from the Sanc-

---

14, 6) Farrar, II, 71.

15, 1) V. 59.

2) The rebuilding of the Temple was not completed until shortly before its destruction. Josephus, *Ant.*, XX, IX, 7. It was not the intention of Jesus that stones should be actually hurled at the woman. Besides, according to the Mosaic Law the execution would have taken place outside the city, Deut. 22, 24.

3) V. 20.   4) See chapter III, 9.

5) Edersheim, *The Temple*, 246.   6) Ex. 13, 21.

tuary was to lighten that which was without." [7]   And indeed this
was a fitting symbolism; for a light was actually to shine forth
from out of Israel.   There were prophecies to this effect.   "The
people that walked in darkness have seen a great Light." [8]   "And
the Gentiles shall come to thy Light and kings to the Brightness of
thy rising," [9] namely, to the Messiah.   We are reminded of the
language of Simeon, whose eyes actually beheld that Light, "a Light
to lighten the Gentiles and the Glory of Thy people Israel." [10]
But the eyes of the people who had gathered at the Feast of
Tabernacles were still unopened, as Jesus, evidently referring to the
illumination ceremony, pointed out: "I am the Light of the world.
He that followeth Me shall not walk in darkness, but shall have
the Light of Life."   Even as Israel of old followed the pillar of
fire to the Promised Land, so he that follows this Light shall be
safely guided to life everlasting.

John 8, 12—20.   **16.**

The reference was only too clear.   Immediately the great declaration was challenged by the ever-present Pharisees.   They charged
Jesus with an idle assertion about Himself.   They maintained that
this great claim lacked proper attestation, to say the least.   "Thou
bearest record of Thyself; Thy record is not true."   But Jesus
replied that the ordinary requirements of law — since they purposed
to enter into the formal aspect of the matter — did not apply to
His witness regarding Himself; for He knew His origin and His
destiny — a Savior coming from God and going to God.   "Though
I bear record of Myself, yet My record is true; for I know whence
I came and whither I go; but ye cannot tell whence I come and
whither I go."   Unacquainted with His true higher position and

Challenged by the Pharisees.   on account of His form of
a servant they had passed
judgment and rejected His Messianic claims.   This they should
not do.   And withal, there was too much judging on their part, as
could be pointed out in the case which had just been dismissed. [1]
Now, in His Savior capacity, He said of Himself: "I judge no
man."   He had come to save and to bless.   However, this principle
did not bar exceptions.   "Yet if I judge, My judgment is true;
for I am not alone, but I and the Father that sent Me."   He wants

15, 7) Edersheim, II, 166.   8) Is. 9, 2.
       9) Is. 60, 2. 3.   10) Luke 2, 32.
16, 1) Vv. 3—11.

to be the Savior of all men; but because so many did not believe
in Him, the Son of the Father and therefore true God, He would
have to be also a Judge. And reverting from the idea of judging
to that of witnessing and to the testimony concerning Himself,
His self-witness was entirely in order and in accord with the Law to
which they continually appealed and which they so frequently disregarded.[2] He is in truth the Light of the world. There are two
witnesses: His own testimony and that of the Father who had
sent Him. — The Pharisees knew perfectly well what and who was
meant. While they themselves transgressed the rule of supported
evidence for an accusation, they in frivolous mockery demanded
witnesses on the spot. "Where is Thy Father?" Calmly Jesus
unveiled to them whence it was that they had put so wicked
a question. "Ye neither know Me nor My Father; if ye had known
Me, ye should have known My Father also." Since they would not
know the Son, the Father, too, would remain unknown to them.
As Jesus spoke these words in the Treasury, within a few feet from
where the august Sanhedrin held its sessions,[3] He would have been
apprehended had it not been that "His hour was not yet come."
That was the reason why "no man laid hands on Him."

John 8, 21—32.   **17.**

Presently we find Jesus teaching a more general audience,[1]
presumably in one of the Temple porches;[2] and His words have
a sad note. He again takes up the subject of His departure[3]
and emphasizes that those rejecting Him will not only vainly seek
Him, but will die in their sins. His departure to the Father seals
the fate of Israel. And is it not true? These many centuries
Israel has sought its Christ and perished in the great sin of rejecting
Him. But the words of Jesus are met with satanic disdain. What
is He talking about? "Will He kill Himself because He saith,
Whither I go, ye cannot come?" Is it by way of suicide that He
wants to put Himself out of their reach? Jesus disregards this
sneering interruption and points out the real cause of the separation
between Himself and them. They are from below, in the worst
sense of the term, while He is from above. And the testimony
which He has given them as the only means of salvation they will

---

16, 2) Deut. 17, 6; 19, 15.
     3) See chapter III, 10. Edersheim, II, 165.
17, 1) V. 22, compared with v. 13.
     2) V. 59.   3) John 7, 33.

not accept. But this the adversaries will not admit, and they do not inquire who He may be, so that they will come to faith in Him and thus gain life and salvation. With quiet dignity Jesus tells them that He is the same as He had said from the beginning that He was and directs them to the divine message which He has received from the Father, through which they will have salvation if they accept it, but which, if they obstinately refuse to believe it, will condemn them. And what He has received from the Father is the truth; for "He that sent Me is true." But that Jesus had been sent by the Father was the very thing they would or could not understand. Therefore Jesus explains: "When ye have lifted up the Son of Man, then shall ye know that I am He and that I do nothing of Myself; but as the Father hath taught Me, I speak these things." After His cru-

The Departure of Jesus with Its Result for Israel.

cifixion and the miracles which would follow — His resurrection, His ascension into heaven, the outpouring of the Holy Ghost on Pentecost, and the establishment of the Christian Church — and, we might add, after the destruction of their city as a preamble to the final Judgment, they would either know and joyfully confess or admit it in grim despair that He had been sent by the Father, that He carried out His will, and that He invariably did what was pleasing in His sight. This announcement made a powerful impression. As a result many were, at least temporarily, brought to faith. And to them, for the purpose of encouraging them to continue in faith, Jesus addresses these beautiful words: "If ye continue in My Word, then are ye My disciples indeed; and ye shall know the truth, and the truth shall make you free."

John 8, 33—59.   **18.**

But hardly had some come to faith in Christ when a number of His hearers were offended at the words He had just spoken. How could He talk of liberty to such as felt that they already were free? "We be Abraham's seed," they claimed, and were called by God to rule over other people, "and were never in bondage to any man." That they had been subject to the Egyptians, Assyrians, Babylonians, and Greeks and were now under the dominion of the Romans they regarded as altogether incidental, because at all times throughout their checkered history they had claimed and practically enjoyed religious independence. But Jesus points out to them that there is a servitude which may, and in their case really did, obtain in spite of their descent from Abraham and of the enjoyment of outward religious liberty, namely, the servitude of sin, to which by nature every human being is subject.[1] "Whosoever committeth sin is the servant of sin." How can a worker of iniquity talk about being free when he is a slave of sin? Of what value is physical descent in a theocracy if in the end one loses his true membership and is cast out? It is only the Son of God who can bring about

Spiritual Liberty and Being Abraham's Children.

spiritual liberty, emancipation from sin and its service. Instead of tracing their ancestry to Abraham, they should have considered Abraham's faith. It is not their physical descent, but their moral condition which is all-important. "I know that ye are Abraham's seed; but ye seek to kill Me."[2] Their conduct showed that the Gospel of freedom which Jesus had proclaimed had not become effective in them.[3] While Jesus was carrying out His Father's will and expressing His Father's thoughts, their reaction betrayed the parentage of one who was their father in truth.

John 8, 33—59.   **19.**

As if to resent the insinuation that they had learned something evil from their high ancestor, the Jews answer: "Abraham is our father." But Jesus replies: "If ye were Abraham's children, ye would do the works of Abraham." "Abraham believed in the Lord; and He counted it to him for righteousness."[1] "But now ye seek to kill Me." There is a difference between physical and

"Ye Are of Your Father the Devil."

true spiritual descent. Although their physical origin may indeed be traced to Abraham, yet they are intent on doing something that Abraham never would have done — to kill "a man"[2] who has proclaimed to them God's own truth. This murderous bent of mind is based upon hostility to God and shows that a paternity other than that of Abraham is theirs. "This did not Abraham." — But now the Jews began to notice that Jesus was speaking of spiritual extraction. And this allusion only increased their anger. Was He alluding to them as idolaters and hinting at idolatrous

---

18, 1) Ylvisaker, 385.   2) John 5, 16. 18; 7, 19.30.

3) Οὐ χωρεῖ ἐν ὑμῖν, "hath no place in you," does not move forward, progress, advance. Compare v. 30 with v. 33.

19, 1) Gen. 15, 6.

2) Ἄνθρωπον, simply used as we might say "person," without reference to the deity of Christ, *sine praeiudicio deitatis.* Bruce sub John 8, 40.

practises that often were connected with idolatry? [3)]   The idea was resented with indignation.   "We be not born of fornication; we have one Father, even God."   The idea was preposterous.   They belonged to the children of Israel in truth.   Whatever else might be said to their discredit, they believed in one God, Jehovah, and had nothing to do with adulterous practises and the worship of idols.   But even the outward worship of one God and conformity to high moral standards was not proof, Christ rejoined, that they were truly spiritual children of God.   "If God were your Father, ye would love Me; for I proceeded forth, and came, from God." "That is the constant argument of Jesus, that, as He came forth from God and was sent by Him, they must have loved and welcomed Him had they been the children of God." [4)]   And this they did not do.   "They would not recognize His speech as divine." There was an unwillingness in them to accept Him and the saving truth He proclaimed, which made them reject the truth He uttered. For this there was but one explanation.   And therefore, since plain language must be used, He told them, "Ye are of your father the devil."   From the beginning of the human race the devil was a liar and a murderer.   Their own murderous intentions and their opposition to the truth only proved their descent from the one who is the origin of all wickedness.   Theirs was a complete perversity as compared with the sinlessness of Jesus.   Owing to their self-righteousness and according to their standards it was easy for them to accuse not only publicans and sinners, but also such as, though walking in the statutes of the Lord, failed to keep all the ordinances and traditions of the elders.   But "which of you convinceth [convicteth] *Me* of sin?"   Their own depravity was so great that, had Jesus "led them into sin, they would have followed, or spoken lies, they would have believed"; [5)]   but now that He spoke the truth, they, because of their corrupt nature, believed Him not.   Manifestly this sad condition was both the result and the evidence of their paternity.   "He that is of God heareth God's words; ye therefore hear them not because ye are not of God."

John 8, 33—59.   20.

To this stinging rebuke the Jews replied with a coarse invective. "Say we not well that Thou art a Samaritan and hast a devil?" Since Jesus refused to admit their true Abrahamic ancestry, they

19, 3) Ex. 34, 15; Lev. 17, 7; Is. 57, 3.
      4) Dods sub John 8, 43.   5) Dods sub John 8, 45.

retorted with the taunt that Jesus was no pure Jew, but a Samaritan heretic and as such Himself a child of the devil. (By the way, this shows how intensely the Jews hated the schismatic Samaritans.) Gently the Lord puts the taunt aside, as it were. "I have not a devil." "The dishonor does not stir His resentment"; for "I seek not Mine own glory." "Nevertheless, on account of His nature [because He is true God] His glory is not to be turned into reproach";[1] for "there is One that seeketh it and judgeth." Those who dishonor the Son of God will one day be judged; and this judgment will be according to His Word.[2] But from this judgment there is an escape in the time of grace: "Verily, verily,[3] I say unto you, If a man keep[4] My saying, He shall never see death." But this death-abolishing claim confirmed the Jews in their opinion that Jesus was demented and demon-possessed. "Now we know that Thou hast a devil. Abraham is dead and the prophets, and Thou sayest, If a man keep My saying, he shall never taste of death. Art Thou greater than our father Abraham, which is dead? And the prophets are dead. Whom makest Thou Thy-

"Before Abraham Was, I Am." self?" Once more Jesus tells them that He was not seeking His own glory. But this is a matter in which the Father is involved, "of whom ye say that He is your God." Now, if Jesus will disavow His knowledge of God and say: "I know Him not, I shall be a liar like unto you." And as far as Abraham is concerned: "Abraham rejoiced to see My day; and he saw it and was glad." The very Abraham in whose parentage they gloried sought salvation through Christ and received it of Him. But the statement about Abraham's seeing the day of Jesus the Jews completely misunderstood. If Jesus claimed that Abraham had seen the days of Jesus, then Jesus must have seen the days of Abraham. A true deduction, but it appeared ridiculous to them in the highest degree. "Then said the Jews unto Him, Thou art not yet fifty years old,[5] and hast Thou seen Abraham?" But even in that sense Jesus solemnly answers the question in the affirmative. "Verily, verily, I say unto you, Before Abraham was, *I am*." No stronger affirma-

---

20,   1) Dods sub John 8, 50.   2) John 5, 23. 24.

3) Notice again that John repeats the ἀμήν. Cp. 1, 51; 3, 5. 11; 8, 51. 58.

4) Τηρεῖν, in the sense of accepting by faith. Compare John 14, 15—24.

5) A round number, sufficiently exact for their purpose and not used to indicate the age of Jesus. Dods *sub loco*.

tion of the eternal existence of Jesus occurs anywhere in Scripture.[6] But this blessed truth is as blasphemy in the ears of His adversaries — claiming equality with the eternal I AM.[7] "Then took they up stones to cast at Him." These they could easily pick up because the unfinished state of the Temple could supply them with such close at hand.[8] But Jesus would not permit Himself to be harmed that way. Unperceived He slipped out of the Temple, "going through the midst of them, and so passed by."

John 9, 1—41.   **21.**

As Jesus "passed by," probably on the next day,[1] at any rate on a Sabbath, He saw a man who was "blind from his birth." We are not told where He met him, but we assume that it was in Jerusalem, in the neighborhood of the Pool of Siloam and the Temple, if not at one of the gates of the Temple itself, where the objects of pity and charity were wont to gather.[2] At the sight of him the disciples of Jesus — who were again in the company of their Master[3] — asked Him: "Master, who did sin, this man or his parents, that he was born blind?" In spite of their long contact with Jesus they were still so thoroughly Judaistic as to think that each particular sickness or sorrow was directly traceable to some particular sin. But Jesus answered: "Neither hath this man sinned nor his parents," as accounting directly for this lifelong affliction. Indirectly of course, it was the result of sin in general. Rather, by means of this affliction "the works of God should be made manifest in him." And therefore the proper question was not where the suffering had come from, but what was to be done with it.[4] In the brief spell of fleeting time works of mercy brook no delay. As applied to Himself as well as to all His followers, Jesus says: "I[5] must work the works of Him that sent Me while

---

20, 6) Dods sub John 8, 58.   7) Ex. 3, 14.

     8) See 15. Josephus, *Ant.*, XX, IX, 7.

21, 1) It is impossible to determine the exact date. But the definite mention that it was a Sabbath (v. 14) rather indicates that it was not the same day on which the Jews tried to stone Jesus. Bruce *sub loco.*

     2) Acts 3, 2. At the Beautiful Gate, the eastern gate of the Temple leading into the Treasury, or Court of the Women. However, the blind man was not begging, because it was the Sabbath-day. Edersheim, II, 178.

     3) There was no direct mention of them in John since the sermon on the Bread of Life in Capernaum, 6, 67. But it is only natural to suppose that they had accompanied the Savior to the Feast of Tabernacles.

     4) Dods sub John 9, 3.

     5) Ἐμὲ δεῖ. Some manuscripts have ἡμᾶς δεῖ.

it is day," that is, while there is still the day of life; for "the night cometh when no man can work." This is in accordance with the purpose of His coming, as explained in His discourse of the previous day.[6] "As long as I am in the world, I am the Light of the world." Neither does Jesus lose any time in putting the proverbial expression of working while it is day into practise and in proving that He is indeed the Light of the world. "When He had thus spoken, He spat on the ground and made clay of the spittle; and He anointed[7] the eyes of the blind man with the clay." Not as if any virtue lay in this particular mode of healing,[8] or as if by this action Jesus in any way passed upon the

Healing of a Man Born Blind.

medical practises and beliefs of the day;[9] but in order to impress upon the afflicted man that the healing came from Him. For the purpose of placing additional emphasis the direction is given: "Go, wash in the Pool of Siloam." From this pool[10] the water was taken for the ceremony of the pouring of water on the last day of the Feast of Tabernacles to symbolize the pouring out of the Holy Spirit. The evangelist adds: "which is, by interpretation, Sent."[11] Thus the living water of the pool is connected with the Water of Life, the Light of the world and the Sent[12] of the Father. Not doubting and without a moment of hesitation the blind man "went his way therefore and washed and came seeing."

John 9, 1—41.   22.

But the miracle led to serious results. At the return of the healed man to his home the neighbors and those who had known him as a blind beggar could hardly believe their eyes. "Is not this he that sat and begged?" While some were certain as to his identity, others doubted on account of his altered appearance, doubts, however, that were scattered by the former blind man's emphatic "I am he." But how did it happen? Thereupon the amazed neighbors made him repeat the story of his cure. A man whom he at the time could not see and who even now was unknown

---

21, 6) 8, 12.   7) Or covered.

8) For in other cases of blindness He did not employ it, *e. g.,* Mark 10, 46 f. Compare also Mark 8, 23, the healing of the blind man at Bethsaida.

9) It is quite unnecessary to adduce citations.

10) See No. 8.

11) Ἀπεσταλμένος, שָׁלוּחַ, *missus.* Compare Is. 8, 6 f. Dods *sub loco.*

12) Gal. 4, 4.

to him, called Jesus, made clay, anointed his eyes, and told him to
go to the Pool of Siloam and wash his eyes, which he did, with
the result that he recovered his sight.[1]   A most astounding cure,

Questioned by His Neighbors.

simplicity itself and yet
a true miracle.   Yet on
account of one particular they felt that something was not quite
in order, and if the marvelous tale did not fail of confirmation,
there was a possibility that the deed itself might lack proper
authorization.   They therefore asked: "Where is He?"   And when
the man answered, "I do not know," they took him to the Pharisees,[2] by whom they had been taught that except in mortal danger
the use of medicine, even the application of spittle on the eyes,
was a breach of the Sabbath if such action was intended as
a remedy.[3]   "And it was the Sabbath-day when Jesus made the clay
and opened his eyes," and the mixing of clay was labor, the work
of a mason, not to mention the order to go and wash himself,
which was an unnecessary piece of work on the Sabbath.   Thus
for dogmatic reasons and out of horror at the neglect of a Sabbath
superstition they entirely overlooked the fact that this was a unique
miracle of mercy.

John 9, 1—41.   23.

Immediately the Pharisees [1] arrange for a hearing.   Again the
miracle is described and its being a deed of mercy disregarded.
Rabbinic wisdom as represented by some of the assembly decides:
"This man is not of God because He keepeth not the Sabbath-day."
The miracle is not denied for the present, but it cannot be a work

Examined by the Pharisees.

of God because it was done
on a Sabbath.   But others
said: "How can a man who is a sinner do such miracles?"   Whether
it was a Sabbath or not, how can such a work be done at all by
a sinner?   "And so there was a division among them." [2]   And
being in a quandary, they asked the blind man his opinion.   To the
best of his knowledge and to the extent of his faith he promptly
answered: "He is a prophet."   Without presuming to enter into
the controversy, he was at least convinced that his benefactor was
of God.

22, 1) Ἀνέβλεψα, looked up.

       2) John 8, 13.   3) Edersheim, II, 182. Farrar, II, 83.

23, 1) Not the Sanhedrin, but an informal, yet apparently responsible
(v. 34) group of a local authority.

       2) Σχίσμα ἦν ἐν αὐτοῖς.

John 9, 1—41. **24.**

More information is needed. Probably it was no miracle at all! A fraudulent agreement between Jesus and the man was now suspected, which was not dispelled until the man's parents had been called. These were showered with questions: Is he your son? Was he really born blind? And if so, "how, then, doth he now see?" The first two questions the parents promptly answered in the affirmative. But as to the next question they shammed ignorance in their own interest and referred the question to their son. "He is of age; ask him; he shall speak for himself." Not as if the parents were ignorant of the miracle or ungrateful to Jesus; it was fear which prompted the answer, because already

Consultation with the Parents. the Jews, as incorporated in the Sanhedrin, had agreed that, if any man confessed that Jesus was the Christ, he should be excommunicated.[1] There were three degrees to this excommunication. The first rebuke, or admonition (*neziphah*), if formally pronounced, lasted thirty days. At the end of that term there was a second admonition (*niddui*), which also lasted thirty days. If the person so visited occupied an honorable position, the sentence was expressed in a euphemistic manner: "Methinks thy companions are separating from thee." And if the culprit was still impenitent, he was solemnly laid under the ban, or final excommunication (*cherem*), the duration of which was indefinite and which, accompanied with curses, entirely cut him off from intercourse with his fellows. Henceforth he was like one dead.[2] No wonder the parents of the formerly blind son dreaded to commit themselves. "This punishment to persons so poor as the parents of a beggar would practically have meant ruin and death." [3] "Therefore said his parents, He is of age; ask him."

John 9, 1—41. **25.**

But "the son was made of sturdier stuff." [1] What did he care about such an excommunication! If he had to choose, he would rather be socially dead than physically blind, not to mention the debt of gratitude which he owed to his Benefactor. Again they called him and said to him: "Give God the praise," [2] that is, tell

---

24, 1) Ἀποσυνάγωγος γένηται, unsynagogued, or put out of the synagog.
    2) See Edersheim, II, 183. 184, or Dods sub John 9, 22.
    3) Dods *sub loco.*
25, 1) Farrar, II, 85.   2) See Josh. 7, 19.

the truth. He was placed under oath, as it were. "We know that this man is a sinner," a desecrater of the Sabbath-day and as such an ungodly man. But the man was unable or unwilling to enter into these speculations. "Whether He be a sinner or no I know not." He knew only one thing, "that, whereas I was blind, now I see." Then they began to subject him to a tiresome cross-examination. "What did He to thee? How opened He thine eyes?" But no more of that! Should he needlessly repeat his testimony just because they had not listened? Or was it that they were wishing to become disciples of Christ? "But no more galling gibe could be flung into their teeth" [3]) than this man's "Will ye also be His disciples?" This was more than they would bear. Expressing their true sentiment in the matter, they began to revile him.

Faith in Christ Confessed. "Cast Out."

"Thou art His disciple, but we are Moses' disciples." Again their championship of Moses and the Law. "We know that God spake unto Moses." But "as for this fellow," [4]) they claimed, "we know not whence He is." Even to the untrained mind of the former blind beggar this wilful ignorance in the face of the undeniable miracle was altogether inconceivable. What astounding ignorance! "Herein is a marvelous thing that ye know not from whence He is, and yet He hath opened my eyes." Should it really be said that a former blind beggar must give these pharisaic doctors a lesson in logic? "Now, we know that God heareth not sinners," but only those that worship Him and do His will. From the miracle which had been performed it was certain that God had heard Jesus. And it was an astounding miracle; for "since the world began, was it not heard that any man opened the eyes of one that was born blind." And therefore this Man is not a Sabbath-defiling sinner, but is from God. For "if this Man were not of God, He could do nothing." But should this miserable beggar, this cursed member of the ignorant mob,[5]) teach *them?* *"Thou* [6]) wast altogether born in sin," reproaching him even for his calamity,[7]) "and dost thou teach *us*," [8]) the pure and godly? Such audacity! And they kicked him out,[9]) not only from the hall, but also from the synagog.

25,   3) Dods *sub loco.*   4) Τοῦτον.   5) 7, 49.
    6) Σύ.   7) 9, 3.   8) Ἡμᾶς.
    9) The word here used is ἐξέβαλον. Compare Luke 6, 22; John 16, 2.

John 9, 1—41. **26.**

But Jesus heard that the man whom He had given his sight had been excommunicated. As He had wished and sought to do, He found him and asked him: "Dost thou believe in the Son of God?" The healed man was a believing Israelite and as such placed his faith in the Messiah, of whom he knew that He was the Son of God. His answer was an admission of this faith, but also an expression of his ignorance as to Messianic identification. "Who is He, Lord, that I might believe on Him?" He did not doubt that Jesus, whom he had already declared to be a prophet,[1] could tell him who the Messiah was. Jesus answered: "Thou hast both seen Him, and it is He that talketh with thee." This blessed revelation was immediately accepted in faith. Here the Light of the world did not shine in vain. Sinking to his knees and worshiping Jesus as God,[2] he exclaimed: "Lord, I believe." Summing up the sig-

His Faith Acknowledged by Christ.

nificance of the miracle, Jesus said: "For judgment[3] I came into the world," that is, to bring to light and to exhibit the actual inward state of men, "that they which see not might see and that they which see might be made blind." Those who are by penitent admission spiritually blind shall receive spiritual sight, while those who presume to have spiritual light, while in reality they are stone-blind, shall be hopelessly darkened. But immediately this oxymoron[4] was attacked. The Pharisees, who were again dogging the footsteps of Jesus, correctly feared that the saying reflected upon them. "Are we blind also?" they asked. Christ's answer was: "If ye were blind, ye should have no sin; but now ye say, We see; therefore your sin remaineth." For penitent sinners there is the light of forgiveness. But to those who bask themselves in the deceptive light of self-righteousness the darkness of non-forgiveness remains. By their rejection of Jesus the Pharisees had shown that they were truly blind. And if the leaders, the teachers, are blind, how can they whom they teach see?

John 10, 1—21. **27.**

From the character which the leaders and teachers of Israel had again displayed in the last few days it was extremely obvious that

---

26, 1) V. 17.

2) Προσεκύνησεν, used in the sense of divine worship.

3) Εἰς κρίμα. Not the act of judging, κρίσις, but the result, κρίμα. Luke 2, 35: "that the thoughts of many hearts may be revealed."

4) Meyer *sub loco.* For the figure see 1 Cor. 1, 18 ff.

they were utterly unfit for their professed work of feeding the flock of God.[1]) It was only too apparent that they were certainly not God's shepherds, having cast out the blind man miraculously healed, judging of Jesus as they did, and excommunicating every one who confessed that Jesus was the Christ. They had climbed into God's sheepfold, but not by the door of the Word and promise by which the Owner, God, had brought His flock into the fold. They were shepherds who had "climbed up some other way" and "attained rule and leadership over God's flock in the same manner and by the same right as a robber and a thief." [2]) This is the truth which Jesus solemnly [3]) explained in a beautiful parable, rather allegory, delivered, probably in the Temple, in continuation of the conversation which arose out of the healing of the blind man. In the East

The True Shepherd of the Sheep.

the flocks are driven at night through a portal into an enclosure which is surrounded by a protecting wall and left in the care of a gate-keeper, or guard. In the morning the shepherd comes to the corral, the gate-keeper opens the door, the shepherd raises his voice, and in the event a number of herds are sheltered in the same fold, the sheep that belong to his own herd will follow him as he calls them by name, and he leads them out. As has been proved by actual test,[4]) sheep will not follow the shepherd's clothes if worn by a stranger, but will flee from him, because they do not know the stranger's voice. Of course, not each detail of the parable must be pressed. The point is that unlike the Old Testament prophets, who pointed forward to Christ, the members of the present hierarchical party, like thieves and robbers, had broken into the herd and assumed authority over the people of God, misleading many, all but the true children of God, who in spite of force or persuasion would not permit themselves to be lured from the voice and promises of God. The parable itself is clear.[5]) What Jesus described happened every day in the Judean hills. But what He allegorically delivered He was compelled to explain. And that does not surprise us; for most of those who heard Him were not of His flock and knew not His voice.

27, 1) Edersheim, II, 188.

2) Edersheim, II, 189.

3) It was exceptional with Him to begin His discourse with a repeated amen.

4) Dods sub John 10, 2.

5) Παροιμία, more exactly, not parable, παραβολή of the Synoptists (because it is not a history), but allegory.

John 10, 1—21. **28.**

For the sake of His hearers and probably also for the sake of
assuring the excommunicated outcast [1] that it was not the Pharisees,
but Jesus who could admit to, and reject from, the fold of God,
the Savior Himself adds the solemn application: "I am the Door
of the sheep." Those who before Him had falsely assumed by their

**Jesus the Door
to the Sheepfold.** own misguiding directions to lead people
into communion with God are thieves and
robbers. But the real sheep of God had
not given heed to their word. Christ is the Door, and only through
Him, if a man enter in, shall he be saved. And led by Him, he
is privileged to enjoy the full pasture of the Gospel. But the thief,
especially the thief in spiritual matters, comes "for to steal and to
kill and to destroy." But Jesus has come for the purpose of giving
full, true, and everlasting life.

John 10, 1—21. **29.**

Continuing the same image, viewed from a different angle,
Christ says: "I am the Good Shepherd." [1] This He is in the
absolute sense, because "the Good Shepherd giveth His life for
the sheep." In contrast with this one Good Shepherd, who lays
down His life for the salvation of the flock, no shepherd deserves
the epithet "good," especially not those hirelings who preach that
which is in their own interest and in the face of danger, seeing
the wolf coming, flee shamefully and desert the sheep. The result
is the slaughter and dispersion of the sheep. But a good shepherd,
even in the literal sense, will fight wolves or thieves at the risk of
his life, just as a conscientious preacher of the Gospel will suffer all,
even martyrdom, rather than become unfaithful to his trust and
disloyal to his charge. And in another respect Christ is the Good
Shepherd, in contrast with all other shepherds, namely, regarding
the intimate knowledge and acquaintance between Himself and His

Christ the Good Shepherd. flock. So close and all-
embracing is that knowledge
and communion as is that between Himself and the Father in
heaven. According to the will of His heavenly Father and for the
salvation of His sheep, this Shepherd, freely and unforced, lays

---

28, 1) Dods *sub loco.*

29, 1) Ὁ ποιμὴν ὁ καλός. "Good" probably in the sense in which we
speak of a "good" painter or a "good" architect. Dods sub John 10, 11.

down His life.[2]   And since this ransom is for the whole world, He wants to gather also other sheep besides those of the house of Israel into His fold.   "And they shall hear My voice, and there shall be one fold and one Shepherd," one holy Christian Church, the communion of saints, scattered throughout the world, in whatever visible Church they may be.   They are all His by the Father's gift and design.   And the chief proof of His Shepherd love is that He will lay down His life for His sheep.   Because of this consummate act of love His father loves Him.   In the laying down of His life is implied that He will take it again.   "No man taketh it from Me, but I lay it down of Myself.   I have power to lay it down, and I have power to take it again."   The sacrifice on the cross must be followed by the return to life; otherwise His entire ministry would have been rendered void.   And in this act of disposing of His life and taking it again, according to the divine plan of salvation, He again is in full harmony with the Father, whose commandment [3] He has received for the salvation of the world.

John 10, 1—21.   30.

The immediate effect of these blessed and comforting truths was another [1] division among the Jews.   Some held that Jesus was mad and possessed of a demon.   But to this insinuation others objected.   His words were

The Effect of the Discourse.

not the usual ravings of demonized persons.   And as to His acts, they were not satanic, not such as are performed by him who is a murderer from the beginning.[2]   And besides, "can a devil open the eyes of the blind?"

29, 2) Bengel (quoted by Edersheim, II, 229) points out a fourfold parallelism in the words of Christ, but of an antithetic character, and with descending and ascending climax: —

Descending		*Ascending*
The hireling	antithetic	I
Is an hireling		Am a Good Shepherd
Careth not for his sheep		Know the sheep
Fleeth		Lay down My life

3) Ἐντολή, authorization as embracing the ἐξουσία both to die and to rise again.

30, 1) V. 16.

     2) 8, 44.

CHAPTER XXI

THE FINAL WITHDRAWAL OF JESUS FROM GALILEE AND THE LATER JUDEAN MINISTRY.

End of October to middle of December, 782 A. U. C., 29 A. D.

Luke 9, 51.[1]   **1.**

After the Feast of Tabernacles, in the autumn of 29 A. D., Jesus seems to have returned once more to Galilee, which province,

Leaving Galilee as a Field of Operations. however, He was soon to leave finally as a field of operations. The days for His taking up [2] as ordained by God [3] were at hand. In fact, the beginning of the end had come as Jesus "steadfastly set His face to go to Jerusalem." But while

---

1, 1) There is an interval of about two months between verses 21 and 22 in John 10, Tabernacles to Dedication, unless (which seems unlikely) this interval is to be placed between John 8, 59 and 9, 1. Though John does not mention the fact, there is little doubt that after His visit of the Temple at the Feast of Tabernacles Jesus returned to Galilee and shortly afterwards took His final departure southward, returning to Jerusalem for the Feast of Dedication, retiring to Perea, returning to Bethany for the raising of Lazarus, withdrawing to Ephraim, and then making His final journey to Jerusalem in the spring of 30 A. D. The intermission between Tabernacles and Dedication seems to be filled in by Luke 9, 51—13, 21. — John speaks of four journeys of Christ to Jerusalem: for the feasts of Tabernacles and Dedication, for the raising of Lazarus, and for the final visits at Bethany. Likewise it seems that there are corresponding breaks in Luke, to be arranged as follows: —

Tabernacles
    John 7, 10—10, 21, followed by Luke 9, 51—13, 21.
Dedication
    John 10, 22—10, 42, followed by Luke 13, 22—17, 10.
Raising of Lazarus
    John 11, 1—54, followed by Luke 17, 11—19, 28 and parallels.
Arrival at Bethany
    John 11, 55—12, 11, followed by Luke 19, 29 and parallels.
    (But for the sequence of this portion of the Lord's ministry there seem to be as many arrangements as there are inquirers. See Andrews, 365—385. After repeated comparisons we have come to the conclusion that the order which we have adopted is preferable.)

2) Ἀνάληψις. The term occurs in the New Testament only here. However, since ἀναλαμβάνεσθαι is the customary term for reception into heaven, Mark 16, 19; Acts 1, 2. 11. 22; 1 Tim. 3, 16, this word ought to offer no particular difficulty. For harmonistic reasons Wieseler offers this explanation: When the days drew to an end in which He found a taking up, reception, in Galilee, He journeyed to Jerusalem to work there. *Synopsis,* 297.

3) Just as in the conception of John the glorification of Christ included the Passion, so in the conception of Luke the assumption into heaven included the crucifixion.

the face of Jesus was set towards Jerusalem, His mind was still
occupied with other things. And the reader of the gospel forgets
all about the cross as he peruses the deeply interesting pages of
intervening events.[4]

Luke 9, 52—56.   **2.**

At His departure from Galilee it was the intention of Jesus
to proceed southward through Samaritan territory. Although there
was no love lost between the Jews and the Samaritans, it was not
an unusual thing for Galileans to cross Samaria in their journeys
to and from Jerusalem.[1] In the beginning of His ministry Jesus
Himself made this journey.[2] And for the purpose of securing
lodging for Himself and His party He sent messengers to a village
of the Samaritans. But these returned with the report that the
villagers declined to receive Him. When Jesus made that early
journey through Samaria, the Samaritans were not only glad to
receive Him, but anxious to have Him stay with them.[3] But now
the circumstances were different. At that time, attended by a few
followers, He abode with them. But now, acclaimed by multitudes,
His face "was as though He would go to Jerusalem." That was

The Inhospitable Samaritans. different. They had heard
                                   something about His being
the Jewish Messiah-King, — misunderstood, of course. And they
would not so much as provide a Jewish Messiah with the ordinary
necessities of life if He were to set up a kingdom in Jerusalem
instead of, as they hoped, restoring and glorifying the worship on
Mount Gerizim.[4] The refusal of the Samaritans to receive their
Master filled the disciples, especially James and John,[5] with the
hottest indignation. Personally convinced, as they were, of the
nearness of the Messianic kingdom, they would now usher it in
with a flare of Sinaitic blaze. "Lord, wilt Thou that we command
fire to come down from heaven and consume them, even as Elias
did?"[6] Thus they seem to justify their fiery proposal with the
example of Elijah. Whether or not the brothers received the name
of Boanerges, or Sons of Thunder, from this circumstance we do

---

1,   4) Bruce *sub loco.*
2,   1) *Ant.,* XX, VI, 1.
      2) John 4, 4.   3) John 4, 40.
      4) See Meyer *sub* John 4, 25 and Luke 9, 53.
      5) Whether they were the messengers, as has been thought by some, is
not apparent from the text.
      6) 2 Kings 1, 10—12.

not know.[7] But Jesus rebuked them and said: "Ye know not what manner of spirit ye are of." The action of Elijah, whom they had seen on the Mount of Transfiguration, is not disparaged, but that was a different matter. As His followers they were not to reflect Sinai and Carmel, but Hermon, Calvary, and His spirit. "For the Son of Man is not come to destroy men's lives, but to save them." To the Samaritans, for the present, the rejection of grace and salvation was punishment enough. And therefore "they went to another village."

Luke 9, 57—62.[1] **3.**

In this period there occurred a repetition of application for discipleship,[2] related by Matthew in connection with the Gadarene journey. As it happens to others in public life, so also in the extended ministry of our Savior there was a recurrence of circum-

Application for Discipleship. stances which gave occasion to a similarity of actions or replies. Jesus was always on the outlook for competent assistants and eager to use such as were available. But in many instances, whether they were invited or whether they presented themselves, these prospects for discipleship were not "fit for the kingdom of God."

Luke 10, 1—12. **4.**

The fundamental rules for those who were privileged to labor side by side with Jesus were laid down in the mission of the Twelve in Galilee.[1] And as others were sent out, they received substantially the same instructions. So also in this time of our Lord's closing ministry, when a group of seventy from the outer circle of disciples received their commission for an extensive "go your ways." From which point these disciples were sent out we are unable to determine. But on account of the sad words uttered over the Galilean cities' rejection of opportunity,[2] to which is added the recent rejection of the Samaritans, we surmise that it was in Southern Galilee and before Christ's crossing of the Jordan into Perea. The immediate purpose of this mission was to make preparation for the reception

---

2, 7) See chapter XI, 7. Mark 3, 17.
3, 1) Compare chapter XIII, 2. Matt. 8, 19—22.
    2) Ἐν τῷ ὁδῷ does not mean on the way to the next village, but in the general period which has been introduced by Luke as the death journey to Jerusalem.
4, 1) Chapter XIV, 5 ff. Matt. 10, 1—42.
    2) Vv. 13—15.

of Jesus in those parts of the land of Israel, especially in Perea and Judea,[3] where He was still comparatively unknown. Neither do we know the reason for the particular number seventy,[4] which is considered by some as symbolic of the spreading of the Gospel in all the world, since the inhabitants of the earth were supposed to have been divided into seventy nations. What surprises us

The Mission of the Seventy.

is the comparatively large number of efficient workers for a temporary mission. They were sent out two by two for the purpose of publicity in the places which the Savior intended to visit. The instructions differed from those issued to the Twelve in this, that they were briefer and that the restrictions about not visiting the Gentiles and the Samaritans were omitted, and less ample miraculous powers seem to have been bestowed upon them.[5]

Luke 10, 13—16.   5.

Though Jesus left faithful hearts behind, it was with sorrow that He started from the scenes of His glorious, but rejected ministry. The base ingratitude of the highly exalted Galilean

The Doom of the Impenitent Cities.

towns moved Him to repeat the woes which He had uttered on a previous occasion.[1] But the disciples should not be discouraged on account of the rejection with which the gracious ministry of Jesus was attended. The Lord assures them as well as every true servant of His: "He that heareth you heareth Me; and He that despiseth you despiseth Me; and he that despiseth Me despiseth Him that sent Me."

Luke 10, 17—24.   6.

The ministry of the Seventy seems to have been of brief duration. Strange things were joyfully reported to Jesus on their return. They were especially elated over the fact, it seems, that they had been able to accomplish more than had been expected or promised. "Lord, even the devils are subject unto us through Thy

---

4,   3) 10, 38.

4) A number of manuscripts read seventy-two, supposed to be a more exact fixing of the number, in accordance with the product 12×6. Meyer sub critical remarks. Or the selection may have been made with reference to the seventy (originally seventy-two) elders of the people. We follow the reading of the *textus receptus,* which has seventy.

5) Matt. 10, 8.

5,   1) Matt. 11, 21—24. Chapter XII, 5.

name." But while Jesus shared the joys of this outer circle of disciples, their report was no news to Him. While they were working, He saw Satan falling. "I beheld Satan as lightning fall from heaven." He who had left his celestial habitation to become the god of this world [1] was falling from the pinnacle of his power. But as the lightning descends in a flash and is suddenly extinguished, so Jesus saw how the foul flash of Satan had reached the end of its course. "For this pur-

The Return of the Seventy.

pose the Son of God was manifested, that He might destroy the works of the devil." [2] And this power of successfully opposing the devil was also transmitted to the disciples of Jesus. Thus they were able to "tread on serpents and scorpions," symbols of Satan, and given power "over all the power of the enemy; and nothing shall by any means hurt you." [3] In the exercise of their duties they could at all times be assured of the protecting hand of God. But lest they be tempted to self-reliance and become overjoyed at their personal success, a warning word is given. The most important point for the individual Christian is not that he has been successful in an engagement with Satan, but that his name is "written in heaven." That is the greatest glory which a Christian can obtain; not that he has accomplished a great deed, be it even the performance of a miracle in the name of Christ, but that his name is inscribed in the Book of Life.[4]

Luke 10, 17—24.   7.

And rejoicing with and over His disciples, Jesus repeated the great "devotional utterance" which He had previously expressed.[1] In the Lord's ministry there were not only seasons of sadness, but also seasons of Savior joy. "In that hour Jesus rejoiced in spirit and said, I thank Thee, O Father, Lord of heaven and earth, that Thou hast hid these things from the wise and prudent and hast revealed them unto babes; even so, Father, for so it seemed good in Thy sight." What the custodians of wisdom, the scribes and

The Joy of Christ.

Pharisees, did not see, the salvation of Christ, was beheld by uneducated disciples, novices and babes, as it were, according to the will and by the revelation of God. Turning to His disciples and addressing them in the same words with which at a previous time the explana-

---

6, 1) 2 Cor. 4, 4.   2) 1 John 3, 8.
    3) Compare Mark 16, 18.   4) Farrar, II, 133.
7, 1) Bruce sub Luke 10, 22. Matt. 11, 25—27. Chapter XII, 6.

tion to the parable of the Sower had been introduced,[2] Jesus impresses upon them in particular the glory of their blessed privilege as followers and believers: "Blessed are the eyes which see the things that ye see; for I tell you that many prophets and kings have desired to see those things which ye see and have not seen them, and to hear those things which ye hear and have not heard them."

Luke 10, 25—37.   **8.**

From the glorious promise of the Gospel as simply accepted by those of childlike faith to a matter of dialectic subtlety as presented by one who represented the prudent and the wise! [1] Just where it was that a certain lawyer, "an expert in Jewish Canon Law," [2] "stood up" for the purpose of involving Jesus in a legal difficulty, we do not know; probably in a synagog, although no reference is given.[3] It was a momentous question which he put to Jesus, concerning life everlasting. About what could and should a man be more concerned? But the question was not asked in good faith; for he *"tempted* Him, saying, Master, what shall I do to inherit eternal life?" His purpose was not to learn something, but to involve Jesus in an unholy debate and to find reason for complaint. And at the bottom was the notion that eternal life is

The Question of the Lawyer.   the reward of merit and works. The only question

was what these works might be. "The idea of sin, guilt, and need of forgiveness had not entered his mind. It was that old Judaism speaking without disguise." [4] Knowing Jesus' principle of appealing to Scripture, he was prepared for a response. The only difference was that, instead of giving the expected Scriptural answer, Jesus parried by asking him a question: "What is written in the Law? How readest thou?" The reply of the legal expert was natural enough. He pointed to the passages which as a part of the daily prayer every devout Jew was supposed to quote in

---

7,   2) Matt. 13, 16. 17.   Chapter XII, 20.
8,   1) V. 21.   2) Edersheim, II, 234.
    3) The silence in the records with respect to direct references of our Savior's teaching in the synagogs as compared with His earlier ministry is striking. Granted that, in the light of John 9, 22, Jesus had in all probability been placed under the ban of excommunication, the exclusion from one synagog did not involve exclusion from all or from the Temple, where a separate door was provided for the excommunicate. Compare Farrar and authorities quoted by him, II, 86. 113.
    4) Edersheim, II, 235.

connection with the words "Hear, O Israel; the Lord, our God, is one Lord," to wit: "Thou shalt love the Lord, thy God, with all thy heart, and with all thy soul, and with all thy strength, and with all thy mind; and thy neighbor as thyself." [5]   What other answer could be given?   Every Jewish child knew the words.[6] They were inscribed upon the threshold of the Jewish homes and inclosed in phylacteries, those little boxes which were suspended from their necks.[7]   From the standpoint of the Law there was no other answer.   Jesus Himself would have given this answer; in fact, on another occasion He did do so.[8]   And therefore Jesus replied: "Thou hast answered right."   But since the Lord was aware that the question was not propounded because the lawyer was interested in the true way to life, He added: *"This do, and thou shalt live."* But the lawyer frustrated Christ's purpose, which was to lead him to examine himself.   In his spiritual blindness he considered this the opening he had been waiting for.   That he loved God with all his heart, soul, strength, and mind, according to a "fourfold analysis of the inner man,"[9] he was fully assured of.   No failure on his part there!   But as to the second part, notwithstanding his correct answer, that he believed, was not so easily settled as the answer of Jesus "This do" seemed to imply.   True, the love of the neighbor was commanded in the Law, but a person must know who his neighbor is.   That gave him the chance to advance the problem under cover of which the tempting question had been introduced in the first place.   "But he, willing to justify himself, said unto Jesus, And who is my neighbor?"   In his opinion "neighbor" was an elastic term.   Had Jesus asked him for a definition, He would no doubt have received a reply in which the term *neighbor* would have been narrowed down to a restricted class of fellow-beings.   For the purpose therefore of showing the lawyer how far orthodox Judaism was from a true understanding, not to mention perfect observance, of the Law, of bringing him to a true knowledge of his sins, as well as of teaching all men of all times a lesson of neighborly love, He told the striking parable of the Good Samaritan.

8,   5) Deut. 6, 4. 5; Lev. 19, 18.

6) And the Rabbis were never weary of quoting the saying of Hillel, who summed up the whole Law in negative form (as compared with the positive statement of Jesus, Matt. 7, 12): "What is hateful to thee that do not to another." Chapter XI, 38. Tobit 4, 15. Edersheim, II, 236.

7) In a false interpretation of Deut. 6, 6.

8) Matt. 22, 37—40.

9) Bruce *sub loco*.

Luke 10, 25—37.   **9.**

"A certain man," probably a Jew, but for the purpose of teaching that the duty of love is independent of race, religion, and color, the man is intentionally presented as an unnamed human being who went down the rapidly descending [1] desert road from Jerusalem to Jericho. Somewhere along this notoriously insecure "Bloody Gorge" [2] the solitary traveler fell into the hands of robbers, who stripped him of his raiment, covered him with wounds, and left him as he was, half dead; and soon he would have breathed his last had not some one come to his help. [3] Now, it happened, by a "providential combination of circumstances" that a certain priest came down that way, which made it seem probable that help would be at hand when most needed. He had very likely returned from his weekly course of service in the Temple to

The Good Samaritan. his home at Jericho. [4] But in spite of the fact that the wounded man was in full view of the priest and presented a sight fit to arouse compassion, "when he saw him," he quickly "passed by on the other side." Likewise an attendant of the priesthood, a Levite, with still cooler indifference, "came and looked on him and passed by on the other side." And why did they pass by? It was due to their wrong answer to the question, "Who is my neighbor?" and the fear lest they make some one the object of their love whom God had probably made the object of His wrath [5] — or simply to lack of love. It probably was the same spirit of quibbling in which nothing was sacred and which would prefer to speculate on the problem "Who is my neighbor?" rather than be spurred on to action by asking, "Whose neighbor am I?" [6] But the unexpected happened. Next a semiheathen Samaritan, of all men most despised and hated by the Jews, as he journeyed, came where the half-dead man was. Of him no Jew, probably not even the suffering man on the roadside, would have expected mercy, nor would he have made him the object of his mercy. It seems that the traveler was on a longer

---

9, 1) From 2,593 above to 820 feet below sea-level.

 2) Then and afterwards infested with marauders.

 3) Bruce *sub loco.*

 4) If Jericho was no priestly city (Meyer), as has usually been taken for granted (since Lightfoot), it was at least the residence of a large number of priests (Edersheim, II, 351).

 5) According to the Jewish view that sickness and misfortune are always the punishment for some grievous sin.

 6) Edersheim, II, 239.

journey [7] than merely from Jerusalem to Jericho. But he did not make haste or business his excuse for passing the unfortunate man by. Neither did he ask who the man was in order to ascertain whether or not he was his neighbor. Nor did he determine within a shade the extent of the maltreated sufferer's actual need. In less time than we have consumed in explaining this he saw him, had compassion on him, went to him, and made preparations to apply medical aid from his traveler's supply. "He bound up his wounds, pouring in oil and wine." On the bandages he poured a mixture of what was commonly regarded and used as a dressing for wounds. And then he lifted him up "on his own beast," which he would otherwise have mounted himself, and shuffled along beside until he arrived at an inn, where he could give him additional care. To all this he attended himself. Business or whatever awaited him at the end of his journey must be deferred. He himself spent the night with the wounded man, who no doubt had a high fever. Not until the next morning, when the patient had sufficiently improved, did he leave his side. Before leaving, however, he extracted from his purse two pence,[8] that is, about twice as much as the laborers in the vineyard received all day.[9] Entrusting these to the innkeeper, he charged him: "Take care of him; and whatsoever thou spendest more, when I come again, I will repay thee." — And now the application: "Which, now, of these three, thinkest thou, was neighbor unto him that fell among the thieves?" The answer is easy enough. All three were bound by the law of love to perform the deed of mercy described, but only one of them did it. And he was a Samaritan. The lawyer was honest enough to answer the question correctly. But lest we say too much in commendation of him, we must add that he was unwilling to take the hated name of the Samaritans on his lips and to give the whole detested nation credit for the kind deed of one. His answer was: "He that showed mercy on him." His periphrase was sufficient admission that a member of a schismatic nation had grasped and observed the true mandate of love where the very men had failed whose official duty it was to interpret the Law and to lead in the worship of God. This, then, was the burden of our Lord's final reply: "Go, and do thou likewise." The Lord, who "knew what was in

---

9,   7) Bruce *sub loco*. "Fully equipped." Also see v. 35.

8) Δύο δηνάρια, about 40 cents. One denarius was ordinarily the daily wage of a soldier or laborer.

9) Matt. 20, 2.

man,[10]) desired to impress this much-needed lesson upon the lawyer that he had failed to show that love to his fellow-men which the Samaritan had practised, that therefore he did not, as he imagined, love his neighbor as himself; much less, then,[11]) did he love God above all things.[12])

Luke 10, 38—42.   **10.**

It is impossible to trace the movements of Jesus in this period of His ministry. But there is hardly any doubt that the continuation of His wanderings, probably between Tabernacles and Dedication and after His final departure from Galilee, brought Him again to Judea, to the little town of Bethany,[1]) just a little east of Jerusalem, from which it was hidden by the Mount of Olives. Here He found hospitality in the home of a certain woman named Martha, who received Him into her house. Whether she was the wife or the widow or some other relative of Simon the Leper [2]) we do not know. The other known members of the household were a sister, Mary, and a brother, Lazarus. The latter, however, is not mentioned in this connection. He is not needed in this picture. Probably he was absent at the time. From the fact that Martha had charge of the household and that she is mentioned first we infer that she was the elder sister. Because the sisters received general sympathy at a later, sad occasion [3]) as well as because Mary used costly ointment for the

The "One Thing Needful."

used costly ointment for the anointing of Jesus,[4]) it is assumed that these disciples were "in easy circumstances and of sufficient dignity to attract the attention in their village as well as in Jerusalem." [5]) We picture to ourselves a stir in this house as the arrival of Jesus was probably announced by some of the Seventy during their mission tour. And especially Martha, being a very kind hostess, was exceedingly busy; she was "cumbered about much serving" and "careful and troubled about many things" in her efforts to provide entertainment that would be both worthy of Jesus and to the credit of her house. Mary, too, was eager to give Jesus a proper reception; but the expression of her devotion was of

---

9,   10) John 2, 25.   11) 1 John 2, 20.

12) Did the Lord here relate a true happening? The story could have happened, but it is usually regarded as a parable. The parable is clear in itself both as to contents and purpose.

10,   1) Compare John 11, 1.

2) Mark 14, 3; Matt. 26, 6.

3) John 11, 19. 33.   4) John 12, 3.

5) Farrar, II, 140. John 12, 9. 10. 17.

a different kind. Jesus arrived. But while Martha was all hustle and bustle and happily engaged in providing as best she could for the material comfort of her distinguished Guest, Mary dropped her work and sat at the feet of Jesus, as Martha thought, idly, and leaving all the troubles fall on her. While Mary listened to the words of Jesus, Martha was in no placid mood. Neither was she backward in expressing her mind. "Just like a bustling housewife, and even if Jesus be present, yes, and even if Jesus came in for a share of the blame!" [6] "Lord, dost Thou not care that my sister hath left me to serve alone? Bid her therefore that she help me." In His answer Jesus was both mindful of Martha's loving service and infinitely tender in supplying the needed correcting word. In no wise would He "pain, but only purify, the faithful heart" to which it was addressed.[7] "Martha, Martha, thou art careful and troubled about many things" — this in grateful recognition of her loving concern for Him. "But" — there is a but — "one thing is needful." After all, in His kingdom the important thing is not food, but the Word; not the body and the house, but the soul and the kingdom of God. "Mary hath chosen that good part, which shall not be taken away from her." Thus Mary is defended, and yet Martha is not repelled. For "Jesus loved Martha and her sister." [8] Nor does the Lord discourage the Marthalike deeds of love done unto Him. That is not the point here. In this instance well-meaning Martha permitted something to keep her from Jesus. While we must place everything at the disposal of Jesus and His Word, there is nothing that should separate us from Jesus, be it time, money, or service. In the proper coordination and relation of values first things must come first. "One thing is needful." This is an absolute truth. For this there is no substitute. Otherwise it would not be the "one thing needful."

Luke 11, 1—4.[1]   **11.**

In their wanderings through Perea it was but natural for the disciples to be reminded of the activities of John. The scenes of his labor brought back to memory his message of repentance, his baptism, his great earnestness and austere life, and especially also his life of prayer. Noticing how Jesus often resorted to prayer, one of His disciples, probably one of the outer circle, who had not

---

10, 6) Bruce *sub loco.*   7) Farrar, II, 142.   8) John 11, 5.
11, 1) Compare Matt. 6, 9—13. Chapter XI, 29.

been with Jesus when He preached the Sermon on the Mount, but had joined Him at a later period or came to Him from the company of John, made the request: "Lord, teach us to pray as John

Christ Again Gives the Lord's Prayer.

also taught his disciples." Except for this notice, although it might have been assumed,[2] we should not have known that John had given his disciples particular instruction in prayer. Jesus gladly consented and repeated in substance the Lord's Prayer which He had already given on the day of the Sermon on the Mount.

Luke 11, 5—13.   **12.**

After Jesus had thus again taught His disciples to pray, He gave them the assurance that their prayers would be heard. They must, however, be instant and persistent in prayer, as He explains in the parable of the Importunate Neighbor. While a certain man was sleeping in his house, he was roused out of his slumber by the unexpected arrival of a friend, who was engaged in a journey. To travel by night in a hot climate is probably "not unseasonable from the traveler's point of view, but a midnight arrival is unseasonable from the standpoint of the people at home." [1] Having "nothing to set before him," he in turn roused his neighbor out of his sleep with the urgent plea to lend him three loaves of bread. But the neighbor protested against this unseasonable request. The door had been barred for the night, the children had retired, and he did not wish to be bothered nor have the whole household disturbed for such a trifling cause. "I cannot rise and give thee." But as the disturber suspected and the sequel shows, it was not so much the inability as the unwillingness of the man to comply with the request of the troublesome neighbor. However, there was no rest for him as long as the knocking continued. We can picture the situation to ourselves as we seem to hear how the urgent pleas were

The Importunate Friend.

repeated. And with this shameless disregard of his neighbor's private comfort and apparent indifference the importunate disturber succeeded in gaining his end. "I say unto you, though he will not rise and give him because he is his friend, yet because of his importunity he will rise and give him," not merely the requested three loaves, but "as many as he needeth." "The difficulty was not in the giving, but in the rising." [2] And this was overcome, if

---

11, 2) Luke 5, 33.
12, 1) Bruce *sub loco.*   2) Edersheim, II, 241.

not because of the mutual friendship, but through the importunity of the pleading neighbor. The point is clear, and the details of the parable need not be pressed. With that persistent knocking going on, the man could not sleep. And in order to be able to go back to sleep, he had to stop the noise. Now, if that slumber-loving sleeper could be forced to yield, how much more will our merciful Father in heaven grant the petitions we address to Him! So important is the lesson of unwearied perseverance in prayer, which may seem to verge on impudence, that the Lord repeats some of the sayings of the Sermon on the Mount.[3] "Ask, and it shall be given you; seek, and ye shall find; knock, and it shall be opened unto you. For every one that asketh receiveth; and he that seeketh findeth; and to him that knocketh it shall be opened." As the loving Father that He is the Lord will, however, not only grant the requests of His children, but will also not deceive them as to the nature of His gifts. Which loving father would give his son a stone when he has requested bread or hand him a serpent when he wants fish? Or if he shall ask for an egg, will he offer him a scorpion? Now, if human parents, whose disposition by nature is evil, will show so much affection for their children, how much more will our heavenly Father grant good gifts, the best gifts, yes, even the Holy Spirit, to them that ask Him!

Luke 11, 14—28.[1]   **13.**

In connection with the healing of a dumb demoniac, which must be placed in this period of the Lord's ministry, the same old blasphemous accusation of demoniacal dispossession by the help of Beelzebub was raised against the Savior as had been done in that portion of the Lord's ministry which we have called the second

The Healing of a Dumb Demoniac. preaching tour, just before the Parables by the Sea. And the Savior made substantially the same reply. "If Satan also be divided against himself, how shall his kingdom stand?" But repeated deeds and sayings in the life of our Savior need not surprise us. Like circumstances bring about like or similar actions, and similar objections are met, as they sometimes must be, with the same arguments. One part of this section, however, is new, though we are reminded of incidents of similar content generally.[2] After

---

12, 3) Matt. 7, 7—10.
13, 1) Compare Matt. 12, 22—30. 43—45. Chapter XII. 13. 16.
     2) Matt. 12, 46—50; Mark 3, 32—35; Luke 8, 19—21.

Jesus had defended Himself against the blasphemous accusation of being in league with the devil, an "honest matron of the large gathering lifted up her voice in blessing on the, to her probably unknown, mother of Jesus." [3) "Blessed is the womb that bare Thee and the paps which Thou hast sucked." The woman meant well. She thought and spoke like a mother who considers herself happy in the possession of a distinguished son. But Jesus points out to her that "true happiness, true blessedness, has a different basis, a different reason." [4) "The felicity of natural motherhood is entirely subordinate to that of discipleship." [5) "Yea, rather," Jesus said, addressing that woman in particular, but voicing a truth intended for the ears of all His hearers, "blessed are they that hear the Word of God and keep it."

Luke 11, 29—36.[1)   **14.**

As the multitudes closed in on Jesus from every side as the result of the healing of the demoniac and His self-defense over against the blasphemous Beelzebub theory, the Lord improved the opportunity to address them all. His cue for the discourse was taken from the request of a sign from heaven.[2) As if miracles were not sign enough! As on the former occasion, Jesus made a veiled reference to His resurrection and again pointed to the sign of Jonas and to what the queen of the South did, who on Judgment Day will condemn the Jews of Jesus' day.[3) From the extreme ends of the civilized earth the queen of Sheba had traveled in

The Sign of Jonas. Parable of the Eye Repeated.
search of the wisdom of a mere man, while here there stood before them one greater than Solomon, whose wisdom they had rejected. Again, the inhabitants of Nineveh repented at the preaching of Jonas; "and, behold, a Greater than Jonas is here." Instead of opposing and obscuring, His listeners should act as a light. This Jesus explains as He repeats the parabolic saying of placing the light on a candlestick and in the parable of the Eye. The reason why so many do not send forth a bright beam of light is because their "eye is evil,"

13, 3) Bruce *sub loco.*
   4) Kretzmann, I, 330.   5) Bruce *sub loco.*
14, 1) Compare Matt. 12, 38—42, chapter XII, 16; 5, 15, chapter XI, 20; 6, 22. 23, chapter XI, 31.
   2) Compare also Matt. 16, 1—4; Mark 8, 11. 12 (chapter XVII, 8); Luke 11, 11.
   3) 1 Kings 10, 1.

because they have no true understanding of God's Word, the heavenly light, in consequence of which their "body also is full of darkness," that is to say, all their works are contrary to the Word, works of darkness. The purpose of a light is to illuminate. And the function of a Christian is to be a light. But in order to serve this purpose, his whole body must be full of light.

15.

Luke 11, 37—54.[1])

While Jesus was still speaking to the people, He received and accepted an invitation of a Pharisee to dine [2]) with him. Why the invitation was extended is not stated, but from the contents of the table-talk it seems that it was not altogether prompted by courtesy.[3]) Jesus went into the house and sat down to meat [4]) without having previously washed [5]) His hands. "And when the Pharisee saw it, he marveled," to say the least.[6]) While Jesus ordinarily observed the regulations of the people, it seems that this neglect was deliberate. In this case non-observance of ceremonial ablutions amounted to a confessional act for the very reason that these ablutions were looked upon as legally binding. There were no direct objections raised, but from the disapproving hints and disgusted glances Jesus must have noticed that the Phar-

Jesus the Guest of a Pharisee.

isee and his company did not distinguish between the Ceremonial and the Moral Law. In their insistence upon externals the Pharisees were without a sense of right and wrong in things that really mattered. Thus the Lord [7]) pointed out that they were most scrupulous about cleansing the outside of the cup and the platter, while the inside and the food were the product of wickedness and plunder. Outside purity was stressed, while the heart was filled with sin. In their insistence upon strict adherence to external purification they entirely overlooked that "He that made that which is without did make that which is within." Why therefore so much stress on the former? And God is especially interested in the

---

15, 1) Compare Matt. 23, 1—36; Mark 12, 38—40; Luke 20, 45—47: Tuesday during Passion Week.

    2) Ἀριστᾶν, ἄριστον. The first of the two customary chief meals of the day.

    3) Compare Luke 14, 1.

    4) Ἀνέπεσεν, ἀναπίπτειν, recline at the table.

    5) Ἐβαπτίσθη, baptized.

    6) Compare Matt. 15, 2; Mark 7, 2, the disciples eating with unwashed hands. Chapter XVI, 13.

    7) Ὁ κύριος. Again, as often in Luke.

spiritual inside, in the purity of the heart. Now, if from a pure and generous heart the Pharisees would give alms from the inside of the cups instead of bothering so much about the outside, then all things would be clean unto them.

Luke 11, 37—54.   16.

This criticism of externalism is followed by a number of woes. Woe unto the Pharisees, who, being so scrupulously careful about paying the tenth [1] of every possible tithable commodity, even of aromatic seeds and fragrant herbs used as condiments or for medicinal purposes, such as mint, rue, anise, or dill, cumin, and "all manner of herb," [2] overlooked such very important matters as impartial and just judgment of their fellow-men and love of God!

Woes upon the Pharisees. Woe unto them for their love of prominence and for their desire to occupy the place of elders and rulers in the synagogs and local courts and to receive the respectful greetings of the people in the market-places! Woe unto them and also unto the scribes, hypocrites, who were like graves without the distinguishing mark of whitewash, so that those passing by could not help stepping on them and Levitically defiling themselves by a contact with the dead! [3] The whitewashing of graves was done every year on the fifteenth of Adar.[4] But in reality the Pharisees with all their falsehood and hypocrisy ought to be whitewashed themselves, so as to warn the people who came into daily contact with them.

Luke 11, 37—54.   17.

As Jesus uttered these strong words in a blanket denunciation of the Pharisees, a professional member of the party, a lawyer,[1] a scribe, spoke up: "Master, thus saying Thou reproachest us also." Up to this point he had been probably secretly enjoying the fearful denunciations of the "silly pietists and woman Pharisees"; [2] but

---

16, 1) Gen. 28, 22; Deut. 14, 23.

2) Compare Matt. 23, 23. Mint, peppermint, flourished all over the mountains in Palestine. Rue was a small shrub with a strong odor. The seeds of anise, or dill, have an aromatic flavor and are used as condiment in cooking and as a carminative in medicine. Cumin, resembling caraway in form and flavor (German, *Kuemmel*), also has carminative qualities and was used for flavoring various dishes, especially during feasts.

3) See Num. 19, 16; Ezek. 39, 15.

4) Meyer sub Matt. 23, 27.

17, 1) Luke 10, 25.

2) Edersheim, II, 212.

now he began to feel that in the attack of Jesus not only pharisaic bigotry and practise, but also the whole system of traditionalism was condemned. This expert on canon law had guessed correctly, for Jesus had called down woes upon the lawyers also. As a result of their findings and interpretations of the Law the lawyers imposed heavy burdens upon the people, but they themselves did not so much as stir a finger to bear them. "Ye lade men with burdens grievous to be borne, and ye yourselves touch not the burdens with one of your fingers." They erected tombs to the prophets with the idea of honoring them, but in reality they continued the prophet-killing work of their fathers. In dealing with Israel, God had perfected a plan as Jesus, the personified Wisdom of God Himself, expressed it: "Therefore also said the Wisdom of God, I will send them prophets and apostles," holy men of God in the Old Testament and the apostles in the New Testament, whom He had

Woes upon the Lawyers.

appointed. But what happened? "Some of them they shall slay and persecute." And what is the divine judgment upon them? Inasmuch as "this generation" had received greater grace than all previous generations of Israel, and since "this generation" had incurred greater guilt in rejecting Christ and His apostles, the blood of all the prophets and martyrs which "was shed from the foundation of the world will be required of this generation, from the blood of Abel," the first martyr, who also was considered a prophet, "unto the blood of Zacharias," the prophet mentioned in the last book of the Hebrew Bible, the Second Book of Chronicles, "which perished between the altar and the Temple." [3] For all these murders the present generation shall be held accountable. But the main responsibility must rest upon the lawyers. They

---

17, 3) According to the arrangement of our Bible the book of the prophet Malachi is the last book in the Old Testament. But the Hebrew arrangement is as follows: Genesis to Second Kings; Isaiah, Jeremiah, Ezekiel; the twelve minor prophets: Hosea to Malachi; Psalms, Proverbs, and the remaining books to First and Second Chronicles. Since the phrase "from the blood of Abel to the blood of Zacharias" is evidently a designation for the blood of the martyrs of the whole Old Testament canon, we have from the mouth of Jesus an implied argument against the apocryphal books of the Old Testament. — Matt. 23, 35 Zacharias is called "son of Barachias." Since Berechiah appears as the father of the *prophet* Zechariah (1, 1. 7), it has been contended that Barachias is a gloss, which through confusion has crept into the text. But the best explanation is that the Barachias of Matthew was either the father or the grandfather of the Zechariah in 2 Chron. 24, 20. According to the latter explanation Barachias would have had two names, Jehoiada Barachias.

were the teachers of the people and the interpreters of the Law. And this leads to the last woe. "Woe unto you, lawyers! For ye have taken away the key of knowledge; ye entered not in yourselves, and them that were entering in ye hindered." The words of prophecy were so clear that the people might have gained the proper understanding themselves. But the leaders stepped in with their false and carnal interpretations and deprived the people of the knowledge of salvation. The words are hard, but true. But instead of leading the opposition to a true appraisal of its own deficiency, the scribes and Pharisees began to be furiously inflamed at Jesus. In a practical admission that Jesus had told them the truth they treacherously lay in wait for Him, seeking for an opportunity to "catch something out of His mouth that they might accuse Him."

Luke 12, 1—12.[1)]   **18.**

While the scribes and Pharisees were pressing upon the Lord vehemently with captious questions after He had left the Pharisee's house, thousands of people gathered,[2)] insomuch that they trod one another down in their desire to hear and see Jesus. Following His custom, the Savior took the opportunity to address the multitudes upon those subjects which for His purposes best fitted their needs. This He did by directing His remarks to His disciples, yet turning at times expressly to the people, so that all could receive the benefit of His teachings. We are unable to trace the trend of thought,[3)] but the opening word is natural enough: "Beware ye of the

Former Sayings Repeated. leaven of the Pharisees, which is hypocrisy!" This reminds us of the departure of Jesus from Dalmanutha when His disciples had forgotten to take bread with them.[4)] The fact that this as well as the following subjects had been treated before need not cause us any uneasiness, because it was for the purpose of emphasis that

---

18, 1) The references for the repeated sayings in this section are given in the notes.

2) Μυριάδων, an "innumerable multitude." These words are not to be taken "hyperbolically." Of probably the "largest crowd mentioned anywhere in the gospels" (Bruce *sub loco*) we have only a fragmentary account. The gospels do not contain a complete Life of Christ as one of the gospelwriters himself admits in his concluding word: "And there are also many other things which Jesus did, the which, if they should be written every one, I suppose that even the world itself could not contain the books that should be written," John 21, 25.

3) Most likely the address has not been reported in full.

4) Matt. 16, 6. 11.   Chapter XVIII, 1.

Jesus repeated those things which He wanted to impress well upon the minds of His followers. The next sayings repeat words of comfort and encouragement, first given in connection with the mission of the Twelve.[5] The word of warning about the terrible sin against the Holy Ghost was already heard on that busy day in Capernaum preceding the Parables by the Sea.[6] And the final word about persecutions and the promised guidance of the Holy Spirit in defense of the truth was likewise included in the instructions given in the mission of the Twelve.[7]

Luke 12, 13—15.   **19.**

A momentary pause in an address of loftiest content is employed by one of the hearers for a request on a purely personal matter. A man who could thus speak with authority would certainly be of service in the one thing which at the time was to him the center of the universe. A very human trait as revealed to many men in public life by those whose horizon is bounded by self. There are always small people in quest of influence for personal reasons. In this case it was an heir in search of some one to help him settle an estate. "Master, speak to my brother that he divide the inheritance with me." Probably he was a younger brother,

Christ Refuses to Divide an Inheritance.

who had not received his share or was not satisfied with the prescribed division of one-third to the younger and two-thirds to the elder brother.[1] But true to the principle that the spiritual must be strictly separated from the temporal, Jesus showed that He was not interested in the case. "Man, who made Me a judge or a divider over you?" He was neither a judge to pass on the merits of the case nor an arbiter to carry out the judgment He would be inclined to make.[2] Very likely the man was a miser at heart. At any rate, Jesus saw fit to add the moral: "Take heed and beware of covetousness." Instead of appealing to Jesus to help apportion his share of earthly goods, he ought to have applied to Him for a portion of the treasures in heaven. For a man's life does not consist in worldly treasures, however much he may possess.

18, 5) Matt. 10, 26—32. Chapter XIV, 8.
    6) Matt. 12, 32. Chapter XII, 15.
    7) Matt. 10, 19. 20. Chapter XIV, 7.
19, 1) Deut. 21, 17.
    2) Bruce *sub loco.*

Luke 12, 16—21.   **20.**

This thought received additional explanation in the parable of the Rich Fool.[1]   The land of a certain man had "brought forth plentifully."   But instead of turning to God in humble gratitude for His rich blessings, the rich man had thoughts only of his own future enjoyment of them, without regard to faithful stewardship before God and his duty to fellow-men less fortunate than he, not to mention the possible loss of wealth and the uncertainty of

The Parable of the Rich Fool. the hour of death.   He thought only of enlarged barns wherein to store up all his fruits and all his goods.   "And I will say to my soul, Soul, thou hast much goods laid up for many years; take thine ease, eat, drink, and be merry."   But as he was thinking about the enjoyment of his possessions for many years to come, he did not even have the possession of days.   In boasting of the morrow, he was blind to the possibilities of even the present day.[2] In the midst of his godless meditations there was a terrible echo from heaven: "Thou fool, this night thy soul shall be required of thee; then whose shall those things be which thou hast provided?"   And the lesson?   "So is he that layeth up treasures for himself and is not rich toward God."[3]

Luke 12, 22—34.[1]   **21.**

The disciples again became the special audience of Jesus.   But we suppose that the multitude also listened as Jesus repeated portions of the Sermon on the Mount.   The section includes the warnings against anxiety about meat and clothing, in which Jesus points to the ravens; "for they neither sow nor reap," and to the lilies, "how they grow; they toil not, they spin not; and yet I say unto you that Solomon in all his glory was not arrayed like one

Repeating Former Sayings. of these."   And since it is God that clothes "the grass, which is to-day in the field and to-morrow is cast into the oven," the admonition is given to seek the kingdom of God, "and all these things shall be added unto you."   Here and there we find a slight variation in expression.   And there is another gem added to the

---

20,   1) Compare Ps. 49, 16—18; Ecclesiasticus 11, 18. 19; 1 Sam. 25, 11.
    2) Prov. 27, 1.
    3) *Εἰς θεὸν πλουτῶν.*   Rich with respect to those treasures laid up with God.
21,   1) Compare Matt. 6, 25—34, chapter XI, 34; vv. 19—21, chapter XI, 33.

string of pearls, as, for instance, when the disciples are encouraged with the words: "Fear not, little flock; for it is your Father's good will to give you the Kingdom." To receive this Kingdom should be the object of all our desires, all is to be sacrificed for it, and its coming is to be eagerly awaited.

Luke 12, 35—40.   22.

In watchful waiting for the Kingdom, "let your loins be girded about and your lights burning," that is, the mantle lifted up and the hem fastened to the belt for instant service, and your lamps lit, as the Lord explains in the parable of the Waiting Servants. Be like faithful servants, waiting for their master, who has gone to his wedding-feast and is expected to return with his bride. When the master returns and knocks at the door, every servant will be

The Parable of the Waiting Servants.

at his place and ready to receive him and give him joyful service. In a happy mood the master will reward such faithfulness in an exchange of roles. Girding himself, he will reward his servants with portions brought from the wedding-feast, especially if he will find them waiting in the second or third watch.[1] "Blessed are those servants." Thus the disciples of Christ should be ready and wait for His return to Judgment. This lesson of readiness is emphasized in another parable:[2] "If the goodman of the house had known what hour the thief would come, he would have watched and not have suffered his house to be broken through." To this the lesson is added: "Be ye therefore ready also; for the Son of Man cometh at an hour when ye think not."

Luke 12, 41—48.[1]   23.

At this point Peter raised the question whether the parable and its lesson was meant for the disciples or for all. The Lord[2] did not answer directly, but the continuation of His discourse indicated that the reference was primarily to believing disciples. The most faithful servants are placed by the master in positions of trust; for instance, the administration of the household and the dealing out of portions of food is entrusted to them. While faithfulness

---

22, 1) See Matt. 14, 25. According to ancient Jewish custom the night was divided into three watches, as compared with the Roman division of four. Compare Mark 13, 35.

2) Compare Matt. 24, 43. 44.

23, 1) Compare Matt. 24, 45—51, chapter XXX, 10.

2) Κύριος again used by Luke instead of the usual Jesus.

in high places is taken for granted, it is sometimes put to a test. And "blessed is that servant whom his lord when he cometh shall find so doing," performing his duty. His reward for faithful service is "that he will make him ruler over all that he hath." But if the servant, trusting in the delay of the master's return, is found beating the male and female slaves, eating and drinking, even

The Parable of the Wise Steward. becoming drunk, at the moment when the master unexpectedly returns, he will receive the punishment which his unfaithfulness deserves. The lord of that servant "will cut him in sunder [3]) and will appoint him his portion with the unbelievers." The punishment is severe, but it is according to the demands of responsibility and trust. The servant who knew his master's will, but failed to do it "shall be beaten with many stripes." On the other hand, however, there is neither an excuse for ignorance. But the offender "that knew not and did commit things worthy of stripes shall be beaten with few stripes." — Thus Peter receives his reply. In the entire matter of sanctification a follower of Christ, especially the trusted disciple, must be alert at all times. The general maxim, which regulates penalty according to responsibility and trust, applies also to the kingdom of heaven. "For unto whomsoever much is given, of him shall be much required; and to whom men have committed much, of him they will ask the more."

Luke 12, 49—53.   **24.**

Great fidelity is required. And this becomes all the more difficult as the truth and the meaning of the Gospel become known. "I am come to send fire on the earth," the fire of a new faith, creating burning enthusiasm among some and fierce antagonism among others, deplorable, but inevitable, and the sooner kindled,

"Suppose Ye that I am Come to Give Peace on Earth?" the better. "And what will I if it be already kindled?" Would that it were already burning! There will be fiery trials; but the disciples should be encouraged at the thought that the Lord Himself will not go out unscathed. "But I have a baptism to be baptized with." The fiery baptism of His Passion looms up before Him with such threatening aspect that He feels Himself "straitened" on every side, both with a fervent desire of its accomplishment and

---

23, 3) Διχοτομήσει, cut asunder with a saw. For this cruel mode of punishment see 2 Sam. 12, 31; 1 Chron. 20, 3; Heb. 11, 37.

with a natural dread of the great ordeal.[1]   And let there be no misapprehension as to the reaction to the Gospel. "Suppose ye that I am come to give peace on earth?"   Jesus is by no means a patron of war, and His Gospel is in every respect a message of peace; yet it will not be peacefully received. To His own question He replies: "I tell you, Nay; but rather division." The preaching of the Word will always act as a separating force. Dissension, strife, and enmity will follow, even in the midst of most closely knitted family ties. "There shall be five in one house divided," father, mother, son, daughter, and daughter-in-law, "three against two and two against three." Of this saddest of conditions in religious life the disciples should be forewarned lest they be offended.

Luke 12, 54—57.[1]   **25.**

A time of discord, conflict, and division, but a dawn of a new era nevertheless. And this period should be viewed in proper perspective, as the Lord points out in again directing Himself to the people. When the clouds came up black from the west, the region of the Mediterranean Sea, this, of course, meant rain; but if the

Discerning the Signs of the Times.

winds blew from Arabia, across the burning deserts, it naturally meant withering heat. "This weather skill any one in the audience might possess." [2]   And still, "ye hypocrites, ye can discern the face of the sky and of the earth; but how is it that ye do not discern this time?" The signs were here, the Messiah had come, and still the eyes of the nation had not discerned it. There was but one conclusion: Of themselves they were unable to judge. They were a shallow lot and without judgment in spiritual things.

Luke 12, 58. 59.[1]   **26.**

It is necessary to be in harmony with the new day, as Jesus explains with a legal scene from every-day life. The lesson on

Conciliating the Adversary.

reconciling the enemy given in the Sermon on the Mount is here used as an admonition to "give diligence" [2] in effecting reconciliation with the adversary by timely repentance, "lest he hale

---

24, 1) Kretzmann, I, 388.   John 12, 27.
25, 1) Compare Matt. 16, 2. 3.
    2) Bruce *sub loco.*
26, 1) Compare Matt. 5, 25. 26.   Chapter XI, 22.
    2) Δὸς ἐργασίαν, a Latinism: *operam da.* Bruce *sub loco.*

thee to the judge and the judge deliver thee to the officer and the officer cast thee into prison. I tell thee, thou shalt not depart thence till thou hast paid the very last mite." [3]

Luke 13, 1—5.   **27.**

We assume that it was in Judea and the time just before the visit of Jesus to Jerusalem for the Festival of Dedication,[1] which possibly was even now in progress,[2] that a report was brought to Jesus of "the Galileans whose blood Pilate had mingled with their sacrifices." It is possible that these countrymen of Jesus had offended the governor by a daring manifestation of liberalistic tendencies, for which the Galileans were nationally known. Of course we do not know, and it might have happened at some other time. But it has been supposed[3] that an attempt had been made to instigate an insurrection during the Feast of Dedication, which festival brought to memory the revolt of the Maccabees against the oppression of foreign masters and the eventual victory of the oppressed. For this Pilate took fearful revenge. In the midst of their sacrifices he caused the rioters to be slain in the Temple, so that their blood mingled with the sacrifices which they intended to present. Nor is this the first time that there had been a massacre in a holy place. Archelaus had slain three thousand Jews during a Passover disturbance thirty years before.[4] The news was brought

The Galileans Slain by Pilate. to Jesus, presumably in the hope that He would be incensed at this outrage against His countrymen, in which some, by the way, have seen the cause of the enmity between Pilate and Herod.[5] Probably Jesus would now join the nationalists in opposition to the hated rule of Rome. But He connects the report with a new admonition to repentance. So sudden a death in the midst of so sacred an act would be popularly regarded as a just divine

---

26, 3) Λεπτόν, half of a κοδράντης, Matthew's word (5, 26), *quadrans,* the smallest Roman coin, equal in value to about ¼ cent. Compare Mark 12, 42. Bruce *sub loco.*

27, 1) See next chapter.

2) Tuesday to Tuesday, 20—27 of December, 29 A. D. Wieseler, *Synopsis,* 435.

3) See Ylvisaker, 476.

4) Josephus, *Ant.,* XVII, IX, 3. Compare also the Pentecost disturbance shortly afterwards under Sabinus. *Ant.,* XVII, X, 2. And on one occasion Pilate actually disguised his soldiers as peasants and sent them to use their daggers freely on the mob. *Wars,* II, IX, 4.

5) Luke 23, 12. Andrews, 394. Kretzmann, I, 339.

punishment for especially wicked deeds which these victims had committed. But Jesus corrects the notion. "Suppose ye that these Galileans were sinners above all the Galileans because they suffered such things?" His listeners would have been inclined to see in such disasters divine punishment for particular sins.[6] But Jesus answers: "I tell you, Nay; but except ye repent, ye shall all likewise perish." And since He kept Himself informed on current events,[7] Jesus could point to another calamity which had taken place in Jerusalem, in which a "tower in Siloam" had collapsed and killed eighteen people. While we know of the Pool of Siloam near Jerusalem,[8] our knowledge of this calamity is contained in the question: "Or those eighteen upon whom the tower in Siloam fell and slew them, think ye that they were sinners above all men that dwelt in Jerusalem?" Probably the hearers supposed that the sufferers were sinners of exceptional guilt. But very emphatically Jesus repeats the former statement: "I tell you, Nay." Contrary to popular expectation some of the best minds in Israel might have been involved in these calamities. The main lesson, however, which Christ desired to teach was: "But except ye repent, ye shall all likewise perish."

Luke 13, 6—9.   **28.**

Repentance is needed for all. And there is time given for repentance. The Lord's long-suffering is great. But at last it will come to an end. This is the earnest lesson taught by Christ in the parable of the Fig-tree planted by a certain man of means in his vineyard, from which he naturally expected fruit. "But he came and sought fruit thereon and found none." Finally he gave it up. The tree had matured. In the ordinary course of nature the time **The Parable of the Barren Fig-Tree.** had fully arrived for it to yield a crop. However, three more years went by, and still there was no sign of fruit. "Then said he to the dresser of the vineyard, Behold, these three years I come seeking fruit on this fig-tree and find none; cut it down; why cumbereth it the ground?" He had waited three years past the time of fruit-bearing to determine whether the fig-tree would do the one thing for which it had been planted. It was not his purpose to raise it to be an ornament or to provide shade. But besides bearing no fruit, the tree occupied valuable space which might be more profitably used. In the face of experience it seemed

---

27, 6) John 9, 2. 3.   7) Bruce *sub loco.*   8) John 9, 7.

useless to waste any more time on its cultivation. But the vine-dresser interceded for the fig-tree, pleading for a fourth year, when he would use all his arts, "dig about it and dung it," in the hope that it might still be coaxed into bringing fruit. "And if it bear fruit, well." But if this last effort should also prove unfruitful, then "cut it down," then remove it and have another tree planted in its place.[1] A few words of explanation. It has been thought that the three years pointed to the three-year public ministry of Jesus.[2] But the best interpretation seems to be to take the three years as the whole period of grace given to Israel in the Old Testament in which the chosen fig-tree was expected to yield fruit acceptable to God. "The fourth year, for which the Vine-dresser, Jesus, pleaded, was the special period of grace, which dawned with the ministry of John, burst into full brightness with the preaching of Jesus, and continued during the ministry of the apostles." [3] "If it bear fruit, well." But we know what happened. The extra time went by, and the fig-tree was cut down, with the destruction of Jerusalem and the dispersion of the race.

Luke 13, 10—17.   **29.**

We have already called attention [1] to the silence in the records with respect to direct references of our Savior's teaching in the synagogs at this time as compared with His earlier ministry. But here again we find Jesus teaching in a synagog on a Sabbath-day. If we are permitted to venture a guess, it was a Judean synagog, probably in the neighborhood of Jerusalem,[2] and probably on the Sabbath before the Feast of Dedication or even on the Sabbath during the Dedication week of 29 A. D.[3] Among the worshipers in the synagog there was a poor woman "which had a spirit of infirmity eighteen years and was bowed together and could in no wise lift up herself." The spirit of sickness which contracted her

28, 1) Luke 13, 29.
      2) Wieseler, *Synopsis*, 235.   3) Kretzmann, I, 340.
29, 1) *Supra,* 8. Luke 10, 25
      2) Possibly at or near Bethany. See next chapter.
      3) In 10, 38 we have traced Jesus to Bethany. This is followed by the teaching of chapters 11 and 12 in "a certain place" (11, 1). There is no movement in these sections. A report is brought of the apparently fresh massacre of the Galileans in Jerusalem, 13, 1. And as we have pointed out (No. 1, this chapter), there are the best reasons for inserting Dedication between verses 21 and 22 of Luke 13. As to the suggestion "even on the Sabbath during the Dedication week," attention is called to the fact that Jesus, for instance, did not spend the whole of the Feast of Tabernacles week in Jerusalem, John 7, 14. Of course there is no certainty. We are merely trying to picture the events to ourselves without taking undue liberties.

body was really a demon,[4] who so paralyzed her muscular powers that she could not so much as raise her head. She was held down in a stooping position, as if bound by chains. The mere sight of her wretched condition was sufficient appeal to the compassionate heart of Jesus. Calling her into His presence, He said to her: "Woman, thou art loosed from thine infirmity." No sooner had He laid His hands on her than she straightened up and glorified God. Thus there is a revelation of that Savior glory as manifested in His usual healing ministry. But the praises of the healed woman were heartlessly cut short by the narrow indignation of the ruler of the synagog "because that Jesus had healed on the Sabbath-day." Under his very eyes a woman, a member of his congregation, had the presumption to be healed on the Sabbath-day. She had not so much as stirred a finger or raised her voice in her own behalf, but "in all the fussiness of official hypocrisy"[5] the ruler of the synagog sees fit to deliver a rebuke as he gets up and speaks *"to the people at Jesus"*[6] about the crime of being healed on a Sabbath-day, when they could just as well have been healed on any other day: "There are six days in which men ought to work" — being healed is work!? "In them therefore come and be healed and not on the Sabbath-day."

The Crippled Woman Healed on a Sabbath.

Luke 13, 10—17. **30.**

To this hopeless stupidity and purely mechanical observance of the Law the Lord[1] replies with an argument which even this rustic official is able to understand. This was not the first time that Jesus had to defend Himself against Sabbath infringements. And we notice that He constantly varied His arguments.[2] Here

---

29, 4) V. 16. Even as in the last analysis all sickness and suffering is caused by sin, which was first brought into the world by the devil.

5) Farrar, II, 114. 6) Bruce *sub loco.*

30, 1) Again Κύριος.

2) Farrar, II, 115. For Sabbath controversies see: —

1. John 5, 10 ff. Compare John 7, 21—24.	His own authority as well as circumcision on the Sabbath.
2. Matt. 12, 1—8; Mark 2, 23—28; Luke 6, 1—5.	Appeal to precedents in Scripture and to Temple-service.
3. Matt. 12, 9—14; Mark 3, 1—6; Luke 6, 6—11.	Appeal to common sense. Sheep fallen into pit.
4. John 9, 1—34.	Man born blind. "Work while it is day; the night cometh when no man can work."
5. Luke 13, 10—17.	Watering ass on Sabbath-day.
6. Luke 14, 1—6.	Ass fallen into pit.

He appealed to the practise of the objector himself, as expressly permitted by rabbinic law.[3] "Thou hypocrite, doth not each one of you on the Sabbath-day loose his ox or his ass from the stall and lead him away to watering?" This was permitted by the Jewish elders, even the drawing of water, provided, however, that the

"Ought Not This Woman be Loosed from This Bond?" water was not carried to the animal. And now the argument: "A daughter of Abraham versus an ass. Bound by Satan for eighteen years versus the thirst of a few hours." [4] "Ought not this woman, being a daughter of Abraham, whom Satan hath bound, lo, these eighteen years, be loosed from this bond on the Sabbath-day?" The argument was irresistible. "All His adversaries were ashamed," while "all the people rejoiced for all the glorious things that were done by Him."

Luke 13, 18—21.[1]   **31.**

The joy of the people at the performance of the miracle on the crippled woman is taken by Jesus as a "good omen for the future." [2] Though the rulers as well as the nation as a whole rejected Him, yet there would remain a "little flock," [3] which even in the face of persecutions would fearlessly receive Him with joyful acclaim. The joy of the people justified the hopes of the Savior on behalf

Parables of Mustard-Seed and Leaven Repeated. of His kingdom, small and insignificant at first, but all-pervading and in the course of time growing into proportions of power. It was probably thoughts such as these which prompted Jesus in this connection to repeat the parables of the Mustard-seed, "which a man took and cast into his garden and it grew and waxed a great tree," and of the Leaven, "which a woman took and hid in three measures of meal till the whole was leavened." "This seems to be the only instance in which parables were connected with synagog addresses as their occasion." [4]

30, 3) Edersheim, II, 225.   4) Bruce *sub loco.*
31, 1) Compare Matt. 13, 31—33; Mark 4, 30—32. Chapter XII, 25.
    2) Bruce *sub loco.*   3) 12, 32.   4) Bruce *sub loco.*

CHAPTER XXII.

AT THE FEAST OF DEDICATION IN JERUSALEM.

Probably December 20—27, 782 A. U. C., 29 A. D.

John 10, 22. 23.   **1.**

We have already stated our opinion [1] that the events related in the preceding pages took place in the neighborhood of Jerusalem, and, we might here add, with Bethany as probable headquarters.[2] According to this arrangement, which fits in with the Evangelist John,[3] there is therefore no reason to conjecture a special journey to Jerusalem for the Feast of Dedication, which was celebrated at this time. It is indeed improbable that Jesus would otherwise have gone up simply because of this feast, because it was one of the minor festivals, and although it was celebrated by many in

The Feast of Dedication. Jerusalem, it might have been observed anywhere else in the land as well.[4] But now, in accordance with the meaning of the feast, since Jesus was the true Judas Maccabaeus and "that faithful Prophet" [5] for whose coming the royalty of the Maccabees was to be held in trust, and since He was the true Deliverer from oppression and the Purifier of the Temple of God from defilement as well as the true Light of Israel and Lamp of David to shine into the darkness, He gives His presence in Jerusalem, though probably only for one day, to this annual octave of enthusiastic patriotic yearning and national joy as well as His testimony to His divine Sonship, in which the visit resulted. The festival itself was not of Biblical origin, but had been instituted by Judas Maccabaeus in 165 B. C., when the Temple, which had been shamefully desecrated by Antiochus Epiphanes, was again dedicated to the service of God.[6] The festival was also called The Lights,[7] from the custom

---

1,   1) Chapter XXI, 29.   2) Luke 10, 38. Chapter XXI, 10.

3) Between verses 21 and 22 in chapter 10.

4) Andrews, 398.   5) 1 Macc. 14, 41. Chapter II, 25.

6) 1 Macc. 4, 52—59. Chapter II, 23. For a general account see Schuerer, I, I, 207 ff. 217. The Temple was rededicated precisely the same day on which three years before, for the first time, the altar had been desecrated by the offering up of heathen sacrifices. A new altar was built of unhewn stone (Ex. 20, 25), while the stones of the earlier altar were laid aside until there would "come a prophet" to show what should be done with them, 1 Macc. 4, 46.

7) *Tὰ φῶτα.* Josephus, *Ant.*, XII, VII, 7.

of illuminating the Temple and the private houses for the duration
of the feast. There was also a chanting of the Hallel,[8] the carrying of palm-branches, and other characteristics of the Feast of
Tabernacles. But while some of the ceremonies may have been
taken over from Tabernacles, it seems that the illumination of the
Temple passed from Dedication into the observance of Tabernacles.
Tradition has it that, when the Temple services were restored by
Judas Maccabaeus, the oil was found to have been desecrated. Only
one flagon was discovered that was undefiled and had been sealed
with the signet of the high priest. The supply was only sufficient
to feed for one day the sacred candlestick, but by a miracle the
flagon was said to have been replenished for eight days, when
a supply of fresh oil was secured.[9] In memory of this the Temple
was ordered to be illuminated the following year for eight days on
the anniversary of its rededication. Hence the eight days, which
were counted from the 25th of Kisleu. For the year 29 A. D.
these days have been calculated [10] to have corresponded with the
20th to the 27th of December, Tuesday to Tuesday. If the Sabbath controversy in connection with the healing of the crippled
woman [11] occurred on the 29th of Kisleu, or the 24th of December,
then Jesus, the Lord of the Temple, may have fittingly spent the
day, which we regard as the last anniversary of His birth, December 25, in the Temple of the Lord.

John 10, 22. 23.　　　　**2.**

At any rate, "it was at Jerusalem the Feast of the Dedication,[1]
and it was winter," [2] that "Jesus walked in the Temple, in Solomon's Porch." [3] Because the weather was cold, He sought the

Solomon's Porch.　sheltering columns on the east side of the
Temple, in front of the Beautiful Gate
and facing the valley of the Kidron.[4] The name of Solomon clung
to these columns either because they were an undestroyed relic of
the old Temple or because they were built of material which had
formed part of the ancient structure.[5]

1, 　8) Pss. 113—118.　　　　9) Edersheim, II, 227.

　　10) Wieseler, *Synopsis,* 435.　11) Luke 13, 14. Chapter XXI, 29.

2, 　1) Τὰ ἐγκαίνια, the feast of renewal.

　　2) Χειμὼν ἦν. Not stormy weather, but the season is meant. Inserted
probably for Gentile readers and to explain why Jesus was teaching under
cover. Dods *sub loco.*

　　3) Στοά, portico, cloister.　　4) Compare Chapter III, 7 ff.

　　5) Josephus, *Ant.,* XX, IX, 7. Farrar, II, 144.

John 10, 24—39.　　　　　3.

At the anniversary of a splendid deliverance wrought by a handful of men the air was mingled with memories of a glorious past and the fervent hope that a similar day, indeed a day of even greater deliverance, might soon arrive. As "the Jews"[1] noticed Jesus walking up and down between the marble columns, they rushed upon Him with the demand to relieve them of their suspense: "How long dost Thou make us to doubt? If Thou be the Christ, tell us plainly,"[2] even now and here in Solomon's Porch. As if He had not already done so! And on many occasions He had testified to the fact by His Messianic works.[3] The trouble was

"If Thou Be the Christ, Tell Us Plainly." not with Him, but with them. "He could not descend to their notions, nor would they rise to His."[4] Still others, who at the outset had probably shared the same false views, had accepted Him as the Christ of God. And yet, in spite of previous rejections and controversies, they would probably even now have acclaimed Him at once if only in a measure He would fulfil their unspiritual hopes. In His reply Jesus first of all defends Himself against the charge that He had not told them the truth concerning Himself. And from His words He appeals to the undisputed witness of the deeds which He had wrought in His Father's name. But their unbelief in view of all evidences was proof that they were not His sheep, "as I said unto you."[5]

John 10, 24—39.　　　　　4.

A shepherd in the form of Judas Maccabaeus would have been followed, but a voice which sounded the Gospel call found no response. The reference to sheep in a figurative sense need not surprise us; for it was made in the same place — and no doubt

"My Sheep Hear My Voice." some of those who heard him now had been present then — where, during the Feast of Tabernacles a few months before,[1] the parables on the relation of the sheep and the shepherd had been spoken. As He had stated then that it was the characteristic of sheep to recognize the voice of their shepherd,[2] so He repeats

---

3,　1) A standing term for the party of opposition.

　　2) Παρρησία, in so many words, devoid of all ambiguity. 16, 29. Dods *sub loco.*

　　3) John 1, 41; 4, 26; 5, 36; 8, 42; 9, 37.

　　4) Farrar, II, 149.　　　5) 8, 47.

4,　1) Chapter XX, 27 ff.　　2) John 10, 4.

here: "My sheep hear My voice, and I know them, and they follow Me." And lest through some carnal interpretation His hearers misunderstand the figure of speech, He adds that He is referring to spiritual things. "And I give unto them eternal life." What He says here is a matter of the Word, the Father, the heart, divine promise, and absolute certainty and assurance of everlasting life. "Neither shall any man pluck them out of My hand." This statement can be so confidently made because the sheep of Jesus are a gift of the heavenly Father, who is "greater than all, and no man is able to pluck them out of My Father's hand." Neither is this a contradiction; for "I and My Father are one." [3]

John 10, 24—39.   **5.**

"I and My Father are one." Jesus had spoken "plainly, and there is no doubt about these words. And in their understanding of them the Jews were no Arians. In these words of Jesus the blind Jews saw more than the anti-Trinitarians see to-day." [1]   And St. Augustine remarks [2] that the word *one* refutes Arianism, which

"I and My Father Are One."

denies the unity of essence, the *homoousion,* and the plural *are* disproves Sabellianism, which denies the distinct persons in the Trinity. Again the Jews, [3] sensing blasphemy, stooped down to seize some of the scattered stones which the unfinished Temple-building supplied, to stone Him. But the "undisturbed majesty of Jesus disarmed them" with the words: [4] "Many good works have I showed you from My Father; for which of those works do ye stone Me?"

John 10, 24—39.   **6.**

In a reply which incidentally confirmed the miracles of Jesus the Jews answered: "For a good work we stone Thee not, but for blasphemy and because that Thou, being a man, makest Thyself

---

4,   3) Ἐγὼ καὶ ὁ πατὴρ ἕν ἐσμεν. Bengel (quoted by Edersheim, II, 229) points out a triplet of double parallelisms in ascending climax: —

Ascending		*Ascending*
My sheep hear My voice	parallel	And I know them
And they follow Me		And I give unto them eternal life
And they shall never perish		And no one shall pluck them out of My hands

5,   1) Bengel, quoted by Dods sub John 10, 30. See also Farrar, II, 147.
     2) As quoted by Meyer and Edersheim.
     3) 8, 59.   4) Farrar, II, 147.

God." They answered as they saw the situation.[1] In their ears the claims of Jesus were nothing short of blasphemy. But, as Jesus points out, it is even possible for ordinary men to be called gods.[2] "For is it not written in your Law, 'I said, Ye are gods'?"[3] The argument is from the lesser to the greater. The reference is to magistrates, through whom the will of God was delivered to the people. If they, in their official capacity as God's representatives,

The Charge of Blasphemy. are called gods, how much greater right has He, then, to be called the Son of God, who has been sanctified and sent into the world by the Father to redeem the world! The quotation used by Jesus is taken from the Book of Psalms, to which He refers as "the Law." This in the Old Testament sense embraced all the canonical writings of the Old Testament,[4] which, by the way, as the divinely inspired Scriptures, "cannot be broken." Returning now to His first argument, about His works, the Lord continues: "If I do not the works of My Father, believe Me not." If they would not credit His statements for His sake, they should at least accept the testimony of His undeniable deeds, not to give Him glory, but that "ye may know and believe that the Father is in Me and I in Him."

John 10, 40—42.   7.

The argument was irresistible. They dared not stone Him. But upon His repeated reference to His personal, essential unity with the Father "they sought again[1] to take Him." They would at least place Him under arrest and have Him examined by the proper authorities. But Jesus, escaping out of their hands, left

Retirement into Perea. the Temple and the city and departed beyond the Jordan, to the place where John had begun His early ministry of baptism.[2] Here he remained for the next few months. After the rejections in Galilee, Samaria, and Judea, Perea was the only region in the land of Israel still open for Him before His final presentation to the nation in Jerusalem at the Passover. Of this Perean period we know

---

6,   1) Kretzmann, I, 470. Lev. 24, 10—17; Deut. 18, 20.

2) Dods *sub loco.*   3) Ps. 82, 6.

4) Dods *sub loco.* Compare 12, 34; 15, 25; Rom. 3, 19; 1 Cor. 14, 21.

7,   1) 7, 30. 44.

2) Πρῶτον, "at first." Dods *sub loco.* Luke 3, 3. Chapter V, 2 ff. Compared with John 1, 28. Chapter VI, 1 ff.

nothing, unless, as we assume, some of the chapters of St. Luke are to be assigned to this period.[3)]   That the stay in Perea was not exactly private can also be seen from the Evangelist John, who tells us that many resorted to Him there.   To many of the inhabitants of this region John the Baptist was not unknown.   As they made comparisons between Jesus and His forerunner, they said: "John did no miracle,[4)] but all things that John spake of this man were true."   And whereas in Jerusalem neither Jesus nor John was generally accepted, the result of the ministry of Jesus in Perea was that "many believed on Him there." [5)]

7,   3) 13, 22—17, 10.   See next chapter.
4) Thus it seems that Jesus did perform some miracles in Perea.
5) See Dods *sub loco.*

CHAPTER XXIII.

THE LATER PEREAN MINISTRY.
AFTER THE FEAST OF DEDICATION TO THE RAISING OF LAZARUS.
Probably January to February, 30 A. D., A. U. C. 783.

Luke 13, 22. **1.**

We remember that the final withdrawal of Jesus from Galilee after the Feast of Tabernacles, in the fall of 29 A. D.,[1] was in reality the beginning of that final journey towards Jerusalem which was to have the cross as its goal. That Jerusalem itself was visited,

Journeying towards Jerusalem. as has just been related, or will be reached again for the raising of Lazarus,[2] does not change the fact that in this whole period "He steadfastly set His face to go up to Jerusalem." But as we have pointed out,[3] while His face was set towards Jerusalem, His mind was still occupied with other things as "He went through the cities and villages," presumably of Perea,[4] "teaching and journeying towards Jerusalem."

Luke 13, 23—30. **2.**

The main occupation of Jesus in this period was teaching, although also a miracle is recorded.[1] And in His teaching He doubtless touched again and again [2] upon the admonition to be prepared for the Day of Judgment and the return of the Son of

"Lord, Are there Few that be Saved?" Man. It was on this journey that some one addressed Him with the question: "Lord, are there few that be saved?" But this was an idle question. Rather than ascertain the number of those attaining salvation, one should be concerned about receiving salvation for himself, which is by far more important. Jesus had not "come into the world to gratify men's curiosity," [3] but to save their souls. For the benefit therefore of the questioner and of others Jesus repeated the saying in the Sermon on the Mount: "Strive to enter in at the strait gate." [4] Heaven is

---

1, 1) John 10, 21, followed by Luke 9, 51. See Chapter XXI, 1.

2) John 11, 17 ff. 3) Chapter XXI, 1. 4) John 10, 40.

2, 1) Luke 14, 1—6. Note also the implication in John 10, 41: "John did no miracle," implying that Jesus did.

2) Compare 12, 40. 59; 13, 9.

3) Ylvisaker, 481. 4) Matt. 7, 13. 14.

pictured as a house with but one door. And he that will not enter through this one door, the door of repentance and faith, will find himself shut out. Moreover, he who does not want to make his entry on the day of grace, while the door is still open, will likewise find himself shut out. As long as the Gospel invitation is heard, the door is still open. It is definitely closed, however, for each individual in the hour of death and for the entire human race when the Lord returns unto Judgment. This is explained in the parable of the Master of the House.

Luke 13, 23—30. **3.**

When an entertainment is given, it is but reasonable for the master of the house to wait for a certain time to receive his guests. When the appointed time has come and he deems that all the guests are, or ought to be, present, he at length rises up and shuts the door, after which no one can be admitted.[1] They who have not heeded the invitation will receive the answer: "I know you not." And should they insist upon recognition, pointing out to the master of the house, as indeed the contemporaries of Jesus could do: "We

The Parable of the Master of the House. have eaten and drunk in Thy presence, and Thou hast taught in our streets," it will help them not. The reason of their exclusion was not because the door was too narrow, but because they would not come in. And now, seeing that the warning of Jesus was true after all, their Judgment Day repentance was too late. "I tell you, I know not whence you are; depart from Me, all ye workers of iniquity."[2] Thus the terrible words uttered against the false prophets in the Sermon on the Mount find a general application here. Judgment Day will be a day of surprise and of gnashing of teeth, when the prophets, the patriarchs, and all their true descendants, "Abraham, and Isaac, and Jacob, and all the prophets," will be found sitting in the kingdom of God and they, who supposed themselves Abraham's sons and the prophets' followers, thrust out. That this would happen the Lord had already said in connection with the faith of the centurion at Capernaum:[3] "Many shall come from the East, and from the West, and from the North, and from the South and shall sit down in the kingdom of God." Thus "there are last which shall be first, and there are first which shall be last."[4] That is, heathen-born believers, for

---

3, 1) Matt. 25, 11. 12. 　　2) Matt. 7, 22. 23.
　 3) Matt. 8, 11. 12. 　　4) Matt. 20, 16; 19, 30.

whom, the Jews thought, there was little or no chance, would be first, while such unbelievers as on account of their birth thought themselves members of the first rank in the kingdom of the Messiah would find no admission at all.

Luke 13, 31—33.   4.

In immediate connection with the foregoing,[1]) and while Jesus was still in the territory of Herod Antipas, presumably in Perea, it happened that certain of the Pharisees approached Him with the warning: "Get Thee out and depart hence; for Herod will kill Thee." Whether they acted as the agents of Herod for the purpose of intimidating Jesus or were stating a fact which had come to their knowledge, or whether they were acting in their own interest, anxious to get rid of the presence of Jesus, it is impossible to ascertain. But in His answer Jesus seems to take the warning at its face value, namely, that of friends warning against a foe, and to keep His own thoughts as to where the craft and cunning lay.[2])

A Warning against Herod. "Go ye and tell that fox, Behold, I cast out devils, and I do cures to-day and to-morrow, and the third day I shall be perfected."[3]) While the fox does not elsewhere in Scripture appear as a symbol of cunning, it seems that Jesus here had the foxlike cunning and knavery of Herod Antipas in mind.[4]) As regards the three days, it seems that they are to be taken as a complete, albeit brief, period of appointed time.[5]) Jesus had come into the world for a purpose, and this purpose He would accomplish. "Nevertheless I must walk to-day and to-morrow and the day following." A termination of His activity is implied. But as regards this, like John the Baptist He would die a prophet's death, not, however, at the hand of Herod, and not at an improper place, as at Machaerus, but, in accordance with the Father's purpose and will, in Jerusalem; "for it cannot be that a prophet perish out of Jerusalem."

4,   1) "The same day."

2) Bruce *sub loco.*

3) *Τελειοῦμαι. Ad finem pervenire,* to come to an end. Meyer *sub loco.* To come to a conclusion in the way appointed by the Father through death on the cross.

4) Bruce *sub loco.* As a destructive force in the Lord's vineyard many commentators point to "the little foxes that spoil the vines," Cant. 2, 15.

5) Like the three years of Luke 13, 7. Compare Hos. 6, 2. Not to be taken as a chronological tag, as Wieseler does, *Synopsis,* 235, who from these words makes the inference that Jesus was still a three days' journey distant from Bethany.

Luke 13, 34. 35.　　　5.

The thought that He was even now on a journey that was to end at the cross caused Jesus solemnly to address the slayer of prophets: "O Jerusalem, Jerusalem,[1] which killest the prophets and stonest them that are sent unto thee, how often[2] would I have gathered thy children together as a hen doth gather her brood under her wings; and ye would not!"[3] On account of such obsti-

"O Jerusalem, Jerusalem!"

nate resistance to the gracious invitation of Christ a word of judgment is pronounced upon the perverted inhabitants. The Temple shall be destroyed and the city left desolate. Judgment for the obdurate, but blessings for the believers, when the true inhabitants of Jerusalem shall see Him again with the eyes of faith and on the day of the revelation of His glory. Jerusalem desolate, Israel dispersed, — and still every believer, whether Jew or Gentile, will be able to say: "Blessed is He that cometh in the name of the Lord."

Luke 14, 1—6.　　　6.

Again the Lord is engaged in a Sabbath controversy.[1] It was on a Sabbath-day that Jesus was invited for a feast into the house of a prominent member of the pharisaic party.[2] The Sabbath feast itself was not a violation of the Sabbath ordinance, provided the food had been previously prepared.[3] Jesus accepted the invitation, although He was aware of a rather strange situation: invited as a friend by a great man among the Pharisees, as if to be held in honor, and yet regarded with suspicion and carefully

---

5, 　1) In the Greek text the word Jerusalem three times in immediate succession: Ἰερουσαλήμ (v. 33). Ἰερουσαλήμ, Ἰερουσαλήμ.

2) Luke reports only one journey of Jesus to Jerusalem during His public ministry. But this word shows that the Synoptists knew of the various journeys John records, although they are not reported in their writings. Ylvisaker, 484.

3) Compare Matt. 23, 37. 38.

6, 　1) 1. The lame man at the Pool of Bethesda. John 5, 10.

2. The disciples in the field of corn. Matt. 12, 2; Mark 2, 24; Luke 6, 2.

3. The man with a withered hand. Matt. 12, 10; Mark 3, 2; Luke 6, 7.

4. The man born blind. John 9, 13.

5. The crippled woman. Luke 13, 14.

6. The man afflicted with dropsy. Luke 14, 4.

2) Ἀρχόντων τῶν Φαρισαίων. Probably a member of the local Sanhedrin. As such the Pharisees had no rulers. This Pharisee may have occupied a position of honor on account of great learning. Hardly a member of the Sanhedrin of Jerusalem if the scene is to be placed in Perea.

3) Ylvisaker, 486. Neh. 8, 10.

watched. Among those present was one, presumably an unbidden guest, yet there by arrangement, who had the dropsy.[4] Because he was there in the plain sight of all and before Jesus, no doubt

The Man Afflicted with Dropsy. it was a trap set for Him. It was thought that Jesus would again venture to offend the popular prejudice by effecting a Sabbath cure or that His miraculous powers might fail in dealing with this inveterate disease. At any rate, it was a case where heartless and unfeeling teachers would cruelly make an object of mercy and his suffering a tool in their hands. But Jesus anticipated any charge of Sabbath healing by submitting to the distinguished company a very simple question: "Is it lawful to heal on the Sabbath-day?" But that was the very question for the answering of which the scene had been laid. "And they held their peace." They could not answer the question in the negative. They knew what the answer of Jesus would be. They felt that it was not only lawful, but *right;*[5] and still, to have made the admission would have amounted to disloyalty to the whole system for which they stood. And so there was an awkward silence. But their very silence was sufficient justification for the merciful action of Jesus. "And He took him [6] and healed him and let him go."

Luke 14, 1—6.   7.

And now the apology. "Which of you shall have an ass [1] fallen into a pit and will not straightway pull him out on a Sabbath-day?" [2] The argument was invincible. It was the appeal to a principle which they had always theoretically admitted. And the healing of a man was far more important than the extrication of

An Irrefutable Argument. a beast from a perilous situation. And besides, it involved less labor. The supreme law was the law of love. And where it was a question of love and mercy, the Sabbath ordinance with respect to bodily labor did not apply. The plot had failed. There was not even an argument. And their very silence was complete proof of the refutation of their contention which they were too "ungenerous to acknowledge." [3]

6,   4) Ὑδρωπικός (ὕδρωψ). The only place in the New Testament where the disease is mentioned.   5) Farrar, II, 120.

6) Ἐπιλαβόμενος. Compare Mark 8, 23. The impressive means employed. Stronger than ἁψάμενος, "touched him," Matt. 8, 3. Meyer *sub loco.*
7,   1) Many MSS. have υἱὸς ἢ βοῦς, a son or (even) an ox, etc. Bruce *sub loco.*

2) Compare Matt. 12, 11.   3) Farrar, II, 121.

Luke 14, 7—11.   8.

The foregoing took place, we may believe, before the meal. The man had been healed and dismissed, and a lesson on true Sabbath observance had been given; but noticing how the guests scrambled for preferred places at or near the head of the table, Jesus saw an opportunity to add another lesson. Not a lesson on table manners, but a lesson on humility on account of the lack of good table manners. Even among their own associates it seems to have been impossible for the Pharisees to deny that they were Pharisees.[1]) In order to teach them a much-needed lesson, the Lord put forth a parable on proper behavior at a wedding-feast. According to a "wiser and better principle of social courtesy"[2]) a guest at a wedding-feast should not strive for the most-honored seat. It may easily happen that among those present there is one who

"Friend, Go Up Higher." is held in higher esteem by the host than the one who otherwise actually was — or assumed that he was — entitled to the seat of honor. What a humiliation it would be to the forward guest if he were compelled by the host to give up his place to the guest of honor and, since all the guests were now seated, to move to the lowest place! A better policy would be to sit down "in the lowest room, that, when he that bade thee cometh, he may say unto thee, Friend, go up higher." Thus true and sincere humility would be honored in the presence of all the guests. Obviously the purpose of the parable is not to teach table manners or to show how in some clever way one may attain honor, but to give a lesson on a great law in the kingdom of God: "Whosoever exalteth himself," for instance, in pharisaic self-glorification, "shall be abased; and he that humbleth himself," that is, he whose humility is a fruit of true repentance, "shall be exalted."

Luke 14, 12—14.   9.

In the last analysis the spirit of pharisaism, whether it be pride, ostentatious almsgiving, self-righteousness, long prayers, pretended sanctity, or even sham humility, was selfishness. And in accordance with the principle of unselfishness and true love of the neighbor

A Word to the Host. Jesus advises His host when making a dinner and inviting guests not always to select these according to the ordinary social standards of intimates, brethren, kinsmen, rich neighbors, and those from whom it might reasonably be expected that they would invite him

---

8,   1) Matt. 23, 6.   2) Farrar, II, 122.

in return, probably even outdo him in hospitality. But with a kind and unselfish heart he should give attention to the poor, maimed, lame, and blind; then he would "be recompensed at the resurrection of the dead."

Luke 14, 15—24. **10.**

At this point one of the guests who was deeply impressed by the words of Jesus, especially by the allusion of a reward in heaven, made the remark: "Blessed is he that shall eat bread in the king-

The Great Supper. dom of God." Probably the expression was the result of momentary enthusiasm.

At any rate, it served to call forth the parable of the Great Supper. A certain man prepared an elaborate banquet and sent out invitations to a large number of guests. At the time of the feast he ordered his servant to make the customary final call: "Come; for all things are now ready."

Luke 14, 15—24. **11.**

But as if by agreement "they all with one consent began to make excuse." In every instance personal interests, which were supported by a good degree of apparent reasonableness, were advanced as an excuse for not attending the feast. Here are a few examples: One had to manage an estate recently purchased and had to go and look it over. "I pray thee have me excused." Another was deeply engaged in an important business transaction, the purchase of five yoke of oxen, and, being now on his way to examine them, could

"I Pray Thee Have Me Excused." not come. "I pray thee have me excused." The mere statement of a third that he had married a wife seemed to be

sufficient explanation why he could not come. Thus the excuses ran in a general refusal. Of course, in the case of a real banquet the offering of such excuses would have been most unusual, especially in view of the free offer, the quality and quantity of the refreshments, the host, and other considerations.[1] But since in this parable, for the interpretation of which we need not go into details, the bulk of the Jewish people are depicted as indifferent to the kingdom of Jesus and to the message of the Kingdom, there is a sequel in the parable in accordance with the truth which the Lord wished to impress upon the guest who had made the above remark.

11, 1) This implied business folly, as though the estate and the oxen had been purchased, as it were, unsight unseen. The view of Wetstein, De Wette, and others. Quoted by Meyer.

Luke 14, 15—24. **12.**

The servant was obliged to report to his master a general rejection of the invitations and an almost unnatural behavior of invited guests. The master of the house was angry. And no wonder, since in the Orient, and elsewhere for that matter, the failure to attend a banquet, even with such apparently reasonable excuses offered, was a high insult. The fact remained that they did not come and that they preferred their affairs to his. Being angry, the master sent out his servant again with the instruction to go quickly into the streets and lanes of the city and to bring in the poor, the maimed, the halt, and the blind. This was done, and many were led into the banquet-hall. We might add that this was done in Israel when the spiritually poor, halt, and blind accepted the Savior's health and salvation of which the scribes and Pharisees did not believe themselves to be in

"Go Out into the Highways and Hedges."

need. But the servant reported to his master: "Yet there is room." As a last resort the master ordered his servant out into the country, along the highways and hedges, saying, "Compel them to come in that my house may be filled." The details of the parables must not be pressed. Not that those out in the country were "lower down socially," but that the house might be filled. As compared with "the Jews in the interpretation," [1] these finally invited guests are represented as without. No implication of a Jewish superiority as such is intended. "For I say unto you [2] that none of those men which were bidden shall taste of my supper." The application to all present was obvious. God will have all men to be saved, and none will be rejected but those who exclude themselves. As applied to the kingdom of God — as there will be surprises as to those admitted, there will be even greater surprises with respect to those who will find themselves cast out. Only recently the Lord had said: "There shall be weeping and gnashing of teeth when ye shall see Abraham, and Isaac, and Jacob, and all the prophets in the kingdom of God and you yourselves thrust out." [3]

Luke 14, 25—27. **13.**

After the meal was over, Jesus again continued on the way which was finally to take Him to Jerusalem and to the cross. As formerly in Galilee, so here He was followed by great multitudes,

---

12, 1) Bruce *sub loco.*

2) Plural ὑμῖν, you (v. 24), as compared with the singular, αὐτῷ, thee, in v. 16.   3) Luke 13, 28.

to whom He spoke. The great number about Him gave Him an occasion to repeat [1] the demands He had made upon those who would follow Him in spirit and in truth. "If any man come to Me and hate [2] not his father, and mother, and wife, and children, and brethren, and sisters, yea, his own life also, he cannot be My

The Cost of Discipleship.

disciple." Surprisingly strong words as compared with the words spoken in connection with the mission of the Twelve, where it was a question of loving less. [3] And still, how true! Love of other interests makes effective discipleship impossible: "He cannot [4] be My disciple." As compared with all other objects of natural love, even life itself, they must be hated so that Christ will be loved alone. True discipleship means the giving up of all else that is deemed precious. And more. Not only the denial of interests, but actual sacrifice and suffering for the sake of Christ. "And whosoever doth not bear his cross and come after Me cannot be My disciple." [5]

Luke 14, 28—30. **14.**

If that is discipleship, then certainly the costs must be counted. You must not only joyfully intend, but carefully consider, firmly resolve, and then follow through and carry out. It is just as with a man who wants to build a tower, a grand house, something to

Building a Tower.

give credit to the builder and distinction to the community. Ordinary prudence will require that he first sit down and count the cost. Will he be able to carry it out? "Lest haply, after he hath laid the foundation and is not able to finish it, all that behold it begin to mock him." In that event, instead of adding a point of interest to the community, he would have reared a monument to his shame.

Luke 14, 31—33. **15.**

Or like a king who feels the urge of combat. Before he risks a battle with a neighboring king, he will first sit down and count how many of his subjects will be available for warfare. [1] While it

---

13, 1) Matt. 10, 37. 38.   2) Μισεῖ.
3) Bruce *sub loco.*   4) Οὐ δύναται.
5) Matt. 16, 24; Mark 8, 34; Luke 9, 23.
15, 1) Some have seen in these words a reference to the war of Herod with Aretas of Arabia as the result of the repudiation of the Arabian king's daughter by Herod and his marriage of Herodias. But this is unlikely. The date given by Schuerer (I, II, 30) for this war is 36 A. D. (after the death of Christ). It seems that the time of the public ministry of Jesus was a period of peace. This, of course, does not prevent the Lord from referring to war.

is not impossible for conquerors to overcome odds at the rate of two
to one, it is as unlikely as it is rare. Therefore, if his army numbers
only ten thousand, while the enemy is approaching with twenty

A King Anxious to Fight.   thousand, common sense will
prompt him to sue for peace,
even though it means humiliation for him, rather than to risk what
in view of unequal numbers points to miserable defeat. Thus they
who would follow Jesus are required to count the cost. Not as if
the costs, prohibitive to natural man, should frighten them from
venturing the expense. That is not the point. As to how the
strong and conspicuous tower of sincere discipleship is to be built
and whence to gain sufficient strength to overcome the two-to-one
stronger enemy, that is a different matter.

Luke 14, 34. 35.   **16.**

And as to the multitudes which followed Him, the Lord is not
so much interested in sudden gains as in the quality of discipleship.
If a man is a disciple at all, he must show the characteristics of
true discipleship. Just like salt, as the Lord explains in repeating

"Salt Is Good."   the illustration used in His Sermon on the
Mount. "Salt is good," that is, as long as
it is salt.[1] But if it has lost its saltiness, then it is good for
nothing, "neither fit for the land nor yet for the dunghill; but men
will cast it out." Mere outward conformity to the divine precepts
of Christian living and sheer formality do not count in the kingdom
of God. "He that hath ears to hear, let him hear." [2]

Luke 15, 1—7.   **17.**

Now we come to a jewel in the gospel account in which God's
love and grace shown a penitent sinner is beautifully portrayed.
In this period of the Lord's ministry as well as at other occasions
publicans and sinners approached Him "for to hear Him." In
accepting these and by telling the following parables, our Savior

"Jesus Sinners doth Receive."   wished to emphasize the
glorious truth that the love
of God embraces every, even the greatest, sinner. But to this
intimate association of Jesus with the outcasts of society the professional guardians of Jewish morality objected. "And the Pharisees and scribes murmured, saying, This man receiveth sinners and

---

16,   1) Matt. 5, 13; also Mark 9, 50. Chapter XI, 20.
    2) Matt. 11, 15; 13, 9. 43; Mark 4, 9; 4, 23; Luke 8, 8.

eateth with them." It seems that it was this last particular, fraternizing with them at table and thus winning their confidence, which was especially loathsome to them. According to their opinion this was carrying the matter of familiarity too far. But this narrow pharisaic faultfinding served Jesus as an occasion for telling the three wonderful parables of the Lost Sheep, the Lost Coin, and the Lost, or Prodigal, Son.

Luke 15, 1—7.   **18.**

The first of these parables, the parable of the Lost Sheep, had been previously told by Jesus,[1] namely, at the close of His Galilean ministry and before His journey to the Feast of the Tabernacles. But at that time His object was to warn against offending the little ones and His earnest concern to restore the erring sinner. Here the point He wishes to emphasize is the joy of God and the holy angels over the conversion of a sinner as opposed to pharisaic ill will. Rather than be offended at Jesus for receiving publicans and sinners, they should rejoice at their entry into the kingdom of heaven. Take, for instance, the case of a man who has a hundred sheep, but loses one of them. It is not so much the pain of diminished possession as the idea of the loss of, and concern for,

The Lost Sheep. the lost member of the flock. This man could easily have afforded to lose one sheep out of his herd; nevertheless he leaves "the ninety and nine in the wilderness," that is, in the unfenced pasture, and, presumably under the care of an assistant, takes immediate steps to find that one lost sheep. After he has found it, probably hungry and thirsty, with its strength practically spent, but fortunately still alive, undevoured, "he layeth it on his shoulders" and carries it to his home rejoicing. Coming home, he gives expression to his joy by calling together his friends and neighbors and saying: "Rejoice with me, for I have found my sheep which was lost." In like manner there is joy in heaven "over one sinner that repenteth, more than over ninety and nine just persons which need no repentance." The latter remark is for the special benefit of the Pharisees and scribes, who were like the rich who have need of nothing, and like the whole, who need no physician.[2] They did not consider themselves lost and condemned sinners and therefore rejected Him who had come to seek and to save that which was lost.

18,   1) Matt. 18, 12—14.
      2) Rev. 3, 17; Matt. 9, 12.

Luke 15, 8—10.   **19.**

Or think of a woman who has lost one of her ten drachmas, or pieces of silver. Now, a drachma in itself is of small value;[1] yet of value to a poor woman who owned only ten drachmas in all. How the woman lost the money is not stated, nor does it matter. But it is assumed that the loss occurred *in the house,* as compared with the sheep that had gone astray.[2] This is a point which the **The Lost Coin.** Pharisees and scribes might incidentally remember. Immediately the woman lights a lamp, sweeps the house, peers into every nook and crevice, and seeks diligently till she finds the lost coin. Having found it, she calls her friends and neighbors and bids them rejoice with her over the recovery of a part of her possessions. Likewise, the Lord tells His adversaries, there is joy in heaven, "in the presence of God" and of His "friends and neighbors," "the angels of God, over one sinner that repenteth." [3]

Luke 15, 11—32.   **20.**

Now the most wonderful parable of all. "Never was there such a world of tenderness compressed into such few immortal words." [1] A certain man had two sons. The younger of them said to his father: "Father, give me the portion of goods that falleth to me." This was a demand for the property which would have fallen to him in due course of time, as founded upon the Jewish law of inheritance: two parts to the elder and one part to the younger son.[2] "And he divided unto them his living." Not that he was compelled to do so, but "that the story might go on." [3] The division of his property before his death was something which the father might, but did not have to do.[4] It seems that this father divided his property among both of his sons [5] in such a way as to reserve a sort of life lease on the portion of the elder son, who **The Prodigal Son.** remained in his service. Not long afterwards the younger son gathered all together and took his journey into an unnamed "far country," for his purposes the farther, the better, and "there wasted his substance with riotous living." This was the spurious independence of a son

---

19, 1) Δραχμή. Used in the LXX as the rendering of "half-shekel." Commonly taken as the equivalent of the Roman denarius, about 20 cents, and equal to the ordinary daily wage of a soldier or laborer.

    2) Edersheim, II, 257.   3) Bruce *sub loco.*

20, 1) Farrar, II, 135.   2) Deut. 21, 17.

    3) Bruce *sub loco.*   4) Edersheim, II, 258.

    5) Διεῖλεν αὐτοῖς.

who was impatient of parental restraint and wished to do as he pleased. It was a sinner's love of the world. But the world "gives a miserable reward." [6] "And when he had spent all, there arose a mighty famine in that land, and he began to be in want." Thus folly and sin are punished by the holy God. Not that the famine was especially created for him; but had he not wasted his substance, he would have been able to weather the storm. "And he went and joined himself to a citizen of that country," literally, he glued himself [7] to one who was not at all willing to engage the miserable wretch, but finally yielded by sending him "into his fields to feed swine." To a Jew a greater ignominy could hardly have been imagined. The scion of a proud race had become the caretaker of an animal whose very name was avoided and spoken of as "another thing." [8] And even in the "foul infamy" of this debasing service the reward was so miserable that for very hunger "he would fain have filled his belly with the husks [9] that the swine did eat; and no one gave unto him," namely, anything better. His new master also felt the pinch of hard times. And "to get a meal of anything, even swine's food, was a treat." [10]

Luke 15, 11—32. **21.**

In this extremity of abject misery the young man "came to himself." [1] Thus recklessness ended in misery and misery in reflection. He who had been the honored son of a respected father and then for a brief spasm the happy host of profligate friends, but now a swine-surrounded wretch, began to meditate. "How many hired servants of my father's have bread enough and to

His Repentance. spare, and I perish with hunger!" And then the resolve, though it involved an effort and pained his pride: "I will arise and go to my father and will say unto him, Father, I have sinned against Heaven and before thee." Not that the possibilities which afterwards occurred suggested themselves to his "befuddled" brain. [2] A reinstatement to sonship was too much to expect. Fully conscious that he had forfeited all filial claims and keenly sensible of his husk food and swine surrounding, he would be sincerely satisfied to be made a bread-fed servant in his father's house.

20, 6) Ylvisaker, 494.　　7) Ἐκολλήθη.
　　8) *Dabhar acheer.* Farrar, I, 427, n. 1.
　　9) Κεράτια, the long, beanlike pods of the carob-tree.
　　10) Bruce *sub loco.*
21, 1) Εἰς ἑαυτὸν ἐλθών.　　2) Ylvisaker, 494.

Luke 15, 11—32.   **22.**

No sooner had the resolution been made than it was carried out. "And he arose and came to his father." What additional misery and privation was involved in his going back to his father as a beggar is not stated. The point is that true repentance must be revealed in deeds of repentance. "And now comes the never-to-be-equaled climax":[1] "When he was yet a great way off, his father saw him." No doubt he had been looking for him. No one would have recognized the ragged stranger as the rich man's son. "But the father's vision was sharpened by love."[2] Instant pity is awakened by the woeful sight. "And had compassion, and ran," — walking was too slow, — "and fell on his neck, and kissed him." Thus the father is again introduced. All these actions were signs of love of a father who was ready to do anything to recover his loss. At this point the son begins the speech which he had already rehearsed before the swine and no doubt repeated along the way: "Father, I have sinned against Heaven and in thy sight and am no

His Return.   more worthy to be called thy son." But it seems[3] that the last clause about making him as one of the servants is repressed by the demeanor of his loving father. The mere fact that his son has returned is to the father a proof of his repentance. And immediately he prepares to restore him to the rights and privileges of a son. We can picture to ourselves the scene. "Make haste!"[4] he calls to the servants who were attracted by the unexpected commotion. "Obliterate all traces of a wretched past! The lost son has returned!"[5] And that they might understand the status of the new member of the household, he tells them: "Off with the rags and get out the robes!" "Bring forth the best robe and put it on him; and put a ring on his hand and shoes on his feet." "Oh, yes, and that fatted calf," he tells them, which is even now standing in the stall,[6] ready to serve us at some future festal occasion, "bring it hither and kill it." "Let us eat and be merry; for this my son was dead and is alive again; he was lost and is found." And if there is joy in heaven at a sinner's return,

---

22, 1) Farrar, I, 428.

    2) Bruce *sub loco.*

    3) Although it appears in some manuscripts.

    4) Some MSS. prefix an expressive ταχύ after "said to his servants": "[Make haste,] bring forth," etc.

    5) Bruce *sub loco.*

    6) Meyer *sub loco:* "The well-known one, which stands in the stall."

so it is most fitting that the return of one as from the dead should be celebrated with feasting and as "with music of angel harps." [7] "And they began to be merry."

Luke 15, 11—32.   **23.**

But the story has a sequel about the elder brother, who, it appears, plays the role of the other lost son. In his attempt to throw a wet blanket over this gala affair he represents the Pharisees in their chilling attitude towards the reception by Jesus of publicans and sinners. While the festival was in progress, the elder son was "in the field." And, we might add, also while the younger son had been wasting his substance with riotous living, the elder son had been in the field. As he now returned to the house, he heard music and dancing. Naturally he did not know what it was all about. The servant to whom he applied for information told him in simple language: "Thy brother is come, and thy father hath killed the fatted calf because he hath received him safe and sound." But

The Elder Brother. with this news the elder brother was not pleased, especially not with the manner in which the returning brother had been received. He was angry at what he considered the unfairness of the whole proceeding "and would not go in." And "therefore came his father out and entreated him." The elder son thought he had a good reason for complaint and made the most of it in a bitter speech. There was much on his mind. He did not like the sound of the music. He was angry with his father for his ready forgiveness of the profligate son. To show such a tender heart was but a sign of weakness. Then there were other things; for instance, he, the elder son, had never been rewarded for faithful service. And then in merciless judgment, saying "the worst in the coarsest way," [1] he dragged up again the forgiven sins of a repentant brother, whom he would not acknowledge as brother. "All these years there was nothing but service and obedience, work and drudgery, for me!" "Yet thou never gavest me a kid that I might make merry with my friends. But as soon as this thy son was come," — he would not call him brother, — "which," as he had guessed correctly, "hath devoured thy living with harlots, thou hast killed for him the fatted calf." It was a son speaking to his father, but it was the language "of a servant" [2] and the expression of pharisaic conception of service

---

22, 7) Farrar, I, 428.
23, 1) Bruce *sub loco*.   2) Edersheim, II, 263.

and reward. But overlooking the self-righteousness of his elder son and justifying his own action of celebrating his younger son's return, the father tenderly replied: "Son, thou art ever with me, and all that I have is thine." Hast thou forgotten? Why this uncharitable desire, this base touch, to make "the worst of sins repented of"? [3] And besides, not only the father's dealing with the younger son, but his dealing with both of his sons was not a matter of service and reward, but of grace and love. Therefore rejoice! "It was meet that we should make merry and be glad; for this thy brother was dead and is alive again; and was lost and is found." — Both this and the two preceding parables were to impress upon the self-righteous Pharisees, who had expressed their dissatisfaction at the reception by Jesus of spiritual prodigals, "publicans and sinners," the glorious truth that God's kingdom is a kingdom of divine grace, mercy and love, in which forgiveness is extended freely to all who, having become ruefully conscious of their lost condition and of their awful plight in the face of a holy and just God, flee for pardon to Him whom the Father had sent into the world to merit this free grace, whom they, however, spurned.

Luke 16, 1—13.   **24.**

Some of the disciples, followers, of Jesus who had just heard the wonderful parable of the Prodigal Son were recruited from just those publicans and sinners to whose reception the Pharisees and scribes had objected. And lest they become overly pleased at the defense of Jesus and negligent in the performance of their duty in the Kingdom, especially in the use of earthly possessions, Jesus set forth the parable of the Unjust Steward. A certain rich man had a steward who was accused unto him, and, he feared, not unjustly, that he was unfaithful to his trust. Calling him into his presence, he said unto him: "What is this I hear of thee? Give an account of thy stewardship; for thou mayest no longer be steward." There was no doubt, it seemed to him, as to the truth of the accusation and the justice of this discharge. But this sudden demand for an itemized account and the notice of his dismissal from a profitable stewardship came to the steward as a thunderbolt from smiling skies. Immediately he deliberated upon a shrewd course of action. There was still some time to do so, and this he turned to good account. "Then the steward said within himself, What shall I do?" By all means something had to be done. There was no note of

23, 3) Farrar, I, 429, n. 1.

sorrow in his meditation, nor was there any desire to amend his ways. To his intensely practical mind it was all a question of doing something to extricate himself from a very unpleasant situation. All possible schemes were rapidly reviewed, only to be as quickly dismissed, especially the two eventualities of manual

Parable of the Unjust Steward. labor and begging. He was too weak to labor and too proud to beg. At last, however, he hit upon a feasible scheme, which would assure him willing reception into the houses of friends. While it was to be admitted that the plan was dishonest and its whole execution based upon fraud and at the expense of his master, yet thus his future would be secured. Be it remembered that for the time being he was still his master's steward, with all legal rights and authorities.[1] Possessing this authority, he was able to summon before him all of his master's debtors who either had bought goods on credit from him or were in arrears with their land rent. The security of his own future depended upon the successful outcome of an intrigue with them. And how he insured their good will for his own best interests, involved them in his own deception and fraud, and secured his own future, all at the master's expense, is shown by a few examples: "How much owest thou my lord?" The reply was: "An hundred measures of oil." The term used is bath, the largest liquid measure among the Jews, corresponding to approximately nine hundred gallons of olive-oil.[2] The amount was not small, and while its value may be roughly given as about fifty dollars, considering the value of money at that time, about twenty cents a day for a laborer or a soldier, the present-day value may safely be computed at over five times the amount.[3] But the steward told the debtor to take his bill [4] showing the amount of indebtedness and take off fifty per cent. "Sit down quickly and write fifty." To another, who owed his master a hundred measures of wheat, about eleven hundred bushels,[5] five to six hundred dollars in value, the instruction was given to deduct twenty per cent. "Take thy bill and write fourscore." In the same manner he dealt with all the various debtors of his master. The diversity of deduc-

---

24, 1) Edersheim, II, 267.

2) *Βάτος.* H. Porter, in *Int. St. B. Encycl.*, 3080. But the expositors are not agreed as to the exact amount. It does not matter. It seems that the size varied in different sections of Palestine, Judea and Galilee. Edersheim, II, 268.

3) Edersheim, II, 269. 4) *Τὰ γράμματα.*

5) *Κόρος.* 10 baths equal 1 kor. Ezek. 45, 14.

tion was merely to make the whole fraudulent proceedings look more like a true account.[6]   There may be some questions asked, but it is assumed that after the day of reckoning, when the steward was shamefully dismissed, he had gained friends who were now themselves involved and that there was now no necessity for him to dig or beg.

Luke 16, 1—13.   **25.**

"And the lord commended the unjust steward because he had done wisely." Though in St. Luke's gospel the word *lord* is frequently used to designate Christ,[1] it seems that here the master of the steward, and not the Lord Jesus, is meant. At any rate, the steward, whom he calls *unjust*,[2] is not commended for his iniquity, but for his worldly prudence. "For," as Jesus explains, "the children of this world are in their generation wiser than the children of light." From the false wisdom of the children of this world in relation to men of their own kind and in regard to their own interests the children of light should learn true spiritual wisdom; and this especially in reference to their own peculiar generation, in their concern about securing their eternal weal and as stewards in the administration of their worldly goods. "And I say unto you, Make to yourselves friends of the mammon of unrighteousness, that, when ye fail, they may receive you into everlasting habita-

The Application.   tions," of course, not after the example of the unjust steward, but by making friends

through deeds of charity. But they should not do this as though by helping the poor they could earn salvation; but because they would thus assure themselves of witnesses at the portals of heaven who in the presence of the Judge will testify to their deeds of mercy and love.[3]   Jesus is not a teacher of immorality, as some have thought as a result of a wrong interpretation of this parable. He that is a faithful steward of earthly possessions, great or small, will receive a gracious reward; he will be placed over greater things, oftentimes receive greater earthly riches and honor, certainly, however, larger spiritual blessings. And he that is unfaithful as a steward of God in the use of his earthly wealth, great or small, has lost the faith; how, then, can he hope to obtain what had been his "own" as long as he stood fast in the faith, the heritage

---

24,   6) Bruce *sub loco.*
25,   1) 7, 13; 10, 1; 11, 39; 12, 42; 17, 5. John 11, 2.
    2) Οἰκονόμον τῆς ἀδικίας.   3) Matt. 25, 35 ff.

in heaven? Finally, repeating a saying of His Sermon on the Mount, Jesus said: "No man can serve two masters; for either he will hate the one and love the other, or else he will hold to the one and despise the other. Ye cannot serve God and Mammon." [4)]

Luke 16, 14—18. **26.**

Jesus had been instructing His disciples, but, it seems, in the hearing of all. Feeling the sting of the concluding saying, the Pharisees, who were lovers of money, showed their anger by turning up their noses,[1)] by sneering, and by deriding Him. This childish behavior caused Jesus to flay their self-righteousness.[2)] As custodians of the Law they justified themselves before men with their outward legality, but their self-righteousness was an abomination in the sight of God. In their proud aloofness from publicans and

The Law has Not been Abolished. sinners they overlooked the fact that the Law and the Prophets had their *terminus ad quem* in John the Baptist.[3)] Since that time the Gospel of the Kingdom has been preached, and penitent sinners have eagerly pushed forward and rushed into it, as it were, by force. Now, this does not mean that the Law has been abolished. The situation is rather this, that it is easier for heaven and earth to pass away than that the smallest turn or stroke of a Hebrew letter should fail.[4)] The commandments are still in force, for instance, the commandment against divorce. "Whosoever putteth away his wife and marrieth another committeth adultery; and whosoever marrieth her that is put away from her husband committeth adultery." [5)]

Luke 16, 19—31. **27.**

If they who appeal to the Law would only heed the Law, "they would find that the Law and the Prophets are a sufficient guide to a godly life." [1)] In a most remarkable fashion Jesus covers a number of points on the Law and the Prophets: worldliness, the service of Mammon, the failure to secure the future, the neglect to make friends of the poor, and the like, in the striking parable of the Rich Man and Lazarus. A certain rich man is presented as clothed

---

25, 4) Matt. 6, 24.
26, 1) Bruce *sub loco.* 16, 14: ἐξεμυκτήριζον. Ἐκ and μύκτηρ, the nose. See Luke 23, 35.
    2) Kretzmann, I, 355.   3) Matt. 11, 12. 13.
    4) Matt. 5, 18.   5) Matt. 5, 32; 19, 9; Mark 10, 11. 12.
27, 1) Bruce *sub loco.*

with the most expensive Egyptian white cotton and covered with the royal purple of Phenician wool.[2]   And his life was a daily feast; for he "fared sumptuously every day."   These details are given, not as if any blame were attached to the possession and enjoyment of wealth as such; for Abraham, who shortly afterwards is introduced as presiding over heaven, as it were, was himself rich and yet was called the friend of God.   However, from the language employed as well as from the trend of the whole story the inference

The Rich Man and Lazarus.

is justified that this particular rich son of Abraham was of a worldly mind and chiefly concerned about the enjoyment of material things.   Such was his manner of life.   In contrast with this unnamed rich man [3] a suffering beggar by the common name of Lazarus is presented.   The name itself probably means "God-help" [4] and is most likely introduced for the sake of convenience in telling the story, because he has to be referred to in the sequel.[5]   As compared with the daily feasting of the rich man, his was a sorry lot.   While servants would be carrying in food and drink for the master's table, friends would probably cast him down [6] at the gate of the rich man's estate, half clothed and covered with ulcers, in order to make it possible for him to satisfy his hunger at least to a small extent and to prolong his miserable existence by means of such scraps as would be cast from the rich man's table.   The position as well as the desire was shared by other creatures, the dogs of the street, who "came and licked his sores."   Whether or not this latter detail was an alleviation or aggravation of the misery we do not know.[7]

Luke 16, 19—31.   **28.**

The beggar died. No more of him here. But the angels came from heaven and carried him "into Abraham's bosom." [1] What happened to the soulless body is passed over in delicate reserve.

27, 2) A probable rendition of βύσσον and πορφύραν.

3) Remembering that the Lord is evidently stating a parable (although some, following Tertullian, think that He is relating history), there is no sense in a tradition which provides a name, Nineue (Sahidic version: *"Cuius erat nomen Nineue"*) for the rich man. See Meyer *sub loco*.

4) Gotthilf, from אֶלְעָזָר, although some have seen in it a "No Help God" from לֹאאֶעָזֶר. See Meyer *sub loco*.

5) Bruce *sub loco*.   6) Ἐβέβλητο.

7) Dogs are otherwise in Scripture not represented as symbols of pity and compassion. Ylvisaker, 501.

28, 1) Εἰς τὸν κόλπον τοῦ Ἀβραάμ. Symbolic language for the blessed abode of departed souls.

But in due course of time the rich man also died "and was buried." Brilliant as was his life, his garments, his table, so also the arrangements that attended his death and burial. But here terminates all his exaltedness before men. As in the case of poor Lazarus, so also in that of the rich man, death did not end all. But there was a difference. The soul of the rich man found itself in hell.[2] The experience is not a mere negative condition or state of death, but he was "in torments" and "with paradise dimly visible, yet within speaking distance."[3] Lifting up his eyes, the rich man could see "Abraham afar off and Lazarus in his bosom." As to the various

In the Hereafter. details, we must remember that they are not "dogmatic teaching, but popular description."[4] No doubt the rich man, a Jew and a son of Abraham, was greatly surprised to find himself in hell, as were probably also the Pharisees among the listeners, for whose particular benefit the story was related, on hearing Jesus making this statement. While there is no furious resentment on the part of the rich man as to a possible injustice because of his consignment to hell, yet, seeing Abraham and recognizing him, he still hoped that the patriarch, his ancestor, could and would do something for him. In a strange dialog the tormented man calls out: "Father Abraham, have mercy on me and send Lazarus that he may dip the tip of his finger in water and cool my tongue; for I am tormented in this flame." Firmly Abraham replies: "Son, remember that thou in thy life receivedst thy good things and likewise Lazarus evil things; but now he is comforted, and thou art tormented." Not that the rich man was damned for the sake of his riches as such or that Lazarus was saved on account of his poverty and misery. Upon the rich man's request that his suffering be alleviated he is told by Abraham that, having on earth given his heart to the things of this world and not to God, he is now getting his well-merited deserts in being tormented ·in hell. And besides he must be reminded that there is "a great gulf fixed, so that they which would pass from hence to you cannot; neither can they pass to us that would come from thence." In those regions there is a great chasm,[5] too wide to be bridged and too long to be outflanked. The disposition of all those entering either abode is fixed and final.

28, 2) ʼΕν τῷ ᾄδη.
    3) Bruce.
    4) Bruce sub v. 23.
    5) Μέγα χάσμα.

Luke 16, 19—31. **29.**

There is no use of his pleading for himself. Dives, as the rich man is often styled after the Latin term used in the Vulgate, must resign himself to his fate. But as he sadly remembers former neglected duties, he continues the dialog with the request: "I pray thee therefore, Father, that thou wouldest send him [Lazarus] to my father's house; for I have five brethren,[1] that he may testify unto them lest they also come into this place of torment." But even this request is denied. "They have Moses and the Prophets," the regular means of grace; "let them hear them." And here we have the answer to the question why Lazarus was saved and Dives awoke in hell. In his misery, poverty, and suffering Lazarus truly had "Moses and the Prophets." With-

"They Have Moses and the Prophets." out them and without the true penitence and saving faith for which the expression stands, regardless of his suffering on earth, he would have found himself alongside of the rich man for continued suffering in hell. And the rich man was not rejected because he was rich, but because he did not heed the Law and the Prophets in repentance and faith. Therefore, as to his five brothers, Abraham says, "Let them hear them." To this the rich man objects: "Nay, Father Abraham; but if one went unto them from the dead, they will repent." However, without entering into the feasibility of sending Lazarus back to earth on this requested mission, the answer is given: "If they hear not Moses and the Prophets, neither will they be persuaded though one rose from the dead." If people will not hear and believe God's saving Word, they will neither be saved "by ghosts." [2] Here the parable as well as the warning of Christ to the Pharisees is abruptly broken off.

Luke 17, 1. 2. **30.**

There is a difference between giving and taking offense. The discussion of the foregoing chapters had been started by the offense which the Pharisees and scribes took at Jesus for receiving publicans and sinners.[1] As Jesus, by doing so, had not only not done wrong, but had acted in accord with His Messianic office, He had not *given* His revilers any offense, but they had unreasonably *taken*

29, 1) A random number, large enough to make the interest in their eternal well-being on the part of a deceased member very intelligible. Bruce *sub loco.*

2) Farrar, II, 127. 30, 1) Luke 15, 1.

offense. The same was true when some one was offended at his neighbor's failure to observe fasting, ceremonial washings, and the like, which really was no sin because these things were not commanded by God, but were only commandments of men. On the other hand, however, as Christ. points out to His disciples, "it is

Offenses. impossible but that offenses will come; but woe unto him through whom they come!" There is a kind of offense which is extremely sinful, namely, that of scandalizing simple believers and especially children, causing them to trip and to fall away from Christ. It were far better for such an offender, as Christ says in a repetition of a former saying,[2] "that a millstone were hanged about his neck and he cast into the sea."

Luke 17, 3. 4. **31.**

Followers of Christ must always guard against giving occasion to some one for stumbling. Moreover, a Christian should exercise brotherly love by admonishing the brother who has sinned against

Forgiveness. him. "And if he repent, forgive him." [1] And on account of the weakness of the erring brother this process may have to be repeated. "And if he trespass against thee seven times a day and seven times a day turn again to thee, saying, I repent, thou shalt forgive him." [2]

Luke 17, 5. 6. **32.**

What Christ here demanded of His followers required an unusual amount of love. And this unusual amount of love presupposes a correspondingly unusual amount of faith.[1] As matters stood, the apostles[2] were unequal to the task and said unto the

The Great Power of Faith. Lord:[3] "Increase our faith." This request gave Jesus an opportunity to enlarge upon the favorite topic, that of the strength of faith. It is not so much a matter of quantity as of quality. "If ye had faith as a grain of mustard-seed, ye might say unto the sycamine tree, Be thou plucked out by the root, and be thou planted in the sea, and it should obey you." [4]

30, 2) Matt. 18, 6. 7; Mark 9, 42.   31, 1) Matt. 18, 5.
31, 2) Compare Matt. 18, 21. 22.   32, 1) Kretzmann, I, 358.
32, 2) Οἱ ἀπόστολοι instead of the usual μαθηταί.
   3) Luke's frequent Κύριος.
   4) Compare Matt. 17, 20; 21, 21; Mark 11, 22. 23. Συκαμίνῳ = συκομορέαν of Luke 19, 4. The fig-mulberry tree. A tree here, a mountain in Matthew and Mark.

Luke 17, 7—10. **33.**

To such efficiency will faith bring the disciples; but they should be warned against the idea of meritoriousness in the sight of God.[1] This is explained in the parable of the Unprofitable Servants. A master who has servants — slaves in those days — plowing in the field or feeding the cattle will not tell them at their return to the house at meal-time to go at once and eat their meal. He will rather

Parable of Unprofitable Servants. make them serve him first. "Make ready wherewith I may sup and gird thyself and serve me till I have eaten and drunken." He does not thank the servant, does he? "I trow not." It is all in

the day's work. So also it is in the kingdom of God. Even if it were possible for the followers of Christ to do their full duty, they would nevertheless in the sight of God be "unprofitable servants." But is God a slave-driver? By no means. There is also a reward for faithful service. But that is not the point here. The purpose of Christ is not to teach in what spirit God deals with His servants, but in what spirit we should serve God.[2]

33, 1) Meyer *sub loco.*
2) Bruce *sub loco.*

CHAPTER XXIV.

THE RAISING OF LAZARUS.

Probably February, 30 A. D.
At Bethany, near Jerusalem.

John 11, 1—4.　　　　　**1.**

It was while Jesus was in Perea, probably in February of
30 A. D., that the news reached Him of the sickness of a member
in a household at Bethany, near Jerusalem, where He had been
hospitably received on a former occasion.[1] His name was Lazarus.[2] We do not know the nature of his sickness, except that he
was in a critical condition, which caused his sisters, Martha and
Mary, to send the message to Jesus: "Lord, he whom Thou lovest[3]
is sick." This is evidently an urgent appeal for the helpful presence
of Jesus, based not upon the worthiness[4] of Lazarus or of his
sisters, but only upon the love of Jesus.[5] We have met the two
sisters before, faithful, serving Martha and attentive Mary. And
"Lord, He whom　　　the evangelist introduces the notice
Thou Lovest Is Sick."　of an act of Mary which took place
　　　　　　　　　　　on a later occasion. "It was Mary
which anointed the Lord[6] with ointment and wiped His feet
with her hair."[7] Evidently the sisters knew where Jesus was to be
found and were confident that the mere notice of their brother's
condition would bring Him to the rescue. They were assured of the
love of Jesus because it is expressly stated that Jesus "loved[8]
Martha and her sister and Lazarus." Jesus, however, gave a puzzling reply: "This sickness is not unto death, but for the glory of

1,　1) Luke 10, 38—42.

　　2) The traditional tomb of Lazarus is still shown in a village on the
southeastern slope of Olivet, nearly two miles from Jerusalem, on the way to
Jericho, now called El Aziriyeh, after Lazarus.

　　3) Φιλεῖς, *amas*. Affectionate love. Natural human affection. Love
as expressed in marks of affection.

　　4) Luke 7, 4.

　　5) The sisters do not say: "He who loves Thee." This, of course,
is also implied.

　　6) Recorded by St. John in the following chapter. Κύριος used in the
narrative. Thus frequently in Luke. See previous chapter, 25.

　　7) John 12, 3. Also recorded by Mark (14, 3—9) and Matthew
(26, 6—13). We notice that John presupposes an acquaintance with the
synoptic gospels. Ylvisaker, 513.

　　8) Here the term ἠγάπα is used; from ἀγαπάω, *diligo*. A higher type
of love, involving will and judgment.

God, that the Son of God might be glorified thereby." The Lord knew that the physical death of Lazarus was imminent, and still His words were true. He would let Lazarus die, so that He could restore him to life and manifest His glory. And therefore, instead of hastening to the bedside of his friend to effect his immediate restoration to health, He purposely decided to wait until [9] Lazarus had breathed his last and to remain "two days still in the same place where He was."

John 11, 5—17.   **2.**

Not until after the death of Lazarus, known to Jesus because of His omniscience, did Jesus announce His intention to His disciples to go to Judea. But the announcement was received with astonishment. The disciples reminded Jesus of His late experience both at the Feast of Tabernacles and at the Feast of Dedication.[1] "Master, the Jews of late sought to stone Thee, and goest Thou thither again?" But to this objection Jesus replies, in the first place, that it was still His day, appointed to Him by the Father, **"Lazarus Is Dead."** in which He must work. "Are there not twelve hours in the day?" And then, continuing in a parable, as long as the day lasts, a man may confidently go forward without stumbling "because he seeth the light of this world." But if a man walks around in darkness, he stumbles "because there is no light in him." As long as His hour had not come in which He should suffer and die, no one would be able to harm Him. After quieting the fears of the disciples as to His safety, and incidentally also of their own, if they had been thinking about that, He speaks about Lazarus again: "Our friend Lazarus sleepeth; but I go that I may awake him out of sleep." Now, Jesus was speaking of the sleep of death. But the reference was misunderstood. "Lord, if he sleep, he shall do well." Then Jesus told His disciples plainly: "Lazarus is dead." Yes, He had permitted Lazarus to die. But in spite of the grief and pain which had been caused, and instead of grieving, He was glad for their sakes that He was not there when Lazarus died. In that case Lazarus would not have died. But now it was His purpose by means of a miracle which He would perform to strengthen their faith.

1,   9) Contrary to the common view that Lazarus died at the time of the arrival of the messenger and that the two days of waiting and two days of travel made up the four days of verse 17. We agree with Ebrard, *Gospel History,* 353.

2,   1) John 8, 59; 10, 31.

And so — "Let us go to him." But the disciples were still bewildered. Whatever might have been the object of the journey of Jesus to Judea, they were convinced that their Master was deliberately walking to His death. At least that was the view of Thomas, called Didymus, or Twin,[2] who was the "pessimist" of the Twelve. Later he appears as the doubting Thomas.[3] "But what else might be said of him, Thomas was no coward." To his mind there was nothing left for Jesus but to die. His is such a sincere and affectionate loyalty that he cannot harbor the thought of allowing his Master to go alone. In addressing his fellow-disciples, he expresses a fearless and undying loyalty in the words: "Let us also go that we may die with Him." "In him unbelief and faith were contending with one another for mastery as Esau and Jacob in Rebecca's womb." [4]

John 11, 18—46.   3.

We do not know from which point in Perea Jesus proceeded to Bethany nor how long it took Him to cover the distance, since it is not stated in the records. Because of the comparatively short distance between any point in Perea and Bethany [1] and on account of the following we assume, however, that Jesus was in no particular hurry. At any rate, when He reached Bethany, "He found"[2] that Lazarus had been four days already in the tomb. According to the custom of the country it is likely that the burial of Lazarus had taken place the same day that he died. Since deep mourning lasted for seven days, the house of Martha and Mary was still the center of the customary demonstration of grief and sorrow. That the family of Lazarus had some standing in the community can be seen from his burial in a tomb and from the visit of many Jews who had come from the near-by [3] capital city to express their condolence. As soon as Martha heard that Jesus was coming, she rushed out to meet him, while "Mary sat still in the house," immersed in grief. When Martha caught sight of Jesus, she called

---

2, 2) $\Theta\omega\mu\tilde{\alpha}\varsigma$ is the transliteration of תְּאֹמָא, and $\delta\iota\delta\upsilon\mu o\varsigma$ means twin. Dods *sub loco.*

3) John 20, 25.   4) Dods sub John 11, 16.

3, 1) From 20 to 75 miles.

2) Presumably by inquiry. A proof of the true human nature of Jesus, corresponding to the proof of His omniscience in verse 14.

3) "About fifteen furlongs off," $\dot{\omega}\varsigma$ $\dot{\alpha}\pi\dot{o}$ $\sigma\tau\alpha\delta\iota\omega\nu$ $\delta\epsilon\varkappa\alpha\pi\acute{\epsilon}\nu\tau\epsilon$. A stadium (furlong) is equal to 606¾ feet and is thus somewhat less than a furlong, which is 660 feet. 15 stadia are about 3,030 yards. *Int. St. B. Encycl.* sub "Furlong."

out to Him: "Lord, if Thou hadst been here, my brother had not died." This was not said to blame Jesus for arriving too late; her words are merely a plaintive lament, issuing from the fulness of her grief-stricken heart. And even now, she goes on to say, correcting her statement, as it were, in accordance with the message of Jesus,[4]

"I Am the Resurrection and the Life."

she is convinced that "whatsoever Thou wilt ask of God, God will give it Thee." This is faith and hope; and still there is something wrong with the statement. "The deity of Jesus was not yet living and real in the consciousness of Martha." For the purpose therefore of leading her to belief in Him as the One who could by His own power raise the dead, Jesus tells her: "Thy brother shall live." But it depends upon how these words are understood. "Martha ventures to take them as a consolatory word of promise relative to the resurrection at the Last Day." [5] It is a beautiful confession in itself: belief not merely in the immortality of the soul, but in the resurrection of the body.[6] But there is no resurrection at all, that is, to life, unless it is based upon Christ. "I AM THE RESURRECTION AND THE LIFE; HE THAT BELIEVETH IN ME, THOUGH HE WERE DEAD, YET SHALL HE LIVE; AND WHOSOEVER LIVETH AND BELIEVETH IN ME SHALL NEVER DIE." Jesus, and Jesus alone, is the Resurrection and the Life. "Believest thou this?" the Lord asks Martha. In reply to a question which implied the expression of an opinion as to the possession of life in spite of physical death the believing heart of Martha supplied an answer which included all: "Yea, Lord; I believe that Thou art the Christ, the Son of God."

John 11, 17—46.   4.

This scene took place before the actual arrival of Jesus in Bethany.[1] After Martha had heard the Word of Life, she hastened back to Mary. On account of the presence of the Jews in her house, of whose enmity against Jesus she was aware, and because she wished to give her sister an opportunity to talk to Jesus alone, she said to her secretly: "The Master is come and calleth for thee." In the conversation reported Jesus had not expressed

---

3, 4) Assuming that the messenger had returned with the message. Ylvisaker, 517.

5) Meyer *sub loco.*

6) Ἀναστήσεται ἐν τῇ ἀναστάσει.

4, 1) Martha had rushed out to meet Jesus, v. 20.

the wish to see Mary. But probably the whole conversation has not been reported, or Martha took it for granted that Jesus would gladly bring comfort to Mary also.[2] Immediately Mary left her sister with the comforting visitors and herself rushed out to meet Jesus. The Jews thought Mary had been overcome by an outburst of grief and sorrow and intended to go to the grave and weep there. They were unwilling to leave her alone without words of sympathy and comfort, and so they rose and followed her.[3] Consequently, when Mary reached Jesus, she had time only to fall down at His feet and to repeat the thought which un-

"Jesus Wept." doubtedly had been the frequent refrain of her plaint in her sorrow: "Lord, if Thou hadst been here, my brother had not died." As Jesus noticed the tears of Mary and the wailing of the approaching Jews, He was filled with anger and displeasure in contemplation of the cause which has brought about all misery and suffering and finally death — sin. "He groaned in the spirit and was troubled." "His intense emotion prompts Him to end the scene." [4] He inquired about the location of the grave.[5] They told Him: "Come and see." He who possessed almighty power now discloses human emotions in a burst of tears. "Jesus wept." [6] He is sorrowful with the sorrowful. Some of the Jews were touched at this manifestation of loving sympathy. "Behold how He loved him!" But others could make nothing of Jesus' tears; His weeping puzzled them. Why had He not healed Lazarus in the first place? Was it unwillingness or inability? It could have been neither. In a half-puzzled, half-mocking way they asked: "Could not this man which opened the eyes of the blind [7] have caused that even this man should not have died?" If He was unable to raise a dead man, how about the other miracles? And if He was unwilling to do so, why the tears?

John 11, 17—46.   5.

The unkind attitude of the Jews towards Jesus as revealed in the remark caused Him to groan again as He approached the grave. This was a cave, whether natural or artificial we do not know,

---

4,   2) Kretzmann, I, 474.

     3) Ylvisaker, 519.   4) Dods *sub loco.*

     5) Either because He wanted those present to accompany Him or because according to His human nature He did not know, voluntarily abstaining from the use of the divine omniscience communicated to His human nature.

     6) **The shortest verse in the English Bible.**

     7) John 9, 7.

and a stone lay upon its mouth. What is supposed to be the tomb of Lazarus is still shown to travelers. Jesus said: "Take ye away the stone." But Martha, who had joined the gathering again, objected: "Lord, by this time he stinketh; for he hath been dead four days." But Jesus replied: "Said I not unto thee that, if thou wouldest believe, thou shouldest see the glory of God?" These words would rather recall what Jesus had said to His disciples in Perea;[1] but the conversation with Martha as recorded [2] was probably abridged. Notwithstanding the objection of Martha, possibly because it was perceived that Jesus had some end in mind, "they took away the stone." Now Jesus speaks a brief prayer of thanksgiving, as if Lazarus had already been restored to life. "Father, I thank Thee that Thou hast heard Me. And I know that Thou

"Lazarus, Come Forth!" hearest Me always; but because of the people which stand by

I said it that they may believe that Thou hast sent Me." It was essential that the miracle He was going to perform be referred to its real source and that all recognize that Jesus was in truth the Messiah sent by God. Crying now with a loud voice that all might hear Him, He gave the command: "Lazarus, come forth!" Scarcely were the words spoken when like a specter there issued from the rocky tomb a figure "bound hand and foot with grave-clothes," long linen wrappings, and with a napkin around the head, "which upheld the jaw that four days previously had dropped in death." [3] Lazarus was restored to life; indeed, as tradition has it,[4] to thirty more years of life and light and love. A dead man had returned to life. But since in the present condition he was unable to walk and was unfit for society, being wrapped in ghastly vestments, the direction was given: "Loose him and let him go." What a sight Lazarus must have presented as he returned to the village! And what an excitement his return to life must have caused as the miracle became known! And still, how true Quadratus,[5] this early apologist and *auditor Apostolorum*, could write during the reign of Hadrian: [6] "But the works of our Savior were always present, for they were genuine: those that were healed and those that were raised from the dead, who were seen not only when they were healed

---

5,   1) V. 4.   2) Vv. 23—26.   3) Farrar, II, 171.

4) Epiphanius, *Haer.*, 66, and Hofmann, *Leben Jesu*, quoted by Farrar, II, 171.

5) 124 or 125 A. D.

6) Quoted by Eusebius, IV, 3. See chapter XII, 1.

and when they were raised, but were also always present; and not merely while our Savior was on earth, but also after His death they were alive for quite a while, so that some of them lived even to our day"! The effect of this stupendous miracle was twofold. Some of the Jews who had come to visit the sisters were convinced of the truth of Christ's words and of His divine power to perform true miracles. They "believed on Him." But others went to the Pharisees and told them what Jesus had done.

John 11, 47—52.   6.

The Pharisees at once took action upon receiving the information. The matter was deemed so important that an immediate meeting of the Sanhedrin seemed advisable. The reality of the miracle could not be denied. But the members of this body refused to believe on Him who had performed it.[1] The general trend of the discussion was that something had to be done. If nothing is done, they assert, to change this impossible situation, then "all men will believe on Him." Jesus would then head a Messianic movement and make Himself king. And this would bring about an intervention by Rome and end their political existence. While the members vainly raged, Joseph Caiaphas, "being the high priest that same year," rose to address them. Not as though the Jews had a new high priest every year, but he was the high priest in that memorable year when Jesus was to die.[2] He was the son-in-law of Annas, who was one of his predecessors in the high-priestly office, and held his office from about 18 to 36 A. D., when Vitellius deposed him.[3] He contemptuously told the council: "Ye know nothing at all." There was only one thing to be done, and that was to select one person — whether innocent or guilty did not

The Prophecy of Caiaphas.   matter, as long as it was expedient for them — as their victim rather than to have the whole nation perish. Thus murderous intention is presented under the guise of concern for the public welfare. No, he did not desire the death of Jesus! But the welfare of the nation made it necessary. The truth, however, was, as he and the members knew, that their own power and influence were at stake. The proposal was as selfish as it was unjust. And "what is morally wrong is politically inexpedient."[4] All things being equal, then, the weal of the nation is worth more of course

---

6,   1) Farrar, II, 174.   2) Ylvisaker, 523.
     3) Schuerer, II, I, 199.   4) Farrar, II, 175, n. 2.

than the life of an individual. But this did not apply. Here it was a case of public benefit, not of public danger, and the life, not of a disturber, but of a benefactor, an innocent man, a popular teacher, a great healer, not to mention that He was the Messiah and the Son of God. And still, as the evangelist points out, in proposing the death of Jesus for the benefit of the people, Caiaphas unwittingly spoke a word of prophecy. In ancient days the high priests communicated to the people the will and counsel of God by means of the Urim and Thummim,[5] lost since the Babylonian Exile. And so here once more, and, it seems, for the last time, a Jewish high priest, albeit by the grace of the Romans and not by the grace of God, unintentionally and unconsciously — like Balaam's ass — revealed a sentence of the gracious will of God. It was indeed expedient that "one man should die for the people"; however, not in the sense of Caiaphas. "And this he spake not of himself, but, being high priest that year, he prophesied that Jesus should die for that nation, and not for that nation only, but that also He should gather together in one the children of God that were scattered abroad."

John 11, 53. 54.   7.

This prophetic utterance of the "bilingual"[1] Caiaphas so influenced the perplexed members of the Sanhedrin that "from that day forth they took counsel together for to put Him to death." But the hour of Jesus had not yet come. Neither was He unaware of the evil plan formulated against Him in the meeting-place of

Retirement to Ephraim.

the Sanhedrin, the Hall of Polished Stones. For the purpose of not precipitating matters He withdrew Himself once more, and for the last time, before the final Passover, at the celebration of which He was to become the true Paschal Lamb. The place of retirement is given as "a country near to the wilderness, a city called Ephraim." There He tarried with the disciples.[2] The place may be located a few miles northeast of Jerusalem, near Bethel, toward the Samaritan border.[3]

6,   5) Ex. 28, 30; Num. 27, 21.

7,   1) Dods *sub loco.*

2) That He spent a few weeks in secrecy is implied in the statement (v. 57) that, if any one knew where He was, he was to inform the chief priests and the Pharisees.

3) Smith, *Hist. Atlas,* 24. About thirteen miles northeast of Jerusalem, in the wilderness of Bethaven. The present village of Taiyibeh. See also Wieseler, *Synopsis,* 291, n. 7.

CHAPTER XXV.

THE FINAL JOURNEY TO JERUSALEM.

Shortly before the Passover of 30 A. D., 783 A. U. C.

Luke 17, 11.   **1.**

There were but a few weeks left of the earthly life of Jesus. These were spent in quiet meditation in preparation for the ordeal before Him. And after He left His retreat in the wilderness of Bethaven, about Ephraim,[1] on His way to Jerusalem, it was by a circuitous route. At the first glance it would seem as if He were turning His back on Jerusalem in a journey which took Him northward through Samaria and then eastward "in the midst of Samaria

"In the Midst of Samaria and Galilee." and Galilee," between the two provinces and on the confines of both, toward the Jordan Valley and Perea.[2] The reason seems to have been that He wished to join a caravan of Galilean pilgrims, probably at some appointed place, on their way to the Passover in Jerusalem. This apparently is confirmed by the later notice that His mother Mary as well as Mary Magdalene, Salome, and many other women went up with Him to Jerusalem.[3] And there was another reason for His journey through the borderlands of Samaria and Galilee: to bring healing to a band of unfortunates who "on the frontiers of two countries had been gathered like froth at the margin of wave and sand to share the misery of both." [4]

Luke 17, 12—19.   **2.**

On the outskirts of an unknown village there met Jesus a company of ten lepers, "which stood afar off." They dared not approach Him, as that would have been pollution. In joyful and

The Ten Lepers. believing recognition of the great Stranger who had happened into their midst they lifted up their voices and cried out: "Jesus, Master,[1] have mercy on us!" The heart of Jesus was immediately thrilled with com-

---

1, 1) John 11, 54. Dods *sub loco.*

2) This seems to be the meaning of the disputed διὰ μέσου of the *textus receptus* or the διὰ μέσον or ἀνὰ μέσον or μέσον alone of other readings. See Andrews, 412.

3) Mark 15, 40. 41; Luke 23, 49. Confirmed also by Matt. 20, 20.

4) Farrar, II, 111.

2, 1) Ἐπιστάτα, a "Lucan expression." 5, 5; 8, 24. 45; 9, 33. 49; 17, 13.

[491]

passion. Quick as an echo the words flashed back: "Go show yourselves unto the priests." The lepers knew the significance of the command. Not as if the priests should heal them, but that they should hasten to request of the local priests an attestation of their cure and the certificate of their restitution to every privilege of social life.[2] "And it came to pass that, as they went, they were cleansed."

Luke 17, 12—19.   **3.**

A most wonderful blessing had been bestowed upon these unfortunate sufferers. For all practical purposes, since it was a case of real leprosy, it was the restoration to life; for had Jesus not miraculously freed them from their dreadful malady, they could not have hoped ever to be cured. But only one, when he saw that he had been healed, turned back, glorified God, and "fell down on his face at His feet, giving Him thanks." And then comes the significant sentence: "And he was a Samaritan." "Once more the Jew suffers by comparison." [1] While the nine benefited Jews were

The Grateful Samaritan.   coldly thankless, the Samaritan returned to Jesus. One would have expected that not even going through fire would have kept them from coming back. Jesus had frequently met ingratitude before, but He could not help being sadly affected by an instance so heartless and cruel. "Were there not ten cleansed? [2] But where are the nine?" Jesus asks in sorrowful surprise. "He came into His own, and His own received Him not." [3] The recognition which He should have received from the children of the Kingdom a despised stranger must bring. But be that as it may, the alien [4] shall not have returned in vain, nor shall his gratitude come short of the blessing it deserved: "Arise, go thy way; thy faith hath made thee whole."

Luke 17, 20. 21.   **4.**

It was clear, even to Jesus' enemies, that He had presented Himself as the Messiah and He had proved it by His deeds; it was only their astounding blindness that made them fail to realize it. But because Jesus asserted that He was the Christ, the impatient and carnal-minded Pharisees wanted to know when the Messianic

---

2,   2) Lev. 13, 2; 14, 2.

3,   1) Compare Luke 10, 33. Bruce, *sub loco.*

     2) The word for healing lepers is "cleanse." To a certain extent being afflicted with this disease also involved ceremonial defilement.

     3) John 1, 11.   4) Ἀλλογενής.

kingdom would come? That is what they were interested in. "When is all this preaching and preparation to end and the *Kingdom*" — such as they expected of course — "to begin?" [1] But as in other of His many encounters with the Pharisees, Jesus points out to them that, as usual, they were wholly mistaken in their point

The Nature of the Kingdom. of view. The kingdom of God does not come in a vulgar, physical sense. "It cometh not with observation." The word used [2] refers to the observation of heavenly bodies, from whose movements one can calculate when an expected phenomenon is to occur. [3] But all attempts at predicting the coming of the kingdom of God in the sense of millennialists or at defining its limits in the sense of exclusive communities must fail. Since the Kingdom is spiritual, also its coming must be invisible. "Neither shall they say, Lo here! or, Lo there! For, behold, the kingdom of God is within you," [4] in your hearts. If you accept Him in faith whom the Father has sent to build up this kingdom in the hearts of men, you will also enter the kingdom above.

Luke 17. 22—37. 5.

Still, on the other hand, there will also be a glorious coming of the Son of Man. The kingdom of God cometh not with observation; not now, but hereafter. However, as to the disciples, for the present there will be days when they will desire the experience of just one day of joy and happiness with their Master, "and ye shall not see it." Deceivers and false Christs will arise and cry: "See here! or, See there!" But they are not to follow or go after them. [1] As for Christ, His final advent will partake of the nature of lightning. But for the present "He must suffer many things and be rejected of this generation." The day of glory for Christ and of judgment upon all unbelievers, however, will certainly dawn, just as the Flood came in the days of Noah and the destruction of Sodom in the days of Lot. [2] As the waters of the Flood covered the "sensualism in the days of Noah and the fire and brimstone from heaven streamed upon the busy wickedness of Sodom," [3] so shall it also be in the day when the Son of Man will be revealed. And the disciples should be warned lest this day burst upon them

---

4, 1) Farrar, II, 136.   2) Παρατήρησις.   3) Bruce *sub loco.*
   4) Ἐντὸς ὑμῶν ἐστιν. For this reason there can be no "coming" of the Kingdom, because, correctly understood, the Kingdom is already here.
5, 1) Matt. 24. 23. 26. 27; Mark 13, 21.
   2) Matt. 24, 37—39.   3) Farrar, II, 137.

unawares. When a hostile army makes a successful assault and the only safety is in sudden flight, there must be no looking back. "Remember Lot's wife!" Thus the Lord incidentally confirms the historicity of the Deluge, the destruction of Sodom, and the

The Day of the Son of Man.

transformation of Lot's wife into a pillar of salt.[4]

He who has only the saving of earthly life and of his temporal goods in mind on that day will lose both these and eternal life with God.[5] Moreover, the Last Day is not only a day of judgment, but also a day of separation. This Jesus explains in a few examples. In that night,[6] of two men in one bed only one will be taken. Two women will be grinding at the same mill; one will be accepted, the other rejected. Two men will be in the field; the one will be taken and the other be left.[7] Persons who were closely associated with one another in this life will on the Last Day be forever separated if one of them is a believer in Christ and therefore heavenly-minded, while the affections of the other during his lifetime were set on earthly things. The warning was not without effect upon the disciples. In awe and fear they asked: "Where, Lord," will this separation take place? But the coming of the Lord is "as little geographical as it is chronological." [8] In a very fitting picture the Lord replies that the Judgment will overtake the ungodly. "Wheresoever the body is, thither will the eagles be gathered together." [9]

Luke 18, 1—8. **6.**

In listening to the words of Jesus about the suddenness of His final coming and the possibility of their being unprepared, the disciples must have felt the need of divine protection and guidance. That is probably the connection between the foregoing and the present section, which treats of prayer. To be instant and even importunate in prayer is certainly a necessity in the last days for all such as intend to heed the warnings about the coming of the Son of Man.[1] In order, now, to teach His disciples the necessity of diligent and unceasing prayer, Jesus tells them a parable about a judge in a certain city "which feared not God, neither regarded

---

5,   4) Gen. 19, 26.   5) Matt. 10, 39.

    6) Hitherto "day." The reference to night suits the illustration. Bruce *sub loco.*

    7) Matt. 24, 40. 41.   V. 36 is considered an interpolation from Matt. 24, 40.

    8) Farrar, II, 138.   9) Matt. 24, 28. Kretzmann, I, 362.

6,   1) Kretzmann, I, 362.

man." Since the Jews had no one-man tribunals as such in those days, we are probably permitted to think of the type of judges such as would be appointed by Herod or Pontius Pilate.[2])   Now, there was a widow in that city with a case which required immediate adjustment. She came to him with the cry: "Avenge me of mine

The Parable of the Importunate Widow.

adversary." What the grievance was is not stated, nor does it matter. Evidently she had a right to demand justice. But the judge took no interest in the case in spite of the fact that she came again and again. Finally, however, he said to himself, though he feared neither God nor man and not for the sake of justice, yet for the selfish reason of ridding himself of a harassing annoyance, "Because this widow troubleth me, I will avenge her." She was making life miserable for him. And if it was not the call of justice, it was the prospect of having the fists of an enraged woman placed below his eyes,[3]) which moved his heart. Thus the shamelessly selfish and utterly unprincipled judge. And the lesson: "Shall not God avenge His own elect," those graciously predestined by Him unto life eternal, who stand in the closest relation to Him and "cry day and night unto Him?" And though He delay His final interposition, yet He will avenge them shortly. But He wants them to cry unto Him. However, with all the temptations surrounding them in the last days and from the standpoint of impotent man, "when the Son of Man cometh, shall He find faith on the earth?"

Luke 18, 9—14.   7.

Among those in the presence of Jesus, if not in His direct following, there were such of a pharisaic disposition, "which trusted in themselves and despised others." To them Jesus spoke a parable about two men who went up into the Temple to pray. That is as far as they went together. Incidentally we notice that, while the worship in the Temple was largely sacrificial, the house of God was also made the place of private prayer.[1]) After taking his stand in the sacred enclosure, before God, the Pharisee offered up what was more an expression of self-congratulation than communion with God, prayer and supplication: "God, I thank Thee that I am not as other men are," [2]) that is, the common herd, "extortioners, unjust,

---

6,   2) Edersheim, II, 287.

     3) Ὑπωπιάζῃ, from ὑπώπιον — ὑπό and ὤψ.

7,   1) Luke 2, 27. 37. Edersheim, II, 289.

     2) The οἱ λοιποί. The *Am ha Aretz,* the people of the soil, from whom he as a Pharisee would be separated.

adulterers, or even as this publican." Plainer words of a thankless thanksgiving could hardly have been spoken. Only one day of the year had been set aside for fasting, the Great Day of Atonement;[3] but he fasted twice a week, presumably on Mondays and Thurs-

The Pharisee and the Publican.
days.[4] The Law required tithes of the herd and of the fruits of the field and trees;[5] but he gave the tenth of all that he possessed or acquired.[6] What, then, was he lacking? In his own mind he was lacking nothing; in truth, however, he was lacking everything: the knowledge of sin, repentance, and realization of the fact that he needed a Savior. On the other hand, the publican, humbly standing aloof, not daring to lift up his eyes to heaven, and smiting his breast in pungent remorse, penitently expressed himself thus: "God be merciful to me, a sinner," literally, "*the* sinner." [7] What a contrast! In his mind the Pharisee was a saint before God and man, and in his heart the publican acknowledged himself a sinner above all others. The judgment of Christ is clear and comprehensive. In the judgment of God the publican, who sought refuge in the grace of God, was absolved. "I tell you, this man went down to his house justified rather than the other." He received the forgiveness and justification which the other claimed. And the general principle, so often enunciated,[8] also applies: "For every one that exalteth himself shall be abased, and he that humbleth himself shall be exalted."

8.

Matt. 19, 1. 2.[1] *Mark 10, 1.*[1]

By this time Jesus was again in Perea, on the journey already begun six months before, when He had definitely given up Galilee

---

7, 　3) If that was the meaning of "afflict your souls," Lev. 16, 29; 23, 27. 　4) Edersheim, II, 291. 　　5) Lev. 27, 30. 32; Deut. 14, 22. 　6) Κτῶμαι. 　　7) Τῷ ἁμαρτωλῷ. 　8) Luke 14, 11; Matt. 23, 12.

8, 　1) Matthew and Mark link up the following with the discourses in Capernaum, after the Transfiguration. But the notice of the departure from Galilee does not preclude the insertion of intervening visits to Jerusalem before this final journey, as supplied by John and introduced between corresponding sections of Luke: —

1. Tabernacles, John 7, 10 ff., followed by Luke 9, 51 ff.
2. Dedication, John 10, 22 ff., followed by Luke 13, 22 ff.
3. Raising of Lazarus, John 11, 1 ff., followed by Luke 17, 11 ff.
4. Final journey, Matt. 19, 1 ff.; Mark 10, 1 ff., joined by Luke 18, 14 ff. As we have seen (No. 1), from Ephraim Jesus went northward, then eastward across the Jordan, and then south through Perea to Jericho, to Bethany, to Jerusalem. See Robertson, *Harmony,* 141, note, and 276—279.

as a field of operations. This journey was now definitely leading Him to Jerusalem and to the cross. As He was approaching His

Returning to Perea. Judean destination by way of Perea,[2] He was attended by multitudes, to whom, as was His wont, He administered the saving Word of Life; and He also performed healing deeds of love.

9.

Matt. 19, 3—12. Mark 10, 2—12.

One of the burning questions of the day between the two rabbinic schools in Israel was the interpretation of the expression "matter of nakedness," or rather, the meaning of a single word, "uncleanness," or "nakedness," in the Mosaic marriage law. "When a man hath taken a wife and married her and it come to pass that she find no favor in his eyes because he hath found some *ervath dabhar* in her,[1] then let him write her a bill of divorcement and give it in her hand and send her out of his house. And when she is departed out of his house, she may go and be another man's wife."[2] In general, the comparatively low estimate of woman may be noted. Hillel and his school explained the passage in the

Concerning Divorce. sense that a man might divorce his wife for almost any reason, while the stricter school of Shammai interpreted the passage as applying to moral delinquency, which, however, was unreasonably extended to include, for instance, the supposed unchastity of appearing unveiled in the streets. "Hillel loosed what Shammai bound."[3] Shammai was right in so far as he permitted no divorce *in foro conscientiae* except for the most flagrant immorality. Hillel was right in that he left an opening for divorce *in foro civili*. While the leaders disputed, the people were perplexed. And besides the theological and moral there was probably also a political aspect. For the bold expression of his view contrary to the practise of a royal adulterer the greatest of all prophets had lost his head. For Jesus to decide in favor of one school under the circumstances would, to say the least, have given mortal offense to the other.

8, 2) The reading of the *textus receptus* in Mark 10, 1 is: Εἰς τὰ ὅρια τῆς Ἰουδαίας διὰ τοῦ πέραν τοῦ Ἰορδάνου.

9, 1) עֶרְוַת דָּבָר, "matter of nakedness," "some uncleanness," *aliquam foeditatem,* Blœsse in irgend etwas.

2) Deut. 24, 1. 2.

3) See Edersheim, II, 333. Farrar, II, 152. Ylvisaker, 444.

10.

Matt. 19, 3—12. Mark 10, 2—12.

Likely for the purpose of placing the Savior in the dilemma of either choosing the unpopular side of Shammai or of exposing Himself to the charge of laxity by siding with Hillel, a tempting question was submitted by the Pharisees: "Is it lawful for a man to put away his wife for every cause?" The latter clause seems to suggest that they expected Jesus to declare Himself in favor of the stricter view. In His response Jesus safely placed Himself upon the authority of the Law. "What did Moses command you?"

"What Therefore God hath Joined Together." But that seems to have been the opening for which they had been waiting. The Mosaic precept is quoted: "Moses suffered to write a bill of divorcement and to put her away." [1] But without quibbling Jesus appealed straight to the highest authority — God's institution of marriage. He who in the beginning "had made them male and female" has said in His Word: [2] "For this cause shall a man leave father and mother and shall cleave to his wife; and they twain shall be one flesh." Thus marriage constitutes an alliance closer than that of parent and child. It is a union which is a unity. "What therefore God hath joined together let not man put asunder."

11.

Matt. 19, 3—12. Mark 10, 2—12.

But does not Jesus thus put Himself in opposition to Moses? "Why did Moses, then, command to give a writing of divorcement and to put her away?" Jesus, however, corrected the misunderstanding. Moses did not command, but only permitted divorce, and this only under certain circumstances and as a concession to

"Except It Be for Fornication." the hardness of their hearts. It was the introduction of a civil measure for the purpose of avoiding greater evils. "But from the beginning it was not so." Only adultery breaks the bonds of matrimony before death in the sight of God. Divorce obtained at the forum of the state is really no divorce, but merely a public declaration of a sinful condition which has already been established.

10, 1) Deut. 24, 1. Since there is a great difference between the term *command* in the question of Jesus and the *suffered* in the reply, this was really a begging of the question.

2) "And said." That is, God said, speaking through the mouth of Adam, Gen. 2, 24.

A husband or a wife may not obtain a divorce unless the other party has committed adultery. "Whosoever shall put away his wife except it be for fornication and shall marry another committeth adultery."

12.

Matt. 19, 3—12. Mark 10, 2—12.

These words were intended as food for reflection for the Pharisees; but what their reaction was the evangelists do not say. But the disciples were dismayed. If that is the meaning of Christ, that except in the case of adultery a man cannot rid himself of an utterly worthless and disagreeable wife, "it is not good to marry." Of a truth, these matters must be considered before entering the state of matrimony. To the remark of the disciples the Lord gives the somewhat dark reply: "All men cannot receive this saying, save they to whom it is given." It seems that the reference is to a person's abstaining from marriage. After all, marriage is "the normal state for normal adults." As to celibacy, there are

Celibacy. three kinds of eunuchs:[1] those who are naturally unfit for wedlock; those who have been mutilated and made eunuchs by men; finally, those who voluntarily make themselves eunuchs "for the kingdom of heaven's sake." But not in the sense of the Church Father Origen, who permitted himself to be mutilated, prompted by an injudicious zeal for the kingdom of God. All three classes, however, are abnormal, even the last, except in extraordinary cases: persecution, great distress, and the like. At all times, even in wedlock, there must be a proper freedom of the heart and emancipation of the will for the service of Christ.[2] As to celibacy, it is neither recommended nor forbidden. "He that is able to receive it, let him receive it." With this final word Jesus again seems to indicate that not celibacy, but marriage, is the normal thing. At any rate, the doctrine which would make the unwedded state a higher degree of Christian perfection is in conflict with the word of God: "It is not good that the man should be alone."[3]

13.

Matt. 19, 13—15. Mark 10, 13—16. Luke 18, 15—17.[1]

As a touching commentary of divine blessing resting upon the institution of matrimony the next incident related by the three

---

12, 1) Εὐνοῦχος, the keeper of the bedchamber in an Oriental harem.
2) 1 Cor. 7, 26—29.   3) Gen. 2, 18.
13, 1) Here Luke again joins Matthew and Mark, whom he had left at the close of the Galilean ministry, before the Feast of Tabernacles, six months

Synoptists is the account of Jesus' blessing little children. "And they brought young children to Him that He should touch them," presumably Perean mothers,[2] though fathers are not excluded.[3] The scene has inspired painters and poets of every Christian age. Was it possibly whispered around that a crisis was at hand and that the departure of Jesus was approaching? At any rate, little children [4] were brought to Jesus that He should touch them and bestow His blessings upon a generation yet to come. But the disciples rebuked those

"Suffer the Little Children to Come unto Me."

that brought them.[5] They did not want their Master to be needlessly troubled and disturbed. But Jesus was much displeased when He saw it and said to His disciples: "Suffer the little children to come unto Me and forbid them not; for of such is the kingdom of God." Children for the Kingdom. The Kingdom is also intended for them; they need it, and it belongs to them. And in a deeper, spiritual sense: the Kingdom for children. For: "Verily I say unto you, Whosoever shall not receive the kingdom of God as a little child, he shall not enter therein." And conferring spiritual blessings upon the little children, "He took them up in His arms, put His hands upon them, and blessed them."

14.

Matt. 19, 16—26. Mark 10, 17—27. Luke 18, 18—27.

As Jesus was again going forth "into the way" which was to take Him steadily nearer to the cross, a young man of wealth and position, presumably a ruler of the local synagog,[1] seems suddenly to have arrived at the conviction that he must by all means apply to the departing Jesus for direction in his quest of the highest good. Determined not to be too late, he came running, and breathlessly kneeling before Him, he addressed to Jesus an all-important question in all sincerity and in terms of genuine respect: "Good [2]

---

previously. From this point the synoptic gospels will be parallel more frequently than they were even during the great ministry of Christ in Galilee. See chapter XIX, 5.

13, 2) On account of βρέφη in Luke. Sucklings, *infantuli ab uberibus pendentes.* Acts 7, 19; 1 Pet. 2, 2. Ylvisaker, 447.

3) On account of αὐτοῖς, masculine, Matt. 19, 13; Mark 10, 13.

4) Παιδία in Matthew and Mark.

5) Compare the remark of disciples concerning the Syrophenician woman, Matt. 15, 23.

14, 1) Ἄρχων — Luke.

2) Some MSS. omit "good." We have followed the *textus receptus.* For critical remarks see commentaries.

Master, what good [3] thing shall I do that I may have eternal life?"
From the standpoint of Jesus the epithet *good* was perfectly proper,
but it was wrong from the standpoint of the ruler. Jesus would
not be reduced to a mere good Rabbi, if indeed the Rabbis were
accustomed to be thus addressed.[4] And even as on other occasions [5] Jesus was unwilling to be called Christ indiscriminately, so
He objects to the above title of honor, unless its implication is fully
understood. As long as the ruler came to Jesus as to one who was

The Rich Young Ruler.

no more than a man, the entire
address, no matter how flatter-
ing, was a mistake. Therefore the correction: "Why callest thou
Me good? There is none good but One, that is, God." It was evident that the youth was not ready to associate "good" with Jesus
and God. As to the question itself, something good certainly must
be done if by *doing* one would obtain everlasting life. The answer
is found in the Law. "If thou wilt enter into life, keep the commandments." A most simple and logical answer; but it took the
man by surprise. He did not expect to be directed to the commandments in general, but rather imagined that this Prophet would
point to some new list of works. Something of this nature was in
his mind when he asked, "Which?" [6] Since there was only one
code in the Moral Law, and since the youth was determined to *do*
something to gain salvation, Jesus directed his attention to the Ten
Commandments and in particular for the purpose of His pedagogy
to the precepts of the Second Table, which, as a true scholar of the
Pharisees, he must have supposed could be most easily kept: "Thou
shalt do no murder, Thou shalt not commit adultery, Thou shalt
not steal, Thou shalt not bear false witness, Honor thy father and
thy mother; and, Thou shalt love thy neighbor as thyself."

15.

Matt. 19, 16—26. Mark 10, 17—27. Luke 18, 18—27.

With the sincerity of an honest heart the young man asserted:
"All these things have I kept from my youth up." At least he
thought he had, as would be expected from one who enjoyed, and
very likely deserved, the honor and respect of his community.

14, 3) Omitted by Mark and Luke.

4) Edersheim, II, 339. Farrar, II, 160. The title was unknown
among the Jews.

5) Matt. 16, 20. Compare also Matt. 9, 30; 12, 16.

6) Ποίας (ἐντολάς); what sort of commandments?

"What lack I yet?" There is an inward want. In spite of his outwardly exemplary life there must have been some inward dissatisfaction; otherwise he would not have asked Jesus that question in the first place. And Jesus, "beholding him, loved him" for his sincerity and moral earnestness and wanted to save his soul. But moral earnestness does not save; it does not suffice. The youth was deceiving himself. Even before the Law, which, he thought, he had kept ever since he became a "son of the Law," there was still much that he lacked. He did not love his neighbor as himself, he did not love God with all his heart, and he was not willing to leave all

"One Thing Thou Lackest."

that he had and to follow Christ. "One thing thou lackest." For the purpose of approaching perfection via the Law there was one test that he might make: "Go and sell that thou hast and give to the poor, and thou shalt have treasure in heaven," that is, inherit eternal life; and then "come and follow Me." Now, Christ was not teaching the purchase of salvation in exchange for voluntary poverty, as some have thought. This was a subjective counsel relative to an individual case. And it was given for the purpose of impressing upon the youth his deficiency. Nor was it lightly given. Moreover, it was a commandment based upon the universal requirement of unconditional self-denial and willing surrender of all for the sake of Christ. The proposal was hopefully made. But the youth was not equal to the sacrifice demanded of him. It was too much. He lacked the knowledge of sin, the godly sorrow of repentance, and faith in the grace of God and Christ. There was a tender spot. With pain in his heart and a frown on his face he walked away "sorrowful, for he had great possessions."

16.

Matt. 19, 16—26. Mark 10, 17—27. Luke 18, 18—27.

The failure of the youth to meet the test saddened Jesus. Looking around at His disciples, He said: "How hardly shall they that have riches enter into the kingdom of God!" The disciples were amazed. But Jesus repeated: "Children, how hard is it for them that trust in riches[1] to enter into the kingdom of God!" It was mildly, yet firmly spoken; it really is impossible for a man to enter heaven as long as he sets his heart upon earthly treasures.

16, 1) The words "for them that trust in riches" are omitted in some leading manuscripts.

"It is easier for a camel [2)] to go through the eye of a needle than for a rich man to enter into the kingdom of God." At this proverbial saying the disciples inquired with increased astonishment:

The Danger of Riches. "Who, then, can be saved?" They must have felt that the warning of Jesus applied to rich and poor alike. Jesus replied that things impossible to human nature are possible to grace. "With God all things are possible." It is not the possession of wealth, whether great or small, that condemns, but the attitude of the heart to wealth; and this regardless of whether the man is or is not in the possession of wealth. Abraham and others were not only rich in goods, but also rich in God. On the other hand, Judas loved money, of which he did not even possess a great amount. While we notice that Christ's tone is much more severe in reference to wealth than to wedlock,[3)] His teaching concerning the possession of wealth is as "little Ebionite as His teaching concerning marriage is Essene." [4)]

17.

Matt. 19, 27—30. Mark 10, 28—31. Luke 18, 28—30.

We are almost jarred by the reaction of the disciples. Peter, probably acting as spokesman for the rest of the apostles, speaks out his mind: "Behold, we have forsaken all and followed Thee. What shall we have therefore?" It was a gain-seeking question. But

The Question of Peter. although Jesus rebuked His disciples on other occasions, this time He has no criticism to offer. Yes, there is a reward, not for the relinquishment of wealth as such, but for the surrender of wealth, home, family, friends, and all for His sake. There will be a harvest of hundredfold increase in the regeneration [1)] of the Son of Man. Then shall the disciples "sit upon twelve thrones, judging the twelve

---

16, 2) Not κάμιλος, a rope, but κάμηλος, a camel, the largest animal in use among the Jews, as the eye of a needle, ῥαφίς, was the smallest known opening. The explanation which makes a small side-gate of a city through which a laden camel might enter with difficulty called "a needle's eye" lacks confirmation. Farrar, II, 163. For the origin of the expression it has been suggested that a camel-driver leaning against his camel and failing to thread a needle with which to sew his sacks might say in comical exaggeration: I might as well try to put the camel through the eye. Bruce sub Matt. 19, 24. Similar expressions, however, are also found in rabbinic writings: an elephant passing through the eye of a needle. Edersheim, II, 342.

3) Matt. 19, 10—12.   4) Farrar, II, 163.

17, 1) Ἐν τῇ παλιγγενεσίᾳ. A new word in the gospel vocabulary, pointing to a general renewal at the end of days. Bruce sub Matt. 19, 28.

tribes of Israel," [2] and share with their Master the eternal dominion of glory. And this reward is not only for the Twelve; but "every one that hath forsaken homes, or brethren, or sisters, or father, or mother, or wife, or children, or lands — with persecutions [3] for My name's sake and the Gospel's [4] — shall receive an hundredfold and shall inherit eternal life." But the idea of merit must be excluded. Moreover, followers must remain faithful unto the end, otherwise "many that are first shall be last and the last shall be first." [5]

Matt. 20, 1—16.   **18.**

For the purpose of teaching His disciples that salvation is full and complete and that the standard of the Kingdom is not merit, but grace, Jesus relates the parable of the Laborers in the Vineyard, also called the parable of the Hours. It was probably in the busy season of grape-gathering that a certain "householder" went forth early in the morning to hire laborers into his vineyard. Agreement as to wages was made on the basis of a denarius, or "a penny a day." According to our money a denarius amounted to only about twenty cents, but at that time it was the ordinary wage for a day's labor. At the third, sixth, ninth, and eleventh hour, counting from six o'clock in the morning, the owner of the vineyard found "others standing idle in the market-place" and sent them out into the vineyard, without, however, stipulating the definite coin or sum, — nothing but the promise: "Whatsoever is right I will give you."

The Laborers in the Vineyard. Up to this point there was no hitch in the proceeding. When the evening arrived, the lord of the vineyard gave instructions to his steward to call the laborers and to pay them off, "beginning from the last to the first." This was a necessary part of the parable, because, as afterwards appears, here is where the complications begin. The order was somewhat strange, but still stranger was the payment. "They received every man a penny," as though each of them had worked all day. To say the least, this arrangement is not the one usually observed between master and men. Nothing is said about the intermediates. But when the first came and saw what the last received, — forgetting the contract, of course, — they naturally expected that they would receive more. But "they likewise received every man a penny." Evidently the full amount of the

---

17, 2) Not to be taken literally. Stoeckhardt (*B. G.,* 218): "The saints made perfect, the great company of the elect."

3) Mark.   4) Mark.   5) Luke 13, 30.

penny as presented by the eccentric master to the one-hour men was not a payment, but intended rather as a bonus, or gift. However, those who had worked all day, not satisfied with this inept liberality, began to express their indignation. Their complaint was excellently put: "These last have wrought but one hour, and thou hast made them equal unto us, which have borne the burden and heat of the day."

Matt. 20, 1—16. **19.**

It is true that the workmen had forgotten the agreement. Still our first impulse is to side with the murmurers. However, this is not a commentary on capital and labor, but a picture of the kingdom of heaven.[1] We must remember that, if we receive salvation at all, it is both a full salvation and is given by grace. In the Lord's vineyard, work is our lifelong duty, and our faithful labors will be rewarded in heaven. But the bountiful reaping that will be our happy lot there will not be given as payment for services rendered, but will be a gift of the grace of God. In the Lord's kingdom salvation is as little ninety-five per cent. as it is one hundred and five, and so there must be no jealousy among Christians nor a pointing to a greater or smaller amount of good works before God. As in other parables, the main point must not be lost sight of, and not all details must be pressed. Singling out one of the murmurers, the master reminded him of the agreement: "Friend,[2] I do thee no wrong. Didst not thou agree with me for a penny?" A man who

"Friend, I Do Thee No Wrong." insists upon right before God loses grace and receives judgment. "Take that thine is and go thy way." As to this giving of a full and unstipulated denarius to each of the laborers, to which "the first" objected, that was both his distinct purpose and his own affair. "Is it not lawful for me to do what I will with mine own?" Instead of being a cause of offense, this act of kindness should have been an occasion for rejoicing. While the goodman of the house was good, the murmurers displayed a jealous heart. "Is thine eye evil because I am good?" Since in the Lord's kingdom work is our duty and grace our reward, there should be neither envy in our hearts with respect to those who are received into the heavenly kingdom although they came to Christ only in the eleventh hour, while we have served Him all our lives, nor a gain-seeking exhibition of our good works before God. The attainment

---

19, 1) V. 1.   2) Ἑταῖρε, comrade. Friendly, but firmly.

of salvation is the same for both saint and sinner. And so, repeating the lesson he had given Peter when he put his question,[3] which suggested the parable, Jesus says: "So the last shall be first and the first last." Indeed, "many be called, but few chosen." [4] Many hear the Gospel. Few heed the call.[5]

20.

Matt. 20, 17—19. Mark 10, 32—34. Luke 18, 31—34.[1]

Again Jesus was on the way to Jerusalem, pressing forward and walking along the path into the deep valley of the shadow of death. His strange manner and His incessant pushing forward caused the disciples to be amazed and others that followed Him to be filled with fear. The very atmosphere seemed to be charged with a foreboding of evil. At last Jesus paused. He beckoned His disciples unto Himself, took them "apart in the way," and again told them about His impending betrayal, arrest, suffering, and death, and about His resurrection. The terrible details are

Death and Resurrection Again Foretold.

all distinctly given: how all the things that are written by the prophets concerning the Son of Man shall be accomplished; how He shall be betrayed[2] to the scribes and priests in Jerusalem, condemned by the Sanhedrin, delivered to the Roman Gentiles, mocked, scourged, spit upon, and —

19, 3) Matt. 19, 27. 30.

   4) Compare Matt. 22, 14. Missing in many manuscripts.

   5) *'Εκλεκτοί*, chosen, not in the sense as though some were were predestined or preordained to damnation. There is no foreordination to damnation; but salvation is by the grace of God and damnation through man's own fault. And, by the way, those who have been chosen from eternity are during their life on earth called by the means of grace. Those who do not heed the Gospel call are not among the elect of God.

20, 1) Compare: —

   1. John 2, 18—22. In connection with the first cleansing of the Temple.
   2. Matt. 16, 21—23; Mark 8, 31—33; Luke 9, 22. At Caesarea Philippi.
   3. Matt. 17, 22. 23; Mark 9, 30—32; Luke 9, 43—45. At the close of the Galilean ministry.
   4. Matt. 20, 17—19; Mark 10, 32—34; Luke 18, 31—34. In Perea.
   5. Matt. 26, 1—5; Mark 14, 1. 2; Luke 22, 1. 2. At Bethany on Tuesday evening of Passion-week.

   2) *Παραδοθήσεται*. The word is used 36 times in the New Testament for the betrayal of Jesus Christ and in addition only three times (Matt. 24, 10; Mark 13, 12; Luke 21, 16) of kinsmen delivering up one another to prosecution. *Int. St. B. Encycl.* sub "Betray."

for the first time the terrible climax is clearly revealed — *crucified.*[3)]
But like a shining light comes also the comforting assurance of the
resurrection: "And the third day He shall rise again." The words
were clear, but the minds of the disciples were so filled with false
Messianic hopes that they passed them by like an idle dream.
"They understood none of these things; and this saying was hid
from them, neither knew they the things which were spoken."

21.

Matt. 20, 20—28. Mark 10, 35—45.

The ignorance of the disciples with respect to the nature of
Christ's kingdom is revealed in an unspiritual request which came
to Jesus soon afterwards from James and John, the two sons of
Zebedee, by means of [1)] their mother Salome, the sister of the
mother of Jesus.[2)] We remember that these relatives of Jesus were
among His most intimate associates and constant attendants. With
an air of mystery they approached Jesus and, kneeling, begged
Him to do them a favor. But Jesus would not commit Himself
before the wish was expressed. "What would ye that I should
do for you?" The mother, speaking for her ambitious sons, requested that in His kingdom they might sit, the one on the right
hand of His throne of glory and the other on the left. It was

**The Ambition
of James and John.** a carnal, selfish request, and it showed
that the nature of Christ's kingdom
was completely misunderstood. In an
Oriental kingdom for persons to be seated to the right and left
of the throne was a token of the highest honor and an evidence
that they were men of the highest rank.[3)] Probably the two disciples had drawn a wrong conclusion from the promise of Jesus
about sitting "upon twelve thrones, judging the twelve tribes of
Israel," [4)] given in connection with Peter's question: "We have
forsaken all and followed Thee; what shall we have therefore?"
Jesus bore gently with their selfishness and error. "Ye know not

---

20, 3) Σταυρῶσαι. Mock, scourge, crucify, all new features.

21, 1) This seems to be the combination of Matthew and Mark. In Mark
it is the sons who petition Jesus, whereas in Matthew it was their mother.
The request was made by the mother, who was the intercessor; but in truth
it was the request of the two disciples, and therefore Jesus directs His reply,
even in Matthew, to them and not to their mother.

2) Mark 15, 40. A comparison with Matt. 27, 56 identifies her as
the wife of Zebedee. From John 19, 25, "and His mother's sister," it is
inferred that she was a sister of Mary.

3) Ylvisaker, 529.   4) Matt. 19, 27. 28. No. 17.

what ye ask." They did not know what Christ's glory was and
how one could become a partaker of it. They sought exaltation
and did not see the step leading to it. "Are ye able to drink the
cup that I shall drink of and to be baptized with the baptism that
I am baptized with?" The reference was to His Passion, the cup
of bitterness,[5] and the billows of the dark waters of death,[6] while
the brothers were probably thinking of a cup of joy[7] or of the
Epiphany glory on the banks of the Jordan.[8] And if indeed by
this time they were sufficiently aroused to grasp the reference to
the Lord's greatest humiliation, they nevertheless imagined, due
to an exaggerated trust in their own ability, that they were able
to drink that cup. "They say unto Him, We are able." Slowly
Jesus then lifted the veil and informed them that there would be
suffering in store for them, but that thereby they could not *earn*
glory. Glory would be theirs, not, however, by way of merit, as in
the case of Christ, but by way of obedience as the lot of followers
to share with Christ, to whom they were joined as Christians. "Ye
shall drink indeed of My cup and be baptized with the baptism
that I am baptized with." The servant is not greater than his
lord.[9] For all Christians there will be more or less tribulation and
persecution, in some instances even bloody martyrdom. But even
this does not merit a seat of honor in heaven. There *are* degrees of
glory in the realms of bliss; the disciples, however, had carnal
conceptions regarding them. Jesus therefore tells them that they
must discard these thoughts. The mighty of this earth, it is true,
give places of honor to their favorites. Not so, however, in His
kingdom. Although James and John belonged to His intimate
circle, they could not for that reason claim any special distinction
in His kingdom, nor would He, in His present state of humiliation,
give them any definite promise. In due time sitting on His right
and left hand "shall be given to them for whom it is prepared of
My Father."

22.

Matt. 20, 20—28. Mark 10, 35—45.

James and John were corrected, and in a deeper sense their
request was granted. As His true followers they shared the bitter
cup of Christ. James was the first martyr among the Twelve.[1]
And John became a companion of Christ's tribulation.[2] In the
Kingdom of Glory they shine as the brightness of the firmament

---

21, 5) Matt. 26, 39.   6) Ps. 42, 7; 88, 7.   7) Ps. 23, 5.
     8) John 1, 33. 34.   9) John 15, 20.
22, 1) Acts 12, 2.   2) Rev. 1, 9.

and as the stars forever and ever.[3] — But "the Ten," filled with the same ambition and jealousies, were indignant at the selfish request of James and John. They were incensed at their secret attempt to secure preeminence for themselves and seats of honor. The offense caused them to quarrel [4] in the presence of Jesus, who was obliged to call them aside and to calm their excited minds. In His kingdom, He told them, highest honor was won by deepest humility. The pyramid of honor was inverted: not the few lording it over the many, but the many, as it were, being lords of

The Way to Glory in Christ's Kingdom.

the few. In this respect His kingdom differed from secular kingdoms. In this world the man who reaches the height of his ambition has achieved greatness by appointing and employing great numbers of inferiors and by making his will their law. "Ye know that the princes of the Gentiles exercise dominion over them and they that are great exercise authority upon them." That was, as they could see from the long history of their own nation, the way of Egypt, Assyria, Babylonia, Persia, Greece, and Rome. "But it shall not be so among you." There is greatness also in the kingdom of Christ. But secular notions of greatness must be turned completely upside down by those who wish to be members of this kingdom here on earth. "Whosoever will be great among you shall be your minister;[5] and whosoever of you will be the chiefest shall be servant [6] of all." Thus a plan for the exercise of "ambition" is proposed which will not offend any of their fellow-men. And for this there is the example of the Master. "For even the Son of Man came not to be ministered unto, but to minister and to give His life a ransom for many.[7]

23.

Matt. 20, 29—34. Mark 10, 46—52. Luke 18, 35—43.

By this time Jesus had left Perea, crossed the Jordan, and was approaching Jericho. In fact, it seems that He had already left the old Jericho and was approaching the Jericho which Herod the

---

22, 3) Dan. 12, 3.

4) Compare Mark 9, 33. 34, after the Transfiguration.

5) Διάκονος, helper, servant.   6) Δοῦλος, slave.

7) Λύτρον. The symbolism is that of prisoners who are liberated upon the payment of a price. Thus the blood of Christ is a ransom, Col. 1, 14; 1 Tim. 2, 6; Acts 20, 28. This ransom was not paid to the devil, but to divine justice, ἀντί, in place, instead — vicarious suffering and death, Ἀντίλυτρον ὑπὲρ πάντων, 1 Tim. 2, 6. Matthew and Mark: πολλῶν. Not restrictive, as if Christ did not die for all, but used in special reference to the great number in whose behalf the sacrifice was made. See Ylvisaker, 530.

Great had rebuilt a generation before.[1)]   As He was accompanied by His disciples and attended by a multitude of Passover pilgrims, two blind beggars, one of whom was Bartimaeus,[2)] acting as spokesman, heard that Jesus was passing by.[3)]   Immediately they cried out: "Have mercy on us, O Lord, Thou Son of David!"   The multitudes resented the noisy clamor as showing disrespect to One who was about to present Himself in Jerusalem as the nation's Messiah.   But the blind men only cried the more: "Have mercy on us, O Lord, Thou Son of David!"   Joshua caused heavenly bodies to halt in their orbits; these blind beggars caused the Sun of Righteousness to stand still.   Jesus did not

Blind Bartimaeus and His Companion Healed at Jericho.

object to the Messianic title with which He had been addressed and ordered the blind men to be called into His presence.   Of a sudden the surrounding throng became most compliant and told Bartimaeus, who probably was so much more prominent than the other one that two of the writers do not even mention the other: "Be of good cheer, rise; He calleth thee." At this Bartimaeus jumped to his feet, cast away his garment, and was led to Jesus.   The heart of Jesus went out to him and to his companion.   For the purpose of forestalling subsequent charges of fraud and to make the blind men express their faith, Jesus asked: "What will ye that I should do unto you?"   Had they been ordinary beggars, or had they believed that Jesus was an ordinary man,

---

23,   1) The old and the new Jericho were not quite two miles apart.   This seems to be the best explanation of the age-long controversy concerning the "discrepancy" between Matthew and Mark as compared with the account of Luke.   Matthew and Mark: "out from Jericho," the old Jericho; Luke: "nigh unto Jericho," the new Jericho, which Herod had rebuilt and named Cypros in honor of his mother.   Josephus, *Ant.*, XVI, V, 2.   *Wars*, I, XXI, 4. 9.   See also *Ant.*, XVII, XIII, 1.   Located at Beit Jubr or Bet Dschabr, just where the road forks to Bethany and Jerusalem.   G. A. Smith, *Hist. Atlas*, VI, 25.   H. Guthe, *Bible Atlas*, II, Map 20.   Zacchaeus had his home, naturally enough, at the custom-house in New Jericho.   Matthew writes for the Christians among the Jews.   It was necessary for him to designate the place just as we find it in his gospel.   Luke writes to Gentile Christians, particularly to those in the Orient.   When they spoke of Jericho, it was the Jericho of the custom-house.   In order to point out the place where the blind men were healed, he had to say that Christ came to Jericho.   Mark, however, drawing his material from Peter, naturally would speak like the Apostle Matthew.   Thus there is perfect harmony where a disagreement would seem to exist.   See James Macknight, *Harmony*, II, 569. 570. Ylvisaker, *Gospels*, 533. 534.   Robertson, *Harmony*, 149.   Andrews, 418. Farrar, II, 181.

2) The son of Timaeus.

3) Matthew mentions two blind men, while Mark and Luke speak of only one, who probably was, and continued to be, the better known of the two.

they probably would have asked to open His purse. But their reply was an expression of their faith. As formulated by Bartimaeus, it gave Jesus the most reverential title: "Lord," Rabboni,[4] "that I might receive my sight." Whereupon Jesus had compassion on them and touched their eyes. "Immediately their eyes received sight," and midst the rejoicing of the multitude they followed Jesus, glorifying God.

Luke 19, 1—10. **24.**

Jesus continued on His way to Jericho, more particularly, New Jericho, an important trade center and customs station and the home of Zacchaeus, a wealthy "chief among the publicans," whose acquaintance we are about to make.[1] Zacchaeus was anxious to see Jesus, the great Prophet of Nazareth, by many acknowledged as the promised Messiah, who was about to go up to Jerusalem and, in connection with the approaching Passover-feast, to present Himself as Israel's King. But being short of stature, he was unable to look over the crowd and therefore, running forward, climbed into the low branches of a fig-mulberry, or sycamore-tree which stood by the road.[2] This action must have exposed him to the ridicule of the bystanders, to whom no doubt he was well known, but by whom he was disliked. His purpose, however, was not curiosity alone. He was in spiritual distress. A secret resolve had come over him. He was in need of peace, which, he felt, he could not obtain by anything he might do. He was filled with a yearning for Him who did not despise publicans and sinners and who had

Jesus Visits Zacchaeus. even elevated one of his hated associates to the rank of an apostle.

We are surprised that Matthew did not bring this incident of Zacchaeus. But probably the very fact that he had been a publican himself moved him, as much as he must have been touched by the action of Jesus, to pass it by in silence. On the other hand, the glorious example of this wonderful Savior love as found in the Gospel of Luke on other occasions[3] was something which this evangelist could not overlook. When Jesus passed under that tree, He paused, looked up, called the publican by name, and told him

---

23, 4) ʽΡαββουνί. Compare John 20, 16. Farrar says, II, 183, that the steps of honor in the title are Rab, Rabbi, Rabban, Rabboni.

24, 1) Zacchaeus, a Jewish name, from זַכַּי, meaning pure, as if describing a particular characteristic. Probably a headman, or overseer, over the local collectors of taxes. Ἀρχιτελώνης. Nowhere else in the New Testament. Bruce *sub loco.*

2) Συκομοραία, a fig-mulberry tree. 3) Luke 15.

to come down.[4] "Zacchaeus, make haste and come down." Jesus
was on His way to Jerusalem. There were still before Him about
fifteen miles of arduous climbing. It was necessary for Him to find
lodging for the night. He would not stay with one of the many
priests who made their home at Jericho,[5] but rather chose to spend
the night in a publican's house. "For to-day I must abide at thy
house." This was more than Zacchaeus could have expected even
in his wildest dreams. But the Lord knew that a change had come
over this formerly thievish publican, that he was penitent and was
concerned about his soul's welfare.

Luke 19, 1—10.   **25.**

Hastily Zacchaeus climbed down the tree and joyfully received
Jesus into his house, not caring for the muttering of those who objected "that He was gone to be guest with a man that is a sinner." [1]
In spite of his name, Zacchaeus, that is, Pure, there is no doubt
that Zacchaeus *was* a sinner in the popular sense. The collectors
of taxes were notoriously dishonest. There was reason for popular
hatred against them as a class and on account of some shady transactions in Jericho against Zacchaeus as an individual. In the collection of duties on balsam, for instance,[2] and imposts on products
that passed between the province of Pilate and Herod Antipas he
was probably not innocent and pure. But listen to his penitent

"This Day is Salvation Come to This House." resolve: "Lord, the half of my goods I give to the poor." This was a general restitution of money
or property fraudulently acquired from persons whom he could
no longer specify. "And if I have taken anything from any man
by false accusation [false charges against taxpayers], I restore him
fourfold." A four- and even fivefold restoration was required by
the Mosaic Law.[3] Jesus recognized the sincerity of this proposal,
voluntarily and sincerely made. Here was a truly penitent and
believing heart. And therefore Jesus said to Zacchaeus: "This day
is salvation come to this house." Others had made much of their
physical descent from Abraham;[4] but here was one of Abraham's
spiritual sons. And as to Jesus' going into Zacchaeus's house,

---

24, 4) Jesus, who had followed Nathanael to the place where he stood,
beneath the fig-tree (John 1, 48), was not ignorant of anything that was
going on.
    5) Edersheim, II, 351.
25, 1) Luke 15, 2.   2) *Ant.*, XIV, IV, 1.
    3) Ex. 22, 1—9; Lev. 6, 2—5.   4) John 8, 33.

that was in accordance with the purpose for which He had come into the world: "The Son of Man is come to seek and to save that which was lost." [5]

Luke 19, 11—28. **26.**

While Jesus rejoiced that He had converted a sinner and Zacchaeus rejoiced that he had found the Savior,[1] the disciples were occupied with thoughts of the kingdom which, they supposed, would now be revealed. There were many indications that a crisis was at hand. On the way to Jericho, Jesus had told His disciples that they were going to Jerusalem, where all the prophecies concerning the Son of Man were to be fulfilled.[2] In the hearing of multitudes and without any objection to it on the part of such as had heard it He had permitted Himself to be addressed with the strictly Messianic title "Son of David," [3] although at other occasions He had purposely discouraged Messianic acclaim.[4] Now the "Son of David" was nigh unto Israel's religious center and the capital of David's ancient kingdom. In addition, the Passover was at hand, from which season the regnal years were counted.[5] There was no doubt that a crisis was at hand. If only the disciples could get the idea of external Messianic world-power off their minds! In order to teach them that the Kingdom of Glory, such as they

The Parable of the Pounds. imagined it to be, was not yet at hand, that He must

first leave the world and receive the royal insignia, and that in the mean while the disciples must faithfully "occupy" till He would come again, He taught them — most likely in the house of Zacchaeus, possibly at meat in the evening — the parable of the Pounds. We need not enter into the discussion of a supposed confounding of this parable with a similar parable recorded later.[6] In accordance with the practise of Herodian princes, ever since Rome had entered into the history of Israel,[7] "a certain nobleman [8]

25, 5) Matt. 18, 11.

26, 1) According to tradition Zacchaeus later became the bishop of Caesarea. (*Clementine Homilies.*) Andrews, 420.

2) Luke 18, 31. 3) No. 22. 4) Matt. 9, 27. 30; 12, 16.
5) Ylvisaker, 537. 6) Matt. 25, 14—30.

7) It is assumed that Jesus and His hearers were familiar with the practise. "A nobleman going into a far country to receive a kingdom" would be utterly unintelligible did we not know that this was actually done both by Archelaus and Antipas in applying for royal dignity in Rome after the death of Herod. *Ant.,* XVII, IX, 3. 4. Here we have one of those unexpected indications of the authenticity and truthfulness of the gospel account. Ylvisaker, 537. Farrar, II, 186, n. 3.

8) Εὐγενής, well-born man.

went into a far country to receive for himself a kingdom and to return." Before leaving, he called "his ten servants"[9] and distributed among them "ten pounds,"[10] with the instruction to do business and trade with them until his return. "Occupy till I come."[11] No sooner had he left, however, than his countrymen sent an embassy after him with the message: "We will not have this man to reign over us." This actually happened in the case of Archelaus after the death of Herod.[12] Nevertheless Archelaus came back from Rome successful, having attained his object, as did the nobleman in the parable. The only difference is that Archelaus was opposed on just grounds, while King Jesus, in the interpretation of the parable, was rejected on unjust grounds.[13] And still in the end He gained His kingdom.

Luke 19, 11—28.   27.

The nobleman in the parable, as stated, was successful in his mission. He received the royal dignity. His first official act upon his return was to summon the servants before him to whom he had entrusted the silver coin. Modestly the first one comes before him with the most successful report: "Lord, thy pound hath gained ten

"Have Thou Authority over Ten Cities."

pounds." For such increase and fidelity there was a splendid reward of a decapolis,[1] or ten cities: "Well, thou good servant; because thou hast been faithful in a very little, have thou authority over ten cities." In like manner a second servant reports: "Lord, thy pound hath gained five pounds." He receives a similar reward, "five cities." There is nothing said about seven of the servants, nor is this necessary.

Luke 19, 11—28.   28.

As a special warning against unprofitableness in the Lord's kingdom a third servant is singled out. As he approaches his master with "slinking gait and whining voice,"[1] he returns the entrusted

---

26, 9) "Ten servants," a round number.

10) Δέκα μνᾶς. The value of what is here rendered pound is uncertain and unimportant. But probably it is significant that, whereas the value of the pound is comparatively small, the importance placed upon fidelity and increase is great. If the Greek silver mina is meant, then the value of the pound is from $17 to $20. If the old Hebrew *maneh,* מָנֶה, is meant, the value is about $32. That there is a reference to a silver standard seems to be indicated in the expression *money,* ἀργύριον.

11) Πραγματεύσασθε ἕως ἔρχομαι. The former verb used only here in the New Testament. Bruce *sub loco.*

12) *Ant.,* XVII, IX, 5. 6.   13) Bruce *sub loco.*

27, 1) Δέκα πόλεων. Bruce *sub loco.*   28, 1) Kretzmann, I, 369.

pound, tied up in a napkin,[2] trying to excuse his failure by blaming the austerity of his master. He was unfaithful, inasmuch as he had not obeyed his lord's command, which was to increase the pound entrusted to him, and therefore he was also unprofitable to him. And that was the point. "Here is thy pound, which I have laid up in a napkin." Fear of the master was advanced as an excuse for his failure. "For I feared thee because thou art an austere man; thou takest up that thou layedst not down and

The Unprofitable Servant.

reapest that thou didst not sow." Out of his own mouth he was condemned. Increase, not mere lazy safe-keeping, was the very purpose of the delivery and the only reason why the money had been entrusted to him. His very behavior showed that he was unfit to serve in any administrative capacity. If he knew of his lord's exacting manner, why, then, did he not act in accordance with his convictions? And if he was afraid to invest the money on his own responsibility, why did he not at least put it in a bank?[3] Then he could have returned it with interest.[4] But he had done neither. And the punishment was: "Take from him the pound and give it to him that hath ten pounds." This would at least give the king the best prospects for gaining a speedy increase.

Luke 19, 11—28. 29.

At this point it seems that Jesus was interrupted. "And they said unto him, Lord, he hath ten pounds." But Jesus points to a truth previously expressed and variously applied:[1] "For I say unto you, that unto every one which hath shall be given, and from him that hath not even that he hath shall be taken away from him." For the sake of his own best interests the king was entirely justified in applying this principle. And in concluding the parable Jesus tells His hearers what the nobleman commanded with regard to those enemies who opposed his rule: "Bring them hither and slay them before me." — The meaning of the parable is: There will also be a kingdom for Jesus. But first He must go into a "far country." In the meantime the disciples, given "pounds" as bearers of the

---

28, 2) Ἐν σουδαρίῳ, handkerchief. John 11, 44; 20, 7.

3) Ἐπὶ τὴν τράπεζαν, upon a (banker's) table.

4) Σὺν τόκῳ. Such transactions were forbidden among Israelites, but were allowed with Gentiles. Interest rates were from 1 to 4 per cent. per month, or from 12 to 48 per cent. per year. Edersheim, II, 463.

29, 1) Luke 8, 18; Matt. 13, 12; Mark 4, 25.

means of grace, should faithfully "occupy" till He returns. Upon His return on the Last Day punishment will be meted out to His open enemies, and an account will be taken of those who according

The Lesson. to their profession were His servants. There will be a reward of grace for the faithful and judgment upon those who have been lazy in their trust. It is required in stewards that a man be found faithful.[2] For such faithfulness there was the example of the Lord. Having thus spoken, He "went on before," possibly on the next morning, and continued His journey to Jerusalem.[3]

29, 2) 1 Cor. 4, 2.

3) As a note of time the expression εἰπὼν ταῦτα is rather vague. We do not know how much time intervened between the telling of the parable and the commencement of the ascent to Jerusalem. It is one of Luke's formulas of transition. Bruce *sub loco.*

CHAPTER XXVI.

ARRIVAL AT BETHANY.

Probably Friday Afternoon before the Week of Passover,
30 A. D. or 783 A. U. C.
March 31 and April 1

Nisan (or Abib)

8	9	10	11	12	13	14	15	16	17

March April

31	1	2	3	4	5	6	7	8	9
Fri.	Sat.	Sun.	Mon.	Tue.	Wed.	Thu.	Fri.	Sat.	Sun.

783 A. U. C.   MARCH   30 A. D.

Sun.	Mon.	Tue.	Wed.	Thu.	Fri.	Sat.
			1	2	3	4
5	6	7	8	9	10	11
12	13	14	15	16	17	18
19	20	21	22	23	24	25
26	27	28	29	30		31		

John 11, 55—57.   **1.**

The Passover was nigh at hand, and the roads were filled with Passover pilgrims, who would probably come to the Holy City a few days before the feast for the sake of purification, some features of which required a week, while others consisted only of trimming the

"The Jews' Passover Was Nigh at Hand."

hair and washing the clothes.[1] Since Jesus had aroused national attention, the main topic of conversation among those who stood about in groups in the courts of the Temple was whether or not He would make His appearance at the feast. That there was room for differences of opinion was due to the fact that the "chief priests and the Pharisees," the Sanhedrin, had given instructions that, if any one knew where Jesus was to be found, he should "show it," so that they might have Him arrested.

John 12, 1.   **2.**

And now we must get our chronological bearing. According to the chronology which we have followed it is the year 30 A. D., or

---

1, 1) According to the general principle of appearing before the Lord ceremonially pure, Gen. 35, 2; Ex. 19, 10. 11; Num. 9, 6 ff.; 2 Chron. 30, 17 ff.

783 A. U. C. Here we receive the notice that six days before the Passover, Jesus arrived at Bethany. According to reliable astronomical calculations the beginning of the Passover on the evening

"Six Days before the Passover." of the 14th day of Nisan in the year of our Lord's crucifixion, that is, the year 30 A. D., corresponded to Thursday evening, April 6, of the Julian calendar.[1] Counting back six days,[2] we arrive at the 8th day of Nisan, or Friday, March 31. In covering the fourteen or fifteen miles between Jericho and Bethany, we assume that Jesus, after spending the night with Zacchaeus, left there early in the morning, so as to arrive at the home of His friends in Bethany before the sunset had commenced the Sabbath hours.[3]

2, 1) We need not take the reader through the extended and complicated investigations which lead to the statement of the result. The interested student is referred to the following: Karl Wieseler, *A Chronological Synopsis of the Four Gospels,* 1865; pp. 307 ff. 435. Samuel J. Andrews, *The Life of Our Lord,* 1891; pp. 421 ff. Oswald Gerhardt, *Der Stern des Messias,* 1922; pp. 124 ff. We are translating a few of the last-named investigator's points in his "Summary of Certain Results" as given on page 139: "The crucifixion of Jesus took place under Pontius Pilate, who was procurator of Syria from 26 to 36 A. D., at a Passover festival. The moon, as the maker of the Jewish month, the law which fixes the Passover meal for the evening of the 14th of Nisan, and the gospel account, which designates Friday as the day of crucifixion, are the reliable principles for the solution of the problem by way of astronomy. In the year to be decided upon (*in dem zu bestimmenden Jahre*) the 14th of Nisan must have fallen on a Thursday, the 15th on a Friday. The latter was the day of death. In considering all possibilities, the principles of astronomical calculations lead to the result, which is accepted by us as a true conception of the Scriptural account, that Friday, the 15th of Nisan, coincided with the 7th of April, 30 A. D., eventually also with the 27th of April, 31 A. D. The date, the 15th of Nisan, 27th of April, 31 A. D., completely lacks historical support. Since it rests upon the conceivably weakest astronomical basis (*auf der denkbar schwaechsten astronomischen Annahme*), it has only mathematical value. It is therefore *astronomically and historically proved* that the day of Golgotha was Friday, April 7, 30 A. D."

2) From Thursday evening, when the Passover lamb was eaten, 14th of Nisan. Lev. 23, 5.

Thursday evening		14th of Nisan	April 6
Wednesday evening	1 day	13th of Nisan	April 5
Tuesday evening	2 days	12th of Nisan	April 4
Monday evening	3 days	11th of Nisan	April 3
Sunday evening	4 days	10th of Nisan	April 2
Saturday evening	5 days	9th of Nisan	April 1
Friday evening	6 days	8th of Nisan	March 31

3) This seems to be the simplest and most natural course of events. While Jesus told the Jewish Rabbis that deeds of mercy and emergency acts were not forbidden on the Sabbath, we do not read that He used the Sabbath for ordinary journeys. Ylvisaker, 542.

3.

(Matt. 26, 6—13.) (Mark 14, 3—9.) John 12, 1—11.[1]

The Sabbath-day was spent in quiet, but for the evening a supper was arranged. It was a festive meal the people of Bethany seem to have arranged in His honor, and they enjoyed the privilege of attending the feast. The place of the banquet is given as the house of Simon the leper. But who this Simon was, whether he was the husband of Martha, the father of Lazarus, or a relative of the family, we do not know. From the expression "house of Simon the leper" we do not even know whether at the time he was alive or dead. But it is quite generally supposed that he was the host at the occasion and that the name "leper" still clung to him because of the malady from which he had previously been cleansed by Jesus. Among those present was the risen Lazarus, almost as much an object of curiosity as the Guest of

The Anointment at Bethany.
Honor Himself. It was really a public affair.

There were many people present, the disciples, the villagers, people from Jerusalem, "and," as John says, "Martha served." Again she was in her peculiar province.[2] "And Martha served." Very likely she had the entire supervision of the feast. Of course, Mary was there, too. It is to her that our particular attention is directed. She sat and thought and gazed, until she finally jumped up to carry out her intention. She had an alabaster flask containing costly

---

3, 1) This anointing has nothing in common with that recorded by Luke (7, 36—50; second preaching tour in Galilee, summer and autumn of 28 A. D.; see chapter XII, 9 ff.), except that here as well as there a woman anointed the Savior's feet and that the name of the host, Simon, which was borne by many Jews, was the same. The account of Matthew and Mark seems to have been brought in parenthetically. It is not to be connected with the "two days" before the Passover (Matt. 26, 2; Mark 14, 1), but with the words "Now, when Jesus was in Bethany" (Matthew) and "being in Bethany" (Mark). The exact time when the anointing took place is not stated. Andrews, 426. And even in John the time is given only in a general way: between Jesus' arrival at Bethany and His entry into Jerusalem. — The following considerations have moved us to place the anointment on Saturday evening: 1. It was the day before Christ's entry into Jerusalem, Palm Sunday, v. 12. 2. The supper was an *evening* meal, δεῖπνον, John 12, 2. 3. Some time must be allowed for preparations and for the coming of people from Jerusalem, which on account of the Sabbath regulations regarding labor and travel would have been out of the question between the sunsets from Friday to Saturday. It is natural to suppose that the report of the arrival of Jesus at Bethany reached Jerusalem on Friday evening and that the people came out on Saturday evening.

2) Luke 10, 40.

Indian spikenard.[3] Her circumstances must have been such that she enjoyed both the possession and the use of wealth. Stepping softly to Jesus, she broke the narrow neck of the jar and poured the valuable contents of the pure and precious nard [4] first over His head and then over His feet and wiped the feet with the long tresses of her hair. In a few moments the atmosphere of the whole house was filled with a delicious odor.

4.

(Matt. 26, 6—13.) (Mark 14, 3—9.) John 12, 1—11.

It was a strange act. Many of those present must have been amazed at this unaccustomed exhibition of lavish luxury. Even making an allowance for the eccentricities of society and wealth, many must have regarded the whole performance as of questionable

"To What Purpose Is This Waste?"

taste. But what does the heart care about cold custom when love would have its way? [1] When the disciples saw it, they were filled with indignation towards Mary. "To what purpose is this waste?" In their opinion Mary's lavish sacrifice might have been devoted to a better purpose. Her costly ointment might have been converted into useful cash, about sixty dollars in our money, for those times an amount large enough to supply at least five thousand hungry people with a bite to eat.[2]

5.

(Matt. 26, 6—13.) (Mark 14, 3—9.) John 12, 1—11.

The most vexed of the disciples was Judas. To his mind there was perfect folly in the "perdition" of so much good money.[1] Money was his dearest treasure. For one-third [2] of the amount this "son of perdition" was ready to sell the Lord Himself. It is the first time that we hear him talk. "Then said one of His disciples,

---

3,　　3) "It was made from the root and the lower stem of a plant, with spikes of purple four-stamened flowers, that grows only on mountain heights in North India. Found there with great difficulty, the nard was carried on camel back up through the passes of Afghanistan and across Persia into the Roman Empire and there regarded as the choicest of all elements in the most perfect ointment." Basil Matthews, *A Life of Jesus*, 380.

4) Ἀλάβαστρον μύρου νάρδου πιστικῆς πολυτελοῦς, Mark 14, 3.

4,　　1) Ylvisaker, 545.

2) 300 denarii, as compared with the 200 denarii in John 6, 7, which were estimated by Philip as required to supply 5,000 persons with a meager meal. Edersheim, II, 358.

5,　　1) Farrar, II, 192. Εἰς τί ἡ ἀπώλεια αὕτη, Matt. 26, 8.

2) Matt. 26, 16. 30 pieces of silver, about $20.

Judas Iscariot, Simon's son, which should betray Him, Why was not this ointment sold for three hundred pence [3] and given to the poor?" But this little touch about giving to the poor was only a veil behind which he tried to conceal the baseness of his heart.

The Reaction of Judas.
He felt as if he had been personally cheated. This act of Mary deprived him, the pilfering treasurer of the apostolic band, of the opportunity to get away with some of the common funds.[4] "This he said, not that he cared for the poor, but because he was a thief and had the bag and bare what was put therein."

6.

(Matt. 26, 6—13.) *(Mark 14, 3—9.)* *John 12, 1—11.*

But Jesus defends Mary. "Let her alone. Why trouble ye her?" Hers was a praiseworthy act. "She hath wrought a good work upon Me." [1] Even luxury and embellishment are permitted when the giver therewith seeks nothing but the glory of God.[2] And as to the poor, they would always be found as objects of the disciples' love. "But Me ye have not always." And, whether Mary

The Defense of Jesus.
understood it or not, her act had a special significance. "She is come aforehand to anoint My body to the burying." By anticipation she actually succeeded to pay Him her last honors, which His body would otherwise not have received. Instead of being criticized for her deed, she should be praised, and her deed will be remembered to the end of days. "Wherever the Gospel shall be preached in the whole world, there shall also this that this woman hath done be told for a memorial of her."

7.

(Matt. 26, 6—13.) *(Mark 14, 3—9.)* *John 12, 1—11.*

In the course of the evening, visitors from Jerusalem had arrived.[1] To them it was a double attraction to see both the Raiser

---

5, 3) *Τριακοσίων δηναρίων*, about twenty cents each. Three hundred denarii would equal about a laborer's wages for three hundred working-days, or one year.

4) *Τὰ βαλλόμενα ἐβάσταζεν.* Made away with what was put therein. Bruce sub John 12, 6.

6, 1) *Καλὸν ἔργον*, a lovely deed. A "nice" deed is a good deed.

2) Ylvisaker, 546.

7, 1) After sundown, when the regulation regarding the "Sabbath-day's journey" was lifted. Compare Acts 1, 12. The distance from Jerusalem to the Mount of Olives is from 1,000 to 1,200 yards, five to six stadia, whereas the distance to Bethany is about fifteen stadia.

of the dead and the raised. "They came not for Jesus' sake only, but that they might see Lazarus also, whom He had raised from the dead." The result was that many saw Lazarus — and believed on Jesus. This was as it should be. But the chief priests in Jerusalem, most of whom were

The Reaction in Jerusalem.

salem, most of whom were resurrection-denying Sadducees, could not bear to have a living witness of life after death and a powerful testimony to the power of Jesus in their neighborhood. When the report reached them, they were moved to the monstrous proposal to "put Lazarus also to death."

CHAPTER XXVII.

PALM SUNDAY.

THE TRIUMPHAL ENTRY INTO JERUSALEM.

April 2, 30 A. D., 783 A. U. C.

Nisan (or Abib)

10	11	12	13	14	15	16	17

April

2	3	4	5	6	7	8	9
Sun.	Mon.	Tue.	Wed.	Thu.	Fri.	Sat.	Sun.

783 A. U. C.			APRIL		30 A. D.	
Sun.	Mon.	Tue.	Wed.	Thu.	Fri.	Sat.
						1
2	3	4	5	6	7	8
9	10	11	12	13	14	15
16	17	18	19	20	21	22
23	24	25	26	27	28	29
30						

1.

Matt. 21, 1—9. Mark 11, 1—10. Luke 19, 29—40. John 12, 12—19.

From the visitors in Bethany on the evening before it must have become known in Jerusalem that Jesus intended to make His appearance in the city on the following day. On the next morning throngs of people streamed from the eastern gates of Jerusalem towards the Mount of Olives to meet Him on the way. According

"Behold, Thy King Cometh!" to their calendar it was the tenth of Nisan, the very day when the Passover lamb was to be selected.[1] But according to God's calendar it was the day when Jesus was to come to Jerusalem as the true Paschal Lamb and to present Himself to the nation as the Redeemer King. "Tell ye the daughter of Sion, Behold, thy King cometh unto thee." At the same time while crowds were streaming eastward on the road to Jericho, Jesus departed from Bethany. He was accompanied by His disciples and a large following of friends. As He was about half-way and approaching the fig gardens of Bethphage, "the House of Figs," [2]

1, 1) Ex. 12, 3.

2) Otherwise unmentioned in the Bible. From several Talmudic references it may be inferred that it was near the Mount of Olives and at the Sabbatical-distance limit east of Jerusalem. *Int. St. B. Encycl. sub loco.*

Jesus sent two of His disciples, possibly Peter and John,[3] with the instruction to proceed to the village, where they would find an ass tied and her unridden colt. "Loose them and bring them unto Me." The underlying idea about the colt "whereon yet never man sat" was that for the intended sacred purpose only an unused animal was to be employed.[4] The possibility of objections to this requisition was taken into consideration. "If any man say aught unto you, ye shall say, The Lord [5] hath need of them; and straightway he will send them."

2.

Matt. 21, 1—9. Mark 11, 1—10. Luke 19, 29—40.
John 12, 12—19.

The two disciples did as they had been told. Everything happened as Jesus had said. They went and found a colt and his mother tied at the gate by the pathway.[1] When untying the animals, the disciples were challenged. The message of Jesus was repeated with satisfactory result. Then the disciples led the ass and the colt to Jesus. A saddle was made of their upper garments and placed upon the animals. Then, as Jesus indicated His choice of **"Sitting upon an Ass."** the mount, they lifted Him upon the colt, after which the triumphal procession began. For this is what it was. Not a triumphal entry into the city according to the fashion of a Roman conqueror, but a humble pomp, so to speak, and unpretentious riding into Jerusalem of the Savior upon the foal of an ass. In after-days it was recalled by the disciples [2] that this unostentatious procession, which supplied the Gentiles with material for stupid jests,[3] was "done that it might be fulfilled which was spoken by the prophets: [4] Tell ye the daughter of Sion,[5] Behold, thy King cometh unto thee, meek, and sitting upon an ass and [6] a colt, the foal of an ass."

1, 3) Compare Luke 22, 8.   4) Num. 19, 2; 1 Sam. 6, 7.

5) Ὁ κύριος in the same sense as used of Christ in the gospels otherwise. Matt. 8, 25. 30, etc. Bruce sub Matt. 21, 3.

2, 1) Δεδεμένον πρὸς τὴν θύραν ἔξω ἔπι τοῦ ἀμφόδου. Tied to the gate or door outside or without on the path that leads from the road or the meeting of the road.

2) Matt. 21, 5; John 12, 16.

3) The Romans indulged in all kinds of sneers against the Jews in connection with the ass: worshipers of an ass's head, and the like, and the Christians came in for their share of them. In the East the ass is not a despised animal. The Rabbis believed that, if the Messiah would not appear floating upon a cloud, He would come riding on an ass as a sign of their faithlessness. Farrar, II, 197.

3.

Matt. 21, 1—9. Mark 11, 1—10. Luke 19, 29—40.
  John 12, 12—19.

No sooner had the procession started than the multitudes, made up of the Galilean Passover pilgrims, the townsmen of the risen Lazarus, and the approaching throng from Jerusalem, who had heard about, and many of whom had witnessed, the raising of Lazarus, started to make a carpet of their upper garments for the path of Jesus. Enthusiasm was at its height. Many cut branches of palm- and fig-trees and spread them on the way. Then, in an outburst of exultation, the disciples began, and the multitudes joined in, the strain which reechoed the great Hallel of Tabernacles and Passover, as also the Gloria of the angels: [1] "Hosanna to the Son of David! Blessed is He that cometh in the name of the Lord; hosanna in the highest!"

"Hosanna to the Son of David!"

4.

Matt. 21, 1—9. Mark 11, 1—10. Luke 19, 29—40.
  John 12, 12—19.

In this happy mood the procession moved onward to Jerusalem. But mingled with the crowd were also some of the Pharisees, to whom the joy of the multitude was as wormwood and gall. [1] Among themselves they had to acknowledge their helplessness. "Behold, the world is gone after Him!" What is the meaning of those Messianic titles and jubilant cries? A few of them took it upon themselves to request Jesus to rebuke His disciples. But His reply was: "I tell you that, if these should hold their peace, the stones would immediately cry out."

"Behold, the World is Gone after Him!"

Luke 19, 41—44.   5.

The joy of Jesus was soon turned into sorrow. As much as He rejoiced over the many sincere hosannas, He was nevertheless pained at the thought that much of the ecstasy was short-lived.

2,   4) Zech. 9, 9, prefaced by Is. 62, 11.

  5) The believing citizens of Jerusalem in general.

  6) This "and" has caused much trouble. Obviously Jesus did not ride on both animals. It has been explained why He rode the colt. Luke gives the answer when he stresses "whereon yet never man sat." It seems that "an ass *and* a colt" is a parallelism, or it is epexegetic "and," in the sense of "and that upon" or "and, to be explicit, upon." Ylvisaker, 549.

3,   1) Ps. 118, 25. 26: "Save me," etc. Luke 2, 14.

4,   1) Farrar, II, 203.

While the true believers would always acknowledge Him as the Son of David, yet He knew that Jerusalem was about to reject its King. And then the terrible consequences. As the awe-inspiring panorama of the ancient city, its surrounding walls, its splendid palaces, the marble pinnacles and the gilded roof of the Temple, suddenly burst into view, He was overcome with sadness and moved to tears. "And when He was come near, He beheld the city and

"He Beheld the City and Wept over It." wept over it." A strange Messianic triumph! Tears and lamentations interrupting the festal cries! If Jerusalem had only known and considered, even now, that day, the things which belonged to her peace! But now they were hid from her eyes. As matters stood, the period of grace for those who had hardened their hearts was already past. Days were to come when enemy hosts would cast a trench about the Holy City, surround her on every side, lay low, level to the ground, her walls, her buildings, and the Temple, in a destruction so thorough as not to leave one stone upon another, and slay her inhabitants. And all this "because thou knewest not the time of thy visitation," as Jesus solemnly declared midst sobs and tears. "Sternly and fiercely, and in less than fifty years, these dire words were literally fulfilled." [1)]

6.

Matt. 21, 10. 11. Mark 11, 11.

Progress was slow. As Jesus finally entered the city, the day was far spent. It was a memorable day. As the black masses poured through the gates in an almost endless stream, the whole city was filled with excitement and alarm. What can this be? "Who is this?" is asked from the windows, the roofs, the streets, and the bazaars. Even Jerusalem, frozen with religious formalism, is moved.[1)] The answer is given: "This is Jesus, the prophet of

Returning to Bethany. Nazareth of Galilee." Thus the word is passed to the homes of the city, to the camps of the pilgrims, to the courts of the rulers, and to the palaces of Pilate, Herod, and Caiaphas. Thus ended the day. After a brief visit in the Temple, merely to look around, but keenly observing the traffic going on within the sacred precinct and listening to the hum of bargaining voices and the clink of gold, but postponing action, it being now eventide, "He went out again to Bethany with the Twelve."

5,   1) Farrar, II, 201.
6,   1) Ἐσείσθη, as if rocked by an earthquake.

CHAPTER XXVIII.

MONDAY OF PASSION WEEK.

April 3, 30 A. D., 783 A. U. C.

Nisan (or Abib)							
10	11	12	13	14	15	16	17

April							
2	3	4	5	6	7	8	9
Sun.	Mon.	Tue.	Wed.	Thu.	Fri.	Sat.	Sun.

783 A. U. C.			APRIL			30 A. D.	
Sun.	Mon.	Tue.	Wed.	Thu.	Fri.	Sat.
						1
2	3	4	5	6	7	8
9	10	11	12	13	14	15
16	17	18	19	20	21	22
23	24	25	26	27	28	29
30						

1.

(*Matt. 21, 18. 19 a.*) [1] *Mark 11, 12—14.*

As Jesus returned to the city on the next morning, He felt hungry. This seems to suggest that He had not spent the preceding night, at least not the latter part of the night, with His friends at Bethany, but rather under the canopy of heaven, in communion with His heavenly Father.[2] At any rate, as He walked along the road on Monday morning with His disciples, He beheld a solitary

The Cursing of the Fig-Tree. fig-tree by the wayside, and although the ordinary season at which figs ripened had not yet arrived, still, seeing its green leaves and vigorous growth, "He came if haply He might find anything thereon." But when He came, He found nothing but leaves. While the ordinary season for the ripening of figs, June, had not yet arrived, we must not suppose that Jesus was ignorant of Palestinian horticulture or unreasonable in being disappointed. Nor, for that matter, is the evangelist,[3] who probably was thinking of the spring or summer fig, wrong in remarking: "For the time of figs was not yet." We are told that at the time of Jesus it was

---

1,   1) From Mark we learn that the incident of the cursing of the fig-tree, Mark 11, 12—14 and 20. 21, and the discussion on the matter took place on two different days, Monday and Tuesday morning. In Matthew the story of the two days is compressed into one, Tuesday morning.
    2) Ylvisaker, 553.   3) Mark.

[527]

not uncommon to see figs and grapes ripening ten months of the year.[4]   And modern writers tell us that early figs, called by the Arabs *taksh,* may be eaten as early as April.[5]   But the tree which Christ approached was hopelessly barren.   It was a fit emblem of a hypocrite.   On it were neither the gleanings of the past nor the promise of the future.[6]   Had it been fruitful the previous year, there would still have been a few of the figs hidden under its leaves.   And had it been fruitful that year, the untimely *taksh* would have appeared.   Since, however, it was both "deceptive and useless," the curse is loudly spoken: "Let no fruit grow on thee henceforward forever."   Presently the fig-tree withered away.   At once the sap ceased to flow from the roots into its branches and leaves, the full effect of which, however, was not seen until the following day.

2.

Matt. 21, 12—16.   Mark 11, 15—19.   Luke 19, 45—48.[1]

Again "the Lord of the Temple entered into the Temple of the Lord."   As in the beginning of His public ministry, three years before, He would now, at the close of it, by forceful demonstration demand the purity of worship.   Already on the day before, after His triumphal entry into the Holy City, He had briefly visited the Temple and looked around.   Again He had noticed that tradesmen for Temple supplies, animals, oil, wine, and salt, and the exchangers of money had entrenched themselves in holy places.   "And He cast out all them that sold and bought in the Temple and overthrew

The Cleansing of the Temple. the tables of the money-changers and the seats of those that sold doves."   The whole worship had been commercialized, and this probably in the manner of modern concessions at fairs and places of amusement, to the advantage of the high priests.   But Jesus cast out all the desecraters of His Temple and, in appealing to Scripture,[2]

1,   4) Josephus, *Wars,* III, X, 8.

5) When the young leaves are newly appearing in April, every fig-tree which is going to bear fruit at all will have some *taksh,* immature figs, upon its branches, even though the time of figs, that is, of the ordinary crop, either early or late, "is not yet."   This *taksh* is not only eaten to-day, but it is sure evidence, even when it falls, that the tree bearing it is not barren. E. W. G. Masterman, in *Int. St. B. Encycl.*

6) Farrar, II, 214.

2,   1) Not to be confused with the cleansing of the Temple at the beginning of our Lord's ministry at the Passover of A. D. 27.   John 2, 13—21. See chapter VII, 1 ff.

2) Is. 56, 7.   From the LXX, with omissions.   And Jer. 7, 11.   Bruce *sub loco* (Matt.).

defended His action with the words: "My house shall be called the house of prayer; but ye have made it a den of thieves." In His holy zeal He would not even suffer the sacred courts to be disturbed by people passing to and fro with vessels and instruments, thus turning them into an ordinary thoroughfare. In this prohibition He agreed with certain rabbinical expressions [3] as to the sacredness of holy places.

3.

Matt. 21, 12—17. Mark 11, 15—19. Luke 19, 45—48.

In opposition to the Temple traffic, Jesus manifested the spirit which shall obtain in His house by healing the lame and the blind who appealed to Him. But the leaders of Israel would not yield, neither listening to His Word nor acknowledging His deeds as divine miracles. When the very children of the Temple, probably employed in the Temple service, continued the hosannas of the day before, the scribes and priests were sorely displeased. They said unto Him: "Hearest Thou what these say?" Again referring

The Hosannas of the Children. them to Scripture,[1] Jesus replied: "Yea; have ye never read, Out of the mouths of babes and sucklings Thou hast perfected praise?" Jesus must have His praise. If the elders refuse to give it, then babes and sucklings will do so. Yes, the very stones must then cry out.[2] But the words of Jesus displeased the chief priests and the scribes all the more. They sought to kill Him; but they feared Him. They had to find a chance to arrest Him when He was not surrounded by a multitude of protecting friends. Unmolested and undisturbed, in spite of the rigorous manner by which He had interfered with their unhallowed gains, He passed another day. In the evening He left the Temple and the city and covered the fifteen stadia [3] to Bethany, where He passed the night.[4]

2,   3) Bruce sub Mark 11, 16.
3,   1) Ps. 8, 2.   2) Luke 19, 40.
    3) John 11, 18, about two miles.
    4) *Ηὐλίσθη*, from *αὐλίζεσθαι*. **To remain in the *aula*, to spend the night.** (Matthew.)

CHAPTER XXIX.

TUESDAY MORNING OF PASSION WEEK.

April 4, 30 A. D., 783 A. U. C.

Nisan (or Abib)

10	11	12	13	14	15	16	17

April

2	3	4	5	6	7	8	9
Sun.	Mon.	Tue.	Wed.	Thu.	Fri.	Sat.	Sun.

783 A. U. C.		APRIL			30 A. D.	
Sun.	Mon.	Tue.	Wed.	Thu.	Fri.	Sat.
						1
2	3	4	5	6	7	8
9	10	11	12	13	14	15
16	17	18	19	20	21	22
23	24	25	26	27	28	29
30						

1.

Matt. 21, 19 b. 20.   Mark 11, 20. 21.[1]

On the next morning Jesus and His disciples returned to the city. They passed by the fig-tree which the Lord had cursed and noticed that it had withered from its very roots. Most likely it was in the same condition on the previous evening, but it would have been too dark to examine it when they passed the spot. It was

The Fig-Tree Withered Away. as if it had been smitten by the hand of death. The disciples marveled at the completeness of the judgment. The miracle probably suggested to them the question how they might accomplish similar deeds. Calling to mind what Jesus had said, they connected the present condition of the tree with the word that Jesus had spoken. Peter, acting as spokesman, expressed the surprise of the disciples: "Master, behold, the fig-tree which Thou cursedst is withered away."

2.

Matt. 21, 21. 22.   Mark 11, 22—26.

In His reply Jesus combined what the disciples needed to know. By unflinching faith they shall be able to overcome the greatest difficulties. It must be faith unmixed with doubt. Not that kind

---

1,   1) See chapter XXVIII, 1.

which made Peter, when he saw a wave coming, begin to sink.[1] Unlimited power is at the trustful believer's command. With neither limitation nor explanation the word applies: "Verily I say unto you, If ye have faith and doubt not, ye shall not only do this which is done to the fig-tree, but also, if ye shall say unto this mountain, Be thou removed, and be thou cast into the sea, it shall be done." [2] These are mighty words, from which nothing by way of interpretation is to be detracted. What believing Christian is going to doubt the truth of the statement? And if he does, he is no believing Christian and is not ready to meet any condition presenting itself. An instrument of divine power is in his possession, regardless of whether or not he ever enjoys its use. Remember,

The Great Power of Faith. however, that this power is not given to presumption, but to faith, absolute, simple, sincere, trustful faith, which gives all glory to God and seeks His glory and trusts in His promises. It is a faith which exercises itself in confident prayer: "What things soever ye desire, when ye pray, believe that ye receive them, and ye shall have them." And He that communes with God in prayer as a believing Christian will desire such things as are well-pleasing to God. His prayer will not be selfish and sinful. For he is a person who fears, loves, and trusts in God above all things and loves his neighbor as himself. At all times a true conciliatory spirit serves as a necessary background. "And when ye stand praying, forgive if ye have aught against any that your Father also which is in heaven may forgive you your trespasses. But if ye do not forgive, neither will your Father which is in heaven forgive your trespasses." [3]

3.

Matt. 21, 23—27. Mark 11, 27—33. Luke 20, 1—8.

The last full working-day of our Lord's public ministry to Israel had arrived. And what a day it was! To judge from the records, it was the busiest day of His life.[1] It was His last day in the Temple, the last day of His teaching, the last warning He gave the Pharisees and Sadducees, and His last call to national repentance.[2] Scarcely had He entered the sacred courts after His

---

2,   1) Matt. 14, 30.

    2) Compare Matt. 17, 20; Luke 17, 6. Chapter XVIII, 12.

    3) Compare Matt. 6, 14. 15.

3,   1) He had another busy day in Galilee, the day of the parables. Chapter XII, 13 ff.

    2) Edersheim, II, 380.

discourse on the way as suggested by the withering of the fig-tree, when He was approached by the chief priests, scribes, and elders. In other words, it was an official delegation of the Sanhedrin, called after the three classes from which the seventy members of the Great Council of the nation were taken. It consisted of chief priests,[3] probably members of the ruling high-priestly nobility and heads of the twenty-four priestly courses, mostly Sadducees; scribes, that is, learned Rabbis and prominent canonists, representing the teaching and legal profession, mostly Pharisees; and rulers, men of wealth and leisure, who represented the laity. Surrounding **The Authority of Jesus Challenged.** Jesus on all sides, they asked the question: "By what authority doest Thou these things, and who gave Thee this authority?" They demanded that He show them His commission authorizing Him to perform the duties of the public ministry, publicly to assume the functions of a Rabbi or prophet, to ride into Jerusalem amid Messianic hosannas shouted, and royal titles attributed to Him, by attendant crowds, and to purge the Temple of the traffickers whom they themselves had probably licensed, at whose presence in the Temple-courts they at least connived, and the like. The Council by no means exceeded its authority by sending a delegation of this kind. It was the duty of this body to watch over the morals and the worship of Israel, especially to pass on the credentials of a prophet, should one arise.[4] But here their purpose was evil, and their plans had already been made. They were not concerned about justice and the right of Jesus to act as He did, but their inquiry was a smoke screen behind which they could make preparations to carry out their murderous resolve. Most likely they thought that Jesus would appeal to His, as they would have it, unproved divine commission, in which event they might easily pass legal judgment upon Him as a false prophet and blasphemer.

4.

Matt. 21, 23—27. Mark 11, 27—33. Luke 20, 1—8.

The answer of Jesus took them by surprise. It was a counter-question: "I will also ask you one thing, which if ye tell Me, I in like wise will tell you by what authority I do these things: the baptism of John, whence was it, from Heaven or from men?" They were caught. Surely they, who had officially inquired into

---

3,   3) Schuerer, II, I, 174 ff.   4) Schuerer, II, I, 186.

the commission of John,[1] were able to answer the question.[2] But no answer came. Besides the fact that John had pointed out Jesus as *the* Prophet, the Messiah, there were the undisputed credentials of John himself. Not that they could not answer the question, but they would not. And why bring up this question of John's baptism now, after John was — as far as they were concerned, fortunately — dead? They were in a complete dilemma. They would not say, so they reasoned among themselves, "From Heaven," because in their hearts they did not believe it. And besides, this

"The Baptism of John, whence Was It?"

would give Jesus the opportunity to ask: "Why did ye not believe him?" Still they could not speak derisively of John and say, "Of men," because the people were persuaded, as even admitted by Josephus,[3] that John was a prophet. To have stated this in the teeth of popular opinion would have endangered their personal safety: "All the people will stone us." And therefore, what they were unable to deny they were nevertheless unwilling to admit. And so they answered: "We cannot tell," we do not know.[4] What an admission by the "incorporate wisdom of Israel"! And what a death-blow to their pretensions! Jesus did not press them on this point. However, to show them that He was not to be taken off His guard, that He owed them no apology, and that their failure to answer absolved Him from the necessity of explaining whence He had His authority, about which by their own confession they were incompetent to judge, He replied: "Neither tell I you by what authority I do these things." For the present the defeated accusers withdrew to the background.

Matt. 21, 28—32.   **5.**

In spite of their pretended piety it was clear from the reception accorded the testimony of Jesus and John the Baptist by the leaders of Israel that they would not enter into the kingdom of God. This Jesus makes clear in the parable of the Unequal Sons, the meaning of which both the multitudes and the members of the Sanhedrin, who were still scowling in the background, could not fail to understand. "What think ye? A certain man had two sons." It appears from the lesson taught that the man in the parable is God, and both sons are members of the chosen race. "And he came to the first and said, Son, go work to-day in my vineyard." The son flatly refused: "I will not." But afterwards he changed his mind

---

4,   1) John 1, 19 ff.   2) Farrar, II, 218.
       3) *Ant.*, XVIII, V, 2.   4) Οὐκ οἴδαμεν.

and went. In the mean while the father approached the second son
and spoke likewise. With all due politeness and in most filial
acknowledgment of paternal authority this son answered: "I go,
sir," but "went not." And now the question: "Whether of the
twain did the will of his father?"

The Parable of the Two Unequal Sons. The answer of the Lord's enemies
was: "The first." Then Jesus pointed
out to them the meaning of their own reply. That is exactly what
happened in His own ministry and in that of John. Despite their
own initial and open shamelessness and brazen-faced disobedience
it was the very publicans and harlots who, repenting, went into
the kingdom of heaven. "They go into the kingdom of God
before you." These despised and hated sinners are "streaming
through the door which is not yet shut." [1]   On the other hand,
the professionally pious and the pretended holy legalists of the
nation, as represented by the blandly promising, but non-performing
second son, would not enter into the kingdom of heaven. Now,
there was John the Baptist, who cultivated strict legal piety like
themselves.[2]   He stood for their own principles of strict righteousness and minute obedience to the Law; yet "ye believed him not."
And even when the effect of his preaching was seen on the publicans
and the harlots, still "ye, when ye had seen it, repented not after-
ward that ye might believe him." They were too proud to learn
from publicans and harlots. The result was that these went into
the kingdom before them.

6.

Matt. 21, 33—44. Mark 12, 1—11. Luke 20, 9—18.

This parable exposes the insincerity of the leaders in Israel and
is followed by one which exposes their open revolt against divine
authority and foreshadows the doom of Jesus. There was a certain
householder who planted a vineyard, placed a hedge around it to
protect it from wild beasts, constructed a wine-press and a pit
beneath it to receive the juices of the grapes, and built a tower for
the laborers and for the storage of the fruit; in short, he did
everything needed to make it a good vineyard and to insure a good
yield of fruit.[1]   Then he leased it out to tenants for a certain
share of the annual crop as payment for the care and the general
management of the vineyard. After all provisions had been made,

---

5,   1) Farrar, II, 221. *Προάγουσιν.* With the word "before you" Christ
still leaves the door open to them for repentance.
    2) Bruce sub Matt. 21, 32.   6,   1) Is. 5, 2 ff.

he went into "a far country." It is assumed that the reference is to a newly planted vineyard and that it would take a "long time," about two or three years, to raise a crop. At any rate, the idea of the total absence of all unreasonableness on the part of the householder is to be conveyed. Not until a sufficient time had elapsed, and at the time agreed upon, he sent his servants to collect the rent. But what happened? The tenants treated the messengers in a most barbarous manner, beating and even stoning them or killing them in some other way. We might have expected the owner to take severe measures immediately; but instead, showing an extraordinarily high degree of good will and

The Parable of the Wicked Husbandmen.

patience, he sent other servants and still others, all of whom, however, received the same brutal treatment. What in ordinary life can hardly be said ever to happen in a parable is made to serve the purpose of truly describing men's conduct in the spiritual sphere.[2] "For the vineyard of the Lord of hosts is the house of Israel and the men of Judah His pleasant plant."[3] At last, "having yet therefore one son, his well-beloved, he sent him also last unto them, saying, They will reverence my son." But the result was the same. "The appearance of the legal heir made them apprehensive of their tenure. Practically the vineyard was already theirs. By killing the heir, the only claimant to it would be put out of the way and so the vineyard become in every respect their own."[4] "Come, let us kill him, and let us seize on his inheritance," thus they reasoned among themselves. They proceeded from the idea that the owner was in a "far country" for an indefinite length of time. It seemed that he was unable to interfere, as indicated by his sending of servants successively. This plainly showed that his only chance of enforcing collection lay in the weak hope of the gentle power of persuasion. And so they let the only son make his approach, who was unaware of the fate which he would meet with. When he arrived, they pounced upon him, cast him out of the vineyard, and slew him.

7.

Matt. 21, 33—44. Mark 12, 1—11. Luke 20, 9—18.

The meaning of the parable is sufficiently clear. God planted the vineyard of the Old Testament theocracy. The hedge is the Law and the covenant, which surrounded Israel and separated the

---

6, 2) Bruce sub Matt. 21, 35.

3) Is. 5, 7.   4) Edersheim, II, 424.

Jew from the Gentile. The wine-press is the Temple with its rituals and sacrifices foreshadowing the supreme sacrifice of the promised Messiah for the sins of all mankind. A tower of civic order or of prophecy was constructed from which the prophetic watchmen could study the approach of Messianic times.[1] The vineyard was let out to husbandmen, even as the management of Israel was entrusted to rulers, teachers, and leaders. At the present

The Meaning.   time these were the high priests and scribes, for the special benefit of whom this parable was related. And so forth. We need not go into details. In due season God sent forth His servants, the prophets, from Moses to John the Baptist, to gather the fruits of love and obedience. But what happened? Jerusalem killed her prophets and stoned those who were sent unto her [2] and became guilty of the blood of all the prophets shed on earth, from the blood of Abel to that of Zacharias,[3] as well as of the blood of John the Baptist,[4] who died a prophet's death. At last God sent His only Son, Jesus Christ. But His appearance made them fearful lest they fail to realize their unlawful desire of getting possession of the vineyard itself. "All men will believe on Him," and "the world is gone after Him." [5] And so they cast Him out of His possession and killed Him.

8.

Matt. 21, 33—44. Mark 12, 1—11. Luke 20, 9—18.

There was no doubt as to the main drift of the parable. In reply to the question what at his coming the owner of the vineyard would do to these husbandmen there could be but one answer: "He will miserably destroy [1] those wicked men and will let out his

"The Stone which the Builders Rejected."   vineyard to other husbandmen." From Jewish lips came the admission that, if God would take His Word and grace from them and give them to the Gentiles, this punishment would be well deserved. As a matter of fact, this very thing, as Jesus points out, had been prophesied in Scripture: "The Stone which the builders rejected, the same is become the Head

---

7,   1) Micah 7, 4; Is. 52, 8; 62, 6.   2) Luke 13, 34; Matt. 23, 37.
      3) Luke 11, 51; Matt. 23, 35.
      4) Mark 9, 13; Matt. 17, 12. See chapter XVIII, 10.
      5) John 11, 48; 12, 19.
8,   1) Κακοὺς κακῶς ἀπολέσαι, badly destroy bad men.

of the corner."[2] This quotation contains the germ of another parable in which the rejected heir becomes the rejected stone of the builders, only, however, in turn eventually to become the accepted Corner-stone of God.[3] Against those who oppose Christ a general and an individual judgment is pronounced. As applied to the nation: "The kingdom of God shall be taken from you and given to a nation bringing forth the fruits thereof." As applied to individuals: "Whosoever shall fall on this stone shall be broken; but on whomsoever it shall fall, it will grind him to powder." We are reminded of the words of Simeon: "Set for a fall and rising again of many in Israel and for a sign which shall be spoken against."[4]

9.

Matt. 21, 45. 46. Mark 12, 12. Luke 20, 19.

The scribes and the Pharisees, of course, saw through the veil of the parabolic language. Their purpose in coming had been to ensnare Jesus, and now for the third time in rapid succession they had been discomfited by Him. The first time it was the implication — only too true — of their rejection of John.[1] Then it was

"They Sought to Lay Hands on Him." the charge of insincerity in the parable of the Unequal Sons. And now in the parable of the Wicked Husbandmen it was the charge of open revolt, unsuccessful in the end and to be followed by the punishment and wrath of God. "They perceived that He spake of them" and intended to apprehend Him on the spot. "But when they sought to lay hands on Him, they feared the multitude, because they took Him for a prophet."

Matt. 22, 1—14. ### 10.

The threat that the kingdom of God would be "given to a nation bringing forth the fruits thereof" is followed by a parable which repeats the truth. It is a reply to the hostile thoughts and plans of Christ's enemies, warning them that, unless they cease their enmity, judgment will come upon them. In its construction this parable closely resembles that of the Great Supper, spoken in

---

8, 2) Ps. 118, 22. 23. From the Septuagint. Bruce sub Matt. 21, 42.

3) As in the case of Joseph, when men thought evil against him, but God meant it unto good, Gen. 50, 20, so here "it is the Lord's doing, and it is marvelous in our eyes."

4) Luke 2, 34.

9, 1) Luke 7, 30.

the Pharisee's house in the later Perean ministry of Jesus.[1] But it differs both as to details and as to the conclusion. The earlier parable was a parable of excuses and of rejected *grace,* while this is — with an addition — more directly a parable of *judgment* upon rejected grace.[2] The kingdom of heaven is likened unto a king who made a marriage for his son. A preliminary invitation is extended to the prospective guests, and an elaborate meal is prepared. At the appointed time a second invitation to the already invited guests [3] is sent out: "Behold, I have prepared my dinner;[4] my oxen and my fatlings are killed, and all things are ready; come unto the marriage." This second invitation seems to accord with Eastern custom.[5] Indeed, we are told [6] that among the distinctions

The Parable of the Marriage of the King's Son.

of the inhabitants of Jerusalem is mentioned that none of them went to a feast till the invitation had been given twice. But in this banquet no details of proper etiquette are overlooked, so as not to offend the most sensitive of the important, the rich, and the powerful of the invited guests. And a most attractive meal is prepared. But instead of showing the king how highly honored they felt at being invited by him and giving themselves the pleasure of being present at such a fine feast, they, making light of it, "went . . . one to his field and the other to his merchandise." [7] Some of them, probably the higher class of invited guests, added insult, even murder, to their indifference. "And the remnant took his servants and entreated them spitefully and slew them." The kingdom of heaven is depicted. The King is God the Father. The Son is Jesus. The banquet is salvation. The guests are the members, the leaders and the led, of the chosen race. The servants are the prophets, the disciples of Jesus, the apostles and evangelists included; and they are slain.[8] Then the parable merges into prophecy: "But when the king heard thereof, he was wroth; and he sent forth his armies and destroyed those murderers and burned their city." As applied to Jerusalem, these armies were led by Vespasian and Titus, and the burning of the city took place 70 A. D.

10, 1) Luke 14, 16—24. Chapter XXIII, 10.

2) Bruce *sub loco.*

3) Καλέσαι τοὺς κεκλημένους, to invite the invited. Bruce *sub loco.*

4) Ἄριστον, midday meal.

5) Esther 6, 14.   6) Edersheim, II, 427.

7) Εἰς τὴν ἐμπορίαν, store.   8) Compare Matt. 21, 35.

Matt. 22, 1—14. **11.**

But the story must go on. The refusal of the Jews to accept the invitation of Jesus shall not retard the extension of the kingdom of God. The king said to his servants: "The wedding is ready, but they which were bidden were not worthy. Go ye therefore **"Go Ye therefore into the Highways."** into the highways, and as many as ye shall find, bid to the marriage." This was done. The servants went out on the Gentile roads and without regard to race, reputation, station, and social position, "bad and good," they swept the roads and the market-places and furnished the wedding with guests. In like manner the Gospel invitation was given: "Go ye into all the world and preach the Gospel to *every* creature." [1]

Matt. 22, 1—14. **12.**

Lest Jesus be accused of anti-Semitic tendencies, there is a sequel containing a warning which concerns all guests, Jews and Gentiles alike. The king was pleased with the success of his plan. As soon as the guests were placed, he entered the banquet hall. While he was passing down between the rows, his eye lighted upon a man without a wedding-garment. There may have been others, but one serves to illustrate the principle. Just how this detail of the parable is to be understood, whether all guests were supposed to come in special wedding-garments or whether they were supplied with suitable vestments by the king, we do not know. The latter is very probable if we suppose that the guests came in from the streets as they were. [1] But the historical accuracy of this assumption has been doubted. [2] At any rate, that those invited should appear in festive attire was a matter of course and demanded by the rules of ordinary etiquette. And the symbolism is complete. How the vest-**The Guest without the Wedding-Garment.** ment is acquired is not the point. It is the necessity of ownership that is stressed. Scripture teaches us elsewhere, and abundantly, that the garment which alone is acceptable before God is the righteousness of Christ. In virtue of the suffering and death of Christ it is a free gift, bestowed upon those who believe. However, this man had thrust himself into the company in rags, and, we might add, in the rags of his own righteous-

---

11, 1) Mark 16, 15.
12, 1) Bruce *sub loco.*   2) See Meyer *sub loco.*

ness. There is no answer to the question of the king: "Friend,[3] how camest thou in hither not having a wedding-garment?" The man was speechless. He had nothing to say. He had no excuse. Before men we like to boast of our high moral standing, but before God all our righteousnesses are as filthy rags.[4] He who as a reward for his pretended piety demands that he be received into heaven insults the grace of God. We must remember that this is a parable of the Kingdom. The man therefore in the parable who appeared without a wedding-garment was cast out. "Then said the king to the servants, Bind him hand and foot and take him away and cast him into outer darkness; there shall be weeping and gnashing of teeth." At the conclusion of the parable the Lord Himself makes the transition to the spiritual sphere.[5]   And again the warning is given: "Many are called, but few are chosen." [6] Many hear, but few heed, the Gospel call.

13.

Matt. 22, 15—22. Mark 12, 13—17. Luke 20, 20—26.

In their attempts upon Jesus' life His enemies did not lack resourcefulness. Since they had failed in their endeavor to question His authority, they tried to bring Him into collision with the civil powers. In evolving their plan, they first of all joined forces with the Herodians.[1] A queer alliance indeed. The Pharisees, as the representatives of the extreme Jewish nationalists and haters of Rome, made common cause with a political party which sought to strengthen the dynasty of Herod by cultivating the favor of Rome.[2] The purpose of this combination was to spy Him out under the guise of an honest inquiry and, if possible, to entangle Him in His talk. This they would do by inveigling Him into some incriminating statement against the government, whereupon they would deliver Him into the hands of the governor. In order to give the whole procedure an appearance of singleness of heart, the Pharisees would not come themselves, but would send a group of their keenest students together with the Herodians, who this time might be expected to come before Him without arousing in Him a suspicion of sinister motives on their part. The impression which

---

12, 3) Ἑταῖρε, a mild way of introducing a rebuke. Meyer sub Matt. 20, 13.

4) Is. 64, 6.

5) Matt. 8, 11. 12; 13, 42. 50; 24, 51; Luke 13, 28. 29.

6) Matt. 20, 16. Chapter XXV, 18.

13, 1) Ἡρῳδιανοί, a Latinism. Mark 3, 6. Chapter X, 34.

2) See chapter XVII, 8.

they evidently designed to make was that a dispute had occurred between them and that they now desired to settle it by referring the matter to an authority such as Jesus was. Their plan was to put Him in a dilemma by asking Him to answer a question about paying tribute to Caesar. Ever since the birth of Christ and the

The Question of Tribute. days of Judas of Galilee [3] this had been a burning question in current politics and in theology. The introduction of the speech of the Pharisees' disciples is cunningly conceived. "Master, we know," everybody knows, "that Thou art true and teachest the way of God in truth." So that infamous accusation that Jesus was in league with Beelzebub was admittedly false! [4] The points which they stressed were His sincerity, His trustworthiness, His fearlessness, and His integrity. "Neither carest Thou for any man, for Thou regardest not the person of men." These were honeyed words. But they left a forked tongue. And in a moment a venomous fang appeared. [5] "Tell us therefore," since Thou art so wise and courageous, "what thinkest Thou?" Thus they tempted Him to commit Himself, while they themselves remained noncommittal. "Is it lawful to give tribute [6] to Caesar?" And without playing a heroic part themselves, the nature of their secretly desired reply seems to be indicated in the final suggestion "or not?" [7] The trap was cleverly constructed. The question — whether for poll-tax or for state purposes — seemed to imply that paying such a tribute conflicted with their duty to God as the only true Head of the nation. [8] Did not the payment of tribute to the Roman emperor or to his representative virtually admit the sovereignty of a stranger over Israel, which in effect was denying the supremacy of God? No matter how Jesus answered the question, it seemed that He would certainly be caught. To answer it

---

13, 3) Luke 2. 1; Acts 5, 37.

4) Matt. 12, 24. See Bruce sub Matt. 22, 16.

5) Farrar, II, 230.

6) Κῆνσον, *censum.* Another Latinism. Φόρον in Luke.

7) Josephus, *Wars,* II, XVI, 4. The speech of Agrippa against the final war. (Niese, II, 386.) Populous, wealthy, and vast Alexandria does not disdain to submit to Roman domination, yet "the tribute (φόρος) which she yields to Rome in one month surpasses that which you pay in a year." — Ἔξεστιν ἡμῖν Καίσαρι φόρον δοῦναι; . . . δείξατέ μοι δηνάριον, Luke 20, 22. 24. The Jews, when accusing the Lord before Pilate, falsely accused Him of "forbidding to give tribute, φόρους, to Caesar," Luke 23, 2. Κῆνσος was a poll-tax and φόρος a payment for state purposes. Madden, *History of Jewish Coinage,* 247.

8) Deut. 17, 15.

in Rome's favor — He had just been hailed as David's Son and Israel's King — would cost Him popular favor, and to answer it in favor of the people would get Him into serious trouble with Roman authorities, which would charge Him with disloyalty to Rome.

14.

Matt. 22, 15—22. Mark 12, 13—17. Luke 20, 20—26.

But Jesus proved that He was indeed true, that He taught the way of God in truth, and did not care for any man. He knew their wicked scheme and said: "Why tempt ye Me, ye hypocrites? Show Me the tribute-money." [1] Under the circumstances, as worshipers in the Temple, their present girdles would probably contain only Jewish coins, without the hated images, the Temple shekel; but they could easily go to one of the money-changers squatted behind his low table by the pillars in the Court of the Gentiles and bring Him a current Roman coin. "And they brought Him a penny." [2] It was the well-known piece of Roman silver coin representing ten units of an earlier bronze standard, the *denarius,* in which metal the annual tribute was paid. In our money it was worth about twenty cents. However, since it represented the average daily amount of a laborer's wages or a soldier's pay, [3] its actual value in buying power must

"Whose Is This Image and Superscription?"

be thought of in corresponding terms. On one side were stamped the haughty features of Tiberius, his Roman nose and scornful underlip, and the inscription: [4] "Tiberius Caesar, son of the divine Augustus, Augustus," and on the other side [5] "Pontifex Maximus," which title, "high priest" or "supreme bridge-builder," made him both the highest civil and the highest religious ruler of the land. The title itself surrounded the enthroned Caesar with his long scepter in his right hand and an emblem of honor in his left. [6] As Jesus looked at the coin, probably turning it in His hand, He

---

14, 1) Νόμισμα. Latinism, *numisma.* The current coin in which the tribute was paid. A denarius (Mark).

2) Δηνάριον, *denarius.* From *as* (*aes*), the original bronze standard. Ten of them, *decem asses,* amounted to one silver denarius. The fourth Latinism: *Herodiani, numisma, census, denarius.*

3) Compare Matt. 20, 2.

4) *TI(berius) CAESAR DIVI AUG(usti) F(ilius) AUGUSTUS.*

5) *PONTIF(ex) MAXIM(us).*

6) For illustration see Bible dictionaries under "Denarius." Ad. Deissmann, *Licht vom Osten,* p. 214. Madden, *Hist. of Jewish Coinage,* 247. Williamson, *Money of the Bible,* 70.

asked the question: "Whose is this image and superscription?" The answer was: "Caesar's." It is assumed that they could read the Latin lettering; if not, there is no doubt that they knew the meaning. Without evading in the least the question about the lawfulness of paying the tribute, Jesus gave a real reply: "Render," [7] give back, "to Caesar the things that are Caesar's." But while the political relation under Caesar must be acknowledged and the obligation which it implies must be observed, [8] at the same time their theocratic duties must not be disregarded. "And unto God the things that are God's." There are duties to Caesar. But there are also duties to God. These must be strictly kept apart. It was their duty to obey and support the government which they after a fashion had chosen; for in the time of the Maccabees the Jews themselves had sought the help of Rome, [9] and after the death of Herod they themselves requested the removal of Archelaus and expressed the wish to be governed by a procurator. [10] Under these circumstances the tax only represented the equivalent for the advantages which they received. To Tiberius they owed tax and submission; but at the same time, in an uninterfered service, themselves they owed to God. By the way, there was no intention on the part of Jesus to restore that erstwhile political status, the "kingdom of God" such as they hoped for. With His simple and true answer Jesus pointed out the correct interrelation of Church and State. — In spite of themselves there was nothing in this guileless wisdom which His enemies could attack. There was no way in which they could "take hold of His words." Amazed and humiliated, they left Him and went their way.

15.

Matt. 22, 23—33. Mark 12, 18—27. Luke 20, 27—40.

A number of Sadducees were present and had witnessed the crushing defeat of the Pharisees and the Herodians. The defeat was not altogether unwelcome to these aristocratic rationalists of Israel because the factions were opposed to each other. But at the same time they looked askance at the success of Jesus. They were not discouraged by the failure of their rivals, and they came forward with the purpose of matching their strength with that of the Prophet of Galilee, with hopes of better success. Only on one

---

14, 7) Ἀπόδοτε.

8) Jer. 27, 4—8; Rom. 13, 1; 1 Pet. 2, 13. 14.

9) 1 Macc. 8, 17 ff. 10) *Ant.,* XVII, XI, 2.

occasion had Jesus come into public conflict with the Sadducees, when, characteristically, they had asked of Him a sign from heaven.[1]　Representing the priestly and ruling classes, they contented themselves with material things, life upon earth.　As long as they had wealth and an honorable position, they were perfectly satisfied with the present order of things.　They were opposed to Jesus because in representing Himself as the Messiah and in teaching about the Kingdom, He threatened to disturb the Sadducean order of a Messiah who was already here.　Like the Samaritans they accepted only the five books of Moses.　As materialists and cold Epicureans they did not include the resurrection of the dead,

The Question of the Sadducees. the immortality of the soul, and the existence of angels and spirits in their theology.[2]　For the purpose of ridiculing the doctrine of the resurrection, known to them as being one of the tenets of Jesus and shared by the Pharisees, they came to Him with one of their stock conundrums and "stale pieces of casuistry" about the seven brothers and the one wife.[3]　It was introduced by an appeal to the ordinance of Moses regarding the levirate marriage.[4]　"Master, Moses said, If a man die having no children, his brother shall marry his wife and raise up seed unto his brother."[5]　Then they submitted, as if it had actually happened, a case in which, upon the death, without issue, of an eldest brother, the six remaining brothers in succession had married his widow, but also had died without issue, with the widow still surviving. And now, "in the resurrection therefore," that is, if there is a resurrection,[6] "whose wife shall she be of them?　For the seven had her to wife."　It was a very clever puzzle.　The Pharisees, who had very materialistic views on the resurrection, some of them holding that a man would rise in exactly the same clothes in which he had been buried, had already to their own satisfaction conceded the wife to the first husband on account of the right of priority.[7]　This, however, in their disputes with one another, the Sadducees would not admit, because to them the fundamental question was still unanswered.

15, 1) Matt. 16, 1.　See chapter XVII, 8; XVIII, 1.

2) Acts 23, 8.　　　　3) Farrar, II, 234.

4) To perform the part of a levir, brother-in-law, by marrying a deceased childless brother's widow.

5) Deut. 25, 5. 6.　　　6) "When they shall arise" (Mark).

7) Farrar, II, 235.　Edersheim, II, 398 ff.　Bruce sub Matt. 22, 28.

16.

Matt. 22, 23—33. Mark 12, 18—27. Luke 20, 27—40.

But if the Sadducees succeeded in baffling the Pharisees with their fairy-tales, they were not able to confuse Jesus. He heard their story to the end. Then He gave them an answer which will forever be remembered. Yes, there is a resurrection. But as concerning its nature "ye do err, not knowing the Scriptures and the power of God." Marriage and the begetting of children is restricted to life in this world. Though love remains in that place of bliss beyond the grave, yet all that is earthly in human relationship is superseded by such conditions as will obtain in heaven.[1] In the resurrection and among those, be it remembered, *"which shall be accounted worthy to obtain that world* and the resurrection from the dead,"[2] there is neither marrying for men nor being given in marriage for women. The relations of time will not apply to things eternal. The resurrected children of God will be like the angels, and matters belonging to the sphere of matrimony will no longer be of concern to them.[3] And as to the question of the resurrection itself, this is plainly taught in Scripture, indeed, already

The Reply of Jesus. in the very Pentateuch which they accepted and which they now marshaled against Him. And in His argument Jesus refrains from quotations taken from the prophetic books of the Old Testament in order to meet them on their own ground. For the purpose of showing their ignorance of Scripture He calls their attention to that passage in the Book of Exodus relating to the burning bush, where God describes Himself to their great lawgiver as "the God of Abraham and the God of Isaac and the God of Jacob."[4] At the time of Moses these patriarchs had been dead a few hundred years, and still God calls Himself their God.[5] Now, personal existence does not cease with death, as the Sadducees had taught. In their relation to men the dead are absent, but in their relation to God they continue to live. How unworthy would the title God

---

16, 1) Cf. Farrar, II, 236.

2) Luke: ἀνάστασις ἐκ νεκρῶν. Not merely a vague immortality of the soul.

3) Jesus does not state that they become angels, but that they are *like* the holy angels in relation to the estate of marriage. Ylvisaker, 576.

4) Ex. 3, 6.

5) The point is not in the εἰμί, "am," for which there is no Hebrew or Aramaic equivalent, but in the relation implied in the title. Bruce sub Matt. 22, 32.

of Abraham, Isaac, and Jacob have been had these fathers been but a handful of scattered bones and crumbling dust, now moldering in the Hittite's cave! [6] "Ye do therefore greatly err." He who calls Himself the God of Abraham is not the God of dust. "God is not the God of the dead, but of the living." — The Sadducees were crushed. "And when the multitude heard this, they were astonished at His doctrine." Even the scribes were constrained to admit that Jesus had spoken well.

17.

Matt. 22, 34—40. Mark 12, 28—34.

In spite of the fact that one of their professional members was constrained to admit that Jesus had spoken well, the defeat of the Sadducees was the occasion for the Pharisees to renew the conflict. While they were pleased to hear that He had muzzled [1] the Sadducees, they themselves had not as yet added any luster to their achievement. A new attack is planned as they gather together. It was decided that one of their number, a legal expert, should act as their spokesman in tempting Jesus with one of the greatest problems of the day: "Master, which is the great commandment in the Law?" What must be its nature to determine the quality of greatness in the legal realm? Now, the rabbinic schools had spun a large accumulation of subtleties all over the Mosaic Law. They had come to the conclusion that there were at least six hundred and thirteen different ordinances: two hundred and forty-eight affirmative precepts, which corresponded to the parts of the human body, and three hundred and sixty-five negative precepts, as corresponding to the days of the year, the total being six hundred and thirteen, the number of Hebrew letters in the Decalog. The same result was reached by other computations of equal value. [2] But of all these ordinances, the light and the heavy, those concerning the Sabbath, sacrifices, meat and drink, fasting, fringes, phylacteries, and ablutions, all equally binding, how was one to find the principle which establishes greatness? And "which is the first commandment of all?"

"Which Is the Great Commandment in the Law?"

16, 6) Farrar, II, 236.
17, 1) 'Εφίμωσεν, from φιμός, a muzzle. Deut. 25, 4.
    2) Farrar, II, 239. Ylvisaker, 578.

18.

Matt. 22, 34—40. Mark 12, 28—34.

Following the example of the legal expert in the introduction of the parable of the Good Samaritan,[1] Jesus points to the recapitulation of the Decalog and the fundamental law of love: "Hear, O Israel, the Lord, our God, is one Lord. And thou shalt love the Lord, thy God, with all thy heart, and with all thy soul, and with all thy mind, and with all thy strength. This is the first command-

"Thou shalt Love the Lord, Thy God." ment. And the second is like, namely this, Thou shalt love thy neighbor as thyself. There is none other commandment greater than these."[2] Love is the fulfilling of the Law.[3] Not as if the commandment of love should be counted as an individual precept, but as indicating the spirit which must underlie all obedience.[4] As referring to their object, God and the neighbor, the words might be divided into two commandments, but their essential demand is the same — love. And therefore "on these two commandments hang all the Law and the Prophets."

19.

Matt. 22, 34—40. Mark 12, 28—34.

Again Jesus won the day. The scribe was intelligent enough to observe and fair enough to acknowledge: "Well, Master, Thou hast said the truth." And then he repeats the twofold command of love. It is not the deed that counts, but the love that prompts the deed. That is "more than all whole burnt offerings and sacrifices."[1] Obedience which springs from love is "better than sacri-

"Thou Art Not Far from the Kingdom of God." fice and to hearken than the fat of rams." When Jesus saw that this expert of Jewish Law had answered as one having sense,[2] He said to him: "Thou art not far from the kingdom of God." Again the Savior throws out the life-line. But was he won? That is recorded in the yet "unread page of history."[3] At any rate, the Pharisees had received their answer. The result was that "no man after that durst ask

---

18, 1) Luke 10, 25—28. Chapter XXI, 8.
    2) Deut. 6, 5; Lev. 19, 18.
    3) Rom. 13, 10.   4) Bruce sub Matt. 22, 38.
19, 1) 1 Sam. 15:22.
    2) Νουνεχῶς, "discreetly."
    3) Edersheim, II, 405.

Him any question," that is, for the purpose of entangling Him in His talk. They were overcome, but unconverted. There was one question which they should have asked: What must we do to be saved?

20.

Matt. 22, 41—46. Mark 12, 35—37. Luke 20, 41—44.

The legalist is to be pitied. He seeks salvation in the Law and cannot find it there; he meets with salvation in the Gospel, but will not accept it. After the Pharisees had questioned Him, Jesus turns the tables on His adversaries and questions them. Not for the purpose of plotting against them as they had plotted against Him, but in order to present to them a Gospel truth, for the last time during His public ministry to call their attention to the difference between the Messiah whom they expected and the Messiah of whom the Old Testament had prophesied, and to convince them of His identity, He directs a question to them. And in order to make it easy for them to answer it, He bases His argument on their own principles of interpretation and supports it with a psalm which they themselves regarded as distinctly Messianic. Gently leading their thoughts from the region of precepts to the realms of promise, He asks them the momentous question: "What think ye of Christ?" First generally and then particularly, as to His descent: "Whose son is He?" Their answer was expected. The Messiah must be David's son. That was the idea of the scribes, carrying along with it the hope of royal dignity and a restored kingdom. They say unto Him: "The son of David." Jesus lets the answer stand. The Messiah was to be a true descendant of David. But at the same

David's Son and David's Lord. time another side of the Messianic relation must be brought out. How, then, does David call Him his Lord, which he does in the Hundred-and-tenth Psalm? That this psalm is of Davidic origin, that it is directly Messianic, and that David when writing it spoke "by the Holy Ghost" are truths on which at the outset both Jesus and His hearers agree. The passage [1] reads as follows: "The Lord (Jehovah) said unto my Lord (*Adonai*), Sit Thou on My right hand till I make Thine enemies Thy footstool." From this passage it is clear that the Messiah Lord is more than David's son, that He is almighty, and that the enemies at whom He strikes and over whom He exercises lordship are greater than

---

20, 1) Exactly reproduced from the LXX. Bruce sub Mark 12, 36.

earthly kings. And still He is David's son! Here is a puzzle: "If David, then, call Him Lord, how is He his son?" Could Abraham have called Isaac, Jacob, or even the illustrious David himself his Lord? And if not, how came David to do so? There could be but one answer: The Messiah is the Son of God and the Son of Man. According to His human nature He is David's son, but according to the divine nature He is David's Lord. But Jesus did not press the point. His believing followers and the "common people," who heard Him gladly, understood. The adversaries, however, had hardened their hearts. "And no man was able to answer Him a word, neither durst any man from that day forth ask Him any more questions." They did not dare to ask any more questions, because then the truth against which they rebelled would have been brought out. And they would not accept Jesus as the Messiah, the Christ.

21.

*Matt. 23, 1—36. Mark 12, 38—40. Luke 20, 45—47
(11, 37—54).*

By their inability to answer the question about David's Son and David's Lord the pharisaic doctors had clearly demonstrated their incompetence as Israel's teachers. Turning again to His disciples, but "in the audience of all the people" and with the Pharisees in the background, Jesus now hurls at them thunderbolts of denunciation. It was His solemn farewell address to all Israel, to its Temple, and to its authorities.[1] The public preaching of Israel's great Prophet was rapidly drawing to its close. It was Tuesday morning of Passion week. Much of the subject-matter of this final Temple discourse had been treated before in the Sermon on the Mount and especially

The Scribes and Pharisees Denounced. at the meal in the Pharisee's house in Perea.[2] It begins with the words: "The scribes and Pharisees sit in Moses' seat." They continued in the office of this great man of God, and as far as they were actually engaged as interpreters of the Mosaic Law, they were right in demanding obedience. But the people should learn to distinguish between their words and deeds. In many instances they exceeded the precepts of the Law. Like sheaves they bound together heavy packloads of rules and themselves did not "move them with one of their fingers." And when they apparently performed good

---

21, 1) Edersheim, II, 406.
   2) Luke 11, 37—54. Chapter XXI, 15.

works, it was for the purpose to be seen of men. Taking certain figurative injunctions literally, they would inscribe certain Bible-texts [3] on pieces of parchment and place them in little boxes, or phylacteries,[4] and tie them to the left arm near the elbow, so that at the bending of the arm they would rest over the heart. Or they would enclose them in frontlets and place them conspicuously on their foreheads between the eyes. In the same manner, so as to attract notice, they would lengthen the tassels, or fringes, of their outer garments, placed there as a reminder of the many command-ments of the Lord.[5] This religious ostentation was followed by social vanity, the desire for seats of honor at tables and in the synagogs and for flattering titles. Long robes covered murderous hearts, and long prayers concealed covetous designs. They loved to have themselves called "Rabbi" and "Father." With a side-glance at His disciples Jesus states that one is their Father, the Father in heaven, and one is their Master, or Teacher, "even Christ," [6] and that they are all brethren. The way to greatness in Christ's kingdom is reached by humility and service; for "whoso-ever shall exalt himself shall be abased." [7]

22.

Matt. 23, 1—36. Mark 12, 38—40. Luke 20, 45—47.

Now Jesus delivered His series [1] of denunciations. "Woe unto you, scribes and Pharisees, hypocrites!" He says, pouring upon them His holy wrath for involving Jerusalem in common sin and causing God to visit His judgments upon it and them. Woe unto them, hypocrites! And play-acting hypocrites they were. Accord-ing to Jewish testimony of ten kinds of hypocrisy in the world nine were found in Jerusalem.[2] 1. Woe unto the scribes and Pharisees for shutting up the kingdom of God by their opposition to Christ! "Ye neither go in yourselves, neither suffer ye them that are enter-ing to go in." [3] 2. Woe unto them for using their prayers as

---

21, 3) Ex. 13, 1—16 (v. 16). Deut. 6, 4—8 (v. 8). Deut. 11, 13—21 (v. 18).

4) Φυλακτήριον, "guard."   5) Num. 15, 37—40.

6) Jesus refers to Himself.   And Matthew, reporting the discourse, refers to the speaker as Christ.

7) Matt. 20, 26; 18, 4; Luke 14, 11; 18, 14.

22, 1) Eightfold in the *textus receptus;* sevenfold if, according to some leading manuscripts, Matt. 23, 14 is to be omitted, the contents of which are found in Mark 12, 40.

2) Farrar, II, 245, n. 1.   3) Luke 11, 52.

a cloak of maliciousness, especially covetousness! "For ye devour widows' houses and for a pretense make long prayers." 3. Woe unto them for their proselytism![4] Being hypocrites and self-righteous, they could not show those whom they were often so extraordinarily zealous to gain as converts from heathenism the true way to heaven; indeed, their proselytes not rarely outdid them in teaching and practising work-righteousness, which made them two-fold more children of hell than themselves. 4. Woe unto them for their hair-splitting trivialities in the manner of oaths![5] It seems that the strangest distinctions were made between oaths and vows that were considered binding and such as on account of their form and some clever evasion were not. But Jesus stresses the sanctity of all proper oaths and vows. Specialization is not to be considered an indication of greater earnestness. People should be

"Woe unto You, Scribes and Pharisees, Hypocrites!" as much in earnest when they say "by the Temple" as when they specify the "gold of the Temple." The best way is to be so truthful and trustworthy as not to be required to say either. Arbitrary trivialities as to form do not make the oath more or less binding. "He that shall swear by heaven sweareth by the throne of God and by Him that sitteth thereon." 5. Woe unto them for extending the Law of tithing to mint, dill, and aromatic cumin[6] while disregarding weightier matters, such as justice, mercy, and fidelity! Truly, this was a practise which reminded one of the proverbial straining of a tiny insect so as not to be defiled[7] and then choking in the attempt at swallowing an unclean camel. The smallest omission of some secondary rule hurt the consciences of the Pharisees while the infringement of some fundamental law made no impression upon them. With respect to tithing we are told that a certain Rabbi had his ass so well trained in piety as to refuse corn from which the tithes had not been collected.[8] 6. Woe unto them for the external cleanness of the cup while the contents were the

---

22, 4) That the Jews were zealous in making converts is the testimony of Josephus and the complaint of classical writers. *Ant.*, XVIII, III, 5; XX, II, 3. 4. Tacitus, *Hist.*, II, V. *Annales*, II, 85. *Apion*, II, 10. 39. Acts 2, 10.

5) Matt. 5, 33—37.

6) Lev. 27, 30. 31. Ἡδύοσμον, ἄνηθον, κύμινον, garden herbs: mint (literally, sweet-smelling), dill, also aromatic cumin (German, *Kuemmel*) with aromatic seeds. Used as condiments or for medicinal purposes. Luke 11, 42. Bruce sub Matt. 23, 23.

7) Lev. 11, 41—43.   8) Edersheim, II, 413.

product of extortion and excess! [9] 7. Woe unto them for white-washing the sepulchers [10] before the Passover season to make them conspicuous, lest an inadvertent approach involve Levitical contamination, while they themselves — with all their outward righteousness — were full of uncleanness and dead men's bones! 8. Woe unto them for erecting and maintaining memorials for murdered prophets and righteous men, lamenting the fact that their fathers were their murderers, while they perpetuated the same murderous spirit in their hearts. [11] This prophet-killing practise resulted in the rejection and the murder of the great Prophet of God. Fill up the measure of your fathers, ye serpents and offspring of vipers! [12]

23.

Matt. 23, 1—36. Mark 12, 38—40. Luke 20, 45—47.

For the purpose of exhibiting this national impenitence, the murdered and rejected Messiah would again send them "prophets and wise men and scribes," the apostles and other messengers of the New Testament. But consistently with their attitude to Christ they would kill, crucify, scourge, and persecute also His messengers.

"The Blood of Righteous Abel unto the Blood of Zacharias." And thus all the accumulated wrath of God would be visited upon them. As heirs of the guilt, and partners of the sin, of their fathers all the blood of the martyred Abel, mentioned first in the Hebrew Bible, to the blood of Zacharias, [1] the son or grandson of Barachias, the prophet named in the last book of the Hebrew Bible, should come upon them. The well-deserved punishment will be swift and complete. "All these things shall come upon this generation."

24.

Matt. 23, 37—39.

In a final lament Jesus addresses Himself to Jerusalem: "O Jerusalem, Jerusalem, thou that killest the prophets and stonest them which are sent unto thee, how often would I have gathered thy children together even as a hen gathereth her chickens under her wings, and ye would not!" [1] It was Christ's final invita-

22, 9) Luke 11, 39—41.
    10) Ezek. 39, 15.   11) Luke 11, 47. 48.
    12) Matt. 3, 7; Luke 3, 7; Matt. 12, 34.
23, 1) 2 Chron. 24, 21; Luke 11, 49—51. Chapter XXI, 20. Jehoiada was probably the grandfather of Zacharias, or he had two names: Jehoiada-Barachias.
24, 1) Luke 13, 34. 35. Chapter XXIII, 5.

tion to Jerusalem to repent. But Jerusalem "would not." Punishment must therefore follow. "Your house is left unto you desolate." It was a sad farewell of Israel's Messiah from Israel's city

"O Jerusalem, Jerusalem!"

and its Temple.[2] But it was a farewell which promised a coming again. "Ye shall not see Me henceforth till ye shall say, Blessed is He that cometh in the name of the Lord." On the Last Day even Christ's enemies will have to confess that He is the Lord, to the glory of God the Father.[3]

25.

Mark 12, 41—44. Luke 21, 1—4.

After the great denunciation just related it was only too clear that the rupture of Jesus with the leaders of Israel was final. But before Jesus took His last leave of the Temple, and while He sat down for a moment to rest His sad heart, an incident occurred which made it possible for Him to leave His Father's house with words of kindness and approval. In one of the courts of the Temple, called the Court of the Women, or the Treasury, were placed thirteen brazen trumpet-shaped receptacles for the various kinds of Temple offerings, as indicated by an inscription.[1] These offerings were contributions for wood, for sacrifices, for incense, and the like.[2] Into these were cast the offerings which helped to furnish the Temple with its splendid wealth. The amount of total contributions may be inferred by recalling the circumstance that at the time of Pompey and Crassus the Temple treasury, after having defrayed every possible expenditure, still contained two thousand talents in money and eight thousand talents in precious vessels and gold. Taking the value of a silver talent at about two thousand dollars, we arrive at a wealth of about twenty million dollars.[3] It was here at the depository of Israel's contributions that Jesus had seated Himself, probably after He had ascended

The Widow's Mites.

the flight of steps which led to the Gate Beautiful from the Court of the Gentiles to the Court of the Women. He "beheld how the people cast money into the treasury; and many that were rich cast in much." The average contributions very likely were of a moderate amount. But considering the large number of worshipers, the total amount which flowed into the Temple treasury must have been

---

24, 2) Edersheim, II, 414.   3) Phil. 2, 11.
25, 1) Bruce sub Mark 12, 41.
    2) Edersheim, II, 387.   3) *Ant.*, XIV, IV, 4; VII, 1.

enormous. Suddenly the eyes of Jesus were attracted by a woman contributor. "And there came a certain poor widow, and she threw in two mites, which make a farthing." [4] The terms used are two lepta, which make a quadrans, the smallest of the brass coins in circulation, eighty of them making one denarius. It took two lepta to make one quadrans, four quadrantes to make one Roman as, and ten of these to make one denarius. And if we take a denarius at about twenty cents in our money, then the two lepta of the widow amounted to about $\frac{1}{2}$ cent. While the contribution was too small to attract the attention of other contributors and the metal itself too impure to have endured for the discovery and identification of modern archeology, [5] it did not escape the notice of Jesus. Calling to His disciples, who were probably at the moment watching the noble and the rich, He pointed out to them the widow. "This poor widow hath cast more in than all they which have cast into the treasury." What the others gave they never felt. They lightly flung in "of their abundance"; "but she of her want did cast in all that she had, even all her living."

26.

John 12, 20—36.

Probably at this point, while Jesus was still in the Court of the Women and was preparing to leave, a message was brought to the inner court from the Court of the Gentiles that certain Greeks "would see Jesus." They were probably proselytes from the Decapolis, Galilee, or some country more remote, of Greek extraction, still uncircumcised, and not yet fully admitted into the Jewish Church, but who attended services in the synagog and participated in the worship of the Temple on the occasion of the great festivals as "proselytes of the gate." [1] Struck by what they had seen or heard of Jesus, they came to Philip, very likely because he understood Greek or because they had seen him at Bethsaida in Galilee, and asked him to arrange a private interview for them with Jesus. It is always a good thing to know some one who knows Jesus. But Philip did not want to take the responsibility of introducing them upon himself and therefore first conferred with his fellow-townsman Andrew, the brother of Peter. Probably his hesitancy was due to the fact that in sending out the Twelve on their

---

25, 4) Λεπτὰ δύο, ὅ ἐστι κοδράντης.

    5) Barton, *Archeology and the Bible,* 165.

26, 1) Andrews, 443. Schuerer, II, II, 316 ff. Ex. 20, 10; Deut. 5, 14; 14, 21; 24, 14; Acts 15, 20, 29; 21, 25.

first mission Jesus had said something about not going "into the way of the Gentiles." [2] If he had any misgivings on this point, they were removed. Together Andrew and Philip made the wish of the Greeks known to Jesus. When Jesus was born, "Chaldeans from the East had sought His cradle, and now Greeks and sons of the West came to His cross." [3] Whether they actually met Jesus is not stated. But, as Jesus told the disciples, no doubt in the hearing of the Greeks, in this request He saw an indication of His

The Greeks who would See Jesus. glorification, which consisted in His being acknowledged by men of all nations, as had been prophesied. The entrance to this glory, however, was reached through His death on the cross. Just as a kernel of wheat, before rising to life, must first fall into the ground and die, so also the road to His glory leads through humiliation. And, in a way, this rule also applies to His followers. "He that loveth his life shall lose it, and he that hateth his life in this world shall keep it unto life eternal." And as to "seeing" Jesus, this requires faith. Jesus must be viewed as a suffering Savior and as a living Lord. And it also entails love and service. "If any man serve Me, let him follow Me." Then those who have sought and properly seen Jesus will be rewarded. "Where I am, there shall also My servant be. If any man serve Me, him will My Father honor."

John 12, 20—36. **27.**

But as Jesus contemplated the painful road to glory, His soul was troubled, and His heart shrank from the idea of death. Still it was His hour, and for this cause He had come into the world. Summoning courage in prayer, He cried: "Father, glorify Thy name." And then for the third time in His life — at His baptism, at His transfiguration, and now — came a voice from heaven, saying, "I have glorified it and will glorify it again." The name of God had already been glorified on countless occasions, and He would glorify it again in the Passion of His Son. The mass of

The Voice from Heaven. people standing by, presumably in the Court of the Gentiles, heard the sound, but did not recognize the voice. They thought it was thundering. Others, recognizing the voice, but not understanding the words, thought that it was an angel speaking to Jesus. He Himself, however, explained that it was for their sakes that this voice had been heard. A critical time, an hour of trial for

---

26, 2) Dods *sub loco.* Matt. 10, 5. 3) Farrar, II, 207.

the world, had come. Now Satan, the prince of this world, was to
be cast out, and this by the paradox of a victory through death
on the cross. "And I, if I be lifted up from the earth, will draw
all men unto Me." Death was to be a source of life. And a cross
was to be the throne around which the believers would gather.[1]
"This He said, signifying what death He should die."

John 12, 20—36.   **28.**

The crowd apparently understood Christ's reference both to
His death and to Himself as the Messiah. But they could not
bring into agreement the idea of death with the prophecies concerning the Messiah and His unending kingdom. "We have heard
out of the Law[1] that Christ abideth forever.[2] And how sayest
Thou, The Son of Man shall be lifted up? Who is this Son of
Man?" This incidentally proves that the title "Son of Man" was

**"How Sayest Thou,
The Son of Man
shall be Lifted Up?"**

associated with the Messiahship,
although in this instance Jesus had
not, as reported,[3] referred to Himself as the Son of Man. Of course,
Christ shall abide forever, but not in an earthly, physical kingdom.
Without going into the details of the Messianic relations, Jesus
admonishes His listeners to use the brief respite during which the
Light is still among them to yield to the influence of the Light,
to believe in the Light, and to become the children of light.[4] And
His warning about the "little while" in which the Light would be
still available was followed by His removal. "These things spake
Jesus and departed and did hide Himself from them."

John 12, 37—50.   **29.**

The last word, a word of invitation and grace, had been spoken
by Jesus in the Temple. But even as His Father's house had been
made a den of thieves, so the glorious truths were dull to blinded
eyes and dead to hardened hearts. "Though He had done so many
miracles before them,[1] yet they believed not on Him." Thus His
whole ministry might be summed up in the complaint of Esaias:
"Lord, who hath believed our report, and to whom hath the arm
of the Lord been revealed?"[2] The fact that so few believed and

---

27, 1) Dods *sub loco.*
28, 1) Here a general term for the Old Testament. Compare John 10, 34.
     2) Ps. 89, 36; 110, 4; Is. 9, 7; etc.
     3) As compared with John 3, 14.   4) Eph. 5, 8; 1 Thess. 5, 5.
29, 1) The evangelist John reports but a few. However, compare
John 20, 30.   2) Is. 53, 1.

that even this failure to accept their Messiah had been foretold, that they simply fulfilled a prophecy, does not excuse the Jews before God and free them from divine punishment. This judgment for unbelief had already begun in the days of Isaiah and was consummated in the days of Christ. The Jews would not believe,

Reflections on the Unbelief of the Jews. and therefore they should not and "could not believe, because that Esaias said again, He hath blinded their eyes and hardened their hearts." [3] — Nevertheless, while the number of believers in Christ was not large, there were at least some. The inherent truth of Christ's teaching compelled response even in those least likely to be influenced. Even among the rulers many believed on Him, but on account of certain excommunication awaiting them they were afraid to confess Him. There were Nicodemus, Joseph of Arimathea, and no doubt others, who, however, were still afraid of criticism and "loved the praise of men more than the praise of God."

John 12, 37—50.   30.

Jesus had left the Temple.[1] But the evangelist's report of the public teaching ministry of Jesus is concluded with a few quotations, statements spoken or repeated by Jesus during the last days of His life as they were addressed to the people in the Temple. The evangelist distinctly calls to mind how Jesus on various occasions cried out and said: "He that believeth on Me believeth not on Me, but on Him that sent Me." Faith in Him may not be divorced from faith in the Father. After all, faith in Him is in accordance with the First Commandment of the Law. He is the

Additional Sayings of Jesus. Light of the world, and he that believes on Him shall not remain in darkness. While it was not the purpose of His coming into the world to judge the world, yet he who rejects Him and His Word condemns himself. "The Word that I have spoken, the same shall judge him in the Last Day." It is not zeal for Himself and His honor which makes Him so insistent, but His eagerness to fulfil the commandment of His Father.[2] And even as the Father's love prompted Him to send Him into the world and as "His commandment is life everlasting," so He, too, during the past three years had told His hearers that He earnestly desired the salvation of all men through faith in Him, the world's Redeemer.

29, 3) Is. 6, 9. 10.
30, 1) John 12, 36.   2) Kretzmann, I, 482.

CHAPTER XXX.

TUESDAY AFTERNOON OF PASSION WEEK.

April 4, 30 A. D., 783 A. U. C.

Nisan (or Abib)

10	11	12	13	14	15	16	17

April

2	3	4	5	6	7	8	9
Sun.	Mon.	Tue.	Wed.	Thu.	Fri.	Sat.	Sun.

783 A. U. C. APRIL 30 A. D.

Sun.	Mon.	Tue.	Wed.	Thu.	Fri.	Sat.
						1
2	3	4	5	6	7	8
9	10	11	12	13	14	15
16	17	18	19	20	21	22
23	24	25	26	27	28	29
30						

1.

Matt. 24, 1. 2. Mark 13, 1. 2. Luke 21, 5. 6.

As far as the Temple in Jerusalem was concerned, the Messiah had come and gone. When Jesus left the Temple after that fearful denunciation of its authorities on Tuesday morning of Passion week, His disciples must have become aware that a terrible crisis had come and that their Master was quitting the Temple forever. And so, leaving it, their thoughts still clung to it with feelings of a pardonable pride. It was a magnificent pile, one of the show-places of the ancient

"There shall Not be Left One Stone upon Another."

world, the rebuilding of which the architectural genius of Herod the Great had begun, in which the builders after forty-six years [1] were still engaged, but whose work, because they had rejected His Son, was "unblessed of God." [2] "Master," one of the disciples exclaimed as Jesus was passing through the gates on the way to the Mount of Olives, "see what manner of stones and what buildings are here!" Look at the stones! Immense blocks! Josephus tells us that the stones used in the Temple were "white and strong, and each of their length was twenty-five cubits, their height was eight, and their breadth about twelve." [3] For building purposes the

---

1,   1) John 2, 20.   2) Farrar, II, 255.   3) *Ant.*, XV, XI, 3.

length of the cubit was about twenty inches. Thus the blocks, measuring about forty by fourteen by twenty feet, must have exceeded anything found in our structures to-day. The disciples would have their Master gaze at the nine gates with two-storied gate towers and with doors thirty by fifteen cubits, covered with thick plates of silver and gold; the last gate, the eastern, over against the Holy House itself, called the Gate Beautiful,[4] or Gate of Nicanor, was made of solid Corinthian brass, was fifty cubits in height, and its forty-cubit doors were covered with plates of silver and gold.[5] The disciples call their Master's attention to the immense wealth with which the Temple was filled, the rich votive offerings which they had again seen, the donations of rulers and kings to the house of God: the large gold table and the two cisterns of gold from King Ptolemy Euergetes of Egypt,[6] the vast clusters of golden grapes, each cluster as large as a man, the gift of Herod the Great,[7] and many other costly gifts. They would have Him gaze at the rising terraces of courts, the Court of the Gentiles with its cloisters and porches, long rows of monolithic pillars of white marble, twenty-five cubits and more in height; above this the flight of fourteen steps which led to the Court of the Women; then the flight of fifteen steps which led to the Court of the Priests, with its immense altar of unhewn stones; and then, once more, the flight of twelve steps which led to the most sacred part of the Temple, the entrance to which, without doors, was seventy cubits high and twenty cubits wide, enclosing under a gold-covered roof the two apartments, separated by an embroidered veil, called the Holy Place and the Holy of Holies and containing on one side of the curtain the altar of incense, the table of show-bread, and the seven lamps and on the other side of the curtain the solitary stone upon which once a year the High priest sprinkled the blood on the great Day of Atonement.[8] This all the disciples would have Jesus "behold," hoping perhaps to change the current of His gloomy thoughts. Once more they turned around. It was a wonderful sight. As viewed under the smiling skies in the bright light of spring, the whole Temple complex from the distance took on the appearance of a glorious mountain, whose snowy summit was gilded by the sun.[9] But Jesus said: "There shall not be left here one stone upon another that shall not be thrown down."

1,   4) Acts 3, 2. 10.
     6) *Ant.*, XII, II, 9. 10.
     8) See chapter III, 6 ff.

     5) *Wars*, V, V, 3.
     7) *Ant.*, XV, XI, 3.   *Wars*, V, V, 4.
     9) *Wars*, V, V, 5.

2.

Matt. 24, 3—14. Mark 13, 3—13. Luke 21, 7—19.

By this time the Mount of Olives had been reached across the valley of Kidron, with the walls of Jerusalem and the Temple in full view. There Jesus sat down for a moment, deeply absorbed in thought no doubt over the words which He had just spoken, and likewise His saddened band of faithful followers, who had been greatly touched by that discourse. There were questions in the minds of all, but the two pairs of brothers, Peter and Andrew, James and John, were more excited than the rest. "When shall these things be," they ask with awestruck voices, "and what shall be the sign of Thy coming and of the end of the world?" [1] There was no doubt in their minds as to the connection of the Speaker with the subject of His discourse. It was also quite natural for them to connect the destruction of the Temple with "the end of the world" and "the coming" of Christ. According to certain prophecies of the Old Testament as well as in the light of the Savior's predictions His final coming might be viewed together with the destruction of Jerusalem as the beginning of the end. [2] As to signs, Jesus tells His disciples there will be such as well as warnings preceding both the destruction of Jerusalem and the end of the world, and these will be of such a nature as to demand watchful minds and courageous hearts.

Prophetic Discourses. The Second Coming. False prophets will arise with the deceptive claim "I am Christ" and will lead many astray. There will be wars and rumors of wars, nations rising against nations and kingdoms against kingdoms. There will be famines, pestilences, terrors, signs from heaven, and earthquakes in divers places. While these things are prelusive both of the destruction of Jerusalem and of Christ's second coming, these things

---

2, 1) Καὶ τί τὸ σημεῖον τῆς σῆς παρουσίας, καὶ τῆς συντελείας τοῦ αἰῶνος; Matt. 24, 3. Παρουσία again in verses 27, 37, 39; nowhere else in the gospels, frequent in the epistles. Συντέλεια τοῦ αἰῶνος in Matt. 13, 39. 49; 28, 20; Heb. 9, 26. The questioners took for granted that the three things went together: destruction of the Temple, advent of the Son of Man, and the end of the current age. Παρουσία (literally, presence, *viz.,* second presence and συντέλεια τοῦ αἰῶνος (end of the world) are the technical terms in the Apostolic Age for the close of the present order of things; and Matthew is the only one of the gospel-writers who uses these terms. See Bruce sub Matt. 24, 3.

2) Dan. 10, 27; 12, 9 ff.; Matt. 16, 27. 28; Luke 17, 23. 24; Matt. 23, 38. 39; Luke 13, 34. 35.

are but "the beginning of sorrows," because "the end is not yet." [3)] This in general; and in particular trials and tribulations will come upon the disciples of Christ. They will be hated, persecuted, excommunicated, arrested, called before governors and kings, tried, imprisoned, beaten, and killed. Some will be called upon to run the whole gamut; others will be allotted only a portion of these painful experiences. But in all these tribulations they should remember that they will suffer all this "for a testimony" against the despisers of the Gospel and for the sake of Christ. And when they would be called upon to give a witness of their faith, they should not be anxious beforehand; "but whatsoever shall be given you in that hour, that speak ye; for it is not ye that speak, but the Holy Ghost." [4)] Trusting in the Lord, they should meet the test; for in spite of universal hatred they would be in God's hand. "There shall not an hair of your head perish." [5)] And even if they lose their life, they shall gain their soul.[6)] And therefore "in your patience possess ye your souls." Indeed, evil days are at hand. Brother will arise against brother, child against father, father against child.[7)] The most intimate family ties will be severed. "And ye shall be betrayed both by parents, and brethren, and kinsfolks, and friends; and some of you shall they cause to be put to death." Iniquity will abound, and the love of many will wax cold. Faithfulness will be required. "He that shall endure unto the end, the same shall be saved." [8)] But in all this darkness there will also be light — the Gospel will be preached.[9)] "And the Gospel of the Kingdom shall be preached in all the world for a witness unto all nations, and then shall the end come."

3.

Matt. 24, 15—22. Mark 13, 14—20. Luke 21, 20—24.

Some signs are given that are especially to precede the final destruction: "When ye shall see Jerusalem compassed with armies, then know that the desolation thereof is nigh." And "Jerusalem shall be trodden down of the Gentiles until the times of the Gen-

---

2, 3) As our chief purpose is to tell the gospel story, the detailed interpretation of these difficult prophecies, those now fulfilled as well as those still to be fulfilled, is beyond the scope of this work.

4) Compare Matt. 10, 19. 20; Luke 12, 11. 12.

5) Compare Matt. 10, 30; Luke 12, 7.

6) Compare Matt. 10, 39; Luke 17, 33; John 12, 25.

7) Compare Matt. 10, 21.

8) Compare Matt. 10, 22.　　　9) Bruce sub Matt. 24, 8.

tiles be fulfilled." Thus it was foretold by the prophet Daniel that "the abomination of desolation" would be seen standing in the Holy Place when the Sanctuary had fallen into heathen hands and the sacrifices to the living God had ceased.[1] The literal fulfilment of this prophecy would be a premonition of the final period. The Christians of course should not yet expect the final Judgment, — that is why the warning is given: "Whoso readeth, let him understand," — but when they would see the Roman armies pouring into the Holy Land, carrying with them instruments of destruction presaging the terrible execution of God's judgment upon Jerusalem, they should seek safety in sudden flight. Let them that are in Judea flee to the mountains. Let them that are in the country not enter the city. Let them that are on top of their houses when the terrifying news comes not take time to carry things out of their

Signs Prelusive of Jerusalem's Destruction.

dwellings. Without looking behind, let them descend and immediately seek the open. Let him that is in the field not return to the house and get his coat. Terrible days of divine vengeance are at hand "that all things which are written may be fulfilled." Under these circumstances, woe unto those women who are about to become mothers and those with infants at their breast! The Christians should therefore pray that their flight will not occur in winter, when the weather conditions are unfavorable for sudden flight, or on the Sabbath, when those who are still binding themselves to Sabbath regulations needlessly endanger their lives. There will be great distress in the land, and God will execute His wrath upon this people. In fact, on account of its significance and effect as well as because of its severity this tragic crisis of Israel will earn for itself a unique distinction as compared with all other calamitous experiences of the whole human race, tribulation "such as was not since the beginning of the world to this time, no, nor ever shall be."[2] It would be a case of God's mills grinding slowly, but with such terrible thoroughness that not one would escape. If the justice of God had not been mingled with mercy, if those days had not been shortened out of loving regard for them that were God's own, and if it had not been for the intercession of those in the mountains and of those who had found refuge beyond the Jordan, in Pella,[3] not one would have escaped the general destruction.

3,   1) Dan. 9, 27; 11, 31; 12, 11.

2) Bruce sub Mark 13, 19.   3) Eusebius, III, v, 3.

4.

Matt. 24, 23—31.   Mark 13, 21—27.   Luke 21, 25—28.

False Christs and false prophets are again referred to.   The Lord has in mind primarily the days preceding the destruction of Jerusalem, the prophecies concerning which, however, immediately merge into those concerning the final wrath to come.   What would people not give for a delivering Messiah in those days!   Christ foresees the coming of such self-styled deliverers.   But "if any man shall say unto you, Lo, here is Christ, or there, believe it not." There shall arise false Christs and false prophets and shall show great signs and wonders, lying satanic wonders,[1] to lead many astray, even, if that were possible, the very elect.   "Behold, I have told you before."   Signs and wonders of such men will be no proof **False Christs.** of their being true prophets if their teaching is contrary to the Word of God.[2]   True believers will not be deceived in the end, even though it be possible to confuse them for a time.   Where Christ is, His elect are.[3]   But they must be on their guard.   Christ is to be found in His Word and not in the dreary wastes of asceticism or in the camps and inner circles of sentimental enthusiasm.   "If they say unto you, 'Behold, He is in the desert,' go not forth; 'Behold, He is in the secret chambers,' believe it not."   As to Christ's final coming, it will not come to pass in such a way that men must search for Him.   "For as the lightning cometh out of the east and shineth even unto the west, so shall also the coming [4] of the Son of Man be."   And His judgment upon the unspiritual cadavers of that day will be as inescapable as His appearance will be sudden.   "For wheresoever the carcass is, there will the eagles be gathered together." [5]

5.

Matt. 24, 23—31.   Mark 13, 21—27.   Luke 21, 25—28.

The period from the destruction of Jerusalem to the final Judgment is but a drama with interludes, to which the first-named calamity is only the initial act.   When the last tribulations have reached their climax, the advent of the Lord will be heralded by appalling signs.   The powers of heaven will be shaken, the sun and moon will be darkened, and stars will fall.   On the earth,

---

4,   1) Deut. 13, 1—3;   2 Thess. 2, 9;   Rev. 13, 13 f.;   2 Cor. 11, 13. 14.
　　2) Gal. 1, 8.　　　　3) Kretzmann, I, 136.
　　4) ῾Η παρουσία.　　　5) Luke 17, 37;   Job 39, 27—30.

among the nations, there will be distress, men fainting for fear and for expectation of the things to come, their fear caused also by the roaring noise of the billows of the sea. It seems that no ordinary eclipses and falling meteors are meant or storms and earthquakes acting in accordance with natural laws, but chaos and the subversion of all powers [1] as a premonition of the end of all things. Earlier signs, eclipses, comets, earthquakes, storms, wars, famines, floods, and the like, must be regarded as a preface to the final catastrophe. And then, amid the uproar of the universe, the great sign, the Son of Man Himself, clothed in majesty and power and accompanied by the heavenly hosts, will appear in the sky. "Then shall appear the sign of the Son of Man in heaven." What this

Signs of the Second Coming. sign is, if indeed there is a reference to any distinctive sign, we cannot say. Whatever it is, it will be self-evidencing. [2] Then "shall all the tribes of the earth mourn," and the vast army of unbelievers and scoffers will tremble in fearful expectation of the descending doom. But all believers, seeing their redemption drawing nigh, will lift up their heads with joy when at the sound of the trumpet the angels will gather the elect from the four quarters of the globe. And of all this the destruction of Jerusalem is but the initial act. As viewed by the Lord, with whom there is no time, the whole intervening period is a time of the coming of the Son of Man. That is why the Lord could in prophecy, without difficulty, pass from "immediately after the tribulation of those days," the days of Vespasian and Titus, to the predictions of the tribulation in the latter days. With the destruction of Jerusalem the curtain falls. [3] Infidels may still scoff at the despised Jesus of Nazareth. If they would but look at the skies, they could probably observe how the speeding vultures of Judgment are cutting in closer and closer with their swift encircling curves. In certain respects there has been no history since 70 A. D., only a wind-up.

6.

Matt. 24, 32—42. Mark 13, 28—33. Luke 21, 29—33.

At this point Jesus continues His eschatological discourse in the form of a parable. With the appearance of young leaves and tender branches in spring the observer does not require much intel-

---

5, 1) Kretzmann, I, 136.
    2) Bruce sub Matt. 24, 30.   3) Bruce sub Matt. 24, 31.

ligence to conclude that summer is near. So also "when ye see all these things come to pass," the signs preceding the destruction of Jerusalem, the destruction itself, and the subsequent recurrence of similar signs, "know ye that the kingdom of God is nigh at hand." And as to the certainty of the fulfilment of "all these things" a final sign is solemnly given. "Verily I say unto you, This generation [1] shall not pass till all these things be fulfilled," [2] or accomplished. But if the Lord here includes, as He obviously does, His final parousia, how, then, is "this generation" to be understood? Was He mistaken? Did He share, or rather give rise to, the later mistaken apocalyptic misconceptions of the time in the belief of the nearness of the Lord? There is much dispute on this point. Most modern scholars insist that *generation* must be taken in the sense of a certain measure of time. But since the parousia of the Lord did not occur within the promised limits of time, unless included by anticipation in the judgment over Jerusalem, then Jesus must have been mistaken in His conviction that His

The Parable of the Fig-Tree.

reappearance would happen within the then living generation. Since this, however, is impossible, some other explanation must be found. Some have thought, for instance, that the prediction refers to the destruction of Jerusalem only, which, however, is obviously not the case; others, that with the destruction of Jerusalem all things have occurred, lacking only the final completion—a forced construction. [3] Other interpretations, associating another idea with the term *generation,* include either all humanity or the Christian Church as the generation of believers which the Lord has chosen. While it is true that the destruction of Jerusalem might be viewed as the beginning of the end [4] and as typifying the final destruction of the world, yet it seems that here a distinctive sign is definitely and solemnly given. In spite of objections from some quarters [5] we prefer to take *generation* as a reference to that wicked and perverse generation, the Jewish race. As an additional and distinctive sign, very obviously so, and in spite of the destruction of the Temple and the dispersion of the nation and the anti-Semitic agitations down to our day, this generation of Christ-rejecting Jewish people "shall not pass till all these things be fulfilled." In the continued existence of this race we have

---

6,   1) Ἡ γενεὰ αὔτη.   2) Γένηται.

3) Of γένηται.   4) See 2.

5) Meyer sub Matt. 24, 34 and Mark 13, 30 — and notes.

a standing proof and a living sermon down to the end of time of the truth of the Word of God. "Heaven and earth shall pass away, but My words shall not pass away." [6]

7.

Matt. 24, 32—42. Mark 13, 28—33. Luke 21, 29—33.

That Christ will return is certain. But the hour is not known. It is foolish therefore by way of computations to attempt predictions. "Of that day and hour knoweth no man, no, not the angels which are in heaven," and, during the days of His humiliation, "neither the Son, but the Father." The period preceding the final coming of Christ will resemble conditions at the time of the Flood.[1] In those days people were eating and drinking, marrying

Watchfulness Urged. and giving in marriage, until the day that Noah entered the ark. No one knew when the threatened catastrophe would take place, indeed, no one believed what Noah said, until the Flood came and took them all away. They cared for nothing but their material affairs. They closed their eyes to the signs of the time and their ears to the voice of the preacher of righteousness.[2] So also in the day of the parousia of the Son of Man. Two men will be in the field; one will be taken, and the other will be left. Two women will be grinding at the mill;[3] one will be taken, and the other will be left. "Watch ye therefore, for ye know not when your Lord doth come." [4]

6,   6) Meyer sub Mark 13, 30 gives the meaning of γενεά as 1. *genus, progenies;* 2. *generatio, genitura;* 3. *aetas, saeculum.* There is no doubt that this word is used in the Greek New Testament for class or people, especially in a bad sense, Matt. 11, 16; 12, 39. 41. 42. 45; 16, 4; 17, 17; 24, 36. Also in Mark and Luke. Always the evil characteristic is stressed. The fact that the word does not signify a comparatively brief span of time is also implied in the prolonged absence of the Lord to meet the requirement in 24, 14, and especially in the note as to the ignorance even as to the approximate date of the Lord's return in verse 36. If the Lord had in mind a period which could be computed with relative certainty as to *terminus a quo* and *ad quem,* thirty to forty years, then the admonitions and parables stressing watchfulness would have lost their point. Qualitatively the Jewish people, and therefore the Jewish race itself, shall not pass away before the final advent of the Lord. Generally speaking, the Jewish race is the same to-day as when the Lord lived upon earth. The Greeks, Romans, Germans, Russians, embraced Christianity, but not the Jews. The legend of the Wandering Jew has its origin in this same basic truth. See Ylvisaker, 617.

7,   1) Compare Luke 17, 26—30. 34—36. Chapter XXV, 5.

2) 2 Pet. 2, 5.

3) Small domestic mills, usually operated by women.

4) Ποίᾳ ὥρᾳ. What sort of hour, early or late. Κύριος ὑμῶν, **Matt.** 24, 42. Jesus here calls Himself Lord. In narrative the title is given to Jesus especially by Luke, chap. 10, 1; 11, 39; 12, 42; etc.

8.

(Luke.)

Matt. 24, 43—51. Mark 13, 34—37. Luke 21, 34—36.[1]

Watchfulness presupposes sobriety. The disciples of Jesus should be on their guard lest at any time their hearts be oppressed by giddiness as the result of drunkenness and the cares of this life

Warning against Surfeiting and Drunkenness.

and so that day come upon them unawares. For as a snare shall it come upon all those sitting on the face of the earth. Strength is to be gained by prayer. At all seasons the Christians should be spiritually awake, making supplication, so that they may be accounted worthy to escape all the things that shall come to pass and to stand before the Son of Man.

9.

(Mark.)

Matt. 24, 43—51. Mark 13, 34—37. Luke 21, 34—36.

Be sleepless and pray, for ye know not when the time is. The exhortation to watch is enforced by a brief parable. The Son of Man is like a man, who, as he set out on a journey to distant parts, "gave authority to his servants," assigned to each of them his particular task, and commanded the porter, or gatekeeper, to watch. During his absence each servant would have his particular duty to

Parable of the Porter.

perform, and a certain responsibility would rest upon him. While it was the special duty of the porter to watch, yet this was the duty of all. "Watch ye [1] therefore, for ye know not when the master of the house cometh." Let no one scoff at the idea of return.[2] The return is certain while the hour is unknown. It may take place during the hours of the day [3] or "at even, or at midnight, or at cock-crowing, or in the morning," according to the Roman division of night-watches.[4] The disciples must watch not only one night, but every night. And what the Lord says to one He says to all: "Watch!" [5]

8, 1) Not strictly parallel, and the order is not stated. General concluding exhortations to watchfulness. Each evangelist brings his own epilog before presenting the Passion history. Our arrangement is in the following order: 1. Luke: Warning against surfeiting and drunkenness. 2. Mark: Parable of the Porter. 3. Matthew: Parable of the Master of the House and the Two Servants. Followed by: Parable of the Ten Virgins; Parable of the Talents; Picture of the Day of Judgment.

9, 1) Ἀγρυπνεῖτε, Mark 13, 33.   2) 2 Pet. 3, 4.   3) Mark 13, 32.

4) See Matt. 14, 25. Chapter XVI, 5. Luke 12, 38.

5) Luke 12, 41.

10.

(Matthew.)

Matt. 24, 43—51. Mark 13, 34—37. Luke 21, 34—36.

Watching for Judgment Day is just like guarding against thieves. If the master of the house had known in which watch the thief were coming, he would have been on guard and would not have suffered his house to be broken through.[1] Thus the believers must constantly be on their guard. Their Master, the Lord of the Church, has placed them in positions of trust. "Who, then, is

Parable of the Master of the House and the Two Servants.
a faithful servant?"[2] It is that rare servant who is steadfastly doing his duty.

He is one of a thousand fit to be placed in charge over his master's estate. On the other hand, the servant who foolishly takes advantage of his master's delay, playing the tyrant among his fellow-servants, eating and drinking with the drunken, will receive due punishment when his master comes upon him unawares. The master of that servant, on his return, "shall cut him asunder[3] and appoint him his portion with the hypocrites; there shall be weeping and gnashing of teeth."[4]

Matt. 25, 1—13.   **11.**

To His solemn discourse on the end of the world and the signs preceding it, Jesus, still addressing His disciples on the Mount of Olives on Tuesday afternoon of Passion week, that last great day of His public ministry, added two memorable parables containing instruction and warning, the parable of the Ten Virgins and the parable of the Talents, and a detailed picture of the Last Judgment. The first of the parables, that of the Ten Virgins, is immediately connected with the foregoing. "Then," namely, at His return for Judgment, "shall the kingdom of heaven be likened unto ten virgins which took their lamps and went forth to meet the bridegroom." Again[1] circumstances connected with Jewish marriage customs are used in the teaching of spiritual truths. But here the marriage supper is not represented as taking place in the

---

10, 1) Luke 12, 39. 40. Chapter XXI, 22.

2) Luke 12, 42—46. Chapter XXI, 23.

3) For this form of punishment see 2 Sam. 12, 31; 1 Chron. 20, 3; Heb. 11, 37. Suetonius, *Caligula,* XXVII.

4) Matt. 13, 42. 50; 22, 13; 25, 30.

11, 1) Compare Luke 12, 35—38; 13, 25. Chapter XXI, 22.

home of the bridegroom in accordance with the usual practise,[2] but is conceived as being held in the home of the bride,[3] from which the bridesmaids set out in the evening for the purpose of meeting the groom. The parable proceeds from the assumption that the bridegroom is somewhere in the distance, so that the precise moment of his arrival cannot be known. But it is known that he will come that night and that the marriage, for which all prepara-

The Parable of the Ten Virgins.

tions have been made, will take place. And so it is perfectly in order that all details for the customary Oriental marriage procession have been arranged. No mention is made of the bride, neither in this parable nor in that of the Wedding Guests,[4] as unneeded for the purpose which Jesus had in mind. Again we remind ourselves of the general canon in the interpretation of parables that the details must not be closely pressed. Ten virgins of the bridechamber, a round number, probably determined by the wealth of the parents, are represented as going forth to meet the bridegroom. "And five of them were wise, and five were foolish." Not as if the equal numbers were intended to represent the proportion in the spiritual sphere; they are merely to show for reasons which will soon appear, that there were prudent and imprudent, thoughtful and thoughtless among them. In setting out to meet the bridegroom, all of them took their lamps,[5] consisting of a wooden staff held in the hand, with a receptacle on top, in which was placed a clay dish or saucer, with an orifice for the reception of oil and the admission of air and a spout for the wick. Now, "they that were foolish took their lamps and took no oil with them." But the wise had oil in their lamps and had taken an extra supply with them. As appears in the sequence, this was a necessary precaution, as for some unknown reason the bridegroom tarried, and therefore proved their prudence. This was the point on which in the application the admonition of readiness hinged. "While the bridegroom tarried, they all slumbered and slept," presumably in some house along the way,[6] in order there to await the approach of the bridegroom. They all slept. This was perfectly natural on account of the long waiting and the extended

---

11, 2) *Int. St. B. Encycl.* Geo. B. Eager sub "Marriage," 1998. Matt. 22, 2 ff.

3) Judg. 14, 10. Bruce *sub loco.* 4) Matt. 22.

5) Λαμπάδας. Barton, *Archeology,* 193. 194. Fig. 131.

6) Meyer sub Matt. 25, 5. On account of ἐξέρχεσθε in verse 6.

delay of the bridegroom and perfectly harmless as far as the wise virgins were concerned, because they were ready. But it was fatal for the foolish virgins. At length, in the middle of the night, the cry was raised by some one not asleep: "Behold, the bridegroom cometh! Go ye out to meet him." Immediately the virgins rose and proceeded to trim their lamps by pulling the wicks forth from the spout so that they might burn with full brightness in the joyous wedding-feast pageant. At this point a startling surprise forced the foolish virgins to make a sad request: "Give us of your oil, for our lamps are gone out." But the wise answered, prompted by sheer necessity and sound prudence: "Not so, lest there be not enough for us and you." Not as if the wise virgins were selfish or ungenerous. You cannot enter heaven on the merits of others. The wise virgins have only the one advice to offer, if indeed it was not — as it seemed it was — too late: "Go ye rather to them that sell and buy for yourselves." By this time very likely the oil merchants were fast asleep, even as at the moment of the Lord's coming the dispensers of grace will have closed their shops. "While they went to buy, the bridegroom came." In a panorama of lights and midst festal joy the bridegroom was escorted to the waiting bride. "And they that were ready went in with him to the marriage." The happy moment had arrived. Naturally, in view of all the opportunities given for making definite arrangements, not unaided by the long delay, all guests were supposed to be within. "And the door was shut."

Matt. 25, 1—13.   **12.**

When it was too late, the other virgins came. Whether or not they succeeded in obtaining oil is of no importance. If they did, it was no longer of any possible use to them, since it could no longer serve the purpose for which it was purchased. The urgent, desperate appeal: "Lord, Lord, open to us!" is met with a solemn "Verily I say unto you, I know you not." The period of eleventh-

"Lord, Lord, Open to Us!" hour repentance cannot be extended beyond the point of lapse. Professing to be members of the bridal party, they ought to have been in the bridal procession. Lapsed membership in the Kingdom of Grace — which has ceased to exist with the coming of Judgment Day — does not entitle one to membership in the Kingdom of Glory. — Without going into details, we might give a brief interpretation of the parable. The bridegroom is Jesus. The feast is heaven. The virgins are the members of the visible

Church. The lamps are faith, fed by the oil of the means of grace. Naturally the wise virgins are such as continued in faith unto the end and therefore were members of the invisible Church, as contrasted with the foolish virgins, who, being without faith, were not. No special significance attaches to the numbers ten and five, the cry, the procession, and the like. Neither is the falling asleep to be represented as a moral shortcoming, for it happened to the wise as well as to the foolish. There is a delay in the bridegroom's coming, even as there is a delay in, but not a failure of,[1] the Lord's return. All the more reason for watchful waking. And that is the point which Jesus makes: "Watch therefore; for ye know neither the day nor the hour," night or day, week, month, or year, "wherein the Son of Man cometh." [2]

Matt. 25, 14—30.   **13.**

Continuing with the same thought of His *parousia,* but linking it up with the duty and work of His disciples during His absence, Jesus tells a parable similar to the one spoken in the house of Zacchaeus at Jericho shortly before His arrival at Bethany in the preceding week.[1] The situation in the kingdom of heaven is, as Jesus points out, that of a man going abroad who called his servants and gave his goods into their charge. In leaving his money with them, he did the best thing he could do under the circumstances, unless he wanted to entrust it to strangers. To one of his servants he delivered five talents, to another two, and to still another one, according to the ability [2] of each. And then he set out on his

The Parable of the Talents. journey. The amount of money entrusted to these servants was considerable. We assume that the reference is to a silver standard,[3] so that one talent amounted to about eleven hundred dollars in our money. But in value a talent amounted to much more. Since one talent was worth six thousand denarii, it covered a day's pay-roll for an army of six thousand men, a denarius being the equivalent of a day's wages for a laborer or a soldier.[4]

12, 1) 2 Pet. 3, 3—9.   2) See Kretzmann, I, 140.
13, 1) Compare Luke 19, 11—28: Parable of the Pounds. Chapter XXV, 25.
    2) Δύναμις.   3) On account of ἀργύριον, silver, in verse 18.
    4) Compare Matt. 20, 2, "penny," denarius. According to this scale:

1 drachma	approximately 1 denarius	17—20 cts.
100 drachmae	1 mina	$17.00—$20.00
60 minae	1 (silver) talent	$1,020.00—$1,200.00

And a gold talent was worth about fifteen times more.

Immediately after his master's departure the first servant, who had received five talents, lost no time in investing his share. He gained another five talents. Likewise the second, who had received two talents. He gained two more. But the third servant, who had received one talent, dug his silver into the ground. The reference of course is to the various commissions in the Kingdom, the wider or narrower fields of activity, and the divers faculties and gifts.

Matt. 25, 14—30.   **14.**

After a long time the master returns. Immediately he arranges a conference with his servants for the purpose of checking over their accounts. The first of them submits his report: "Lord, thou deliveredst unto me five talents. Behold," [1] as if inviting him to count the money, "I have gained besides them five talents more." A gain of one hundred per cent.! "Well done, thou good and faithful servant," the master replies. "Thou hast been faithful over

"Well Done, Thou Good and Faithful Servant!"

a few things, I will make thee ruler over many things." It is not the money that is stressed, but faithfulness. A rich master is speaking, to whom a few talents more or less are as little things. But seeing the capacity [2] of the servant, he would make more extensive use of his faithful efforts in what he considered a limited sphere. "Enter thou into the joy of thy lord." With this expression the Savior directs the carnal-minded disciples to heavenly things.[3] The second servant submits a similar report and receives a corresponding reward.

Matt. 25, 14—30.   **15.**

The third servant now steps up and makes his speech. "Lord, I knew thee that thou art an hard man." Guided by this opinion of a master who was hard to please, who struck a hard bargain, who reaped where he had not sown and gathered where he had not winnowed, and fearing lest he lose the talent itself and displease the master all the more, he had hidden his talent in the ground. No, he was not dishonest! "Lo," behold,[1] as if likewise inviting him to count the money, "there thou hast that is thine." Just as if the mere safe return of the money were the sole purpose for which the master had entrusted the funds to him! But the servant's own

---

14, 1) Ἴδε.   2) Δύναμις.

3) Χαρά. Not feast, but joy. Salvation as the "joy of the Lord."
15, 1) Ἴδε.

words condemned him. We are rather surprised at this servant. He was a disappointment. From him, as judged by the yield frequently returned by such of his class in the Kingdom, the unfavored and those handicapped by the lack of fortune and opportunity at the outset, we should have by comparison expected a return of — let us say — an additional talent and one half or a gain of at least one hundred and five per cent., just to show that he was not to be outdone. But instead he had proved himself

"Thou Wicked and Slothful Servant!" a small man in every respect. Such, however, sad to say, are also found in the Kingdom. If that was the idea he had of his master, whose character he had altogether misjudged in that he spoke of him as one who reaped where he had not sown and let his servants slave without offering them any inducement, and if he himself was too much afraid to risk trading with his master's money, then why did he not, without trouble for himself and with profit to his master, put it in the bank? "Thou oughtest therefore to have put my money to the exchangers." [2] Now he was not only useless to his master as a servant, but what he said in defense of his conduct was preposterous. "Take therefore the talent from him and give it unto him which hath ten talents." This would at least give the master some prospects of a speedy return. In this manner of dispensing justice the general rule applies: "Unto every one that hath shall be given. From him that hath not shall be taken away even that which he hath." [3] The general lesson is clear. The whole Kingdom with all its reward will come to faithful servants. The *Kingdom* for servants. But *Servants* for the Kingdom. In the end the useless and unprofitable servant, like the useless fig-tree, "cumbereth the ground." [4] He will be cast out into outer darkness, where "there will be weeping and gnashing of teeth." [5]

Matt. 25, 31—46. **16.**

With an illuminating word picture of the final Judgment the Lord closes His prophetic discourse on the Mount of Olives, leaving an urgent exhortation impressed upon the hearts and minds of His disciples to be ever watchful and faithfully waiting for the

---

15,   2) Τραπεζίταις. See Luke 19, 23. Chapter XXV, 27.

      3) Luke 8, 18; Matt. 13, 12; Mark 4, 25.

      4) Luke 13, 7.

      5) Matt. 24, 51; 8, 12; 13, 42. 50; 22, 13.

coming of the Son of Man. As time passes into eternity, the Son of Man, accompanied by the host of holy angels, shall return in the fulness of His heavenly glory. Immediately there shall be assembled in perfect attendance all the members of the human race, "the living and the dead," the willing and the unwilling, those

The Last Judgment. who were prepared and such as were not prepared to meet their Judge. At the same time a separation will be made, not according to sex, age, color, birth and rank, and the like, but "as a shepherd divideth his sheep from the goats." Evidently the reference is to the sheep that hear His voice [1] and the proverbially stubborn goats. In other words, the separation will be according to whether a person was a believer or an unbeliever in this life. "And He shall set the sheep on His right hand, but the goats on the left." With this separation, in which the believers will receive the place of honor, being placed at "His right hand," the Judgment is already rendered, and the subsequent sentence is only the confirmation of an act already in the past.

Matt. 25, 31—46.   17.

A hearty welcome is extended to the righteous by the Son of Man, who now speaks of Himself as King: "Come, ye blessed of My Father, inherit the Kingdom prepared for you from the foundation of the world." The promise of a glorious inheritance, which excluded every consideration of merit, made by the one-time lowly Jesus of Nazareth to His once despised and persecuted little flock, is true after all! Come nearer and enjoy glory and the blissful state of the Kingdom! And what is the reason of this wonderful gift? All this as a gracious reward for every-day, simple little deeds of love. "For I was an hungred, and ye gave Me meat;

"Come, Ye Blessed of My Father." I was thirsty, and ye gave Me drink; I was a stranger, and ye took Me in; naked, and ye clothed Me; I was sick, and ye visited Me; I was in prison, and ye came unto Me." Not as if the believers were saved by these deeds; these deeds of love are mentioned because by them their faith was attested. In surprise the righteous reply: "Lord, when saw we Thee an hungred and fed Thee? or thirsty and gave Thee drink? When saw we Thee a stranger and took Thee in? or naked and clothed Thee? Or when saw we Thee sick or in prison and came unto Thee?" Surely the King must be mistaken! Of such high honor of personal service

16, 1) John 10, 27.

they had been altogether unaware. But, as Jesus points out, all deeds of love performed in faith are considered as done unto Him. "Verily I say unto you, Inasmuch as ye have done it unto one of the least of these My brethren, ye have done it unto Me."

Matt. 25, 31—46. **18.**

From those on His right the King turns to those at the left. By the way, He had placed the sheep at *His* right hand [1] and the goats at the left.[2] Then He had turned to those on *His* right. And now He addresses those on the left. Before God there is no predetermined "left hand," meaning eternal damnation, but only a "right hand," signifying life everlasting. It is really an upsetting of God's plan that "any should perish." [3] Since, however, men wilfully transgressed His commandments, would not heed His warnings, but set Him at defiance and despised His Word of Grace, punishment became necessary, justice must be executed. Sternly the Judge addresses Himself to those at the left: "Depart from Me, ye cursed, into everlasting fire, prepared for the devil and his angels." It is an awful sentence. The Judge takes no pleasure in its pronouncement, and He is most particular in the choice of His words. He does not say: "Cursed of My Father"; for they brought the curse upon themselves. Neither does He say: "prepared from the beginning of the world." God's original plan did not call for the damnation of any one. The "left hand" was a later addition, prepared only for the devil, but in time was reserved and kept ready for occupation by such as followed his leading. According to the same standard by which those at the

"Depart from Me, Ye Cursed, into Everlasting Fire."

right hand were adjudged the blessed of the Father those at the left are now condemned. As in the case of the righteous nothing was said of martyrdom and heroic acts, so in this case, by contrast, there is no mention of murder or heinous crimes. Nor is there a chance given for many of them to point with pride to the erection of hospitals and institutions, to the creation of funds, endowments, and memorials to the honor and glory of their name. This was not discussed. It was the neglect of true charity and the small deeds of Christian love which testified to their lack of faith and love of Christ. Of course, there is a chorus of protests: "When saw we Thee an hungred, or athirst, or a stranger, or naked, or sick, or in prison, and did not minister unto Thee?" But Jesus replies:

18, 1) Ἐκ δεξιῶν αὐτοῦ.   2) Ἐξ εὐωνύμων.   3) 2 Pet. 3, 9.

"Verily I say unto you, Inasmuch as ye did it not to one of the least of these, ye did it not to Me." There was no faith, and therefore there could be no outflow of faith — love, love of Christ and of their fellow-men for Christ's sake. Such love as they showed did not spring from faith, but was unsanctified love such as is found in natural man. "And these shall go away into everlasting punishment, but the righteous into life eternal." Everlasting life for the believers, unending torment for the damned. There is no happy last-minute reversal of judgment in a supposed restoration of all things. Neither is there an annihilation of the wicked. The words are clear. The absolute idea of eternity with respect to the punishment in hell cannot be removed by toning down the force of the word *eternal* [4] to age-long, but not everlasting, and *punishment* [5] to pruning, so as to leave room for hope of an ultimate delivery from "the everlasting fire." Scripture is Scripture.

19.
Luke 21, 37. 38. [1]

From the Mount of Olives it was but a short distance to the home of Jesus' friends at Bethany, where He spent the night. It was from this place, as we have seen, that He started early in the morning to instruct the waiting multitudes in the Temple. With His departure from the Temple on that memorable Tuesday, however, and His prophetic discourses on the Mount of Olives this glad ministry had at this particular point already come to an end.

Return to Bethany.

20.

Matt. 26, 1—5. Mark 14, 1. 2. Luke 22, 1. 2.

The Lord's public work was finished. With His arrival in Bethany on Tuesday evening He saw fit to repeat the sad announcement of His impending death, at the same time giving the exact time and manner of its occurrence. According to the Jewish calendar it was the twelfth day of the month of Nisan, two days before the Feast of Passover, or the seven days of Unleavened Bread, which began on the evening of the fourteenth day of

18, 4) Αἰώνιος.   5) Κόλασις.

19, 1) Without strict regard to actual sequence at this place the evangelist gives a summary of the Lord's activity of the final week. Otherwise it would seem that he is out of agreement with the two other Synoptists, as appears from Mark 13, 1. 3 and Matt. 24, 1. 3, where we are told that Jesus had already left the Temple, without apparently entering it again. — Curiously four cursive manuscripts have placed the section of the woman taken in adultery, John 7, 53—8, 11, after Luke 21, 37. 38. Ernst von Dodschuetz, *Einfuehrung in das Gr. N. T.,* 29.

Nisan.[1] This Passover was to be distinguished as no Passover ever celebrated before. It was to be the Passover in which the Lamb of God was presented, and all the Old Testament types of Christ, the sacrifices, the Passover, the lamb without blemish, the sprinkling

Jesus Again Predicts His Death.

of blood, the passing over, and of all the ceremonies of the Old Testament worship were to be fulfilled. This Jesus knew. And therefore, before dismissing His disciples for the night after what would seem according to the records the most crowded day of His public life,[2] He turned to them with the prediction: "Ye know that after two days is the Feast of the Passover, and the Son of Man is betrayed to be crucified." [3]

20, 1) Ex. 12, 1—27; Lev. 23, 5, 6,

2) It is probably of interest in this connection to make a comparison of the records of a few busy days in the life of our Lord.

THE DAY OF THE SERMON ON THE MOUNT.

Matthew	Mark	Luke
5, 1—48	3, 13—19	6, 12—49
6, 1—34		
7, 1—29		
8, 1		
112	6	37 verses. Total verses, 155.

THE DAY OF THE PARABLES IN GALILEE.

Matthew	Mark	Luke
12, 22—50	3, 20—35	8, 4—25
13, 1—53	4, 1—41	
8, 18—27		
90	55	21 verses. Total verses, 166.

TUESDAY OF PASSION WEEK

Matthew	Mark	Luke
21, 19—46	11, 20—33	20, 1—47
22, 1—46	12, 1—44	21, 1—38
23, 1—46	13, 1—37	22, 1—2
24, 1—51	14, 1—2	
25, 1—46		
26, 1—5		
214	96	87 verses. Total verses, 397.

3) There were many references in the records to His death. At this time we remind ourselves of the following predictions: —

	Matthew	Mark	Luke	John
1. At the first cleansing of the Temple				2, 19—22
2. At Caesarea Philippi	16, 21—23	8, 31—33	9, 22	
3. At the close of the Galilean ministry	17, 22—23	9, 31—32	9, 43—45	
4. On the final journey to Jerusalem	20, 17—19	10, 32—34	18, 31—34	
5. Two days before the final Passover	26, 2—5			
(6. Thursday night	26, 31. 32	14, 27. 28)		

THE LIFE OF CHRIST.

37

21.

Matt. 26, 1—5. Mark 14, 1. 2. Luke 22, 1. 2.

At the same time while Jesus was talking the betrayal process had already begun. An important meeting was being held in Jerusalem. In unholy assembly the members of the Sanhedrin were gathered in the palace [1] of Caiaphas, the high priest. It was Caiaphas who had already settled the fate of Jesus with these words: "It is expedient that one man should die for the people." [2] The events of the last few days seemed to make it clear that he was right. Under his leadership Pharisees, Sadducees, Herodians, priests, scribes, Rabbis, lawyers, and elders were all united in an alliance of destruction. Of the meeting itself and of the discussions we know nothing. However, we have some information as to the conclusions reached.

The Rulers Plot Jesus' Death.

These included a number· of points: that Jesus must be put to death; that there must be no delay; that He must be arrested at a time when He would not be surrounded by a protecting crowd; that the whole thing must be slyly handled; and that on account of His popularity the murder had best be postponed until immediately after the Passover in order to give the multitudes a chance to disperse and especially to give the enthusiastic Northern pilgrims a chance to return to their homes. But after all, in spite of their determination, one point still remained unsettled, and that was *how* they might put Him to death. While they were still discussing ways and means, an event occurred which at once altered their conclusions and made possible the immediate capture of Jesus without the tumult which they feared. [3]

21, 1) Not in the Temple, the regular meeting-place of the Sanhedrin in the Hall of Polished Stones, which would be closed by this time, but in the near-by palace of Caiaphas.

2) John 11, 50.

3) *(Matt. 24, 6—13; Mark 14, 3—9.)* (Compare John 12, 1—11.) *The anointment of Jesus in the house of Simon the Leper.* Here follows in the order of Matthew and Mark the anointing of Jesus at Bethany in the house of Simon the Leper. The incident is probably related by the Synoptists at this point for the purpose of completing their narrative and for the reason that the base deed of Judas brought back to their minds one of the immediate motives of the betrayal, namely, the resentment of Judas at what he pretended to believe was a waste of money, in connection with an incident in Bethany, of which, however, they had as yet not informed the reader. The account is now brought in parenthetically. While we try to satisfy ourselves with this explanation, we must admit that it does not remove all difficulties. Probably the anointing *did* take place here. In that event some explanation must be found for the transposition in John. For it is not Matthew and Mark, but *John* who pointed out the resentment of Judas. See chapter XXVI, 3.

22.

Matt. 26, 14—16. Mark 14, 10. 11. Luke 22, 3—6.

While the members of the Sanhedrin were still deliberating on ways and means of ridding themselves of the hated Jesus of Nazareth, Judas Iscariot, one of the Twelve, came with an offer to betray his Master. Ever since the rebuke administered to him by Jesus in connection with the anointing at Bethany, related by Matthew and Mark at this juncture, there had been something on his mind. But was it only the loss of the three hundred denarii which, he claimed, might have been "given to the poor," but upon which he would have laid his hands, which prompted him to commit that most awful crime? Was it the well-nigh irresistible attraction of the prospects of making a paltry gain? Was it in a fit of uncontrolled passion for the purpose of seeking revenge because Jesus had called him to task? Was it the petty jealousy of small circles which deeply resent even the smallest inequality in the distribution of favors? Or was it that as almost the only true Judean among the apostles he was sorely disappointed at the failure of Jesus to fulfil the Jewish Messianic hopes? Or was it his purpose to force Jesus, if He really was no pretender, to prove His Messianic claims? And if He was no pretender, could He not easily save Himself by a miracle and give him a chance to make a little money besides? But to account for the conduct of Judas is like trying to fathom a bottomless abyss. Satan had entered into his heart. This statement of our Lord best explains his awful state. Otherwise it would have been unthinkable for one of the twelve chosen apostles to present himself to the sworn enemies of Jesus with the proposition to betray Him and to deliver Him into their hands.[1] Naturally there was some discussion among the members of the Sanhedrin when they were approached by Judas. There were questions. Who was Judas? Just what did he know about Jesus? How long had

Judas Bargains for the Betrayal of Jesus.

he been in His company? Was it really true that Jesus made the claim that He was the Messiah? And where did He keep Himself when He was not surrounded by protecting hands, or rather, when and where could they come upon Him when He was not surrounded by a multitude of friends? But Judas was not willing to talk as yet. "What will ye give me, and I will deliver Him unto you?" There was some more dis-

---

22, 1) The term used is παραδίδωμι.

cussion. Finally an agreement was reached. We can picture to ourselves the scene — hushed tones, pleased gestures, wicked smiles, flickering lights. The plan appealed to the scribes and the officers of the Temple police, the "captains," [2] whose aid would be needed to carry out the plan. And the price? "And they covenanted with him," or rather they placed or deposited, [3] and probably actually weighed out, "thirty pieces of silver," [4] the price of a slave. [5] It was the amount which as a fine, for instance, was collected when an ox had wounded a slave. [6] If the money was taken from the Temple treasury, as seems likely, then the payment was made in shekels, probably even carefully weighed out, true to form, — the most iniquitous thing done in the most orthodox way. [7] For a miserable purse Judas sold his Lord. For a sack of jingling coins he sold his soul. In our money the sum amounted to a little less than twenty dollars, but considering the comparative value of money, representing at that time in wages at least four months of a working-man's pay, — it was enough to attract the avarice of Judas. [8] As a pledged traitor a chosen apostle of Jesus left the assembly under the agreement to inform the members of the Sanhedrin of the first opportunity to arrest Him in the absence of the usual circle of protecting friends.

22, 2) Στρατηγοί, Acts 4, 1.

3) Ἔστησαν, from ἵστημι.   4) Τριάκοντα ἀργύρια.

5) Gen. 37, 28. Joseph was sold for twenty pieces of silver. Compare Zech. 11, 12. 13.

6) Ex. 21, 32.   7) Bruce sub Matt. 26, 15.

8) According to the scale: —

A day's wages (Matt. 20, 2)	1 denarius ("penny")	17 to 20 cents
1 denarius (approximately)	1 drachma (Luke 15, 8)	16 cents (circa)
2 drachmas (Matt. 17, 24)	1 half shekel	33 cents (circa)
	(Ex. 30, 13; 38, 26)	
4 drachmas (Matt. 17, 27), or stater	1 shekel	66 cents (circa)

4 denarii = 1 shekel.

30 shekels = 120 denarii.

120 denarii, or 30 pieces of silver, pay for 120 working days. According to our standards, at least, $400 to $500. This amount was large enough to attract the avarice of Judas.

See Edersheim, II, 477, and Bible dictionaries.

CHAPTER XXXI.

THURSDAY AFTERNOON TO THURSDAY NIGHT OF PASSION WEEK.

PASSOVER AND THE INSTITUTION OF THE LORD'S SUPPER.

April 6, 30 A. D., 783 A. U. C.

A. U. C.	779	780	781	782	783
A. D.	26	27	28	29	30
Age of Jesus	30	31	32	33	34
Passovers		I	II	III	IV

Nisan (or Abib)

10	11	12	13	14	15	16	17

April

2	3	4	5	6	7	8	9
Sun.	Mon.	Tue.	Wed.	Thu.	Fri.	Sat.	Sun.

783 A. U. C.   APRIL   30 A. D.

Sun.	Mon.	Tue.	Wed.	Thu.	Fri.	Sat.
						1
2	3	4	5	6	7	8
9	10	11	12	13	14	15
16	17	18	19	20	21	22
23	24	25	26	27	28	29
30						

1.

Matt. 26, 17—19. Mark 14, 12—16. Luke 22, 7—13.

We have no records for the movements of Jesus for the Wednesday of Passion week. Doubtless even on this day the people in Jerusalem waited for His appearance in the Temple,[1]

Wednesday. even as — since their agreement with Judas — the priests and Pharisees looked out for Him with sinister aims. But He did not come. During this day the Lord most likely remained in seclusion in Bethany, probably once more to enjoy the free communion with God which He had so earnestly sought in the midst of His active ministry and to strengthen Himself for the ordeal of His suffering and death.

1, 1) Luke 21, 38.

2.

Matt. 26, 17—19. Mark 14, 12—16. Luke 22, 7—13.

It was some time during the next day, Thursday, the fourteenth of Nisan, probably in the afternoon, that the disciples came to Jesus with the question: "Where wilt Thou that we prepare for Thee to eat the passover?" Strictly speaking, the Passover Festival began on the evening of that day. But because by noon of this day, the fourteenth day of Nisan, or Abib, all traces of leaven had to be removed from the houses and no leavened bread must be eaten until the evening of the twenty-first,[1] it was already called "the first day of the feast." At this point we remind ourselves that the Passover Festival was instituted in commemoration of the deliverance of the Israelites from the destroying angel when all the first-born of the Egyptians were slain.[2] It was distinguished chiefly by the eating of a roasted male Passover lamb, one year old, without blemish, between the two evenings[3] of the fourteenth and fifteenth

The Preparation of the Paschal Meal. of Nisan by one or two families,[4] — according to the size; for none of the meat was to be left over,[5] — with un-leavened bread and bitter herbs. Originally the lamb to be sacrificed, which was selected on the tenth of the month, was slaughtered at home by the father of the household or the servant appointed for this task. But later it was slain by the worshiper in the Temple under the supervision of the twenty-four courses of priests, by whom the blood was caught up in a golden bowl and in one jet was emptied upon the altar.[6] While this was going on, there was a threefold blast from the silver trumpets of the priests, and the Great Hallel[7] was chanted by the Levites, with responses by the people. The tallow, kidneys, liver, and tail were burned as sacrifices unto the Lord. Bound up in its skin, the lamb was then carried to the house where the feast would be prepared. The number of animals slain each Passover was enormous; and from the

---

2,   1) Ex. 12, 18; Deut. 16, 1.

2) Ex. 12, 27.   3) Ex. 12, 6, marginal reading.

4) Ex. 12, 4. Later it became customary for not fewer than ten nor more than twenty to participate in one meal.

5) Ex. 12, 10.

6) Edersheim, II, 487; Temple, 191. Other voluntary festive sacrifices were made, which, if the paschal lamb did not suffice, were added to it. These were called the first *chagigah*, festive sacrifice. E. Robinson, *Greek Harmony*, 213. Edersheim, II, 484; Temple, 186.

7) Psalm 113—118.

number of sacrifices we can make an estimate of the immense throng gathered in Jerusalem for the annual Passover. In the time of Nero, who held the Jewish nation in contempt, the governor of Syria, Cestius, tried to convince the emperor of the city's strength. He instructed the chief priests, if by any means possible, to take a census of the population. They simply counted the lambs slain at a Passover Feast, 255,600, and multiplied the number by ten. Thus they were able to report for the city a Passover population of over two million and a half.[8]

3.

Matt. 26, 17—19. Mark 14, 12—16. Luke 22, 7—13.

But to return. In a heated oven the lamb was roasted intact over a glowing fire. Not a bone of it should be broken. And in the evening, now the fifteenth of Nisan,[1] the roast was placed on the table. Other parts of the menu included unleavened bread, bitter herbs, probably a salad of cucumbers and lettuce, besides a dish containing vinegar and salt water, with a sauce prepared of various fruits, and wine mixed with water, in proportion of one to two.[2] On the next day, still the

The Passover Festival.

fifteenth, there were special sacrifices, the second *chagigah,* in which thank-offerings from the flock and herd were made and eaten.[3] On the third day, the sixteenth of Nisan, the first-fruits of the barley-harvest were brought to the Temple and waved before the Lord to consecrate the harvest.[4]

2,   8) Josephus, *Wars,* VI, IX, 3.

3,   1) Because according to Jewish interpretation of the history of creation the day belonged to the previous night. For rabbinic references see Edersheim, II, 469, note. It is distinctly stated that the Passover began with the darkness on the fourteenth of Nisan.

2) One part wine, two parts water. Edersheim, *Temple and Its Services,* 202 ff.; or Edersheim. *Life and Times of Jesus,* II, 485. Even the poorest must have "at least four cups, though he were to receive the money for it from the poor-box."

3) Andrews, 471; Edersheim. *Temple,* 186. It was this *chagigah,* says Edersheim, which the Jews were afraid they might be unable to eat if they contracted defilement in the judgment hall, John 18, 28. But the term *Passover* was probably used by John to denote the whole festival, in this case the whole remaining festival, since the eating of the paschal lamb was by this time presumably already past.

4) And other sacrifices were made, Lev. 23, 5—14. No distinct reference to this by the evangelists. "The morrow after the Sabbath," in Lev. 23, 11, is not the weekly Sabbath, but the day after the fifteenth of Nisan, the festival Sabbath, regardless on whatever day of the week it might fall. According to the rule, though it were a Sabbath, the grain was cut down on the evening before, Friday evening, the 15th, though the Sabbath had actually begun. Edersheim, *Temple,* 221 ff.

Thus the first few days. And the last day of the Passover, the same as the first, was again a day of holy convocation and was observed as a Sabbath. The intervening days were minor festivals, for which, however, minute rules as to the kind of labor allowed were laid down.[5]

4.

Matt. 26, 17—19. Mark 14, 12—16. Luke 22, 7—13.

This, then, was the holy festival for which the pilgrimage to Jerusalem had been made. It was one of the three holy festivals on which all male Israelites were commanded to appear before the Lord.[1] And since the disciples did not know where Jesus desired to eat the passover, they asked for instructions as to the place where preparations should be made. Under the circumstances the supper could have been held in Bethany; for it seems that for ecclesiastical purposes Bethphage and Bethany were included by the Rabbis as parts of Jerusalem.[2] But it was the intention of Jesus to eat the passover in Jerusalem. Two disciples, Peter and John, were singled out and given definite instructions, one of the pair known for deepest feelings and the other as a man of very quick action. Soon we shall see them together again. Judas is listening.

"Where Wilt Thou that We Go and Prepare?"   "Go ye into the city, and there shall meet you a man bearing a pitcher of water. Follow him."

If the purpose of this mysterious instruction was to keep the knowledge from Judas[3] lest the last meal with the institution of the Holy Supper be interrupted and Jesus' last retreat betrayed before all had been said and done, even down to the last prayer in Gethsemane, then these words are a wonderful combination of fore-knowledge and prudence. It is not that some arrangements between Jesus and some friends in Jerusalem had been previously made. The Lord is here giving His disciples a most remarkable proof of His omniscience and omnipotence. To carry water in the East is commonly considered a woman's work. While a man might be seen with a water-pitcher, the chances were extremely remote. A traveler and his friend were walking in Nazareth towards the

---

3,   5) Edersheim, *Temple*, 225.

4,   1) Ex. 23, 14. 17.

    2) Edersheim, II, 480.

    3) Bruce sub Matt. 26, 18; and others.

Virgin's Fountain a few years ago, when suddenly the friend, who had been a resident in Palestine for over thirty years, exclaimed: "See that man. He is carrying a water-jar. Only once have I seen that done as long as I am living in Palestine." [4]

5.

Matt. 26, 17—19. Mark 14; 12—16. Luke 22, 7—13.

The instruction of Jesus continues: "And wheresoever he shall go in, say ye to the goodman of the house, The Master saith, Where is the guest-chamber where I shall eat the passover with My disciples?" The time of the Master was at hand — for the celebration of the Passover and also in a larger sense. The man, who evidently was a believer, would understand. He would place at the disposal of Jesus and His disciples a large upper room,[1] a spacious hall, from which all leaven had been removed, large enough to **"The Master Saith, Where Is the Guest-Chamber?"** accommodate a number of guests and furnished with tables and couches.[2] Who he was, Joseph of Arimathea or the father of John Mark [3] or a disciple of Christ unknown to us, does not appear. The two disciples went forth and found everything as Jesus had said and did as they had been told. In the city they met a man, most likely a servant, carrying a water-pitcher, and followed him to the house where he was going. Then they talked with the landlord, delivered the message, secured the room, provided themselves with the lamb, went up to the Temple, offered the necessary sacrifices,[4] joined in the hallelujahs and responses, carried the lamb back to the upper room, and made all arrangements for the Passover.[5]

4,   4) A photograph was taken on the occasion and included in Basil Matthew's *Life of Jesus* opposite p. 416. See p. 413.

5,   1) 'Ανάγαιον or ἀνώγεον = ἀνά-γαῖα, γῆ = above the earth.

2) 'Εστρωμένον, from στρωννύω, furnished; not paved. See Schirlitz *sub voce.*

3) Acts 12, 12; 1, 13.

4) There is a tradition, of little importance, however, and of questionable reliability, that John was a priest and wore the sacerdotal plate. Eusebius, *H. E.,* V, XXIV, 3.

5) The traditional site of the upper room where the paschal supper was eaten — the *Coenaculum* — is on the western hill, generally known as Mount Zion, near the traditional house of Caiaphas. It is a room in a mosque known as Neby Daud. It was early held that the apostles were assembled in the same room at Pentecost when the Holy Ghost descended upon them, Acts 1, 13; 2, 1. For traditional claims see Andrews, 498.

6.

Matt. 26, 20. Mark 14, 17. Luke 22, 14—18.

It was on the evening of Thursday when, according to Jewish reckoning, Friday, the fifteenth of Nisan, had begun, that Jesus, accompanied by the Twelve, made His way to Jerusalem. After completing the arrangements for the Passover supper, Peter and John seem to have rejoined their Lord. Nothing is said of the mother of Jesus, the mother of James and John, and other women, although on the following day we meet them again. While they belonged to the party of the Galilean Passover pilgrims, yet probably because His hour of suffering had come, Jesus had tenderly left them behind. As the party climbed up to the city, it was already growing dark. From the rear, bright and full, the Passover moon was rising in the star-sown sky. Soon they came to the designated house, where an outside staircase led up to the upper room. Lighted lanterns hung from brackets on the wall. They went in. The sandals were taken off and left by the wall near the door. The door was closed. And the Passover supper began.

Jesus on the Way to the Passover Meal.

7.

Matt. 26, 20. Mark 14, 17. Luke 22, 14—18.

According to the later rituals the Passover meal followed a certain order. How much of the details were observed by Jesus the evangelists do not state. The characteristic features of the feast, however, are known from the gospel account. The meal was opened by the head of the house, who filled a goblet of wine, took it in his hands, and consecrated it with words of thanksgiving and prayer. "Blessed art Thou, Jehovah, our God, who hast created the fruit of the vine." The first cup of wine was then drained, and each washed his hands. On this particular evening the washing of the disciples' feet was evidently connected with the washing of hands. Then the table was brought forward, on which were placed the unleavened bread, the bitter herbs, the side-dishes, the paschal lamb, and — if for a larger company the flesh of a small Eastern lamb did not suffice for a complete meal — the flesh of an additional sacrifice, which was called the first *chagigah*. In order that the guests might not be disturbed, the divans, or couches, were placed on three sides of the table only. One side was left

The Ritual of the Passover Feast.

open. As the eating began with a benediction, a second cup of wine was poured out. A very interesting ceremony now took place. The youngest member present inquired into the meaning of the feast. Then followed the *haggadah,* or instruction, by the father or the host regarding the meaning of the feast. The first part of the Hallel [1] was then sung, a blessing repeated, the Passover lamb was eaten, a third cup, "the cup of blessing," was drained, the rest of the Hallel was sung,[2] a fourth cup of wine was drunk, and the ceremony ended by the singing of a hymn of praise.[3] The meal had to be concluded by midnight. What remained of the lamb was burned.[4]

8.

Matt. 26, 20. Mark 14, 17. Luke 22, 14—18.

This was really the first Passover, and also the last, of which Jesus partook together with the full number of His apostolic band. At the first Passover of His ministry His twelve apostles had not yet been gathered,[1] neither at the second, if, as we assume, the Unnamed Feast was a Passover.[2] And the third Passover Jesus did not attend. At that time, after the death of John the Baptist, He was in the utmost parts of Galilee, in the borders of Tyre and Sidon, where of course no sacrifices could be made.[3] And so it is with peculiar significance that Jesus opened the feast with the announcement: "With desire have I desired to eat this passover with you before I suffer." No more

"With Desire have I Desired to Eat This Passover with You before I Suffer."

festival dinners would He enjoy with His disciples until the perfection of the Kingdom was attained. Again the reference to suffering, which, of course, the disciples did not understand. They had ears only for the Kingdom, concerning which, however, they continued to entertain conceptions of their own. As the Host of the day Jesus opened the feast by filling a goblet of wine, over which the customary prayers were spoken, and passed it along with

---

7, 1) Pss. 113 and 114.
   2) Pss. 115—118.
   3) Ps. 136.
   4) Ex. 12, 10. Detailed descriptions are found in Edersheim, II, 496 ff.; *Temple,* 204 ff. Ylvisaker, 648 ff. Farrar, II, 290 ff. Andrews, 484.
8, 1) Chapter VII.
   2) Chapter VIII.
   3) Chapter XVI.

the same thought: "Take this and divide it among yourselves. For I say unto you, I will not drink of the fruit of the vine until the kingdom of God shall come." [4]

(Luke 22, 24—30.) [1]   **9.**

Imagination loves to reproduce the probable details of the solemn scene. And if we compare the notices of ancient Jewish customs with the fashions still existing in the changeless East, we can feel quite confident as to the general nature of the arrangements. These are, however, unlike those with which the genius of Leonardo da Vinci and other great painters have made us familiar. [2] The couches, or cushions, each large enough to hold three persons, [3] were arranged in the form of an elongated horseshoe around three sides of one or more low wooden tables, each one scarcely higher than a stool. The seat of honor was probably the central position on the first couch, to the right of the servants as they approached the open end of the table. [4] The

The Arrangement of the Paschal Table.

Talmud formulates the position of guests as follows: The worthiest lies down first, on his left side, with his feet stretching back. The next worthiest reclines behind him at his left hand. The third worthiest lies beside the one who had lain down first (at his right), so that the chief person is in the middle (between the worthiest guest at his left and the less worthy one at his right hand). [5] From the gospel narrative we know that John occupied a place to

---

8, 4) Namely, again, after this meal, from henceforth, until —. Luke 22, 18, compared with Matt. 26, 29. Not to be taken as an absolute refusal on the part of Jesus to partake of wine. This is a gratuitous implication on the part of Meyer. See Meyer *sub loco* and editorial remarks under pages 540 and 556. The drinking of wine was an essential part of the Jewish Passover Feast.

9, 1) Luke places the reference to the traitor and the disciples' dispute about rank after the institution of the Lord's Supper. But it seems that he does not insist upon strict chronological order in this place. Possibly for the purpose of completing his account, he brings in both incidents before passing on, without, however, claiming that his order must be followed against the order of Matthew and Mark as compared with John. We are reminded of the circumstance that Luke at other times completes his account of logically related subjects, even though the chronology may be disturbed; for instance, in Luke 1, verses 65 and 66 belong after verse 79; in Luke 5, verses 1 to 11 probably belong after 4, 31, as compared with Matthew and Mark. See also the question: "Did Judas receive Holy Communion?" in this chapter, 14.

2) Farrar, II, 278.

3) Called *triclinia,* couches for three. But sometimes used for four or five.

4) John D. Davis, *Bible Dictionary.*   5) Edersheim, II, 207.

the right of Jesus, so that his head could at any moment be placed upon the breast of his Friend and Lord.[6]   He would therefore have received the second place of honor among the guests.   At the left and back of Jesus lay the man of Kerioth, as we infer from a few details of the meal, that of dipping his hand into the dish

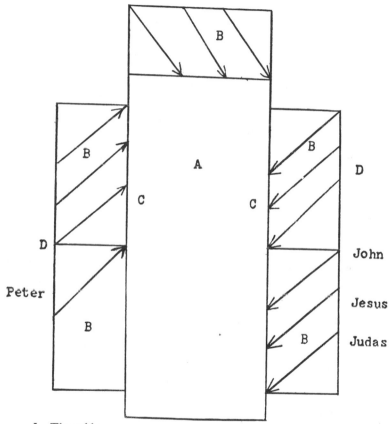

A. The table.

B. The *triclinia,* or divans, on which the guests reclined on their left side, with their

C. Heads pointing towards the table and their

D. Feet stretching back towards the floor.

with Jesus, receiving the sop directly from Him, and other indications which point to a position close to the Lord.   According to the arrangement prescribed by the Talmud it seems that he really occupied a place at the Passover table first in honor.   It is probable that

9,   6) John 13, 23.

he boldly claimed and obtained the chief seat at the table next to the Lord. His place was at the end of the row. It was called among the Romans the *locus consularis,* as being a place of honor at the head of the table next to the host. Since it was on the open side of the couch, it was chosen in order that, if a consul happened to be present, he might be able to receive communications, sign documents, or transact business without the least inconvenience. This arrangement explains how Jesus, beginning at the end, could hand the sop to Judas first without attracting the particular attention of the others. The position accounts for the circumstance that, when Judas, desirous of ascertaining whether his treachery was known, dared to ask, "Is it I?" and that, when the Lord answered in the affirmative, no one — except John and probably Peter across the table— knew what had been said.[7] Peter, we assume, in accordance with his character, after the Lord had rebuked the disciples for striving to be uppermost, claimed for himself the place across from John, at the *foot* of the table. From there he could easily give a hint[8] to John across the table to ask Jesus who the traitor was.[9]

(Luke 22, 24—30.)   **10.**

It may be that the very act of taking their seats started the contention among the disciples as to their respective places. In hearing the reference to the Kingdom, they had thoughts only of the trappings of royalty and of the order of precedence observed at kingly courts. The question had

Contention among the Disciples as to Rank.

been brought up and settled before.[1] Gently the Lord tells them that it was the custom of Gentile kings to exercise lordship and to give themselves flattering titles, such as Euergetes and Benefactor.[2]

9,   7) Matt. 26, 25, compared with John 13, 24. 29.

8) Probably more by signs than words, like Zechariah in Luke 1, 22, διανεύων.

9) John 13, 24. Of course, there is no certainty in the matter. Our only interest is in helping picture the scene. For details see Edersheim, II, 493 ff., compared with p. 207 ff. and other writers. Farrar, II, 278. Andrews, 485. 486. Geo. B. Eager in *Int. St. B. Encycl.* under "Meals"; likewise the article under "Meals" in Davis, *Bible Dictionary;* and article "Triclinium" in *Encycl. Brit.*

10, 1) Luke 9, 46, after the Transfiguration; Matt. 20, 25—28 and Mark 10, 42—45, after the request of James and John to sit at the right and left in the kingdom of Jesus.

2) For instance, Ptolemy Euergetes of Egypt and others. Deissmann, *Licht vom Osten,* 215. A Syrian coin has been found, issued by King Antiochus VII (138—127 B. C.), with the inscription: (Money of the) King Antiochus Euergetes. George C. Williamson, *Money of the Bible,* p. 33.

"But ye shall not be so. But he that is greatest among you, let him be as the younger, and he that is chief as he that doth serve." He points to His own example. His whole life has been one, not of being served, but of serving. However, since as His disciples they have faithfully shared His trials, He graciously promises them that they shall share His glory in the kingdom which His Father has appointed unto Him. They are to participate in His Messianic glory, eat and drink at His table in His kingdom, and sit on twelve thrones, judging the twelve tribes of Israel.[3]

John 13, 1—20.[1]   **11.**

For the purpose of teaching His disciples a lesson of humility, Jesus performed for them a service which otherwise would have been the task of the lowest servants. He knew that His hour had come. He also knew what Judas had in mind and that His glorification was by way of suffering and death. But love having been the key-note of His whole life, He decided to display this love to those who had been His particular friends to this very hour.

10, 3) The defection of Judas not taken into account, Matt. 19, 28.

11, 1) *Did Christ eat the passover?* Some think certain expressions in the Gospel of St. John show that Jesus did not eat the passover, thus hopelessly contradicting the other gospels. Did Christ eat the passover? Or to put the question in another form. On what day of the month, the 14th or the 15th day of Nisan, was Jesus crucified? It is clear from the four gospels that the crucifixion occurred on the same Jewish day as the eating of the meal recorded by all four evangelists. But was this the passover meal or not? It is agreed that the crucifixion took place on a Friday and that the meal was eaten on the evening before, our Thursday; but was this the 14th or the 15th of Nisan? If Jesus was crucified on the 14th, the day when the Passover lamb was slain, then the meal of the previous evening must have been an anticipatory supper, and then, of course, He did not eat the passover at all. A great controversy once raged in the Church about this matter. At that time the point was that Christ did not eat the passover, because otherwise, it was thought, the idea would have been lost that He Himself became the true Paschal Lamb. And since then the question has been taken up and kept alive for the purpose of discrediting the gospel account. — 1. *The Paschal Controversy.* The gist of the second-century paschal controversy was whether the day commemorating the death of Christ would always have to be the 14th of Nisan, or whether it would always have to be a Friday. According to the latter view the day of Christ's crucifixion would always fall on a Friday and the day of His resurrection on a Sunday. But according to the former, "Good Friday" might fall on a Tuesday and "Easter Sunday" on a Thursday. Polycarp of Smyrna, appealing to the Apostles John and Philip, clung to the Asiatic practice of observing the 14th day of Nisan, but could not persuade Anicetus, bishop of Rome, to adopt his view, nor could the latter persuade Polycarp to abandon his. While the Latin churches held the view that Jesus ate the passover on the evening of the 14th and was crucified on the 15th, the Eastern churches took the position that Jesus Himself became the Passover Lamb (with His death) on the 14th. As emphasizing the date, regardless of the day, the name of Quartodecimanians later clung to the adherents of this view. However, the Roman practise, which made the Sunday of the Resurrection the center of the whole Easter Festival, gradually prevailed and was officially adopted by the Council of Nicaea in 325 A. D. The Greek churches, while admitting that Jesus died on a Friday and rose on a Sunday, nevertheless still hold that He did *not* eat the passover. But these arguments are subjective and do not affect the question of fact. See Eusebius, V, XXIII. XXIV. *Nicene and Post-Nicene Fathers*, Vol. I, notes 241 ff. — 2. *The Testimony of the Synoptists.* a. Jesus predicted that His death would occur on the fast of the Passover, Matt. 26, 2; Mark 14, 1; Luke 22, 1. As to the terms Passover and Unleavened Bread, one always includes the other. b. The Jewish authorities decided not to put Jesus to death during the feast, Matt. 26, 5; Mark 14, 2. But after the offer of Judas this decision was changed. c. It is expressly stated that the disciples Peter and John were sent on the first day of Unleavened Bread to make preparations for eating the passover and that on the evening of that day Jesus ate the passover with His disciples, Matt. 26, 17. 20; Mark 14, 12. 17; Luke 22, 7. 14. 15. Now, the first day of Unleavened Bread was the 14th, and the evening was the 15th. There is no question about this. d. Jesus Himself calls it Passover, Luke 22, 15. It has been assumed that, when there was a Sabbath following Passover, the Pharisees advanced the meal (by what right?) to Thursday evening (Jewish Friday), while the Sadducees (less scrupulous about the Sabbath) ate their passover on Friday evening (Jewish Saturday) and that Jesus, following pharisaic practise, accordingly ate the Passover meal on Thursday evening in anticipation of the Passover meal which should have been held on Friday evening (after His death). For a somewhat similar solution see a recent work by P. Feine, *Jesus.* — 3. *The Testimony of John.* A number of passages are produced to show that John is in conflict with the Synoptists. But a careful examination of these passages proves that this is not the case. a. *John 13, 1.* "Now, *before* the feast of the Passover." This expression refers to the whole festival, in this case to the whole remaining festival. b. *John 13, 2.* "*Supper being ended.*" But as John himself explains, not strictly so. The supper was still in progress, as can be seen from the expressions "riseth from supper," v. 4, "was set down again," v. 12, "leaning on Jesus' bosom," v. 23. The Revised Version adopts the text "during supper." c. *John 13, 27.* "*That thou doest, do quickly.*" It is claimed that the supper of John 13 was not the Passover meal and that Judas should quickly make preparations for it, it being assumed that the "feast" of v. 29 was the Passover. But it is clear that the disciples were thinking of the whole festival, the second day, the third day, etc., of which this supper was only a part, while Jesus was no doubt referring to the betrayal. d. *John 18, 28.* "They themselves entered not into the palace that they might not be defiled, but *might eat the passover.*" Strictly speaking, they had already eaten the passover. Again the expression "to eat the passover" refers to the celebration of the whole festival. e. *John 19, 14.* "*Now, it was the Preparation of the Passover.*" Not the 14th day of Nisan, but an expression to designate the day of the week. A common expression for Friday, Passover Friday. Preparation has long been the regular name for Friday in the Greek language, caused by New Testament usage. Friday is still called Preparation in modern Greek. Friday is called the Preparation for the Sabbath, just as in German Saturday is called *Sonnabend* because of its being the day before Sunday. f. *John 19, 31.* "For that Sabbath-day was an high day." Not that the 15th was a Saturday, that Christ was crucified on the 14th, and that the annual Passover and the weekly Sabbath coincided in that year, which easily might have happened. But it was a "high day" because it was a Sabbath, because it was a second holiday, and because, in addition, it was the day when the sheaves of the first-fruits were offered. — For a detailed discussion of the problem see: A. T. Robertson, *Harmony of the Gospels*, 279 ff.; Edw. Robinson, *Greek Harmony of the Gospels*, 241 ff.; Sam. J. Andrews, *The Life of Our Lord*, 461 ff.; John Ylvisaker, *The Gospels*, 637 ff.; Karl Wieseler, *Chronological Synopsis*, 208 ff. 363 ff.

It was while this meal was in progress, at supper-time,[2] that Satan had taken full possession of Judas Iscariot, Simon's son, prompting him, likely after he had overheard a remark made by Jesus as to His intention after the Passover meal, to betray Jesus by bringing this information to the high priests. But nevertheless, without interfering with his plan, though He had full knowledge of all these things, and obediently submitting Himself to the humiliation and pain which the next few hours would bring, Jesus rose from the supper, which had just begun with the first cup, and did a most

Washing the Disciples' Feet.

peculiar thing. Quarreling about their respective places at the table, the disciples had failed to wash their feet, or rather to have them washed, as befitted men of rank about to enjoy, as they supposed, a royal banquet! This was the work of slaves! Since no one therefore in this small assembly of expectant rulers and generals volunteered to perform this service, the King Himself left His couch, put aside His outer garments, wrapped a towel around His waist, poured water into a basin, and without a word, probably starting with Judas,[3] stepped up behind the couches, and, as though He were the lowliest servant, began to wash the feet of His disciples and to dry them with a towel. Awe and shame sealed their lips until Jesus came to Peter, who had probably drawn up his feet and could hardly repress his emotions. To the half-indignant question: "Lord, dost Thou wash my feet?" Jesus replied: "What I do thou knowest not now, but thou shalt know hereafter." But Peter persisted: "Thou shalt never," till the end of time, "wash my feet!" But here Jesus revealed to Peter the harm he would do his soul by false humility: "If I wash thee not, thou hast no part with Me." Even as Jesus had spoken many parables, so now, in the washing of His disciples' feet, He, as it were, performed a parable. It was clear to Peter that Jesus was pointing to some connection not conditioned by mere external washing of feet. These words of Jesus suddenly changed the whole current of Peter's thoughts. Have no share with Jesus? Heaven forbid! And then he shot into the other extreme. In that case,

---

11, 2) V. 2. Δείπνου γενομένου, not "after supper." Compare vv. 4 and 12. "Supper having arrived," not, "Supper being ended." If we read γινομένου, the meaning is substantially the same; "supper arriving," at supper-time." See Dods *sub loco.*

3) The view of Chrysostom, as quoted by Andrews, 483, and Meyer *sub loco.*

if that is what Christ meant, then, Peter said, "Lord, not my feet only, but also my hands and my head." Once more, however, Jesus must correct His impulsive disciple. Correctly understood, "He that is washed needeth not save to wash his feet, but is clean every whit." In other words, as a believing disciple and by virtue of the redemption of Christ, Peter was clean already, and he was in need only of daily spiritual cleansing, daily sanctification, corresponding to the daily washing of feet in physical life. Otherwise the disciples were clean every whit, only that the sanctification of their lives must continue as symbolized by the washing of feet. In making this declaration, however, Jesus made an exception: "But not all!" Jesus knew who would betray Him. And he that rejects Christ, refusing to be washed of his sins by Him, and therefore is not justified before God naturally excludes himself from sanctification.

John 13, 1—20.   **12.**

After Jesus had finished His lowly task, He again slipped into His outer garments and went back to His place at the table as the Head of the household. The disciples were still watching in questioning silence as He explained His action: "Know ye what I have done unto you?" They regarded themselves as privileged persons and therefore desired to occupy seats of honor in the Kingdom, — and now the King had washed their feet! As their Lord and Master, He tells them, He has given them an example, namely, an example of humble service and brotherly love. As their Lord

The Washing Explained. has done unto them, so they should do unto others. Not in literal imitation, as if the disciples should now make it a daily or yearly practise to wash one another's feet. That would be a pharisaic interpretation of their Master's example. No; they should make a general application of this divine exemplar: love and serve one another. "Verily, verily,[1] I say unto you, The servant is not greater than his lord, neither he that is sent greater than he that sent him." [2] This important principle of Christianity applies to every follower of Christ as well as to His apostles. And "if ye know these things, happy are ye if ye do them."

12, 1) We have already pointed out, chapter VI, 20, John 1, 51, etc., that the double ἀμήν, verily, does not occur in other parts of the New Testament; but in John we find it twenty-five times, and only as spoken by Jesus.

2) Compare Matt. 10, 24; Luke 6, 40.

John 13, 1—20. **13.**

The discourse continues with another allusion to Judas, who, though one of the chosen Twelve, was, sad to say, not one of the elect. To him the words of blessing do not apply. Not that he had been preordained to be "the son of perdition," — no one is predestinated unto eternal damnation; — he was lost only because he rejected Christ. By his betrayal of the Savior he assisted in bringing about the fulfilment of Scripture. This is what Jesus now refers to as He quotes the following prophecy: "He that eateth bread with Me," that is, who enjoys the distinction of utmost intimacy and friendship, "hath lifted up his heel against Me." [1] The choice of Judas as an apostle had been made in good faith,

An Allusion to Judas. but at the same time with full knowledge of what would happen. It is not for us to dispute with the omniscient God because of His inscrutable ways, which are past finding out.[2] And now, since that most heinous crime would be committed and had been divinely predicted, Jesus made an announcement of it for the very purpose of strengthening the faith of His disciples in His Messiahship. "Now I tell you before it come that, when it is come to pass, ye may believe that I am He." But treason perpetrated by one of their number should not discourage them from performing their duty. In spite of the defection of one they have the most glorious promise for their apostleship: "Verily, verily, I say unto you, He that receiveth whomsoever I send receiveth Me; and he that receiveth Me receiveth Him that sent Me." [3]

14.

Matt. 26, 21—25. Mark 14, 18—21. (Luke 22, 21—23.)[1]
John 13, 21—30.

The presence of a traitor at His table caused the Lord to become troubled in spirit. Even as David's heart was filled with sadness when his nearest friend and trusted counselor became his

13, 1) Ps. 41, 9.

  2) Rom. 9, 20 (marginal reading) ; 11, 33.

  3) Matt. 10, 40; Mark 6, 37; Luke 9, 48.

14, 1) *Did Judas receive Holy Communion?* That depends upon when the identity of the betrayer was revealed and whether or not the order of Luke is to be adopted. According to Matthew and Mark the traitor was revealed during the Passover meal and before the institution of Holy Communion. According to John, who does not mention the Lord's Supper, it was during the meal which we believe to have been the Passover supper. Jerome, Augustine, Chrysostom, Quenstedt, and others believe that the disclosure was made

bitterest foe,[2] so it was with David's Son. "Verily, I say unto you, One of you which eateth with Me shall betray Me." While it is true that "the Son of Man goeth as it was determined," still that does not relieve the instrument of wickedness of his responsibility. "Woe unto that man by whom the Son of Man is betrayed! It had been good for that man if he had not been born." At these words the eyes of the disciples fell and their hearts misgave them. None of them felt safe now. Glancing from one to another, they could read shame and self-distrust in one another's eye. Each was not thinking of his fellow-disciple, but only of himself as he sadly asked: "Lord, is it I?" Still leaving the special person undetermined, Jesus said: "It is one of the Twelve that dippeth with Me in the dish." The reference very likely was to the dish of bitter herbs, the *charoseth,* a gravylike sauce of a muddy color, made of figs, dates, vinegar, and spices, in which the cakes of unleavened bread were dipped to remind the celebrants of the Passover of the burning of bricks in Egypt.[3] Into this common dish Jesus may have

The Traitor is Revealed.

dipped a morsel of bread and passed it along. But this sign would not make the matter sufficiently clear to the anxious questioners, unless Judas, who occupied the first place at the table, was the first one to receive the sop, for which, however, we have no

---

after the words of the institution were spoken and that Judas therefore took part in the first Communion service. The *Formula of Concord* likewise seems to support this view (*Solida Declaratio, Concordia Triglotta,* 33. 60, pp. 982. 992). But the opposite view is held by many scholars: McKnight, Meyer, Tischendorf, Robinson, Robertson, Ebrard, Wieseler, Edersheim, and others. See Stoeckhardt, *B. G.,* 265. Our arrangement is not prompted by doctrinal interests. Whether or not Judas received the Lord's Supper, the doctrine concerning this Sacrament remains the same. The argument of St. Paul stands that such as are known to be unworthy communicants should not be permitted to partake of Holy Communion, 1 Cor. 11, 28. 29. But suppose that Jesus, though knowing all things, nevertheless permitted an unworthy communicant to partake of the very first Communion, our argument is that He did so, 1) because He would not pass public judgment upon Judas as long as his sin was generally unknown; 2) because the betrayal, while fully decided upon by Judas, had not yet been actually committed. Ministers of the Gospel, therefore, who do not know the hearts, must content themselves with what seems to make it evident that the person whom they admit to the Sacrament is a worthy communicant. In endeavoring to bring Luke into agreement with Matthew and Mark and also with John, we are prompted by the considerations that Luke does not insist upon strict chronological sequence of his particular arrangement and that at other places he has permitted strict chronology to be disturbed by the connection of incidents which were logically joined, cf. section 9 above. See Stoeckhardt, *B. G.,* 265. Ylvisaker, *Gospels,* 654 ff. Andrews, *Life of Our Lord,* 493.

2) Probably Ahithophel. Ps. 41, 9, compared with 2 Sam. 15, 12. 31. 34, etc. Farrar, II, 285.

3) Edersheim, II, 506. Bruce sub Matt. 26, 23.

certain proof. At any rate, the disclosure was not generally evident, even as we are not certain of the detailed sequence of events. It may have been at this point that Peter, who was probably reclining across the table from John, beckoned to the disciple "whom Jesus loved," who was "leaning on the bosom of Jesus," that is, to the right of the Master, to find out from Him who the betrayer was. We assume that this disciple, who does not name himself, was John. Quietly Jesus gave the sign: "It is he to whom I shall give the sop when I have dipped it." [4] This He proceeded to do. Very likely already before this, when the rest had raised their voices, Judas also, to keep up an appearance of innocence, had joined in the question: "Master, is it I?" [5] Then came the reply, no doubt made in a low voice: "Thou hast said." It was another effort of the loving Jesus to save the soul of the traitor. "When He had dipped the sop, He gave it to Judas Iscariot, the son of Simon." In giving the betrayer's full name and parentage, John, as it were, made a formal arraignment. Jesus knew. Judas knew; but he was dead to the final warning of Christ; Satan had entered his heart. Likewise Peter and John knew. But not the rest. For when Jesus, seeing that the fate of Judas was sealed, began to direct events Himself by telling Judas: "That thou doest, do quickly," the other disciples did not know what it was about. This final word was spoken loud enough for all to hear; the disciples, however, thought that Jesus was giving Judas some instructions as the company's treasurer for to-morrow's sacrifices or that he was to make some offering for the poor.[6] When Judas had received the sop, he slipped off from his couch, an appalling figure, and rushed out into the night.

John 13, 31—35.   **15.**

With the departure of Judas the atmosphere seemed cleared. It was a critical moment. The hour of the Lord's Passion had now arrived. The betrayal was the first step, which led down into the deepest humiliation; but it was also the first step to glorification. "Now is the Son of Man glorified, and God is glorified in Him." After the accomplishment of His life-work the Son of Man would soon be glorified by His Father. Only a little while longer

---

14,   4) In Matthew and Mark the term refers to the dish; in John, to the contents.

   5) Matthew.

   6) Not to make preparation for the Passover supper, which was now past. See 3. The second *chagigah*.

the Master would remain with those whom He affectionately addressed as "little children," or boys.[1]   Soon the intimate association which they had all enjoyed would cease.   As Jesus had told the Jews at the Feast of Tabernacles that they would seek Him when

Upon the Departure of Judas, Jesus Indicates His Glorification.

it was too late and that whither He went they could not go,[2] so also the disciples, He said, would seek Him after His departure

with a sad and longing heart.   Still they should not be discouraged. He would leave, but they would follow.   He would go, but He would come again.   And in the mean while: "Love one another."

16.

Matt. 26, 26—29.   Mark 14, 22—25.   Luke 22, 19. 20.
1 Cor. 11, 23—26.

We now come to the most solemn part of the night, the institution of the Lord's Supper.   It is beyond the limits of this present work to delve into all the questions and controversies which, sad to say, have gathered around the plain and simple words of this sacred institution.   And still it would not be quite honest if we were to pass them by altogether.   It was in the same night in which Jesus was betrayed, and "after supper," [1] when the Passover meal as such had come to a close.   The reporters are the Synoptists Matthew, Mark, and Luke, while the absence of John is made up

The Institution of the Lord's Supper.

by the narrative of St. Paul, who vouches for it that he "received of the Lord" [2] that which he relates.   From the expres-

sion "cup of blessing" [3] some have thought that the institution of the Lord's Supper came after the third cup, when the Passover meal as such had been brought to a close, while others think that it came after the fourth cup, which preceded the singing of the final hymn.[4]   This does not matter.   While there was a connection with the Old Testament Passover, still there is the indication that

---

15, 1) The expression is frequent in 1 John; in John's gospel only here. Dods *sub loco.*

2) John 7, 34; 8, 21. 24.

16, 1) Paul and Luke: μετὰ τὸ δειπνῆσαι.

2) Παρέλαβον ἀπὸ τοῦ κυρίου.

3) 1 Cor. 10, 16: ποτήριον τῆς εὐλογίας.

4) Compare Matt. 26, 30; Mark 14, 26.   Findlay sub 1 Cor. 10, 16 in *Exp. Greek N. T.*   Meyer sub Matt. 26, 27.   The third cup was technically called "the cup of blessing" from the standpoint of the Jewish ritual, but from the Christian standpoint probably the fourth cup would be meant.

Matthew	Mark	Luke	Paul
And as they were eating. Jesus took bread, and blessed it, and brake it, and gave it to the disciples, and said, Take, eat; This is My body.	And as they did eat, Jesus took bread, and blessed it, and brake it, and gave it to them, and said, Take, eat; This is My body.	And He took bread, and gave thanks, and brake it, and gave it to them, saying, This is My body, which is given for you. This do in remembrance of Me.	For I have received of the Lord that which also I delivered unto you, that the Lord Jesus the same night in which He was betrayed took bread; and when He had given thanks, He brake it and said, This is My body, which is broken for you. This do in remembrance of Me.
And He took the cup, and gave thanks and gave it to them, saying, Drink ye all of it; for this is My blood of the new testament, which is shed for many for the remission of sins.	And He took the cup; and when He had given thanks, He gave it to them; and they all drank of it. And He said unto them, This is My blood of the new testament, which is shed for many.	Likewise also the cup after supper, saying, This cup is the new testament in My blood, which is shed for you.	After the same manner also He took the cup when He had supped, saying, This cup is the new testament in My blood.
But I say unto you, I will not drink henceforth of the fruit of the vine until that day when I drink it new with you in My Father's kingdom.	Verily I say unto you, I will drink no more of the fruit of the vine until that day that I drink it new in the kingdom of God.		This do ye, as oft as ye drink it, in remembrance of Me. For as often as ye eat this bread and drink this cup, ye do show the Lord's death till He come.

the Lord's Supper was the inauguration of a new covenant, or testament,[5] and that the Old Testament Passover had forever ceased.[6] Even as with the sacrifice of Christ all other sacrifices ceased, so also the Lord's Supper was not a sacrifice, but a feast, an eating and drinking. In the fourfold account we notice that Mark follows Matthew and Luke follows St. Paul. But in calling attention to this particular, we are not suggesting that or showing how the evangelists copied from one another. The text used in our churches does not strictly follow any of the four separate versions, but is an adaptation from the fourfold account of an ancient liturgy. While it is true that none of these versions gives us the very words of Christ, because He spoke Aramaic, still we must remember that the Lord saw fit to transmit His words to us in Greek. And therefore, if at this or that point there is an argument about certain terms, there can be no question as to whether we should follow uninspired conjectures or the inspired records. And what do the records state?

17.

*Matt. 26, 26—29.   Mark 14, 22—25.   Luke 22, 19. 20.
1 Cor. 11, 23—26.*

As the disciples were still sitting and eating at the Passover table, — the meal having naturally been interrupted by the discussion about Judas, but now resumed, — Jesus took bread. The reference is evidently to unleavened bread; but since in the fourfold account the term is simply bread,[1] it is quite clear that for future practise the unleavened character need not be stressed. Next Jesus gave thanks to God and invoked a blessing upon the bread.[2] The ancient Jewish prayer over the bread was: "Blessed be Thou, our God, King of the universe, who bringest forth bread out of the earth." [3] From the expression "when He had given thanks" the name Eucharist clings to the Holy Supper. Then He brake the bread, most likely for the purpose of distribution. Beyond this no significance is to be attached to this action; for even if the expression "which is broken for you," considered by many an early gloss, is authentic, we must remember that no bone was broken

---

16, 5) Καινὴ διαθήκη.

6) After the eating of the Passover lamb no one was at liberty in that night to eat anything more. Meyer sub Matt. 26, 26.

17, 1) Ἄρτος.

2) Εὐλογήσας, Matthew and Mark; εὐχαριστήσας, Luke and St. Paul.

3) Kretzmann or Meyer sub Matt. 26, 26.

either of the prototype, the paschal lamb,[4] or of the antitype, Jesus.[5] Then He gave the consecrated bread to the disciples with the invitation: "Take, eat."[6] A remarkable statement, however, is added. "This," namely, that which ye are to take and eat, "is My body, which is given for you." The reference was clearly to the body which was to die on the cross and to the unspeakably great benefit which was to come to them through His vicarious

"This Is My Body." suffering and death. The words are clear, and yet their meaning has been questioned in many different ways. So many questions have been raised by human reason. Does the little word *is*,[7] which in every language under the sun stands for real existence, here suddenly acquire a symbolic significance, or did the Lord really mean to invite His disciples while physically sitting in their presence to partake of His body? What did the disciples think? Certainly they must at the moment have interpreted the words in a figurative sense, if indeed they interpreted them at all. Thus many reason. However, the disciples were simple believers, not much given to speculation. And even if they had been, it does not matter what they thought. We do not know how much or how little they were able to grasp. Nor does it concern us in the least. Our faith is not based upon what fallible men may think, but upon the Word of Christ. According to the highest critical standards the truthfulness of the record cannot be questioned. And from the account it is clear that in the Holy Supper Christ has promised His true body and blood to all partakers of this Sacrament. To say that the word *is* denotes only a symbolic existence is juggling with the language. Even in figurative language, for instance, in "The Lord *is* my Shepherd," the word *is* does not lose its force. But, on the other hand, to say that the bread has been changed to Christ's body is going beyond the words of the institution as explained by Paul: "For as often as ye eat this bread." The bread is still bread. From the words of institution it cannot be proved that the consecrated bread is changed into the body of Christ (transubstantiation) or that the bread and the body form a third substance (consubstantiation). There is no proof for the assertion that by means of the consecrated elements the natural body of Christ is communicated to the recipients in the same natural manner as the physical elements

---

17, 4) Ex. 12, 46.   5) John 19, 36.

6) Λάβετε, φάγετε.   7) Ἐστίν.

by way of consubstantiation. Without speculating, simple faith believes that both the bread and the true body of the Lord are received with the mouth, the former in a natural, the latter in a supernatural manner. That in this memorial of Christ a new order of things is intended and at the same time the establishment of an inseparable, most intimate, relation between Him and the partaker is effected is indicated in the words "This do in remembrance of Me."

18.

Matt. 26, 26—29. Mark 14, 22—25. Luke 22, 19. 20.
1 Cor. 11, 23—26.

The distribution of the bread was followed by the taking and the blessing of the cup. The usual word of blessing spoken over the cup, as transmitted to us, was as follows: "Blessed is He who created the fruit of the vine." [1] The expression *cup* [2] naturally refers to the contents of the cup. That there was wine in the cup is clear from the history of the Jewish Passover. The wine in the cup is the means of conveying the atoning blood of Christ, at the point of being shed. And because through the shedding of His blood a new covenant is to be established, Jesus calls the cup, by virtue of its contents, the new testament in His blood. This cup He now offers to His disciples with the invitation to drink its consecrated contents. "Drink ye all of it," — which they did, [3] —

"This Is My Blood of the New Testament." "for this is My blood of the new testament." What has been said before about the term *is* in connection with bread and body applies also to wine and blood. — With the next words, as reported by Matthew, the purpose and the benefit of the shedding of Christ's blood is already given: "which is shed for many for the remission of sins." [4] The expression *for many* is not to be understood as if the Lord desired to say that He would not die for all; He merely emphasizes that His work is not done for a few, but for many, all mankind constituting a mighty host. From the words "for you," [5] "shed for you," "shed for many for the remission of sins," [6] it is certainly clear that the Lord's

---

18, 1) Meyer sub Matt. 26, 27.

    2) Ποτήριον.

    3) Mark.

    4) Τὸ περὶ πολλῶν ἐκχυνόμενον εἰς ἄφεσιν ἁμαρτιῶν.

    5) Ὑπὲρ ὑμῶν.

    6) Περὶ πολλῶν ἐκχυνόμενον.

Supper is in a special sense a Sacrament and a means of grace. It is not a mere ceremony, only a solemn memorial, but it actually gives and imparts to the believing, worthy communicant the forgiveness of sins.

19.

Matt. 26, 26—29. Mark 14, 22—25. Luke 22, 19. 20. 1 Cor. 11, 23—26.

In the concluding words as reported by Paul two truths are stressed. "This do ye, as oft as ye drink it, in remembrance of Me." In the first place, unlike Baptism, this Sacrament is to be received not only once. In the second place, at each celebration of it, until Judgment Day, there is an inseparable relation between the partaking of Holy Communion and its being a witness and testimony of the atoning death of Christ. Not that the Lord's Supper is a repeated sacrifice. "For as oft as ye eat this bread and drink this cup, ye do show the Lord's death till He come." As the Passover of the Old Testament was a remembrance of the exodus of Israel from Egypt and a testimony to the protecting hand of God, so this paschal feast of the New Testament is to be a testimony of the Lord's redeeming death and a reminder of His coming to Judgment. And as the Passover strengthened Israel for its long journey through the wilderness, so the Lord's Supper cheers and comforts the children of God in the New Testament on their pilgrimage through this vale of tears, incidentally pointing to the end of the journey and to the happy reunion and the marriage supper of the Lamb in the heavenly kingdom. "But I say unto you, I will not drink henceforth of the fruit of the vine [1] until that day when I drink it new with you in My Father's kingdom." [2]

"For as Often as Ye Eat This Bread and Drink This Cup."

19, 1) Ἐχ τοῦ γεννήματος τοῦ ἀμπέλου. Technical name for the Passover cup.

2) Here follows in the order of Luke: —
The traitor is revealed   Luke 22, 21—23
The contention of the disciples   Luke 22, 24—30

A strict chronological order does not seem to have been intended by Luke at this place. See 9 and 14.

CHAPTER XXXII.

THURSDAY NIGHT OF PASSION WEEK —
FAREWELL DISCOURSES.

April 6, 30 A. D., 783 A. U. C.

Nisan (or Abib)

10	11	12	13	14	15	16	17

April

2	3	4	5	6	7	8	9
Sun.	Mon.	Tue.	Wed.	Thu.	Fri.	Sat.	Sun.

A. U. C.	779	780	781	782	783
A. D.	26	27	28	29	30
Age of Jesus	30	31	32	33	34

783 A. U. C.   APRIL   30 A. D.

Sun.	Mon.	Tue.	Wed.	Thu.	Fri.	Sat.
						1
2	3	4	5	6	7	8
9	10	11	12	13	14	15
16	17	18	19	20	21	22
23	24	25	26	27	28	29
30						

1.

*Matt. 26, 30—35. Mark 14, 26—31. Luke 22, 31—39.
John 13, 36—38.*

After the singing of the paschal hymn,[1] or, in this case, the first Christian Communion hymn, Jesus and His disciples passed out of the upper room to the streets of Jerusalem, across the brook of Cedron, to the Garden of Gethsemane, on the slopes of the Mount of Olives. While the hour cannot be determined, it was most likely quite late at night. But some time between the departure from the guest-chamber and the actual arrival at Gethsemane,

"I will Smite the Shepherd." Jesus announced the dispersion of the Twelve and three denials of Peter and delivered the great farewell discourse as recorded in the Gospel of St. John, the precise order of which, however, cannot really be determined.[2] Before the institution of the

---

1, 1) Probably Ps. 136.

2) Variously placed by the different harmonists. The order which we have followed is prompted by the desire to avoid wherever possible all transpositions. In this place we notice that A. T. Robertson, who consistently follows the order of Mark in his *Harmony of the Gospels,* so as even to give him first place in the parallel columns, for the first time allows a transposition in the gospel of Mark.

Holy Supper Jesus made a reference to His departure. "Yet a little while I am with you." And then the disciples would seek Him. But "whither I go ye cannot come." [3] The statement had left a question in Peter's mind. And now, to prepare His disciples for the matter at hand, Jesus gives the warning: "All ye shall be offended because of Me this night." In the next few hours events would happen which would cause all the disciples to become offended at Jesus. His great humiliation would not at all agree with their Messianic conception. The result would be the fulfilment of the prophecy: "I will smite the Shepherd, and the sheep of the flock shall be scattered abroad." [4] A bright future, however, is added to dispel the gloom: "After I am risen again,[5] I will go before you into Galilee." But Peter did not agree with his Master. He resented the implication as to general apostolic weakness. "Whither goest Thou?" The Lord would not needlessly excite His disciples by plainly telling them of His death, for He still had much to tell them to which He wished them to listen undisturbed.[6] "Whither I go thou canst not follow Me now, but thou wilt follow Me afterwards." Thus the Lord pointed out to Peter in a veiled manner his future martyrdom.[7] But Peter answered: "Why cannot I follow Thee now?" Suppose his Master *did* refer to death, could he not also say with Thomas: "Let us also go that we may die with Him?" [8] And he added: "I will lay down my life for Thy sake." And as to being offended, or scandalized, Peter was willing to concede that such a thing could happen to the rest, but not to him.[9] "Though all men shall be offended because of Thee, yet will I never be offended."

2.

Matt. 26, 30—35. Mark 14, 26—31. Luke 22, 31—39. John 13, 36—38.

Peter thought he knew himself. But the heart is a deceitful thing. And the Lord, who loved him and knew his weakness, had made him the object of special prayer. "Simon, Simon, behold, Satan hath desired to have you[1] that he may sift [you] as wheat." Satan was not satisfied with Judas only; if at all possible, he would have them all. In the process of sifting, where that which is not

1,   3) John 13, 33.   4) Zech. 13, 7.
     5) See chapter XXX, 20.   6) Dods sub John 13, 36.
     7) John 21, 19.   8) John 11, 16.
     9) Bruce sub Matt. 26, 33.
2,   1) Plural, ἐξητήσατο ὑμᾶς.

wheat is cast out, Satan would have Peter and his companions. "But I have prayed for thee that thy faith fail not." There would be an onslaught; but Satan's victory would not be final. "And when thou art converted,[2] strengthen thy brethren." Peter's fall

"Before the Cock Crow Twice." and repentance are both foretold, the latter being necessary before he could again become an apostle of Jesus. But Peter still objects: "Lord, I am ready to go with Thee both into prison and to death." Peter was willing, but he did not know himself. He was ignorant both of his own weakness and the exact nature of his Master's fate. The reference to dangers ahead is quite definite, but there is a big difference between prison and death. Without arguing the point, Jesus gives Peter a definite warning: "Verily I say unto thee, That this day, even in this night, before the cock crow twice, thou shalt deny Me thrice."[3]   But the announcement was vehemently protested by Peter: "If I should die with Thee, I will not deny Thee in any wise." And in this he was joined by the other disciples.

3.

Matt. 26, 30—35. Mark 14, 26—31. Luke 22, 31—39. John 13, 36—38.

But in their overconfidence the disciples had probably overlooked one thing. Their previous safety from vicious attacks and temptations lay in the protecting hand of the Lord. But other times were now at hand. When the Lord had previously sent them forth without provisions and means of defense, "what did ye lack?" Their reply was: "Nothing." But now the relation was changing. In figurative language Jesus tells His disciples that they would need supplies and means of defense. "He that hath a purse, let him take it and likewise his scrip," or bag. "And he that hath no sword, let him sell his garment and buy one." Bitter enmity would

---

2,   2) Matt. 18, 3.

3) Mark gives the more exact wording as coming probably from Peter himself. The warning may have been repeated in the conversation as reported by the other evangelists. "Before the cock crow," πρὶν ἀλέκτορα φωνῆσαι, of Matthew may also be taken as a watch of the night. Compare Mark 13, 35. Cocks are not mentioned in the Old Testament. The fowl was probably introduced into Palestine after the Exile, likely from Babylon. Even if the fowl was not permitted to be kept in Jerusalem on account of possible Levitical defilement, the prohibition would not have applied to the Romans occupying the near-by judgment-hall of Pilate and Fort Antonia in the Temple complex. See Edersheim, II, 537, n. 1. Bruce sub Matt. 26, 34.

have to be expected. Preparation was necessary. "The sword is the one thing needful." [1] If their Master is a "crucified male-factor, what can the followers expect"? As for Him, the words of prophecy "And He was reckoned among the transgressors" [2] must be fulfilled. This cannot be changed now. And He was, oh! so desirous to carry out His Father's loving decree to save all mankind through the vica-

"He that Hath No Sword, Let Him . . . Buy One."

rious suffering and dying through Him, His beloved Son. [3] But once more the words are understood in a grossly material sense. After the manner of their countrymen these Galileans had provided them-selves with two long knives or swords, which were concealed under the upper garment. [4] And Peter carried one of them. "Lord," they call out, "behold, here are two swords." The reply of Jesus is brief: "It is enough." In fact, too much for the purpose He had in mind. But there is no use going into this matter again. Enough for the present of misunderstanding and attempts at disenchant-ment! [5] Events will soon teach where instruction has failed.

John 14, 1—31.   **4.**

The hearts of the disciples were troubled on account of their Master's repeated references to His departure; for this departure was incompatible with their worldly Messianic views. And there-

Jesus Comforts His Disciples in an Extended Farewell Discourse.

fore Jesus comforted them in an extended farewell discourse. While it was true that He would depart to the Father, there to prepare a place for them, still He would come again. This the disciples knew, for they had been sufficiently instructed; but for the present "they did not know that they knew," inasmuch as for the moment it had slipped their minds. [1]

John 14, 1—31.   **5.**

That this was the case was clear from the way Thomas spoke: "Lord, we know not whither Thou goest; and how can we know the way?" Just like Thomas. He was willing to believe, but he wanted to be shown. His difficulty was that, not knowing the goal,

---

3,   1) Bruce sub Luke 22, 36.   2) Is. 53, 12.   3) Ps. 40, 7. 8.
        4) Edersheim, II, 537. Josephus, *Wars,* III, III, 2.
        5) Bruce sub Luke 22, 38.
4,   1) Kretzmann, I, 489.

the destination, he could not know the way. What was Christ driving at? What was the goal? And which was the way to it? In the reply of Jesus both the way and the goal are disclosed. "I am

Interrupted by Thomas. the Way and the Truth and the Life. No man cometh unto the Father but by Me." Believing in Christ is both seeing and approaching the Father. He Himself was the Jacob's Ladder to heaven, on the top of which stood the Father.

John 14, 1—31.   **6.**

These words interested the practical-minded Philip. Immediately he had made some calculations. He considered the possibility of actually receiving a physical glimpse of God. "Lord, show us the Father, and it sufficeth us." Thus he uttered the universal human craving of faith based upon the evidence of physical sight. It is the effort of material sight to behold the invisible God. Always there persists the feeling that something more might be done to make God known than has been done. "We walk by faith and not by sight," is what Paul tells the Corinthians.[1] And Jesus gently points out to Philip that to have seen Him as manifested in His words and works is to have seen the Father. And if the disciples were tempted to doubt His works, faith might have the evidence of greater works in personal experience. By preaching the Gospel, they would cure the spiritually sick and awaken the spiritually dead to everlasting life. "Not as though Jesus had not converted men by His preaching. But the great work of the New Testament, the gathering of the Christian Church through the

Interrupted by Philip. preaching of the Gospel, did not really begin until after Pentecost." [2]

Doing these "greater works" would also be seeing the Father. Then there is also the evidence of unlimited power in the promised answer to prayer. Of course, this power is qualified by faith and by obedience to His commandments. Finally, there is the evidence of the Holy Spirit, the other Comforter, the Paraclete, or Advocate,[3] even the Spirit of Truth, whom the Father will send. The Son was sent into the world. Not so the Holy Spirit; He is sent to believers. This the disciples know because He has His abode in them. And in view of His promised coming as a Representative of Christ the disciples would not be

---

6,   1) 2 Cor. 5, 7. See Dods *sub loco.*
     2) Kretzmann, I, 490.   3) *Παράκλητος.*

left comfortless or orphans in this world. While it is true that the unbelieving world, which only saw what fell within the range of outward vision, would henceforth see Jesus no more, supposing that He had been permanently removed when He was laid in the grave, the disciples should see Him on account of this comforting presence and enjoy with Him the fellowship of life. And not only on the day of the advent of the Holy Spirit, on Pentecost, but throughout the whole Christian era the believers would enjoy His blissful indwelling in their hearts.

John 14, 1—31.   7.

At this point in the discourse, which we can touch but briefly and which, even if we tried to enter upon it more fully, we could not hope to fathom, Jesus was again interrupted. This time by Judas, not Iscariot. On the roster of apostles he appears as Judas, Thaddaeus, Lebbaeus, and Jude of James.[1] Of him there is "a plurality of names and a paucity of knowledge." By this time it was clear that the manifestation referred to was not along the expected Messianic lines. What arrested the attention of Judas was that the manifestation was not to the world, but to believers only. In expressing his thought, which was no doubt also the thought of the rest, he asks, "How is it," what is the reason, what has happened, "that Thou wilt manifest Thyself unto us and not unto the world?" He still held to the opinion that Messianic glory would somehow be in the nature of a great demonstration and with much display of temporal power. Once

Interrupted by Judas. more Jesus patiently explains. Together with the Spirit He Himself and the Father will dwell in those who love Him. When He is no longer bodily present with them, the Paraclete, the Holy Spirit, whom the Father will send in His name, will bring all these things to their remembrance. He will be His Representative. The Lord's Messianic mission was not to bring temporal power, but spiritual peace. To bring His work to conclusion, He was going to the Father by means of suffering and death. He would have to meet the last onslaught of the prince of this world and ruler of death; but on account of His sinless nature Satan would have no claim upon Him. Still He would go out to meet him in battle and submit to his sting of death. Not as if He were crushed by the

---

7,   1) See chapter XI, 14.

machinations of Satan; He would go voluntarily in order that the world might know that He was doing it out of love and in obedience to the gracious and saving will of God. Since this was the purpose of His coming into the world, there was not at all, as Judas thought, a change in His Messianic program. And thinking about it, and since the hour of His suffering was rapidly drawing near, the summons was given: "Arise, let us go hence."

John 15, 1—27.   8.

Just what the occasion was that prompted the Lord to continue His discourse by presenting Himself as the true Vine, whether it was the fruit of the vine in the paschal meal or a vine growing in the courtyard or the symbol of the vine on one of the Temple gates, we do not know. In the Old Testament, Israel is represented as a vineyard planted by God to bring forth fruit.[1] But Christ represents Himself as the true Vine, the Father as the Husbandman, and the disciples as the branches. The most intimate relationship exists between Christ and all those who believe in Him. By accepting His Word, His saving Gospel, the believers cling to Christ as a branch does to the vine. His Word brings them in

Christ the True Vine.   close communion with Him, — "if My words abide in you." And as the branches receive sap and vigor from the vine, so that they can grow and bring fruit, so the believers, who without Christ can do nothing pleasing unto God, through His Word obtain spiritual strength and willingness to bear fruit, yea, much fruit, to abound and be fruitful in every good work, to the glory of the Father. Moreover, if they abide in Christ, they have the glorious privilege of asking of the Father in prayer what they will and may be assured that it shall be done unto them. — The Lord then reminds His disciples of the unspeakable love He has shown them and will show them by laying down His life for them and all men. This should prompt them to keep His commandments, particularly to love one another as He loves them.

John 15, 1—27.   9.

From the relation of the disciples to one another Christ now turns to their relation to the world. Because He has chosen them out of the world, they will be hated by the world. This is to be

---

8,   1) Is. 5, 1—7; Ps. 80, 8—14.

expected. "The servant is not greater than his lord.[1] If they have persecuted Me, they will also persecute you." The mere fact that the disciples of Jesus afterwards professed their faith in Him constituted a capital offense in the eyes of His enemies. To speak the very name was a crime in the eyes of the law.[2] "But all these things will they do unto you for My name's sake,[3] because they know not Him that sent Me." And that was their own fault. If Jesus had not proved to them by His preaching and by His astounding miracles that He was the Son of the Father and the promised Redeemer of the world, if He "had not done among them the works which none other man

The Relation of the Disciples to the World.

did," they could not have been faulted for not believing in Him. "But now they have no cloak," or excuse, "for their sin" of unbelief. However, by rejecting and hating Him, they also hated the Father who had sent Him into the world. It was an almost incredible blindness and obduracy. This hatred and rejection was foretold in the Old Testament. "But this cometh to pass that the word might be fulfilled that is written in their Law, They hated Me without a cause." [4] And therefore they would persecute His disciples and followers, too. — But there is also an encouraging note. The Comforter shall come and testify, in whose effective witness the apostles are to join. "Ye shall also bear witness because ye have been with Me from the beginning."

John 16, 1—33.   10.

Jesus comes back to the subject of persecutions. As viewed in the light of fulfilment one such prediction would have been sufficient. It was, however, for the purpose of saving His disciples from being offended that these repeated predictions were made. Not only would they be excommunicated, or unsynagogued,[1] but whoever killed them would deem this a religious service to God. This fanatical blindness was of course due to ignorance of Christ and of God; but the disciples were forewarned lest they be taken

---

9, 1) Matt. 10, 24; Luke 6, 40.

2) Persecutions for the "name," *nomen ipsum,* in the Roman Empire. See E. G. Hardy, *Christianity and the Roman Government,* p. 87.

3) Διὰ τὸ ὄνομά μου.

4) "Their Law" is here, as in chap. 10, 34, used of the Old Testament Scriptures as a whole. Not a direct quotation; but similar expressions are found in Ps. 69, 4 and 35, 19. Dods *sub loco.*

10, 1) Ἀποσυνάγωγος γένηται. John 9, 22; 12, 42.

unawares. There had been suggestions of persecutions before,[2] but the reason why Jesus had not previously made definite and full predictions regarding the experiences the apostles would have when they no longer would enjoy His visible presence was that until this eventful day He had not considered it necessary. But now the time for His departure had come. The apostles, however, were so sadly absorbed in the thought of separation from their beloved Master and its consequences to them that they did not pause to inquire: "Whither goest Thou?" That is, they thought only of the fact of His departure and did not inquire into the purpose, and the benefit to them and the world, of His going to the Father, of His suffering and death, His resurrection, and finally His ascension. Viewed from that angle, it was certainly expedient for them that

Persecutions. Jesus went away; for otherwise they would not have had a Savior, there would have been no pouring out of the Holy Spirit, no coming of the Comforter, and there would have been no Christian Church. As regards the advent of the Comforter, that will be an event of supreme importance; for "He will reprove the world of sin and of righteousness and of judgment." This the Lord explains. The world stands accused of sin, namely, of the one chief sin, the rejection of the Gospel and therefore its refusal to believe in Christ as the Redeemer; and the Holy Spirit convicts it of this damning sin. He will convict it also of righteousness; that is, He will cause it to be proclaimed in all the world that by His fulfilment of the Law in the sinners' stead and by the shedding of His holy, precious blood Christ has merited for all men the righteousness which alone avails before God and that therefore he who spurns this righteousness has no hope of salvation. Lastly He convicts the world of judgment, "because the Prince of this World is judged." Since Christ has destroyed the works of Satan, this arch-enemy of mankind is condemned, his doom is sealed, and all who nevertheless follow him will be equally doomed. — Many things remained to be said, but due to their present depression of spirits and insufficient measure of spiritual knowledge the disciples could not bear them now. The Holy Spirit, however, the Spirit of Truth, who would soon be poured out upon them and whose essential function was to guide them, would lead them into all truth, which would make them infallible teachers of the Church.

10, 2) Matt. 10. 17. 18; Mark 13. 9; Luke 21. 12. 13; etc.

John 16, 1—33.   **11.**

Only a little while, Jesus continues, during the few hours of darkness in the tomb, He would be hidden from them. But the disciples did not understand. "What is it that He saith, A little while? We cannot tell what He saith." Jesus therefore explains what He means. They will weep and lament at the supposed loss of their Master, but the world, His enemies, will rejoice. "Ye shall be sorrowful, but your sorrow shall be turned into joy." An illustration is added of the pain suffered by a mother at the birth of a child. But upon the delivery of the child the anguish is turned into joy. So the sorrow of the disciples because of His announced departure, His suffering and death, will after "a little while," after His resurrection, be turned into joy that nothing will be able to take from them; for they will rejoice over the heavenly treasures that He will bring from the grave. And "in that day," after the outpouring of the Holy Spirit, all the questions which they would like to ask Him now will be answered. Then, after fully understanding His person and His work, they will address all their **"A Little While."** prayers to the Father in His name, which they have not done until now; and since they will receive what they ask for in His name, their joy will be full. They will pray the more confidently when He, through the Holy Spirit, will no longer speak in parables to them, but make God's entire wonderful counsel of salvation fully clear to them. Jesus moreover assures them that He need not first conciliate the Father in order that He may be willing to listen to their petitions, since in consequence of His work of redemption He is already reconciled to them, yea, loves them. — After these enlightening and comforting words of the Lord the disciples not only reaffirmed their faith in Him as the Son of the Father, but also intimated that all He had ever taught them had been understood by them now. Jesus, however, forewarned them that their faith would be put to a severe test. When His hour of suffering would come, they would all be scattered and, what is worse, cowardly desert Him. This dark hour of the beginning of His Passion was to be premonitory of the manifold tribulation they and all His followers would have to suffer throughout their lives, yet with this comfort to sustain them that they have peace with God through Him who has overcome the world and Satan.

John 17, 1—26.　　　　**12.**

After Jesus had finished His great farewell discourse, He lifted up His eyes to heaven and poured out His soul to God in words of infinite tenderness and love. The seventeenth chapter of St. John has been called the great sacerdotal prayer,[1] because the Lord on the very threshold of His Passion presents Himself to the Father as the true High Priest, making intercession for His disciples and for all such as would at some future time be joined to Him in faith. Where the words were spoken, whether in the upper room or in the courtyard or in some retreat on the way to Gethsemane, — hardly in the Temple, — the evangelist does not indicate.[2] It is quite possible that the whole farewell discourse was spoken as the disciples rose from the table, strapped on their sandals, stepped

The Great Intercessory Prayer.
out on the balcony, and were standing in the courtyard, very likely, "as He came out and went, as He was wont, to the Mount of Olives."[3] A party of twelve could not have conveniently talked together in the streets.[4] We can scarcely imagine that the discourse was uttered while they were passing through the narrow streets of Jerusalem,[5] and surely the prayer was not spoken then. As to the prayer, no more blessed or exalted voice was ever heard in earth or heaven. Plain and simple though it sounds, yet it is so deep, rich, and wide that none can fathom it.[6] Spener, a devout preacher, never ventured to preach upon it because he believed that its true understanding exceeded the ordinary measure of faith; but he caused it to be read to him three times on the evening before he died.[7] It naturally divides itself into three parts.

John 17, 1—26.　　　　**13.**

In the first place Jesus prays for Himself. It is at the culmination of His whole life's work and at the hour in which He went forth to suffering and death that He approaches the throne of

For Himself.
heaven with the words: "Father, the hour is come." He asks the Father to glorify His Son that the Son may glorify Him. The work of redemption which the Father gave Him to perform can now be considered accomplished,

---

12,　1) By David Chytraeus. Ylvisaker, 687.
　　2) See Meyer sub John 14, 31; 15, 1.
　　3) Luke 22, 39.　　　　　4) Dods sub John 14, 30.
　　5) Edersheim, II, 511.　　　6) Meyer, quoting Luther, p. 475.
　　7) Meyer sub John 17, p. 475.

and He asks the Father to lead Him through to glory and permit Him again to enjoy the undiminished glory which He shared with Him in heaven before the world began. It is a prayer for His own glorification as man, which glorification, however, will also redound to the benefit of men.[1] It is glorification linked up with the salvation of men. "This is life eternal, that they might know Thee the only true God, and Jesus Christ, whom Thou hast sent." [2]

John 17, 1—26.   **14.**

In the second place Jesus prays for His believing disciples who have accepted Him as the Messiah sent by the Father. Setting aside the unbelieving world, He makes the disciples the object of His prayer because they are His own. "I pray for them; I pray not for the world, but for them which Thou hast given Me; for they are Thine." Not as if He were praying against the world. For afterwards [1] He prays for all who to the end of the world will be brought to faith in Him by means of the Word. He prayed for His enemies at His crucifixion.[2] But since God's work has already been manifested to His disciples, He feels a certain responsibility for them. Viewing Himself as already gone from the world, thus depriving His disciples of His visible presence, He realizes that they are in need of His protection. In praying for them, He has two important objects in mind. "Holy Father, keep through Thine own name those whom Thou hast given Me that they may be one as We are." That is, keep them in true faith and in the

For His Disciples. confession of the saving truth that in no wise the spiritual union may be disturbed. While He was with them, He personally kept them in the faith. "Those that Thou gavest Me I have kept, and none of them is lost but the son of perdition, that the Scripture might be fulfilled." [3] We have already pointed out that Judas was not deliberately chosen for the purpose of playing the role of traitor.[4] He was chosen in good faith, but he turned traitor, and thus Scripture was fulfilled.[5] This prayer in behalf of the disciples is uttered

---

13, 1) Kretzmann, I, 503.

2) We notice that Jesus here solemnly in the third person speaks of Himself as Jesus Christ, the promised Messiah. See Mark 9, 41.

14, 1) V. 20.   2) Luke 23, 34.

3) John 18, 9; 13, 18; Ps. 69, 4; 109, 8; Acts 1, 20.

4) Chapter XXXI, 13.

5) Υἱὸς τῆς ἀπωλείας. The form "son of perdition" is in accordance with Hebrew usage. Compare 2 Thess. 2, 3; Is. 57, 4; Matt. 23, 15.

while He is still in their presence to assure them of His interest
in them. They will now be left in the world. The world will hate
them because they are not of the world. His prayer is not that
the Father would take them out of the world, but that He would
keep them from evil.[6] "Sanctify them through Thy truth; Thy
Word is truth." All the more should they be separated from all
that is impure and consecrated to God and His service because as
His apostles they are to be sent out into the world. As He brought
the sacrifice by which He made atonement for their sins, sanctified
and consecrated Himself for them in His divine office of Savior, so
they must dedicate themselves to the task of being His witnesses.

John 17, 1—26.   **15.**

Finally the Lord includes all future believers in His prayer.
"Neither pray I for these alone, but for them also which shall
believe on Me through their word." He prays that they may be
one in the Father and in Him and in loving union and communion
with one another. There should be no disruptions and discord
among them, already for the reason that Christian testimony and
unity may serve as a visible testimony that Jesus was sent of God.
The very existence of the Christian Church and the sincere love
and godly walk of the Christians should act as a missionary agency,
so "that the world may know that Thou hast sent Me and hast
loved them as Thou hast loved Me." And as Christ has received
glory from the Father, so there shall be glory for all those who
believe in Him. "Father, I will that they also whom Thou hast
given Me be with Me where I am." All the greater is His boldness
in making this request because the believers are a gift of God's

For All Believers. love and because the Father loved the Son
before the foundation of the world. In
conclusion He appeals to the justice of the Father as the basis
of His assurance. The world does not know God, but the believers
know that Christ was sent by God to redeem the world, and they
accept Him as their Savior. According to God's justice therefore
the believers must not share the fate of the unbelieving world; but
as the Father loves the Son, so He cannot but love those who believe
in Him and let them dwell with Him forever and behold His glory.
And as Christ has made known the name of God during His three-
year public ministry, so He will continue to do, even after the

---

14, 6) Ἐκ τοῦ πονηροῦ. "Evil" may be neuter or masculine in the sense
of "the Evil One." 1 John 2, 13; or Matt. 6, 13.

withdrawing of His visible presence, namely, by the Spirit of Truth, whom He will send. Thus the end and crown of all will be "that the love wherewith Thou hast loved Me may be in them and I in them." This was the final amen. As the last tones of this divine prayer were dying away, the Lord led His disciples into the "moonlit silence of the Oriental night" [1] in quest of that place of final seclusion which was to precede His willing death.

15, 1) Farrar, II, 304.

CHAPTER XXXIII

THURSDAY NIGHT TO FRIDAY MORNING OF PASSION WEEK.

AGONY IN GETHSEMANE, BETRAYAL, ARREST, AND TRIAL BEFORE JEWISH AUTHORITIES.

April 6 and 7, 30 A. D., 783 A. U. C.

A. U. C.	779	780	781	782	783
A. D.	26	27	28	29	30
Age of Jesus	30	31	32	33	34

Nisan (or Abib)

10	11	12	13	14	15	16	17

April

2	3	4	5	6	7	8	9
Sun.	Mon.	Tue.	Wed.	Thu.	Fri.	Sat.	Sun.

783 A. U. C.			APRIL			30 A. D.
Sun.	Mon.	Tue.	Wed.	Thu.	Fri.	Sat.
						1
2	3	4	5	6	7	8
9	10	11	12	13	14	15
16	17	18	19	20	21	22
23	24	25	26	27	28	29
30						

1.

Matt. 26, 36—46. Mark 14, 32—42. Luke 22, 39—46. John 18, 1.[1]

It was the night in which Jesus was betrayed. Whether it was one of the Eastern gates, north or south of the Temple area, through which the Savior left the city of Jerusalem on His way across the brook of Kidron [2] to His retreat on the slopes of the

---

1, 1) Matthew and Mark narrate the Lord's announcement of Peter's denial as if it had taken place after they had left the upper room and were on their way to the Mount of Olives; Luke and John, as taking place before they had left the room. For our arrangement see chapter XXXII, 1. 12. John does not mention the agony in Gethsemane. It is, however, implied in the reference to the cup which the Father had given Him to drink, John 18, 11, compared with the prayer to remove the cup recorded by the Synoptists in the present section.

2) At other times the brook over which David had fled before Absalom, 2 Sam. 15, 23, was only a dry ravine, but at this time of the year it was filled with water, τοῦ χειμάρρου τῶν Κέδρων, John 18, 1. (The meaning of the term for brook is "winter flowing," and the expression Kidron is variously explained as "of the cedars," "to become black," and "a spot for enclosure of cattle.") See Dods sub John 18, 1.

Mount of Olives, we do not know. The place was called Gethsemane, or Oil Press, and probably was a small garden or orchard
connected with some near-by olive-press, from which it received its
name. What to-day is pointed out as the site of the sacred spot,
a walled-in enclosure, containing eight old olive-trees, is about

**The Agony of Jesus
in Gethsemane.**
seventy steps square. The location
is probably approximately correct,
although the gnarled old olive-trees
can hardly be those of the time of Jesus.[3] From the expression "as
was His wont" [4] we assume that it was a spot frequently used by
Jesus as a retreat and that it was the property of an unknown man
who was a friend of the Lord. It was a quiet resting-place, very appropriate for retirement and prayer, perhaps also for sleep, used as
such before this and known to the disciples, also to Judas, who was
soon to make his appearance. After Jesus had passed through the
entrance of the garden, He pointed out a certain spot for eight
of His disciples to sit and rest, while He Himself advanced with
Peter, James, and John a stone's cast farther for the purpose of
praying. It was fit that the three disciples who had been witnesses
of His glory, when He raised the daughter of Jairus [5] and when
He was on the Mount of Transfiguration,[6] should now become
witnesses of, and a source of comfort in, His agony,[7] but also
because Peter had vehemently assured Him of his loyalty [8] and
the sons of Zebedee had so confidently professed their ability to
drink His cup.[9]

2.

*Matt. 26, 36—46. Mark 14, 32—42. Luke 22, 39—46.
John 18, 1.*

It was the hour of trial. As a real man Jesus felt the need of
a few intimate friends. Anticipating the pain of the coming
struggle, He announces: "My soul is exceeding sorrowful, even
unto death." [1] But soon the society of His most trusted friends
was more than He could bear. Before Him was a struggle in
which He must engage alone. Casting Himself forward a little,
but being still in their hearing and asking them to watch with Him

---

1,   3) E. W. G. Masterman, in *Int. St. B. Encycl.* under "Gethsemane."
   4) Luke 22, 39.   5) Mark 5, 37.   6) Matt. 17, 1.
   7) Ἀγωνία, Luke 22, 44. Here only in the New Testament. From
this word comes the expression "agony in the Garden." Bruce *sub loco*.
   8) Matt. 26, 35.   9) Matt. 20, 22.
2,   1) Ps. 42, 6.

in this bitter hour, He fell upon His knees and prayed: "Abba,
Father! O My Father, all things are possible unto Thee; if it be
possible, take away this cup from Me; nevertheless not My will,
but Thine, be done." The three evangelists here, as so often, supplement each other. Obedient to the will of the Father, yet trembling with fear, the holy Son of God shudders as He comes in
close contact with death. And there was also the onslaught of
Satan, the powers of dark-

"Father, if Thou Be Willing, Remove This Cup."

ness.[2] It was a terrible
struggle, in which our sal-
vation was at stake. But we must not intrude too closely upon
the awful scene. The Savior's prayer was heard by the Father
because He was satisfied with His beloved Son's submissive obedience. During His agony there came an angel from heaven,
strengthening Him and encouraging Him to carry out the work of
redemption, probably by picturing to Him the glorious result of
His substitutionary suffering. But for the present the struggle
went on.[3] When He was in great agony, "His sweat was as it were
great drops of blood falling down to the ground." It is Luke, the
physician, who reports the rare phenomenon of the bloody sweat.
When one is under the pressure of supreme agony or fear, not only
the waters of perspiration, but also blood oozes through the pores.
It is reported that under certain psychological or physiological conditions other such actual cases of bloody sweat have occurred.[4]
And even if there were no instances of bloody sweat in the medical
records, the historical character of this phenomenon would nevertheless come under the same category as that of the angelic
strengthening.

2,   2) Luke 22, 53.

3) As Luke alone mentions the appearing of an angel, it is not certain
where this should be inserted in the accounts of Matthew and Mark. Some
place it between the first and second prayer, believing that the angel came at
this juncture to strengthen Him for that still more terrible struggle, when
He was sweating great drops of blood. Others think the death agony and
the sweating of blood took place before the appearance of the angel, indeed,
that he was sent by the Father after this culmination of the Lord's soul-
suffering had been reached, although narrated after it. The latter would not
have been contrary to the practise of Luke, as may be seen from other sections
of his gospel. See chapter XXXI, 8. Andrews, 502.

4) H. L. Luering, in *Int. St. B. Encycl.*, under "Sweat." Edersheim,
II, 540, n. 3. Vv. 43. 44 are missing in some codices. Ὁ ἱδρὼς αὐτοῦ ὡσεὶ
θρόμβοι αἵματος. Θρόμβοι, clots, not drops, of blood. Here only in the
New Testament. A lump, or curd, of blood. Nowhere else used in the
sense of drops. But the disciples may have seen this mark of agony as clots
of blood on His forehead or on the ground.

3.

Matt. 26, 36—46. Mark 14, 32—42. Luke 22, 39—46. John 18, 1.

Rising from prayer, the Savior returned to His three disciples and found them asleep. To have heard one word of encouragement from their lips would have been music to His soul.[1] There was pain in His heart when He shook the slumberers, addressing Himself especially to Peter: "Simon, sleepest thou? Couldest not thou watch one hour?" It seems that the term "one hour" is a proverbial expression, without reference to the particular time. The disciples were aroused, but hardly sufficiently to heed the admonition: "Watch and pray that ye enter not into temptation." The "fiery Sons of Thunder" and the would-be valiant Peter were fast asleep. What the other eight disciples were doing does not appear. Most likely they, too, were asleep.[2] The hour was late, and the disciples were tired. Of course, they were as compassionate, tender-feeling, and sad as they could be under the circumstances; but deep grief is apt to relax the tension of the nerves, with the result that such a person involuntarily falls asleep. And that is exactly what happened; they were "sleeping for sorrow," as Luke states. It is true that children cry themselves to sleep; but sleep in this case was also a mark of in-**The Sleeping Disciples.** difference and a result of disregard of warnings, although the loving Lord put the best construction upon the behavior of His disciples by saying: "The spirit is willing, but the flesh is weak." Again Jesus retired and prayed: "O My Father, if this cup may not pass away from Me, except I drink it, Thy will be done." Once more the devil had made his onslaught, but failed. And in spite of the chilly evening[3] the disciples were sleeping again. Their eyes were heavy with unseasonable sleep, and they knew not how to excuse themselves. For the third time Jesus left them and prayed. And for the third time He returned, this time completely strengthened and triumphant. He now aroused His disciples with the words: "Sleep on now and take your rest."[4] No longer was He in need of their watchful interest. Still, "it is

---

3, 1) Ylvisaker, 698.

2) As inferred from Luke, who does not mention the three.

3) John 18, 18.

4) Not ironically or sarcastically, hardly interrogatively. See Bruce sub Matt. 26, 45.

enough!" [5])   Arise!   Awake!   "The hour is come.   Behold, the
Son of Man is betrayed into the hands of sinners.   Rise up, let
us go!   Lo, he that betrayeth Me is at hand!"

4.

*Matt. 26, 47—50. Mark 14, 43—46. Luke 22, 47. 48.
John 18, 2—9.*

While Jesus yet spake, Judas approached with a multitude
composed of Roman soldiers from the cohort [1]) stationed in the
garrison of the castle of Antonia, members of the Temple guard,[2])
Jewish leaders, and private citizens.   It was a motley band.   The
Roman soldiers of course were regularly armed with swords, but
also, as at other times, with staves,[3]) for the purpose of keeping
order against possible Passover disturbances.   The Temple guard
was unarmed, but probably in this case these members of the
Levitical police were deputized to assist in the arrest of Jesus, to
resist possible interference, and were supplied, if not with swords,
with cudgels and, in spite of the full moon, with torches and
lanterns.   As to the exact progress of events there is some diversity
of opinion.[4])   Whether the multitude mentioned by the Synoptists

The Betrayal of Judas. was in addition to the arresting
party, itself a large number, or
not, is of little importance.   Since Judas had brought the word
earlier in the evening, there had been hasty conferences in Jerusalem.   Messengers were sent to and fro, from the palace of
Caiaphas to the hall of Pilate.   Orders were issued and dispatched
to the castle of Antonia and to the Temple guard.   The forces of
darkness were busy.   Rumor was naturally very active in throwing
out hints about a riot which would be ready to break out at any
moment.   And all this while the suspected rioters, the disciples of

---

3,   5) One of those puzzling expressions of Mark for which many explanations are given.   Bruce *sub loco.* Ἀπέχει, *sufficit.*   "I have conquered in
the struggle.   I no longer need your sympathy." Etc.

4,   1) Λαβὼν τὴν σπεῖραν, John 18, 3.   Cohort, the tenth part of a legion,
about 600 men.   Under the command of a χιλίαρχος, tribune, or master of
a thousand, John 18, 12.

2) The servants of the high priests, led by the captains of the Temple,
στρατηγοὺς τοῦ ἱεροῦ, Luke 22, 52.   They had no independent criminal jurisdiction outside the Temple area.   The Sanhedrin, not possessing the power
of the sword, had of course neither soldiery nor a regularly armed band at
command.   Edersheim, II, 541; II, I, 187.   However, see Schuerer, II,
I, 187: "Possessed the right of ordering and making arrests."

3) Josephus, *Wars.* II, IX, 4.

4) In fitting the account of John in before or after the kiss as recorded
by the Synoptists.

Jesus, were fast asleep. — Soon a band of mixed forces was making its way to the Mount of Olives. A signal had been agreed upon for the establishment of the identity of Jesus. As soon as He would be singled out, the guard was to seize Him and lead Him away; and Judas had said "safely." [5] He might slip out of your hands! This He had done at other times.[6] Here we have one of the involuntary traces of the secret terror and misgivings of Judas.[7]

5.

Matt. 26, 47—50. Mark 14, 43—46. Luke 22, 47. 48.
John 18, 2—9.

We picture the scene to ourselves as follows. Judas is in advance of the crowd. He hastily approaches Jesus. He is in sight of the armed band, a short distance in the rear. He is a traitor. His part is to play the hypocrite, to deceive Jesus and the disciples, perhaps coming in the nick of time to warn Jesus of the danger which was even now threatening at His heel. He advanced and greeted Jesus with the title "Hail, Master!" so as to be heard by the rest.

"Judas, Betrayest Thou the Son of Man with a Kiss?" "And kissed Him." Not only did he give Him the customary Oriental greeting, which included a kiss, but he actually covered Him with kisses.[1] In all innocence — apparently. But it was a signal to those now at his heels. Jesus suffered the indignity. But He showed that He was not in ignorance of the meaning of what would otherwise have been the usual greeting. "Friend," comrade, "wherefore art thou come?"[2] Is it for this purpose that thou art come? "Judas, betrayest thou the Son of Man with a kiss?" Judas had betrayed Jesus to His enemies, but he had also betrayed himself.

6.

Matt. 26, 47—50. Mark 14, 43—46. Luke 22, 47. 48.
John 18, 2—9.

At this point, it seems, the notices of John come in. The signal had been given in plain sight of the advancing band. But Jesus Himself took matters in hand. "Whom seek ye?" They answered: "Jesus of Nazareth." To the title by which He was

---

4,   5) Ἀσφαλῶς. Mark 14, 44.

6) Luke 4, 30; John 8, 59.   7) Farrar, II, 319, n. 1.

5,   1) Κατεφίλησεν.

2) Ἑταῖρε, ἐφ᾽ ᾧ or ἐφ᾽ ὅ — πάρει; See commentaries.

commonly known Jesus responded: "I am He." By this time
Judas was standing with the party to which he actually belonged.
Struck by the majesty of the word "I am He" they fell to the
ground. While they were still "cowering and struggling," [1)] Jesus,

"Whom Seek Ye?" permitting them to rise, again asked
them: "Whom seek ye?" Once more
they replied: "Jesus of Nazareth." Thus Jesus forced them to
make their mission public. He would not suffer Himself to be
taken and put away, as it were, on the sly. But He stated the terms
of His arrest. "I have told you that I am He. If ye therefore
seek Me, let these go their way." Jesus would permit Himself to
be taken, but the disciples must go free, and this in fulfilment of
the sacerdotal prayer: "Those that Thou gavest Me I have kept,
and none of them is lost." [2)] Then they laid their hands on Jesus
and took Him.

7.

Matt. 26, 51—54. Mark 14, 47. Luke 22, 49—51.
    John 18, 10. 11.

This was too much for Peter, who by this time was wide
awake. When he and others saw the enemies step forward to lay
unholy hands on Jesus, they cried out: "Lord, shall we smite with
a sword?" They had only two swords,[1)] but they would not have
their Lord delivered into the hands of His captors without a blow.
Without waiting for the reply of Jesus, Peter drew forth his sword
and with an ill-timed blow slashed off the right ear of a man named
Malchus, who happened to be the servant of the high priest. Peter
thought he was able to protect Jesus with physical force, and it was
his intention no doubt to cleave the servant's head. But in resort-
ing to violence, he made an ordinary rioter of himself besides
making the case look bad for Jesus. Jesus could not afford to
implicate Himself in this rash deed of an impassioned disciple.
Peter did not realize what he was doing. In offering resistance to
those who were on the point of arresting Jesus, he was blocking
salvation for himself. Jesus reprimanded him by saying: "Put up

Peter's Untimely Zeal. thy sword into the sheath. The
cup which My Father hath given
Me, shall I not drink it?" The sword has its place, but not here.
By his action Peter had provided a just cause for the sword to be
turned against him. "For all they that take the sword shall perish

---

6,   1) Farrar, II, 322.   2) John 17, 12.
7,   1) Luke 22, 38.

with the sword." Jesus did not need this kind of assistance, especially not in this case, when it meant resistance to lawful government. If it were God's will that His Son should be rescued, it could be done in different ways. "Thinkest thou that I cannot now pray to My Father and He shall presently give Me more than twelve legions of angels?" Not merely out of twelve disciples two protecting swords, but for each of the twelve disciples more than six thousand angels, according to the standard of the Roman army. "But how, then, shall the Scriptures be fulfilled that thus it must be?" By his rash act Peter would harm the cause of Christ besides frustrating salvation for himself. The damage must be repaired. With the words "Suffer ye thus far," [2] meaning probably, Just a moment, please! or, Forget about this single act of resistance! Jesus touched the ear of Malchus and healed him.

8.

Matt. 26, 55. 56 a. Mark 14, 48. 49. Luke 22, 51—54 a. John 18, 12.

After Jesus had called His bellicose disciple to order, He turned to the crowd which closed in on Him to make the arrest. Already some of the elders, chief priests, and Temple officials in the crowd were coming forward to gaze on Him with "insulting curiosity." [1] But Jesus had one more word to say before He permitted His holy and unresisting hands to be placed into disgraceful bonds: "Be ye come out as against a thief with swords and staves?"

"Be Ye Come Out as against a Thief with Swords and Staves?" Was He one of those Sicarii that infested the country in the final struggle with Rome? [2] Neither was he a robbing bandit, nor was He hiding from justice. "When I was daily with you in the Temple, ye stretched forth no hands against Me." The point is not that they did not make the attempt, but that His behavior and speech were without reproach and that He did not have to slink into hiding like a common thief. But this is done, namely, His submission to the present disgrace, "that the Scriptures of the prophets might be fulfilled." And even as their nature agreed with the hour of the night, so it was their hour and the power of darkness.

7, 2) Ἐᾶτε ἕως τούτου.
8, 1) Farrar, II, 324.
2) Josephus, *Wars*, VII, I, 1.

9.

Matt. 26, 56b. Mark 14, 50—52.

These fatal words to His captors quenched the last hope in the minds of the disciples. They realized that the announcements of Jesus about His capture had to be literally understood. Then they, all of them, also the fiery Peter, the loving John, the stolid Thomas, left Him and fled. Jesus was now entirely alone. Another drop was added to the bitter cup.[1] And still, for the present He was not entirely alone. There remained an unknown and interested witness, a certain young man, as some think, the Evangelist Mark,

The Disciples Flee. by whom this incident has been recorded. It is like a "monogram in the corner of the picture." [2] When the band went to the Mount of Olives, he was for some reason or other found in the crowd. Assuming that he was a disciple of Jesus, he had received notice of the movement to arrest Him and was apparently aroused from sleep, for he had nothing but a linen sheet [3] cast about his naked body. Attention was attracted, or suspicions were aroused, on account of this curious guise. He was seized by the linen cloth. Whereupon the terrified stranger left the linen cloth in the snatching hands and fled away naked. After this Jesus, with His hands tied to His back, was left absolutely alone.

10.

13. 14.
John 18, 19—23.[1]

Surrounded by Roman soldiers and followed by Jewish emissaries, Jesus once more went forth into the night, but this time like a sheep led to the slaughter, over the Kidron, through one of

---

9,   1) Bruce sub Matt. 26, 56.

2) Bruce sub Mark 14, 52.   3) Σινδών.

10, 1) The Jewish trial comprised three stages: the preliminary examination by Annas, the informal trial by the Sanhedrin, and the formal trial after dawn. With these are related the denials of Peter and the suicide of Judas. Each of the four gospels records the denials of Peter, but the details differ considerably, as must be the case where various reports point out certain features and pass over the rest. Of these three stages of the trial John apparently gives the first stage, Matthew and Mark give the second stage fully and mention the third only briefly, while Luke mentions the last part of the Jewish trial. — Between verses 14 and 19 and following verse 24 John records the denial of Peter. Likewise the other three evangelists insert the incident into their account, Matthew and Mark as running through the second stage of the trial and Luke as preceding that of the final session. In separating the trials and throwing together the denials, we are following the lead of the gospels in an attempt to give a combined arrangement of the progress of events. We must, however, confess our inability to arrange exactly all circumstances into a complete program. See A. T. Robertson, *Harmony of the Gospels,* notes on pages 209 and 212.

the eastern gates, and up the slopes of the city. The strange procession reached its destination at the palace of Caiaphas, the high priest, which at this time seems to have been occupied by the two "prime movers in the black iniquity," [2] Annas and his son-in-law Joseph Caiaphas. We are bearing in mind that Judea was under Roman rule and administered by Pontius Pilate, who usually resided at the seaport Caesarea,[3] but during the annual Passover deemed it expedient to establish his headquarters in the ancient palace of Herod.[4] It was the policy of Rome to flatter its conquered nations

Jesus First Brought before Annas. with a semblance of self-government and to be tolerant, especially in matters of religion.[5] In general, there were but two rules which had to be strictly obeyed, proper regard for the *pax Romana* and the payment of taxes. Thus in Judea the ancient ecclesiastical tribunal, the honorable Council of the Seventy,[6] was still permitted to try all religious offenses and to punish offenders. In the matter of serious offenses and where the verdict was a sentence of death, the case had to be retried by the governor; and the carrying out of the sentence of the Sanhedrin, if it was confirmed, devolved upon him. In the present case it was at the instance of the Sanhedrin, as led by Caiaphas, the acting high priest, that Jesus was arrested. But as a matter of fact his father-in-law, Annas, a man of seventy, who had been high priest himself twenty years before and after him five of his sons and one son-in-law, was still the power behind the throne.[7]

13. 14.
John 18, 19—23. **11.**

In ancient days the high-priesthood was an office for life;[1] but since the days of Herod and the Roman rule the dignity had been degraded from a permanent and sacred religious office to a "temporary secular distinction." [2] Josephus tells us that from

10, 2) Farrar, II, 328.

   3) *Ant.*, XVIII, III, 1. *Wars*, II, IX, 2, etc.

   4) *Wars*, II, XIV, 8; XV, 5.

   5) Stalker, *Trial and Death of Jesus*, 16.

   6) On the Sanhedrin and the high priests see Schuerer, II, I, 163 ff.

   7) Annas, 6—15 A. D.; Eleazer (son), 16 and 17 A. D.; Caiaphas (son-in-law), 18—36 A. D.; Jonathan (son), 36 and 37 A. D.; Theophilos (son), 37 A. D.; Matthias (son), 41 A. D.; Annas (son), 62 A. D. Schuerer, II, I, 198 ff.

11, 1) Ex. 29, 9. 29.   2) Farrar, II, 329.

the days of Herod the Great to the taking of Jerusalem there were twenty-eight high priests in one hundred and seven years.[3] No longer did the high priests rule by the grace and in the fear of God, but by the grace of the Romans and in their own interest. As to Caiaphas, it was he who, being used by the Lord as His instrument to speak a divine prophecy, had given the counsel "that it was expedient that one man should die for the people." [4] Both he and Annas, including their families, were cold, haughty, and

The House of Annas.   worldly Sadducees,[5] an able, but an ambitious and arrogant race.[6]

The Talmud preserves a sort of street ballad which characterizes the popular hatred against this infamous house: "Woe is me for the house of Annas! Woe is me for their whisperings" (snakelike hissings and secret denouncements)! "For they are the high priests and their sons the treasurers; their sons-in-law are Temple officers, and their servants beat the people with their staves." [7] Jealous of their power and fearful of losing it, they were filled with deadly hatred against the great Miracle-worker and popular Teacher, who a few days previous had for the second time cleansed the Temple and "interfered with their illicit and greedy gains." And there was good reason why Annas, who is remembered by his own people as the head of "a viper brood," should strain to the utmost his cruel power to "crush a Prophet whose actions threatened to make him and his family wholly contemptible and comparatively poor." [8]

13. 14.   **12.**
John 18, 19—23.

To Annas, Jesus was brought first. This gave him a chance to subject the Savior to an initial investigation, and it allowed time for the Sanhedrin to assemble. Of course, this session was not quite legal. The midnight meetings of the Sanhedrin, which were illegal, and other features of the Passion history recorded by the gospel-writers are sometimes pointed to as proofs that not all the statements of the gospel-writers are historically correct. But in the proceedings against Jesus, which were a mockery and a shameful perversion of all justice, such an illegal course of action is rather to be expected. Since there was an opportunity of getting rid of

---

11, 3) *Ant.,* XX, 10.   4) John 11, 49. 50.
    5) *Ant.,* XX, IX, 1.   6) Stalker, 18.
    7) Quotation from *Jesus of Nazareth* by Joseph Klausner, a Jewish writer from Jerusalem, p. 337.
    8) Farrar, II, 335.

Jesus before the festal Sabbath,[1]) the members of the Sanhedrin were in trouble and in haste. Imagine what might happen if Jerusalem awoke in the morning and found the popular Teacher in the hands of His unpopular enemies! At all events He had to be accused, tried, condemned, and delivered into the strong hands of the Romans

Preliminary Investigation. before morning and before the multitudes had learned what it was all about. While messengers scoured the city for an urgent midnight meeting, Annas asked Jesus of His disciples and of His teaching.[2]) The purpose of the question was to ensnare Him into some incriminating statement and to advance some charge of secret sedition and unorthodox teaching. Jesus replied — and for all His calmness His answer contained a stinging rebuke —: "I spake openly to the world. Why askest thou Me? Ask them which heard Me." Thereupon a miserable underling, probably seeing an indignant blush on the high-priestly face, struck Jesus in the mouth, saying: "Answerest Thou the high priest so?" The face which angels behold in wonder is struck by a contemptible slave! [3]) But without a trace of temper Jesus reproved this impudent transgressor: "If I have spoken evil, bear witness of the evil; but if well, why smitest thou Me?" Jesus was well aware that the high priest was a "ruler of the people," [4]) and He had only given him, respectfully, but firmly, a reply such as his questioning deserved.

13.

Matt. 26, 59—66.[1])   *Mark 14, 55—64.*[1])   *Luke 22, 54 a.*[1])
    57   *53*
John 18, 24 a.[1])

In the mean while the Sanhedrin had been assembled. Into its august presence, the members seated in a semicircle around the high priest, Joseph Caiaphas, and his two clerks, whose duty it was to count the votes, Jesus was led.[2]) The seventy members themselves, with the high priest as the seventy-first, were made up of Sad-

---

12, 1) Mark 14, 2. The murdering of Jesus during the feast was at first regarded as out of the question.

    2) Stalker, 19.   3) Farrar, II, 336.   4) Ex. 22, 28.

13, 1) The account interspaced with the denials of Peter.

    2) The regular place of meeting was the Hall Gazith, the Chamber of Hewn Stone, in the Temple buildings. We must regard this meeting in the palace of Caiaphas as an exception to the rule. For meetings of the Sanhedrin see Schuerer, II, I, 190 ff.; Edersheim, II, 553 ff.; James Stalker, *The Trial and Death of Jesus Christ*, 20 ff.

ducean priests, non-professional elders, and pharisaic Rabbis or scribes. Ordinarily, in judicial trials, witnesses are on hand. But in this case witnesses had to be found. And though many witnesses came, their witness did not agree. Many were called to testify

Jesus Led before the Sanhedrin. against Jesus, but the fiasco grew worse and worse. This would not do! If incriminating evidence could not be obtained in any other way, false witnesses must be sought, whose accusations would be of such a nature as to justify the High Council to pass a verdict of death upon Jesus.

14.

Matt. 26, 59—66.   Mark 14, 55—64.   Luke 22, 54 a.
*   57   53*
*   John 18, 24 a.*

At length two witnesses were brought into approximate agreement, out of which, it was hoped a successful charge could be constructed. As this was an ecclesiastical court, Jesus had to be charged with having taught false doctrine and at the same time having offended against the Moral Law, so as to make it a misdemeanor punishable by the civil court. Thus the testimony against Jesus centered upon a statement made in the early days of His public ministry about destroying the Temple and in three days building it again.[1] But while one witness twisted the words to refer to the physical Temple, the other possibly testified that the

False Witnesses. reference was made to a temple built without hands. Just how the statement should constitute a criminal offense, except if it was argued that Christ had spoken of demolishing a public building of the city, the Temple, does not appear. The fact of the matter was that the words of Jesus were neither a command to destroy nor a promise to restore the Temple of Jerusalem after its destruction, but a veiled reference to His death and resurrection. At any rate, it was as clear as day, even to the high priest, that out of these words a successful charge of blasphemy preferred against the Prisoner before them could not be constructed. Jesus looked on in absolute silence while His disunited enemies confuted one another's testimony. Mark these silences of Jesus! There will be more as the trial proceeds. As the carefully prepared "arrows of perjuries" fell at the Savior's feet,[2] it looked as if the enemies would fail for the lack of a few consistent lies.

14, 1) John 2, 19.   2) Farrar, II, 340.

15.

Matt. 26, 59—66. Mark 14, 55—64. Luke 22, 54 a.
        57   53
John 18, 24 a.

Overcome with a paroxysm of anger lest, after all, his thirst for blood go unslaked, the high priest sprang to his feet. "Answerest Thou nothing? What is it which these witness against Thee?" But Jesus held His peace. Reduced almost to utter despair and fury, the high priest now took one more arrow from his quiver of unrighteousness. It concerned not what properly belonged to the sphere of the court, what the Defendant had done, but what He was, at least what He claimed He was, as had been consistently reported to the high priest and as he most likely had himself ascertained in his interview with Judas.[1] "I adjure Thee by the living God that Thou tell us whether Thou be the Christ, the Son of God." As this concerned a holy and eternal truth, this question had to be answered. Apparently Jesus recognized the right of the high priest to put Him under oath. At least He saw that silence at this point would have been construed as a withdrawal of His claims. Decidedly and solemnly He therefore answered: "Thou hast said; I am." [2] For the moment His accusers were His judges.

"Whether Thou Be the Christ, the Son of God." But some day He would be theirs. For He adds: "Hereafter shall ye see the Son of Man sitting on the right hand of Power and coming in the clouds of heaven." What was that? "Power?" "Clouds of heaven?" [3] Even from the standpoint of their false conception there could be no mistaking as to these Messianic references. It has often been stated that Christians claim for Christ what He did not assert of Himself. But here we have a straightforward, properly witnessed affidavit of the deity of Christ.[4] If Jesus was the Messiah, then He was the Son of God. And if He was the one, He was the other *ipso facto.* And if He was the Son of God, then He was also God. This clearly, incontrovertibly, follows. But what appears as the most glorious truth to the believing heart was as blasphemy in the horrified ears of the Sanhedrin. The cry of "Blasphemy!" reverberated through the sacred hall. In holy horror the high priest rent

---

15, 1) Luke 22, 4.
    2) $\Sigma \grave{v}\ \epsilon \tilde{\iota} \pi a \varsigma = {}' E \gamma \acute{\omega}\ \epsilon \tilde{\iota} \mu \acute{\iota}$, I am, in current usage.
    3) See Ps. 110, 1; Dan. 7, 13.
    4) Stalker, 25.

his clothes.[5] "What need we any further witnesses? Ye have heard the blasphemy. What think ye?" he exclaims. Obviously it was not blasphemy for a man to call himself the Messiah in a country where a Messiah was expected, unless of course he did so falsely. And that was the point which here at the outset was taken for granted. "He is worthy of death!" He is a *ben maveth*, a son of death! was their impassioned reply.[6]

16.

58   1)   54   1)
Matt. 26, 69—75.   Mark 14, 66—72.   Luke 22, 54 c—62.[1]
           15—18 1)
   John 18, 25—27.

Now we come back to what happened in the mean while. After the first panic of Christ's capture in the Garden of Gethsemane and the flight of the disciples two of them, Peter and another, had so far recovered as to steal behind the moving mass.[2] It was only when the band was nearing its destination, the palace of the high priest, that they pushed forward, a disciple, presumably John, entering with Jesus into the courtyard, Peter, however, remaining behind until such time as admission for him could be procured. Let us try to picture to ourselves the scene. Where our houses look out into the street, an Oriental house looks upon an open, yet enclosed inner court, reached through an arched passage, which is usually guarded and watched. When the arresting party arrived with their Prisoner, the gate was opened, the whole party admitted, including the disciple whom we may surmise to have been John, who was acquainted with the high priest. But Peter was shut out. As the

The Denials of Peter. sequel shows, it would have been better had his exclusion been final.

It seems that John occupied a higher social level than the rest of the Twelve. Since the Gospel of St. John is rich with details of the Judean ministry of Jesus, it has been claimed with a good degree of likelihood that he had spent quite a bit of his time previous to his discipleship in Jerusalem, perhaps as the youthful

---

15, 5) As may be seen from 2 Kings 18, 37 the rending of garments as an indication of unusual provocation was indulged in above all on hearing any utterance of a blasphemous nature.   That part of the Law which forbade the high priest to rend his garments had reference merely to mourning for the dead, Lev. 10, 6; Cf. also 21, 10.

   6) Lev. 24, 15; Deut. 18, 20. Death was the penalty for blasphemy and for a false prophet. Bruce sub Matt. 26, 66.

16, 1) For arrangement see note 10, 1.   2) Stalker, 32.

representative of his father's prosperous fish business in the capital city.[3] At any rate the disciple in question was known to the high priest, also to the servants at the gate, because shortly after he had entered the palace, he went out to the maid that kept the door and brought Peter in. It was a friendly act. And still it was an ill turn which he did his fellow-disciple. Neither of these two disciples had any business to be there. John did not enter as the disciple of Jesus, but as the friend of the high priest. And as to Peter, it was his purpose to see the end; but thus he was led into temptation. After he had been admitted, John, it seems, hurried across the court into the hall where Jesus was, to witness the proceedings. Not so Peter. He did not feel at home in that strange, big house. He felt more at ease among the servants; but even there he was out of place.

17.

58   54
Matt. 26, 69—75. Mark 14, 66—72. Luke 22, 54b—62.
15—18
John 18, 25—27.

It was long past midnight by this time, and the spring air was cold and chilly. In the center of the court the servants had built a fire to warm themselves and were now standing with others around the coals of fire. It was this miscellaneous group that Peter resolved to join. But he did not "belong." He was in danger, though in another sense than he had supposed. It was not bodily peril. That would have been an eventuality which his fiery nature would have been able to cope with. But he did not anticipate dangers to his soul. Yet that was the very danger lurking in the shadows at the fire. No doubt the fireside rang with jests about the Prisoner who had been captured. Peter was silent. He did not interrupt their conversation. He simulated disinterest and indifference. It is when least expected that temptation like a wild **The First Denial.** animal sneaks up and strikes a sudden blow. Already in the darkened archway Peter's pretended indifference and betraying restlessness had attracted the portress by whom he had been admitted. As a hypocrite Peter was a failure. When the gatekeeper was relieved by another maid, she stepped closer to the fire to verify her suspicious intuition concerning Peter. She fixed upon him an earnest gaze.

16, 3) The view of Nonnus, an Egyptian scholar, writing about 400 A. D. He wrote a paraphrase on the Gospel of St. John. B. Matthew, 447.

No, she was not mistaken! With a flash of recognition she exclaimed: "And thou also wast with Jesus of Nazareth!" What an honor! To what greater praise could mortal man ever aspire? What better inscription could be engraved on the tombstone of a Christian's grave than the words: "He was also with Jesus of Nazareth"? At another time Peter himself would have desired none better. But here he was taken off guard. A mask had suddenly been torn from his face. But instead of taking himself in hand, since the mask did not fit him anyhow, and confessing before all, he denied, lamely saying: "I know not what thou sayest." How easily, how quickly, Peter glided and fell!

18.

58   54
Matt. 26, 69—75.   Mark 14, 66—72.   Luke 22, 54 b—62.
15—18
John 18, 25—27.

For a while Peter was at rest. None pursued the subject broached by the portress. No one bothered him. But he felt uneasy and warm. There was a fire burning within him. Quietly he slunk away from the glowing embers to the arch-covered entrance of the open court. He suddenly felt in need of refreshing air. Just then the crowing of a cock "smote unheeded on his guilty ear." [1] But it did not occur to him that Christ had said: "Verily I say unto thee, That this day, even in this night, before the cock crow twice, thou shalt deny Me thrice." [2] And not only that. If he only had heeded the warning! But he did not. That

The Second Denial. is the way of sin. Such is our miserable human nature. You may talk all you want to about human nature, since the Fall it is a miserable human nature. A second maid replaced Peter's first accuser. At that moment she probably was talking with a number of men. Pointing Peter out to them, she came forward and said: "This fellow was also with Jesus of Nazareth." Poor Peter! Again he was felled to the ground by the gentle touch of a "woman's hand." And how often a woman's "jeering laugh and saucy tongue" have made a man feel ashamed of his highest and holiest possessions! This time it took more than a mere denial to set Peter straight in the eyes of those servants. "He flung at her an angry oath." He denied with an oath and said: "I do not know the man!" This was the second denial. [3]

18, 1) Farrar, II, 347.   2) Mark 14, 30.   3) Stalker, 37.

19.

58   54

Matt. 26, 69—75. Mark 14, 66—72. Luke 22, 54b—62.
15—18
John 18, 25—27.

No sooner had this false oath passed Peter's lips than cold shivers rushed down his back. By this time an hour had passed. Turning on his heels, he returned to the fire. He was now completely wild. He was boiling with conflicting emotions, and his mouth was out of control. Before he had been silent. Now he would talk. Assuming an air of defiance, he threw himself into the conversation, outdoing all the rest in coarse and noisy talk. He would show them that he had not been with Jesus of Nazareth. But before he knew it, he was fatally betrayed by his rough "Galilean burr." [1] "Surely thou also art one of them," the scoffing firesiders insisted, "for thy speech betrayeth thee." Galilean speech was defective as to the pronunciation of the gutturals. But Peter would show them! He would also be very careful lest his *sh* sound like a *th*.[2] When you are with the Romans, you must do as the Romans, is an old proverb. But the more Peter tried, the less he succeeded. A Christian cannot twist his mouth to speak the lan-

The Third Denial. guage of the devil. And the more he tries, the more he becomes a laughing-stock for the devil. In spite of his oaths and denials Peter was utterly despised. A kinsman of the wounded Malchus, whose ear Peter had slashed off in the Garden, stoutly asserted that he had been with Jesus in the Garden. In the face of such evidence, how could Peter deny? And still he made one more awful effort. "Then began he to curse and to swear, saying, I know not the man." This was the third denial. How easily, how quickly, and how deeply Peter had fallen! If he could not bear to be teased and vexed by maids, how could he defend himself when an overpowering group of ruffians would pile in on him? And immediately as his shameless curses were still quivering in the air, the cock crowed, and the word of Jesus had been fulfilled: "Before the cock crow twice, thou shalt deny Me thrice." But repentance for Peter? Not yet. To his denials he had added curses and oaths. As far as

---

19, 1) Farrar, II, 348.

   2) Making ש sound like ת. Meyer sub Matt. 26, 73. **Something on the order of saying** *share* **for** *chair* **and** *ting* **for** *thing.*

he was concerned, he had done his part and tried his best to fill the whole courtyard with foul and infernal fumes. He had for the time being thoroughly lost his faith. "Like a raging bull in the arena he was stabbed from every side." [3]   He became blind with fury, rage, and shame.

20.

58   54
Matt. 26, 69—75.   Mark 14, 66—72.   Luke 22, 54b—62.
        15—18
John 18, 25—27.

But there is a sequel. It was the Lord Himself who brought about Peter's return. "I have prayed for thee that thy faith fail not." [1]   Not even the second crowing of the cock, which ought to have struck into his conscience like a charge of dynamite, brought Peter to his senses. Peter called to mind the word that Jesus had said unto him. And it was the look which the Lord employed for this purpose. "And the Lord [2] turned and looked upon Peter," likely as He was conducted across the court from Annas to Caiaphas. But what a look! It was as if an "arrow had pierced

"And He Went out and Wept Bitterly." His" fallen favorite's "inmost soul." [3] Then Peter remembered, not before. There was pain in that look, disappointment, and reproach, but also understanding, kindness, grace, forgiveness, and unspeakable love. With his heart filled with unbearable pain, Peter cast down his tear-stained eyes, and flinging the fold of his mantle over his shame-flushed face, [4] like Judas he rushed out into the night. Gone, forgotten, were his foolhardiness, his fears, enemies, denials, curses, oaths, and perjuries, and something else had filled his heart. He rushed out into the night, but not into the "unsunned darkness of miserable remorse," [5] the midnight of hopeless despair, but into the "darkness of repentance" preceding the morning dawn. [6] "And went out and wept bitterly."

19, 3) Stalker, 38.

20, 1) Luke 22, 32.

2) Κύριος in narrative. Thus in many places in Luke.

3) Farrar, II, 349.

4) Ἐπιβαλών. Another one of those puzzling words in Mark's vocabulary. The choice is between "thinking thereon" or "covering his head and flinging himself out." Bruce *sub loco*. We prefer the latter.

5) Farrar, II, 350.

6) Lange, quoted by Farrar, II, 350.

21.

(Matt. 26, 67. 68.)[1] (Mark 14, 65.)[1] Luke 22, 63—65.

And now let us return to Jesus. The foul work of the night had been accomplished. It needed but the technicality of a few hours' adjournment to make the sentence entirely legal and binding. According to Jewish law an acquittal could be immediately made, but a capital sentence could not be definitely pronounced until the following day.[2] A court of law is supposed to be a place of dignity, where even the condemned is treated with respect. But in this court all forces of evil were united to cover Jesus with shame. During the remaining hours of the night He

Jesus Maltreated during the Night. was left in the coarse and cruel hands of the guard. To make play of their victim and to while away their time, masters and servants alike beat Him with sticks, struck Him with the palms of their hands, and spat in His face. So fertile was their infernal imagination that they even invented some sort of game to scoff and mistreat Him. In allusion to His claim of being the Messianic prophet they threw something over His head and struck Him again and again with the words: "Prophesy unto us, Thou Christ, Who is he that smote Thee?" Yes, there are terrible things in the heart of man. We can hardly conceive how such shameless insults could be borne so meekly and patiently by our Savior. "The claw of the dragon was in His flesh and its foul breath in His mouth." [3]

22.

Matt. 27, 1. Mark 15, 1a. Luke 22, 66—71.

After a brief reassembly of the whole Sanhedrin in an early-morning official session the tentative sentence of the nightly meeting was speedily confirmed. Again the question was asked: "Art Thou the Christ?" and again Jesus gave an answer, somewhat indirectly, but still in the affirmative: "If I tell you, ye will not believe. And if I also ask you, ye will not answer nor let Me go." [1] What is the use of extending the argument? But again Jesus pointed to a speedy change of position from humiliation to exaltation. "Here-

---

21, 1) The account of Matthew and Mark was interrupted by the narration of Peter's denials.

2) Schuerer, II, I, 194. 3) Stalker, 30.

22, 1) The last phrase of the *textus receptus*, "nor let Me go," is omitted in leading codices.

after shall the Son of Man sit on the right hand of the power
of God." The reference was only too clear. Eagerly grasping
at the handle offered by these words, they pressed Jesus for a direct
answer: "Art Thou, then, the Son of God?" Jesus answered this
question with an afirming formula: "Ye say that I am." The

**Formally Condemned
by the Sanhedrin.**
judges were satisfied with the reply.
"What need we any further witness?
For we ourselves have heard of His
own mouth." The chairman raps for order. "What think ye?"
The votes are taken and counted. Beginning with the youngest,
each judge stands up in turn.[2] With the noble exception of Joseph
of Arimathea [3] and Nicodemus, possibly also of Gamaliel, the
votes are all for condemnation. "He is a *ben maveth!* He is
guilty of death!"

22, 2) Schuerer, II, I, 194.

    3) Luke 23, 51. If he was absent from the meeting, as some think,
then Mark 14, 64, "All condemned Him to be guilty of death," is to be
interpreted as "all those present."

CHAPTER XXXIV.

FRIDAY OF PASSION WEEK.
"SUFFERED UNDER PONTIUS PILATE."

April 7, 30 A. D., 783 A. U. C.

A. U. C.	779	780	781	782	783
A. D.	26	27	28	29	30
Age of Jesus	30	31	32	33	34

Passovers				I	II	III	IV

Nisan (or Abib)

10	11	12	13	14	15	16	17

April

2	3	4	5	6	7	8	9
Sun.	Mon.	Tue.	Wed.	Thu.	Fri.	Sat.	Sun.

783 A. U. C.   **APRIL**   **30 A. D.**

Sun.	Mon.	Tue.	Wed.	Thu.	Fri.	Sat.
						1
2	3	4	5	6	7	8
9	10	11	12	13	14	15
16	17	18	19	20	21	22
23	24	25	26	27	28	29
30						

1.

Matt. 27, 2. Mark 15, 1 b. Luke 23, 1. John 18, 28 a.

"Suffered under Pontius Pilate." With these words the Christian Creed forever not so much places the whole blame for the suffering of Jesus on Pontius Pilate as fixes the time when this supreme event of the world's history took place. For if any one was very anxious, if not to spare the agony of Jesus, at least to save

Jesus Brought before Pilate. His life, it was that Roman — Pontius Pilate. The sentence of death had been passed on Jesus by the Sanhedrin, the highest ecclesiastical court in the land. Gladly would these Jewish judges have carried out their sentence, presumably by stoning,[1] but it was not in their power. A capital sentence had to be confirmed by the provincial governor, in this case Pontius Pilate. This he did in the end. And so he was indeed guilty of the death of Christ, though, as Christ said,[2] not in the

---

1,   1) Lev. 24, 11—16.   2) John 19, 11.

same measure as the Jews, especially the chief priests and rulers. The beginning of the governorship of Pilate coincided about with the beginning of the ministry of John the Baptist. He had been in office long enough to become thoroughly acquainted with the most difficult race which the experienced officials of Rome ever had to manage. Neither did he like His subjects nor they him. And so there was no love lost between them. His usual residence was at sea-washed Caesarea, itself a little Rome.[3] But the pomp and the perils of the Passover Festival, when the heaving lava of glowing patriotism was ever apt to leap into eruption, yearly summoned him to the "capital of a nation which he detested and the headquarters of a fanaticism which he despised." [4] At such times, especially when accompanied by his wife, he would occupy the gorgeous palace which the architectural genius of the first Herod had reared.[5] It was a luxurious abode, overlooking Jerusalem to the southwest of the hill on which the Temple was built.[6] In front of it extended a broad pavement, locally called Gabbatha,[7] flanked by porticoes and columns of marble. And here, in the open and from a raised platform, the trials were conducted on account of the prejudice of the Jews against entering the Gentile ruler's house. Besides, now, in the season of Passover, when every trace of leaven had to be removed, there was all the more reason to guard against ceremonial defilement. In this Pilate had to yield to his subjects' scruples, though secretly, in his heart, he cursed them. But before proceeding with the account of the civil trial of Jesus, a terrible thing is related which happened about the same time that Jesus was led to Pilate.

2.

Matt. 27, 3—10. (Acts 1, 18. 19.)

When Judas saw that with the leading away of Jesus to Pilate the Savior's fate was sealed, his brains reeled at the thought of what he had done. He "repented himself." [1] It was not godly sorrow, however, which worketh repentance to salvation, but the

---

1,   3) *Ant.*, XVIII, III, 1. *Wars*, II, IX, 2.   Acts 23, 33.

4) Farrar, II, 364.

5) *Wars*, II, XIV, 8; XV, 5. Edersheim, II, 566.

6) *Wars*, I, XXI, 1; V, IV, 4.

7) John 19, 13.

2,   1) Μεταμεληθείς, from μεταμέλομαι. Used in Matt. 21, 29. 32; 2 Cor. 7, 8; Heb. 7, 21.   The usual word for repent in the Scriptural sense is μετανοέω. Edersheim, II, 573.

sorrow of the world, which worketh death,[2] being without faith in Him who can save to the uttermost. Instead of prostrating himself at the feet of his Savior, Judas despaired and went to the associates of his crime. The miserable thirty shekels in his girdle in which his heart had delighted were now as thirty serpents in his bag. With wild eyes, a haggard face, and an indescribable pain in his heart he brought back the silver, "the reward of iniquity," [3] to the partners of his crime. At least that was his intention, and he wanted to remove as far as possible the terrible divine curse laid upon his atrocious crime: "Cursed be he that taketh reward to slay an innocent person." [4] With a wild cry he broke into a confession of his sin: "I have sinned in that I have betrayed the innocent

Remorse and Suicide of Judas. blood." Here we have out of the mouth of the traitor a confession of his treachery as well as incidentally a testimony to the innocence of Jesus. But the guilty priests were not interested in a sinner's return. "What is that to us? See thou to that." The bargain had been made, the money had been paid, and they owed him nothing, not even sympathy. Judas now had no friends, no partners, no Savior, no peace — only thirty pieces of silver. And the sight of them filled him with utter disgust. Where the interview of Judas with the priests and elders took place, whether in the Hall of Polished Stones or in the palace of Caiaphas, we do not know. — Now follows the act of a desperate man. What did he care! With fire in his eyes he rushed forward to the Sanctuary, through the Court of the Women, up the flights of stairs, through the Court of Israel, as far as — if not into — the Court of the Priests.[5] There he stopped. He bent forward and with all his might hurled the shekels into the Holy Place.[6] And then, with the empty girdle still in his hands, he rushed out of the Temple, out of the city, across the Valley of Hinnom,[7] up the slopes of the mountain, and straight into the gnarled branches of a tree overhanging a rock. "And hanged himself." Falling headlong, the branch probably breaking from the weight, "he burst asunder in the midst, and all his bowels gushed out."

2,   2) 2 Cor. 7, 10.   3) Acts 1, 18.   4) Deut. 27, 25.

5) Edersheim, II, 574.

6) Ναός. Bruce and Meyer *sub loco.*

7) According to tradition to the south of Jerusalem, somewhat to the west, and above where the Kidron and Hinnom valleys merge. Edersheim, II, 577. Andrews, 526.

3.

Matt. 27, 3—10. (Acts 1, 18. 19.)

In the mean while there was staged in the Temple a piece of hypocrisy in its most repulsive form. In certain respects the heirs of Judas, the priests and elders in the Temple, were scrupulous men. While the murder of an innocent man was not against their code, the possible infraction of a legal statute filled their hearts with consternation. They were not interested in the remorse of Judas. "What is that to us? See thou to that!" they cried out when their partner in sin confessed his crime. They would not accept those shekels from Judas. Of course they were forced to pick them up; however, they would not return the coins to the sacred treasury,

The Potter's Field. or Corban; for — this much they admitted — it was blood-money. "It is not lawful for to put them into the treasury because it is the price of blood." [1] Finally it was decided to use the money for some charitable purpose. A parcel of ground was purchased, perhaps a worked-out clay pit and still called the potter's field, and used as a burying-ground for pilgrims who happened to die at Jerusalem. On account of the association another name afterwards clung to it: Aceldama, or The Field of Blood. In a remarkable way there was also a prophetic correspondence: "And they took the thirty pieces of silver, the price of Him that was valued, whom they of the children of Israel did value, and gave them for the potter's field, as the Lord appointed me." [2]

4.

*Matt. 27, 11—14. Mark 15, 2—5. Luke 23, 2—5.
John 18, 28 b—38.*

It may have been about six o'clock on that memorable April morning that a dignified procession, no doubt followed by a thrill-seeking throng, was seen approaching Pilate's palace at an unusual hour. The matter was urgent and had to be completely dispatched

---

3,   1) An extension of Deut. 23, 18. See Bruce *sub loco. Wars*, II, IX, 4. A disturbance was caused in Jerusalem because Pilate expended "that sacred treasure which is called Corban upon aqueducts."

2) Zech. 11, 13; Jer. 18, 2; 19, 2; 32, 6—15. Matthew does not name Zechariah, though he quotes him three times: 21, 5; 26, 31; 27, 9. But it was a common saying among the Jews that Zechariah had the spirit of Jeremiah. Farrar, II, 359, n. 1. "Ridderwold believes that the prophecy of Zechariah refers to a prophecy in Jeremiah, chapter 19, and that, because the prophecy in Zechariah is fully understood only by the light shed upon it in Jer. 19, therefore Matthew says that the words are from Jeremiah, although they are found in Zechariah." Ylvisaker, 720.

before sundown on the day which had just begun. The long-bearded and wise-looking judges, probably headed by Caiaphas himself, would not enter into the Praetorium, or Judgment Hall,[1] "lest they should be defiled, but that they might eat the passover";[2] and so Pilate went out to them. They were afraid of coming in

Jesus before Pilate the First Time. contact with leaven, which in this season would be found in a Gentile's house; but they did not shrink from the shedding of holy and innocent blood. Disturbed in that early hour, Pilate was in no pleasant mood, although he knew that disturbances might be expected at the Passovertide. In a half-necessary condescension he accommodated himself to what he considered the puzzling superstition of a hated race. As he ascended the tribunal, no doubt accompanied by secretaries and guarded by bronzed representatives of the power of Rome, he cast one haughty look over the priestly notables and the turbulent mob. Noticing also a bound victim in their midst and, observing, in spite of the bonds, some unexplainable glint of glory, he immediately demanded: "What accusation bring ye against this man?"

5.

Matt. 27, 11—14. Mark 15, 2—5. Luke 23, 2—5. John 18, 28 b—38.

The question took the Jews by surprise. It almost seems as if they had expected Pilate to accept their verdict and to sign the bill of execution, as we would say, unsight unseen. This manner of dispensing justice was sometimes observed by provincial governors, either out of indolence or in blind reliance upon the native courts. Especially, as in this case, in religious matters, which a foreigner was not expected to understand, it was not always the unreasonable course to pursue.[1] "If He were not a malefactor, we would not

---

4, 1) Most likely the royal palace of Herod the Great, which by this time had become state property. It occupied the highest part of the southwest hill, near the northwest angle of the ancient city, now traditionally called Zion. It is needless to point out how greatly this view of the site of the Pretorium must modify the traditional claims of the Via Dolorosa, the whole course of which depends on the theory that the Pretorium is identified with Castle Antonia, located on the northwestern corner of the Temple complex. Edersheim, II, 566. Farrar, chap. 60. See "Pretorium" in *Int. St. B. Encycl.*

2) The phrase "eat the passover" is to be understood as referring to the observation of the whole festival or to the sacrifices of this particular day, the second Chagigah, and not to the Passover meal itself, which, as we have seen, was already eaten on the 14th of Nisan, the evening before. See chapter XXXI, 3. 11, and references.

5, 1) Stalker, 50.

have delivered Him up unto thee," is the somewhat offended reply. But this morning Pilate was in no yielding mood. He would not give the sanction of his tribunal to their dark decree. He would not be the executioner where he had not been the judge.[2] Very

"Judge Him according to Your Law."

well, "take ye Him, then, and judge Him according to your law." If you do not want me to take up the case, you must be satisfied with what the law allows. This meant that they would have to impose excommunication, fines, imprisonment, forty stripes save one, or other punishments. This, however, would not at all have satisfied their thirst for blood, and the sentence upon which they had agreed would not have been executed. Revealing their infernal desires as well as acknowledging the power of Rome, they were forced into the humiliating confession: "It is not lawful for us to put any one to death." [3] And even if they had had the right to inflict capital punishment, it was decreed in the counsel of God as well as foretold by Jesus Himself that He was to die, not by stoning or by strangulation, but by the Roman mode of executing a criminal, by crucifixion. "And shall deliver Him to the Gentiles to mock and to scourge and to crucify Him." [4]

6.

Matt. 27, 11—14. Mark 15, 2—5. Luke 23, 2—5. John 18, 28 b—38.

And therefore, since Pilate was determined to retry the case, the accusers were forced to formulate definite charges, upon doing which they hoped their sentence would be confirmed. A flood of vehement accusations, unprovable, however, by witnesses, was poured forth, out of which at last three distinct charges emerged. First, this Jesus of Nazareth was perverting the nation. Secondly, He forbade to pay the imperial tribute. Thirdly, He set Himself up as Christ the King. The fourth charge, blasphemy, for which really the Sanhedrin had pronounced the death-sentence upon Him,

The Charges against Jesus.

was not even mentioned. They knew too well that, if they had advanced this charge here, they would have been sneered out of court. The first, a rather vague charge, "We found this fellow perverting the nation," Pilate passed by. If they had told the truth, they would probably have stated that He was making too many disciples and that they were afraid the whole nation

---

5,　　2) Farrar, II, 367.　　　3) *Wars*, II, VIII, 1.　　　4) Matt. 20, 19.

would accept His false teaching. Pilate knew perfectly well "that for envy they had delivered Him." [1] Likewise the second charge, "forbidding to give tribute to Caesar," Pilate ignored. If it had been true, that would have been a crime. But the government of Pilate was too well organized not to know that this accusation was a flagrant lie. The very opposite had been taught by Jesus. There must have been a smile on the governor's face at the prospect of this sudden zeal for the paying of the Roman tribute. Should it really be true that the *pax Romana* was actually becoming popular on this Palestinian soil? It was the third charge which attracted his attention: "Saying that He Himself is Christ, a king." Discounting the ungrasped Messianic reference for the present, — if it was true that He was setting Himself up as king, a possible rival to gloomy Tiberius, this accusation certainly had to be investigated. Not as if he had any particular worries in this respect; but it must not be charged against him that he was sleeping on the job.

7.

Matt. 27, 11—14. Mark 15, 2—5. Luke 23, 2—5.
John 18, 28 b—38.

Just how much Pilate was acquainted with the career of Jesus we do not know. It is certain that he was not altogether ignorant of it. On the previous evening he had granted a Roman guard to assist in His arrest. [1] Then there was the dream of his wife, Procula, which seems to show that there had been a conversation in his house about that "young enthusiast who was bearding the fanatic priests." [2] Now the charge that He was "Christ, a king." We assume that during these proceedings Jesus was, probably with a guard, within the walls of the Pretorium. Leaving the impatient Sanhedrin and the raging crowd, Pilate retired into the Judgment Hall. In that hall he stood face to face with Almighty Power. "Art Thou the King of the Jews?" he asked. But that depends upon how the royalty of Jesus is understood. In His reply the Savior is cautious. "Sayest thou this thing of thyself, or did others tell it thee of Me?" "Am I a Jew?" is Pilate's disdainful reply. "Thy own nation and the chief priests have delivered Thee unto me. What hast Thou done?" What a shame — and what a charge! Israel's own people had rejected Israel's King.

6, 1) Matt. 27, 18; Mark 15, 10.
7, 1) Chapter XXXIII, 4.   2) Stalker, 53.

And what had He done? Done? He had done all things well, performed works of mercy, love, power, — and still He was now a prisoner, standing at the bar of justice. A just judge should not ask that question. A prisoner ought to be considered innocent until his guilt is proved. In answering Pilate, Jesus reverts to his first question. Yes, He is a king. But no rival of Tiberius.

The King of Truth. For in that event His servants would fight for Him. And still a king. But His kingdom "is not of this world." In giving the explanation, He had used the word *kingdom*. At this point Pilate broke in and said: "Art Thou a king, then?" "Yes," Jesus answered, "Thou sayest that I am a king. To this end was I born, and for this cause came I into the world, that I should bear witness of the truth. Every one that is of the truth heareth My voice." So that's it — a king! However, not a king of men, but a king of hearts and of the truth. Truth! Truth? But "what is truth?" What has he, a "busy, practical Roman governor, to do with such abstractions"! [3] At this, almost persuaded, like Agrippa, Pilate rushed out. So near the fountain and yet so far from the life-giving stream. This idea of non-earthly royalty he set aside as completely unreal. Too bad, he thought. What "a high-souled, but altogether impractical dreamer"! But this much was certain: whatever He was, He was not guilty of death. Pilate went out to the impatient Sanhedrin and pronounced an emphatic and unhesitating acquittal. "I find no fault in Him at all."

8.

Matt. 27, 11—14. Mark 15, 2—5. Luke 23, 2—5. John 18, 28 b—38.

The judge had arrived at his conclusion. He was satisfied that Jesus was no dangerous character. To his mind He was probably only a man with a fixed idea. And now, what ought to have followed? The unjust verdict of the Sanhedrin ought to have been reversed, the Prisoner released, and, if necessary, protected by a Roman guard. And why was this not done? Leaving out of consideration for the moment the "determinate counsel" of divine mercy that Jesus should die for the sins of the world, we cannot but say that Pilate, with all his bold swagger, was a coward and did not have the courage to resist the bold and influential accusers. This they knew. They were confident that, if they would insist that their verdict be upheld, they would see the fulfilment of their

---

7,   3) Farrar, II, 370.

foul design. An incident in the previous official life of Pilate may best explain.[1] Some years before, as recently arrived governor, with a supply of new ideas, Pilate resolved to move the headquarters of the Roman army from Caesarea to Jerusalem. Resolved and done. Roman legions with clanking swords, shining helmets, armored breastplates, and military ensigns, to which were affixed the Roman eagles and the effigy of the imperial master, were seen in Jerusalem. And who was there to resist? But to the popular

The Weakness of Pilate.

mind it was sanctioning idolatry to permit these images in the Holy City and was considered a gross insult and desecration. There was no objection to the image of Tiberius on the denarius, especially if sufficiently multiplied. Neither was there resistance to the blades on the end of the hilt and the spears on the shaft. But there was serious objection to the gilded ornaments on the tip of the military ensigns. Soon a noisy delegation rushed down to Caesarea with well-spiked protests against the introduction of idolatrous images into the Holy City. And besides, what was the idea of sneaking them in at night-time, as had been done? Furthermore the delegation reminded Pilate that, when former governors made their entry into the city, it was without those idols on the top of the poles. Pilate refused to listen. He was still a new governor, and he had to learn. For five days he refused. Finally he was so irritated that he gave the order to disperse the noisy mob and, if necessary, to cut off their heads, since there was no other way of silencing their mouths. "All right!" they cried and stretched forth their necks, saying that they would rather die than have their city defiled. In the end Pilate had to have the images of his imperial master carried out of Jerusalem and stored in a warehouse at Caesarea. Such was the governor, and such were the people with whom he had to deal. For the sake of a principle and the effigy of his master he could not afford to arouse a revolution and to wreck the revenues of a tribute-producing province.

9.

Matt. 27, 11—14. Mark 15, 2—5. Luke 23, 2—5. John 18, 28 b—38.

The words "I find no fault in Him at all" were but a signal for the release of an angry clamor. Charges and accusations were hurled from every direction. "And the chief priests accused Him

---

8, 1) *Wars*, II, IX, 2. 3. *Ant.*, XVIII, III, 1.

of many things." Pilate, hopelessly in the air, weakly turned to Jesus Himself: "Answerest Thou nothing? Behold how many things they witness against Thee." But Jesus, with His life at stake, was the only calm person in the assembly,[1] and He "answered nothing, so that Pilate marveled." Suddenly, however, in the midst of the confusion, a way out of the difficulty seemed to open itself to Pilate. He heard the word Galilee. "He stirreth up the people,

"He Stirreth Up the People, . . . Beginning from Galilee." teaching throughout all Jewry, beginning from Galilee to this place." The mention of Galilee was intended to excite prejudice against Jesus, because Galilee was a hotbed of insurrection. But to Pilate's mind there was suggested a way of ridding himself of the terrible responsibility in the present case and at the same time of flattering Herod, who was present in Jerusalem for the Passover. This he could do in accordance with the Roman law by transferring the Prisoner to him, to whose jurisdiction Jesus of Nazareth, as a resident of Galilee, belonged.[2] Glad to get rid of this detestable business, he sent the Prisoner and His accusers down the hill to the near-by ancient Maccabean palace in which Herod used to reside on his visits to the capital city. It lay lower down on the eastern slope of the southwest hill, where at a later time, as Josephus expressly says, Herod Agrippa II and his sister Bernice were living.[3]

Luke 23, 6—12. **10.**

In order to understand the following, we must briefly review a bit of Herodian family history.[1] After the death of Herod the Great his dominions were divided by Rome among three of his sons, so as thus more effectually to keep the country under control. Archelaus received Judea, soon to be taken from him at the request of the people themselves and to be administered by Roman governors, of whom Pontius Pilate was fifth in line. Philip received

Herod Antipas. Iturea and the northern regions. And Antipas received Galilee and a strip of land east of the Jordan, and at this time, after thirty years, Philip and Antipas were still enjoying their possessions. Like his father, Herod Antipas was a builder. Also corrupt. But otherwise he lacked his father's ability, and his reign was drowned in debauchery and blood.

9, 1) Stalker, 63.   2) Stalker, 63.
   3) *Wars*, II, XVI, 3. See "Pretorium" in *Int. St. B. Encycl.*
10, 1) Compare chapters IV and XV.

He took a fatal step when he entered into an intrigue with Herodias, his niece, another brother's, Herod Philip's, wife, which brought about the death of John the Baptist and a war with Aretas of Arabia and in the end cost him his tottering throne.

Luke 23, 6—12.   **11.**

When that stern wilderness preacher of repentance, John the Baptist, began to set fire to the country, Herod Antipas was interested and invited him to his palace and heard him gladly, until John said: "It is not lawful for thee to have her," Herodias. That was carrying the matter of repentance too far. And especially did Herodias "have it in" for him. We know what happened. On the king's birthday Herodias's daughter by a former marriage, Salome, danced before a drunken crowd. The king was pleased with her unchaste performance and promised to give her anything that she might ask, up to one half of his kingdom. "And he sware unto her." The "young witch, well drilled by her mother in the craft of hell," asked for the head of John the Baptist on a charger [1]

The Death of John the Baptist. and was not refused. The executioner was sent to John in the dungeon. "No time for preparation is given nor needed." [2] A few minutes, and it is all over. The guard returns. And Herodias receives her "ghastly dish." [3] This awful crime filled the country with horror. Herod's own mind was haunted by the specters of an impenitent remorse. When the fame of the great Galilean Prophet reached him, he thought it was none other than John the Baptist risen from the dead. Feeling the hatred of his subjects, he turned more and more to foreign customs. His court was distinguished for Roman and Greek imitations and affectations. And especially the professional conveyors of pleasure, the charlatans and fakers of the day, jugglers, and the like, were welcome at his court. [4] His annual visit to the Passover at Jerusalem was altogether conventional and was not inspired by devotion, but by hope of amusement.

Luke 23, 6—12.   **12.**

When Herod saw Jesus, he was exceeding glad. It was an excitement. And then, because Jesus was sent to him by the proud Pilate, it was a compliment. Indeed, we are told that as a result of this unexpected attention the erstwhile enemies became friends.

11, 1) Stalker, 66.   2) Edersheim, I, 674.
     3) Edersheim, I, 674.   4) Stalker, 67.

But most of all his delight was increased by the hope that this great Galilean miracle-worker would entertain him with two or three choice miracles for his particular benefit. And why not? This was a prisoner's chance to influence him, a king, in his favor. No doubt he thought Jesus would grasp the opportunity to show, as he regarded it, His skill. Thus he revealed his estimate of the person of Christ. At once he addressed Jesus in the friendliest manner and "questioned with Him in many words." We can

Jesus and Herod. imagine his welcoming smile. In his eagerness he altogether forgot the purpose for which Pilate had sent Him. But Jesus answered him nothing. Herod, however, did not notice it and went rambling on.[1] He liked to hear himself talk. He had views on religion and wanted to voice them. He had theories to ventilate, puzzles to propound, and remarks to make. "Then he questioned with Him in many words." Just imagine. The most shallow, silly drivel is poured into the suffering ears of the silent Son of God! "But He answered him nothing." At last Herod had exhausted himself. He waited for Christ to speak. He waited. But Jesus never uttered a word. Silence continued. At last the old chatterer grew angry. But Jesus did not utter a word. "He was silent that the word of John the Baptist might continue to ring in his ear." [2]

Luke 23, 6—12.   **13.**

The king is through speaking. And now the accusers begin. "And the chief priests and scribes stood and vehemently accused Him." The same old charges were poured out, and this time, it seems, into receptive ears. Then the corrupt satellites around the debased throne chimed in. "And Herod with his men of war set Him at naught," that is, they treated Him with the insolence of studied contempt. Mocking His harmless innocency and ridiculing His candidacy for the Messianic throne, they threw a shining robe over His holy shoulders. And midst ribald laughter and cruel in-

Mocked and Set at Naught. sults Herod sent Him back to Pilate, whose friend, as a result, he now became. Just what the cause of the previous enmity had been cannot be ascertained. Most likely it was the jealousy of a native prince harbored against a foreign ruler. Some commentators think that it was on account of the Galileans whose blood Pilate had mingled with their sacrifices.[1] But the records do not

---

12, 1) Stalker, 68.   2) Stalker, 72.   **13,** 1) Luke 13, 1.

state that the friendship brough about by such unholy circumstances endured for a long time. Enmity against Christ and His Church does make strange bedfellows and friends. A thousand times better it would have been for both Pilate and Herod had they sought and retained the friendship of Jesus.

Luke 23, 13—16.   14.

Pilate's hope of disposing of the case put before him by sending Jesus to Herod was in vain; for before long the Prisoner was brought back to the royal palace. While Herod had treated Jesus with shameless disdain, Pilate still treated Him with genuine respect. Yet he could plainly see that the verdict of Herod agreed with his own, namely, that whatever views might be held as to the teaching and person of the Galilean Prophet, He at least was not guilty of death. This point was now definitely established by Pilate's own observation and confirmed by expert advice, for as such naturally the action of Herod would be interpreted as coming from a native prince.[1] There was now for Pilate absolutely no excuse for a delay of favorable action. But what did he do? He still followed the policy of all weaklings, that miserable policy of stalling for time. When the fate of Jesus was once more placed into his unhappy hands, he called together the chief priests and the rulers and the people for the purpose of making an important announcement, always probably hoping that something, he knew not what, might turn up. At last he began his speech. "You have brought this Man unto me as one that perverteth the people. I have examined Him before you and have found no fault in Him at all. Then I sent Him to Herod. By the way, there is nothing to the

Returned to Pilate. rumor at all that Herod and I are not on speaking terms. Herod examined Him. And the result is the same. And therefore," he continued, still thinking hard, "therefore," — therefore what? "And therefore," you would expect him to say, "I am going to release Him; and I warn you by the power of Rome and the terrible anger of Tiberius not so much as to disturb a single hair of His head." But instead he offered a proposition in defiance of all logic and justice: "I will therefore chastise Him and release Him." Was there a more unjust proposal ever made: on the one hand, to inflict a severe punishment as a "sop to their rage" and then to release Him as a tribute to justice?[2] And yet this proposal was thoroughly char-

---

14, 1) Stalker, 76.   2) Stalker, 77.

acteristic of the man who made it as well as of the system which he represented. The spirit of imperial Rome was ever the spirit of compromise, so as ultimately to gain its end. And nine times out of ten it worked. Scores of officials throughout the empire were even now successfully conducting their administration along these very lines. "Only to Pilate fell the sinister distinction of applying the base system to an altogether unexpected exception to the rule." [3] In proposing to have Jesus, though innocent, chastened, Pilate cut himself loose from all principles of justice. But he hoped thus to guide his course safely to the point at which he aimed. In this he was fatally deceived. The impulse of his own false beginning could end only in his own wreck and ruin. Only by means of right can you achieve right. You cannot do one thing wrong in the hope of making another thing right. It cannot be done.

15.

Matt. 27, 15—18. Mark 15, 6—10. John 18, 39.

It seems that in the eager pursuit of temporizing measures there was opened another avenue of hoped-for escape. Up to this point the actors assembled on the stage of Christ's trial were still comparatively few as compared with the masses that now appeared on the scene. And it was just by means of this mob of Jerusalem as against the leaders with whom he had been dealing that Pilate hoped to extricate himself from a dilemma. His knowledge that it was for envy that Jesus had been delivered by the leaders he hoped to turn to good account. It was the custom of the Roman governors, as a contribution to the Passover joy of the people, to release a prisoner whom they would. There were generally plenty of political prisoners on hand, rebels against the detested power of Rome, but for that reason popular heroes.[1] And for once the annual demand to have a prisoner released was welcome to Pilate.

"Jesus or Barabbas?" Here was the plan. He would give them the choice of freeing either a robber and leader of sedition, who in a late uprising had committed murder, Barabbas,[2] or Jesus, who but a few days before had been the hero at a popular demonstration. As an aspirant to

---

14, 3) Stalker, 77.   15, 1) Stalker, 82.

2) Literally, son of the father. The Syriac variant with double *r* (Barrabban) would mean son of a Rabbi. Jerome, in his commentary on Matthew, says that in the Hebrew gospel the word was interpreted *filius magistri eorum.* Origen mentions that in some MSS. this man bore the name of Jesus Barabbas, which makes the contrast of character all the more striking. See commentaries under Matt. 27, 16.

Messiahship, he imagined, Jesus would be the very person they should want. It was seemingly a good plan. He thought he could not go wrong. And still, taking into consideration the Person and the issue, failure was the only outcome in which this plan could result. You cannot gamble with justice. It was an utterly unjust thing for Pilate to do because the proposal treated Jesus as if He were guilty and already condemned, which was not the case. And furthermore, it staked the life of an innocent man upon the voice of the people in the hope that the *vox populi* would be *vox Dei*, the voice of the people the voice of God, which is not always the case.[3]

Matt. 27, 19. **16.**

Not that Pilate did not know better nor that he was unwarned. It was about this time that a distinct warning came to him from Procula,[1] his loving wife. As a good wife of a husband who was in need of sound advice she sent a messenger to tell him of a terrifying dream she had just had about the Prisoner and to warn him not to have anything to do with that just Man. And how did she know about Him? That is not stated. But we must remember that Jesus was nationally known and no doubt had been the subject of many a conversation in the palace. On the evening before

The Message from Pilate's Wife. Pilate had put a Roman guard at the disposal of the high priest to assist in His arrest. The matter was probably mentioned between him and his wife. And with the thoughts of Jesus, Procula went to sleep. Now, we are not going to talk about dreams. The person that pays much attention to dreams pays attention to himself. But we can be assured that the hand of God was in this dream and that in the message both the hand of God and of a loving wife were outstretched to save Pilate from a doom to which he was hastening.[2] Pilate, who as an educated Roman will have remembered Caesar's death and Calpurnia's dream,[3] must have been impressed. Gladly would he have yielded if it had not been for that secret streak of cowardice.

15, 3) Stalker, 85.

16, 1) The name given to her by tradition. Claudia Procula, or Procla, is said to have been a Jewish proselyte at the time of the death of Jesus and afterwards to have become a Christian. Her name is honored along with Pilate's in the Coptic Church, and in the calendar of saints honored by the Greek Church her name is found against the date of October 27. *Int. St. B. Encycl.*, under "Pilate."

2) Stalker, 81.

3) That the pediment of their house fell and that her husband was stabbed in her arms. Suetonius, *Iulius*, LXXXI.

17.

Matt. 27, 20. 21. Mark 15, 11. Luke 23, 17—19.
John 18, 40.

There was a brief interval, which was put to good use by the
priests and the scribes. Since Pilate had appealed to the mob, they,
too, would appeal to it. And they knew the mob better than Pilate.
They persuaded the people and moved them to do their bidding.
All they had to do was to employ a simple political trick, as old as
politics, and pass the word on as to which of the two was Pilate's
choice. And then, as far as the mob was concerned, the matter
was safe. Picture to yourselves the scene — the holy, undefiled, sin-

Barabbas is Chosen. less Son of God standing with a
scowling thug on that high tribunal!
Words fail to describe the contrast, as great as heaven and the
bottom of hell. "For the Holy, the Harmless, for Him whom
a thousand hosannas had greeted five days before, not a word of
pity is heard." [1] And then, as the choice is made which is to
decide the fate of the Redeemer and forever confirm the tragic
truth of the natural depravity of the human heart, a thousand,
ten thousand hands are pointed, and ten thousand voices raise the
cry of "Barabbas!"

18.

Matt. 27, 22. 23. Mark 15, 12—14. Luke 23, 20—23.

And so, in spite of manipulations, the matter had come to the
worst. After a last brief moment of hopeful suspense the choice
of Barabbas must have been a staggering blow to Pilate. He had
staked all on the choice of the people and lost. His testimony to
the innocence of Jesus, his repeated appeals to the people's conscience, his outrageous expedient of having Him whom he had
pronounced innocent cruelly scourged, to satisfy His bitter enemies,
in order to save Him from crucifixion, all had been in vain. "What
shall I do, then, with Jesus, which is called Christ?" he asked in

"What shall I Do, helpless despair. This is a question
then, with Jesus?" which every believer asks and properly
answers. Probably Pilate had hoped
for the answer: Release Him, too. How willingly would he have
complied with such a request! "What will ye, then, that I shall
do unto Him whom ye call the King of the Jews?" The appeal to
their Messianic as well as to their national aspirations left them

---

17, 1) Farrar, II, 378.

untouched. Quick as an echo the answer was flashed back: "Crucify Him!" As with wild vehemence the hideous yells rent the air, Pilate now became fully aware that this bloodthirsty pack of accusers were in dead earnest in their clamor for blood. What the governor had considered "a loophole for escape was a noose into which he had thrust his neck." [1] He was lost. There was no use of his pleading any longer.

Matt. 27, 24. 25.[1]   19.

When Pilate saw that he could prevail nothing, he did a most unusual thing. Calling for a basin of water, he washed his hands before the multitude and said: "I am innocent of the blood of this just person; see ye to it." In itself it was a most impressive act,[2] but in the case of Pilate it was a farce. Blood and guilt are

Pilate Washes His Hands. not washed off so easily. And Pilate's hands were covered with blood. Instead of washing his hands, he ought to have used them;[3] he ought to have refused to perform a deed of which he himself disapproved. Pilate was guilty. Still, back of it all was the sinner-saving will of God. Pilate, coward that he was, was afraid of heaping guilt upon his soul. But the people were not. His pitiful plea of mercy for Jesus — for that is what it was — was

---

18, 1) Stalker, 87.

19, 1) Our arrangement in bringing this incident at this point (following Stalker, Cadman, Kerr, J. M. Wilson, Edersheim, Stevens and Burton, Robinson, Davis, and others) rather than at the usual dramatic close, is prompted by the desire to follow the natural order of the combined account (without transposition) and to avoid the arrangement which would presumably have Jesus scourged twice: John 19, 1, followed by verses 2—15 in John, as compared with the arrangement which would make Matt. 27, 26 and Mark 15, 15 follow John 19, 15. Our arrangement follows this natural order: —

Matt. 27, 24. 25			
26	Mark 15, 15	Luke 23, 24. 25	
26	15		John 19, 1
27—31 a	16—20 a		2. 3
			4—7
			8—11
			12—15
31 b	20 b	26 a	16

2) Reminding us of the rite prescribed in Deut. 21, 6 f. of marking the freedom from guilt of the elders of a city where untracked murder had been committed. The expression is Jewish, 2 Sam. 3, 28; Ps. 26, 6; 73, 13. Pilate may have known of the custom, although we find allusions to some such custom also among the heathen; but it was all the more forceful as appealing to the Jews. See Edersheim, II, 578.

3) Stalker, 87.

met with a hideous howl of hell. "His blood be on us and on our children." Madder cries were never uttered, and profaner curses were never heard — and remembered with a vengeance. Some thirty years more, and judgment was pronounced upon Jerusalem's noblest and best. A few years more and a forest of crosses bore mangled Jewish bodies in sight of the spot where Jesus had been nailed to the cross.[4] "The soldiers out of rage and hatred amused themselves by nailing their prisoners in different postures; and so great was their number that space could not be found for the crosses nor crosses for the bodies." [5] And ever afterwards the Jewish wanderers, from century to century and land to land, have borne the curse which they have invoked upon themselves and on their children.

20.

Matt. 27, 26. Mark 15, 15. Luke 23, 24. 25. John 19, 1.

Pilate's various attempts to save Jesus had come to naught. There was now no other course open to him than to hand Him over to the tormentors. In presenting the intense suffering of our Savior, it is not necessary to dwell upon every detail until each sentence drips with blood, as used to be the custom in a more realistic age, as long as we remember that it was a real suffering, a vicarious suffering, and in true penitence meditate on the cause — our sins. The people had spoken, but the voice of the people is not always the voice of God. And now Pilate had to yield to the popular storm. He released Barabbas and delivered Jesus to be scourged.[1] This terrible punishment, from which Roman citizens

Barabbas Released and Jesus Scourged.

were exempt,[2] was ordinarily the preliminary to crucifixion and other forms of capital punishment. Woe unto him upon whom it was inflicted! It meant that he was doomed to die. It was a punishment so terrible that the mind revolts even at the description of it.[3] The victim was stripped and tied in a bent position to a pillar, and then blows were laid on the naked back with leathern thongs, weighted with jagged edges of bone and lead. Scourging as practised by the Romans [4] was

---

19, 4) Edersheim, II, 578.   5) Josephus, *Wars*, V, XI, 1.

20, 1) $Φραγελλώσας$, Matthew and Mark. A Latinism from flagello. John: $ἐμαστίγωσε$. The same term used by Josephus in *Wars*, V, XI, 1. Bruce sub Matt. 27, 26.

    2) Acts 22, 25.   3) Farrar, II, 379.

    4) As to the beating, or whipping, of a culprit sanctioned by the Mosaic, Law, see Deut. 25, 2. 3; 2 Cor. 11, 24.

so merciless and fierce that the victim generally fainted and often died.[5] The reason why Pilate tolerated this torture before the last and deciding word had been finally spoken apparently was that he was still hoping to save Jesus, thinking that by causing Him to undergo so much suffering he would arouse the pity of even a hitherto furious mob; and then he would set Him free. But if these were his hopes, they were as futile as his measures were heartless and unjust.

21.

Matt. 27, 27—31 a. Mark 15, 16—20 a. John 19, 2. 3.

Assuming that Jesus was condemned and that He was their victim, whom they might treat as they pleased, the soldiers now took Him in hand. They led Him away within the court and called together the whole band.[1] In civilized countries all possible measures are taken, — and sometimes this is even overdone, — to spare suffering to a murderer condemned to death. But with the Roman soldiers, who were inured to bloodshed and delighted in the bloody sports of the arena, the opposite was the case. If they had not been permitted to treat a condemned criminal roughly, so as to cause him additional pain and humiliation, they would have considered themselves deprived of their greatest fun. The trial of Jesus was over. The Passover celebrated in Jerusalem meant nothing to these soldiers. And so they would have a Roman holiday of their own. Somehow the fact had penetrated their barrack-schooled brains that the drift of the charge against Jesus was that He pretended to be a king. And so their horse-play took the

The Crown of Thorns. form of a mock coronation.[2] In staging their heartless ceremony, the hardened ruffians treated Jesus as if they were creating a successor to the aged and suspicious incumbent of the purple who at the time was hiding his gloomy features at Capri.[3] A king must wear the purple. And so they tore Herod's gift, the shining robe, from His bleeding shoulders and threw over Him a cast-off officer's coat.[4] He must have a crown. And so one of them pulled a few sharp-needled twigs off a near-by bush and plaited them into

---

20, 5) For a horribly realistic picture see Eusebius, IV, XV, 4.

21, 1) Σπεῖρα, at most a cohort of 600 men. At Passover time a large guard would be at hand. Bruce sub Matt. 27, 27.

2) Stalker, 92. 3) Farrar, II, 387.

4) Matthew, "scarlet"; Mark and John, "purple." Probably the color was actually scarlet, but the purpose of the mockery was to convey the idea of purple.

a laurel of thorns.[5]   He must also have a scepter.   And thus
a reed [6] was thrust into His rope-tied hands.   The royal outfit was
now complete.   And now their newly made king must be duly
saluted.   As to the proper royal address, the only time when they
had seen that made was at Rome in the circus, when they had seen
gladiators approach the imperial presence with the greeting *"Ave,
Caesar, morituri te salutant!"*   And so they advanced, one after the
other, and, bending low, said: *"Ave, Caesar!*   Hail, King of the
Jews!"   And then, passing from unshamed mockery to savage
cruelty midst outbursts of coarse laughter, they struck Him over
the head with the cane which His hand was unable to hold.   And —
must we repeat it? — they covered His face with spittle.[7]

John 19, 4—7.   22.

What a spectacle!   Putting an end to this misery for the
present, Pilate led Jesus forth.   Hoping the sight of the scourged
Prisoner would content the Jews, he brought Him out that they
might see Him and that He might have another opportunity of
pronouncing Him guiltless.   Pointing to Jesus, who was still wearing the mock symbols of royalty and was covered with blood, he
burst out into that famous "involuntary exclamation which has
thrilled untold millions of hearts": [1] "Behold the Man!"   Painters
have chosen this moment of extreme humiliation when Jesus came
forth, bleeding from cruel stripes, His back lacerated, wearing the
scarlet robe and the crown of thorns, the weariness of deathly
agony pictured in His sleepless eyes, as the one to portray the Man
of Sorrows.[2]   And many a priceless canvas bears the title "Ecce
Homo!   Behold the Man!"   Two words fell from Pilate's lips
which the world will never forget: "What is truth!" and "Behold
the Man!"   One may be taken as the answer to the other.   "What

"Behold the Man!"   is truth," heavenly truth, the will of
the Father, and the way to life may be
beheld only in the Man Christ Jesus.   Let the whole world turn
to Him and with a truly penitent and believing heart "behold the
Man."   It was an outcry to move the hard hearts to mercy; but it
only awakened a fierce uproar of bloodthirsty screams: "Crucify

---

21,   5) As regards the particular species of thorn, nothing definite is known.
  6) קָנֶה — κάλαμος, canna, cane.   Probably a reed or cane walking-stick.
Is. 36, 6.
  7) Stalker, 93.
22,   1) Farrar, II, 382.   2) Stalker, 103.

Him, crucify Him!" The mere sight of the suffering Jesus, even in these unspeakable depths, seemed only to add fuel to their infernal flames. Pilate pleaded with them. But again he missed his guess. There was no voice of compassion, but only the "howling refrain of their wild liturgy of death." [3] At his wit's end, Pilate cried out in utter disgust: "Take ye Him, for I find no fault in Him at all." What an admission from a Roman judge, and what a wretched subterfuge to attempt to escape the responsibility by shifting the blame to the Jews! Now the enemies felt safe. They saw that they had the governor completely in their power. Now they could even come out boldly with their real charge against Jesus, which hitherto they had kept carefully concealed. "We have a law,[4] and by our law He ought to die, because He made Himself the Son of God."

John 19, 8—11.   **23.**

What was that? "Son of God?" When Pilate heard these words, terror filled his superstitious soul. Immediately he left the yowling multitude and took Jesus with him to the interior of the Judgment Hall. There he asked Him with a mixture of awe and terror: "Whence art Thou?" For the fourth time [1] since the trial began Jesus retired into majestic silence. We can but guess at the purpose. He could not say that He was not the Son of God. And in this connection to have said that He was, would have been interpreted by Pilate in a grossly pagan sense.[2] And so He said nothing. And besides, it was too late now. Pilate had heard enough. Almost angrily he broke out: "Speakest Thou not to me?

"Whence Art Thou?" Knowest Thou not that I have power to crucify Thee and power to release Thee?" But Jesus soon set him straight on this point. Talking about power! Why didn't he show it? And what about justice, truth, innocence, and conscience? And as to power, in reality he had none except the governmental powers given to him from above. And he should be very careful not to abuse this power. Of course, he had been compelled to conduct this trial; yet he would not be excused for the miscarriage of justice. He would still be guilty, although the prosecutors, Caiaphas, "he that

---

22, 3) Farrar, II, 383.

    4) Referring probably to Lev. 24, 16.

23, 1) Before Caiaphas, Matt. 26, 63; Mark 14, 61; before Pilate, Matt. 27, 12; Mark 15, 4; before Herod, Luke 23, 9; and here, John 19, 9.

    2) Stalker, 106.

delivered Me unto thee," and the members of the Sanhedrin, had "the greater sin." Thus with "infinite dignity and yet with infinite tenderness did Jesus judge His judge," who just a few minutes before had given Him over to be tortured.[3]

John 19, 12—15.   **24.**

Pilate returned. He was still intent upon releasing the Prisoner. For the third [1] and last time since the beginning of that memorable trial on that early Good Friday morning, from about six to seven A. M.,[2] Pilate ascended the tribunal erected on the pavement called Gabbatha. And this time he was determined to carry out his purpose at all hazards. A crisis had come, and the frantic rioters could plainly see that there was fire in his eyes. But in his speech he never got beyond his opening words. For once he was willing to connive at their guilty and ill-concealed royalistic aspirations. "Behold your King!" But again he failed. For once the enemies of Rome would not have their disloyalty to the dearly beloved government of Rome flung into their face! Loyalty? Patriotism? Why, they even threatened Pilate with his! "If thou **"Behold Your King!"** let this man go, thou art not Caesar's friend. Whosoever maketh himself a king speaketh against Caesar." Pilate could not take the part of Jesus and retain the friendship of Caesar. This was plain language. "But shall I crucify your King?" The reply is: "We have no king but Caesar." If Tiberius had only heard this! How was that for patriotism as coming from that hotbed of insurrection? That settled it for Pilate, for the priests, for the people,

---

23, 3) Farrar, II, 385.

24, 1) At the beginning of trial, after the return of Jesus from Herod, and now.

2) "And it was the preparation of the Passover." The term "preparation," παρασκευή, was the usual appellation of Friday, the day of preparation for the weekly Sabbath. Here the addition of "the Passover" indicates that it was the Friday of Passover Week. Compare Matt. 27, 62; Mark 15, 42; Luke 23, 54; John 19, 31. 42. "Preparation" is still the name for Friday in modern Greek. As regards the question whether it was the 14th or the 15th day of Nisan, see chapter XXXI, 11. The time is given as "about the sixth hour." It appears that John, who wrote in Asia Minor after the destruction of Jerusalem, makes the day begin at midnight, as the Greeks and Romans did. In the language of the Roman court it was about 6 A. M., the time set for the beginning of the trial. Mark says that it was the third hour when they crucified Him, Mark 15, 25. Thus, according to Jewish time, the crucifixion took place about 9 A. M. (For a full discussion see Andrews, 545 ff.) We might add that the reading τρίτη for ἕκτη, third for sixth hour, is found in some manuscripts. See Nestle-Dobschuetz, p. 2.

for one and for all. Nothing would stop the crucifixion now. That *was* the last straw. "If thou let this man go, thou art not Caesar's friend!" At the terrible name of Caesar, Pilate trembled. At all events there must be no complaint lodged against him at Rome. Rather the loss of an innocent life, yes, a thousand lives, than the loss of the friendship of Caesar. And what about that hypocritical loyalty to Caesar? "We have no king but Caesar!" Indeed, how true! Pilate took them at their word; henceforth they would have no Savior, no Redeemer, no Friend, no King — but Caesar!

CHAPTER XXXV.

FRIDAY OF PASSION WEEK.
"CRUCIFIED."

April 7, 30 A. D., 783 A. U. C.

A. U. C.	779	780	781	782	783
A. D.	26	27	28	29	30
Age of Jesus	30	31	32	33	34
Passovers		I	II	III	IV

Nisan (or Abib)

10	11	12	13	14	15	16	17

April

2	3	4	5	6	7	8	9
Sun.	Mon.	Tue.	Wed.	Thu.	Fri.	Sat.	Sun.

783 A. U. C.   APRIL   30 A. D.

Sun.	Mon.	Tue.	Wed.	Thu.	Fri.	Sat.
						1
2	3	4	5	6	7	8
9	10	11	12	13	14	15
16	17	18	19	20	21	22
23	24	25	26	27	28	29
30						

1.

Matt. 27, 31 b. Mark 15, 20 b. Luke 23, 26 a.
John 19, 16. 17 a.

The trial of Jesus was over. The death warrant was signed. Once more the Savior was "unrobed and robed." [1] The mock purple was torn from His wounded shoulders and the crown of thorns from His bleeding brow. And with the order *"Ibis ad crucem!* Away to the cross!" or some similar phrase,[2] Jesus was

Jesus Led to the Cross. immediately led away. Cruci- fixion was not a Jewish mode of punishment. In Rome it became deplorably common after the time of Julius Caesar. Particularly does it seem to have charac- terized the government of Rome in Judea. There was a merciful law of Rome in existence that some time must pass, from two to ten days, between a capital sentence and its execution; but either it did not extend to the provinces, or it did not apply to Jesus "because He had made Himself king." [3] On account of the

1,   1) Edersheim, II, 582.
    2) Andrews, 543.   3) Stalker, 131.

[662]

approaching Passover Sabbath there was no time to be lost. The terrible preparations, the cross, the hammer, and the nails, were soon made. Naturally the Roman soldiers were in charge. According to all appearances it was a perfectly proper public Roman execution. As always, the cross was borne to the place of execution by Him who was to suffer on it. The procession was led by a centurion. In this case it was a man whom tradition remembers by the name of Longinus.[4] He was preceded by one who proclaimed the nature of the crime, as indicated on a wooden slate. The cross itself appears in varied form. As an instrument of torture it first was a single pale,[5] the *crux simplex,* after which it assumed the following forms: the so-called St. Andrew's cross,[6] the *crux decussata;* the Egyptian, or St. Anthony's, cross,[7] the *crux commissa;* the later Greek cross;[8] and the Latin cross, or *crux immissa.*[9] It was the latter on which, we believe, the Savior died. This form would most readily admit of affixing the board over the head with the threefold inscription of the accusation on the cross. But at any rate it was not, and could not have been, the massive and lofty structure of considerable weight with which thousands of pictures have made us familiar.[10] We need not enter into the intrinsically improbable story of the discovery of the true cross by Helena, the mother of Constantine, in 326 A. D.[11]

2.

Matt. 27, 32. Mark 15, 21. Luke 23, 26 b.

Jesus is now on the way to the cross. In modern Jerusalem there is a street, running roughly northeast to southwest, from the castle Antonia on the northwestern corner of the Temple complex to the Church of the Holy Sepulcher, which is pointed out

---

1,   4) Andrews, 562. Becoming a believer, he was afterwards said to have been the bishop of Cappadocia.

5) |
6) ✕
7) T
8) +
9) † Andrews, 550.   10) Farrar, II, 393.

11) Related by the early church historians: Socrates, I, 17; Sozomenus, II, 1; Rufinus, I, 7; and Theodoret, I, 18. It is very significant that Eusebius, in his *Life of Constantine,* III, 26—28, whose writings carry more weight than those of the above-named together, omits the story. It is apparently but a version of the old Edessa legend, which tells of an identical discovery of the cross, under the very same circumstances, by the wife of the Emperor Claudius, who is said to have been converted to Christianity by the preaching of Peter. The Jews generally burned the crosses. See H. E. Dosker, in *Int. St. B. Encycl.,* under "Cross."

as the veritable Via Dolorosa along which the procession passed. But this is doubted by many investigators. We must remember that ancient Jerusalem, even more than ancient Rome, is buried beneath the rubbish of centuries.[1] If, as we assume, Jesus was buried outside of the present city walls and somewhere near the traditional Holy Sepulcher, — if the Pretorium, as we take it, was at Herod's palace, — the way ran north and south and not roughly east and west. But, of course, if the Pretorium is to be identified with the castle Antonia, which, however, many refuse to admit,

The Via Dolorosa. then the street ran southwest along the traditional way. The traditional site of Christ's crucifixion and death, however, over which the Church of the Holy Sepulcher is built, is inside the present walls. This does not agree with the requirement that Jesus, condemned as a malefactor, had to, and did, suffer crucifixion without the city gates.[2] But this argument is met with the claim that the place was outside the walls at that time. The opinions are about equally divided. Then there is the opinion which places the crucifixion to the south, across the Valley of Hinnom. But there is a rapidly growing agreement that the place was on the northern end of the Temple hill, near the Damascus Gate, and without the city wall, the southern face of which hill, with holes in the rock, looks much like a skull. This place at least fulfils all conditions.[3] But after all it does not matter. The important consideration is not the place, but the cause and purpose of Christ's death and the truth of His resurrection. The straining endeavors of ages have found locations for a number of events which are said to have taken place on the Via Dolorosa: the place where the fainting Jesus made an impression with His shoulder in the stone wall when He fell, the house of St. Veronica, who wiped the bleeding brow of Jesus with a handkerchief, and the like.[4] We can discard these incidents as later disturbing embellishments. Two incidents, however, are recorded in the gospel history as having occurred on the way to the cross.

2,   1) Stalker, 132.

2) Lev. 24, 14; Num. 15, 35. 36; Deut. 17, 5. — John 19, 17; Matt. 28, 11; Heb. 13, 12.

3) For the various arguments see E. L. Wilson, *In Scripture Lands,* 223 ff.; Andrews, 575 ff.; and E. W. G. Mastermann, under "Golgotha," in *Int. St. B. Encycl.*

4) The story of Ahasuerus, the Wandering Jew, doomed to wander till the second coming of Christ because he taunted Jesus as He leaned against his door when passing it, bearing the cross. According to the legend he struck Jesus a blow and commanded Him to go on, to which the Lord replied, "I go, but thou shalt wait till I return." In a fantastic representation of an individual it is the tragic fate of the Jewish race. Stalker, 143.

3.

Matt. 27, 32. Mark 15, 21. Luke 23, 26 b.

It will be readily understood that Jesus, after the agony and tortures of a sleepless night, broke down [1] under the load of the cross. Even if pity did not move the Roman soldiers, they naturally would object to hindrance and delay. They helped themselves out of the difficulty by making a military requisition. An inhabitant of Cyrene, a city in North Africa, south of Crete, who presumably

Simon of Cyrene. was in Jerusalem on a Passover pilgrimage [2] and at the moment was coming into the city from the country,[3] was pressed into service and compelled to bear Christ's cross. His name was Simon, and afterwards, most likely on account of his Christian connection, he was familiarly known to Mark and other Christians as the father of Alexander and Rufus.[4] But there can be little doubt that the connection of the whole family with the Christian Church was the result of this incident in the father's life.

Luke 23, 27—31. **4.**

While Jesus was betrayed by Judas, denied by Peter, forsaken by the disciples, accused by false witnesses, condemned by the Sanhedrin, struck by the servants, reviled by Herod, lashed by the soldiers, sentenced by Pilate, all men, He was now lamented by at least one section of the community. While we have not forgotten the part which women played in the denials of Peter, it is quite significant that there is no instance of direct hostility of women in the gospel records against Jesus. Women followed Him, served Him, remembered His sayings, sat at His feet, called after Him, ministered unto Him of their substance, washed His feet with tears, anointed His head with oil, testified to His innocence during His trial, stood under His cross, and came to embalm His body. And now, while their husbands, brothers, and fathers were hounding Him to death, they bewailed and lamented Him.[1] All this of course is a strong testimony to the character of Jesus as well as a credit to the so-called weaker sex. But while women were, and

---

3, 1) See Mark 15, 22: φέρουσιν αὐτόν; carry Him. "They bring Him."

2) Compare Acts 2, 10.

3) Not necessarily "field," as if he had been working in the field and was now returning from labor.

4) These names are too common to enable us to identify them with those of the same name in Acts 19, 33; 1 Tim. 1, 20; Rom. 16, 13.

4, 1) Stalker, 147.

still are, some of the most faithful followers of Jesus, and while
their tears were natural and in some respects a genuine expression of
their sympathy, Jesus would have none of them. Mere sympathy
with the condemned Christ almost certainly involves an admission
of guilt on His part. And shedding tears without repentance implies a view of Him and His Passion which is essentially the opposite

The Lamentation of the Daughters of Jerusalem.

of that which His innocent suffering for us sinners should
effect in us. The weeping of
those women was at best an emotional outburst of womanly feeling.
Turning to them, Jesus says: "Daughters of Jerusalem, weep not
for Me, but weep for yourselves and for your children." He warns
them of the wrath which awaits them and their children and their
race. When the day of punishment will come to strike an impenitent race, it will strike men, women, and children alike. In
those days childlessness will be a blessing and barrenness an advantage. "Blessed are the barren and the wombs that never bare
and the paps which never gave suck." So terrible will be the affliction of those days that the people will call upon the mountains and
hills to fall upon them to hide them from the wrath of Almighty
God. "Then shall they begin to say to the mountains, Fall on us;
and to the hills, Cover us."[2] For if such terrible punishment as
they are now about to witness is meted out upon One who is Himself
innocent, but upon whom the Lord hath laid the iniquity of us all
that He might atone for the sins of the world, what will happen
to the guilty if they themselves are exposed to the burning fire of
the wrath of God? "For if they do these things in a green tree,
what shall be done in the dry?"

5.   38.

*Matt. 27, 33—38. Mark 15, 22—28. Luke 23, 32—34.
John 19, 17 b—24.[1]*

At this point we are informed that there were also two others,
malefactors, led [2] with Jesus to be put to death. They were rebels
and thugs of the lowest stamp. As far as the Romans were concerned, it was all in a day's work. There were always prisoners on
hand, robbers, bandits, and, as dissatisfaction with the powers that
be grew, especially such as rebelled against the government of

---

4,   2) Hos. 10, 8; Is. 2, 19.

5,   1) A close examination will reveal a few apparent discrepancies in the
order of events; but there are no contradictions.

2) Mark says φέρουσιν, as if Jesus were half carried, borne, to the
cross. Mark 15, 22.

Rome.[3]) If it had not been for the popular choice, no doubt Barabbas would also have been included in the procession. It is true that Pilate had been more than usually interested in the case of Jesus. But, after all, He was only one of many. His execution could be made part of that of other victims scheduled for that

The Arrival at Golgotha.

day. And so it happened that three condemned prisoners were marched out to the fatal spot. It was called Golgotha, or, in its Latin form, Calvary, that is, a Skull. Whether or not it had received its name from the fact that it was the usual execution ground, we do not know. Presumably it was called thus on account of its skull-like shape. It is constantly referred to as the hill of Golgotha or Mount Calvary, though the gospels speak of it merely as a place. While we picture it to ourselves off the highway to the north of Jerusalem, just outside the Damascus or St. Stephen's Gate, near Jeremiah's Grotto, nothing definite is known. All that we know of Golgotha, and all that God willed us to know, is that it was without the city gate.[4]) The representation of a skull in pictures at the foot of the cross refers to an old legend that the cross of Jesus rested on Adam's grave.[5])

6.   38.

Matt. 27, 33—38. Mark 15, 22—28. Luke 23, 32—34.
John 19, 17 b—24.

It was a merciful custom to give those led to crucifixion a medicated cup of sour wine mixed with some narcotic like wormwood or myrrh so as to deaden consciousness. This charitable office is said to have been performed at the cost of wealthy ladies in Jeru-

The Myrrh-Mingled Cup.

salem.[1]) The stupefying potion was probably freely taken by the two malefactors. It was offered also to Jesus. But as soon as He had tasted it and noticed its character and the purpose for which it was offered Him, He would not drink of it. Just as He declined the tears of the daughters of Jerusalem, so He now refused their cup. He preferred "to look death straight in the face."

5,   3) The brigands in the time of Felix. The banditti, the so-called *sicarii*, who committed murder daily in broad daylight with their short, curved daggers, especially in the festival seasons, from the time of Nero onward to the end of the last Jewish war. *Wars*, II, XIII. 2. 3.

   4) Heb. 13, 12.

   5) First mentioned by Origen, 185—253 A. D., who lived in Palestine for twenty years.

6,   1) Edersheim, II, 590.

7.   *38.*

*Matt. 27, 33—38. Mark 15, 22—28. Luke 23, 32—34.
John 19, 17 b—24.*

"And when they had crucified Him," or "where they crucified Him," — thus two evangelists in a participial phrase, and the other two in an equally passing manner, relate the terrible deed. And so we, too, turn our heads in horror as the huge nails "tear their way through the quivering flesh." [1] It was a terrible death. "Let it never," says Cicero,[2] "come near the body of a Roman citizen; nay, not even near his thoughts or eyes or ears!" As a method of dispatching condemned criminals from life to death it was a most

Crucified. inhuman means of execution, whose only purpose must have been to strike horror into the hearts of witnesses, to torture the victims, and to make death as painful and lingering as was humanly endurable. The crosses were erected so that the cross of Jesus was reared in the midst, and those of the malefactors were placed one on the right hand and the other on the left. Thus was the prophecy of Isaiah fulfilled that "He was numbered with the transgressors." [3] And in the midst of this infinite horror a voice cries out; it was a cry not of agony, as might have been expected, nor a cursing scream, but a fervent petition of the suffering Savior, for His enemies, His first word on the cross: "Father, forgive them, for they know not what they do."

8.   *38.*

*Matt. 27, 33—38. Mark 15, 22—28. Luke 23, 32—54.
John 19, 17 b—24.*

It was the third hour, that is, at nine o'clock in the morning, as Mark informs us, that the crucifixion of Jesus took place.[1] According to common Roman custom the clothes of the unrobed

**The Parting of
Christ's Garments.** victims, it seems, fell to the quarternion [2] of soldiers whose duty it was to guard the crosses. This was a precaution, taken to prevent the possibility of rescuing the crucified. At the request of Josephus to Titus, in the last Jewish war, three men who had been crucified were taken down alive. But in spite of all possible efforts to save them two of them died.[3] The soldiers

---

7, 1) Farrar, II, 401.   2) Quoted by Stalker, 163.

  3) Is. 53, 9. 12; Luke 22, 37; Mark 15, 28. The passage in Mark appears in the *textus receptus,* but is omitted in many manuscripts.

8, 1) Raising a harmonistic problem as compared with John 19, 14. See chapter **XXXIV**, 24.

  2) Acts 12, 4.   3) *Vita,* 75.

at the cross of Jesus decided to divide the head-gear, the outer garment, the girdle, and the sandals of the unrobed Jesus among themselves. But for the more valuable seamless inner garment, or *chiton,* which was woven in one piece from top to bottom, they decided to cast lots. To tear it would have been to spoil it. "Let us not rend it," they said to each other, "but cast lots for it whose it shall be." How this was done we do not know, probably by casting dice. Thus unwittingly they contributed to a fulfilment of Scripture: "They parted My raiment among them, and for My vesture they did cast lots." [4]

9.   *38.*

Matt. 27, 33—38. Mark 15, 22—28. Luke 23, 32—34. John 19, 17 b—24.

Above each of the crosses was placed an inscription, on which was stated the charge on the strength of which the sufferers had been condemned. The title could be plainly seen, and it was indeed read by many because the crosses were conspicuously placed off the highway and near the city. In the case of Jesus, the title,

I. N. R. I.   it seems, had been drawn up under the special direction of Pilate. It ran in the three languages of the ancient civilized world. One of these was certain to be known to every one in the assembled multitude: local Hebrew, or Aramaic, the common language of the Eastern world; popular Greek, the language of culture throughout the Roman Empire; and official Latin, the language of camp and court. The title was supposed to state the charge, but at the same time it made public a sacred truth:

JESUS OF NAZARETH THE KING OF THE JEWS.[1]

Officially Jesus was crucified as a rebel, the judicial verdict being that He was executed because He had made Himself king of the Jews. But as the chief priests and leading Jews studied the superscription, it suddenly flashed upon them that in the particular wording the charge against Jesus was really an insult on the part of Pilate and the Roman government heaped upon them. King of the Jews? And crucified? It was as clear as day that Pilate and

---

8,   4) Ps. 22, 18. LXX version quoted verbatim. Dods sub John 19, 24.

9,   1)   ישוע הנצרי מלך היהודים

IHCOYC O NAZΩPAIOC O BACIΛEYC TΩN IOYΔAIΩN

IESUS NAZARENUS REX IUDAEORUM

THE TITLE ON THE CROSS, BASED UPON THE TEXT OF JOHN.

Rome were serving public notice that this is what would happen to every one that would become a Jewish king. Why this insult? Had they not that very day professed their loyalty to Rome? And besides, they had not even acknowledged Jesus as their king! Immediately they rushed to Pilate and demanded a change in the obnoxious title. "Write not," they demanded, " 'The King of the Jews,' but that 'He said, I am the King of the Jews.' " A slight change, but still in agreement with Pilate's sentence and, understanding 'King' as the 'Messiah' and 'Son of God,' in accordance with the finding of the Jewish court. But here was Pilate's chance to get even with them for forcing him in the morning to act against his will. His courage, which had so rapidly melted away at the name of Caesar, had now returned. He dismissed the priestly notables with a curt and contemptuous reply: "What I have written I have written." And Jesus was indeed in the true sense the King of the Jews, the promised Messiah, and the Son of God.

10.   **39.**

Matt. 27, 39—44. Mark 15, 29—32. Luke 23, 35—37.[1]

The people stood there and gazed. But some of them, probably some of the many false witnesses of the previous night, as they passed by the cross, ridiculed Jesus, wagged their heads,[2] and said: "Ah, Thou that destroyest the Temple and buildest it in three days, save Thyself and come down from the cross!" Likewise the scribes, chief priests, elders, and rulers were not ashamed to disgrace themselves with taunting cries: "He saved others, Himself He cannot save. If He be the King of Israel, let Him now come down from the cross, and we will believe Him. He trusted in God;[3] let Him deliver Him; for He said, I am the Son of God."

Mocked and Ridiculed by Passers-by.

And if these unholy ecclesiastics did not consider it beneath their dignity to heap insults upon a silently suffering and dying man, no wonder that the coarse soldiers, probably as they sat down to their midday lunch, in coarse brutality drank to Him as they gulped down their cheap sour wine and even mockingly asked Him to pledge them in return.[4] It was the basest mockery of His royalty when they flung at Him the taunt: "If Thou be the King of the Jews, save Thyself." Yes,

---

10, 1) Not in the exact order of Matthew and Mark, but it need not disturb us in the least.

2) Ps. 22, 7.   3) Ps. 22, 8.

4) Edersheim, II, 594. Luke 23, 36.

even the poor wretches who were crucified with Him, at least one of them, joined in this shameful abuse. Reproachfully they demanded of Him to save Himself and them if He were really the Christ.

Luke 23, 39—43.   **11.**

The priests, the scribes, the rulers, the soldiers, and, as a class, even the robbers on the cross joined in the mockery of Jesus. But there was an exception. Some think that one of the malefactors, whom tradition remembers as Dysmas, first joined in the reproaches, but soon spoke out his inmost mind;[1] rather, the Spirit of God had wrought in him a true and sincere sorrow of heart on account of his sins. Turning to the other malefactor, whom tradition has given the name Gestas,[2] the "good robber"[3] rebuked him for his blasphemous remarks: "Dost not thou fear God, seeing thou art in the same condemnation?" And then followed the wonderful

The Penitent Thief. confession: "And we indeed justly, for we receive the due reward of our deeds. But this man hath done nothing amiss." These words are a testimony to the innocence of Jesus and also a dying thief's confession of faith in the crucified Christ, for he adds: "Lord, remember me when Thou comest into [4] Thy kingdom." In spite of death Thou art going to Thy kingdom, and may I go there to be with Thee at the resurrection of the dead! To this intense appeal the Lord replies: "Verily I say unto thee, To-day" — not to-morrow or the following day or on the Last Day, at My second coming, but to-day — "shalt thou be with Me in paradise."[5] Death is a door through which he must pass; but as to his soul his last day upon earth is to be his first day in heaven.

John 19, 25—27.   **12.**

Many voices were raised to mock Jesus, and still there were hearts in the crowd that painfully beat in sympathy and deepest sorrow. Conspicuous among this heart-stricken group were the

---

11, 1) Farrar, II, 410.

2) Andrews, 554. Edersheim, II, 598. The names Titus and Dumachus are also found. Apocryphal New Testament, I. Infancy, VIII, 2—8.

3) *Bonus latro.*

4) The traditional text reads "in." The prayer then means: "When Thou comest as King to earth again, may I be among those whom Thou shalt raise from the dead to share its joys!"

5) A synonym for heaven in 2 Cor. 12, 4.

women that had followed Jesus from Galilee.[1)]   While the disciples were in hiding, at least most of them, these women followers exposed themselves to attack and shame.   First of all, there was the mother of Jesus, the Virgin Mary, a sword now passing through her soul at this horrible sight.[2)]   Then there was Salome, the sister of Mary.[3)]   It quite answers to John's method that he should refer to the second member of the small congregation under the cross of Jesus, his own mother Salome, only indirectly as "His mother's sister"; for in speaking of himself, he never mentions his name and even does not mention his brother.[4)]   The third member of the group is Mary, the wife of Cleophas, or Clopas, and, as we suppose, the wife or widow of Alphaeus, or Clopas, the brother of Joseph.[5)] And, besides the reporter, Mary Magdalene, out of whom the Lord had cast out seven devils,[6)] completes the group.[7)]   If our identifica-

Jesus Commends His Mother to John. tion is correct, then not only Salome, the sister of Mary, but also Mary, the wife of Clopas, Joseph's brother, would in a certain sense have been the aunt of Jesus and their sons His cousins.   Thus we notice among the twelve apostles five cousins of the Lord: James and John, the sons of Salome and Zebedee, and the three sons of Alphaeus, or Clopas, and Mary, James, Judas, and Simon.   Jesus was filled with loving concern for His own even in death.   When His eye fell upon His mother and the disciple "whom He loved," He entrusted His mother to him as a sacred charge.   "Woman,"[8)] He said to her, "behold thy son."   Henceforth John was to take His place as a providing son. And to John He said: "Behold thy mother."   If John was His mother's nephew, as we feel confident he was, then it was but natural that Jesus should entrust her to him rather than to one of the sons of His foster-father's brother.   The charge was accepted.

12,   1) Matt. 27, 55.   2) Luke 2, 35.

3) Mark 15, 40; Matt. 27, 56.

4) Weiss, I, 366, n. 1.   Meyer sub John 19, 25.

5) Luke 6, 15. 16 and Acts 1, 13, compared with Matt. 27, 56. Matt. 13, 55. 56.

6) Luke 8, 2.   But not to be identified with the unknown sinner of Luke 7, 37.   See chapter XII, 9. 11.

7) This is our view.   But, of course, there are others.   A change in punctuation reduces the number to three women: 1. His mother. 2. His mother's sister, Mary, the wife of Cleophas.   This view, besides eliminating Salome, would place two Marys into one family.   3. And Mary Magdalene. We need not here go into the whole question again.   See Andrews, 111 ff. Edersheim, II, 602 ff.   Dods and Meyer sub John 19, 24.   For Joseph and Mary, Alphaeus and Mary, Zebedee and Salome, relation and family, see chapter IV, 43.   For James, Judas, and Simon see chapter XI, 13.

8) In Greek not a term of disrespect.

Immediately John led her away from this scene of unutterable horror to the shelter of his home.[9] Except the notice that Mary continued with the early Christians in Jerusalem in prayer and supplication,[10] this really completes the story of Mary, the mother of Jesus. A few hours later we do not find her with the group consisting of Mary Magdalene, Mary, the mother of James and Joses, and Salome, the mother of James and John, and other women, "beholding afar off." [11]

13.

46 a.

Matt. 27, 45—50 a. Mark 15, 33—37 a. Luke 23, 44—45 a.[1] John 19, 28—30 a.

It was high noon by this time, and now an unnatural darkness swept over the guilty world. It cannot have been an ordinary eclipse of the sun because it was the season of the Paschal moon.[2] The fifteenth day of Nisan was the very day when the first full moon coincided with the period of the vernal equinox, making impossible an eclipse of the sun. The

Darkness from Noon to 3 P. M.

darkness continued from the sixth to the ninth hour,[3] from noon until three o'clock, and extended, if not over the whole earth, at least far over Judea and adjoining lands. Neither was it a sand-storm, for it was a darkness [4] as if the sun were actually eclipsed,[5] without the phenomenon of a lunar intervention. Scripture tells us nothing about the last three dark hours. "The awful darkness of the bright noonday sun in spring may well have overawed every heart into an inaction respecting which there was nothing to say." [6]

12, 9) *Εἰς τὰ ἴδια* does not necessarily mean that John had a house in Jerusalem.

10) Acts 1, 14.   11) Matt. 27, 55. 56; Mark 15, 40. 41.

13, 1) Luke introduces the rending of the veil in the Temple at this point, v. 45 b, which, however, probably occurred later. The arrangement of this section seems to be as follows: —

The darkness	Matthew	Mark	Luke
"Eli, Eli"	Matthew	Mark	
"I thirst"			John
It is finished"			John
A loud cry	Matthew	Mark	Luke
"Father, into Thy hands"			Luke

2) For that reason an eclipse mentioned by Phlegon in the 202d Olympiad, 29—32 A. D., is out of the question. Wieseler, Syn., 353 ff.

3) This is the first reference in Matthew to the time of day. Bruce sub Matt. 27, 45.

4) *Σκότος*.

5) *Τοῦ ἡλίου ἐκλιπόντος*, a well-attested reading in Luke 23, 45. Bruce sub loco.

6) Farrar, II, 414.

THE LIFE OF CHRIST.

43

14.   46 a.

Matt. 27, 45—50 a. Mark 15, 33—37 a. Luke 23, 44—45 a.
John 19, 28—30 a.

It was as if the voice of heaven were making itself heard through nature. A silent gloom made it appear as if even the earth and the sun were bewailing the ignominious death of the Son of God. Jesus drank the deepest dregs of the cup of humiliation and sank into the "fathomless depth of suffering, into which we cannot enter." [1] It was a suffering beyond all human endurance; it was possible for Him to endure it only because He is the Son of God. At the end of the third hour He broke the silence which He had maintained during that dread darkness by bursting forth into that awful, mysterious cry: *"Eli, Eli, lama*

"Eli, Eli, Lama Sabachthani?" *sabachthani?"* that is to say, "My God, My God, why hast Thou forsaken Me?" [2] The suffering Savior was made to feel the full weight of the sins of the world. Even God, whom in the last fearful moments of His extreme agony He addressed in His own familiar Aramaic, had forsaken Him. God forsaken by God! It is a mystery which eternity alone will solve. Christ felt the full measure of the wrath of God against sin and all the pain and anguish of hell deserved by every sinner. But He did not despair. Nor did He succumb. There was strength and glory in His suffering. This can be inferred from His very words, a quotation from a prophecy which contains a picture of His whole Passion, from extreme distress to supreme glory at the completion of the work of redemption. It was in His most intense anguish that His thoughts turned to that great Messianic psalm, the twenty-second, which begins with a cry of deepest agony and ends in praise.

15.   46 a.

Matt. 27, 45—50 a. Mark 15, 33—37 a. Luke 23, 44—45 a.
John 19, 28—30 a.

Amid the darkness and the muffled noise of the milling mass the words were not understood. Even if they had been, they would have been misunderstood. Some, very likely catching only the first word of the cry, thought that Jesus was calling upon Elias for

14, 1) Edersheim, II, 605.
    2) Ps. 22, 1.

help. And indeed, from their standpoint it did seem as if the
precursor of the great and terrible day of Jehovah [1] were in some
way connected with this marvelous phenomenon.   At the very
moment the bright spring sun was shrouded in an impervious dark

"Behold, He Calleth Elias!"   veil. According to a current view the coming again
of Elijah was intricately mingled with the coming of the Messiah.
At that time revelations of divine wrath must be expected.   "The
sun shall be turned into darkness and the moon into blood before
the great and the terrible day of the Lord come." [2]   The heavens
would come down and touch the mountains, and in some awful
form Elias, who went up by a whirlwind into heaven, [3] would make
his reappearance, riding upon pillars of smoke, this or something
similar would happen.   Of course, these vague anticipations were
unfulfilled.   Both Elijah [4] and the Messiah had already come.
And the latter was at that very moment hanging on the cross.

16.   *46 a.*

*Matt. 27, 45—50 a. Mark 15, 33—37 a. Luke 23, 44—45 a.
John 19, 28—30 a.*

At the cry of Jesus, for help as was thought, some one ran to
the vessel containing the posca, or sour wine, of the Roman soldiers.
The mouth of the vessel was filled with a sponge, which served as
a cork. [1]   And it was probably also at this moment that Jesus,
"knowing that all things were now accomplished," in order that

"I Thirst!"   the scripture, a word of prophecy, might be fulfilled, [2] broke into the only cry expressive of
physical suffering: "I thirst!"   Instantly the sponge was soaked
to the wine and placed upon the end of a hyssop reed [3] and
raised to the parched lips of the dying Savior.   But even this simple
act of pity, which Jesus did not refuse, was the occasion of mocking
remarks.   All right! Let Him be refreshed! they said.   "Let us see
whether Elias will come to take Him down."   It seems that even
he who performed the act of mercy joined the rest in uttering these
unloving words. [4]

15, 1) Mal. 4, 5.   2) Joel 2, 31.
     3) 2 Kings 2, 11.   4) Matt. 11, 14. Mark 9, 13.
16, 1) Farrar, II, 417.   2) Ps. 69, 27.
     3) The plant has not been definitely identified. Dods sub John 19, 29.
     4) Mark 15, 36.

17.

46 a.

Matt. 27, 45—50 a. Mark 15, 33—37 a. Luke 23, 44—45 a.
John 19, 28—30 a.

Elias did not come! There was no *deus ex machina*, no Elijah, no angel, no deliverer! It was the will of God that the Savior should drink the cup and be made perfect through sufferings.[1] After Jesus had taken the drink, not "on account of a spurious thirst for the sake of a constructed fulfilment," on the contrary, a real need contributing to a true fulfilment, Jesus now announced

"It is Finished!"   to the world the completion of His work. It was not the gasp of a dying man, but as a proclamation of victory Jesus uttered the exultant cry: "It is finished!" Finished was His suffering for the sins of mankind, finished His redeeming work! All the things that were written in the Old Testament Scriptures concerning the Messiah were now fulfilled.[2] At an end at last were the well-nigh unending mockery and endless shame. All things were now accomplished. The battle had been fought, the Serpent had been crushed, sin had been conquered, redemption was effected, and the walls of separation between man and God were removed.

18.

46 a.

Matt. 27, 45—50 a. Mark 15, 33—37 a. Luke 23, 44—45 a.
John 19, 28—30 a.

And then, once more crying out with a loud voice, not in the manner of a dying man,[1] with the words of a psalm on His lips,[2] the Savior commended His spirit into the hands of God. "Father,

"Father, into Thy Hands I Commend My Spirit."   into Thy hands I commend My spirit." Death did not come to Jesus, but Jesus came to Death.[3] Even as He had come forth from the Father and gone into the world, so He here for "a little while"[4] cut Himself off from physical life and went to the Father.

17, 1) Heb. 2, 10.

2) Luke 24, 44; Acts 3, 18.

18, 1) Still, impiously and contrary to the word of Christ "I lay down My life; . . . I lay it down of Myself," John 10, 17. 18, some writers state that Jesus died of a ruptured heart. See Bruce sub Matt. 27, 50.

2) Ps. 31, 5.

3) In the language of an early Christian hymn. Quoted by Edersheim, II, 609.

4) John 16, 16.

CHAPTER XXXVI.

FRIDAY OF PASSION WEEK.

"DEAD AND BURIED."

April 7, 30 A. D., 783 A. U. C.

A. U. C.	779	780	781	782	783
A. D.	26	27	28	29	30
Age of Jesus	30	31	32	33	34
Passovers		I	II	III	IV

Nisan (or Abib)

10	11	12	13	14	15	16	17

April

2	3	4	5	6	7	8	9
Sun.	Mon.	Tue.	Wed.	Thu.	Fri.	Sat.	Sun.

783 A. U. C. APRIL 30 A. D.

Sun.	Mon.	Tue.	Wed.	Thu.	Fri.	Sat.
						1
2	3	4	5	6	7	8
9	10	11	12	13	14	15
16	17	18	19	20	21	22
23	24	25	26	27	28	29
30						

1.

Matt. 27, 50 b. Mark 15, 37 b. Luke 23, 46 b. John 19, 30 b.

"And gave up the ghost." With these words the evangelists describe the death of the Savior. They do not use the word *died*, which would describe a passive condition, but a phrase which distinctly asserts an act. Indeed, the Savior died. "O sorrow dread, our God is dead!" It was a true death in every respect. But at the

"And Gave Up the Ghost." same time Christ's death was a voluntary resignation of His life in accordance with His own words: "I lay down My life that I might take it again. No man taketh it from Me, but I lay it down of Myself; and I have power to take it again." [1] It was a distinctly voluntary sacrificial act. "He gave up His life because He would, inasmuch as He would, and as He would." [2] And still it was death. It was the cold hand of death that touched

---

1, 1) John 10, 17. 18.   2) St. Augustine.

His brow. There is real sorrow when a noble life is softly and peacefully pillowed in death. But there never was such a pitiful sight as when this great Sufferer, whose life had been spent in perfect obedience to His Father's will and in loving service of man and who suffered and died for the redemption of sinful mankind, bowed His head on the cross. Dead. But He died that we might live.

2.

Matt. 27, 51—56. Mark 15, 38—41. Luke 23, (45 b).[1]
47—49.

Strange phenomena attended the death of Christ. "Behold, the veil of the Temple was rent in twain from the top to the bottom." This is spoken of first as being a most significant token, especially to Israel. Reference is to the veil which separated the Holy from the Holy of Holies in the Sanctuary, which was made "of blue and purple and scarlet and fine twisted linen, of cunning work."[2] From a rabbinic source we learn that its dimensions were sixty by thirty feet and that it was of the thickness of a palm. In the exaggerated language of the time it was so heavy that it required three hundred priests to handle it.[3] This veil was now rent in twain, which exposed the Holy of Holies to the vulgar eye. Here was a clear indication that the Old Testament with its high

The Phenomena Accompanying the Death of Christ. priests and typifying sacrifices was now a thing of the past. There was now no more need of an intervening screen and mediating high priests; for by virtue of the atoning blood of Christ all sinners have free access to the throne of God.[4] The rending of the veil must have taken place about the time when the priests in the Temple were making preparations for their evening sacrifice. How it happened we do not know. But all of a sudden the priests were able to gaze into that awful emptiness of the most holy enclosure into which hitherto the high priest alone had been permitted to enter, and that but once a year. With unprivileged eyes to have gazed on the dwelling-place of God must have seemed to them a terrible portent. Indeed, we are told of strange portents which appeared forty years before the destruction of Jerusalem. The mysterious extinction of the

---

2,   1) The rending of the veil is introduced by Luke in connection with the darkness.

    2) Ex. 26, 31.

    3) Edersheim, II, 616.   4) Heb. 9, 8 ff.; 10, 20.

chief light in the golden candlestick, the supernatural opening of themselves of the great Temple gates, and the shattering of a vast beam over a Temple lintel [5] may have been distorted versions of the strange phenomena attending the death of Christ.

3.

Matt. 27, 51—56. Mark 15, 38—41. Luke 23, (45 b).
47—49.

And there were other signs. "The earth did quake, and the rocks rent." As a result, graves were opened, and dead bodies of departed saints returned to life. This does not mean that "in the confusion of an unnatural darkness, to which was added the terror of an earthquake, bewildered minds imagined that they saw the disimprisoned spirits of the dead." There was an actual restoration to life of departed saints. Through

Resurrected Saints. His death Christ "hath abolished death and hath brought life and immortality to light." [1] Who they were the evangelists do not state. Whether they had recently died or had been long dead does not matter. "Many bodies of the saints which slept, arose, and came out of the graves after His resurrection, [2] and went into the Holy City, and appeared unto many." In spite of its monstrous wickedness Jerusalem was still called the Holy City, [3] because it harbored the Sanctuary of God. Of these resurrected saints nothing further is known.

4.

Matt. 27, 51—56. Mark 15, 38—41. Luke 23, (45 b).
47—49.

The long darkness, the loud voice, the Savior's sudden death, and the earthquake were not without effect. The leader of the executioners and of the Roman guard, the centurion, whom tradition remembers as Longinus, [1] now came forward with a wonderful confession. Many a sad scene of horror must he have seen in his day, — it was a cold and an inhuman age, — but none like this. It is assumed that he had witnessed all, from the trial before Pilate, probably even from the arrest in the Garden, to the end. There

---

2,   5) Ylvisaker, 752. Edersheim, II, 610.

3,   1) 2 Tim. 1, 10.

   2) Μετὰ τὴν ἔγερσιν αὐτοῦ. The only place in the New Testament where the term ἔγερσις is used. Active rising of Christ. The usual word is ἀνάστασις. See Bruce sub Matt. 27, 53.

   3) Is. 48, 2; 52, 1; Neh. 11, 1; Matt. 4, 5. Meyer sub Matt. 4, 5.

4,   1) Andrews, 562.

was only one conclusion at which he could arrive. Jesus was not guilty, even as Pilate had repeatedly stated, and He was actually what He professed to be and for the profession of which He was condemned. "Certainly this was a righteous man" [2] and "the

"Truly, This Was the Son of God!" Son of God." [3] It was a Christian confession, and it was the truth. Tradition has it that later he was bishop of Cappadocia. [4] And not only the centurion was impressed, but also "they that were with him watching Jesus," the Roman guards, who had previously derided Jesus, "feared greatly" and joined in the confession. Likewise many of the multitude, beholding the things which were done, returned to Jerusalem, smiting their breasts. We may hope that as a result many of them afterwards espoused the Christian faith.

5.

Matt. 27, 51—56. Mark 15, 38—41. Luke 23, (45 b). 47—49.

Only a small congregation of faithful followers remained. "All His acquaintance" that followed Him from Galilee stood afar off. But only women followers are named, such as had ministered unto Him and followed Him from Galilee to Jerusalem. Among these was Mary Magdalene. Then there was Mary, the

The Women Followers. mother of James the Less and Joses. [1] Also Salome, the wife of Zebedee and mother of James and John. And there were others. Mary, the mother of Jesus, who appeared with Salome and the two Marys, the wife of Cleophas and Mary Magdalene, under the cross, [2] is not mentioned. It is assumed that John, who is silent at this point, had removed her from this scene of horror and himself left the cross for a few minutes after Jesus had committed His mother to his charge.

John 19, 31—37.   6.

As the darkness receded from the completed sacrifice on Calvary, the reappearing April sun was fast approaching the evening of the Sabbath, which began at six o'clock. In general, there was a law that the body of a criminal should not be left hanging unburied

---

4,   2) Luke.   3) Matthew and Mark.
     4) Andrews, 562, n. 4. Stalker, 293.
5,   1) See chapter XI, 13. Of this Joses nothing further is known. His name appears (Mark 6, 3 and Matt. 13, 55) among the "brethren" of Jesus.
     2) John 19, 25.

overnight.[1] And now, since it was the Day of Preparation, that is, Friday, and the next day was both a Sabbath and the second Paschal Day and therefore a high day and the day when the wave-sheaf was offered to the Lord,[2] there was all the more reason to have the corpses removed. They who had not regarded the murder of the Messiah a pollution of the Passover were now concerned about the sanctity of the Passover Sabbath. Official application was therefore made to Pilate for an order to have the legs of the crucified

The Crurifragium. victims broken and their bodies taken down. Ordinarily, according to Roman custom, the bodies would have decayed on the cross. And if the bodies were taken down, precaution was taken by means of the so-called crurifragium that this was not done as long as the crucified were still alive. Now, crucifixion was a slow death, the sufferers living at least twelve, sometimes as long as forty-eight hours before death set in. Thus by means of a club or hammer, followed probably, as some think,[3] by the stroke of a sword or the thrust of a spear, an end was quickly put to what remained of life. Pilate had no objection to the request and therefore granted it. The soldiers came, probably from both sides, and broke the legs of the malefactors first; but when they came to Jesus, they found that He had already died. Unwittingly they observed a regulation of the Passover lamb, whose antitype Jesus was, and contributed to the fulfilment of a prophecy: "A bone of Him shall not be broken."[4]

John 19, 31—37.   7.

But in order to make certain of the death of Jesus, one of the soldiers forced the head of his spear into His side. "And forthwith," says St. John, attesting the truthfulness of his account, "came there out blood and water." This puzzling effusion has caused much discussion.[1] It is said that this phenomenon would naturally take place, but only if a crucified person died of rupture of the heart. But it is best not to make an attempt at a physiological explanation. Why speak of the physical cause of the death of Christ? What happens and ordinarily does not happen with corpses can hardly be applied to the sacred and uncorrupted[2]

6, 1) Deut. 21, 23.
    2) Lev. 23, 11—14. See chapter XXXI, 3. 11.
    3) Edersheim, II, 613.
    4) Ex. 12, 46; Num. 9, 12; see also Ps. 34, 20.
7, 1) For the various views see Andrews, 567 ff.   2) Ps. 16, 10.

body of Christ. John himself offers no explanation. He merely stresses the remarkable fact, assures the reader that his is a truthful account, and points to a fulfilment of Scripture: "They shall look on Him whom they pierced."[3] "And he that saw it bare

The Spear-Thrust. record, and his record is true; and he knoweth that he saith true that ye might believe." Quite naturally the passage lends itself to symbolical interpretation. From the riven side of Jesus there spring forth the cleansing water and the redeeming blood.[4] The beautiful saying has come down from the Fathers that from the side of Jesus, as from the open door to life, have flowed forth the holy Sacraments of the Church.[5] At any rate, there is no doubt that Jesus truly died.[6]

8.

Matt. 27, 57—60. Mark 15, 42—46. Luke 23, 50—54. John 19, 38—42.

For the present the members of the Sanhedrin were not concerned about the burial of Jesus. As long as His dead body was removed from the cross so as not to defile the land,[1] especially in this sacred season, they would have been satisfied if together with the bodies of the malefactors it had been cast into some nameless grave. But some one else was interested in His burial, one whose strange attention in the matter could not be easily brushed aside.

Joseph of Arimathea. On that memorable pre-Sabbath afternoon one of their aristocratic associates came out boldly before Pilate and "craved the body of Jesus." His name was Joseph of Arimathea. The place, a Jewish city, is otherwise unknown.[2] He was a man of wealth and high character and a distinguished member of the Supreme Council of Jerusalem. In the trial of Jesus he had not consented to the wicked counsel, he himself looking for the kingdom of God. In fact, he

---

7,   3) Zech. 12, 10.

4) John 7, 38; 1 John 1, 7.   5) Ylvisaker, 754.

6) The incident of the water and the blood is also brought into connection with the disputed passage of the three witnesses in 1 John 5, 6—8. To the witness of the Spirit there is added the witness of the water and the blood.

8,   1) Deut. 21, 22. 23.

2) Some identify it with Ramathaim-zophim, the Ramah of Ephraim and the birth- and burial-place of Samuel, 1 Sam. 1, 1. 19; 25, 1; others, with, it seems, greater likelihood, identify it with the Ramah in Benjamin, a few miles north of Jerusalem, which for a time belonged to Samaria, but later was joined to the province of Judah, 1 Macc. 10, 38; 11, 28. 34. Hence "a city of the Jews."

was a secret disciple, but hitherto had failed openly to profess his faith on account of fear of the Jews. But now, in a bold avowal of his love, he asked for permission to bury the body of Jesus.

9.

Matt. 27, 57—60. Mark 15, 42—46. Luke 23, 50—54. John 19, 38—42.

Two things must have strangely impressed Pilate. In the first place, that this man of standing, whom an apocryphal Gospel [1] even calls a "friend of Pilate," should make this request. Did he not belong to the very number of judges who had so urgently insisted upon the death of Christ? And in the second place, Pilate

Pilate Gives Permission to Bury Jesus.

was astonished that Jesus was already dead. Calling to him the centurion, he asked him "whether He had been any while dead." The centurion assured him that Jesus was certainly dead; for otherwise he and his guard would still be out there watching the crosses. And when Pilate had learned that all was in order, he immediately assigned the body of Jesus, probably with some degree of satisfaction, to this "counselor of honorable estate."

10.

Matt. 27, 57—60. Mark 15, 42—46. Luke 23, 50—54. John 19, 38—42.

The time was growing short. Joseph wasted no moments, while he still had a chance before the closing of the shops, to purchase a long fine piece of linen cloth. And immediately another man came forward. We have met him before, another member of that august body which had passed sentence upon Jesus. It was

Nicodemus.

none other than the Pharisee who had come to Jesus by night — Nicodemus. [1] It was he who at a later time had asked the unholy plotters: "Doth our Law judge any man before it hear him?" [2] If he was present at the trial of Jesus, we may hope that he likewise dissented from the death-

---

9, 1) The Gospel of St. Peter. Legends of a later origin claim that Joseph was sent by the Apostle Philip from Gaul to Britain in 63 A. D. and that he built an oratory at Glastonbury, that he brought the Holy Grail to England, and that he freed Ireland from snakes. C. M. Kerr, in *Int. St. B. Encycl.* under "Joseph of Arimathea."

10, 1) John 3, 1. See chapter VII, 5.
    2) John 7, 50—52.

sentence. He made his appearance with a costly compound of myrrh and aloes [3] for the embalmment of Jesus. The supply was bountiful, about a hundred-pound weight, [4] testifying both to his riches [5] and to the great measure of his love of Jesus.

11.

Matt. 27, 57—60. Mark 15, 42—46. Luke 23, 50—54. John 19, 38—42.

Whether these two Jewish dignitaries had previously been closely associated we do not know. But deeds of love and charity are in need of no introduction. Close by the place of crucifixion was [1] a court or garden belonging to Joseph. In its enclosure he had a new and unused tomb, hewn out of the solid rock for his own future use. "Wherein was never man yet laid," which there-

Jesus Laid in Joseph's Tomb.

fore was fresh and clean. The Sabbath was so near at hand that the embalmment could be only temporary and hasty. Between layers of the aromatic preparations Joseph and Nicodemus wound the limbs and the body, from which the vital parts had not been removed, in long strips of linen cloth, after the manner of the *Jewish* burial customs. [2] And likewise a separate cloth, or napkin, was wound around the head. The sun was sinking behind the western hills. As the Day of Preparation, that is, Friday, came to a close and Sabbath dawned, [3] they rolled a great stone to the door of the sepulcher and departed.

12.

Matt. 27, 61. Mark 15, 47. Luke 23, 55. 56 a.

For the moment nothing more could be done. Only a few of the faithful women who had followed Jesus from Galilee to Jerusalem, remained in the neighborhood to see where His body was laid. They could hardly be expected to come forward when

---

10, 3) Ps. 45, 8.

4) The λίτρα (*libra,* or pound) was rather over eleven ounces avoirdupois. Dods sub John 19, 39.

5) Compare Is. 53, 9: "Made His grave with the rich."

11, 1) But probably there is no significance in the ἦν, "was," as if the place was no more in existence when John wrote his gospel.

2) John 19, 40. This for the purpose of informing the reader that the body of Christ was not disemboweled. The Egyptians also wrapped the mummies; but when *they* embalmed the dead, the intestines were removed. Ylvisaker, 756.

3) Luke 23, 54. The sunset of Friday evening was the dawn of Sabbath.

they observed that two distinguished members of the Sanhedrin had taken matters in hand. They noticed, however, that the body had not yet been properly and completely embalmed. Among

Women Followers Witness the Burial.
them were the same that have previously been mentioned: [1] Mary Magdalene and the other Mary, the wife of Alphaeus, or Clopas, and the mother of James and Joses.[2] And a few other women. They decided to hurry home now and to provide spices and ointment that they might be at hand early Sunday morning to complete their service of love.

Matt. 27, 62—66.　　　**13.**

And now Sabbath and rest. For all, but not for the enemies of Christ. Because of their uneasy consciences awful misgivings still vexed them in spite of the Savior's death on the cross; especially probably since they had seen two of their own number attend to the burial of the slain Jesus of Nazareth, harassing suspicions were aroused within them. And neither was there rest for Pilate. From the standpoint of the Jewish recorder it was already "the next day that followed the Day of the Preparation." But according to our division of time it was probably still the same day, that is, Good Friday, the evening of the Sabbath which had just begun. Again Pilate was disturbed by a delegation. What else might be said of this representative of the power of Rome, it must be stated to his credit that at all hours of the day he was on the job. From the early hours of the morning to late at night he was in his office,

The Guard at the Grave of Jesus.
as it were, in the interest of a disliked *pax Romana* on this unthankful Palestinian soil. The relentless enemies of the slain Jesus were still persecuting the object of their still unspent venom even after death. "Sir, we remember," they said, with a contemptuous reference to the unnamed object of their hatred, that this "deceiver [1] said while He was yet alive, After three days I will rise again." [2] Of course, there was no danger of His returning to life, but the attempt might be made to supply a fictitious fulfilment of His prediction. "Command therefore that the sepulcher be made sure until the third day lest His disciples come by night and steal His body and say to the people, He is risen

---

12, 　1) See chapter XXXV, 12; XXXVI, 5.
　　2) Mark 6, 3; Matt. 13, 55.
13, 　1) Πλάνος, vagabond.　　2) Matt. 12, 40.

from the dead; so the last error shall be worse than the first." In a contemptuous manner Pilate gave them permission to do anything they liked in the matter. "Ye have a watch;[3] go your way, make it as sure as ye can." A guard was placed at their disposal. The stone was sealed. This was probably done by stretching a cord across the stone at the mouth of the sepulcher and then fastening it to the rock on both ends by means of sealing-clay.[4] And all precautions were taken to prevent theft — and resurrection.

14.

Matt. 28, 1. Mark 16, 1. Luke 23, 56 b.

The next day, Saturday, was spent by the disciples in a sad and miserable silence. They were as a flock of scattered sheep whose shepherd had been slain. Not until late in the afternoon,[1] when **Saturday.** the Jewish Sabbath verged on the first day of the week, that is, Saturday evening, did the two Marys, Mary Magdalene and the other Mary, the mother of James and Joses, venture out for a brief glimpse of the guarded grave, after which, together with Salome, they completed the purchase and preparation of spices and ointment for the task which they intended to perform early the following day.

13, 3) Or else imperative: "Have your watch!" Ἔχετε κουστωδίαν. Notice also the Latinism, which would be quite natural in the case of Pilate. Bruce *sub loco*.

4) Meyer *sub loco*.

14, 1) Matt. 28, 1: "In the end of the Sabbath, as it began to dawn toward the first day of the week." Ὀψὲ δὲ σαββάτων, "now late on the Sabbath-day" (Revised Version). This phrase once gave much trouble, but the usage of the vernacular *Koine* Greek amply justifies the translation. The visit of the women to inspect the tomb was thus made before the Sabbath was over (before 6 P. M. on Saturday). But the same Greek idiom was occasionally used in the sense of after. See Robertson, *Grammar of the Greek New Testament in the Light of Historical Research*, p. 645. The distance from Jerusalem or Bethany to Golgotha was not more than a Sabbath-day's journey. The spices could be purchased after sundown either in Bethany or Jerusalem. It must be remembered that the Jewish first day of the week began at sundown on our Saturday. A. T. Robertson, *Harmony of the Gospels*, 239, n.

CHAPTER XXXVII.

THE RISEN AND EXALTED SAVIOR.
RESURRECTION TO ASCENSION.

From Sunday, April 9 (Nisan 17), to Thursday, May 18,
30 A. D., 783 A. U. C.

783 A. U. C.   APRIL   30 A. D.

Sun.	Mon.	Tue.	Wed.	Thu.	Fri.	Sat.
						1
2	3	4	5	6	7	8
9	10	11	12	13	14	15
16	17	18	19	20	21	22
23	24	25	26	27	28	29
30						

Matt. 28, 2—4.   **1.**

We have now arrived at the most important chapter of this book. If this chapter is not true, then all the rest might as well have been left unwritten. St. Paul says:[1] "If Christ be not raised, your faith is vain; ye are yet in your sins. Then they also which are fallen asleep in Christ are perished." If the Christian religion applies only to this life, then its professors "are of all men most miserable."[2] Then the Christian religion would have value only as a philosophy of life, and a sorry one at that, as compared

The Resurrection of Jesus. with a looser moral standard, which would make most out of the enjoyment of material things. "Behold, these are the ungodly, who prosper in this world; they increase in riches."[3] Make a list of a half dozen of the most distinguished men living in the world to-day, and hardly one of them is distinguished for his Christian faith. "But now is Christ risen from the dead."[4] The most comforting "but" in all Scripture. Upon it everything depends, our hope of heaven, and from it everything follows. And since our faith is based upon the Biblical account of Christ's resurrection, we can proceed with our story. Neither need we be ashamed of this faith. Every honest and unprejudiced scholar has had to confess that the resurrection of Christ is a fact. Judged merely from the standpoint of authenticity, the gospels have proved themselves in every respect thoroughly reliable and trustworthy records of

---

1, 1) 1 Cor. 15, 17. 18.   2) 1 Cor. 15, 19.
       3) Ps. 73, 12.   4) 1 Cor. 15, 20.

[687]

history. The writer is here not quoting the opinion of others. This very book is the result of an extended and detailed study on the historicity of Jesus. But we cannot enter into the subject here. The whole life of Jesus is a proof of His resurrection. Then there is the transformation of the disciples at the outpouring of the Christ-sent Holy Ghost and the existence and preservation of the Christian Church.

Matt. 28, 2—4.   **2.**

Apparently the sealed and guarded grave of Jesus had been left undisturbed until the first faint streaks of that great Easter dawn. Even then, without thoughts of a possible resurrection of Him whom they loved, a group of pious mourners were on their way to do the last sad honors to a highly esteemed Dead. But in the mean time wonderful

The Earthquake and the Rolling Away of the Stone.

things had happened at the grave of Christ. There was another earthquake, a great shaking of the earth, coincident with the coming down from heaven of an angel of the Lord, who rolled away the stone and sat upon it as the guardian of an opened and empty grave. The appearance of his countenance was as lightning and his raiment as white as snow. At this dazzling appearance the frightened and trembling keepers became as dead men, and when they recovered from their stupor, they took to their heels and fled.

3.

Matt. 28, 5—7. Mark 16, 2—7. Luke 24, 1—8. John 20, 1.

It was very early on Easter Sunday morning, while it was still dark, that a band of grief-stricken followers left their quarters in Jerusalem or Bethany on their way to the sepulcher for the purpose of completing the work of embalmment. These included Mary Magdalene, the other Mary, the mother of James, Salome, Joanna, the wife of Chuza,[1] and others, whose names have not passed into history, but which are recorded in the Book of Life. The grief-stricken mother of Jesus is not mentioned. Probably her very sorrow caused her to be left behind. It seems that Mary Magdalene played the same part among the women that Peter assumed among the men. For the moment, however, stormy Peter as well as the leaderless group was still in hiding. As this devoted band of

---

3,   1) Luke 8, 2. 3; 24, 9. Chuza probably was the court official whose son Jesus had healed by the word spoken at Cana. See chapters XII, 11; VII, 21.

women with their burden of precious spices made their way through the glimmering dawn, they anxiously inquired among themselves:

Women Going to the Grave. "Who shall roll us away the stone from the door of the sepulcher?" After all, they were only weak women, and the slab may have weighed from three to five hundred pounds. But as they approached the grave, probably as the first rays of the rising sun were breaking over their shoulders, they could see that the stone had already been rolled away. It was probably at this point, without going any farther and fearing the worst, that Mary Magdalene rushed back to inform Peter and John of what she had seen.

4.

Matt. 28, 5—7. Mark 16, 2—7. Luke 24, 1—8. John 20, 1.

As the perplexed women pushed forward, they indeed found the stone removed, but, what was more, the grave was empty and the body gone. Moreover, looking up, they found that they were not alone. They were struck with a nameless fear as they beheld first one and then another angel in dazzling apparel. The latter, who probably acted as spokesman, had apparently seated himself "to the right" and on the stone without. Pointing to the empty tomb, the heavenly messenger preaches the first Christian Easter

"Why Seek Ye the Living among the Dead?" sermon. It treats of the dying Savior and the living Lord. "Fear not ye! Ye seek Jesus of Nazareth, who hath been crucified. Why seek ye the Living among the dead? He is not here. He is risen, even as He said. Remember how He spake unto you when He was still in Galilee [1] that the Son of Man must be delivered up into the hands of sinful men and be crucified and the third day rise again. Behold the place where they laid Him. Go quickly and tell His disciples, especially Peter: He is risen from the dead. And, lo, He goeth before you into Galilee. There ye shall see Him, as He said unto you. Lo, I have told you."

5.

Matt. 28, 8—10. Mark 16, 8. Luke 24, 9—11.

Trembling with fear and joy and probably forgetting all about the now unneeded precious ointment, the women fled from the tomb. They said nothing to any one along the way because they

---

4, 1) Mark 8, 31.

were afraid. But before they reached the city, Jesus Himself met them with the greeting "All hail!" Immediately they took hold of His feet and worshiped Him. They were overawed by His sudden

Jesus Appears to the Women.
appearance. But Jesus said: "Be not afraid" and added what they had already heard from the angel: "Go tell My brethren that they go into Galilee, and there shall they see Me." With their hearts and minds bursting with news of such paramount importance, they went to the Eleven [1] and to the circle of waiting friends. But even to them the extremely strange, though, if true, welcome, news appeared as an idle tale.

6.

Luke 24, 12. John 20, 2—10.

By this time Mary had already brought her report to Peter and John: "They have taken away the Lord out of the sepulcher, and we [1] know not where they have laid Him." For how else could she explain it? This startling news was too much for Peter and John. It induced them to run off at once. Now followed an extraordinary race to the grave of Christ. At first the disciples ran together, side by side. But soon the younger and nimbler John outran Peter and won the race. He came first to the sepulcher. But there he hesitated. He could not make up his mind to enter, but, stooping down and peeping in, he noticed the linen clothes

Peter and John Rush to the Grave of Christ.
which had been wound around the body of Christ, but did not go in. By this time the impulsive Peter had arrived. There was not a moment's hesitation. He entered and examined. And what he saw was significant. He saw the linen wrappings lying there, but found that the napkin which had been wrapped about the head of Jesus was not with the other linen, but was lying by itself and fallen together, as it were, in itself. Peter's remarkable discovery was communicated to John, who now entered and saw and believed. Just what did Peter see which caused him to wonder? What did John see and believe? What is there so significant about these linen wrappings [2] — in three verses

---

5, 1) Called the Eleven, although at the moment Peter and John may have been absent.

6, 1) John 20, 2. The plural proves the presence of other women with Mary, as related by the Synoptists. When alone, she uses the singular "I know not," etc., in John 20, 13. See Dods *sub loco.*

2) Ὀθόνια.

they are mentioned three times — which was to these disciples an indisputable proof that not a removal of the body, as had been feared by Mary, but rather that a resurrection had taken place?

7.

Luke 24, 12. John 20, 2—10.

Most commentators of this passage satisfy themselves with the explanation that it was the *order* found in the grave which forced upon the disciples the conviction that the body had not been stolen by friends nor removed by enemies, but that a resurrection had taken place. Without the thought of foisting his views upon others, the present writer is of the opinion that John says much more. Christ had risen with a glorified body, not only divesting Himself of the linen wrappings, but passing through them, even as He afterwards passed through closed walls and doors,[1] leaving the linen wrappings as an empty shell fallen together and undisturbed. This agrees with what John says in particular about the napkin.[2] He saw it lying, not on the heap with the other linen, as you would expect to find it when a man had taken off his clothes, but "by itself," in its own place, namely, on that particular place which had been occupied by the head, but the head was gone. We are told that it was "wrapped together in a place by itself," literally, in *one* place by itself.[3] That is, it was now still wrapped together just as it had been wound around the face and head, but the head was gone. In other words, the grave-clothes, the linen wrappings, the napkin,

The Linen Cloth and the Napkin.

had not been touched or unwound or disturbed since they had been placed about the sacred body of our Lord by Joseph and Nicodemus and were still lying there in the same place, but crumpled together like an empty shell. But the body was gone. Lazarus could not rise that way. He came up, bound hand and foot with grave-clothes, his face bound with a napkin, and Jesus had to say: "Loose him and let him go."[4] We have here a most wonderful proof of the bodily resurrection of our Lord.[5] Standing and gazing at the evidence before their very eyes, Peter and John came to the knowledge of the truth. It certainly is a remarkable fact, which aids in making

---

7,   1) Luke 24, 36; John 20, 19.

    2) Σουδάριον.

    3) Χωρὶς ἐντετυλιγμένον εἰς ἕνα τόπον.

    4) John 11, 44.

    5) See articles in *Lehre und Wehre,* 1914, 159 ff.; 1927, 167 ff.

the story trustworthy, that it was not the belief based on Old Testament Scripture and on Christ's own prediction that He would rise from the dead which led them to expect it, — in a way preparing the ground for resurrection stories, — but the evidence that He had risen from the dead led them to the Scriptures, to a right understanding of the Messianic prophecies as well as to a recollection of what Jesus had taught them. The resurrection of the Lord! We are not dealing with an invention or a delusion, with a vision or a fraud, but with history, written by eye-witnesses, yes, a fact which was unexpected and a startling surprise to the eye-witnesses themselves. It was not that hope which they had entertained in their hearts had paved the way for a belief in the resurrection of the Lord; rather, what they had beheld with their own eyes, the empty grave and the crumpled linen, convinced them that their beloved Master had taken His life again, as He had told the Jews He would and as had been prophesied in Scripture, all of which had hitherto been an enigma to them.

8.

Mark 16, 9[1]*—11. John 20, 11—18.*

In the mean time, Mary, who had followed Peter and John to the grave, stood without, hopelessly weeping. But to her, from whom had been cast out seven devils,[2] was to go the honor of the first private interview with the risen Lord. As she peered into the tomb with tear-filled eyes, she beheld the figures of two angels in white. They were sitting, one at the head and the other at the feet, where the body of Jesus had lain. To their question "Woman, why weepest thou?" she gives the reply: "Because they have taken away my Lord, and I know not where they have laid Him." At that moment, probably hearing a footstep, she turned back and saw Jesus.[3] But so altered was His appearance from the suffering figure she had last seen stretched on the cross that she did not know that it was Jesus, not even when He addressed her: "Woman, why weepest thou? Whom seekest thou?" Supposing Him to be the gardener or caretaker, as the only one likely to be present on the premises in that early hour, Mary said to Him: "Sir, if Thou

---

8,　1) This is not the place to enter into a discussion of the disputed close of Mark (16, 9—20). Though missing in many manuscripts, it is found in others. Present in Tatian's *Diatessaron.* And it is included in an important and very ancient uncial, the Washington (Freer) Manuscript, Codex W. Robertson, *Studies in the Text of the N. T.,* p. 100.

　2) Luke 8, 2.　　　3) Dods sub John 20, 13.

have borne Him hence, tell me where Thou hast laid Him, and I will take Him away." It almost seems as if she thought the removal due to a change of mind on the part of Joseph of Arimathea as a possible encumbrance of the ground. Jesus addresses her with one word: "Mary!" Recognizing the Master now, she gives utterance to her great surprise in an exclamation betokening highest respect: "Rabboni!" "Oh, my Master!" [4] Saying this, she may have made a forward movement. [5] But Jesus checked her. "Touch Me not," He said; "for I am not yet ascended to My Father." Not as if Jesus could not be touched. He had just permitted the friends of Mary to touch His feet in adoration. He later offered His body to the touch of the doubting disciples in proof that He was no spirit. [6] But that was different. The prohibition in this case was because His resurrection did not yet mean His return to visible fellowship with His disciples. [7] This was reserved for a later time; and even then He would no longer hold intercourse with them fully in the same manner as in His former state of humiliation. "But go to My brethren and say unto them: I ascend unto My Father and your Father, and to My God and your God." Patiently wait for the time when, in heaven, all who believe in Me will forever enjoy a most intimate, blissful communion with Me. — With a cry of joy Mary added her testimony to that of her friends: "I have seen the Lord!" But as yet the weeping disciples disbelieved.

The Appearance to Mary.

Matt. 28, 11—15.   9.

While the women delivered the message of the risen Lord, a few of the guard reported to the Sanhedrin, to whom Pilate had made them responsible, what had happened at the tomb of Jesus. "They came into the city and showed unto the chief priests all the things that were done." This report included the shaking of the earth, the appearance of the angel, the moving of the stone, their own seizure with a paralytic fear, and the empty tomb. The matter was considered important enough to be deliberated upon at a session of the highest native court. The matter was solemnly discussed, and the only way that seemed open to them to save their reputation and to prevent the people from believing in Jesus was to resort

---

8,   4) Compare Mark 10, 51: ʹΡαββουνί. The steps of honor in the title are said to be: Rab, Rabbi, Rabban, Rabboni.

5) Dods *sub loco.*   6) Luke 24, 39.   7) Dods *sub loco.*

to a lie. Thoroughly understanding the value of silver,[1] these
worthy judges were not slow in spreading it with a free and easy
hand. The distribution was accompanied with the instruction:
"Say ye, His disciples came by night and stole Him away while we

The Report of the Guard. slept." Of course, in spreading this report, the soldiers
incriminated themselves. It was well known that the ordinary military punishment for falling asleep on the watch was death. But aid
was promised if the story should lead to complications. "And if it
come to the governor's ears, we will persuade him and secure you."
The soldiers took the money. They might then have submitted
a true report to the governor. But it seems that they did as they
had been told. And whatever else might be said of the theft theory,
we know that ever since those days it has not failed to make its
threadbare rounds.

10.

Mark 16, 12. Luke 24, 13—32.

On that same Sunday afternoon "two of them," not of the
Twelve, but of the larger circle of disciples, were on their way to
a village named Emmaus, which was situated sixty furlongs, or
stadia, from Jerusalem.[1] It is now quite generally identified with
Kalonieh, lying about five miles to the northwest of Jerusalem, on
the road to Joppa.[2] The two disciples were having a lively discussion about the happenings of the last two days, when Jesus drew
near and asked them why they looked so sad and talked about
matters that seemed to trouble them very much. "But their eyes
were holden that they should not know Him." One of them was
Cleopas, otherwise unknown.[3] Many commentators have thought
of Luke himself as the other. If this was the case, then each of
the four gospels would, like a picture, bear in some obscure corner
the indication of its author:[4] Matthew, who alone among the
evangelists uses the epithet "the publican" in mentioning his name;
Mark, the young man "who fled from them naked"; John, the

9,   1) Bruce *sub loco.*
10, 1) One stadion about 600 feet; 60 stadia about 6 miles.

2) Josephus, *Wars,* VII, VI, 6. Schuerer, I, II, 253, n. 138. The
claims of Amwas, called Nicopolis in *Soz.* V, XXI, and the seat of an
episcopal see in the third century, about fifteen miles from Jerusalem, do not
satisfy the requirements of sixty stadia.

3) Not identical with Clopas (A. V., Cleophas) of John 19, 25.

4) Edersheim, II, 638.

disciple "whom Jesus loved"; and the other disciple on the way to Emmaus.[5] It was the companion of this unknown disciple who turned to Jesus with a touch of surprise: "Art Thou only a stranger in Jerusalem and hast not known the things which are come to pass in these days?" Jesus asked them: "What things?" And then they told Him. The one supreme topic of the hour was concerning Jesus of Nazareth, a prophet mighty in deed and word, whom the chief and popular rulers had condemned to death and crucified. But they had hoped, evidently misunderstanding the Messianic prophecies, that He would redeem Israel. They had probably dreamed of the overthrow of the Romans and the reestablishment of David's throne; but all their hopes had come to naught. He was dead. And besides all this, it was now the third day since these things had come to pass. And still a story was making the rounds, "women's talk," of an empty tomb, of visions of angels, who had told them that He was alive. Certain of the brethren had made an investigation at the tomb and had found that what the women had reported about the tomb's being empty was true. "But," the speaker added, probably with a significant shrug, "but Him they saw not."

The Two Disciples on the Way to Emmaus.

11.

Mark 16, 12. Luke 24, 13—32.

The Stranger listened in silence until the speaker had finished. Now it was His turn to speak. He reproached the two men for their dull intelligence and slowness of heart to believe all that the prophets had spoken. "Ought not Christ to have suffered these things and to enter into His glory?" And then, beginning with Moses and all the prophets, He led them to a true understanding of Scripture's prophecies concerning Himself. By this time Emmaus was reached. But Jesus "made as though He would have gone further." They pressed Him to stay, stressing the late hour, which, however, was not their real reason. "Abide with us; for it is toward evening, and the day is far spent." His teaching had impressed them, and they were anxious to learn more. "And He went in to tarry with them," at least for the evening meal. "And it came to pass, as He sat at meat with them, He took bread, and blessed it,

"O Foolish Men and Slow of Heart to Believe!"

10, 5) Matt. 10, 3; Mark 14, 52; John 21, 20; Luke 24, 18.

and brake, and gave to them." This is not a reference to the Lord's Supper. It was when He acted as their host, saying the table prayer and distributing the food, which they had so often seen Him do before, that "their eyes were opened and they knew Him." But when this point was reached, which included positive identification, the truth and proof of His resurrection, and, incidentally, the opening of Scripture and comprehension of the true significance of His Messianic work, "He vanished out of their sight." As soon as they recognized Him, He was gone. Looking at each other in questioning surprise, they could read in each other's eyes the same question together with its answer: "Did not our heart burn within us while He talked with us by the way and while He opened to us the Scriptures?"

12.

Mark 16, 13. Luke 24, 33—35. (1 Cor. 15, 5.)

That same day, but in circumstances and in a manner unknown to us, the Lord appeared to Peter. He is the first of the apostles mentioned to whom was given the privilege of beholding the risen Lord. And he needed this interview, for he was burdened by

The Appearance to Peter. a deep sorrow over a grievous sin. It was a special interview, far removed from inciting jealousy in the hearts of the other disciples;[1] it was vouchsafed him by the risen Savior because of His loving concern for him, as shown in the words which He spoke to him not many hours before his denial: "I have prayed for thee that thy faith fail not,"[2] on account of which the angel at the tomb had received the divine charge to say to the women: "Tell His disciples *and Peter.*"

13.

Mark 16, 13. Luke 24, 33—35.

It was impossible for the two disciples at Emmaus to keep the good news for themselves. Rising from their unfinished meal, they hastened to inform their brethren in the city. When they arrived, they heard of the risen Lord's appearance to Peter. They found the Eleven and those gathered with them. Probably Peter was arguing with the rest. Since the sad decrease of their number

---

12, 1) Which has supposedly, among other things, caused a change to be made in the original close of Mark. On account of Luke 24, 34. Rohrbach, quoted by Bruce under Mark 16, 9—20. In that case the removal ought to have begun with Mark 16, 7. "Tell His disciples and *Peter*"!

2) Luke 22, 32.

the apostles are now called the Eleven. But in reality, as we shall presently see, there were only ten, because Thomas was not with them.[1] The doors were closed for fear of the Jews.[2] The sub-

The Two Disciples Report to the Eleven.
ject of their conversation of course was the risen Lord. We can imagine Peter surrounded by nine of his col-
leagues and engaged in a lively debate. The two pilgrims who had gone from Jerusalem to Emmaus and just had returned were admitted. Immediately they added their testimony to that of Peter: "The Lord is risen indeed." But Thomas was not the only doubter. Even as the two rehearsed their story, the others disbelieved.

14.

Mark 16, 14.[1] Luke 24, 36—43. John 20, 19—25.

On that Sunday evening as the disciples were still discussing the happy news about the risen Lord, Jesus Himself appeared with the greeting: "Peace be unto you!" But the disciples were terrified and supposed that they beheld a spirit. Jesus upbraided them for their unbelief and their hardness of heart because they had not believed those who had brought the joyous report of His resurrection. "Why are ye troubled?" He asked them. And why are such anxious doubts in your hearts? "Behold My hands and My

The Appearance on Sunday Evening.
feet, that it is I Myself. Handle Me and see; for a spirit hath not flesh and bones, as ye see Me have." Jesus was
able to prove that He had certainly risen from the dead. Even while He spoke, He showed them His hands and His feet. And while joy and doubt were still struggling in their hearts, He asked them: "Have ye any meat?" And in order to assure them that,

---

13, 1) John 20, 24.　　　2) John 20, 19.

14, 1) Here follows in Codex W a remarkable interpolation (after v. 14): "And they defended themselves, saying: This world of lawlessness and unbelief is under Satan, who does not suffer those unclean things that are under the dominion of spirits to comprehend the power of God. On this account reveal Thy righteousness now. They said [these things] to Christ. And Christ replied to them: There has been fulfilled the term of years of the authority of Satan, but other dreadful things are drawing nigh [even to those] for the sake of whom as sinners I was delivered up to death in order that they might return to the truth and sin no more; in order that they might inherit the spiritual and incorruptible glory of righteousness which is in heaven. But go ye into all the world," etc. The first few lines of this insertion had been previously known in a Latin translation from Jerome (*Against Pelagians*, 2, 15), who states that he had seen the lines in some Greek manuscripts. See *Biblical World*, March, 1908, p. 206. A. T. Robertson brings the Greek text in *Studies in the Text of the New Testament*, p. 100.

though since His resurrection He had a glorified body, being no longer in the state of humiliation, it was still a true human body,[2] He ate a piece of broiled fish and of a honeycomb [3] in their presence.

15.

Mark 16, 14. Luke 24, 36—43. John 20, 19—25.

"Sir, we would see Jesus," with this request certain Greeks had approached Philip a few days before Jesus' crucifixion.[1] This same request was in the minds of the disciples. "Then were the disciples glad when they saw the Lord." Their sorrow was "turned into joy." [2] To the proof of His resurrection Jesus now adds a sermon. Again He addresses them: "Peace be unto you." He now prepares them for their mission of peace. "As My Father hath sent Me, even so send I you." Even as He had become the Father's Apostle, so they should become the apostles of Christ. The purpose of His labors upon earth was to procure the forgiveness of sins. The blessings of the completed work of redemption should now be brought to others in the proclamation of the Gospel. The Holy Spirit, with whom He had been anointed without measure,[3] He now bestowed upon them. Symbolizing the transmission, and conveying to them, of the Spirit of God, He breathed on them and said: "Receive ye the Holy Ghost. Whosoever sins ye remit, they are remitted unto them; and whosoever sins ye retain, they are retained." Not until Pentecost, however, when the Holy Spirit would be poured out upon them and they would be endued with power from on high, were they definitely and publicly to begin their work of peace. Nor is the Office of the Keys an authority conferred upon only certain individuals, a privileged class, or to be an arbitrary power,[4] but it accompanies, rather, is an outflow of, the Gospel; absolution is "the application of the general Gospel promises of forgiveness to individual persons." [5] By the preaching of the Gospel and the administering of the Sacraments, heaven is opened and sins are forgiven to all who believe; but the sins of those who reject the means of grace are retained.

"Whosoever Sins Ye Remit."

14, 2) Luke 24, 39 ("flesh and bones") ; John 20, 27; Phil. 3, 21.

3) The phrase about the honey is missing in leading manuscripts.

15, 1) John 12, 20.   2) John 16, 20.

3) Ps. 45, 7; Is. 61, 1; Acts 10, 38.

4) Compare Matt. 16, 19.   Chapter XVIII, 5.

5) *Christian Dogmatics*, p. 459.

16.

Mark 16, 14. Luke 24, 36—43. John 20, 19—25.

On this Sunday evening Thomas, called Didymus, or Twin,[1] one of the Twelve, "was not with them when Jesus came." Why, we do not know. When the other disciples told him, "We have seen the Lord," he would not believe them. It was not wilful rejection of a divine truth on his part, but he feared that his fellow-apostles had become victims of hallucination. Nothing short of

Thomas Is Absent. the testimony of his own physical senses would convince him. He is called Twin.

It was common in those days, as seen in the example of Cephas or Peter, to have corresponding Hebrew and Greek names. He was willing to believe — under certain conditions. And he stated the terms: "Except I shall see in His hands the print[2] of the nails and put my finger into the print of the nails and thrust my hand into His side, I will not believe."

John 20, 26—29. **17.**

A week had passed and with it the Passover festival and the Days of Unleavened Bread.[1] But the disciples were still in Jerusalem. While they continued to assemble privately, the expression "for fear of the Jews" no longer occurs. That apprehension had for the present passed away. Once more Jesus appeared with the greeting: "Peace be unto you!" This time Thomas was present.

The Appearance after Eight Days. He had not entirely separated himself from the "apostolic band." Nor had he become an outright agnostic; for otherwise his associates would not have tolerated his presence. Immediately the Lord directed Himself to His doubting disciple. Thomas had demanded proof. And proof could be given. "Then saith He to Thomas, Reach hither thy finger and behold My hands; and reach hither thy hand and thrust it into My side; and be not faithless, but believing."

John 20, 26—29. **18.**

Whether Thomas actually availed himself of the opportunity to satisfy his physical senses we do not know. At any rate, he was convinced. He burst forth into that most wonderful con-

---

16, 1) See chapter XI, 12.   2) Type, *τύπον.*
17, 1) According to our chronology April 6—13, 783 A. U. C., or 30 A. D., Nisan (or Abib) 14—21. This Sunday would bring us to April 16, 30 A. D.

fession: "My Lord and my God!" [1)] Thomas no longer doubted.
His confession has become the confession of the Christian Church:
"My Lord and my God!" Many years later, in Pliny's letter to
Trajan, the Christians are described as singing hymns to Christ as
God.[2)] But Thomas was also corrected. "Be not faithless, but
believing." He should have believed the testimony of the other
disciples, of his Master, and of Scripture.[3)] "Thomas, because
thou hast seen Me, thou hast believed. Blessed are they that have

"My Lord and My God!" not seen and yet have believed." This does not mean
that we should close our eyes and believe anything and anybody.[4)]
Faith must be based on reliable testimony. But it is wrong to say,
as the rationalists do, that the testimony of the Word of God is
not a sufficient basis for our religious teachings, that these teachings,
to be acceptable, must be approved by our reason or be confirmed
by the verdict of our own senses and observation. Even in the
natural sphere it is unreasonable to reject the testimony of witnesses.
Most of us have not seen the regions of the North Pole and the
land of the midnight sun, where, so we are told, the sun does not
set for weeks and months. Yet it would be foolish for us to
deny — just because we have not seen — that this is actually the
case. How much less should we refuse to accept the unerring
testimony of the Word of God!

John 20, 30. 31.   **19.**

Here follows the first close of John's gospel, in which we are
informed that Christ performed many unrecorded miracles. "Many

Unrecorded Miracles. other signs truly did Jesus in the
presence of His disciples which are
not written in this book." Such as have been recorded are "written
that ye might believe that Jesus is the Christ, the Son of God, and
that, believing, ye might have life through His name."

John 21, 1—14.   **20.**

A pause must have occurred in the appearances of the risen
Savior, which may have caused the disciples to return to Galilee,
where He had promised to see them.[1)] In the group of disciples

18, 1) For other confessions of disciples made at various times see chapter
XVIII, 5.
2) *Letters*, X, 96. A. D. 112.
3) Stoeckhardt, *Bibl. Gesch. d. N. T.*, 324.
4) 1 John 4, 1; Matt. 24, 4. 5.
20, 1) Matt. 28, 7; Mark 16, 7.

gathered by the Sea of Galilee we find Peter, Thomas,[2] Nathanael, of whom we are informed at this place that he was of Cana, James, John, and two others whose names are not given. For the moment they were without a final commission and without a common purse.[3] For three years they had followed Jesus, going on their errands without purse and scrip, never, however, lacking anything;[4] but now we may suppose them to have been in straitened circumstances. Quite naturally we can imagine them discussing ways and means of procuring a livelihood and finally joining Peter when he said: "I go a-fishing." This for the present seemed to them the only way of making an honest living. But they did not succeed in catching any fish. After getting their boats and nets, probably long unused, in order and setting forth one evening, they toiled all night, but took nothing. The next morning Jesus stood on

The Appearance beside the Sea of Galilee.

the beach; but they did not know it was Jesus. He called to them: "Lads,[5] have ye caught no fish?"[6] It was as if a fish merchant were asking them about their catch. "No," was their despondent reply. The voice came back: "Cast the net on the right side of the ship, and ye shall find." They probably supposed that the Stranger had been making observations from the shore and had noticed a shoal or signs of fish.[7] They followed the direction and dropped their net. "And now they were not able to draw it for the multitude of fishes." It was a miracle. The incident was so remarkable that the miraculous draught of fishes of earlier days was called to their minds.[8] Immediately the beloved disciple, John, whispered to Peter: "It is the Lord!" Instantly, though only half dressed,[9] Peter threw himself into a fisher's blouse and jumped into the sea. He swam the hundred yards or so[10] to the shore, leaving the disciples to drag the fish. On the shore, preparations for a meal were already found: wood-

---

20, 2) We are glad to see Thomas with the disciples, happily cured of all doubt.

3) Farrar, II, 441.   4) Luke 22, 35.

5) The familiar παιδία, boys, or lads.

6) Παιδία, μή τι προσφάγιον ἔχετε; Προσφάγιον really means a side-dish. In that sense fish was the ordinary side-dish eaten with bread. And the word was commonly used in the meaning of fish. Dods *sub loco.*

7) Dods *sub loco.*   8) Luke 5, 1—11.

9) One might have on the χιτών, the inner garment, and still be called naked. Dods *sub loco.*

10) Ὡς ἀπὸ πηχῶν διακοσίων, about 200 cubits. Πῆχυς, cubit, 16—18 inches.

fire, bread, and broiling fish. When the disciples approached, Jesus called out: "Bring of the fish which ye have now caught." There was to be a meal for all. Slowly they dragged in the strained, but unbroken net, containing exactly one hundred and fifty-three good-sized fish. We need not seek a mystical meaning in this number.[11] It simply means that the fish were large, that the catch was remarkable, that the net was unbroken, and that Simon and John were real fishermen, who would not make a haul without noticing the size and counting the number of the fish. Assuming the part of host, Jesus now invited the disciples: "Come and dine." As they gathered around the fire for their morning meal, with Jesus breaking the bread and distributing the fish, they could not help realizing that it was the Lord. But none "durst ask Him, Who art Thou? knowing that it was the Lord." This was the third time since His resurrection that Jesus appeared to a group of disciples.

21.
John 21, 15—23.

After the meal Jesus took up a matter with Peter, whom, however, He addressed by his original name: "Simon, son of Jonas, lovest[1] thou Me more than these?" There was a painful reference in the words "more than these."[2] Peter replied: "Yea, Lord; Thou knowest that I love Thee."[3] Jesus said to him: "Feed My lambs." For the second and third time came the same question: "Lovest thou Me?" and likewise Peter's answer: "Lord, Thou knowest that I love Thee," and now both times the Lord's command: "Feed My sheep." When the Lord put the question the third time, evidently wishing to remind Peter of his triple denial, Peter was grieved. Deeply humbled and greatly distressed, he replied: "Lord, Thou knowest all things. Thou knowest that

---

20, 11) Some of the Fathers understood 100 for the Gentiles, 50 for the Jews, and 3 for the Trinity. Jerome says that there are 153 varieties of fishes. And other like inventions. See Meyer or Dods sub John 21, 11.

21, 1) Ἀγαπᾷς.

2) Matt. 26, 35; Mark 14, 29.

3) Φιλῶ. Jesus used the word ἀγαπᾷς. Peter said φιλῶ. The Vulgate distinguishes by using the term *diligis* and *amo*. But probably there is no difference in the words. Different terms used for euphonic reasons. The distinction is usually made that ἀγαπᾶν is based on judgment and esteem and φιλεῖν on the affection of the heart. If the two words differed in meaning to the extent of giving each a special significance, it could not be said that Peter was grieved because Jesus had said φιλεῖς a third time; for Jesus had not used the same word three times. He said ἀγαπᾷς twice in succession and φιλεῖς the third time. — The same applies to the term *feed*. The first time Jesus said βόσκε, the second time ποίμαινε, the third time βόσκε. The function is the same. Dods *sub loco*.

I love Thee." By commanding Peter to feed both His lambs and His sheep, the Lord reinstated him in the apostleship and commissioned him to preach the Gospel to young and old. But His

"Feed My Lambs. Feed My Sheep." threefold question showed him as well as his fellow-apostles that love to Him is essential for the proper performance of the ministry. And their love would be put to a severe test. In the case of Peter the statement was made: "Verily, verily, I say unto thee, When thou wast young, thou girdedst thyself and walkedst whither thou wouldest." Formerly his will was his law, limited only by his ability to carry it out. But in the service of Christ not the principle of will and choice, but the principle of obedience and submission applies. "But when thou shalt be old, thou shalt stretch forth thy hands, and another shall gird thee and carry thee whither thou wouldest not." What the Lord here alluded to is explained by the evangelist: "This spake He, signifying by what death he should glorify God." Tradition has it that during the reign of Nero Peter died on the cross.[4] With the words "Follow Me" Peter was again officially called to be the Lord's apostle. He was not made the highest incumbent of the apostolic office, with supreme authority and dominion over all the other apostles or with the right to fleece the herd, but with the duty laid upon him to join the other shepherds in the work of feeding the lambs and sheep of Christ. "Feed My lambs. Feed My sheep. Follow Me."

John 21, 15—23.   **22.**

As Peter rose to follow Christ, thinking probably about the pangs of his predicted martyrdom, he turned and noticed John, his own intimate companion and the disciple whom Jesus loved, slowly following them. Curiosity prompted him to ask the question: And what about him? "Lord, what shall this man do?" In seeking to know the future of another disciple, Peter was clearly overstepping his ground. Mysteriously Jesus replied: "If he tarry till I come, what is that to thee? Follow[1] *thou* Me." *Your*

Prediction Concerning John. business is to follow Me, not to meddle in the affairs of others.[2] The answer led to the wide misapprehension prevalent in the early Church that John was not to die until the second coming of Jesus. Quietly the evangelist corrects the error by quoting the

---

21, 4) Eusebius, II, XXV, 5; III, I, 1.   Crucified head downward.
22, 1) Σύ μοι ἀκολούθει.   2) Dods *sub loco.*

exact words of Jesus. He points to the hypothetical form of the remark. "Jesus said not unto him, He shall not die; but, *If* I will that he tarry till I come, what is that to thee?" John *did* outlive all the other apostles. In fact, he lived to see the destruction of Jerusalem and the terrible overthrow of the Jewish nation, which might be taken as the beginning of Christ's return.[3]

John 21, 24. 25. **23.**

At this point we may as well bring the account of John to a close. In a final note the apostle defends the truthfulness of the record he has offered. He has not written on the basis of questionable sources, but he knows, and others who join him in the certificate know with him,[1]

The Close of John's Gospel.

that his testimony is true. When he had attained to a very old age, living probably in Ephesus,[2] there were still other Christians of venerable age and of highest integrity who were able to certify the truth of his account. Incidentally he affirms that, if all the sayings and miracles of Jesus were to be recorded, the world, as one might say, could not contain the books.

24.

Matt. 28, 16—20. Mark 16, 15—18. (1 Cor. 15, 6.)

It may have been in connection with His appearance by the Sea of Galilee that Jesus designated the particular mountain in Galilee where He would meet all those who loved Him for a final general assembly. Where the mountain was we do not know. Most likely it was a place, such as the Mount of Beatitudes or some other height, made familiar by former occasions. If we may bring in the testimony of St. Paul at this place, it was a large assembly. "He was seen of above five hundred brethren at once, of whom the greater part remain unto this present, but some are fallen asleep."[1] When Jesus made His appearance, some worshiped Him, while others still doubted. And it seems that the reference is to some of the Eleven.[2] When Jesus made His appearance in Jeru-

---

22, 3) Compare Matt. 16, 28; Mark 9, 1; Luke 9, 27.

23, 1) Οἴδαμεν.

2) Eusebius, III, I, 1. According to tradition he lived until the reign of Trajan, 98—117 A. D. Eusebius, III, XXIII, 4; XXXI, 3. Jerome says he died in 98, a hundred years old.

24, 1) 1 Cor. 15, 6. St. Paul wrote these words about twenty-five years after Christ's resurrection.

2) Matt. 28, 16. 18.

CODEX WASHINGTON. (W)

Now in Smithsonian Institution, Washington, D. C. Fourth century.
Mark 16, 12—17.

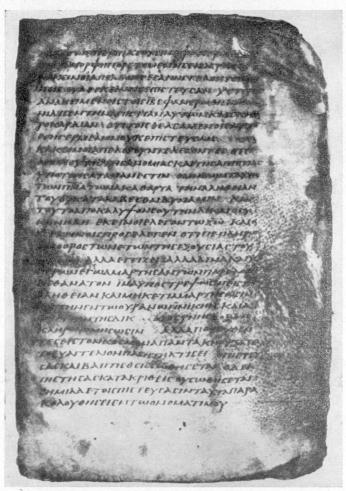

"Go ye into all the world and preach the Gospel to every creature."
Mark 16, 15.

---- ΠΟΡΕΥΘΕΝ   πορευθέν-
ΤΕΣΕΙΣΤΟΝΚΟΣΜΟΝΑΠΑΝΤΑΚΗΡΥΞΑΤΕ
τες εἰς τὸν κόσμον ἅπαντα, κηρύξατε
ΤΟΕΥΑΓΓΕΛΙΟΝΠΑΣΗΤΗΚΤΙΣΕΙ
τὸ εὐαγγέλιον πάσῃ τῇ κτίσει

(Beginning after interpolation in seventh line from the bottom.)

salem, it was Thomas who doubted. But Thomas was cured of
all his doubts. We are expressly told that he was with the seven
assembled at the Sea of Tiberias.[3] But on the occasion under

**The Great
Mission Command.**
discussion some of the others expressed
doubt. The disciples did not doubt the
resurrection of Jesus, but the doubt
seems to have concerned the identity of Him who stood before
them. The doubt of the disciples is rather a testimony to the
truth of the inspired record. The disciples were not credulous,
and the very fact that Jesus had to remove their doubts proves
beyond a doubt that He truly rose from the dead.[4] As Jesus
came closer to them, however, He removed all fear and uncertainty.
It was a most solemn occasion; for now He issued His great
mission command, the Great Commission: "All power is given unto
Me in heaven and in earth. Go ye therefore and teach all nations,
baptizing them in the name of the Father and of the Son and
of the Holy Ghost; teaching them to observe all things whatsoever
I have commanded you. And, lo, I am with you alway, even unto
the end of the world."

25.

Matt. 28, 16—20. Mark 16, 15—18. (1 Cor. 15, 6.)

The making of disciples, according to this great mission command, is effected by two means of grace: by "baptizing them
[all nations] in the name of the Father and of the Son and of
the Holy Ghost" and by "teaching them to observe all things
whatsoever I have commanded you"; in other words, by "preaching
the Gospel to every creature" and administering the Sacraments as

**The Institution of the
Sacrament of Holy Baptism.**
the means of grace. Here
we have the institution of
the *sacramentum initiationis,*
the Sacrament of Initiation, of the Christian Church. In the Great
Commission of our Lord "baptizing" is mentioned previous to
"teaching," or "preaching." But this is not to be taken as a command that baptism must at all times precede instruction. Still
less reason is there to conclude that instruction must always precede
baptism, for instance, in the case of children. And these are not
excluded, because the Lord says: "Teach all nations, baptizing
them."

24.　3) John 21. 2.
　　4) Lenski, *Eisenach Gospels,* 705. Walther, *Brosamen,* 121.

26.

Matt. 28, 16—20. Mark 16, 15—18. (1 Cor. 15, 6.)

Likewise the way of gaining salvation is briefly shown. "He that believeth and is baptized shall be saved; but he that believeth not shall be damned." When a sinner hears the Gospel of Christ, he must accept it as true, as meant for him, and he must appropriate its promises to himself. The Holy Spirit graciously operates on the heart of the hearer through the Gospel and kindles this faith.

Way of Salvation. He kindles it also through Baptism; for Baptism is "the washing of regeneration and renewing of the Holy Ghost, which He shed on us abundantly through Jesus Christ, our Savior, that, being justified by His grace, we should be made heirs according to the hope of eternal life." [1] But Jesus does not say: "He that believeth not *and is not baptized* shall be damned"; therefore it is unbelief only that damns. In other words, an unbaptized person may be saved. But though "saving faith may exist with lack of Baptism, it cannot exist with the contempt of it." [2]

27.

Matt. 28, 16—20. Mark 16, 15—18. (1 Cor. 15, 6.)

And signs are to follow. "And these signs shall follow them that believe: In My name shall they cast out devils; they shall speak with new tongues; [1] they shall take up serpents; and if they drink any deadly thing, it shall not hurt them; they shall lay hands on the sick, and they shall recover." These signs are given not only to the apostles or other preachers of the Gospel, but to "them that believe." And all these miracles actually were performed within the pale of the Christian Church. But a few points must be remembered. In the first place, these signs were given for a purpose, as a testimony, to prove the truth of the Gospel and to establish it in this or that locality, especially at the time of the nascent Christian Church. In the second place, the words of Jesus are by no means a promise that each individual believer shall be able to perform a sign whenever he feels the urge. [2] In the great

---

26, 1) Titus 3, 5—7.

2) The unbaptized malefactor on the cross as compared with the Baptism-despising Pharisees. Luke 22, 43; 7, 30.

27, 1) Not ecstatic glossolalia, incomprehensible utterances, 1 Cor. 12, 10; 14, 2, etc., but the much more wonderful speaking of previously unknown languages to the praise of God and the spiritual welfare of benighted souls, as in Acts 2, 4 ff. See Meyer sub Mark 16, 18.

2) Ylvisaker, 783.

mission command the disciples were not primarily commissioned to become, as it were, miracle-mongers, but were commanded to baptize and to teach. And if necessary for their work, for the establishment of the Gospel and for the glory of God, miracles

Signs. would follow. In making this statement, we are on safe ground. An appeal to Mark 16, 17. 18 cannot be made for all kinds of healings and speaking of tongues. And if the particular signs are more uncommon in our day than they were, for instance, in the early Christian Church, it is partly due to insufficient faith, partly, however, or rather largely, also to the circumstance that they are no longer needed; after all these centuries of Christian preaching in all the world there is no particular need of signs "confirming the Word." We have "Moses and the Prophets." And "let them," all men, "hear them." "If they hear not Moses and the Prophets, neither will they be persuaded though one rose from the dead." [3] But at the same time, Christians always have this promise of divine protection: "Lo, I am with you alway, even unto the end of the world." And this promise concludes the Gospel of St. Matthew.

(1 Cor. 15, 7—9.) **28.**

There were appearances of the risen Christ in addition to those recorded in the gospels. St. Paul relates that after the appearance to the five hundred "He was seen of James." But he does not tell us which James it was. Positive identification is impossible. But it is believed that it was not the brother of John and son of Zebedee, who met a tragic death by the sword at the hands of Herod Agrippa I as early as 44 A. D. [1] The reference is likely to that James whose mother, Mary, is called the mother of James and wife of Cleophas, or Alphaeus, and also called the brother of our

Appearances to James and Paul. Lord. [2] This James, also called the Less, either on account of his stature or in order to distinguish him from James, the son of Zebedee, is quite generally identified as the head of the church of Jerusalem in the Apostolic Age. [3] And it was probably the circumstance of his future high position which accounts for the fact that the risen Lord granted him a special interview. [4] Likewise

---

27, 3) Luke 16, 29—31.
28, 1) See chapter XI, 7.
   2) Luke 24, 10; John 19, 25; Gal. 1, 19. See chapter XI, 13.
   3) Acts 12, 17; Gal. 1, 19; Acts 15, 13. 19; 21, 18; etc.
   4) See G. G. Findlay under 1 Cor. 15, 7 in *Exp. Greek N. T.*

Paul, the great Apostle to the Gentiles, had the honor of a special appearance. Modestly Paul refers to this appearance [5] in the words: "Last of all He was seen of me also, as of one born out of due time. For I am the least of the apostles, that am not meet to be called an apostle because I persecuted the Church of God."

29.

Luke 24, 44—49. (Acts 1, 3—8.)

783 A. U. C.			MAY		30 A. D.	
Sun.	Mon.	Tue.	Wed.	Thu.	Fri.	Sat.
	1	2	3	4	5	6
7	8	9	10	11	12	13
14	15	16	17	[18]	19	20
21	22	23	24	25	26	27
28	29	30	31			

Forty days had passed since the resurrection of Jesus on Easter morning. Referring again to our calendar, this would bring us to Thursday, May 18, 783 A. U. C., or 30 A. D. The day had arrived for Jesus to be taken up into heaven.[1] It seems that Jesus had directed His disciples in Galilee to return to Jerusalem. At any rate, we find the Eleven assembled in Jerusalem and Jesus with them. It is as if the former days had returned. Jesus is in the midst of an address.[2] It is a farewell discourse. The Savior is speaking as though He were already parted from His disciples. "These are the words which I spake unto you while I was yet

The Last Appearance in Jerusalem.

with you." He reminds them that all the things which they had witnessed, His entire work, His suffering, death, and resurrection on the third day, were necessary that the entire Scriptures, the Law of Moses, the Prophets, and the Psalms, should be fulfilled in Him. And pointing to the prophecies, He opened their understanding of Scripture. This was necessary because they were to be His witnesses. The contents of their testimony among all nations, beginning at Jerusalem, was to be

---

28, 5) Acts 9, 5. 6: 26, 14 ff.: 1 Cor. 15, 8. Or was there another appearance? 1 Cor. 11. 23: "For I have received of the Lord," etc.

29, 1) Even from Luke it is clear that the ascension of Jesus did not take place on the same day of the week as His resurrection; for the same writer explains in the Book of Acts (1, 3) that Jesus showed Himself alive for forty days after His Passion.

2) Separating Luke 24, 44 from the foregoing.

repentance and the remission of sins. A glorious message, but also a stupendous task. It is true, what the injunction demanded of them was beyond their strength; but the Holy Ghost would make them equal to the task. In "breathing on them," [3] He had already conferred upon them a portion of their required spiritual equipment; but they were soon to receive the full measure of the Father's promise.[4] "Tarry ye in the city of Jerusalem until ye be endued with power from on high." A spiritual baptism was soon to take place. "For John truly baptized with water; but ye shall be baptized with the Holy Ghost not many days hence."

30.

Luke 24, 44—49. (Acts 1, 3—8.)

It was thus that Jesus, not only on this occasion, but also on others in the period of the glorious forty days, spoke to His apostles of the things pertaining to the kingdom of God. But hitherto they had cherished a mistaken Messianic hope. Again they had heard something about the Kingdom, and now the Lord spoke also of the baptism with the Holy Ghost, which they correctly, and still in a false interpretation, had connected with Messianic times.[1] Linking the promise of the Spirit and the reference to the Kingdom with earthly dominion, the disciples asked: "Lord, wilt Thou at

"Ye shall Be Witnesses unto Me unto the Uttermost Part of the Earth."

this time restore again the kingdom to Israel?" Jesus had not been speaking of the "kingdom of Israel," but of the "kingdom of God." Immediately He checked their nationalistic hopes: "It is not for you to know the times or the seasons which the Father hath put in His own power." They were always thinking of power,[2] authority, dominion, and glory. But the power which the Lord had in mind for them was the power [3] of the Holy Ghost. "Ye shall receive power after that the Holy Ghost is come upon you." That was the power which they were to receive — the ability to become effective witnesses for the Gospel of Christ. "Ye shall be witnesses unto Me both in Jerusalem, and in all Judea, and in Samaria, and unto the uttermost part of the earth."

---

3) John 20, 22.
4) Is. 44, 3; Joel 2, 28.
30, 1) Joel 2, 28. 29, compared with 30. 31.
2) 'Εξουσία.
3) Δύναμις.

31.

Mark 16, 19. 20. Luke 24, 50—53. (Acts 1, 9—12.)

Read that last sentence once more. Was there a more sublime utterance ever made? Under any other circumstances the words could be disposed of as sheer grandiloquence, but here they were uttered by One whom we have followed from the manger to the regions beyond the grave and of whom it can be truly said that not once "was guile found in His mouth." [1] And besides, they are the heritage of Him whom we are about to behold ascending to the portals of heaven. "Ye shall be witnesses unto Me both in Jerusalem, and in all Judea, and in Samaria, and unto the uttermost part of the earth." And after He had thus spoken, He led His disciples out until they were over against Bethany — past the scene of His triumphal entry into the city of Jerusalem, past Gethsemane and the site of His suffering, to one of the slopes of the

The Ascension. Mount of Olives overhanging the village of His now no longer to be visited friends. There was nothing more to be done beyond bidding His disciples farewell. The work He had come to do was accomplished. And the future of the Church was provided for. "But the Comforter, which is the Holy Ghost, whom the Father will send in My name, He shall teach you all things and bring all things to your remembrance, whatsoever I have said unto you. Peace I leave with you, My peace I give unto you. . . . Let not your heart be troubled, neither let it be afraid." [2] And He lifted up His hands and blessed them. And it came to pass, while He blessed them, He was taken up, the eyes of the disciples following Him higher and higher, until a cloud received Him out of their sight. It was the ascension of Christ into heaven, the coronation of the heavenly King, who "is gone up with a shout, the Lord with the sound of a trumpet." [3] He sat down [4] at the right hand of God, there to assume the rule, also according to His human nature, over all creatures and especially to govern and to protect His Church and finally to lead it to glory.

32.

Mark 16, 19. 20. Luke 24, 50—53. (Acts 1, 9—12.)

We have come to the close of the gospel records and to the end of our book. But the complete story of Christ has not been told. The ascension of our Lord was followed by the founding of

---

31, 1) 1 Pet. 2, 22.   2) John 14, 26. 27.   3) Ps. 47, 5.
4) Ἐκάϑισεν — καϑίζω. The same term in Luke 4, 20.

the Christian Church, whose Head was and is and ever will be the ascended and ever-living Lord. There is another chapter, still incomplete, of the life of Christ, which takes us to Judgment Day, to be followed by the chapter on the eternal joy and glory of all the saints with Christ in heaven. With worshiping hearts the disciples gazed at what seemed to them a disappearing Lord. Suddenly two angels in white apparel stood by them and said: "Ye

Conclusion. men of Galilee, why stand ye gazing up into heaven? This same Jesus which is taken up from you into heaven shall so come in like manner as ye have seen Him go into heaven." And since that is the case, the separation from their departed Master was not a cause for sorrow, but an occasion of great and undiminished joy. The disciples returned to Jerusalem. Joyfully they entered upon their work, went forth and preached everywhere, praising and blessing God. — There are many "Lives of Christ." And as we lay aside our books and finish our task of love and joy, may we hope that the reader also will finish the perusal of these pages with a sense of joy. Lift up your heads with joy. "This same Jesus which is taken up from you into heaven shall so come in like manner as ye have seen Him go into heaven."

"TO WHOM BE GLORY FOREVER!"

BIBLIOGRAPHY.

LIST OF AUTHORITIES CHIEFLY USED IN WRITING THIS BOOK.

The references to page or chapter as given in the notes follow the year, edition, or publisher of the respective book as indicated in this list.

Andrews, Samuel J.: *The Life of Our Lord upon the Earth.* Charles Scribner's Sons. New York. 1891.

Apocryphal New Testament. The Worthington Co. New York. 1890.

Arndt, W.: *Does the Bible Contradict Itself?* Concordia Publishing House. St. Louis. 1926.

Augustine: *Harmony of the Gospels.* In *Nicene and Post-Nicene Fathers.* The Christian Literature Co. New York.

Barton, George A.: *Archaeology and the Bible.* American Sunday-school Union. Philadelphia. 1933.

Bentwich, Norman: *Josephus.* The Jewish Publication Society of America. Philadelphia. 1914.

Blunt, A. W. F.: *Israel in World History.* Oxford University Press. London. 1927.

Bowman, S. L.: *Historical Evidences of the New Testament.*

Brandes, Georg: *Jesus: A Myth.* Albert and Charles Boni. New York. 1926.

Breasted, J. H.: *The Conquest of Civilization.* New York. 1926.

Broadus, John A.: *A Harmony of the Gospels.* A. C. Armstrong and Son. New York. 1893.

Browne, Lewis: *The Graphic Bible.* The Macmillan Company. New York. 1928.

Bruce, Alexander B.: "The Synoptic Gospels." In *The Expositor's Greek Testament.* George H. Doran Company. New York.

Burton, E. D. and Goodspeed, E. J.: *A Harmony of the Synoptic Gospels.* Charles Scribner's Sons. New York.

Cadman, Jas. P.: *A Critical Harmony of the Gospels.* Fleming H. Revell Company. New York. 1885.

Case, Shirley Jackson: *The Historicity of Jesus.* University of Chicago. 1912.

Catholic Encyclopedia. The Robert Appleton Company. New York.

Cobern, C. M.: *The New Archaeological Discoveries.* New York. 1917.

Crafer, T. W.: *The Didache, or the Teaching of the Twelve Apostles.* The Macmillan Company. New York. 1920.

Dallmann, William: *Jesus.* Northwestern Publishing House. Milwaukee. 1914.

Dau, W.: *Harmony Outline Based on Chemnitz, Leyser, Gerhard.* Concordia Seminary Lectures. St. Louis. 1912.

[713]

Davis, John D.: *A Dictionary of the Bible.* George H. Doran Company. New York.

Deissmann, Adolf: *Licht vom Osten.* J. C. Mohr. Tuebingen. 1923.

Dobschuetz, Ernst von: *Eberhard Nestle's Einfuehrung in das griechische Neue Testament.* Vandenhoeck and Ruprecht. Goettingen. 1923.

Dods, Marcus: "The Gospel of St. John." In *The Expositor's Greek Testament.* George H. Doran Company. New York.

Ebrard, J. H. A.: *The Gospel History.* T. and T. Clark. Edinburgh. 1863.

Edersheim, Alfred: *The Life and Times of Jesus the Messiah.* Longman, Green and Company. New York. 1923.

Edersheim, Alfred: *The Temple, Its Ministry and Services.* Ira Bradley and Company. Boston. 1881.

Ellis, W. T.: *Bible Lands To-day.* D. Appleton and Company. New York. 1927.

Encyclopaedia Britannica, The. Britannica Company. New York.

Eusebius: *Church History.* In *Nicene and Post-Nicene Fathers.* The Christian Literature Company. New York. 1890.

Expositor's Greek Testament, The. George H. Doran. New York.

Farrar, F. W.: *The Life of Christ.* E. P. Dutton and Company. New York.

Fuerbringer, L.: *Theologische Hermeneutik und Einleitung.* Concordia Publishing House. St. Louis. 1912.

Gebhardt, Oscar De: *Novum Testamentum Graece.* Bernhard Tauchnitz. Leipzig. 1912.

Geikie, Cunningham: *The Life and Words of Christ.* Appleton. New York. 1896.

Gerhardt, Oswald: *Der Stern des Messias.* Deichert. Leipzig. 1922.

Gibbon, Edward: *Decline and Fall of the Roman Empire.* Porter and Coates. Philadelphia.

Glover, T. R.: *The Jesus of History.* Associated Press. New York. 1917.

Goguel, M.: *Jesus the Nazarene — Myth or History?* D. Appleton and Company. New York. 1926.

Graetz, Heinrich: *History of the Jews.* The Jewish Publication Society. Philadelphia. 1891.

Gregory, G. C.: *Text and Canon of the Greek New Testament.*

Guthe, Hermann: *Bibelatlas.* H. Wagner and E. Debes. Leipzig. 1926.

Hardy, E. G.: *Christianity and the Roman Government.* The Macmillan Company. New York. 1925.

Harris, Rendel: *The Twelve Apostles.* W. Heffer and Sons. Cambridge. 1927.

Hauber, E. D.: *Harmonie der Evangelisten.* In the Greek-German *Original-Bibel.* Zuellichau. 1740.

Henry, Matthew: *Commentary.* Fleming H. Revell Company. New York.

Hill, J. Hamlyn: *The Earliest Life of Christ.* Tatian's *Diatessaron.* T. and T. Clark. Edinburgh. 1894.

Hurlbut, Jesse Lyman: *A Bible Atlas.* Rand McNally and Company. New York.

International Standard Bible Encyclopaedia, The. Howard-Severance Co. Chicago. 1915.

Jewish Encyclopedia, The. Funk and Wagnalls Company. New York.

Josephus. With an English Translation by H. St. G. Thackeray. In *The Loeb Classical Library.* G. P. Putnam's Sons. New York. 1926.

Josephus, Selections from. By H. St. G. Thackeray. The Macmillan Company. New York. 1919.

Josephus. Translated by William Whiston. Charles Griffin and Company. London.

Kenyon, M. A.: *Our Bible and the Ancient Manuscripts.* Eyre and Spottiswoode. New York. 1903.

Kerr, John H.: *A Harmony of the Gospels.* American Tract Society. Boston.

Klausner, Joseph: *Jesus of Nazareth.* The Macmillan Company. New York. 1929.

Kretzmann, Paul E.: *Popular Commentary of the Bible.* Concordia Publishing House. St. Louis. 1921.

Lenski, R. C. H.: *The Eisenach Gospel Selections.* Lutheran Book Concern. Columbus. 1916.

Lightfoot, J. B.: "The Lord's Brethren," in *St. Paul's Epistle to the Galatians.* Macmillan and Company. London. 1874.

Lodder, W.: *Die Schaetzung des Quirinius bei Flavius Josephus.* Doerffling and Francke. Leipzig. 1930.

Ludwig, Emil: *The Son of Man.* Boni and Liveright. New York. 1928.

MacCoun, Townsend: *The Holy Land in Geography and History.* F. H. Revell. New York. 1897.

Macknight, James: *Harmony of the Gospels.* London. 1809.

Madden, F. W.: *History of Jewish Coinage.* London. 1864.

Matthews, Basil: *A Life of Jesus.* Richard R. Smith, Inc. New York. 1931.

Meyer, H. A. W.: *Commentary on the New Testament.* Funk and Wagnalls. New York. 1884.

Milligan, G.: *Words of the New Testament.*

Milman, H. H.: *The History of Christianity.* Harper and Brothers. New York. 1861.

Milman, H. H.: *History of Latin Christianity.* Sheldon and Company. New York. 1860.

Morison, Frank: *Who Moved the Stone?* The Century Company. New York. 1930.

Mosheim, J. L. von: *Institutes of Ecclesiastical History.* New York. 1869.

Myers, Philip Van Ness: *General History.* Ginn and Company. Boston.

New International Encyclopaedia, The. Dodd, Mead, and Company. New York. 1914.

Pieper, Franz: *Christliche Dogmatik.* Concordia Publishing House. 1924.

Philostratus: *The Life of Apollonius of Tyana.* In *The Loeb Classical Library.* G. P. Putnam's Sons. New York. 1917.

Ramsay, W. M.: *The Bearing of Recent Discovery on the Trustworthiness of the New Testament.* London. 1915.

Ramsay, W. M.: *Was Christ Born at Bethlehem?* Hodder and Stoughton. London. 1898.

Renan, E.: *Life of Jesus.* Little, Brown, and Company. Boston. 1924.

Robinson, Edw.: *A Harmony of the Gospels in Greek.* Crocker and Brewster. Boston. 1845.

Robinson, T. H.; Hunkin, J. W.; Burkitt, F. C.: *Palestine in General History.* Oxford University Press. London. 1929.

Robertson, A. T.: *A Harmony of the Gospels.* George H. Doran. New York. 1922.

Robertson, A. T.: *Luke the Historian in the Light of Recent Research.* Scribner's Sons. New York. 1920.

Robertson, A. T.: *Studies in the Text of the New Testament.* George H. Doran Company. New York. 1926.

Sanders, H. A.: *Facsimile of the Washington Manuscript of the Four Gospels.* The University of Michigan. Ann Arbor. 1911.

Sanders, H. A.: *The Washington Manuscript of the Four Gospels.* The Macmillan Company. New York. 1912.

Schirlitz, S. Ch.: *Griechisch-deutsches Woerterbuch zum Neuen Testament.* Giessen.

Schuerer, Emil: *A History of the Jewish People in the Time of Jesus Christ.* T. and T. Clark. Edinburgh. 1905.

Schweitzer, A.: *The Quest of the Historical Jesus.* A. C. Black. London. 1911.

Sharman, H. B.: *Records of the Life of Jesus.* George H. Doran Company. New York.

Shepherd, William R.: *Historical Atlas.* Henry Holt and Co. New York. 1926.

Sitterly, C. F.: *Praxis in Manuscripts of the Greek Testament.* Eaton and Mains. New York. 1898.

Smith, G. A.: *Atlas of the Historical Geography of the Holy Land.* Hodder and Stoughton. London. 1915.

Smith, W. W.: *Students' Historical Geography of the Holy Land.* George H. Doran Company. New York. 1924.

Souter, Alex.: *Text and Canon of the New Testament.* 1913.

Stalker, James: *The Life of Jesus Christ.* Fleming H. Revell Company. New York.

Stalker, James: *The Trial and Death of Jesus Christ.* Hodder and Stoughton. New York.

Stanley, A. P.: *The History of the Jewish Church.* Charles Scribner's Sons. New York. 1884.

Stevens, Wm. A.; Burton, E.: *A Harmony of the Gospels.* The International Committee of Y. M. C. A. New York. 1903.

Stoeckhardt, G.: *Die Biblische Geschichte des Neuen Testaments.* Concordia Publishing House. St. Louis. 1898.

Strauss, D.: *Life of Jesus.* New York. 1855.

Suetonius: *The Lives of the Caesars.* In *The Loeb Classical Library.* The Macmillan Company. New York. 1914.

Tacitus: *The Annals.* Translated by Arthur Murphy. E. P. Dutton Company. New York.

Tacitus. With critical notes by Charles Anthon. Harper and Brothers. New York. 1877.

Tacitus: *History of the Jews.* In Whiston's *Josephus.* Charles Griffin and Company. London.

Tatian: *The Diatessaron.* Translated by J. Hamlyn Hill. T. and T. Clark. Edinburgh. 1894.

Thackeray, H. St. J.: *Selections from Josephus.* The Macmillan Co. New York. 1919.

Thorburn, T. J.: *Jesus, the Christ.* T. and T. Clark. Edinburgh. 1912.

Tholuck, A.: *Die Bergpredigt Christi.* Hamburg. 1833.

Tholuck, A.: *Die Glaubwuerdigkeit der evangelischen Geschichte.* 1837.

Weiss, B.: *Introduction to the New Testament.*

Weiss, B.: *The Life of Christ.* T. and T. Clark. Edinburgh. 1883.

White, H. J.: *Select Passages Illustrative of Christianity in the First Century.* Society for Promoting Christian Knowledge. London. 1918.

Wieseler, Karl: *A Chronological Synopsis of the Four Gospels.* Cambridge. 1864.

Williamson, Geo. C.: *Money of the Bible.* Revell. 1894.

Wilson, E. L.: *In Scripture Lands.* C. Scribner's Sons. New York. 1890.

Wislicenus, W. F.: *Der Kalender.* B. G. Teubner. Leipzig. 1914.

Ylvisaker, John: *The Gospels.* Augsburg Publishing House. Minneapolis. 1932.

Zahn, Th.: *Introduction to the New Testament.* Edinburgh. 1910.

Zorn, C. M.: *Der Heiland.* Northwestern Publishing House. Milwaukee. 1907.

APPENDICES.

NOTES ON PLATES.

Codex Washington. (W.) Between pages 100 and 101.

A most remarkable manuscript. Probably the chief treasure in the National Library (Smithsonian Institute), Washington, D. C. It was purchased by Mr. C. L. Freer of Detroit from an Arab dealer in Gizeh, near Cairo, in December, 1906. It dates from the fourth century. It does not contain the story of the woman taken in adultery, John 7, 53—8, 11, which is also missing in Aleph, (ℵ) B, A, C, and others. But it does contain that other famous disputed passage at the close of Mark's gospel; and not only this passage, but a most remarkable, though uncanonical, reading besides, which goes to show that Mark 16, 9—20 certainly was an integral part of the original text. The page containing Luke 2, 1—12 is reproduced from the facsimile edition by Professor Sanders of the University of Michigan. The last line brings us the name of the Savior — *"which is Christ the Lord."* But the order is reversed. It reads: *"Which is the Lord Christ."* Notice the abbreviations used for the Lord Christ: $\overline{KC}$ $\overline{XC}$, with superinscribed bar.

Codex Vaticanus. (B.) Between pages 172 and 173.

The chief treasure in the Vatican Library. Probably one of the fifty Bibles prepared by Eusebius for Constantine the Great. Together with the Codex Sinaiticus it is universally regarded as the oldest and the best manuscript of the Greek New Testament. It is placed in the beginning of the fourth century. There are no accents, breathings, or punctuations, though it was corrected and retraced by later hands. The page is a copy of the phototype edition of Rome, 1889. It contains John 2, 16—3, 17. The first word is "sold" and the last is "world," KOCMon. Three columns.

Codex Alexandrinus. (A.) Between pages 282 and 283.

Dates from the fifth century. Supposed to have come from Alexandria. In 1627 it was sent as a gift of the Patriarch of Constantinople to Charles I. Now in the British Museum. The page is taken from the autotype facsimile edition issued by the British Museum in 1880. The Eusebian sections appear in the margin. The page contains Luke 6, 42—7, 16. The first word, "hypocrite," can easily be deciphered. The last word on the page is "all." But the scribe had to squeeze the letters ΠΑΝΤΑC together to get them on the line. Two columns.

Codex Sinaiticus. (ℵ.) Aleph. Between pages 330 and 331.

This is the famous uncial manuscript found by Tischendorf at St. Catherine's Monastery on Mount Sinai in 1859. For a long time in the former Imperial Library at Leningrad, but in December, 1933, acquired for the British Museum and now preserved there. Fourth century. The page is

taken from the St. Petersburg facsimile edition of 1862. It contains Matt.
10, 17—11, 5. It starts in the middle of the word "beware" and ends in
the middle of the word "preached." Eusebian sections in the margin. Four
columns.

Codex Washington. (W.) Between pages 704 and 705.

This page contains also the apocryphal addition to Mark in Codex W,
following Mark 16, 14 and beginning with the first letters of line nine and
continuing to the middle of line seven from the bottom: —

κἀκεῖνοι ἀπελογοῦντε λέγοντες ὅτι αἰὼν οὗτος τῆς ἀνομίας καὶ τῆς
ἀπιστίας ὑπὸ τὸν σατανᾶν ἐστιν ὁ μὴ ἐῶν τὰ ὑπὸ τῶν πνευμάτων ἀκάθαρτα
τὴν ἀλήθειαν τοῦ θεοῦ καταλαβέσθαι δύναμιν. διὰ τοῦτο ἀποκάλυψόν σου
τὴν δικαιοσύνην ἤδη· ἐκεῖνοι ἔλεγον τῷ Χριστῷ. καὶ ὁ Χριστὸς ἐκείνοις
προσέλεγεν ὅτι πεπλήρωται ὁ ὅρος τῶν ἐτῶν τῆς ἐξουσίας τοῦ σατανᾶ, ἀλλὰ
ἐγγίζει δινὰ καὶ ὑπὲρ ὧν ἐγὼ ἁμαρτησάντων παρεδόθην εἰς θάνατον ἵνα
ὑποστρέψωσιν εἰς τὴν ἀλήθειαν καὶ μηκέτι ἁμαρτήσωσιν· ἵνα τὴν ἐν τῷ
οὐρανῷ πνευματικὴν καὶ ἄφθαρτον τῆς δικαιοσύνης δόξαν κληρονομήσωσιν.

("And they defended themselves, saying, This world of lawlessness and
unbelief is under Satan, who does not suffer those unclean things that are
under the dominion of spirits to comprehend the power of God. On this
account reveal Thy righteousness now. They said [these things] to Christ.
And Christ replied to them, There has been fulfilled the term of years of the
authority of Satan, but [other] dreadful [things] are drawing nigh, and let
those for the sake of whom, as sinners, I was delivered up unto death return
to the truth and sin no more in order that they might inherit the spiritual
and incorruptible glory of righteousness which is in heaven." And v. 15:
"Go ye into all the world," etc. The last words on this page are "in My
name," v. 17.)

The first few lines of this insertion had been previously known in
a Latin translation from Jerome (*Contra Pelag.*, 2, 15), who states that
he had seen the lines in some Greek manuscripts. Jerome was in Egypt,
the ancient home of W, in 386 A. D. See *Biblical World*, March, 1908,
p. 206. Text also in Robertson, *Studies in the Text of the N. T.*, 100.

THE DISTINCTIVE MIRACLES OF JESUS.

(Besides this list numerous miracles were performed which have not been particularly described.)

#		Matthew	Mark	Luke	John	Chapter
1.	The water made wine. Cana				2, 1—11	VI, 21
2.	The healing of the nobleman's son. Cana				3, 46—54	VII, 22
3.	The infirm man at the Pool of Bethesda. Jerusalem				5, 2—13	VIII, 3
4.	The miraculous draught of fishes. Capernaum			5, 1—11		IX, 11
5.	The healing of a demoniac. Capernaum		1, 21—28	4, 31—37		14
6.	The healing of Peter's mother-in-law. Capernaum	8, 14.15	29—31	38.39		21
7.	The healing of a leper. Galilee	8, 2—4	40—45			X, 4
8.	The paralytic healed. Capernaum	9, 2—8	2, 1—12	5, 12—15		10
9.	The man with a withered hand. Galilee	12, 9—14	3, 1—6	6, 6—11		29
10.	The centurion's servant. Capernaum	8, 5—13		7, 1—10		XI, 43
11.	The raising of the widow's son. Nain			11—17		XII, 1
12.	The blind and dumb demoniac. Capernaum	12, 22—37				XIII, 5
13.	The stilling of the tempest. Sea of Galilee	8, 23—27	4, 35—41	8, 22—25		7
14.	The Gadarene demoniacs	28—34	5, 1—21	26—40		13
15.	The raising of the daughter of Jairus. Capernaum	9, 18—26	22—43	41—56		14
16.	The woman with the issue of blood. At the same time	9, 18—26	22—43	41—56		17
17.	Two blind men healed. At or near Capernaum	27—31				18
18.	The dumb demoniac. At or near Capernaum	32—34				
19.	The feeding of the five thousand. Bethsaida	14, 15—21	6, 35—44	9, 12—17	6, 5—13	XVI, 5
20.	Jesus walking on the water. Sea of Galilee	24—34	47—53		16—21	XVII, 2
21.	The daughter of the Syrophenician woman. Tyre	15, 21—28	7, 24—30			6
22.	The healing of the deaf-and-dumb man. Decapolis	30—31	32—37			7
23.	The feeding of the four thousand. Decapolis	32—38	8, 1—9			
24.	The blind man near Bethsaida		22—26			
25.	The demoniac boy at Mount Hermon	17, 14—18	9, 14—27	9, 37—43		XVIII, 2
26.	The stater miraculously provided. Capernaum	24—27				11
27.	The man born blind. Jerusalem				9, 1—41	XIX, 3
28.	The healing of the dumb demoniac. Perea			11, 14—28		XX, 21
29.	The crippled woman. Perea or Judea			13, 10—17		XXI, 13
30.	The man with the dropsy. Perea			14, 1—6		29
31.	The raising of Lazarus. Bethany				11, 1—46	XXIII, 6
32.	The ten lepers. Border of Samaria and Galilee			17, 12—19		XXIV, 1
33.	Blind Bartimaeus and his companion. Jericho	20, 29—34	10, 46—52	18, 35—43		XXV, 2
34.	The fig-tree cursed. Near Jerusalem	21, 18—20	11, 12—20			XXVIII, 1; XXIX, 1
35.	The healing of the ear of Malchus. Gethsemane			22, 50.51		XXXIII, 7
36.	The second miraculous draught of fishes. Sea of Galilee				21, 1—14	XXXVII, 19

"And many other signs truly did Jesus in the presence of His disciples which are not written in this book." John 20, 30.

Compare:	Matt. 4, 23	Mark 6, 56	Luke 4, 40	John 2, 23
	9, 35		5, 15	3, 2
	11, 21		6, 17	4, 45
			7, 21	20, 30
			10, 13	21, 25

THE PARABLES OF OUR LORD.

The limits between parable, simile, and metaphor are not strictly defined. Often there is scarcely any difference. In a technical sense the word *parable* ordinarily signifies a complete, howbeit imaginary, story. But etymologically the word signifies the placing of two or more objects together for the sake of comparison. In a wider sense the public preaching of our Lord assumed the general characteristic of speaking in parables. "All these things spake Jesus unto the multitude in parables; and without a parable spake He not unto them," Matt. 13, 34. The following list is submitted with the explanation that it does not confine itself to parables in the strictly technical sense and that it does not exhaust the parabolic sayings of our Lord.

	Matthew	Mark	Luke	John	Chapter
1. The sons of the bridechamber	9, 15	2, 19. 20	5, 34. 35		X, 23
2. A new patch on an old garment	16	21	36		24
3. New wine in old wine-skins	17	22	37—39		25
4. The blind leading the blind			6, 39		XI, 35
5. The mote and the beam	5, 3—5		41. 42		35
6. The light of the world	14—16	4, 21. 22	8, 16. 17		XI, 20; XII, 22
7. The salt of the earth	5, 13	9, 50	14, 34. 35		XI, 20; XIX, 8; XXIII, 16
8. The wise and foolish builders	7, 24—27		6, 47. 48		41
9. The children in the market-places	11, 16. 17		7, 31. 32		XII, 4
10. The two debtors			7, 40—42		10
11. Satan's kingdom	12, 25—29	3, 23—27			14
12. The return of the evil spirit	43—45				16
13. The sower	13, 3—9	4, 3—9	8, 5—8		19
14. The seed growing of itself		26—29			23
15. The tares	24—30				24
16. The mustard-seed	31. 32	30—32	13, 18. 19		25
17. The leaven	33		20. 21		26
18. The hidden treasure	44				29
19. The pearl of great price	45. 46				30
20. The net	47—50				31
21. The householder	51—53				32
22. Things defiling a man	15, 10—20	7, 15—23			XVI, 16
23. The unforgiving servant	18, 23—35				XIX, 13

	Matthew	Mark	Luke	John	Chapter
24. The Good Shepherd				10, 1—21	XX, 27
25. The good Samaritan			10, 30—37		XXI, 9
26. The importunate friend			11, 5—13		12
27. The rich fool			12, 16—21		20
28. The waiting servants			35—40		22
29. The wise steward			41—48		23
30. The barren fig-tree			13, 6—9		28
31. Seats at a wedding-feast			14, 7—11		XXIII, 8
32. Feast for the poor			12—14		9
33. The great supper			15—24		10
34. Building a tower			28—30		14
35. A king going to fight			31—33		15
36. The lost sheep	18, 12—14		15, 3—7		18; XIX, 9
37. The lost coin			8—10		19
38. The prodigal son			11—32		20
39. The unjust steward			16, 1—13		24
40. The rich man and Lazarus			19—31		28
41. The unprofitable servants			17, 7—10		XXIII, 34
42. The importunate widow			18, 1—8		XXV, 6
43. The Pharisee and the publican			9—14		7
44. The laborers in the vineyard	20, 1—16				17
45. The pounds			19, 11—28		25
46. The two sons	21, 28—32				XXIX, 5
47. The wicked husbandmen	33—41	12, 1—9	20, 9—16		6
48. The rejected building-stone	43—45	10. 11	17. 18		8
49. The marriage of the king's son	22, 1—14				10
50. The fig-tree	24, 32—34	13, 28—30	21, 29—32		XXX, 6
51. The porter		35			9
52. The master and the thief	43. 44				10
53. The two servants	45—51				10
54. The ten virgins	25, 1—13				11
55. The talents	14—30				13
56. The sheep and the goats	31—46				16

THE GENEALOGY OF CHRIST.

Old Testament	Matthew 1, 1—17	Luke 3, 23—38 (In reversed order)
Adam (Gen. 5, 3 ff.; 1 Chron. 1, 1 ff.)		38. 1. Adam, which was the son of God (1)
Seth		2. Seth
Enos		3. Enos
Cainan		37. 4. Cainan
Mahalaleel		5. Maleleel
Jared		6. Jared
Enoch		7. Enoch
Methuselah		8. Mathusala
Lamech		36. 9. Lamech
Noah		10. Noe
Shem		11. Sem
Arphaxad (Gen. 11, 13 ff.)		12. Arphaxad
——		13. Cainan (inserted in LXX and in Luke)
		35. 14. Sala
Salah		15. Heber
Eber		
Peleg	1. The book of the generation of Jesus Christ, the Son of David, the the Son of Abraham.	16. Phalec
Reu		17. Ragau
Serug		18. Saruch
Nahor		34. 19. Nachor
Terah		20. Tharah
Abraham (1 Chron. 1, 34)	2. 1. Abraham begat	21. Abraham (2)
Isaac	2. Isaac	22. Isaac
Jacob	3. Jacob	23. Jacob
Judah (1 Chron. 2, 1 ff.)	4. Judah and his brethren	33. 24. Judah
Pharez (Ruth 4, 18 ff.)	3. 5. Phares and Zara of Thamar	25. Phares
Hezron	6. Esrom	26. Esrom
Ram	7. Ram (many ancient authorities, א BLX, etc., insert) =	27. Aram
——		28. Admin
Amminadab	4. 8. Aminadab	29. Aminadab
Nahshon	9. Naasson	32. 30. Naasson
Salma	5. 10. Salmon	31. Salmon
Boaz	11. Booz of Rachab	32. Booz
Obed	12. Obed of Ruth	33. Obed
Jesse	6. 13. Jesse	34. Jesse
David	14. David, the king (counted twice)	31. 35. David
	1. David the king	
Solomon (1 Chron. 3, 1 ff.)	2. Solomon of her that had been the wife of Urias	36. Nathan
		37. Matthatha
		38. Menan
Rehoboam	7. 3. Roboam	30. 39. Melea
Abia	4. Abia	40. Eliakim
Asa	5. Asa	41. Jonan
Jehoshaphat	8. 6. Josaphat	42. Joseph
Joram	7. Joram	43. Juda
Ahaziah (1 Chron. 3,	——	44. Simeon
Joash 11. 12)	——	29. 45. Levi
Amaziah Omitted in Matthew =		46. Matthat
Azariah, or Uzziah (Is. 1, 1)	8. Ozias	47. Jorim
Jotham	9. 9. Joatham	48. Eliezer
Ahas	10. Achaz	49. Jose
Hezekiah	11. Ezekias	28. 50. Er
Manasseh	10. 12. Manasses	51. Elmodam
Amon	13. Amon	52. Cosam
Josiah	11. 14. Josias begat	53. Addi
Jehoiakim, or Eliakim = (omitted) (2 Kings 24, 6)	——	54. Melchi
	Jechonias and his brethren, about the time they were carried away to Babylon	
	12. And after they were brought to Babylon	
Jehoiachin, or Jechoniah (Jer. 22, 24)	1. Jechonias begat	27. 55. Neri

Old Testament	Matthew 1, 1—17	Luke 3, 23—38 (In reversed order)
Pedaiah (Salathiel) (3) (1 Chron. 3, 17)	2. Salathiel (Ezra 3, 2; 5, 2)	56. Salathiel
Zerubbabel (1 Chron. 3, 19)	3. Zorobabel	57. Zorobabel
Meshullam = Rhesa?		58. Rhesa
(Hananiah=Joanna?)		59. Joanna
	13. 4. Abiud = father or grandfather (4) of Jud or Juda = ?	26. 60. Juda (4)
		61. Joseph
		62. Semei
		63. Mattathias
		64. Maath
		25. 65. Nagge
		66. Esli
		67. Naum
	5. Eliakim	68. Amos
	6. Azor	69. Mattathias
	14. 7. Sadoc	24. 70. Joseph
	8. Achim	71. Janna
	9. Eliud Eus. *II. E.*, I, 7.	72. Melchi (5)
	15. 10. Eleazar	73. Levi
	11. Matthan m.=Estha (?) m.=	74. Matthat
	12. Jacob = step-brothers? =	
	16. 13. Joseph, the husband of Mary of whom was born (7)	23. 75. Heli (m. Anna?)
		76. (Mary) == Joseph (6)
	14. JESUS, who is called Christ	77. JESUS (8)

NOTES.

1. "Which was the son of God." This refers to the ultimate source to which also the human ancestry of Jesus is traced.

2. B. Weiss, in his *Life of Christ*, I, 220, sees an "artistically planned" arrangement in the order of Luke: —

3×7 from Adam to Abraham
2×7 from Isaac to David
3×7 from Nathan to Salathiel
3×7 from Zerubbabel to Jesus

11×7 or in all 77 generations from Adam to Christ

3. Pedaiah and Salathiel were brothers. Because Zerubbabel is called son of Salathiel in Matthew and Luke, a levirate marriage or adoption is commonly supposed, and Ezra 3, 2 and 5, 2 are followed. With Zerubbabel the pedigree of Christ in the Old Testament becomes obscure and passes out. See Ebrard, *The Gospel History*, 149—163. E. Robinson, *Greek Harmony*, 184 ff.; Andrews, 62 ff.

4. See R. D. Wilson in *Int. Stand. Bible Encycl.*, under "Serubbabel."

5. Africanus in Eusebius seems to confuse Matthat with Melchi, 72 with 74. For tradition see Andrews, *Life of Our Lord*, 62 ff.

6. There is a remarkable reference to Mary as the daughter of Heli in the Talmud. See Weiss, *Life of Christ*, I, 221, note. Louis M. Sweet, in *Int. St. B. Encycl.*, under "Genealogy of Christ," 1198.

7. Joseph did not "beget" Jesus. Of whom "was born," ἐγεννήθη. In all other cases "begat," ἐγέννησεν. This is a proof of the Virgin Birth.

8. Jesus, "being, as was supposed, the son of Joseph," but in reality the maternal grandson of Heli.

THE FAMILY OF JESUS.

The purpose of this graph is not to pretend wisdom where Scripture is silent, but to help picture to ourselves the life of Him who for our salvation became incarnate and lived among men.

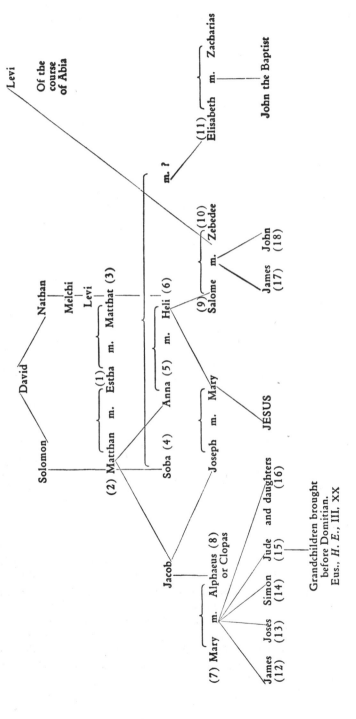

NOTES.

1. **Estha.** "By Estha then (for this was the woman's name according to tradition) Matthan, a descendant of Solomon, first begat Jacob." Eus., I, VII, 8.

2. **Matthan.** According to another (late) tradition Matthan had two daughters, Anna and Soba, and a son, Jacob. Anna was the mother of Mary and Soba the mother of Elisabeth. Quoted by Andrews, 57; also in *Cath. Encycl.* under "Elizabeth," V, 387. The source is also given: Nicephorus Callistus, quoting Hippolytus, *Hist. Eccl.*, II, III.

3. **Matthat.** Eusebius, quoting Africanus, says that Estha, after the death of Matthan, married Melchi. But it seems Matthat is meant. He refers to him as Melchi, the third from the end. But in the present texts of Luke, Melchi is given as the fifth from the end. It is suggested (Westcott and Hort's *Greek Testament*, Appendix, 57) that Levi and Matthat were missing in the text of Africanus. It is impossible to suppose that in such an investigation as this Africanus could have overlooked two names by mistake if they had stood in his text of the gospels. McGiffert in Eusebius, I, VII, note 6.

4. **Soba,** the mother of Elisabeth and sister of Anna, the mother of Mary. See 2.

5. **Anna,** the mother of the Virgin Mary. Apocryphal *Gospel of the Birth of Mary*, 1, 1. *Protevangelion*, 2, 1. Of Bethlehem. Married to Heli, or Joachim, of Nazareth in Galilee.

6. **Heli.** Of Nazareth. According to the *Gospel of the Birth of Mary*, 1, 1, and the Gospel of James, or *Protevangelion*, 1, 1, his name was Joachim. The name God, Jahve, was substituted for Elohim. Joachim = Eliachim = Eli or Heli. Anna and Heli were the parents of Mary.

7. **Mary.** The Mary in the gospels, called the wife of Alphaeus or Clopas, John 19, 25. Mary, the mother of James and Joses, Matt. 27, 56.

8. **Alphaeus,** or Clopas, the brother of Joseph. Eus., III, XI, and IV, XXII. See chap. IV, 43.

9. **Salome,** sister of Mary, John 19, 25, as compared with Matt. 27, 56 and Mark 15, 40.

10. **Zebedee.** The father of James and John. There is a tradition which makes him a priestly descendant of Levi. Eus., III, XXXI, 3, "Genealogy of the Twelve Apostles." See also R. Harris, *The Twelve Apostles*, 98.

11. **Elisabeth,** cousin to Mary, Luke 1, 36.

12. **James.** The Apostle James the Less. See chap. XI, 13. Early head of the Jerusalem church.

13. **Joses,** Mark 6, 3; Matt. 13, 55. Otherwise unknown.

14. **Simon.** The Apostle Simon Zelotes. "Became bishop after James the Just and fell asleep and was buried there at the age of 120 years." Hippolytus on "The Twelve Apostles." *Ante-Nicene Christian Library*, IX; Hippolytus, II, 131; likewise Eus., III, XXXII. Symeon, the son of Clopas, suffered martyrdom at the age of 120 years, while Trajan was emperor.

15. **Jude,** the Apostle Thaddaeus, or Lebbaeus. See chapter XI, 10. His grandchildren were brought before Domitian. Eus., III, XX, 2.

16. **Daughters.** The sisters of Jesus, Mark 6, 3.

17. **James.** The well-known Apostle James. Killed by Herod Agrippa, Acts 12, 2.

18. **John,** the apostle and evangelist.

THE PHYSICAL APPEARANCE OF JESUS.

In Ps. 45, 2 we read: "Thou art fairer than the children of men," and in Is. 53, 2: "He hath no form nor comeliness; and when we shall see Him, there is no beauty that we should desire Him." But from these or other passages of Scripture, which refer either to the glory or shame of Christ in His work of redemption, we must not infer great physical beauty nor exceptional deformity in the external appearance of our Lord.

Aside from the consideration of His divine nature there is no doubt as to the superior intelligence, the attractive personality, the commanding figure, and the oratorical ability of Jesus. He who could attract and hold the attention of multitudes and minister unto them, especially in His work of healing, must have enjoyed certain favorable physical qualities, at any rate, a voice which could make itself heard and understood in an audience of thousands. Yet, in spite of the supreme distinction of His person and office, the external appearance of Jesus was in every respect that of fallen and sinful man. That there was really nothing remarkable about His appearance may probably be gathered from the fact that a betrayer was engaged to point Him out, that — in addition to other reasons — Mary Magdalene mistook Him for the gardener, and that the disciples on the way to Emmaus as well as the apostles at a later occasion failed to recognize Him. As a true human being "He endured the common, or general, infirmities of men." He lived and walked, He was hungry, thirsty, tired, happy, or sad just as other men. But of any personal illness, such as a siege of sickness or of any physical deformity or defect in body or limbs, there is no record.

Precious works of art may stimulate the imagination, but as to height, weight, and other details of the physical appearance of Jesus nothing definite is known. The earliest pictorial representations, such as the Vine, or the Lamb and the Fish in the catacombs, are purely symbolic. On account of their largely Jewish extraction the first Christians and witnesses of Palestine were not much given to pictorial representation. An ancient brass figure, however, erected at Caesarea Philippi, attracted considerable attention as the supposed representation of Christ's healing of the woman with the issue of blood, Matt. 9, 20. This is the statue which Eusebius saw and which Julian the Apostate is said to have destroyed. (Eusebius, VII, XVIII, 3. Sozomenus, V, XXI.) Eusebius also speaks of likenesses of Peter and Paul as well as of Christ Himself, said to have been painted by St. Luke. Of these not a trace, not even an early description, has remained. The apocryphal accounts of the miraculous impression on the napkin of Veronica, the likeness of Christ sent with the famous letter to Abgarus, the ruler of Edessa, and the like, must be considered unreliable tradition.

A detailed description of the appearance of Jesus, though not older than the twelfth century, is of considerable interest for the history of Christian art. It is in the form of a letter supposed to have been composed by a certain Roman officer, Publius Lentulus, and is addressed to the senate of Rome. While the remarkable document is no doubt based upon earlier tradition, it can hardly be accepted as genuine. None of the church historians from Eusebius (fourth century) to Evagrius (sixth century) mention it. The first time it appears in the pages of history is in the *Historia Ecclesiastica* of Nicephorus, who flourished in Constantinople about 1325 A. D.

"There has appeared in our times," he quotes from that letter, "a man of great virtue named Jesus Christ. He is a man of tall stature, good appearance, and a remarkable countenance, such as to inspire beholders both with love and awe. He has wavy hair, rather dark and shining, flowing over the shoulders, and parted in the middle of the head after the style of the Nazarenes. [It seems that Nazarites, or Nazirites, is meant. But Jesus was no Nazirite.] His forehead is smooth and perfectly serene, His face is free from wrinkle or spot and beautiful with a moderate ruddiness, and He has a faultless nose and mouth. His beard is full, of an auburn color like His hair, not long, but parted. His eyes are quick and clear. His aspect is terrible in rebuke, placid and amiable in admonition, and cheerful, without losing its gravity. He has never been seen to laugh, but often to weep. His stature is erect, and His hands and limbs are beautiful to look upon. In speech He is grave, reserved, and modest. He is fair among the children of men." *

---

* Quoted in *McClintock and Strong's Cyclopedia sub* "Jesus Christ." Also in Farrar, II, 464. Compare also Pieper, *Christl. Dogmatik*, II, 82—84, and Mueller, *Christian Dogmatics*, 261.

THE MACCABEAN FAMILY.

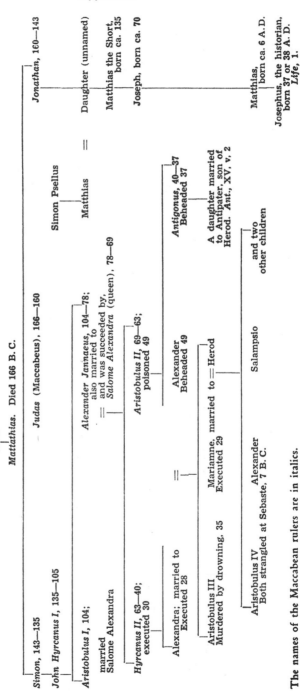

(Jehoiarib, 1 Chron. 24, 7)

Asmoneus   (Hashmon of the course of Jehoiarib.

Simeon   *Ant.*, XII, vi, 1. 1 Macc. 2, 1)

John

Mattathias.   Died 166 B. C.

Simon, 143—135

John Hyrcanus I, 135—105

Judas (Maccabeus), 166—160

Jonathan, 160—143

Aristobulus I, 104; married Salome Alexandra

Alexander Jannaeus, 104—78; also married to *Salome Alexandra* (queen), 78—69 and was succeeded by,

Simon Psellus

Hyrcanus II, 63—40; executed 30

Aristobulus II, 69—63; poisoned 49

Matthias =

Daughter (unnamed)

Matthias the Short, born ca. 135

Alexandra; married to Executed 28

Alexander Beheaded 49

Antigonus, 40—37 Beheaded 37

Joseph, born ca. 70

Aristobulus III Murdered by drowning, 35

Mariamne, married to = Herod

A daughter married to Antipater, son of Herod. *Ant.*, XV, v, 2

Alexander Both strangled at Sebaste, 7 B. C.

Aristobulus IV

Salampsio

and two other children

Matthias, born ca. 6 A. D.

Josephus, the historian, born 37 or 38 A. D. *Life,* 1.

The names of the Maccabean rulers are in italics.

THE HERODIAN FAMILY.

Antipas, governor of Idumea
Antipater, procurator of Judea, 47—43 B. C.
m. Cypros

HEROD THE GREAT
King of Judea, 37—4 B. C.

Wives

1. Doris of Jerusalem
2. Mariamne I, the Asmonean; executed 29 B. C.
3. Mariamne II, daughter of Simon the High Priest
4. Malthace, the Samaritan
5. Cleopatra of Jerusalem

And five other wives

And six other children

Phasael

Joseph

Pheroras

Salome
m. to 1. Joseph
2. Costobarus
3. Alexas

Bernice

Antipater
Executed 4 B. C.

Aristobulus   Alexander
Both executed 7 B. C.
m. Bernice

Salampsio

Herod Philip
m. Herodias

Antipas
Tetrarch of Galilee
Mark 6, 17
Banished A. D. 39
m. 1. D. of Aretas
2. Herodias

Archelaus
Ethnarch of Judea,
Matt. 2, 22
Deposed A. D. 6

Herod Philip
Tetrarch of Trachonitis and Iturea
Luke 3, 1
m. Salome

m.

Cypros m.

Herod
King of Chalcis
m. Bernice

Agrippa I
Acts 12, 1
m. Cypros

Herodias
m. to 1. Herod Philip
2. Antipas

Salome

Herod Agrippa II
Acts 25, 13; 26, 32

Bernice
Acts 25, 23
m. to 1. Herod, King of Chalcis
2. Polemon of Cilicia

Drusilla
Acts 24, 24
m. to 1. Azizus
2. Felix

For a greater number of details see: 1. *Ant.*, XIV, 1, 3; *Wars*, 1, VIII, 9. Parents, brothers, and sisters of Herod. 2. *Ant.*, XVII, 1, 3; *Wars*, 1, XXVIII, 4. Wives and children of Herod. 3. *Ant.*, XVIII, v, 4; *XIX*, IX, 1; *Wars*, II, XI, 6. Descendants of Mariamne.

THE COURSE OF ABIA.

(See p. 60.)

The eminent chronologists J. J. Scaliger (1540—1609) and S. Calvisius (1556—1615) were the first to call attention to the fact that the notice of the course of Abia may serve as a chronological tag. But they were quite uncertain as to the *terminus a quo* and especially also as to the *terminus ad quem*, that is, as to the starting-point of their calculation and as to the year of the birth of Christ. They arbitrarily supposed that, when Judas Maccabeus restored the Temple-worship on the 25th of Kislev, corresponding to our month of December, in 165 B. C. (1 Macc. 4, 52), the course of Jehoiarib began its service, according to 1 Chron. 24, 7, and that the other courses succeeded in turn. Counting forward (from which day of the Julian calendar we do not know), they arrived at the 28th day of July, 750 A. U. C., or 4 B. C., as the day on which the course of Abia retired from office in the days of Zacharias. This calculation makes the birth of Christ occur in September or October, 3 B. C. (after the death of Herod), a well-nigh impossible date.

In the calculation everything depends upon the supposed year of the birth of Christ and also on the assumed regularity of the weekly succession of priestly courses. By availing themselves of a reliable Talmudic tradition, J. A. Bengel (1687—1752) and others were able to make a more accurate calculation, at least as far as the *terminus a quo* is concerned. According to a Talmudic statement (*Bab. Taanith*, 29 a) the Temple was destroyed on a Saturday evening, 8—9th of Ab, corresponding to our 4—5th of August, in 823 A. U. C., or 70 A. D., just when the course of Jehoiarib had entered office. On this date there is a pleasing amount of agreement. Josephus tells us (*Wars*, VI, IV, 1. 5) that the Temple was first set on fire on the 8th of Ab and completely destroyed on the 10th. It is almost absolutely certain that for many years previously the various priestly courses had been succeeding one another in unbroken regularity (*Ant.*, VII, XIV, 7). Counting back (27,244 days), we arrive at October 1 to 7 in 748, or 6 B. C., for the course of Abia. This agrees almost exactly with Wieseler, Andrews, and others, who arrive at October 3 to 9, and with Greswell, who has decided upon September 30 to October 6.

Now let us see what happens if we extend our calculations back to Scaliger's uncertain starting-point, the 25th of Kislev, in 165 B. C., or 589 A. U. C. The writer is quite authoritatively informed (by Dr. Jacob Mann of the Hebrew Union College, Cincinnati) that "it is difficult to ascertain with which date of the Julian calendar the 25th of Kislev, 165 B. C., corresponds. We can only say that it fell approximately in December, 165 B. C." It seems that astronomical calculations are not available. But in assuming the regular weekly succession of priestly courses, what will be the result for December, 165 B. C.? Which of the twenty-four courses will be on duty for the last few weeks of the year? Will by any chance the course of Jehoiarib, the first on the list, be on duty in the month of December? We remember that it was on this *assumption* upon which Scaliger based his calculation. A remarkable thing happens. Counting back (58,100 days) from the 1st of October, 6 B. C., the day on which we suppose that Zacharias began his service, or (85,344 days, exactly 508 sacerdotal cycles) from the 4th day in August in 70 A. D., when the first course entered service at the destruction of the Temple, we arrive precisely at December 6 for a tentative date for the 25th of Kislev in 165 B. C., with the Maccabean course of Jehoiarib, the first in order, on duty for the rededication of the Temple. This is, to say the least, a most remarkable coincidence. Thus we have a probable date for the 25th of Kislev, 165 B. C., an incidental proof for the regularity of the weekly succession of the priestly courses and, since we are quite certain as to the year, a confirming bit of evidence for the probable time of the birth of Christ. At any rate, our findings are in complete harmony with the chronology which we have adopted. (See Karl Wieseler, *Chronological Synopsis,* 121—124; S. J. Andrews, *Life of Our Lord,* 13. 14; and Edersheim, *Jesus, the Messiah,* I, 135; II, 705.)

BUSY DAYS IN THE LORD'S MINISTRY.

	Matthew	Mark	Luke	Chapter
1. The Day of the Sermon on the Mount. (Number of verses, 155.)	5, 1—48 6, 1—34 7, 1—29 8, 1	3, 13—19	6, 13—49	XI, 18—42
2. The Day of the Parables. (Number of verses, 166.)	12, 22—50 13, 1—53 8, 20—27	3, 20—35 4, 1—41	8, 4—25	XII, 12 to XIII, 6
3. Tuesday of Passion Week. (Number of verses, 397.)	21, 19—46 22, 1—46 23, 1—46 24, 1—51 25, 1—46 26, 1—5	11, 20—33 12, 1—44 13, 1—37 14, 1. 2	20, 1—47 21, 1—38 22, 1. 2	XXIX, 1 to XXX, 20

SABBATH CONTROVERSIES.

	Matthew	Mark	Luke	John	Chapter
1. The Infirm Man at the Pool of Bethesda. — Christ appeals to His own authority and at a later occasion to the practise of circumcision on the Sabbath. Compare John 7, 21—24				5, 10—19	VIII, 9
2. The Disciples Plucking Grain on the Sabbath. — Christ appeals to precedents in Scripture and to Temple service	12, 1—8	2, 23—28	6, 1—5		X, 27
3. The Man with a Withered Hand. — Christ appeals to common sense. The sheep fallen into a pit	12, 9—14	3, 1—6	6, 6—11		X, 30
4. The Man Blind from His Birth. — "I must work while it is day; the night cometh when no man can work"				9, 1—34	XX, 21
5. The Crippled Woman Healed on a Sabbath. — The watering of an ox or ass on a Sabbath			13, 10—17		XXI, 30
6. A Man Healed on the Sabbath Who Had the Dropsy. — The ass fallen into a pit			14, 1—6		XXIII, 7

CHRIST DISTINCTLY PREDICTS HIS DEATH AND RESURRECTION.

	Matthew	Mark	Luke	John	Chapter
1. In Connection with the First Cleansing of the Temple				2, 19—22	VII, 3
2. At Caesarea Philippi	16, 21—23	8, 31—33	9, 22		XVIII, 6
3. At the Close of the Galilean Ministry	17, 22. 23	9, 31. 32	9, 43—45		XIX, 2
4. On the Final Journey to Jerusalem	20, 17—19	10, 32—34	18, 31—34		XXV, 20
5. On the Tuesday of Passover Week. (Death.)	26, 1. 2				XXX, 20
6. Thursday Night. (Resurrection.)	26, 31. 32	14, 27. 28			XXXII, 1

Besides these there are other references: John 3, 14; Matt. 9, 15; John 6, 51; Matt. 16, 4; Matt. 12, 40; Luke 11, 29.

THE INNOCENCE OF JESUS

AS BROUGHT OUT DURING HIS TRIAL
AND DEATH ON THE CROSS.

Judas. (When he returned the thirty pieces of silver.)
"I have sinned in that I have betrayed the innocent blood." Matt. 27, 4.

Pilate. (At the beginning of the trial, after he had asked the question: "What is truth?")
"I find in Him no fault at all." John 18, 38; Luke 23, 4.

Pilate. (After the return of Jesus from Herod.)
"I, having examined Him before you, have found no fault in this Man." Luke 23, 14.

Herod. (As reported by Pilate.)
"No, nor yet Herod." Luke 23, 15.

The Wife of Pilate. (While the people were considering the choice of "Barabbas or Jesus?")
"Have thou nothing to do with that just Man." Matt. 27, 19.

Pilate. (After the choice of Barabbas.)
"Why, what evil hath He done? I have found no cause of death in Him." Luke 23, 22.

Pilate. (Washing his hands.)
"I am innocent of the blood of this just Person." Matt. 27, 24.

Pilate. (Twice; immediately before and after speaking the words: "Behold the Man!")
"Behold, I bring Him forth to you that ye may know that I find no fault in Him." John 19, 4.
"Take ye Him and crucify Him; for I find no fault in Him." John 19, 6.

The Penitent Thief. (On the cross.)
"This Man hath done nothing amiss." Luke 23, 41.

The Centurion. (After the death of Christ.)
"Truly this was the Son of God." Matt. 27, 54.
"Truly this man was the Son of God." Mark 15, 39.
"Certainly this was a righteous man." Luke 23, 47.

CONFESSING CHRIST.

John the Baptist.
"Behold the Lamb of God!" John 1, 29. 36.

Andrew.
"We have found the Messias." John 1, 41.

Philip.
"We have found Him of whom Moses and the prophets did write." John 1, 45.

Nathanael.
"Thou art the Son of God." John 1, 49.

The Disciples.
"Of a truth Thou art the Son of God." Matt. 14, 33.

Peter.
"Thou art that Christ, the Son of the living God." John 6, 69.

Peter.
"Thou art the Christ, the Son of the living God." Matt. 16, 16; Mark 8, 29; Luke 9, 20.

Thomas.
"My Lord and my God." John 20, 28.

COMPARATIVE VIEW OF THE DATES ASSIGNED TO THE BIRTH, BAPTISM, AND DEATH OF CHRIST.

See also the table in Wieseler's *Chronological Synopsis.*

	Birth	Baptism (According to the chronology by which the year 1 A. D. is made to correspond with the year 754 of the founding of Rome, A. U. C.)	Death
Irenaeus, born ca. 120	3 B. C.		
Tertullian, born ca. 150	3 B. C.		
Clement of Alexandria, born ca. 150	2 B. C.		
Eusebius of Caesarea, born ca. 280	2 B. C., January 6	29 A. D.	32 A. D.
Epiphanius of Salamis, born ca. 315			
Julius, Bishop of Rome 337—352			
Jerome, born 331	3 B. C., December 25	29 A. D.	32 A. D.
Luther, Martin 1483—1546	4 B. C., December 25	30 A. D., January 6	34 A. D.
Baronius, Caesar, born 1538	3 B. C., December 25	29 A. D., January 6	32 A. D., March
Scaliger, J. J., born 1540	2 B. C., Sept.—Oct.	29 A. D.	33 A. D., April 3
Calvisius, S., born 1556	3 B. C., Sept.—Oct.	30 A. D.	33 A. D., April 3
James Ussher, born 1581	5 B. C., December 25	27 A. D., November 8	33 A. D., April 3
Bengel, Johann A., born 1687	4 B. C., December 25	29 A. D., February	30 A. D., April 7
Hug, Johann L., born 1765	1 B. C., February	28 A. D., September	33 A. D.
Macknight, James 1809	6—5 B. C., September	25 A. D., December—January	29 A. D., April 15
Ideler, C. 1825	7 B. C., December	29 A. D., February—March	31 A. D., April 26
Paulus, H. E. G. 1828	3 B. C., February	26 A. D., autumn	29 A. D.
Robinson, E. 1845	5 B. C.	29 A. D.	33 A. D.
Ebrard, J. H. A. 1850	4 B. C., February		
Wieseler, Karl 1864	4 B. C., February	27 A. D., spring	30 A. D., April 7
Farrar, Frederic W. 1874	5—4 B. C., December 25	27 A. D.	30 A. D.
Edersheim, Alfred 1883	4 B. C.	28 A. D., winter	29 A. D.
Weiss, B. 1883	5 B. C., December	27 A. D., January	30 A. D., April 7
Cadman, J. P. 1885	5 B. C.	28 A. D.	30 A. D.
Schuerer, Emil 1890	5 B. C.		
Andrews, S. J. 1891	5 B. C., December	27 A. D., January	30 A. D., April 7
Broadus, John A. 1893	8—6 B. C.	26 A. D.	29—30 A. D.
Ramsay, Wm. M. 1898	5 B. C., December	27 A. D., January	30 A. D., April 7
Kerr, John H. 1903	5—4 B. C.	27 A. D.	30 A. D., April 7
Ylvisaker, John 1905	5 B. C., autumn	27 A. D.	30 A. D.
Orr, James 1915	6 B. C.	26 A. D.	29—30 A. D.
Armstrong, W. P. 1915	6—5 B. C.		
Robertson, A. T. 1922	7 B. C., spring	26 A. D.	30 A. D.
Gerhardt, O. 1922	5 B. C., December 25 (?)	27 A. D., January 6 (?)	30 A. D., April 7
Davis, J. D. 1924	5 B. C., December 25	27 A. D., January	30 A. D., April 7
Fahling, A. 1936	(749 A. U. C.)	(780 A. U. C.)	30 A. D., April 7 (783 A. U. C.)

In view of the fact that the extreme limit of the dates of the birth and death of Christ as given by all chronologists ranges from 34 B. C. ([1] to 8 A. D. — birth) to 35 A. D. (death), the general agreement of the investigators presented in this table is remarkable.

INDEX OF SCRIPTURE-TEXTS.

TOPICAL INDEX.

MAP
OF THE
HOLY LAND

SCALE OF MILES

0   9   18   36   54

Mediterrane

RIVER NILE

LAKE
MENZALA

EGYPT

ANCIE

DESERT OF SHUR